Don't Learn my Son no Sums

A School and its Village

Steve Ward

2009

First published in 2009 by
Yardstick Publishing
6 Yew Tree Close
Bishop Sutton
Bristol
BS39 5UG

Reprinted November 2010

ISBN: 978-0-9563997-0-0

Cover design by Alan Reynolds

The cover is based on a painting from the late 1800s by an unknown artist. The original hangs over a friend's mantelpiece.

Printed and bound by
Short Run Press Ltd.
Bittern Road
Sowton Industrial Estate
Exeter
EX2 7LW

To the children of Bishop Sutton School past, present and future; also to my own children Peter, Catherine and Andrew, two of whom were pupils at the school.

CONTENTS

ACKNOWLEDGEMENTS

My sincere thanks to everyone who so happily delved into their pasts and their attics and gave me their help, encouragement and permission to reproduce their photographs and documents. I could not have written this book without these kind souls, and I apologise if I have inadvertently omitted anyone:

Clare Anning (Red Maids' School Development Office, Bristol), Lynda Bills (headteacher of Bishop Sutton School) and her staff (especially Diane Dimmock), Les Bown, Janet Bradbrook, Geoff Brent, Philip Brent, Joan Bunney, Monica Castle, Olive and Dick Chapman, Wendy Childs, Bettina Cohn, Wendy Compton, Joan Davidge, Teresa and Delvin Dowling, Marie-Louise Hales (clerk to Chew Magna Parish Council), Pauline Heron, Isobel Hill, June Hingley, Cynthia Holman, Peter James, Pete Marsh, Malcolm Mellish, Eunice Ogborne, Eunice and Fred Ottewill, Heather Pool, Julian Pool, Eric Price, Victor Pritchard, Ken Rapps, Marjorie Reed and family, Ann Saunders, Mark Savage, Eunice Spencer, Audrey and Gordon Stuckey, Eileen Stuckey, Colin Symes, Jenny Tatham, Jean Veale, Sheila Walker, Sean Watts, James Welsh, Freddie White, May Woodward, Jane and Chris Woolley.

Some contributors have sadly passed away since I spoke to them, and my condolences go to their families.

I am most grateful to the following archives, libraries and organisations:

Somerset Record Office and Somerset Studies Library in Taunton, Bath Record Office, Bath Reference Library, Bristol City Record Office, Bristol Reference Library, Wells Library, Church of England Record Centre, Barclays Bank (for information on their branch in the village), Bristol Rovers Football Club, Chew Magna Parish Office, Department for Children Schools and Families, and the Parliamentary Archives.

A thousand thanks too to Anne Collier, my daughter Catherine and my wife Janet for their arduous yet vital job of proof-reading. The cover would have been a mere shadow of its current self without the expertise of my friend Alan Reynolds. And none of the book would have been possible without the support of my wife.

The names against photographs of pupils and teachers are the consensus views of very many individuals. Many of the documents illustrated in this book are old and scruffy and have had to be 'remastered'. This has occasionally and unfortunately resulted in some loss of clarity.

There are inevitably many people from whom I should have sought information, and I did not. I apologise if anyone feels left out – it was simply not practicable to talk to everyone.

Mother told me that she could not get her Boy to School because his teacher did call him a bunch of rags and the children did make fun of him.

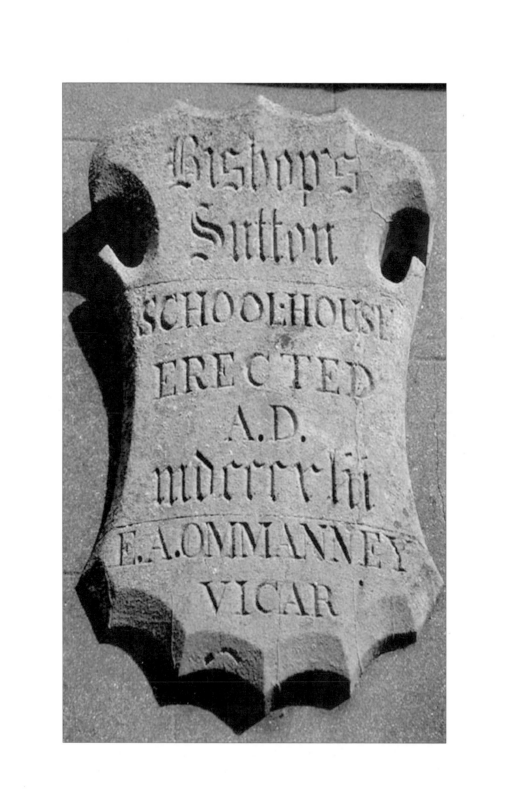

THE EXPLANATORY BITS

INTRODUCTION

This is a story of scary sums, attack by mob, happy children and stressed teachers. It's about Bishop Sutton School and its village but it could have its echo in many semi-rural, partly hidden away and traditionally not very affluent parts of the country. It's the smell of wet clothes drying in front of the open fire, the football match on the rec, the feeling in your tummy when you don't know your sums, the bluebells in the fields. It's about waiting with a sticky ha'penny clutched tightly in your hand for the sweet shop to open.

John Betjeman said that childhood is measured out by sounds and smells and sights before the dark hour of reason grows. Historian Edward Gibbon reckoned that history was little more than the register of the crimes, follies and misfortunes of mankind, and Henry Ford thought it was more or less bunk. So if you have no interest in crimes, follies and misfortunes (and successes, joys and pleasures), all of which feature here strongly, then you've wasted your money. And it's one up to Gibbon and Ford.

I am fascinated by the social history of the place where I live and where my children went to school. There were old records begging to be explored, old maps and plans to be pored over, people to be spoken to, logbooks to be read. I have been tingled and saddened and amused by descriptions of how it used to be 'in the good old

days'. But as with researching family history, you start off with the well-intentioned discipline of tracking, say, your mother's side, and then you stumble across a bit of a scandal involving Aunt Maud. So you meander down that turning. Before you know where you are, you've got several turnings on the go, so I offer no apologies for diverting occasionally from the main road to explore a bridle path.

The school was built in the early 1840s. The logbooks, which are so rich in information, run from 1872 to the present day, but I have read nothing after 1979. This is for two reasons: it was in that year that the headmaster retired who had led the school since 1958 after it had ceased to be 'all-age', and the late '70s were at least one full generation ago. So I shouldn't have stepped on too many toes. There is a preponderance of information for the period 1872 to the 1930s. I can offer no apology: it's just the way it is. More recent logbooks and records are much less descriptive, but that's partly made up for by the personal reminiscences which are nearly all from the post-1930 period. In a village where memories are long and families inter-related, I've occasionally used initials to avoid causing unwitting upset.

It's been said that the past is a foreign country, but it's a place to which all of us have travelled. We remember its customs, we recognise its highways and byways. We know people there. This book is the past of Bishop Sutton School and its village. That past contributes, in no small measure, to the present and to the future.

I hope and believe that the historical details are accurate and that I have not ventured too far into the realms of subjectivity or flippancy. I welcome corrections from those more knowledgeable than I. All individuals and sources have been quoted in good faith and with permission, but I will happily rectify any accidental omission in any future edition. I'm sure that my writings will jog memories and prompt the discovery of other photographs and clippings in dusty musty lofts.

Time for part of a song[a]:

> I remember, I remember the place where I was born,
> Where the morning glories twine around the door at early morn.
> I've forgotten, I've forgotten how long I've been away,
> But I'd like to wander back again down the lane to yesterday.

Before you wander, you should know that I've tried to organise the book in such a way that you can dip in and out, using the chapter headings as a guide to the bits you might find the most interesting. I start with social and historical context for both village and school, meander through buildings, teachers and lessons, and end with ailments and childhood and war. Words or phrases in italic print are direct quotations. 'Sic' is Latin for 'yes I know it's spelt wrong or the grammar's appalling, but that's what it says in the records'.

I hope you enjoy reading it as much as I've enjoyed researching and writing it. If the worst comes to the worst, you can always use it as a doorstop.

LOGBOOKS, STANDARDS AND LANGUAGE

The school's logbooks are the glue that sticks this book together. They are aided and abetted by the Punishment Book, the School Board Minute Books and Copy Letter Books, Parish Council (henceforth abbreviated to 'PC') records, church documents and sundry paperwork.

So what are these logbooks? The inside cover of the earliest one states: *This book was received into the school on October 14th 1872, until which time no record of the work had been kept. After the visit of HM Inspector on July 29th, the children were all moved into their Standards[b] for the next examination. On August 15th the children went to the vicarage in Chew Magna to join the children of that school in a feast given annually by Sir E. Strachey of Sutton Court; on the 16th August the school was closed until the 16th September for the harvest. When the school was reopened, one monitor was added to the staff of teachers, four girls have since been admitted and two boys and three girls have left.* As the Rev. Edward Aislabie Ommaney had been responsible for having the school built, it's understandable that he wanted to sign the first logbook. So he did, adding the comment: *the school is under good influence. New desks will be put up when the building is enlarged …*

----

[a] Composed by Andrew Sterling and Harry Von Tilze.

[b] 'Standards' are a bit of an enigma. In the 1870s those children who attended school started at the age of 4 or 5 and generally stayed in the infant class until they were 7. They were then steadily introduced to more formal work and divided into six Standards according to their ability. If they passed the exam that the inspector set for each Standard, they went on to the next Standard. Standard I demanded an ability to read from a textbook including some words of more than one syllable, to write a few simple words from dictation, to do simple addition and subtraction of numbers consisting of not more than four figures (simple?), and to know their tables up to times 6. Many children left school after reaching Standard IV, a level of attainment supposedly within the reach of an average 10-year old. For decades after this system disappeared around the 1920s and the class (or form) structure that we know today became commonplace, the words 'Standard' and 'class' (or 'form') were often used interchangeably.

more books and reading cards are needed. The needlework wants attention.

(Extract from the New Code of Regulations for 1872,)

"The Principal Teacher must make at least once a week in the Log Book an entry which will specify ordinary progress, and other facts concerning the School or its Teachers—such as the dates of withdrawals, commencements of duty, cautions, illness, &c.—which may require to be referred to at a future time, or may otherwise deserve to be recorded.

"No reflections or opinions of a general character are to be entered in the Log Book.

"No entry once made in the Log Book may be removed or altered otherwise than by a subsequent entry.

"The summary of the Inspector's Report, and any remarks made upon it by the Education Department, when communicated to the Managers, must be copied *verbatim* into the Log Book, with the names and standing *(certificated Teacher of the —— Class, or Pupil Teacher of the —— Year, or Assistant Teacher)* of all Teachers to be continued on, or added to, or withdrawn from the School Staff, according to the decision of the Education Department upon the Inspector's Report. The Correspondent of the Managers must sign this entry, which settles the School Staff for the year.

'The Inspector will call for the Log Book at every visit, and will report whether it appears to have been properly kept. He will specially refer to the entry made pursuant to Article 39, and he will require to see entries accounting for any subsequent change in the School Staff. He will also note in the Log Book every visit of surprise (Article 12), making an entry of such particulars as require the attention of the Managers."

Logbook 1899
'No reflections or opinions of a general character are to be entered...'

The first logbook, 500 pages, covered the 27 years from 1872 to 1899. The second, of a similar size, managed to cover the 58 years from 1899 to 1957 when headmaster Reginald Bailey retired and the senior pupils were transferred to the new Chew Magna Secondary Modern School. Entries steadily became shorter, and the books became less of a 'Dear Diary'. By the 1960s premises and administration formed the main topics of discussion. Part of a third book covered the years to 1979[c]. Until 1949 the logbooks were written exclusively in quill or fountain pen. Ballpoint dipped its toe in the water on 4 July 1949. Perhaps it was Mr Bailey's birthday and he'd been given one as a present. Anyway, he didn't like it and he reverted to old-fashioned ink from 5 July 1949 to October 1955, in which month he used biro for a whole three days. But then back to fountain pen. It wasn't until the

----
[c] The anoraks amongst you may like to know that headmistress Hassell (logbook 1872 to 1875) wrote an average of 14 pages per year, headmaster Jones (1875 to 1878) 12 pages per year, Mr Northam (1878 to 1881) 12, Mr Hawkins (1881 to 1882) 17, Mr Hill (1882 to 1883) a hefty 35, Mr Brown (1883 to 1897) 17, Mr Wightman (1897 to 1931) a paltry eight, and Mr Bailey (1931 to 1957) only nine. Mr Price (1958 to 1979) found enough to write about to fill 12 pages a year.

mid-'60s that the headmaster ventured to use ballpoint pen most of the time.

Bishop Sutton brass band outside The Red Lion, 1924

What have I found by way of records pre-1872? Only isolated references in censuses, maps or church documents, so the period 1842 to 1872 perforce remains murky. This is a shame. The records are all in English, with a dash of Latin to trap the unwary. But they reflect a changing English: gramfer or gramfy (granddad), daddy gramfers (woodlice), holidaymaking (*many children are away holidaymaking*). There are words whose spellings or meanings have altered. The village name itself was not immune. The apostrophe – Bishop's Sutton – died out, at least as regards the school records, around 1875. Perhaps it was realised that the time would come when people would commonly forget whether it should come before or after the 's' or, indeed, whether it should come at all. Far safer to leave it out. The language was more stilted in the 1800s, yet more varied and descriptive. It wasn't unusual, for example, to find 'children', 'scholars' and 'pupils', all with their own nuance, in the same paragraph. There were certainly no 'kids'. The same writer would switch randomly between 'show' and 'shew' until well into the second half of the 20th century. What we now consider to be the American 'vacation' was routinely used alongside 'holiday' until the mid-1930s, and intermittently even until the 1960s. Not only that, but the standard transatlantic 'write a person' (instead of 'write to a person') was normal until the 1960s: *I wrote the architect* and *I have written the clerk*. In 1956 the chairman of the PC referred to *the sidewalk of the High Street*. 'Secretary' didn't fully replace 'correspondent' until the 1970s. 'I am of opinion that' rather than 'I am of the opinion that' was the usual form until the early 1900s. 'Respecting' (uniformly abbreviated to 're' from around 1900, rather than the earlier 'resp.') was the norm instead of 'regarding' or 'concerning' or 'with reference to'. There were surprisingly early usages of what we might assume to be modern concepts: in October 1889, for example, the School Board applied for 'Kindergarten materials'.

The word 'office' was a formal euphemism for 'toilets', and was used throughout the school records until the 1940s.

CAN'T THEY WAIT TILL ALL THE OLD PEOPLE HAVE DIED OUT?

Pre-decimal money was a quintessentially British eccentricity that set us apart from Johnny Foreigner who could only count in tens, hundreds and, if you were an Italian sifting through your lire, thousands. Decimal Day in February 1971 put paid to a thousand years of British coinage, yet the occasion passed with nary a mention in the school logbook. When referring to £sd, some books show the current decimal equivalent in brackets. As there are plenty of people around who were unselfconsciously spending their money pre-1971, I have chosen a different tack. A direct comparison is, in any event, meaningless in view of rising (and, occasionally, falling) prices over the years, so I have generally left untranslated any sums quoted in the records.

As a rough guide, £1 in 1840 (and in 1900, despite wages having almost doubled during the intervening sixty years) was equivalent to some £77 in 2009. A penny in 1840 was equivalent to about 32p in 2009, £1 in 1950 around £25 now, and £1 in 1980 about £3 now. Average male earnings in the 1840s were less than £50 a year, rising to a heady £90 by 1900. Even by 1950 they were only around £500, but by 1980 up to £7,500, and some £25,000 now. Women working full time would have earned appreciably less, at least until the 1980s.

The coins generally available throughout much of the pre-decimal period covered by the logbooks were:

- farthing (¼d), a small copper coin which clung determinedly to life until 1957. Half farthings (of which there were 1,920 to the £) were minted until 1856, but rarely used.

- halfpenny (½d), a slightly larger copper coin withdrawn in the mid-1960s.

- penny (1d), a large copper coin; there were 12 to the shilling, 240 to the pound.

DECIMAL CONVERSION CHART

	1d	2d	3d	4d	5d	6d	7d	8d	9d	10d	11d
0	½	1	1	1½	2	2½	3	3½	4	4	4½
1/-	5	5½	6	6	6½	7	7½	8	8½	9	9	9½
2/-	10	10½	11	11	11½	12	12½	13	13½	14	14	14½
3/-	15	15½	16	16	16½	17	17½	18	18½	19	19	19½
4/-	20	20½	21	21	21½	22	22½	23	23½	24	24	24½
5/-	25	25½	26	26	26½	27	27½	28	28½	29	29	29½
6/-	30	30½	31	31	31½	32	32½	33	33½	34	34	34½
7/-	35	35½	36	36	36½	37	37½	38	38½	39	39	39½
8/-	40	40½	41	41	41½	42	42½	43	43½	44	44	44½
9/-	45	45½	46	46	46½	47	47½	48	48½	49	49	49½

50 NEW PENCE   10/-

*Conversion charts, given out with petrol,
with corn flakes, and on the bus*

- threepenny bit (3d), a tiny silver coin replaced by a 12-sided nickel-brass affair from the late 1930s.

- groat (4d), a silver coin confusingly of the same size and thickness as a silver 3d, only produced until 1855, rarely seen after about 1900, and the subject of a most distressing episode involving a girl at the school.

- sixpence (6d), or 'tanner', a slightly larger silver coin.

- shilling (1s or 1/-), or 'bob', a larger silver coin, replaced from 1968 by the 5p coin of same size and post-decimal face value; there were 20 to the pound.

- two shillings (2s or 2/-), or florin, larger than a shilling, replaced from 1968 by the 10p coin of same size and post-decimal face value.

- half a crown (2s.6d or 2/6), or two shillings and sixpence, or 'half a dollar', or 'two and a kick', larger than a florin and withdrawn on decimalisation.

- crown (5s or 5/-), a very large silver coin which ceased to be in common usage after the late 1930s, although persisting until recent times as a commemorative coin.

- half sovereign (10s or 10/-) and sovereign (£1), both small gold coins. Neither showed the denomination, and the minimal difference in size led to ample confusion, especially in the dark. The 10/- and £1 bank notes introduced by the Treasury in 1914 – known as 'treasury notes' until well into the 1950s – quickly replaced their gold equivalent; the 10/- note was replaced by the 50p coin of same value from 1969.

- guinea (£1.1s.0d), one pound and one shilling; not minted since 1813, but the term remained in common use until very recent times and was considered more 'refained' than a pound: tradesmen were paid in pounds, but craftsmen or professionals in guineas. It was a tradition in the legal world that a barrister would invoice in guineas but keep only the pounds, giving the shillings to his clerk.

The complexity of the pre-decimal monetary system – the bane of foreign visitors to the UK and of American soldiers lending us a hand in the war – meant that children spent a disproportionate amount of school time mastering it. With 12 pennies to the shilling and 20 shillings to the pound there were more than enough different fractions to worry about, some of them quite vulgar. I myself recall spending ages in primary school chanting: "12 pence one shilling, 18 pence one and six, 20 pence one and eight, 24 pence two shillings, 30 pence two and six, 36 pence three shillings, 40 pence three and four" and so on, right up to 100 pence, stopping at each sixpenny, tenpenny and one shilling mark.

Sixpence: 1883, 1887, 1922, 1947, 1967 (actual size)

There's sufficient knowledge still of imperial units to render it unnecessary to translate them into metric, although equivalents are given for some of the more esoteric ones such as the beguiling 'rod, pole or perch', being 5½ yards.

ABBREVIATIONS

The following abbreviations can be found throughout this book:

CEO	County Education Officer or Chief Education Officer
CV	curriculum vitae
CVS	Chew Valley School
DS	Domestic Science
HMI	His (Her) Majesty's Inspector or Inspection
LEA	Local Education Authority
MP	Member of Parliament
p.a.	per annum
PC	Parish Council
PE	Physical Exercise or Education
PT	Physical training, or pupil teacher
RDC	Rural District Council
RI	Religious Instruction
UDC	Urban District Council
WI	Women's Institute
'	(e.g. 2') foot or feet
"	(e.g. 6") inch or inches

CHAPTER ONE

BISHOP SUTTON

WILD OATS, PEDLARY AND TASTEFUL ERECTIONS
(BUT NOT IN BISHOP SUTTON)

Bishop Sutton is a thriving community of some 1,500 souls. At the time of writing in 2009, it has a post office and general stores, a butcher's, a hairdresser's, two pubs, two car repair workshops, several small businesses, no lime kilns and hardly any effluvia. It's more or less equidistant from the historic centres of Bath, Bristol and Wells. The PC keeps the footpaths, hedgerows and pavements spick and span (well, spickish and spannish), and the Local Authority in Bath fills some of the potholes. There's a football club, tennis club and a raft of societies and associations

The fortunes of commercial concerns in the village have waxed and waned. There are those who remember the days – not so long ago – of two bakers, a draper, a haberdasher, several grocers, three petrol retailers and pubs aplenty. And lime kilns. And

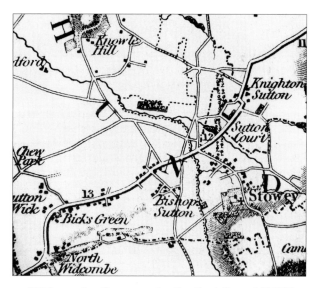

1822 map by Greenwood, after the toll road (A368) was constructed. Note the name Bick's Green rather than Wick Green.

effluvia. At one time there were smithies, a part-time doctor's surgery, a car-hire business, a haulier and a half-hearted attempt at a branch of Barclays Bank. Plus a colliery or two.

There was, and is, a well-respected primary school with around a hundred happy, well-adjusted and well-educated children. It's been there for longer than anyone can remember, and predates Holy Trinity Church (1848). It's the early 1840s where this story starts. Or thereabouts: a spot of geographical and social comparison is always useful, especially when embroidered by a bit of whimsy and a dose of envy.

Bishop Sutton in the early 1800s was a motley collection of groups of houses – most of which fell into the 'humble' classification – built around small farms and ramshackle coal pits. For 'humble', read 'squalid'. It wasn't even a village. It was simply 'Bishop's Sutton Tything', being the southern extremity of Chew Magna parish. It was rather a non-place contrasted with surrounding villages of greater antiquity. As we shall see.

For much of the period covered by this book, families tended to be large and almost

Church Lane in the 1950s, looking north from the right-angled bend.

everyone left school at 14 or earlier. There was little choice in what you did for a living. Homes had no electricity, very few had running water, and cooking was done over a coal fire. There weren't many inside toilets, and a fair few houses didn't even have an outside one worthy of the name. Roads were dusty, muddy or under several inches of water. For most of the population it was a hard daily grind, always short of money, few treats and no holidays. Many older people remember it as the best time of their lives. It was the era of the rag and bone man giving out goldfish in exchange for a bundle of rags, and of the oil man selling paraffin, candles, chalk (for the miners to mark their trucks) and black lead for grates. The knife grinder sat astride his tricycle sharpening knives or scissors. The hearse was drawn by four black horses with plumes of black leather attached to their halters. Mirrors and steel knives were covered up if thunder was expected. Les Bown (at school from 1944 to 1953) remembers the corn waving in the sun up Church Lane.

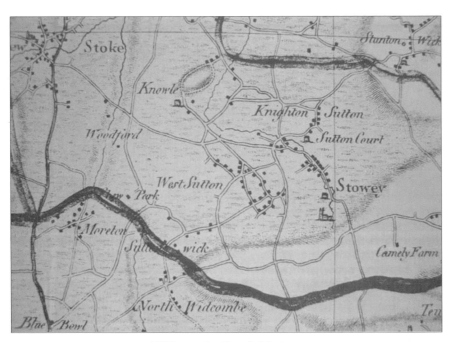

1782 map by Day & Masters.
A shame about the thick black line that somebody has drawn on!
Note the terminology 'West Sutton'.
Compare against the 1822 map on page 7, on which the new toll road is shown carving across the lanes south and west of Sutton Court.

Sheila Walker (née Rapps, at school from 1936 to 1942) can set the scene far more descriptively than I:

My mother cooked on a primus stove and a coal range in the living room in winter. There was a large stone boiler in one corner of the kitchen, fuelled by coal and used every Monday for washing day and for heating the bath water. A large iron mangle, turned by hand, was used to get excess water out of the clothes. If the weather was fine, the washing was hung in the garden to dry, otherwise in a tin shed outside. We had oil lamps until electricity came to the village in 1936. No-one had a fridge but used the walk-in larder in the kitchen. Everyone shopped at Lovells[1] no-one had transport to go elsewhere. A local farmer delivered milk each morning, travelling round on a horse and cart; he hung the churn on a wooden yoke over his shoulders and the milk was tipped direct into the customer's jug. There were two good family bakers who delivered daily with delicious cakes at weekends for those who could afford them. Everyone knew one another, and many were related. We were free to wander where we wished, with few fears for our safety. At the age of four I would wander in the fields near my home with my dog, often I could hear the trains at Clutton three miles away, the countryside was so quiet. We loved picking mushrooms and blackberries, and I invariably won a prize for the wild flower competition at Bishop Sutton August Flower Show. We dammed streams, made dens and climbed trees. There was so little traffic that we could stretch a rope across the road for skipping. Early film shows in the village were on a large screen on the back of a lorry in the Village Hall. Occasionally a travelling concert party would put on a Variety Show with rather doubtful talent.

Customs and practices have changed. Business have closed or changed hands. Hovels have been demolished or converted. The village roads are lined with cars. But the school is still there. The children are different, and the teachers no longer cane 5-year olds for wetting their pants. But much of the building looks much the same from the outside as it ever did.

That was the whimsy. Now to the envy.

Before prodding the social history of the school, it's illuminating to see just what competition Bishop Sutton faced back along (as some are wont to say hereabouts). The compilers of gazetteers and tourist guides – in so far as the few tourists that there were dared step foot outside Bath, Wells or Bristol – knew a thing or two about the art of describing and had a delightful way with the English language. So delightful, in fact, that a quick journey to the land that they portrayed is irresistible. Readers who have little time for the mildly amusing may happily skip the next couple of pages, for they'll find nothing about the school.

Bishop Sutton made one of its very first guest appearances as a collection of hamlets in John Collinson's 1791 'History and Antiquities of Somerset' in which he afforded the briefest of mentions to *Sutton Wick, North Wick, Sutton North (otherwise known as Knighton-Sutton and Sutton-Milities from its having been anciently possessed by the knightly family of the St Loes[2]).* But he waxed quite lyrical about Stowey: *consisting of about 20 houses, most of which are thatched, and so surrounded with lofty elms and other wood as not to be seen at any distance. In a lane near the Church a spring rises, and flows along the west side of the street in its way to the river at Pensford ..., of a very petrifying quality* [and forms] *slight incrustations around sticks and other bodies which it passes over. It is very remarkable, however, that no person who drinks frequently of this water was*

----

[1] The Lovells were major local employers and benefactors who owned the mill and most of the shops, and built several state-of-the-art houses. The family name was given to a new road at the Cappard's Farm development.

[2] As in Newton St Loe, near Bath.

ever known to have the stone or gravel. So travel to Stowey, all ye who wish to be gravel-free.

When Bishop Sutton School was built, the ink was barely dry – comparatively speaking – on W. C. Oulton's comprehensive two-volume 1805 tome snappily entitled 'The Traveller's Guide or English Itinerary: Containing accurate and original Descriptions of the Counties, Cities, Towns, Villages, Hamlets &c and their exact Distances from London: (eight lines of title omitted) The whole comprising a complete Topography of England and Wales, (six lines of title omitted) and every other useful Information, equally calculated for the Man of Business and the inquisitive Traveller'. After digesting the title, the reader would be forgiven for wanting a little lie-down before sampling the contents, but you can see what Bishop Sutton was up against with some of Mr Oulton's 'accurate and original' descriptions:

Kaynsham, Keynsham or Cainsham: Market town distant from London 113 miles, 4 furlongs. It is a popular tradition that this town owes its name to Keyna, a British virgin who lived in the year 490 AD … Some time of the spring every year, the river here swarms with millions of little eels, scarcely as big as goose quills, which the people catch on the top of the water with small nets; and by an art they have, make them scour off their skins, when they look very white, and then make them into cakes, which they fry and eat. In other counties they are reckoned a delicacy.

Harptree, East: On a neighbouring hill there are several mines of lapis calaminaris; among which are found some manganese and beautiful sparry concretions. The stone here is a mossy pebble, rounded, by water, from the size of a pea to that of an orange, in a strong cement, which takes a good polish.

Chelwood: An insignificant place, but remarkable for the following singular occurrence which happened in the year 1759. On opening a grave to inter a corpse, an oak coffin was taken up, in which a person who died of the smallpox had been buried 50 years; the coffin was so firm as to admit its being taken out whole; but the sexton having forced his spade through the lid, there issued from it a very noxious effluvia. The corpse that was going to be interred having been a person of some eminence in the parish, the funeral procession was attended by a great number of the inhabitants; there were many amongst them, who, never having had the small-pox, were infected by inhaling the putrid stench, 14 of whom sickened immediately, and in three days several others; but, although the attack was so very violent, the pox proved of so favourable a kind that only two persons died[1].

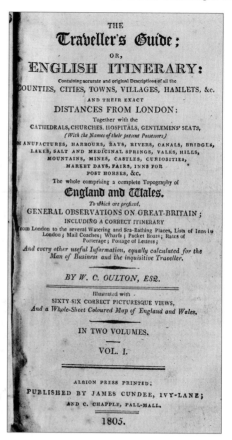

Mr Oulton's Guide, 1805

No-one would ever write about Bishop Sutton in such romantic terms. Bishop Sutton had no concretions, no recipes for skin-free eel cakes, not even a pox-harbouring

----
[1] Reminiscent of the famous newspaper headline: 'Small Earthquake in Chile, not many Dead'.

churchyard. It was only in the field of noxious effluvia that Bishop Sutton could hold its own.

Hunt & Co.'s 1850 'Directory of North Somerset' examined Chew Magna: *This place is of considerable extent, and is the residence of many opulent persons, whose mansions are generally erected with much taste.* The opulence of the persons didn't extend to Bishop Sutton, so Hunt & Co. ignored Bishop Sutton. In 1855, when our school was over ten years old, W. G. Blackie PhD was busy penning his 'Imperial Gazetteer, a General Dictionary of Geography, Physical, Political, Statistical and Descriptive, compiled from the latest and best authorities'. Again, Bishop Sutton was unworthy of mention, but Mr Blackie did find space in his 2,600 pages to damn neighbouring villages with faint praise: *a portion of the* [Chew Magna] *inhabitants are employed in the manufacture of stockings ... Chewton Mendip's inhabitants were chiefly employed in the mines, and governed by laws peculiar to themselves ... in Pensford there was a small market on Tuesdays, but so trifling that we cannot call it a market town; fairs May 6 and November 8 for cattle, sheep and pedlary.*

Bishop Sutton never made it into the bucolic world of Edward Hutton's 1924 'Highways and Byways of Somerset' either, although he did lyricise of Chew Magna: *one of the quietest places in a county that seems the very home of eternal summer.* Mr Hutton also revelled in his encounter with Chew Stoke Church: *one of the altars within, in the old days, was dedicated, we are told, to Maid Uncumber, otherwise St Wilgefort, not a very orthodox Saint we might suppose, for she was invoked by wives who wanted to get rid of their husbands; her favourite offering was of course wild oats.* He thought Compton Martin 'beautiful', and East Harptree 'interesting and pretty', but the closest he got to Bishop Sutton was Sutton Court, where *John Locke* (philosopher) *often stayed with his friend Mr Strachey.* More of the various Misters Strachey later. And in a sentence that has you cancelling the holiday in Tuscany: *there is nothing in England lovelier than the views and vistas of the hills here, where the enchanted valleys lead up into the blue Mendips.*

Tasteful erections in Chew Magna, pedlary in Pensford and wild oats in

Chew Stoke: Bishop Sutton just wasn't in that league. We have to wait until 1903, when Frederick A. Wood penned his 'Collections for a Parochial History of Chew Magna', to find anything vaguely descriptive about the place:

The tything of Sutton Episcopi or Bishop Sutton lies to the south of Knowle Hill and embraces the land from the river Chew on the west to the western slopes of Camely Down on the east. The land is generally good, but it is very marshy between the Chew and the village of Bishop Sutton. It is crossed by a small brook comprised of two branches, one rising near White Cross on the slopes of the hill above the village, and one other in Stowey, on the edge of the grounds of Stowey Court. It is called Norbrook or Hollow Brook, and is the chief cause of the marshland near Denny. The tything has an area of 1,365 acres and is the largest division of the Chew Magna parish.

HOSE CLOTH, OBADIAH, VIOLENT FOOTBALL, AND A WALK ROUND THE VILLAGE

This doesn't profess to be a history of the village – and does, I fear, lose its way every so often as a history of the school – but it is useful context to look at the villagers and their businesses over the years, at least in so far as they had an impact on the children. The 'useful context' also takes in a circumambulation of the village and the reminiscences of former pupils.

Others have spent a lot of time ascertaining that very little has actually been written about Bishop Sutton – if only because there wasn't really a Bishop Sutton to write about – apart from isolated mentions in Domesday of 'Sutton Episcopi'[1] owned by the Frenchman Giso (whose day job was Bishop of Wells), of villagers having the right to let their poultry peck on The Batch, of minstrels minstrelling at Wicks Green (or, as an 1822 map would have it, 'Bick's Green'), and of wills. The wills have absolutely no relevance to Bishop Sutton School, but are too curious to be ignored. In 1522 Alice Athassell left 4d to the *pore man's box* and *a red peticote and a whom* to her lucky daughter-in-law Agnes Athazell. Note the change of spelling. No, I don't know what a whom is. As Alice is unlikely to have bequeathed her womb, she may have suffered from a speech impediment and meant a 'loom'. In 1568 William Athele from Sutton Wick left *a hose cloth of puke died alredii* to his son Henry. Thoughtful of dad to have pre-dyed his puke trousers.

Fast forward 270 years, when plans were being made for a proper school to replace the infants' school (about which only a little is known). The night of Sunday 6 June 1841 saw the first general census. The population of Bishop Sutton tything was found to be 733 (380 males and 353 females). There were 53 children aged 11 to 14 and a staggering 284 aged 10 or under. 46% of the village population was under 15. Detailed addresses weren't given and individuals' occupation or status was often not quoted. Of those that were, most men were coal miners, agricultural labourers or farmers. There were also smiths, publicans, shopkeepers, masons, a tailor, a butcher, a baker (but no candlestick maker), a thatcher, an engineer, two cordwainers (i.e. shoe makers as opposed to cobblers, who were shoe repairers) and several of 'independent' status. There were a few 'yeomen' (the traditional meaning of which was a smallholder of common birth who cultivated his own land): Robert Ricketts (65), the father and son team James (89) and James (50) Challenger (and the 40-year old wife Betty of, presumably, the latter), the Hassell family (John and Ann, both 34, and their six children aged from 2 months to 12) and the Elms family (George, 40, Elizabeth, 39, and four children aged 4 to 10). The

----
[1] Just think how a name like Sutton Episcopi would have enhanced local house prices.

largest family in the village were the Babers, farming at Spring Farm in Sutton Wick: Robert was 45, Elizabeth 36, with eleven children from 10 months to 21. If the children were all Elizabeth's, then she would have had their first baby at around 15. This wouldn't necessarily have set tongues wagging as it wasn't until 1885 that the Age of Consent was raised from 13 to 16. Numerous families had seven or more children. The oldest inhabitant was the above-mentioned James Challenger at 89, followed by Isaac Templar (80) and his wife Martha (79), both of 'independent means'. Runner up was 75-year old George Clothier, who was still working as an agricultural labourer. The most common surnames were Filer and Harvey (eight households each), followed by Coles, Withey, Hassell, Fear, and Veale.

Spring Farm, where the largest family in the village lived in 1841. The last occupants, before the farm was demolished and submerged under the Lake, were the Hassell family.

By the time of the 1851 census – which gave more detail than its predecessor – the population had risen slightly to 776, of whom only some 40% were under 15. Over half of the adult males were working on the land, and a quarter in the coal industry. Few married women worked outside the home and only around 14% of the adult females were officially employed. No-one under the age of 11 was listed as actually having a job, but they didn't all attend school: of those aged 5 to 10, only 65% of the girls and 70% of the boys were classed as scholars. The girls' employment prospects were worse than the boys': fewer than half of the 11 to 20-year old females had any recorded work. Most of those who had were servants, dairymaids or dressmakers, although some worked on the farm as 'farmer's daughters'. Only three households had three or more housekeepers, suggesting that there wasn't much wealth about. The array of occupations from 1841 was augmented in 1851 by the odd charwoman and clerk, two journeymen (being tradesmen who had served their trade apprenticeship and mastered their craft, not bound to serve a master but hired by the day), a basket maker, a dealer, a nurse, a 73-year old 'monthly nurse' (a woman attending during the first month after childbirth), a toll collector, a haulier, a rope maker and a hay dealer. The cordwainer was still waining his cord. There was an annuitant (a recipient of a pension) and a lawyer. John Dixon was the man that no self-respecting community should be without: an annatto and mustard manufacturer. He probably imported the seeds of the annatto bush[1] and ground them to produce a dye for foodstuffs such as cheese.

One inhabitant in three over the age of 60 was a pauper. There were 29 single people (commonly widows or widowers) listed as the head of the household, but only four individuals actually lived by themselves. One in five households had other relatives living with them; one household in ten had lodgers or boarders, mainly agricultural labourers or coal miners. Coles, Fear and Veale had fallen away in the surname popularity stakes, to be replaced by Travis, Perry and Sage. The Filers were languishing badly, but there were still a lot of Harveys. The largest family was the Chiswells with eleven children aged between 1 and 20 born to Annie (40) and her husband Harding, a 'master blacksmith' (also 40). By 1861 daughter Agnes had died, but they had acquired the exotically named Fannybella, born in 1854.

1861 census enumerator William Veale counted 131 inhabited houses, 21 uninhabited, and one in the throes of being built. The population had slumped to 612, but tidily divided itself as to 306 males and 306 females. Cord was no longer being wained. The most common activities were coalmining (45 workers), general labouring (33) and agricultural labouring (35, to which could be added 42 farmers, farmer's boys or farmeresses. For the first time, there was a 'police constable', who lived at an unspecified address at Knowle (Hill), but close to the Baptist Chapel: James Larcombe (27) with his wife Elizabeth (26) and their two young children. The oldest Bishop Suttonians were William Fear and Isaac Tombs (both described as agricultural labourers despite being, respectively, 84 and 83) and Sarah Collins, also 83. The Fears and the Hassells were now all-conquering with 14 households between them. The 1861 census was the first to list the place of birth: 400 of the 612 inhabitants were from 'Chew Magna' (which probably largely meant 'Bishop Sutton', which was still in Chew Magna parish). A combination of Dundry, Chew Stoke, Clutton, Compton Martin, the Harptrees, Stanton Drew, Stowey, Hinton Blewett, Chewton Mendip, Paulton and 'Widcombe' (being North or South Widcombe, not the one in Bath) mopped up another 100 people. Most of the remainder were from other villages within a 20-mile radius. Surprisingly, only three people had been born in Bristol, and two in Bath. Nine were from South Wales.

By the time of Kelly's 1861 Directory, Bishop Sutton merited its own mention. But only a little one. The tything was listed as comprising the Chapel of Ease (so called because worshippers no longer had to travel to Chew Magna), several coalpits and various important people: Joseph Ashman was licensee at The Red Lion, S. C. Bryant was a grocer, John Collins and John Slocombe were shopkeepers, Joseph Cook and Samuel Travis were coal proprietors, William Travis a blacksmith, William Shepherd a butcher, and Miss Hassell the schoolmistress.

By the time of the 1871 census, the population was 610 (306 males and 304 females) across 143 inhabited houses. Ten houses were empty. Farming was still the largest employer, but the number of agricultural workers had almost halved since 1851. The number of farmers had also dropped in twenty years from 21 to 15 as a result of amalgamations. Spring Farm, for example, had grown by some 25 acres, Sutton Wick Farm by six, and Bishop Sutton Farm on Church Lane by ten. In 1851 the smallest farmer had been listed as owning four acres, but by 1871 the smallest owned 20 acres. Mining was still the second largest occupation. The oldest child still at school was 13; the youngest, Hugh Dowling, only 3. He was listed as living with his widowed mother Ruth (38), who also took in the 4-year old 'boarder'

----
[1] Bixa orellana, for anyone who may have forgotten.

Henry Harvey, who may have been an orphan. Plenty of children were working, including Sarah Millard (12) as a live-in domestic servant with the Gray family at Spring Farm. 12-year old Mary Gibbs was likewise engaged with the Mapstones at The Butcher's Arms and 11-year old Fanny Sammuel similarly for her 63-year old grandfather George Wines, a pit labourer. 12-year old George Harris was a 'coal miner' living with his grandfather Joseph Harris (67), a 'late coal miner'. Edwin Harvey (13) was an agricultural labourer from Blaina in Monmouthshire. His father Alfred (36) hailed from Bishop Sutton, so must have moved away for a time to find work. Or a wife. By 1871 more heads of household had the surname 'Harvey' than any other. The men were outliving the women by some margin: the most senior citizen was Albert Veale at 85 ('no occupation'). There were two epileptics, a lunatic and a cripple. One person was blind and another was deaf. The curate was William Holmes (48), born in Ireland and thus the most 'non-local' villager. He lived at Bonhill Villa with his wife Katharine Jane (42), six children aged between 2 and 13, and a 17-year old servant girl. The 1872 edition of Kelly's Directory described his Church *as a neat edifice, consisting of nave, chancel, south aisle, north porch, and turret with one bell.*

Bishop Sutton mill, probably taken in the 1920s

By 1881 the enumerator's handwriting had improved but the population was down to 588 (301 males, 287 females). New occupations included a brick and tile maker, a coal weigher, railway porter, engine driver and laundress. The 1870 Education Act – see later – was in full force, and virtually all children below the age of 14 were at school, although 13-year old William Harvey worked as an agricultural labourer. Several 4-year olds were listed as 'scholar'.

An 'army pensioner' warrants a small paragraph all to himself. Charles Etler was 59 and born in Stowey. His wife Hannah was only 35 and hailed from Woolwich. Their children present a gazetteer of an army man's life: Edward (12) was born in Melbourne (Australia), Orvinia (10) in Islington, Caroline (9) in Sheerness (Kent), Florence (7) in Aldershot, Henry (3) in Westminster, Emily (2) in Shorncliffe (Kent) and Adeline (6 months) in Bishop Sutton.

The men were still outlasting the fairer sex. At 75, Eliza Harris shared the ladies' joint first prize with Elizabeth Coles. Elizabeth lived with her husband John, also 75 and an agricultural labourer, at 'Stitch in Shord'. The ladies had some way to go to beat 80-year old Francis Veale (agricultural labourer), let alone 87-year old Charles Fear, a widower and 'formerly a farmer'.

By the 1883 edition of Kelly's, Bishop Sutton had spread its favours round a bit: it fell within the Clutton Poor Law Union, the Temple Cloud County Court Division, the Frome Parliamentary Constituency, the Chew rural deanery, the Bath archdeaconry, and the Bath and Wells diocese.

The 1891 census was the first to incorporate street names. They included Cabbage Stump Lane (i.e. Church Lane), Kennards Cottages (four two-up two-downs on the same alignment and covering much the same area as today's Midway and Cornerways on Church Lane, but 30 yards or so to the west), Water Lane (leading southwestwards from Chew Park House to Stratford Bridge and now under the Lake), Coalpit Road (the main road through the village), Yew Tree Cottages (where Yew Tree Close is now) and Sutton Cottages (at the top of Sutton Hill Road where Rose Cottage now stands). The population had fallen to 544 (267 males, 277 females), 171 of whom (31%) were below the age of 15. In 1851 it had been 40% and in 1841 46%. The occupations were more or less unchanged, although someone – perhaps a census supervisor – had crossed through all the 'collier' entries, and written 'coalm.'. For the first time since 1841 the women overtook men in the longevity stakes. The oldest inhabitant was pauper Maria Faux (82) of 9 Cabbage Stump Lane (possibly one of a cluster of cottages at the right-angled bend). Lucinda Sheldon of 1 Kennards Cottages was the next oldest, although some way behind at 75. In the column headed 'Deaf-and-Dumb, Blind, Lunatic, Imbecile or Idiot', one person was listed as 'subject to fits from childhood'; there was one 'cripple', one 'cripple from childhood' and one imbecile. It seems there was no official Village Idiot.

The 1901 census is the latest readily available at the time of writing. The population was 560 (with 30 more men than women), of whom around 200 (36%) were under the age of 15. Apart from 13-year old James Price of 'Upper Sutton', who was described as a grocer's errand boy, everyone seems to have been at school who should have been. The ladies' age supremacy from 1891 hadn't lasted long: in 1901 there were four octogenarians, none of whom was of the female variety. Richard White of 'Stitchingshord' was 82, a widower and on outdoor relief (i.e. obtaining Poor Law relief in his own home rather than in the workhouse). His next-door neighbour Richard Gibbs ('retired coalminer', living with his wife Mary, 77) was also 82. There must have been something in the Stitchings Shord soil. 81-year old Henry Morgan (agricultural labourer) was kept in trim by his 32-year old 'domestic servant' Ada Harris in Church Lane (no longer referred to as Cabbage Stump Lane). No more than five doors away – the house number wasn't given – lived 81-year old William Tovey, a retired coalminer. Rare for coalminers to have lived much into their 60s, let alone 80s. William Stallard, farming at Mountain Ash Farm, was also 81 and lived with his 62-year old wife Charity.

Two listings testifed to the symmetry of Mother Nature. The Wyatt family of Upper Sutton consisted of Mark (30, a journeyman baker), his wife Blanche (29) and their children Charles (8), Annie (7), Thomas (6), Blanche (5), Reginald (4), Ellen (2) and Alfred (8 months). The Wyatts may, in time, have caught up with Jesse Lovell and his wife Sarah's unbroken boy-girl-boy-girl sequence across no fewer than ten children, albeit not as evenly spread: 34, 30, 26, 24, 21, 20, 19, 18, 17, 15.

Who lived where and did what? Former pupils remember so much and the logbooks (predictably) say so little, perhaps mindful of the warning of Dick Chapman (at school from 1926 to 1935): in Bishop Sutton you have to be very careful whom you put down, as everyone is someone's cousin.

BISHOP'S SUTTON is an ecclesiastical parish formed March 23, 1876, out of the parish of Chew Magna, and is 9 miles south from Bristol, 4½ south-west from Pensford station, and 2¾ west from Clutton station, on the North Somerset branch of the Great Western railway, in the Northern division of the county, hundred of Chew, Temple Cloud petty sessional division, Clutton union, county court district of Temple Cloud, rural deanery of Chew, archdeaconry of Bath and diocese of Bath and Wells. The church of the Holy Trinity, erected in 1848, is a building of stone, in the Early English style, consisting of chancel, nave of four bays, south aisle, north porch and a western belfry containing one bell: there are sittings for 300 persons. The register dates from 1876. The living is a vicarage, annexed to that of Stowey, February 13, 1877: tithe rent-charge £171; joint gross yearly value £180, in the gift of the Bishop of Bath and Wells, and held since 1835 by the Rev. James Samuel Hill, of London University, who resides at Stowey. Here is a Wesleyan chapel. The population in 1881 was 644; rateable value included with Chew Magna. Sexton, Edwin Fear.

Board School (mixed), under the jurisdiction of the Chew Magna School Board, for 120 children: average attendance, 100; Ebenezer Brown, master

POST OFFICE.—James Andrews, postmaster. Letters arrive from Bristol via Pensford at 9.30 a.m.; dispatched at 3.30 p.m. week days only; Chew Magna is the nearest money order & telegraph office; postal orders are issued here, but not paid

CARRIER TO BRISTOL.—Noah Gibbs, tues. thurs. & sat. from his house

Arter George, Redland villa
Bower Mrs
Dendy Richard

COMMERCIAL.

Andrews James, grocer, Post office
Baber Edward, farmer
Bishop Sutton Coal Co. (George James, manager)
Daunton Georgina (Mrs.), Red Lion p.h
Dean Clement, farmer

Dendy Richard, annatto manufacturer
Elmes James, farmer
Fear Edwin, shoe maker
Ferris George, blacksmith
Gibbs Noah, carrier
Harris James, shopkeeper
Harris John, farmer
Hassel Edward, farmer
Hill John, beer retailer
Kennard Joseph Weston, grocer & draper & musical instrument dealer

Lovell Jesse, grocer & miller (steam)
Manning Richard, farmer
Mapstone George, beer retailer
Mapstone Isaac, farmer
Melhuish George, beer retailer
Perry James, beer retailer
Sheldon George, blacksmith
Shepherd William, cattle dealer
Sims Joseph, carpenter
Treasure James, carpenter

Kelly's Directory 1899

Any examination of villagers must start with the Lovells, who had pretty much all the local commerce (with the exception of a small shop at the far end of the village) tied up from around 1870 to 1945. Paterfamilias Jesse Lovell was born on the Mendips in 1847, worked from the age of 12 in a lead mine there for sixpence a day, married Sarah Watts in 1867 and moved to Bishop Sutton. As outlined above, he was unstinting in his marital duties. He started his commercial career with a chest of tea which he divided out into small bags and sold. With more trade, he bought a pony and cart and expanded further. In the 1870s he purchased Cappard's Farm from a Miss Travis, built stables and started slaughtering for his butchery business, supplying nearby villages with fresh meat. At about the same time, he bought five small cottages at the crossroads, pulled them down and built the corn mill, which soon did a roaring trade delivering flour to bakers; roaring enough by the 1920s to merit a telephone (Chew Magna 26). Before long, the family was operating a butchery and grocery business within the mill complex. The retail butcher's was through the packing rooms at the end of a passageway leading from the grocery store and next door to the Lovells' own kitchen. On the left was the housekeeper's room where the servants met for their cuppa, and on the right a pantry led through to the main house, meaning that the workforce was passing to and fro amid the customers. To add to the hubbub, children were sometimes allowed to hobnob with the housekeeper's parrot. A loading bay opened out onto the bottom of Sutton Hill Road, and Ken Rapps (at school from 1928 to 1938) recalls the day when a Foden lorry was reversed in, fatally crushing Mr Dowling, who lived on The Batch and who was deaf.

As the Lovell children came of age, they were all given a position of responsibility; when they married, Jesse bought or built houses for them in the village. Walter ran the Bristol warehouse (but, according to the school records, resigned as a school manager in 1909 and left the neighbourhood), Ernest ran the grocery business (and at the time of the 1923 Kelly's Directory lived at The Elms, Sutton Hill Road) and Joseph-Wesley ran the colliery. Lilian (who was married to the Rev. Scurrah, a Methodist minister; some children thought the name was Squirrel) ran the draper's and kept a huge box of dressing-up clothes for events such as the Annual Fête and Flower Show. Another daughter and her husband ran the post office.

Jesse and Sarah Lovell and children in the 1890s

Jesse had purchased the colliery (including some 40 cottages which housed the workers) in 1908 with his sons James, Fred, Ernest, Walter, Joseph-Wesley and Arthur. He sold it in 1924 so that he could concentrate on the mill. He bought more horses and wagons and – unfortunately for aforementioned Mr Dowling – the Foden steam lorry. Feed milling continued until 1945 when the mill was sold together with the wholesale business: first to the Orchard Family, who only owned it for a year, and then to Hateley and Company. The business declined and the mill closed in the 1960s. By 1970 the only traces of machinery left were some boiler mountings, two pairs of horizontal grinding stones, the remnants of sieving machines and blenders, and a few bits of elaborate elevators and conveyors. Although the machinery had been cooled by water pumped from what is now a sunken area to the immediate east of Southlea on the other side of the main road, the mill itself had never been water-powered. In the 1970s the building was partly demolished and partly converted to storage and living accommodation. The monkey puzzle tree – long a landmark for the village, and wistfully remembered by older villagers – disappeared.

Jesse's wife Sarah died when he was 86. He still had a bit of life in him, and he married her sister. He died in 1940, leaving six sons and six daughters. He had been a member of the PC and served on the School Board. The family's standing in the village was such that when son Arthur[1] was very ill, the road was covered with sawdust to deaden the sound of traffic. When Bath was bombed, Lovell's lorries and drivers helped in rescuing people from the ruins.

----
[1] The 1923 Kelly's Directory listed Arthur as living at Highland House on The Batch; the 1931 edition at Sunnymead on Sutton Hill Road, south of the Church Lane junction.

Sheila Walker recalls meeting Jesse quite often as he proceeded to Chapel. He had a white beard and was immaculately dressed in top hat and tails. He always stopped to say hello and would produce two small but exquisitely hot peppermints from his waistcoat pocket for Sheila to take to Church.

The Lovells were Bishop Sutton society at a time when there were few big houses in the village. They received the deference and respect that they doubtless deserved. But they were 'trade' and their home was attached to their business, so they weren't in with the hierarchy such as Lord Strachey, or with the Ushers. Major Usher – whose family was connected with Usher's Beers – lived at Redlands. Sheila Walker reminisces that she was sometimes invited to have tea and play in the nursery with the Major's daughter Anne, who was a year younger. On the appointed day, Sheila would come out of school feeling very proud to see a chauffeur-driven limousine waiting for her at the kerb. Nanny presided over the nursery and Nina the maid would arrive with tea laid out on a silver tray. There were delicious chocolate cakes, and Sheila would have loved to dare take one home for her mother. She recalls with nostalgia the nursery rocking horse. To a 7-year old, it seemed as big as a real horse.

Communal village existence – throughout the country and not only in Bishop Sutton – was formalised by an almost military ranking which subconsciously enabled people to assess their position in relation to others, so that they could either doff their cap to their betters or patronise those lower down the social scale. Yet whilst working people would willingly extend the customary courtesies, they were seldom subservient; they 'knew their rights' and were prepared to stand up for them, as was often clear from the school records. Status was put aside when it came to cricket, football or singing in the choir.

One proud representative of working people in the village was Edwin Harvey. Known to the world as 'Evvy', he is remembered with wry respect and affection by numerous former pupils. He was born on 13 December 1915 in Church Lane. His grandfather was a blacksmith; his father Edward was born in Old Pit Cottages opposite The Butcher's Arms and took up the trade. The School Admission Register shows that Edwin started school on 16 September 1919 and left on 20 December 1929. He began work at Lovells' mill, carrying one-hundred-weight bags of meal (about 50 kg) on his back out to the steam lorries. After a long bout of rheumatic fever – reputedly from lifting the sacks – he helped out at the family smithy and eventually acquired land which he farmed with his brother Jim, both in the village

The Harvey brothers in the 1930s

and at Whitchurch. Evvy would travel to his more far-flung acres on his tractor along the A37.

There is one particularly endearing and self-deprecating story, which Evvy himself would gleefully recount. For such a powerful man, he had a deep-seated fear of mice. On one notably icy day, one such critter had taken refuge in a cupboard under Evvy's sink. In order to extract the beast without running the risk of actually touching it, he threw a bowlful of water at it. The mouse shot out, discovered how cold the kitchen floor was, did a prompt U-turn and ran back into the cupboard. "Don't thee tell I a mouse do 'ave no brains" was how Evvy would always end his tale. The stories are legion about Evvy driving up Park Street in Bristol on his tractor to see his accountant, Evvy helping to put a fire out at the Scout Hut during the war, Evvy and his father persuading children to pump the bellows at the blacksmith's after tantalisingly showing them a shiny sixpence on a high shelf. And then omitting to give them the sixpence. Ken Rapps recalls the elusive tanner, but he also recalls Evvy and his father happily making hoops for the boys. One-time post office proprietor Harold Lyons, who had served overseas in the Forces, donated his false teeth to his longstanding friend Evvy, who had allegedly simply said, "I want they teeth". Evvy would then proudly announce to anyone who'd listen that his teeth had travelled the world. He died in 2003, missed by several generations of villagers who'd known him since they were young.

Harold Lyons and his false teeth

The Strachey (or Strachie) family were hugely important to the school and to the village for much of the period covered by the school logbook. The spelling was changed from 'Strachey' to 'Strachie' around 1900. The family lived at Sutton Court and Stowey Mead. Sutton Court was originally built around 1312 by William de Sutton, and the battlemented walls were considered to be amongst the oldest in England. Kelly's Directory of 1839 described the Court as *a noble pile, the tower and court wall of which date from the reign of Edward II; the manor house was added to the tower previous to the time of Henry VIII; a chapel and great parlour were added in 1558 by Elizabeth Hardwick[1], whose husband Captain St Loe, dying without heirs, left his estate to* her. John Strachey acquired Sutton Court in 1650. As an example of the august circles in which the family moved, Sir Henry Strachey (1736 to 1810) had been a clerk at the War Office, was with Clive in India, had a private zoo and was a Commissioner for Peace to the American Colony Revolt.

But moving hastily to more recent times: Sir Edward Strachey (1812 to 1901) married Mary Addington Symonds and they had three sons (Edward, John St Loe, Henry) and a daughter, Frances. The first son, Edward (Eddie, 'Old Lord Strachie', 1858 to 1936), was knighted to become Sir Edward, the First Baron Strachie, and kept himself much to himself. He lived at Sutton Court and is remembered as being 'old fashioned gentry', proud and inaccessible. The early logbooks bore witness to the fact that he was nobody's fool and was quite prepared to stand up for what he thought was right, as we shall see later with regard to prosecutions for children's nonattendance at school. Mrs Olive Chapman (née Tibbs) recalled that he wore

----

[1] A well-connected lady, in 1549 she and her husband had bought the land on which Chatsworth House in Derbyshire now stands.

white gloves and always let tradesmen keep the change. Kelly's Directory suggested that when he wasn't at Sutton Court, he could be found at 27 Cadogan Gardens, London SW3, or in a plush armchair in the National Liberal, Brooks' or Travellers' Clubs.

The third son, Henry (Harry, 1863 to 1940), was a scoutmaster and a friend of Baden Powell. He lived at Stowey Mead and led a much simpler life than his older brother. He was an accomplished artist and painted the war memorial at the Methodist Chapel and the murals in Stowey Church. He is remembered by former pupils for his generosity, his Scouting and for painting nude boys. Dick Chapman recalls that Sir Henry once had a new Austin Seven. Dick's chums would creep up behind when he was about to drive off, and hold on to the back bumper. After a few minutes they'd let go and the car would leap forward. Sheila Walker recalls that Sir Henry would buy shoes for poor boys and regularly gave children rides in his car. Sounds risky nowadays, but no-one thought it inadvisable then.

An Austin 7, but not Sir Henry's

His nephew (Old Lord Strachie's son) was unimaginatively also called Edward (or Teddy or Eddie, 'Young Lord Edward', 1882 to 1973) and was the Second Baron Strachie. Like his father, he lived at Sutton Court and, like his uncle, he featured strongly in the school records. In contrast to his dad, he involved himself in the lives of his tenants and the community at large, despite being separated from his wife, which was normally a big no-no in social circles in those days. For many years he was chairman of the school managers and would come to school each month to hand out salaries from the Education Authority. A logbook entry from July 1963 was one of numerous similar over many years: *Lord Strachie called at the school lunch time today … he spent ½ hour watching the meal being served*. It was sadly never recorded whether he partook of stodgy semolina or whether he returned home for canapés and port.

Sutton Court, from a 1700s engraving

Everywhere Lord Strachie went, his Great Dane, Prince, was sure to go. He (lord, not dog) kept a benevolently watchful eye on things at the school, invigilated exams and, using his height to good advantage, regularly told boys off. Colin Symes remembers – perhaps repentantly – that he regularly checked children's books. Marjorie Reed (née Treasure, last headmistress at Stowey School and a pupil at Bishop Sutton School from 1924 to 1934) recalls that as clerk-cum-secretary to Stowey School, Lord Strachie would bring her salary of £15 every month, accompanied by Foula. Golden Labrador Foula preceded Great Dane Prince. He (lord, not dog) found Marjorie a house when she got married. Lord Strachie would give parties for both Stowey and Bishop Sutton Schools and would present a Christmas tree from his estate. Marjorie recalls one year when he wrapped a plate up and put it on the tree as a special present for her.

The affection in which this unaffected gentleman was held, and his numerous accomplishments for the village, can best be summed up by the Stowey Sutton PC minute book entry of 23 May 1973: *Before the start of the meeting, everyone stood in silence for a few minutes in memory of Lord Strachie who had died the previous week. Lord Strachie was one of the first councillors to serve on the Parish Council when the parish of Stowey Sutton came into being in 1949 … He continued to serve on the Council until May 1970 when he was forced to retire on medical grounds. He was always available to give assistance and advice and was aptly described in the press as the 'kindly peer'.* What the minutes didn't say, but Mair Price did (in a fondly reminiscent way), was that if managers' meetings were going on a bit, Lord Strachie would pointedly examine his watch and bring things to a close by announcing assertively that 'there's something on the wireless'. Dick Chapman reflects that he would 'provide stuff for children. A real gentleman'. On the day of his death, his erstwhile housekeeper Sarah Pritchard wrote 'today, Lord Strachie died, and so did Sutton Court'[1].

It wasn't, of course, just the Lovells, the Ushers, the Strachies and Evvy Harvey. There were between 500 and 1,000 other inhabitants at any one time, many of whom are recalled by former pupils. The following, in no particular order, are snippets from those recollections:

Les Bown calls to mind Mr and Mrs Williams who lived in a cottage down Ham Lane: a little old couple, they would bake Les and his mother an apple. The Brown brothers lived 'down Stitchenham' next door to the Walkers (they of 16 boys and their own football team). One of the Browns was astonishingly tall and could lie in bed and hang his feet out of the window. Also in Stitchings Shord Lane, in a not-very-salubrious cottage, lived Obadiah. He couldn't lie down and had to sleep in a chair. Children would chant 'Obadiah jumped the stile', simply out of childish delight at the rhyme rather than for any intrinsic connection with a field entrance. Mr Jutsum at Rose Cottages at Top Sutton grew his own tobacco but it was too green to smoke. Gramfy Alvis wore his wellies on the wrong feet. Miss Thring lived next to Gordon House by the post office. She had spent time abroad and her house was full of oriental knick-knacks. She got on the bus one day and after a few yards said, 'Driver, stop, I've left my little case behind'. She got off the bus, fetched her brown bag and got back on again. Her lodger was cartoonist Reg Bass, who drew the pictures on Tate and Lyle sugar bags. Ken Rapps recalls that as well as drawing

----

[1] When Edward died, the estate passed to Charles Townley Strachey, fourth Baron O'Hagan. He had married Princess Tamara, daughter of His Serene Highness Prince Michael Imeritinsky of Menton, France (born in St Petersburg 1900, died in Nice 1975). They were well connected, were the Stracheys (or Strachies).

posters for village events, Reg penned a cartoon of trumpeter and bandleader Leslie Hutchinson (1906 to 1959) and got it signed.

The Walker Brothers football team in the 1940s

When the drapery at the crossroads came onto the market in the early 1900s, Jesse Lovell bought it and built up its trade. He then sold it to the Hateley family who sold it to Dick Chapman after the Second World War. Dick expanded into dyeing and dry cleaning, hardware, home perms, footwear and boot repairs, nuts and bolts. He had a good feeling for the agricultural trade, and spotted that he could save farmers a journey into Bristol by stocking barbed wire, milk filters, strainers and anything else they might want. This included shotgun cartridges, with which Dick supplied abattoir owner Mr Potter. In the 1960s Pauline Heron (née Dowling, at school from 1944 to 1953) bought the shop and sold children's clothes, knitting wools etc. The shop has been a hairdresser's for many years, but if you look carefully when the sun is shining in a certain direction, you can still make out the words 'Chapmans Drapery' above the windows.

After the Hateleys sold the drapery, they ran what remained of the mill they'd bought from Lovells, being a small retail grocer's on the site of what is now the Millennium Garden, with the front door opening directly onto what was then a very narrow road. The warehouse behind the shop sold wholesale groceries. The shop closed in 1964 and the building remained derelict for many years before eventually being demolished for road-widening in the early 1970s.

The shop at Sideways, near the Chapel, was run in turn by the Dury and the Montgomery families, although owned for many years by the Lovells. At the time of the 1901 census the property was occupied by John Montgomery (47) and his wife Georgina (41), 'fishmongers', and their six children. A door (now bricked up, but the outline of which can still be seen alongside the window) opened straight onto the narrow pavement and during the Second World War had a sign AIR RAID WARDEN above it. Exactly when the business first opened and when it finally closed – probably early 1950s – is unknown, but it features strongly in former pupils' recollections. A sweet shop and tobacconist's, it also sold the Green 'Un and Pink 'Un sports papers, which children were sent by their dads to buy. "Oh and while you're down there, get me five Woodbine." Sheila Walker well remembers borrowing pennies (or, in extremis, ha'pennies) for sweets. The shop played an important role in Ken Rapps' childhood: it had a dartboard. He also played Sevens there for pennies. Gambling with coin was illegal, and Ken reflects ruefully on the occasional raids by the police who came out from Temple Cloud, that being the closest station. Somewhere at the back of the small shop, children would throw rings onto hoops. The ice lorry would drive slowly past and sling a block of ice out onto the pavement without stopping.

The post office had been established in the village in 1853, probably on the other side of the road to where it is now, in part of what later became the Lovell mill complex. The postmaster in 1869 was John Collins Junior, and in 1872 Mrs Elizabeth Collins. Kelly's Directory of 1872 stated: *letters from Bristol, viâ Pensford, delivered at 10.30 am, despatched at 2.15 pm*. If you wanted more than stamps, you had to go to Chew Magna, which was the nearest Money Office. James Andrews took over in 1875, handing the business in 1883 to Jesse Lovell himself, who handed it back in 1889 to James Andrews who was already operating a grocery business on the premises. Although Mr Andrews was by then allowed to issue postal orders, he couldn't encash them, which implies that only a small quantity of money was kept on the premises. Telegraph business was taken on in 1892, and money order and Savings Bank Office business on 2 January 1893. The village and its commercial concerns were prospering, and by 1897 Mr Andrews was handling Express Delivery, parcels, annuities and insurance. He also opened on Sunday mornings from 8 till 10, but only for telegrams. Kelly's listed his daughter Agnes (27) as the 'telegraph and postal clerk'. In the 1930s the business belonged to Mr Watts, who had a house built at the end of the lane next to Sideways. Harold Lyons and his false teeth then took over. Sheila Walker recalls that the post office started selling ice cream after the war, at about which time a 'Stop Me And Buy One' van would also come round on Sundays and annoy the grown-ups with its merry little Greensleeves tune.

Continuing along the northern side of the main road, we come to what was the school's nearest shop. Now a private house, it had been a shop for a hundred years or more. It was never spacious in latter years, but at one time it was smaller still. At the 1901 census it was occupied by James Harris (41), grocer, and his wife Emma (41). An agency of Barclays Bank was established next door on 18 August 1922, operating hours 11.30 am to 3 pm (Fridays only), and run by manager Mr W. R. Wadham from the main Corn Street branch in Bristol. The hours were changed in August 1923 to 10 am to 2 pm (Fridays only). The branch closed on 30 September 1924, and the village would not have a bank again. The premises formed a part of the Lovell property empire, were subsequently bought by the Dury family, then by Mabel Withey and, in the 1960s, by Mr Munn. Mr Miles then took the shop on, but sold it in 1971 to Mr and Mrs Stuckey, previously of Sutton Farm. Gordon Stuckey had been running a newspaper delivery service from a van for several years before buying the shop.

Barclays Bank at Dury's shop: established 1922, closed 1924.
One of the ladies is believed to be a Mrs White. The porch still
exists, although altered. To the right of the building is a lane
leading to yards at the rear. The railings disappeared shortly after
the outbreak of World War Two. The building to the left became
Stuckey's shop.

Joan Bunney (née Challenger, at school from 1942 to 1952) recalls being sent to the shop with the family's wartime ration book. The shop assistant would mark the book, Joan would take it home, her aunt would rub out the markings and send Joan back for more oranges. Joan says they always seemed to fall for it. Eunice Ogborne (née Montgomery, at school from 1923 to 1932) remembers earning half a crown a week for her part-time job there. Next to the shop is Wren Cottage, to where Les Bown moved when he was 15. It was 'unfit for human habitation', he says.

Stuckey's in the 1970s, with Wren
Cottage to the left

The Lovells owned most of the business premises in the village, and therefore shared in the profits. Mr Lovell wasn't keen on competition. In October 1892 the clerk to the School Board wrote to a Mr J. Boley in Bishop Sutton: *Replying to your letter card this morning, I beg to inform you that the statement which you say Mr Jesse Lovell is circulating about my price for soap is untrue. I have not charged 1/- per bar, but elevenpence and for <u>one</u> bar only had during the last school year. You are mistaken, it is not illegal for officers of a School Board to supply goods for the use of* *the schools. The Act applies to monitors of the School Board only. Thanking you for bringing the matter to my notice. I beg to remain Yours Faithfully, W. E. Milton.* The 1891 census listed John Boley as a commercial traveller residing at 'Hill View House (Local Reform Lodge)', near Stowey Quarry. He was presumably in the soap business.

After that little diversion, our circumambulation lands us, more or less, at The Red Lion. It was The Red Lion – a pub since at least 1846 when it was noted in the Church Rates Book as being run by Mary Bush – that was at the heart of village celebrations. The forecourt was where parades started, where stalls and entertainments were traditionally set out, where Armistice Day remembrances were held, and where children gathered. Joan Davidge recalls that the pub, for over a hundred years in the ownership of the Dury family, would lay on Boxing Day and May Day sandwiches.

The monkey puzzle dominates the scene. The photo can be dated to 1934 (or later), as that was when the concrete telephone kiosk was installed: at the left of the main road, a few yards beyond the telegraph pole.

A brief excursion into the realm of pubs is warranted at this juncture because (a) they're interesting and (b) they feature regularly in children's recollections and, occasionally, in the school's records. Not until 1886 was the sale of beer to children under the age of 13 outlawed, although they had been banned from buying spirits since 1872. For a long time after 1886 it was standard practice for youngsters to call at a pub to take beer home.

But we're getting ahead of ourselves. It was cheaper and quicker to get drunk on gin than on beer and in an attempt to reduce gin drinking, laws restricting the sale of beer were steadily relaxed from 1800 onwards. Under the 1830 Beer Act, any householder could pay two guineas for a licence for selling beer or cider on his premises, and local magistrates no longer had a say in who was granted a licence. As a further incentive, all duty on beer was abolished. In the first 12 months after the passing of the Act, 30,000 beerhouse licences were taken out across England

and Wales. Hogarth's 'Gin Lane' quickly became a thing of the past. Astoundingly high though the number of licences was, the figure excluded cider houses, which were regarded as beyond the law. The high point for beer consumption in Britain was 1876 with an average of 275 pints downed annually by every man, woman and child. Consumption of spirits had peaked a year earlier at a mere 10.4 pints per head of population. These were government revenue figures and therefore probably understated. By way of comparison, the figure for 2006 was a paltry 180 pints of beer or lager per year per person, plus 2.3 pints of spirits. So binge-drinking is hardly a recent phenomenon, at least among adults. A fascinating fact – and apologies to readers who pedantically point out that it happened long before our school was a twinkle in the Rev. Ommaney's eyes – is that in the late 1700s, when water was considered generally unsafe, most people in towns drank beer. To make it more palatable for children, it was sweetened. With lead.

The Red Lion in the early 1950s. The building set back to the right is the old Legion Hall, demolished in the 1990s.

Before we move from the national general to the Bishop Sutton specific, it's worth looking at what was afoot in nearby towns. Newspapers from 1882 reported that in Bath in that year there were 175 licensed victuallers (innkeepers), 96 beerhouses and 29 licensed grocers for a population of some 40,000. The Bath Temperance Society sanctimoniously stated that *this was in the extraordinary proportion of one to every thirty houses, to which must be added innumerable cider houses throughout the city*. Bristol papers reported the startling figures collected by a team of temperance workers, also in 1882, who manfully and womanfully stood outside all the Bristol pubs one winter evening between 7 and 11 o'clock. 54,074 men entered, 36,803 women, 13,415 children. A total of 104,292 from a population of 206,503. Perhaps not the most scientific of surveys: some people may have gone into more than one pub, it may have been a particularly cold night when the warmth of the pub fire was enticing, but nevertheless! The Temperance Movement was at its peak. During a two-week campaign in Bristol, American Temperance advocate Mr R. T. Booth distributed 36,678 'abstinence ribbons' and took 21,193 pledges of teetotalism. To the (short-lived) relief of publicans in Bath, his intended visit there in November 1882 was cancelled as he was ill. But the campaign went ahead without him in the Assembly Rooms, where a 200-strong choir sang for 16 consecutive nights. Pledges taken amounted to 6,651 and ribbons were pinned on 10,663.

Back to the thirsty people of Bishop Sutton. The 1871 census listed, in a village of 610 souls, at least five pubs and beer sellers: The Red Lion, The Royal Oak, The Colliers' Arms ('The Colliers') at the corner of Church Lane and Sutton Hill Road, The Butcher's Arms ('The Butchers'), The Live and Let Live, and possibly also The Park Street. Large though the number of alcoholic establishments was, most 'decent' people frowned on pubs, 'nice' women wouldn't generally venture into them, especially alone, and the Methodists kept a very respectable distance. In addition to the pubs, cider would have been widely available at many farms. A lot of cider was knocked back, and not only by adults. It was traditionally fermented in a wooden cask; a dead rat was partly immersed head down in the liquid, suspended by its tail from a string tied across the top of the cask. When the body disassociated itself from the tail, the cider was ready to drink. But only after the larger pieces of rotting rodent had been strained off.

Colliery Road, Bishop Sutton, in the very early 1900s, as seen from the current Village Hall car park. Note the pit wheel in the background. The cottage at the centre of the picture, with the wooden porch, is the current no. 5, Wick Road. The plaque (which still exists) below the roof between the two bedroom windows reads 'I + T, B + S 1846'. Mont's Lane runs to the left alongside the cottage. The row of houses set back from the road has either been demolished, or substantially altered to form the terrace that is there now.

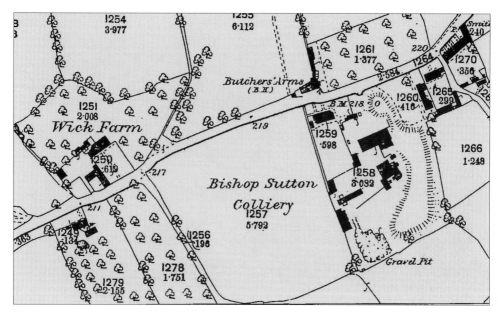

Ordnance Survey 1885

Between The Red Lion forecourt and the Church Lane junction was a short terrace of small dwellings. A compulsory purchase order was served on them in summer 1956, and they were gone by the end of the year. Attached to them at a right angle were cottages – the buildings largely still exist – on Church Lane. In the 1930s Marie Filer lived in the end cottage with the corrugated tin roof, Thora Matthews in the middle one, and Mrs Griffiths in the L-shaped part. See photographs on following pages.

Next door to the school to the west was Myrtle House (built in 1895 and sometimes referred to as 'Myrtle Cottage'), subsequently renamed Bois Pont and then Copperstacks. The 1901 census listed the occupants as the Treasure family, being Tom (41, carpenter and wheelwright), his wife Henrietta (50) and his children Wilfred (14, carpenter's apprentice), Herbert (11), Clifford (9) and Samuel (2). Herbert subsequently took over the carpenter-cum-builder-cum-undertaker-cum-school-caretaker-cum-general-factotum family business, having learned a trade as a wheelwright during the Great War. He had an allotment behind the house, which features elsewhere in connection with the school's expansion over the years. His daughter Marjorie became Mrs Reed, the last headmistress at Stowey School. If Bishop Sutton School wanted something in the early days, then it was off to Mr T's. Marjorie remembers him bonding wheels in a shed adjoining the school, helped by a hired miner from Pensford. Eric Price (at school from 1951 to 1958) recalls that the large shed alongside Myrtle House and adjacent to the school railings was referred to as 'Mr Treasure's sawmills'. The 'shed' is now a two-storey stone building, and probably predates the house itself.

c1930

Top: the three cottages between The Red Lion forecourt (background, left) and the junction with Church Lane (foreground, right). Note the unusual overhanging roof. Only one door was onto the main road; the other two were at the back. Part of the front wall has been retained alongside the main road. The windows of the building set back on the extreme right of the photo are the right-hand windows on the lower picture.

Bottom: the cottages at the bottom of Church Lane; the building largely still stands. The building at the left is the back of the terraced row in the upper picture.

c1930

The top photo is a closer view of the cottages at the bottom of Church Lane; the building largely still stands.

The bottom picture shows the extension to the right.

Just into Church Lane, past the terrace of bungalows built in 1938, was a piggery. A bit further along on the left, and next to what is now part of Sutton Park but where, until the 1960s, stood the Mellishes' farmhouse, is Mendip View, where Janet Bradbrook lived. Janet (née Harvey) was at the school from 1944 to 1950. On the other side of the road were allotments – some former pupils describe them as waste ground – which stretched down to the back of the school. Alongside was a dead-end

Kennard's Cottages, off Church Lane, 1890s

unmade track leading to Kennards Cottages, built by Colin Symes' forebears. Janet remembers the end one as being in a very sorry state and the water from the well was none too savoury. May Woodward (née Cottle, at school from 1935 to 1939) recalls that a Miss Veale, the Toveys and the Chidzeys lived in the cottages in the late 1920s. Miss Veale moved to the middle house on the corner of Ham Lane, and the Chidzeys moved to Harptree. One of the cottages, previously empty, was given to the evacuee Brassett family (or Bassett or Blissett or Brassick) comprising a mother and several children, one of whom was called Teresa. The evacuees didn't stay long – they found the soil floors and the total lack of toilet facilities quite beyond the pale – and moved to part of what is now Rose Cottage at Top Sutton. Kennards Cottages may also have housed another evacuee family, the Robinsons. At the right-angled bend on Church Lane, on the left going up, was a small cluster of cottages where the Harris family lived. One Mr Harris was a cattle dealer who drove his cows – on foot – to Knowle on Wednesdays, placed them in a field overnight and herded them on to Bristol Cattle Market the next day. The only remaining building now forms Church Cottages.

The Royal Oak ('The Oaks') was near the bottom of Sutton Hill Road. The property is now known as Oak House, but was formerly Four Seasons. The 1861 census listed Isaac Dagger (66) as beerhouse keeper on 'Sutton Hill' – which must have been the tavern in question – with his wife Mary Ann (64). Ten years later the pub was being run by Frederick Gover (36) and his wife Beatrice. By 1901 the occupier was William Dury (48), his wife Elizabeth (50), two children (11, 18) and servant Maud Tovey (13). Dick Chapman recalls that his Grampy Montgomery used to make bread in the outhouse adjoining the pub and taught Millie Tibbs how to bake. The pub closed in the 1920s.

In the late 1800s Charles Tucker of Vine House on Sutton Hill Road owned several carthorses for hauling stones from Stowey Quarries to be placed in lay-bys for subsequent breaking down into smaller pieces for road mending.

The next pub presents a small mystery. When the 1871 census enumerator came north down Sutton Hill Road, he turned left into what is now Church Lane, and listed the first property as 'Park Street'. Is that what he thought Church Lane was called – perhaps not being able to bring himself to write 'Cabbage Stump Lane' – or was it an aberration on his part, or was it an earlier or alternative name for The Colliers which, according to the plaque on the current site, dated back to 1785? In any event, the enumerator noted that it was run by wheelwright and beerhouse keeper James Hill (54) and his wife Mary (53). Peter James (at school from 1939 to 1945), who lived at nearby Rose Cottages, remembers being sent by his dad to The Colliers for cigarettes. The pub was then kept by Lettie Hill, and the last landlord when it closed in the late 1960s was Mr Patch. The hoop for tethering horses is still fixed into the outside wall. Mr Patch's relative Harry Patch died on 25 July 2009 at the age of 111, and was the last surviving British soldier to fight in the First World War.

The Colliers, Top Sutton, in the early 1960s

One of the three fuel retailers in the village was The Lodge on the opposite side of the main road from the school and some 50 yards westwards. Originally owned by the Gibbs family, it was from there – according to Kelly's 1882 Directory – that John Gibbs had a thrice-weekly carriership business, taken over (as per the 1901 census) by Noah Gibbs, who operated a parcel run to Bristol and a coach and car-hire business in the years before the Second World War. It was also from there that Mrs Lily Gibbs sold fish and chips; trade was brisk after film shows at the Village Hall. The Brent family subsequently bought the garage business, although not the premises: Fred Brent couldn't be doing with the mine shaft on the site. Colin Symes recalls that The Lodge sold only petrol, sweets, cigarettes, batteries. There were no motor repairs.

For most of the period covered by this book, there were two bakers in the village: Tibbs' and Montgomery's ('Mont's'). The former were 'Church', the latter 'Chapel', which sometimes had a bearing on who bought their bread where. Tibbs' was at The Barton (an old word for an enclosed yard), a row of cottages set at right angles to the main road alongside The Lodge. The outlines of the bricked-up window onto the main road, and the door a few yards along the lane, can still be seen. Montgomery's was on the right-hand side of Mont's Lane leading off the main road between Montrose Cottage and The Laurels. Tibbs' closed in 1968, but Montgomery's continued well into the 1990s. Both firms operated daily deliveries at one time, initially with a horse and cart. The Montgomery cart was reportedly more up-market: it had a roof. Tibbs' used to give free loaves to the poor: one family would take theirs away in a long bolster. Marjorie Reed recalls that Nelson Tibbs was on his rounds one day and saw Cyril Chidzey causing trouble by the bakery, so he took his horsewhip to him. Several pupils recall going to Montgomery's for penny buns during their lunch break. No-one seems to remember Tibbs' in that way, despite its being closer to the school. Perhaps that's why the children didn't go there: the risk of prying eyes!

Montgomery's bakery, early 1900s

And somewhere there was the mysterious Live and Let Live and/or The Stockland Inn. The Live and Let Live merited a mention only in the 1871 census, when it was run by William Dury and his wife Mary Ann. It appears to have been in the vicinity of The Butcher's Arms, although not necessarily on the same side of the road. There's anecdotal evidence that it was along Mont's Lane and was popular with miners. According to the deeds, the 150-year old Brent family house (on the same lane) used to be The Stockland Inn, which was probably the earlier name for the Live and Let Live. Stockland End Lane led from the top of Mont's Lane, past the back of the Brents' house, to the right-angled bend on Church Lane.

One pub outside our patch but frequented by teenagers from Bishop Sutton in the early 1950s was The Sun at Newtown, now re-named The Pony and Trap.

Most shops would deliver their produce, first by horse and cart and then by van or small lorry. Milk and bread came daily, and anyone who lived some distance from the road would place a wooden box on the verge. Some families obtained their milk from the nearest farm, the children dropping an empty jug off on their way to school and collecting it, full, on their way home. Les Bown recalls that as milkman Stan Hoddinott (of red fiery hair) lugged his crate from one front door to the next, he'd whistle and his horse would dutifully lumber along the road to the next gate. Children would wait until Stan was out of sight, imitate his whistle and watch the horse plod its way up Church Lane. At Christmas, Stan would get tipsy from all the drinks and leave his horse to find its own way home.

At one time, the Dowling family sold fruit and flowers from a house on the school side of the main road, more or less at the junction of where Hillside Gardens are now.

The 1871 census listed George Ferris as the village blacksmith; the family was to acquire some notoriety in the eyes of headmaster James Northam. The Harvey forge was to the east of the school near the junction of Church Lane; when a horse was tied up for shoeing, it would stick out into the road. After World War II, Coventry-based tractor maker Harry Ferguson offered to supply farmers with a tractor and all the implements for £1,000. The 'Ferguson System' did blacksmiths no favours, as farmers began to swap their heavy horses for tractors. To survive, smithies and forges came to rely on the sale and repair of bicycles. Once that trade waned, many forges mutated into motor garages, selling petrol and car accessories, sometimes cars themselves, and venturing into car hire and coaches. They would sell and recharge accumulators[1] for radios. One such business was Brents. Geoff Brent explains that his father Fred had learned the blacksmith and farrier trade from George Ferris's son Vic. Fred bought the Ferris business in 1930 and diversified into bicycles and motorbikes. Vic had sold petrol from two pumps in a hedge at a small pull-in at the side of the road, but Brents soon found the equipment to be inadequate for what was becoming a very busy A368, and in 1938 the holes for two 500-gallon tanks were dug. By hand. In 1936 the first hire car was bought: an eight-seater Austin 12. The first coach was purchased in 1950. With a 28 hp engine and a maximum speed of about 30 mph, it cost £650 and could hold 25 seated passengers and as many standees (as per those dreadful notices on Bristol buses) as could cram inside. A trip to Brighton before the motorways would take five hours – much as it can now with the motorways – and there was no heater. Brents took on the school-trip trade which, in the 1950s, produced a net income of around £1 a day. The car hire business ended in 1972.

Geoff Brent in the 1950s

----
[1] The first valve radios were powered by a lead-acid accumulator (the forerunner of batteries), a metal box about 8″ x 3″ x 6″ attached to the radio by a cable. The accumulator was recharged at a radio shop or a garage. The first mains-powered radio reached the market in 1925, but accumulators remained common until well after the Second World War.

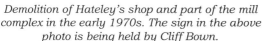
Demolition of Hateley's shop and part of the mill complex in the early 1970s. The sign in the above photo is being held by Cliff Bown.

Newspapers were delivered at one time by Rolf Harvey who walked from Pensford twice a day for his round. Charles Bown operated a photographer's business in the late '40s and early '50s. Unfortunately he only had a push-bike, restricting him to just one or two engagements a day, whereas his car-owning competitors in other villages could manage several. Ken Rapps remembers a piano tuner, completely blind, who walked from either Clutton or Temple Cloud. Wendy Compton (née Hudson, a pupil at the school from 1942 to 1952) had a paper round; the Bristol Evening post brought just 29 daily copies for her to deliver.

Numerous former pupils remember Kellaways, the smallest shop in the village, and one of the few businesses before the mid-'40s that wasn't part of the Lovell empire. Adjacent to The Butcher's Arms, it was run by Sid and Joyce Kellaway and sold all sorts, opening at lunch time and closing around 10 pm. If Mrs K happened to be serving in the pub, you'd have to wait until she was free. It shut in the 1970s. The 1901 census didn't list the Kellaways, but stated The Butcher's Arms as being occupied by George Mellish (37), 'beer retailer and farmer', Caroline (34), 'grocer', and their four children. The Kellaways may have simply continued the tradition of a pub-cum-grocery business.

Pit Cottages (or Old Pit Cottages or Pit Row) was a row of three or four tidy little houses at right angles to the main road near what is now Old Pit Garage. Eric Price believes that in the 1950s they were home to the Berry, Griffiths, and Ogborne families. At one time, the cottage nearest the main road was occupied by Colin Symes's wife Josephine's grandfather Lewis Collier, a winder at the pit who died when he was only 50, apparently from a disease caught unloading cargoes at Avonmouth. The cottages were pulled down in the late 1950s. The Old Pit Garage (confusingly on the site of the New Pit) was established in 1946 by Eric Price's father, Doug. Eric recalls that the volume of traffic heading for the coast – especially at weekends and on bank holidays – was such that the garage would be serving petrol (National Benzole) until 11 at night. The petrol side of the business closed in the 1970s. On a visit to the old colliery site in the '70s, retired miners G. Travers, J. Small and H. Lyons were shown not only 'Doug's Den' (a large collection of ironwork, paperwork, coalwork and general ephemera) but also the 'nuclear fallout shelter' which Doug had adapted for local civil defence purposes from one of the lower chambers of the old mine buildings. The old colliery has been the site for many years of Doug's yellow submarine which may – or may not – have been the one immortalised by The Beatles. It had once made the voyage partway to Nova Scotia.

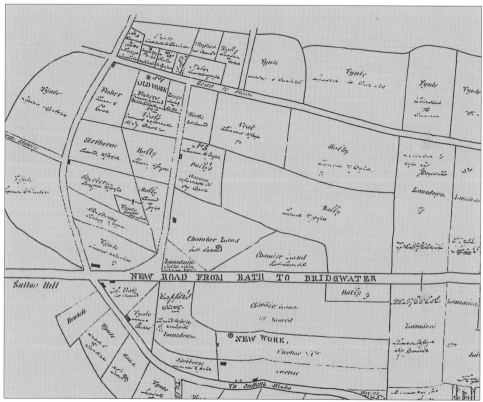

Coalmining map from the early 1800s. North is at the bottom.
Sutton Hill is the road running up from the crossroads, not to the left, as marked.
The road leading up from the words 'NEW ROAD' is Church Lane. The road along the
bottom of the map (Stitchings Shord Lane) is marked 'To Sutton's Weeks'.
Bishop Sutton School would be built just above the word 'BRIDGWATER'.

Old Pit Garage takes us, not altogether accidentally, to the village collieries.

The last mine closed in 1929 but had been working only intermittently for several years before that. Few can remember it in its heyday. Not that 'heyday' is the most appropriate word, as the mine scarcely bore comparison with those at Radstock or Midsomer Norton, let alone South Wales or Yorkshire. Mining in Bishop Sutton was never very profitable; the seams were narrow (the thickest only about a metre, and most around 60 cm) and interrupted by geological faults. The workings flooded easily. The coal wasn't of the best quality and was sold only locally or, further afield, for smelting lead or burning lias stone to produce lime for farms and for the building trade. Mining was nevertheless the main single employer in the area for the first eighty-odd years of the school's existence, villagers were proud of their local pit, and a cursory history wouldn't go amiss. Perhaps surprisingly, one of its few mentions in the logbook was when the hooter wasn't working and the children were late for school. After the mine closed, the rusty machinery featured in many a children's game.

The Old Pit (originally also known as Sutton Top Pit or Upper Sutton Pit) was off Church Lane, close to its junction with Sutton Hill Road. The shaft was 132 metres deep and the cage held four men. Wages in 1852 were from 1s.6d to 2s.3d a day: just enough to allow the colliers to frequent the eponymous pub next door before taking a few coppers home to their wives. The manager of the Old Pit, Robert Blinman Dowling, had The Elms built for himself and his family at the bottom of Sutton Hill Road. The house backed on to part of the mine complex, and next door was The Coal Barton (coal yard). Den Hill's family, last farmers at Yew Tree Farm (where Yew Tree Close is now) had once farmed Coal Barton Farm. After over fifty years of chequered production, the Old Pit finally shut in 1855.

In 1845 Samuel Travis, of a High Littleton mining family, came to Bishop Sutton as a colliery bailiff. He rented two adjoining fields to the north of the main road at Capper's Orchard[1] and sank two shafts, the deepest being some 300 metres, working with a two-man cage. Travis Pit was closed about 1865, but in 1913 Jesse Lovell bought the site so that he could reopen one of the shafts for use as an emergency exit from his New Pit – see below – and constructed an underground rail trackway between the two. After the Lovell family had struggled for some years to turn a profit at the New Pit, they contemplated reopening Travis Pit for any remaining coal, but decided against. The Bishop Sutton Rescue Team used Travis Pit for their routine practices.

So to the main pit, the New Pit or Sutton Pit. For those of you who've lost your bearings, the New Pit was behind where Old Pit Garage now stands. The mine opened around 1820, faced immediate difficulties because of flooding, and had to close on several occasions. The veins of coal varied from only 30 cm to 90 cm and

The New Pit c1910

had eccentric names such as Peacock, Stinking, and Cathead. There were two shafts, each 1.2 metres in dia-meter, one for pumping out water and for ventilation, and the other for coal winding and for the cage that raised and lowered the men. When it was all sold in the 1850s after some exp-ansion by the previous proprietors, it comprised the New Pit, the site of the Old Pit, a beer house (perhaps The Live and Let Live) and numerous cottages. In 1908, after a series of owners, the Lovell Partnership bought that part of the complex comprising the New Pit site and some of the cottages. By 1921 the New Pit was producing some 8,000 net tons of coal a year at a price of £1.11s.3d a ton, but a strike that year led to a reduction in the workforce from 150 to 100 and a 5% reduction in wages. Even with production on

----
[1] The name alternated over the years between Capper's and Cappard's.

three shifts, Lovells couldn't make a profit and they sold out in 1924 to the Bishop Sutton Coal Co. Ltd, who were confident enough of success to install a telephone (Chew Magna 34). But not enough people were ordering by phone and 1925 production fell to 4,338 tons. The May 1926 General Strike brought everything to a standstill again, and this at a time when coal was fetching only 16s.7d a ton. By 1928, after costly work had been undertaken to expand the tunnels, production increased to around 9,500 tons but the price sank to 15s.5d a ton. The new coal was soft and friable and the ground above the seams treacherous. Short-time working became frequent: to warn men not to attend the next shift, three blasts were given on the colliery hooter. The pit was losing money fast, receivers were brought in and the mine finally closed in 1929. The remaining miners travelled on foot or by bike to Bromley or Pensford Pits, and some even to Radstock.

An industry that never made much money – but which was a main employer and had a firm place in villagers' hearts – was no more. All in all there are thought to have been some 18 shafts in the area since records began in the early 1700s: eight near Stowey Lands, two on The Batch, one at the back of The Red Lion, two near what was Tibbs' Bakery, two at the top of Church Lane, two near The Old Pit Garage and one by The Redlands. Now there's nothing left apart from some half-hidden slag heaps and a bit of rusty machinery. And some gert big holes. But what did continue for a long time was the miners' (and miners' descendants') 'bag coal' or free allowance. Married workers underground (and some married surface workmen) received three hundredweight a week (about 150 kg) for life, and some miners were given rent-free homes.

SOMERSETSHIRE.

TO BE SOLD BY AUCTION,

BY MR. HENRY BLINMAN,

BY ORDER OF THE TRUSTEES FOR SALE,

At the Red Lion Inn, in Bishop Sutton, on TUESDAY, the 15th day of June, 1852,

At THREE o'Clock, for FOUR in the Afternoon, Precisely, (Unless an acceptable offer be made in the meantime by Private Contract,)

THE

SUTTON OLD COLLIERY,

WITH ITS STEAM ENGINES, MACHINERY, AND PLANT,

AND RICH VEINS OF COAL AND MINERALS,

Under Three Hundred Acres of Land ;

ALSO A COMFORTABLE RESIDENCE, AND TWELVE COTTAGES,

AND A

COMPACT FARM AND LANDS,

In the following or such other Lots as may be fixed at the time of Sale, and subject to conditions to be then produced :—

Going, going, gone in 1856

Mining was a nasty horrible dangerous job, however much romance may have been attached to it since. The building of the school in 1842 coincided with the Government's Shaftesbury Commission into the industry, which reported: *the men work in a state of perfect nakedness, and are in this state assisted in their labours by females of all ages, from girls of 6 years old to women of 21, these females being themselves quite naked down to the waist*. The report went on: *Any sight more disgustingly indecent or revolting can scarcely be imagined – no brothel can beat it*. They'd clearly done their research diligently, these men of the Commission. After 1842 women and children under 10 were forbidden by law from working underground.

Bishop Sutton miners c1920.
The only man recognised is Mr Daunton, third from left on front row.

The opening of the school coincided with the passing of the Hours of Labour in Factories Act of 1844, drawn up shortly after Karl Marx's comrade Friedrich Engels had described the long and toilsome days of the British miners:

Working for 12 or more hours at a stretch, frequently undertaking double shifts so that they could spend 26 hours without coming to the surface, having no set times for meals but eating when they could. Their children, mostly over 8, but sometimes little more than 4, were employed underground in opening and shutting ventilation doors as well as carting lumps of coal in heavy wheel-less baskets and tubs. It is a very common occurrence for children to come home from the mine so exhausted that they throw themselves on to the stone floor in front of the fire. They cannot keep awake even to eat a morsel of food. Their parents have to wash them and put them to bed while they are still asleep. Sometimes the children actually fall asleep on the way home and are eventually discovered by their parents late at night. Nearly all miners were physically stunted, and most were bandy-legged or knock-kneed or had some spinal or other deformity. Among both boys and girls puberty was delayed, often until the 18th year. Diseases of the lungs and heart, internal pains, indigestion and the distressing complaint known as black spittle were all widespread, and life expectancy was very low.

There's no record of women ever having worked in Somerset mines, but had Bishop Sutton's children ever been so employed? The 1871 census for the village had described 12-year old George Harris as a 'coal miner', but he would almost certainly have been working above ground. It's unlikely that things were quite as bad here as were depicted by Engels, but mining was nevertheless not for the faint-hearted.

What do former pupils recall of this once great industry? Peter James's father worked at Sutton Pit but got a job at Folly Farm after the General Strike in 1926, moving to Bromley Pit until that closed in 1957. Peter remembers taking his father on his motorbike to Bromley to feed the pit ponies one Christmas in the mid-'50s.

Ken Rapps can still hear the clank-clank of clogged feet walking to Bromley, where his Uncle Tommy James was a blacksmith. Dick Chapman recalls being nearly scalded to death when he was about 4. His father had a horse and cart and hauled bag coal, and Dick would often play at the pit. One day a boiler burst near a rhine (ditch) and boiling water gushed into the yard where he was playing. A miner scooped him to safety. The surface machinery and outbuildings survived for many years after the pit closed and were a magnet for the children, who would climb into boilers, crawl along flues and peer up smokestacks. Jean Veale (née Montgomery, at the school from 1929 to 1939) played in the sawdust there. Predictably there was a coal round in the village, and Ken Rapps recalls that Mrs Easter ran a horse and cart: she was up front, black as the ace of spades. After Bishop Sutton Colliery closed, she brought the coal from Bromley.

Just to finish the coal thing off: during World War II, the large tip at Pensford caught fire. Hundreds of men were drafted in from around the area, including from Bishop Sutton, to put it out for fear of attracting German bombers.

Mellish farmhouse, Church Lane (near current Sutton Park). Douglas Mellish's grandparents – George and Caroline Mellish – moved here in the 1920s from Ham Farm.

WATERLESS IN SLAP ARSE LANE

"Are we never going to get to the school?" I hear you ask. Yes, but not just yet. You've still got sewage to trudge through, plus electricity and street lighting. Oh, and street naming. But I do like to think that it all goes towards a fuller understanding of the schoolchildren's home village.

We start with electricity. There wasn't any. Well, not until 1936 in the village and, according to the logbook, 12 May 1938 at the school. Quite frankly, 1936 was a bit late to be connected to the mains: Bishop Sutton really had been living in the Dark Ages.

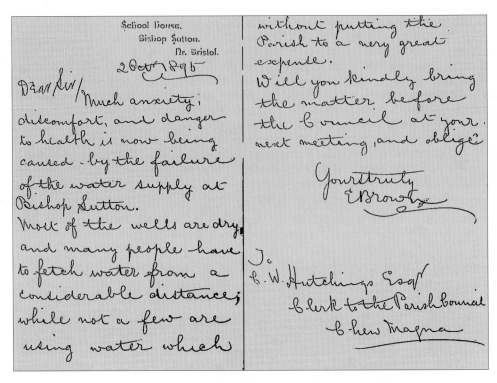

School House.
Bishop Sutton.
Nr. Bristol.
2 Oct 1895

Dear Sir,
Much anxiety, discomfort, and danger to health is now being caused by the failure of the water supply at Bishop Sutton. Most of the wells are dry, and many people have to fetch water from a considerable distance; while not a few are using water which without putting the Parish to a very great expense.

Will you kindly bring the matter before the Council at your next meeting, and oblige

Yours truly
E Brown

To
C. W. Hutchings Esq
Clerk to the Parish Council
Chew Magna

A watery complaint from Headmaster Brown in 1895

A public supply of water had come late too, but at least it arrived here before it did in Chew Magna, where the (property-owning) ratepayers had campaigned agin it, arguing that it would be an unreasonable drain on their rates, and couldn't the (non-property-owning) poor make do with the pumps sprinkled around the village? The PC had been concerned for many years that the local water wouldn't pass a clarity test, and a Mr Tucker (supposed expert in all things aqueous) reported to the councillors in October 1895 *that the water supply of Bishop Sutton was very prejudicial to health and suggested that a spring in Strawberry Wood[1] could be utilised*. The PC did what PCs are good at and appointed a committee. It consisted of Messrs Tudball, Morgan, Lane, Tucker, Hutchins and the Rev. J. Galbraith. In December 1895 the six gentlemen took themselves off to *the springs at Strawberry Wood and Heel Well … and found a plentiful supply of water*. So far, so good. In the meantime Bristol Water Works representative Mr A. J. Alexander had told the School Board *that the said Company would be prepared to supply standpipes at Bishop Sutton at a charge of £10 per annum each, and £2 each rent of meter (maximum supply to be 25,000 gallons each quarter) and £10 each for erecting same*. Mr E. Strachey reported to the Board that he was quite willing to *grant the use of the piece of ground called Strawberry Wood to the Council for the purpose of the supply of water to Bishop Sutton at a rent to be agreed*.

While all this was going on, parishioners were becoming increasingly impatient. What they really really wanted was a reliable supply of clean water. They petitioned the PC in July 1896 but, with apparently flagrant disregard for their wishes,

----
[1] On the eastern side of Sutton Hill Road, about 100 yards past Hillside House.

councillors wrote to householders the following month, essentially saying 'if you haven't got a proper supply of water, then get one'. This, from the minutes of their meeting in October 1897: *considering the small number of houses in the village of Bishop Sutton without a supply of water … resolved that a public supply of water is not needed for the village.* By June 1901 – with elections coming up – the Council had a pragmatic change of view and felt that *the present supply of pure drinking water at Bishop Sutton is insufficient. Jesse Lovell and others proposed that Bristol Water Works undertake to supply water from their mains; Jesse Lovell and others are prepared to guarantee to the District Council that they will pay for the erection of a stand pipe in a convenient spot in Bishop Sutton. Minimum average supply of 200,000 gallons but no more.* This was the same Jesse Lovell who, as we shall see, had agreed to supply water to the school in July 1887 but had presumably not done so.

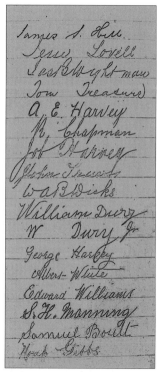

Villagers petitioning for water in 1901

Back to the school. In July 1900 the Board wrote to Mr Alexander: *in consequence of the confirmed scarcity of good drinking water at Bishop Sutton, and the great difficulty and inconvenience the Master has in obtaining from a distant neighbour a bucketful daily for the use of the School and School House, I am directed by my Board to ascertain if the Bristol Water Works Company would supply the Bishop Sutton School premises with water from their mains and, if so, what the possible costs?* Reply not known. 'Distant neighbour' was a touch of poetic licence on the Council's part, but the situation at the school was clearly dire nevertheless. Twenty years on, there was still a problem in the wider community, and the PC recorded in October 1921 that *Mr Moody brought forward the question of the scarcity of water in the village … and also the great number of unemployed who are unable to obtain work in the parish at the present time, and taking into consideration the government subsidy was of the opinion that this was an opportune time for carrying out the above work.* The unemployed were not to be so employed.

Nothing to do with the school and hardly anything to do with water, but in one of those occasional examples of wonderful Dad's-Army English eccentricity, the PC's January 1959 meeting was enlivened by Councillor D. G. Price's reassurance that *he had a siren available at his garage which could be sounded off to warn parishioners by a series of call signals that a service was being withdrawn: one signal for water, two for electricity etc. It was agreed to enquire from the local police whether such a warning would contravene any bye-laws.* The clerk noted at the May meeting that *the police confirmed that they would have no objection, but there were certain human characteristics which should be made known. The Parish Council decided not to proceed on this item.* Doug Price's siren remained unwailed.

So much for incoming water, what about the outgoing variety? Sewage was a particular challenge. The PC had formed a committee in the early 1890s to examine *the various properties which drain into the open ditch at Bishop Sutton … and decided that the best remedy would be for the owners to construct cesspits to receive their sewage. Notices to that effect were sent to the owners of the various properties viz[1] Messrs F. Spencer, H. Morgan, Jesse Lovell, Benjamin Wyatt, Wm Dix, Fras Weaver, Job Harvey, Isaac Mapstone, Mrs Harvey, the Royal Charity Trustees … The primary cause of complaint was pollution of the well on premises owned by Bristol Charity Trustees and occupied by H. Symonds.*

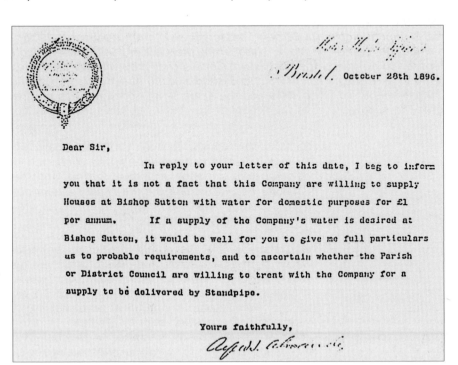

Letter from Bristol Water Works 1896

The 1891 census listed Mr 'Simmons' at 13 Cabbage Stump Lane (Church Lane), probably somewhere near The Colliers. The committee found that *all have done the best they could under the circumstances by disconnecting their privies from the stream and using bones and dry earth, but the drainage and slops still drain into the stream, which (in dry weather is very small) flows under their back yards and is covered in some places with loose flags and owing to the size of the yards which are only about 7' or 8' wide, it is impossible to construct cess pits. We suggest that the stream should be diverted to the other side of the road and thus give them room to construct pits.* That was in 1894 or thereabouts. In August 1898 the PC noted *a complaint respecting several alleged nuisances existing at Bishop Sutton through the closets belonging to G. Sheldon and the adjoining houses, James Harris and adjoining houses, William Elmes and adjoining houses emptying into the brook. Sanitary Inspectors to be called in.* The 1891 and 1901 censuses suggest that these were houses at the top of Sutton Hill Road near the Church Lane junction. The open ditch was the infamous one running down the western side of Sutton Hill Road and disgorging its reeking contents hither and thither, and particularly near the school. It was so awful (a) that children loved to play in it, and (b) that it will be looked into again later on.

----
[1] Latin abbreviation for 'videlicet', meaning 'namely'.

Street lighting has also been a bone of contention over the years. At the PC meeting in February 1964, headmaster and councillor Tom Price *successfully moved that the South West Electricity Board be invited to estimate the cost of a comprehensive lighting scheme to cover the Parish in readiness for the meeting next month ... it is expected that this will be the best attended Parish Annual Meeting for many years. Local opinion is known to be divided on the installation of street lighting. The outcome is unpredictable, for Bishop Sutton is in the commuter belt and the number of new residents nears the stage at which it can outnumber the native vote.* The native vote? Quite what came of that is anyone's guess, but in April 1969 *Somerset County Council refused the PC's request for the lighting of the main road through the village.* There are still many villagers who prefer the darkness and the clarity of the night skies.

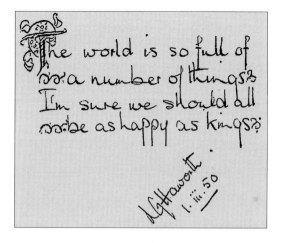

From Ann Saunders' autograph book 1950

Street naming was controversial too. But first, a bit of background. In his 1903 work 'From Collections for a Parochial History of Chew Magna', Frederick A. Wood researched some meanings. Bonhill comes from 'ban', meaning 'high land'. Denny is from the Old English 'denu', meaning 'valley' (hence 'dene'). Gold Cross, where four lanes meet, was probably originally marked by a gilt cross, possibly in the form of a crucifix. Stitchings Shord Lane is particularly pregnant with derivations. 'Shord' is a gap in a hedge or a field with no easy access from adjacent land. 'Stichen' or 'stitchen' comes from the Old English 'stiga', a pathway. That particular lane has, over the years, been Sti(t)chenshord, Sti(t)chenshort and, most commonly, Sti(t)chenham. Evvy Harvey's native vote turned it into something vaguely resembling Stchnshrrrd. Street names have changed over the years. Cabbage Stump Lane and Slap Arse Lane (either Bonhill Road, or the lane up to The Batch, depending on who you talk to) have sadly gone, but there have been other changes. At a PC meeting in February 1965 *it was unanimously agreed to recommend to the RDC that the estate behind Church Lane should be named High Mead Gardens.* In July 1966 Lakeside Close was re-named 'Rushgrove Gardens'. Councillors retreated in May 1968 from their *insistence that Rushgrove Gardens (a name chosen by the developers and favoured by the new residents) be re-named Blinlands Mead.* In December 1967 came the bizarre yet unanimous decision that *the name Church*

Road should remain and not be changed to Church Lane. Hands up, those villagers who abide by that decision of their democratically elected councillors.

And finally, from a newspaper report from March 1965:

Stowey Sutton PC believes that the names of new housing estates in the village should retain local links. At the March meeting, the Council received a letter from Clutton RDC in connection with the estate called Lake View on the development plan, asking if it would continue to be known by that name. "I understand the people who live there are now referring to it as St Helen's Close" said the clerk. "It appears that the builder gave it that name in memory of his wife, who died", said Lord Strachie. "It is a nice sentimental idea, but it has nothing to do with the village. Ideally, names should have some local connection", said the chairman Mr Douglas Price. Mrs A. R. Hanny said "we already have two Lake Views in the village". Lord Strachie: "It could be very confusing to have

Stowey Sutton
Estate names 'should keep local links'

another". When Mr L. Hammond suggested asking the residents of the estate which name they would like, Mrs Hanny said "we cannot possibly do that, it would get hopelessly complicated". It was unanimously agreed to adopt the chairman's suggestion and recommend the name Hillside Gardens.

PC meetings can be so exciting.

Pen-and-ink drawing of The Colliers c1885

CHAPTER TWO

THE LEGAL SIDE OF THINGS: FROM WORK TO SCHOOL

We're finally there. Well, almost. The school itself. But before skimming over the various Education Acts which, in one way or another, led to the school system we know today, we need a quick foray into the Factory Acts. In no small measure, it was these that enabled children to go to school and remain there for longer than a few years.

Parliament's first ever legislation in the field of work was The Factory Health and Morals Act of 1802. Covering cotton and woollen mills, it had absolutely no impact on Bishop Sutton but as it was passed less than two generations before the current school was built, it gives an insight into the social thinking of the time. The preamble and some of the provisions are just too good to be missed: *It hath of late become a practice in cotton and woollen mills … to employ a great number of male and female apprentices, and other persons, in the same building, in consequence of which certain regulations are now necessary to preserve the health and morals of such apprentices*. Gosh. Put male and female apprentices under the same roof, and there's no saying what will happen. The Act stated, in summary, that every apprentice was to be given two complete suits of clothing with appropriate underwear, stockings, hats and shoes, and that they must not work before 6 in the morning and after 9 at night and for more than 12 hours a day. Male and female apprentices were not to share the same room, and there were to be absolutely no more than two to a bed. On Sundays they were all to be instructed in the principles of the Christian religion, and all rooms in factories were to be lime-washed twice a year and ventilated.

Althorp's Factory Act of 1833 introduced two hours of compulsory schooling every day for children under the age of 9, but only in parishes with a school. This was the first time that children of all backgrounds in England and Wales[1] had (theoretical) access to education. Children from 9 to 13 could no longer work more than 42 hours a week and children from 13 to 16 an exhausting 69 hours a week. For the first time, inspectors were employed to enforce the laws.

----
[1] Most parishes in Scotland had had their own school since around 1700, paid for by a tax on landowners or by fees for parents who could afford them.

Then came the Mines and Collieries Act of 1842, the year in which Bishop Sutton School was being built. The Act banned all boys under 10 (and all women and girls) from working underground, and no-one under 15 was allowed to work winding gear. Safety guards had to be fitted to machines. On the other hand, the Act actually reduced the minimum age for working in factories to 8. But that was all right, as children of those tender years (and their pals up to the age of 13) were now prevented from working more than 6½ hours a day. Boys aged 13 to 16, and all women, could work up to 12 hours a day. The intention had also been for children under 8 to attend schools to be built out of the local Poor Law rates and for those aged 8 to 13 to receive a part-time education, but those elements were quickly scotched by Nonconformists incensed by the stipulations that the schoolmaster must be a member of the Church of England and that the school managers were to include the parson and two of his churchwardens. Interestingly, that's just how it would turn out at Bishop Sutton School.

As a quick aside, it's worth (a) looking at the evidence given to the Children's Employment Commission of 1842 by the agent for the Countess of Durham's Collieries, and (b) bearing in mind that by this time our school was in the throes of construction. The evidence from Durham included the following:

I believe that employing children in coal mines is perfectly consistent with good health. They earn good wages. Working on the night shift does no harm, the air and ventilation are the same at one period as at another. Have never heard of boys injuring themselves down pits from the nature of work, only by accidents. I do not think any change in hours of work is necessary for children. Would not object to a law preventing children from working before 10 years of age but would rather leave it to the manager to accept or refuse them. Any such law would be unfair on parents with large families. I do not think that working in the pit means that boys are incapable of having lessons after a day's work.

Six and a half hours underground, then a few hours of sums and grammar. Great.

There was to have been an 1843 Factory Act, but it failed on the back of religious dissent, the Nonconformists again objecting to headmasters having to be of the Church of England faith and children having to be taught the catechism and go to church on Sundays. But by 1844 the parliamentarians were eventually getting somewhere; perhaps they had read in the papers about the opening of Bishop Sutton School and been enthused by it. Graham's Factory Act of that year provided for all children from 8 to 13 to attend an approved elementary school for three hours a day, five days a week. The Factory Act of 1847 limited children under 18, and all females, to a 58-hour working week. After 1868 it was illegal to employ children under 8 in agricultural gangs. The Factory Act of 1874 made it illegal to employ children anywhere under the age of 9 unless it was on a part-time basis.

This was all good stuff, but it's questionable how effective it was. There were few inspectors, and fines were too low to have any real impact on employers. Few people had birth certificates, and parents who wanted their offspring to work would lie about the child's age. Mill and factory owners, farmers, magistrates and other influential people often didn't believe in the reforms and did their level best to obstruct them.

Of the children employed in Bishop Sutton in the 1840s, the majority would have been in agriculture. Many parents probably didn't see child labour as a bad thing if, indeed, they even thought about it. Reading and writing were not needed to lug straw around and dig potatoes. Furthermore, agricultural work – very dependent on the weather, on good harvests and on the price of produce – was precarious and badly paid. One wage per family was insufficient, and a farm labourer's wife and children generally had to work to supplement his meagre income. But Bishop Sutton may nevertheless have been ahead of the game: there is some evidence of a small infants' school (at the top of Church Lane) predating the building of the current school.

The Factories and Workshops Act of 1878 raised the minimum working age to 10 in non-textile factories and workshops, and gave birth to a 'half-time system' combining employment and education. This survived, with modifications, until the early years of the 20th century. Agriculture and domestic service were excluded. The system is immortalised in the song 'Poor Little Hauve Timer' by the Lancashire folk group The Oldham Tinkers:

> Where is our John, stood all forlorn,
> Who used to get up at break of morn,
> Spend 'alf a day working and 'alf on a form (a school bench),
> Poor little half timer!
>
> It ne'er did him good, sighing and sobbing.
> He stuck out his chest like little cock robin,
> But sitting in school, his head would keep nodding.
> Poor little half timer!
>
> He had no time to comb his locks,
> For looking around to find his socks.
> Under his arm, his breakfast box.
> Poor little half timer!

Educators, be they church or secular, had always laboured under the unfortunate fact that their mission did not enjoy popular appeal. There were many who were unconvinced of the advantage of schooling, especially if it had to be paid for, and even more especially if it was to be at the taxable expense of the rich. Education was commonly seen as a disturbing influence that bred discontent and dissidence. The revolutions that swept Europe from the late 1700s to the mid-1800s reinforced a widespread reluctance in England and Wales to educate the poor and the dispossessed. There remained an ingrained view that whilst education might civilise, it might also encourage the poor to question their station in life. Teaching pauper children to read, write, speak properly, dress neatly and wash now and again was to criticise them. Moreover, the poor often resented what they saw as interference.

In 1842 it was estimated that National Schools in Suffolk reached only 10% of the rural population, while nationally it was nearer 39%. It is likely that Somerset was similar to Suffolk. Bishop Sutton was lucky indeed: it had just gained a school. The Government's Newcastle Commission of 1861 revealed a deplorable state of affairs: fewer than half of Britain's children had been at school in 1858. In 1861 there were more than 11,000 parishes in England and Wales without any kind of educational facility. And Bishop Sutton wasn't even a parish, but merely a tything in the parish of Chew Magna. Thank goodness Chew Magna had had an enlightened vicar.

> **THE**
> **WORKMENS COMPENSATION**
> **ACT 1897**
> **NOTICE IS HEREBY GIVEN** THAT IN ALL CASES WHERE AN ACCIDENT MAY OCCUR TO ANY PERSON IN THE EMPLOY OF THIS COMPANY BY REASON OF HIS LEAVING HIS PROPER WORK AND BEING IN ANY PLACE OR INTERMEDDLING WITH ANY WORK MACHINE OR THING OTHER THAN THAT OR THOSE IN ABOUT OR FOR WHICH HE IS THEN EMPLOYED BY THIS COMPANY SUCH PERSON WILL BE DEBARRED FROM OBTAINING COMPENSATION UNDER THE ABOVE ACT
>
> BY ORDER
> HARTFORD WORKS   JNO WYNNE
> MAY 1899   SECRETARY

A more protective attitude towards children steadily began to challenge the earlier view of them as little adults. The age of consent in England and Wales was raised from 13 to 16 under The Criminal Law Amendment Act of 1885, and The National Society for the Prevention of Cruelty to Children (NSPCC) was founded in 1889. The restrictions imposed on child labour by the various Factory Acts brought an opportunity to educate children, but the central problem remained the need for their labour. Families needed the income and farmers needed the workers. As Norfolk Schools Inspector Rev. Beckett rather unchristianly put it, the farmers' great objection to education was that *the labourer would become capable of understanding his rights, and that instead of being a mere piece of machinery or a slave forgetting his sorrows and cares in the beer mug, he would start to think for himself and become independent, sober and respectable*. In other words, the poor should know their place. Furthermore, the Victorians' dominant laissez-faire theories meant that direct intervention by the State in the field of education was to be discouraged. The powers that be were generally quite happy to leave education – voluntary or otherwise – to the private sector.

Things did gradually begin to change. Illiteracy started to be viewed as a hindrance by factory owners who wanted to put up notices saying 'Work Harder'. Civil and church authorities found the increase in juvenile delinquency and moral destitution – not to mention drunkenness – disturbing. Benefit was seen in allowing at least a modicum of instruction.

Sunday Schools were the catalyst. Founded in 1780 by Robert Raikes in Gloucester, they soon spread to every corner of the land. Why? For six days a week children had been kept busy in the factory, the mill or the field, and on the Sabbath they were deplorably free to behave like the young hoodlums they were thought to be, so any scheme that would keep them usefully occupied and therefore under control met with almost unanimous approval. Especially by parents who welcomed a bit of peace and quiet of a Sunday morning. Sunday Schools quickly showed not only that universal education was possible, but also that it could act as a steadying influence rather than a disruptive one. The latter point was persuasive in helping to overcome prejudice in high places and, perhaps more importantly, Sunday Schools raised hopes of better prospects amongst the hitherto hopeless and helpless poor.

Sunday School medal (actual size) found buried in Joan Davidge's back garden in The Barton, Bishop Sutton. Apparently made of copper, it dates from 1930. The effigy is of Robert Raikes. The Welsh inscription reads 'A DAU CAN MLWYDDIANT GRUFFYDD JONES' (For two hundred years: Griffith Jones).

The foremost educational visionary was Joseph Lancaster who, in 1798 at the age of 20, opened a day school in Borough Road, Southwark, London. The inscription over the door was *All who will may send their children and have them educated freely*. The cost was negligible for those who could afford to pay, and free for those who couldn't. From an initial mere handful, the numbers on roll increased to 800 in six years. Lancaster emphasised that £200 a year would provide a sound education for a thousand children[1]. A penny a week a head. Such a businesslike figure couldn't fail to appeal, and public interest was quickly aroused.

----
[1]   1d x 52 weeks (less holidays) x 1000 at 240d to the £.

Lancaster's monitorial system, whereby the more advanced pupils taught the beginners, enabled one teacher to control almost any number of children by means of instruction by rote. Lancaster was received by King George III, who promised his patronage. This was presumably on a morning when His Royalness was not barking at the moon in the belief that he was a cocker spaniel. The Society for Promoting the Lancasterian System for the Education of the Poor was formed in 1808, and gained the support of prominent evangelical and nonconformist Christians such as William Wilberforce, the slavery abolitionist. In 1814 the Society was renamed the British and Foreign School Society, and throughout the 19th century set up 'British Schools' on non-sectarian principles. The Society is still in existence.

But hell hath no fury like the Church of England scorned. In 1811 it formed a powerful rival in the Church of England National Society, and the decisions of its inaugural meeting were uncompromising: *the National Religion should be made the foundation of National Education, and should be the first and chief thing taught to the poor, according to the excellent Liturgy and Catechism provided by our Church.* By offering grants on the sole condition that development was to be fostered along religious lines, the Society funded the construction, enlarging and equipping of school rooms, and was a driving force in most Church of England (and Church in Wales) schools, which became known simply as 'National Schools'. These were not necessarily grand: the common standard can be gauged by a contemporary estimate that *a room 35' by 21' will house 120 children.* The observations regarding religion and premises are illuminating when read in the context of the National Society's grant of £30 to Bishop Sutton's School in 1843 (about £2,300 in today's money).

The National Society never forgave Joseph Lancaster for being a Quaker. He was accused of plagiarism by the established church, having allegedly copied the ideas of the Rev. Andrew Bell, who hadn't actually founded a school at all. In the end, the maligned Lancaster had to leave the country, penniless, subsequently to meet a messy end under a Manhattan tram. Bell, on the other hand, became a prebendary of Westminster, had his portrait hung in Lambeth Palace and left a fortune of over £120,000. All was fair in Christianity.

We're getting ahead of ourselves again. Education reform was moving in tandem with social legislation. In 1807 Samuel Whitbread MP had proposed a new Poor Law on behalf of the country's 200,000 pauper children. That's not the interesting bit, unless you were a pauper child. The interesting bit is that the Law would provide every child aged 7 to 14 with two years' education, fee-based for those whose parents could afford it and paid for by the parish for those who couldn't. Whitbread thought that such schooling would reduce crime and pauperism. The measure received the half-hearted assent of the Commons but was summarily rejected by the Lords, where the Archbishop of Canterbury denounced it as leaving the parish clergy with too little control. It was furthermore seen as too expensive and likely to encourage people to question their social lot and shy away from manual work. Memories of guillotines in France were too recent for the upper classes to want to give their social inferiors any fancy ideas.

In 1833 independent radical MP John Roebuck (Member for Bath) stood up in the Commons to say that education would teach people how to be happy and that it would result in less violence, mischief and political unrest. He argued his case from the example of the 'most enlightened' countries in Europe, being France and Prussia (most of which was to become Germany), which had already accepted a 'happiness doctrine'. Roebuck took his reputation in both hands and moved *that this House proceed to devise a means for the universal and national education of the whole people*, urging that the State had a positive duty to all its subjects. Both sides of the House considered this notion utterly preposterous. The motion was withdrawn, but by way of consolation, Parliament did vote its first, historic, educational grant: a whole £20,000. This was in the year that MPs granted £50,000 to improve the Royal Stables. But large oaks from small acorns grew, and applications for financial aid were soon pouring in from the Church of England National Society and the British and Foreign Schools Society, each eager to claim their sixpennuth. In 1839 the Government appointed a Special Committee of the Privy Council (under secretary Dr Kay) to oversee the distribution of school grants. That committee paved the way for what would become the future Board of Education, one of whose first proposals was a training college for prospective teachers. Defying another howl of outrage from the Church of England, 22 voluntary training colleges had been established by 1845, so following the precedent set by Scotland and many continental countries. In 1846 a pension scheme for teachers came into being, and a training scheme for pupil teachers was introduced.

The money paid out by the Government in grants rose to over £100,000 a year by 1847 and to more than £900,000 in 1859, a truly huge sum. But it was still too little to meet the demand for new schools (or, in many areas, for any schools), and critics from across the political spectrum were becoming alarmed that education in England and Wales was falling yet further behind that of other nations. The Prussian system in particular was held up as a shining example.

Bishop Sutton c1960

In the second half of the 19th century, crime and pauperism were on the increase in Britain, as were riots, strikes and social unrest. Despite an Empire on which the sun never set, Britain's commercial and manufacturing supremacy was falling back, and the Government came to associate political stability and economic prosperity with education of the masses. Schooling was imperative if we were to keep up with the best. But reactionary change was also in the air. The forward-looking Dr Kay was replaced in 1859 by the dictatorial Robert Lowe, vice president of the newly formed Education Department. Mr Lowe's book 'Primary and Classical Education' had stated: *the lower classes ought to be educated to discharge the duties cast upon them. They should also be educated that they may appreciate and defer to a higher cultivation when they meet it, and the higher classes ought to be educated in a very different manner in order that they may exhibit to the lower classes that higher education to which, if it were shown to them, they would bow down.* In other words, one school for the cap-doffing poor, one for the superior rich, and ne'er the twain shall meet. Much of 'Authority' was constitutionally incapable of understanding the lower orders or of regarding them as anything other than a nuisance: the lower orders were what they were simply because they were undeserving and inferior in every way. Britain was an impossibly class-ridden society. With a few praiseworthy exceptions, the Victorian middle and upper classes had an almost mystical veneration for money and a disdain for those without any.

As a sop to those die-hards who preferred to see the children of the lumpen masses remain totally uneducated, Lowe set about making schools more efficient. Under his Revised Code, each pupil was subjected to a tough yearly examination conducted by Her Majesty's Inspectors. Whether or not the pupil earned a capitation grant for the school – payment by result – depended on performance and proficiency in the three Rs and, to a lesser extent, on attendance. For grant purposes, nothing else mattered: enterprising teachers might indulge in such flights of fancy as History or Music, but woe betide them if anything went wrong at the inspection because they'd frittered their scholars' time away. Within a few years Lowe managed to undo most of his predecessor's work, and by 1865 the total parliamentary grant to schools had dropped to £636,000. Criticism steadily grew; the system was modified in 1867 and abolished in 1904. But Lowe was quite unrepentant. He might not have made education better, but he had made it cheaper: *Those for whom this system is designed are the children of persons who are not able to pay for their teaching … we do not profess to give these children an education which will raise them above their station and business in life, that is not our object.*

The Reform Act of 1867 gave the vote to some 1,500,000 men of the 'upper' working-class (being male adult householders and male lodgers paying £10 a year for unfurnished rooms). Women were naturally excluded. The Government's worry was that the working class (whether upper or lower) was prone to socialist tendencies and was illiterate. This was a time when votes could be bought, and voters who couldn't read were more susceptible to being bribed. A lack of education was therefore endangering democracy.

In 1869 Lowe disappeared from the scene, and in 1870 William Edward Forster MP introduced his long-awaited bill that would put education on the English and Welsh map. But before we get too tinglingly excited, let's not forget that Bishop Sutton had had a primary school since the early 1840s. It had had a small infants' school for an unknown number of years before that. Schools in several local villages predated Bishop Sutton's. The Chew Valley was almost certainly better educated than the urban poor.

Mr Forster, vice president of the Education Department, stressed the need for action: *We must not delay. Upon the speedy provision of elementary education depends our industrial prosperity. If we leave our work-folk any longer unskilled, notwithstanding their strong sinews and determined energy, they will become over-matched in the competition of the world.* He went on: *Civilised communities are massing themselves together, each mass being measured by its force, and if we are to hold our position among the nations of the world, we must make up the smallness of our number by increasing the intellectual force of the individual.* William Gladstone himself opined that German successes in the Franco-Prussian War (which broke out in 1870) seemed, among much else, to award a marked triumph to the cause of systematic popular education. Mr Forster told Parliament that *our object is to complete the present voluntary system, to fill up gaps, sparing the public money where it can be done without, procuring as much as we can the assistance of the parents, and welcoming as much as we rightly can the co-operation and aid of those benevolent men who desire to assist their neighbours.*

A SCHOOL-BOARD PERPLEXITY.

Active Member (to Mother of numerous "Irregulars" and "Absentees"). "JOSEPH IS JUST TURNED THIRTEEN, AND THEREFORE 'CLEAR;' SIMON, YOU TELL US, IS SICKENING FOR THE MEASLES, AND MARY IS GONE INTO THE COUNTRY TO NURSE HER AUNT'S BABY. WHAT WILL YOU HAVE TO SAY RESPECTING PETER AND JAMES?"

Mother of "irregulars" and "Absentees". "PLEASE, SIR, THEY BE TWINS. CAN'T YOU ALLOW 'EM AS ONE, AND LET 'EM DO HALF A DAY EACH?"

Active Member is puzzled. Orders Mother to stand aside, and requests Clerk to refer to Mr. Forster's Act "for law bearing on point."

> *The perceived difficulties, as depicted by Punch in 1874, posed by the Education Act 1870*

The Act required the establishment of elementary (primary) schools nationwide, not to replace or duplicate those already there but to supplement those already being run by the churches, private individuals and guilds. These publicly administered schools were to be paid for partly out of the rates and partly out of taxation, and were to be governed by some 3,000 locally elected School Boards responsible for raising sufficient funds for maintenance. These schools would be called 'Board Schools', and in Chew Magna and Bishop Sutton that term replaced the earlier 'National School', to be replaced again after 1903 by 'Council School'. The Boards could charge a weekly fee not exceeding ninepence, and were empowered to pay the fees of the poorest children. The Government hedged on the question of compulsory attendance. It had to; there simply weren't enough places in schools. The Act left it to those School Boards that did have enough space – as appears to have been the case at Chew Magna and Bishop Sutton – to decide whether or not to employ Attendance Officers to force children to go to school from the ages of 5 to 11. The local Board did so decide. The headmaster at Chew Magna School, who clearly didn't have enough work to fill the day job, seized his opportunity in July 1878 and sent off his application. The Board asked the Education Department if *it will sanction the appointment of the schoolmaster as School Attendance Officer.* 'No', was the reply.

The attempt to keep everyone religiously content made the Act very cautious. A sop to the secularists was the clause that no religious catechism or religious formulary distinctive of any particular denomination should be taught in schools which receive rate aid. In essence, Religious Instruction was to become an integral part of the school curriculum but was not compulsory, and the curriculum was to be non-denominational. The Conscience Clause was introduced, enabling parents to withdraw their children from lessons on religion. A cleaner managed to lose the Conscience Clause at Bishop Sutton.

> **4. The term "Public Elementary School" is defined by the Elementary Education Act, 1870, sec. 7, which is as follows :—**
>
> " Every elementary school which is conducted in accordance with the following regulations shall be a public elementary school within the meaning of this Act; and every public elementary school shall be conducted in accordance with the following regulations (a copy of which regulations shall be conspicuously put up in every such school) ; namely,
>
> "(1.) It shall not be required, as a condition of any child ,being admitted into or continuing in the school, that he shall attend or abstain from attending any Sunday school or any place of religious worship, or that he shall attend any religious observance or any instruction in religious subjects in the school or elsewhere, from which observance or instruction he may be withdrawn by his parent, or that he shall, if withdrawn by his parent, attend the school on any day exclusively set apart for religious observance by the religious body to which his parent belongs :

The Conscience Clause

Overall, room for improvement, but even if the State was not able or minded to take over all the schools, it had made itself responsible for some. But children invariably still left at the age of 10 or thereabouts unless they were considered particularly bright or useful to the smooth running of the school or had parents whose pockets were deep enough to pay for further education. The Act was in force before Bishop Sutton School logbook was introduced, and there's therefore no knowing whether it was greeted with any local fanfares. But the red carpet was certainly rolled out a hundred years later. Headmaster Mr Price wrote in July 1970: *Open Day was held at school this afternoon and evening. A special exhibition was held to celebrate the centenary of the 1870 Education Act and which showed something of the history of the school and village over the past 100 years. Many people attended and the exhibition was extended to a second night to enable as many people as possible to visit.*

The 1870 Act didn't necessarily give England and Wales an educational service worthy of a world power. But further reforms did follow in reasonably quick succession, although change was incremental rather than far-reaching. Mundella's Elementary Education Act of 1880 made schooling compulsory up to the age of 10. The Elementary Education (School Attendance) Act of 1893 raised the formal leaving age to 11, and an 1899 Act raised it to 12. The Education Act of 1900 stipulated that no-one under the age of 14 could be employed without a certificate, although once children had reached the age of 12 they could generally work half-time provided they passed the Labour Exam (a basic competence test) or had notched up 300 school attendances in the previous five years. The Bishop Sutton records show that in July 1896 the Board made *a Special Note of the case of Thomas Bates who, on being summoned, was dismissed by the Magistrates because any child who has passed the 4th Standard and is 12 years of age has a right to claim as a half-timer, and the Magistrates state the Boy has the right to claim it whether the School Board grant a Labour Certificate or not*. In September 1908 the school managers noted that *several children are applying for half time and others just 13 are at home without an exemption certificate*.

The absence of real reform in the secondary sector meant that education in 1900 was generally only up to primary level. Britain was now lagging seriously behind France and Germany, where partial secondary education had been in place for many years. Compulsory attendance at primary level was nevertheless finally here to stay. The labourers of the future gradually became more literate and thus gained access to new ideas.

Then came what was arguably the best legislation of all: the Assisted Education Act of 1891, which made government grants available to all schools, thus enabling them to stop charging for basic elementary education. The 'school pence' disappeared. The dramatic effect at Bishop Sutton School will be examined later.

The Balfour Education Act of 1902 abolished School Boards and replaced them with school management committees overseen by statutory Local Education Authorities (LEAs) which would organise funding, employ teachers and allocate school places. The Act also provided for the funding of secondary schools out of local rates with the help of grants from central government. A scholarship scheme made it possible for clever children from poor backgrounds to attend secondary schools, although not for many years was there much evidence if its having changed the practice in Bishop Sutton whereby you left school at 14 (at the latest) unless your parents had the money to send you to a fee-charging establishment of further education.

With payment by results abolished, no more school pence, far more children at school and proper training in place for teachers, primary schools (still called 'elementary schools') were becoming brighter, happier places. The Code of Regulations for 1904 advised: *The purpose of the Public Elementary School is to form and strengthen the character and to develop the intelligence of the children entrusted to it, and to make the best use of the school years available in assisting both boys and girls, according to their different needs, to fit themselves, practically as well as intellectually, for the work of life*. Furthermore, *teachers should arouse in them a living interest in the ideals and achievements of mankind*. Nature walks were introduced, outdoor visits, school journeys, daily PE and organised games. When

King George III had asked Joseph Lancaster in 1808 how he could handle so many scholars at a time, he was told: *In the same way that Your Majesty's armies are governed, by the word of command.* That 'sit-still-stop-talking-hands-behind-your-head' discipline of frosty-faced schoolmarms and sergeant-major headmasters was a long time a-dying, but the 1904 Code did set a distinct change in educational tone, and pupil-teacher training centres attached to some secondary schools led to a gradual upgrading in instructional methods.

The physical condition of volunteers for the Boer War (1900 to 1902) and the Great War (1914 to 1918) was causing alarm in high places, with many politicians and militarists believing that it might ultimately lead to Britain's imperial downturn. It was felt that children's health would be improved if they remained longer at school, where teachers could keep an eye on them. The Minister of Education, Liberal MP Herbert Fisher, raised the standard leaving age to 14 in his Education Act of 1918. There was provision for this to be 15 at the discretion of local authorities, although that seemed not to have been applied in Somerset. Half-time schooling was abolished. The 1918 Act also allowed for medical inspection, nurseries and (very haphazardly) for pupils with special needs.

We were can-canning our way through the Roaring Twenties, and adopting a more modern outlook. The 1926 report 'The Education of the Adolescent' by Sir Henry Hadow (1859 to 1937) was the first to examine primary education in any detail. It prioritised activity and experience rather than rote learning (which, over the years, had resulted in a monotonous routine of repetitive chanting), and was radical in examining the specific needs of children with learning difficulties. The report also recommended limiting class sizes to a maximum of 30. In 1931 came his follow-up report 'The Primary School', influenced by the educational ideas of Swiss psychologist Jean Piaget (1896 to 1980) who had advocated a style of teaching based on children's interests. Note the official use of the word 'primary'. Hadow wanted schools to be divided as to infants (5 to 7), juniors (7 to 11) and seniors (11 to 14 or 15). The reports did not lead to many tangible improvements, but they did succeed in bringing primary education into the limelight.

The Education Act of 1936 set the scene for an increase in the school leaving age to 15 on Monday 4th September 1939, but the instigators of the Act could not have foreseen that Hitler would invade Poland the Friday before. The proposals had to be postponed. The war ensuing from Hitler's actions was to result in the destruction of one fifth of Britain's schools in air raids, including many in Bristol and Bath.

A Consultative Committee Report of December 1938 confirmed the policy of a clean break at 11, and pressed for three types of secondary school: Grammar, Modern and Technical High. The last two were to have workshops and laboratories, be in direct contact with the world of industry and commerce, and provide an education suitable for children of a practical rather than academic bent. Admission was to be via the same entrance exam as for grammar schools, the final allocations being made after an interview and after consulting the pupils' record cards. Needless to say, there was insufficient money for all the new buildings that would be required and, in any event, the war intervened. Many of Herbert Fisher's hopes from his 1918 Act would remain unrealised. Almost three quarters of children between the age of 11 and 14 in all-age schools (including, possibly, at Bishop Sutton) were receiving no advanced instruction, but merely a repetition of what they had already been taught below the age of 11. Almost a quarter contrived to leave school before they were 14. As few as 7% nationally managed to reach such grant-aided secondary schools as did exist. The number of young people going on to university was pitiful: fewer than eight students out of every 10,000 in the early 1930s, and of these only a fifth were girls. The comparative figures for France for that period were rather higher at some 11 students out of 10,000, and in Germany around 20.

With the 1870 'Primary Education for All' Act and the 1891 'No More School Pence' Act now a distant memory, the one that's nowadays affectionately regarded as the most far-thinking is Rab Butler's Education Act 1944. Conservative MP Richard Austin Butler ('Rab', or Baron Butler of Saffron Walden to his friends) was Minister of Education in Winston Churchill's coalition government of 1940. The Act reflected the conviction that education was of vital social and economic importance to both the nation and the individual. Broadly welcomed by MPs of all persuasions, the Act would supersede all previous educational legislation and, in the exalted tones of the time, *would be a measure of reform from which no person, young or old, should consider himself excluded*. LEAs were to have particular regard to provision *for pupils who have not attained the age of 5 years*. In other words, nursery schools for all. Parents were not to be compelled to send their children to such schools, but it was hoped that *most would avail themselves of the opportunities* and that *mothers would be persuaded of the advantages of nursery education*. The instigators of the Act envisaged pleasant, readily accessible centres situated in every village and housing estate so that mums could drop in for an informal cuppa and, if they wanted, lend a helping hand. It was stated in the Act - perhaps a tad patronisingly – that anterooms or annexes where parents could *meet and discuss their family problems and affairs and receive advice would be used to great advantage … many newly-weds are appallingly ignorant both before and after the happy event, and mothercraft and marital relations are not so sacrosanct as to be beyond the pale of further education*. Once you get over the 1940s English and the lack of 21st century political correctness, it's interesting to muse on just how much (or little) of that provision is in now place, well over 60 years later.

Bishop Sutton post office, 1950s

The Butler Act made scant reference to primary education itself, other than to state that class sizes were to be reduced to a maximum of 30 – an echo of the 1926 Hadow Report – although MPs refused to be drawn into any commitment on timing. In raising hardly any questions on primary schools, Parliament was taking primary education very much for granted and appeared little interested in it. French philosopher Jean-Jacques Rousseau (1712 to 1778) had philosophised that 'le plus dangereux intervalle de la vie humaine est celui de la naissance jusqu'à l'âge de douze ans'[1], but MPs seemed unconvinced.

The Butler Act formalised the proposals of the 1938 Consultative Committee Report for a tripartite system of free secondary education. This was the German format that the victorious Allies supported in 1945, and which was to contribute in no small measure to Germany's post-war Economic Miracle. Britain was to have three types of school: grammars for the more academic pupil, secondary moderns for the less academic, and technical schools for those who wanted a specialist practical education. Allocation would be by the 11-Plus exam. It was the responsibility of LEAs to see that these three types of secondary schools were made available and free to all. But the concept brought with it an air of unreality. Mr and Mrs Middle Class would probably have preferred Johnny to go to a grammar school where he could study French and Chemistry and wear smart blazers and play tennis with well-spoken children from Acacia Gardens, although Dad did harbour a sneaking suspicion that as Johnny was rather good at Meccano, he might be better off at a technical school. Mr and Mrs Upper Class retained the right to send Annabella to a private school, and Mr and Mrs Working Class often still had to be convinced of the merits of any sort of academic upbringing, so a secondary modern was their default expectation.

It was all pretty irrelevant anyway, as the country couldn't afford it. The technical schools that performed so well elsewhere in Europe were allowed to fall quietly by the wayside, leaving just the grammars and the secondary moderns, with children's future being largely dictated by an 11-Plus which proved contentious from the start. The school leaving age was to be raised to 15 without exception from 1 April 1945 and to 16 at an unspecified later date. The raising to 15 was postponed to April 1947 due to a shortage of teachers, and it wasn't until 1972 that the leaving age was increased to 16 (by Edward Heath's Conservative Government).

The Education Act of 1944 Act saw to it that religion would continue to play a large part in State schools, where the day had to begin with a single act of collective worship, albeit with provision for separate assemblies for Roman Catholics. Religious Instruction (RI) would follow a non-denominational syllabus agreed by representatives of the clergy, LEAs and teachers. Although parents could withdraw their children from RI if they wished, religious and spiritual values were still viewed as being of paramount importance. The decisions made in 1944 retain their impact today, when HM inspectors still gently berate schools without a single collective act of worship.

Last but not least, the Act also provided for milk and hot meals.

So far, so good. In theory. The full provisions of the Butler Act didn't quite make it to the Chew Valley (or to many other rural areas), where there would be no secondary school for many a long year, and where children would remain in 'all-age' schools until it was time to leave. Furthermore, for a working-class child to get to a grammar school was one thing – and generally a difficult thing for children from Bishop Sutton where there was little tradition of secondary education – but thriving there could be quite another. The slump of the 1930s had seen fewer working-class children in grammar schools (which were scholarship-based or fee-paying), as economic hardship had left their families less able to accept the places offered. A

----
[1] 'The most dangerous period of human life lies between birth and the age of twelve'. Rousseau went on to say: If the infant sprang in one bound from its mother's breast to the age of reason, the present type of education would be quite suitable, but its natural growth calls for quite a different training'.

further disincentive was the cost of uniforms. All this meant more places for middle-class children, whose parents had largely escaped the unemployment associated with the Depression and could more easily pay. The relative beneficiaries of the 1944 Act were the children of professionals and businessmen: denied the right to buy grammar school places, they won them instead by examination, and at no cost. It was calculated that by 1950 around 60% of the children of professionals and businessmen could expect to get to grammar school, compared with 10% of children from the 75% of the population who were considered to be working class. The position was worsened by the difficulties often encountered by working-class children in staying the pace: lack of privacy and a quiet room at home for homework, and relative scarcity in the grammar schools of their own peer group. It was even more challenging, of course, for working-class children to reach university. In Bishop Sutton, it was actually rare for anybody at all to reach university, regardless of their background: so rare that it merited a mention in the logbook. Former pupil Peter James graduated in June 1955, and headmaster Bailey wrote to him: *Hearty congratulations … .I do not know if we have ever had an old scholar of this school receive a University degree before, I expect in this you have made history and we are proud of you. Mrs Bailey joins with me in sending you all good wishes for the future.*

1944 was when fundamental changes could have been forced through Parliament. The country had come through a devastating war, it had entered the technical and atomic age with a vengeance, voters had high expectations and had given Labour a landslide victory in the expectation of social improvements. Why weren't private schools abolished? Why did the Government stick with 11 as representing the end of primary education? That age was more to do with administrative convenience and tradition than with the realities of children's development. There was to be no change nationally in 1944. There was no real change at Bishop Sutton until September 1947, when headmaster Mr Bailey *asked for an additional teacher so that a proper break can be made at 11+ and the Seniors then taught in two groups.*

1951 saw the introduction of single-subject 'General Certificate of Education' (GCE) qualifications – Ordinary ('O') Level and Advanced ('A') Level – to replace the earlier general School Leaving Certificate and Higher School Certificate. O-Levels were sat at 16, but generally only by pupils in grammar schools and private schools. A-Levels were for those in grammar schools who wished to stay on into the sixth form until the age of 18 and study three or four subjects in greater depth. In secondary modern schools the opportunity to take such exams was rarely available: in 1964 some 70% of children across the country were at secondary moderns and yet only 318 (!) of those children were put forward for A-Levels. In the '50s and early '60s most pupils left school with no formal qualifications whatsoever. Harold Wilson's Labour Government introduced the Certificate of Secondary Education (CSE) in 1965, which would stand alongside O-Levels and A-Levels and would provide a suitable goal for a wider ability range. The new examination was graded from 1 to 5, with 1 regarded as equivalent to O-Level grade C or above, and 4 being pitched at average attainment for the whole age group.

Comprehensive schooling had been introduced by a very few LEAs in the 1950s: in contrast to the tripartite system – in reality, the bipartite system – it was intended to suit pupils of all abilities. The Labour Party, which had always been lukewarm about selective education at 11-Plus, wanted to go much further, and in July 1965 Education Secretary Tony Crosland wrote Circular 10/65, which has been described as the most far-reaching piece of paper in the history of education. The circular did not order LEAs to go comprehensive but 'requested' them to do so. New government money for expanding and improving buildings was conditional thereon. The writing was on the wall for grammar schools, of which there were some 1,500 in the mid-'60s.

Then came the 1967 Plowden Report 'Children and their Primary Schools', compiled by the Central Advisory Council for Education (England) into Primary Education and named after the chair of the Council, Lady Bridget Plowden (1910 to 2000). It observed that new skills were needed in society: *the qualities needed in a modern economy extend far beyond skills such as accurate spelling and arithmetic … they include greater curiosity and adaptability, a high level of aspiration …. .* Parents were to be more involved in schools, and 'child-centred' education was to be the norm. Although later denounced by traditionalists as a symbol of Sixties permissiveness, the report paved the way for what is still seen as mainstream thinking in primary education. It argued, for example, in favour of giving extra resources and staff to schools in deprived areas, something now long accepted as part of government policy.

For those of you who assume it's always been around, the National Curriculum didn't exist until the Conservatives introduced it as part of their Education Reform Act of 1988. The National Literacy Strategy was introduced by Labour in 1997. Both initiatives were to try to address the increasingly strident concerns that education in England and Wales wasn't up to the standards achieved elsewhere in the world. Readers who've stuck with this chapter from the beginning will know that such concerns were first being raised at least 150 years ago!

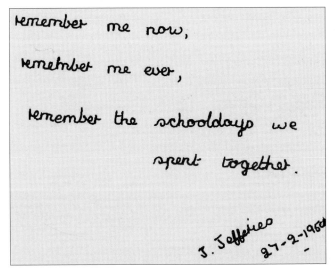

From Ann Saunders' autograph book 1950

CHAPTER THREE

THE BUILDINGS

> Warning: the next 15 pages or so ('Building the school', and 'Who owned
> what, when and why?') are heavy on detail and Old English. Feel free to
> skip to 'Overcrowding, flooding, and cement up to your knees' if it's more
> the light-hearted and scurrilous that you're after.

BUILDING THE SCHOOL

Hurrah. It's time to look at Bishop Sutton School itself.

Queen Victoria was on the throne, the British Empire was
burgeoning, missionaries were hell-bent on civilising darkest Africa,
universal penny postage had been invented and there was a
general air of enlightenment about the place. Children were no
longer going up chimneys and were rarely going down pits, and
education was very slowly being recognised as something of
benefit for the poor as well as the rich. Bishop Sutton was about to
get a proper school.

The earliest document to come to light – thank you, Church of
England Record Centre – is an application dated 28 August 1843 for financial
assistance towards building *a School House at Bishop Sutton for 100 boys and girls*.
A bit late, as the school may have already been built, but we'll come on to that
inconvenient detail. The application was signed by Edward Aislabie Ommaney (*Vicar
of Chew Magna cum Dundry and secretary to the Building Committee*). We shall
probably never know why he decided to build a school, but Bishop Sutton should be

Application dated 28 August 1843

forever grateful that he did. And 'Aislabie Ommaney' does have a very distinguished ring about it. Born at Mortlake, London, on 13 September 1806, he graduated from Exeter College, Oxford ('Exon Oxon') with a 3rd class BA Honours degree in 1827 and obtained his MA in 1831. Made a deacon in 1829, he was ordained vicar of Chew Magna in 1841, and was described in Kelly's Directory of 1861 as 'Lord of the Manor'. He died in Bath on 21 January 1884.

The Rev. Ommaney affirmed at the top of his application that the school had *not yet* [been] *united to the National Society*, to which it seems that the application was posted. He stated that the population of the catchment area of the proposed school was 900 in 1841 and went on to say: *It can scarcely be said that there exists any regular school in* [the] *district, there was a small Infant School of about 20 children which, being no longer supported, will be merged in the new school. No Sunday Church School.* (As will be seen, there was a Methodist Sunday School, but as the Rev. Ommaney was Church of England, he clearly chose to ignore it.) The vicar may also have exaggerated the catchment area: the 1841 census listed 733 people in the Bishop Sutton Tything.

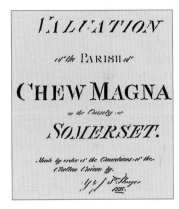

1838 Survey of Chew Magna

It wasn't easy tracking down the whereabouts of that 'small Infant School', and note anyway the vicar's use of the past tense 'was'. The 1838 Survey of Chew Magna eventually provided the key. A beautifully bound leather volume, painstakingly written in copperplate, the Survey listed the owners and occupiers of all the properties and plots in the parish, with areas, rentable values and rates charged. And, most pertinently, the plot numbers under the tithe apportionment system[1]. Listed against owner Robert Blinman Dowling[2] and occupier William Withy were 25 perches (756¼ square yards or some 690 square metres) at plot number 1467, described as 'Infant School'. Plot 1467 was at the triangle formed by the junction of Sutton Hill Road and the northern side of Church Lane and was shown on the map as the site of a building. That building – or at least part of it – was The Colliers' Arms which, according to the modern plaque on the cottages into which the pub was converted, was built in 1785. Was the infant school in a back room or in adjoining premises? By 'no longer supported', did the Rev. Ommaney mean that there were now too few parents sending their little tots there or, more likely, that the Church was no longer financing the school?

----

[1] Tithe apportionments had been prepared under the 1836 Tithe Act, which commuted most tithes in kind (e.g. so many bushels of corn to be given to the church) to fixed rent charges; for this purpose a large-scale map of each parish was drawn up and the apportionment for each plot of land assessed.

[2] Listed in Kelly's Directory of 1839 as a commissioner for the care and maintenance of public highways, he was also the manager of the Old Pit and therefore an important man in the parish. Furthermore, he owned Tithe plots 1468 ('Coal Works', being the Old Pit colliery behind The Colliers), 1469 (a large plot of land to the east of plot 1467 and stretching northwards in the direction of The Red Lion) and 1478 (the small triangular corner plot that still exists at the junction of the main road and the western side of Church Lane).

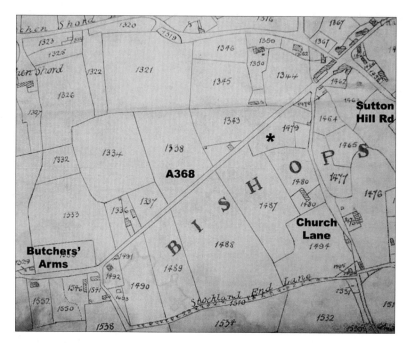

Sturge's Tithe Apportionment map 1840. Captions have been superimposed for ease of orientation. Plot 1479 (marked with an asterisk) is near the junction of the A368 and Church Lane.

There was one solitary school-related reference in the 1841 census of Bishop Sutton Tything. Maurice Batten (55 and 'independent') lived with his son Samuel (20, agricultural labourer) and daughter Martha at 'Wick' (Sutton Wick); the census enumerator was no more specific than that. Martha was 15 and was listed as 'school mistress'. The Batten family was possibly related to the building and plumbing Battens who did a lot of work for the school in the second half of the 20th century. Was Martha Batten in charge of the infant school? Was there perhaps another small school at Sutton Wick?

Who owned the land on which the new school was to be built? The plot in question was numbered 1479 on the Tithe Apportionment map, and extended eastwards to Church Lane. The only property on it (according to the map) was a building on Church Lane, now Plum Tree Cottage. The land was owned by Alderman Whitson's Charity and had been one of the plots sold a couple of decades before by Red Maids' School in Bristol. The following extract from 'Apparelled in Red, The History of the Red Maids' School' by Jean Vanes, reproduced by kind permission of Clare Anning of Red Maids' School, gives more background than we need here, but there's some deliciously detailed gore that deserves to be savoured:

The establishment of the [Red Maids'] school dates back to 16 September 1634 when the retiring mayor of Bristol, Matthew Warren, and the aldermen decided to set up a small committee … 'to consider of a meet woman with twelve young girles to be setled for a beginning in the new Hospitall of Mr Alderman Whitson's guifte' … John Whitson, founder of the hospital of Red Maids, was born at Clearwell in the Forest of Dean in around 1557. On 16 March 1622, nearing death, he enfeoffed all his lands and properties to a group of his trusted friends and 'their heirs and assigns for ever' … Having survived a stabbing on 7 November 1626, when he was sitting in Court to settle a dispute, and the knife passed through his nose and cheek into his mouth, he died of a fall from a horse on 25 February 1629, when 'his head pitched on a nail that stood on its head by a smith's shop'. From time to time, more lands were purchased, including around Bishop Sutton (possibly as early as 1708, and again in the 1790s) and extending towards the River Chew. The rents from these lands contributed towards the building of a new School for the Red Maids in 1656. By 1819 the Whitson Charity was amassing substantial monies from lands, including £549.11s.3½d from Dundry, Littleton and Chew Magna

'Chew Magna' would have included Bishop Sutton. Some of these lands were sold in the early 1840s. Two morals of this story: always enfeoff your land before you die, and don't fall off your horse outside a smithy.

The land on which the school was built was described in the 1838 Survey of Chew Magna as *house and orchard* occupied by William Sheppard. The plot measured 4 acres, 2 roods and 17 perches (some 4.6 acres), but only a fraction was used for the school: an 1844 Transfer Deed referred to *half an acre* consisting of an orchard. The July 1842 Rate Book for Chew Magna showed the site as still owned by the Charity and let to Mr Sheppard, with annual rates of 13 shillings. The adjacent plot to the south, numbered 1480, was owned by John Bally and occupied by *Isgar Walter and others*. The Tithe Apportionment map of 1840 shows what appears to be a row of cottages (or a long barn) at the southern end of plot 1480, which may have been or become Kennards Cottages. At some stage, at least part of the above land passed to the Mapstone family who were the owners around the turn of the century when the school wished to extend its territorial empire to the south. According to the 1842 Rate Book, Alderman Whitson's Charity also owned 8 ac 2 r 20 p of land somewhere in the vicinity, which they let to Benjamin Mapstone. That remained the case until at least July 1844, but between then and the next Rate Book of January 1845 the lessee changed to James King, who himself owned a considerable 21 ac 2 r 34 p of land somewhere in the village under the name of Barfoots. None of these Rate Books or, indeed, the Churchwarden's Accounts, mentioned the school at all.

By way of quick diversion, a fascinating entry in the Chew Magna Vestry Meeting[1] book for 2 August 1844 is worth repeating verbatim, although its relevance is mainly to the Church that would be built in 1848 next door to the school in Bishop Sutton.

At a vestry held on this day pursuant to Notices affixed on the Church and Chapel doors for the purpose of obtaining the consent of the inhabitants to the erection of a Chapel at Bishop Sutton ... moved by Mr R. Mullins and seconded by Mr R. Collins that in the opinion of this Vestry it is highly desirable that a District Church or Chapel be erected in Bishop Sutton to afford the inhabitants of that distant portion of the Parish better opportunity of attending Divine worship. The cost of the erection of such Church or Chapel to be defrayed by Voluntary Subscription ... Proposed by Mr A. Danger (? - handwriting open to interpretation) and seconded by the Rev. Mr G. Hutchins that a Burial Ground be attached to the Church or Chapel in order to prevent the expence (sic) and inconvenience incurred by the inhabitants of this District in bringing the dead for interment at Chew Magna and that the churchwardens be empowered to purchase out of the Church Rate sufficient portion of land adjoining the site of the proposed Chapel for the above purpose, [signed] *E. A. Ommaney, Chairman.*

As a further aside, in 1865 a Vestry meeting considered *the propriety of assisting persons to emigrate* – it was decided that no, they couldn't, not without a special rate having been set for that purpose – and resolved *that John Fear be the sexton of*

----
[1] Vestries were effectively the precursors to PC meetings and involved themselves in the setting of rates, the foisting of paupers onto other parishes and 'to consult on the other parish business'.

Bishop Sutton at a salary of £6 per annum. But of the building of Bishop Sutton School, nothing at all, despite the fact that its founding father was the Rev. Ommaney, the chairman of the Vestry members. Perhaps there are other records waiting to be discovered.

So back to the Rev. Ommaney's application form, which went on to state that the statutory space allowed for each child was 6 square feet and the 100 boys and girls were to be accommodated in one room to be used for 'daily school' as well as Sunday School. The fee was to be 1d per week, paid quarterly[1]. The estimated annual cost of the headteacher was £35, to be met *by subscription from myself and two or three other individuals amounting at present to £25.* The building was to be 34' long by 18' wide[2], 10' 5" high *to the wall plate* and 15' *to the collar beams.* It would have *a tie beam roof.* The initial description of materials to be used indicated that the foundations were to be *existing stone work.* The south wall was to be *taken down and rebuilt of rubble stone work – other walls existing.* The roof was *to be repaired – consisting of old work* (indecipherable word) *with collar beams and is to have platter* (indecipherable word) *ceiling* (indecipherable word) *to collar – beams in very dilapidated state.* That initial description in the application form had, however, been crossed out and revised notes were written on the reverse: *foundation – a course of thick slabs of sandstone, then lias; the floor – Baltic fir; walls – lias; roof – Baltic fir, slated, with lath and plaster inside.*

The school was to be for the *purpose of educating the Poor in the principles of the Established Church.* The total cost was calculated at £376.1s.10d including £20 for the land, £32.16s.6d for the architect, all legal expenses, labour and materials. Although the application incorporated the printed proviso that the cost of the School House must not be included in the estimate, the Rev. Ommaney explained that it could not be separated out as *no subscriptions* [had been] *given specially to the School House.* Of the required sum, £215 had been raised *by subscriptions,* nothing by *Collections after Sermon,* no donations, £120 *by borrowing from funds which ought to be applied to the building of the Chapel,* leaving a shortfall of £41.1s.10d.

The form – dated 28 August 1843 – confirmed that the building *has been conveyed to the following Trustees, viz the Vicar, Churchwardens and overseers of Chew Magna.* Yet the actual transfer deed was dated 23 January 1844.

The application was accompanied by a copy letter (also dated 28 August 1843): *Rev. Sir, In reply to your letter of August 17th* (which doesn't seem to have survived; this is a great pity as it could have provided useful background)*, I beg to return the papers properly filled up in regard to the School and School House at Bishop's Sutton in this parish. I must add that the bills are already paid by borrowing from the general fund subscribed towards the building of a Chapel in that district, but we hope to replace the sum borrowed in order to carry out that object as soon as possible.* The letter is signed *I am, Rev. Sir, your obedient servant E. A. Ommaney.* Worthy of note, perhaps, is that the church authorities decided that financing the school was more important than financing the church. The form and letter arrived at the National Society (or perhaps The Committee of Council on Education) on 29 August 1843. It was allocated case number 838, and the summarisers amended some of the details: they described the school as 'S & D'

----

[1] 1d per week paid quarterly amounted to around one shilling per school term. This was a considerable sum, and many parents would surely have paid weekly or even daily.

[2] This accords to the guideline from the very early 1800s for National Schools, which suggested 35' by 21' for 120 children, or 6¼ square feet per pupil

(whatever that meant) and increased the number of children to 102. They changed the estimated expenditure to £372.1s.10d, with the *probable grant from Committee of Council* to be '£51?' (the question mark appears on the document), leaving a *deficiency of £106.1s.10d*. The summarisers also highlighted a comment that *£120 more has been apportioned to the school but is borrowed from the Chapel building fund and must be repaid. No Church accommodation as yet provided. Wants the Bishop's signature.*

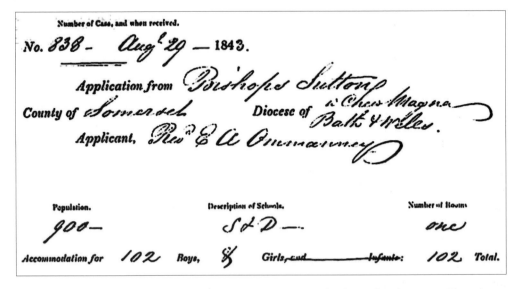

There was the further remark: *The school is already built.* Indeed it was. The plaque above the school door still proudly quotes 'mdcccxlii' (1842). The school was built using the remains of an existing building, as suggested in the application form and in the 1838 Survey of Chew Magna (which referred to 'house and orchard').

The back of the application form indicated that £30 cash was granted on 7 September 1843. 'Trustees' (unnamed) signed it as a 'draft deed' on behalf of the 'Committee'. There were to be at least two further versions of the form, allocated National Society case numbers 2/838 (22 September 1843) and 3/838 (7 October 1843).

Next in this rather confusing chronological sequence was a letter dated 21 September 1843 from E. A. Ommaney to the Secretary of the National Society:

Rev. Sir, I beg to acknowledge with many thanks the receipt of your's (sic) of the 12th announcing the intention of your Committee to grant the sum of £30 towards the Bishops Sutton (sic – no apostrophe) school in my parish, and I now forward the draft of the Deed of Conveyance for your approval; unfortunately I cannot accept your suggestions (and there's no record of what they were!),
as the Charity trustees are only authorized by their Act to convey land to the parties therein mentioned, but I think that every precaution has been taken to insure (sic) the carrying on of the School under the direction of the Clergy, and for the maintenance of the principles of the Church. The Deed of Conveyance has been already signed by 19 out of the 21 Trustees so that it would be difficult to effect any alterations in it now. The Committee of Council on Education have, as you will see, approved of the Deed, but I fear their object is rather to please all

parties than to give sound Education in the principles of the Church of England[1]. Please to return the Draft as soon as you can. I remain Rev. Sir Your obedient servant E. A. Ommaney.

A 'Form of Certificate' dated 5 October 1843 was drawn up by the Rev. Ommaney:

Grant to the school at Bishops Sutton £30 voted 7 September 1843. We the undersigned promoters of the school at Bishops Sutton in union with the National Society hereby certify: 1st, that the new schoolhouse in aid of which the National Society was pleased to grant £30 is completed in a satisfactory and workmanlike manner, being built of the proper dimensions and in all respects according to the statement forwarded to the Society. 2nd, that the amount of private subscriptions has been received, expended and accounted for; and that there does not remain any debt, charge or claim of any kind, except what will be liquidated by the grant made by the National Society, the payment of which is now prayed for. 3rd, that the site of the Schoolhouse has been conveyed with a good legal tenure and has been duly conveyed to the Trustees, and the deed enrolled in Chancery so as to secure the building for the purpose of educating the children of the poor according to the principles of the National Society. 4th, that a draft of the Trust Deed has been submitted to the Society, and that no change has been made since it was approved. In testimony whereof we affix our signatures and request the payment of the sum appropriated to the School at Bishops Sutton aforesaid. Chew Magna, Bristol October 5th 1843. [signed] E. A. Ommaney, Vicar.

£30 is granted towards the building of the school, 1843

----
[1] We've already seen that the National Society was established on the premise t*hat the National Religion should be made the foundation of National Education, and should be the first and chief thing taught to the poor, according to the excellent Liturgy and Catechism provided by our Church.* The Transfer Deed of 1844 – see later – would seem to echo that premise, so it's difficult to see where the vicar's concerns lay.

Accompanying the certificate was a copy letter written by the vicar on 5 October 1843:

Rev. Sir, I herewith forward the usual application for the grant voted to the Bishop's Sutton school by your Society and thank you much (sic) for your kind aid. As my curate is now absent, my name is the only one appended to the certificate and if it is informal (sic), pray return it. With regard to the draft of the Conveyance of the land, I quite agree with your remarks that it might have been better drawn to meet our views[1], but the Bristol Corporation[2] from whom the land was purchased bound me to use this form. I have the honour to be Yours faithfully, E. A. Ommaney.

Part of the Trust Deed of January 1844

Nothing then until the Trust Deed of 23 January 1844:

We Richard Smith (plus some 20 other gentlemen) all now or late of the City of Bristol Trustees appointed by an Order of the Lord High Chancellor of Great Britain bearing date the nineteenth day of October one thousand eight hundred and thirty six in pursuance of the provisions of a certain Act of Parliament passed in the fifth and sixth years of the reign of His late Majesty King William the Fourth intitulo, an Act to provide for the regulation of Municipal Corporations in England and Wales of the estates and property of a certain Charity called The Red Maids School or Alderman Whitson's Charity under the authority of an Act passed in the fifth year of the reign of Her Majesty Queen Victoria intitula, an Act for affording further

----

[1] This concern would seem to refer back to the comments that the vicar had made in his letter of 21 September 1843.

[2] Synonymous, for these purposes, with Alderman Whitson's Charity.

facilities for the conveyance of sites for schools (cont'd)

Roughly translated: We are lots of people who were appointed in October 1836 as trustees of various things, including the Red Maids' School or Alderman Whitson's Charity.

(cont'd) *and so far as we lawfully can or may, do hereby in consideration of the sum of forty pounds to us paid, grant, authorise and convey to the Reverend Edward Aislabie Ommaney clerk vicar of Chew Magna with Dundry annexed in the County of Somerset and Richard Mullins Gentleman Daniel Fevier churchwardens of the said parish of Chew Magna and William Morris carpenter George Sage yeoman William Thomas carpenter and Robert Baber yeoman overseers of the said parish of Chew Magna all that piece or parcel of ground containing by measurement half an acre situate at Bishop Sutton in the parish of Chew Magna aforesaid being to southwest and or part of a certain orchard now in the occupation of Mr William Sheppard and numbered (with other premises) 1479 on the map accompanying the apportionment of the rent change in lieu of the tithes of the said parish of Chew Magna which said premises are delineated in the map shown in the margin hereof* (cont'd)*

Roughly translated: In exchange for £40, we will convey all our rights to half an acre of land in Bishop Sutton to various people jointly. The land consists of part of a site (including an orchard) currently occupied by William Sheppard and numbered 1479 on the tithe map.

(cont'd) *and all our right title and interest to and in the same and every part thereof to hold unto and to the use of the said Edward Aislabie Ommaney* (etc) *and their successors for the purposes of the said Act and to be applied as a site for a school for poor persons of and in the Tything of Bishop Sutton in the said Parish of Chew Magna and for the residence of the School Master of the said School and for no other purpose whatever the said school to be under the general management and control of the said Parish of Chew Magna and their successors and to be at all times open to the Inspector or Inspectors for the time being appointed by Her Majesty in Council in conformity to the Order in Council of the tenth day of August one thousand eight hundred and forty,* (cont'd)

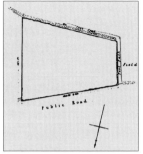

'The map in the margin hereof': small, barely legible and rather pointless

Roughly translated: These people and their legal successors are to use the site for a school for poor people in Bishop Sutton and for a School House for the headteacher, and for no other purpose. The school is to be managed and controlled by Chew Magna Parish, and can be inspected at any time by Her Majesty's inspectors.

(cont'd) *and it is hereby declared that the Instruction at the said School shall comprise the following Branches of School Learning, namely Reading, Writing and Arithmetic, also Geography, Scripture, History and (in the case of girls) Needlework* (cont'd)

Self explanatory.

(cont'd) *and it is hereby further declared that it shall be a fundamental regulation and practice of the said School that the Bible be daily read therein by the children and that all children in the said school shall be educated therein in the principles of the Christian religion according to the doctrines and discipline of the United Church of England and Ireland. The said education to be under the superintendance and direction of the said Minister and churchwardens,* (cont'd)

Roughly translated: It is absolutely crucial that the children must read the Bible at school every day and be taught the principles of the Christian religion as laid down by the Church of England

(cont'd) *and each of the said parties hereto of the first part doth hereby for himself his heirs exors and admors only, but not for the others or other of the said parties hereto of the first part or the acts deeds and defaults of the others or other of them but for his own acts deeds and defaults only covenant promise and agree to and with the said Minister Churchwardens and Overseers that they the said parties hereto of the first part have not nor hath any or either of them done or executed or been party or privy to any act deed matter or thing whatsoever whereby or by reason or means whereof the said premises hereby assured or any part thereof are is can or shall or may be impeached charged incumbered or prejudicially affected in title estate or otherwise howsoever* (cont'd).

Very roughly translated: Everyone who has signed this document confirms that he has the legal ability to do so, that there is no reason why he cannot do what the document expects him to do, and that he is not gaga.

(cont'd) *In witness whereof the said parties hereto of the first part have hereunto set their hands and seals the twenty third day of January in the year of our Lord one thousand eight hundred and forty four, Richard Smith (plus his 18 acquaintances). Signed sealed and delivered by the above in the presence of M. Brittan Solicitor Bristol, S. J. Mancher Secretary to the Bristol Charity Trustees. And be it remembered that on the eighth day of July in the year of our Lord 1844 the aforesaid James Cunningham came before our said Lady the Queen in her Chancery and acknowledged the Deed aforesaid and all and every thing therein contained and specified in form above written and also the Deed aforesaid was stamped according to the tenor of the statutes made for that purpose – enrolled the ninth day of July in the year of our Lord one thousand eight hundred and forty four.*

Roughly translated: Many people signed it on 23 January 1844 and had it witnessed. On 8 July 1844 James Cunningham went to London to see the Queen in her chancery – that was probably a bit of poetic licence on the part of the draftsman – and it was registered and made legal on 9 July 1844. The Trust Deed had been born.

This all begs a few questions: Nothing was shown on maps, so what exactly was the house already on the site? Did the school only take in the poor, as stipulated in the Transfer Deed and, if so, where were the non-poor to be educated? When did the school stop insisting that the children read their Bible daily? On which day did the school actually open for business, who was the headteacher, and how many pupils were there?

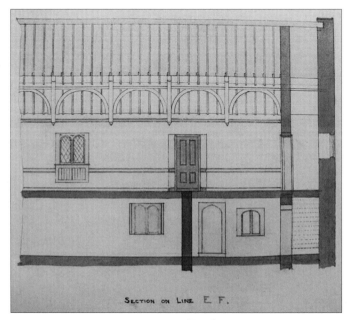

Section on Line E F.

From an 1878 plan

WHO OWNED WHAT, WHY AND WHEN?

In the Chew Magna parish archives are the minutes of the meeting held in the Vestry Room on 13 June 1873 to *consider a Notice received from the Education Department respecting the condition of the Schools in this Parish and to adopt measures for supplying the deficiencies in School accommodation*. The chairman of the meeting was the Rev. M. A. L. Simmons. It was decided *that the Parishioners in Vestry having heard read the requirements of the Elementary Education Department under the Act of 1870, elect to carry out the requirements and to conduct the Schools under the Voluntary principle rather than under the School Board System and compulsory rate. Carried unanimously.* The minutes were written on a scrappy piece of paper, but a passable copy is shown on the next page.

What does the Vestry decision mean? It covered both Chew Magna and Bishop Sutton but, staying with the latter, it suggested that as the school built by the Church in 1842 and financed by voluntary subscription as per the August 1843 application for a grant and run by Church overseers was doing very nicely as it was, there was no need to take up the provisions in the 1870 Education Act for an elected School Board and for financing via compulsory rates. What were the reasons for this decision? One might have been that under the Trust Deed that founded Bishop Sutton School, *it shall be a fundamental regulation and practice of the said school* [that] *the Bible be daily read therein by the children*. This was stricter than stipulated in the 1870 Act and thus gave the desired degree of local control to the vicar. The assembled gathering *resolved that a Committee be formed for the purpose of carrying out the foregoing resolution and it consist of the following gentlemen … .* The fact that there were 61 of them, any five of whom could form a quorum, gave ample opportunity to skip meetings. The 61 represented what must have been all of the great and good of Bishop Sutton and Chew Magna, and included such luminaries as the Rev. Ommaney, the Rev. Simmons, the Rev. Orr, George Arter, Jesse Lovell, Thomas Dowling, Isaac Mapstone, Strachey Senior Edward Bart., Henry Strachey and Thomas Hardy (presumably not the Thomas Hardy). Uncle Tom Cobleigh was left out. In the scarcely conceivable event that this vast multitude should prove insufficient, they granted themselves *the power to add to their number.* George Arter would act as Honorary Secretary.

It wasn't to be long before the esteemed gentlemen changed their minds about this subscription malarkey, and two years later decided that the Education Act provisions of 1870 to elect a School Board, charge fees and receive money from the rates did have their advantages after all and would be adopted.

In January 1875 a Mr Wilkinson (probably representing the vicar and churchwardens of Chew Magna, in whose name the premises vested) attended a meeting of the school managers *and offered to grant a long lease of the Bishop Sutton School House and premises at a yearly rent of £6 for five days a week from 6 am to 6 pm.* The managers could not *give so large a rent as £6 p.a., but will be willing to take a transfer of the School House and premises at Bishop Sutton for a term of 50 years at a rent of £2.10s.0d p.a., the Board paying all rates and taxes and keeping the premises in repair and insured against fire … . Mr W accepts the terms offered, but suggests that term be 21 years not 50. Clerk was directed to reply, must be for 50 years.* The Board then explained the position to the Department of Education in Whitehall.

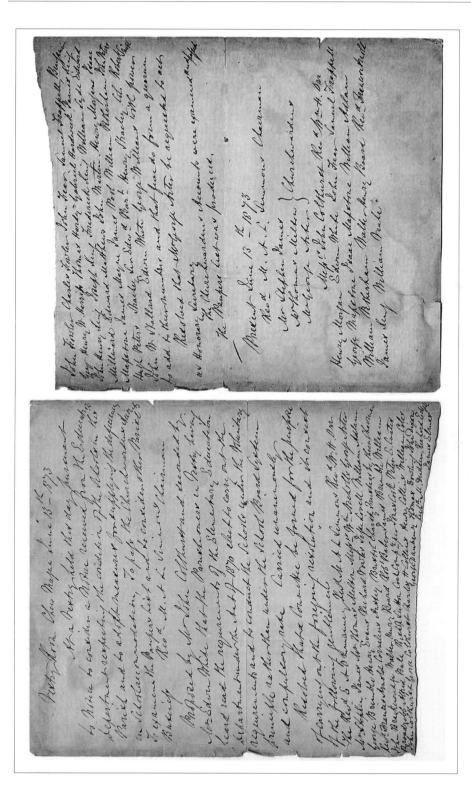

Minutes of Vestry Room meeting on 13 June 1873

But how strange. George Arter and the Rev. Ommaney (and possibly others as well) were members of the School Board and had been named on the Trust Deed. You'd think they'd have remembered that the buildings were vested in the vicar who, after all, was Edward Aislabie himself. Anyway, *Messrs Brittan and Sons of Bristol* [were] *requested to act as solicitors to the Board in obtaining a transfer of the schools and leases of the school buildings*. This transfer document would become the Memorandum of Arrangement. So what was it?

Extracting the unconscionably high number of wherefores and wherebys and one parts and second parts, the content can be loosely summarised as follows: various important people, including the vicar and managers of the Bishop Sutton National School, resolved that the school should fall within the provisions of the 1870 Education Act. The document referred back to the Deed of 23 January 1844 which had transferred the half acre to the vicar and churchwardens of Chew Magna. But the Deed hadn't provided for a subsequent transfer to anyone else, so at a meeting in March 1875 *all the annual subscribers to the School* agreed to a retrospective transfer of the school from the vicar and the churchwardens to the Board. This transfer was sanctioned by the Education Department on 30 June 1875, and would be backdated to 29 October 1874. Quite where that date came from is lost in the mists of paperwork. On 10 July 1875 the Board's seal was well and truly affixed, and the Rev. Ommaney and friends would no longer have to dig deep into the pockets of their cassocks to fund the school. All this happened only two years after a Chew Magna Vestry meeting had decided unanimously that it wanted nothing to do with a School Board.

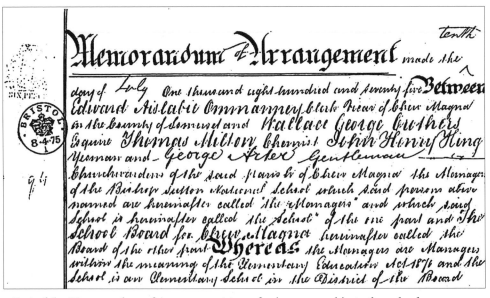

Part of the Memorandum of Arrangement transferring ownership to the school managers, July 1875

There were conditions attached. The Board only had the right to occupy the school for 30 years – not 50 years – from 29 October 1874 *from 6 o'clock in the morning to 6 o'clock in the evening on every day of the week except on Saturday and Sunday, Christmas Day, Ash Wednesday, Good Friday and Ascension Day*. If the school was to be used outside those hours, then it had to be left in good order. The schoolmaster's house was available to the Board for 24 hours a day. The Board had to pay rates and taxes, and had to keep the buildings insured against fire *in the sum of £500 at least*.

The Board presented the clerk *with a gratuity of £5 in consequence of the extra work thrown upon him* during the weeks leading up to the Agreement. That fiver had been well deserved. There had been acrimonious to-ings and fro-ings, culminating in a comment in the managers' minute books in February 1875: *The Board is not aware of any special reason, or in fact, of any reason at all, why a rent of 50/- (£2.10s.0d) should be paid … . The matter has been discussed on various occasions and it was only after much hesitation that the Board agreed to the request of Mr Ommanie (sic) (who was supposed to be the sole trustee of the property) or his representative that a rent should be paid if the Education Department would sanction it, which always appeared to be doubtful.* There were disagreements between the Board members, some of whom had been members of the old school management committee. Also in February 1975, Mr Nickolls (a member of that committee) had written to solicitors M. Brittan and Sons: *I return all the papers you sent me this morning. I have determined personally to take no further part except as a member of the School Board; all communications therefore please address to the clerk of the Board, W. W. H. White … . You must get Mr Ommaney or someone else to take the necessary action for the managers, but it strikes me that the managers have no power to let the school buildings, they do not belong to them, but to the vicar, churchwardens and overseers under the Trust Deed. The Board is willing to pay a rent of 50/- a year at Bishop Sutton as there is a teacher's residence there.*

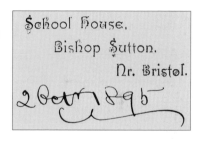

In December 1898 it was decided that a proper infants' room was needed, but this entailed sorting out the lease. The Board wrote to the Education Department with a question: *The school premises were leased to the School Board from 10 July 1875 by the Vicar and Churchwardens as Managers. The Vicar and one Churchwarden died some years since, and another has left the neighbourhood. Now only two of the original Managers remain in the parish. In the event of the School Board finding it possible to provide the increased accommodation by enlarging the present school and requiring an extension of the existing lease, who would be the legal party to treat with for the same, the surviving three Managers named in the agreement of 10 July 1875 or the present Vicar and Churchwardens as trustees?* The Education Department was content with the second option and the Board resolved in January 1899 *to retransfer the premises under Section 24 of the Elementary Education Act 1870*[1] *to the School Managers under the Trust Deed dated 23 January 1844, viz the Minister and Churchwardens of the Chew Magna Parish.* The trustees played ball and wrote to the Board: *We, the undersigned, being the trustees under a Trust Deed bearing date the 23 January 1844 of the site of Bishop Sutton School … do hereby*

----
[1] Section 24 stipulated *that where any school or any interest therein has been transferred by the managers thereof to the school board … in pursuance of this Act, the school board … may, by a resolution passed as hereinafter mentioned, and with the consent of the Education Department, re-transfer such school or such interest therein to a body of managers qualified to hold the same under the trusts of the school as they existed before such transfer to the school board, and upon such re-transfer may convey all the interest in the schoolhouse and in any endowment belonging to the school vested in the school board.*

consent to the building of an addition to the said school premises ... for the purpose of increased school accommodation ... and further, in view of this additional building, we hereby consent to the extension for the term of 30 years beginning from the date of the new lease on the same conditions as those of the present lease ... which will terminate on 9 October 1904. The Board met on 5 February 1900 to affix its seal and to be told that *disinfectants are being freely used in and about the offices* (toilets).

The Red Lion c1960

Preliminary negotiations as to how the lease could best be renewed in 1904 had coincided with the passing of the Balfour Education Act of 1902 which abolished School Boards and replaced them by LEAs and local school management committees. In 1903, the new school managers for Bishop Sutton attempted to summarise the background, but managed merely to add murk to a continuing lack of clarity.

On the 10th day of July 1875 it (the master's house and the 'old portion' of the existing building) *was transferred to the Chew Magna School Board in pursuance of Sec. 23 of the Elementary Education Act 1870 and was transferred to the Managers on the 5th day of February 1900[1], but is still under the control of the Board.* [The] *Form of Transfer dated February 5 1900 says the Board shall during 30 years from the 5th February 1900 have the exclusive use at all times of every teacher's residence forming part of the School House and also the exclusive use of the rest of the School House on every week day from 6 o'clock in the morning until 6 o'clock in the evening on every day of the week except for Saturday, Sunday, Christmas Day, Ash Wednesday, Good Friday and Ascension Day. Provided always that the Board may also have the exclusive use of the rest of the School House for the purpose of an evening School during any two evenings in the week as the Board may from time to time*

----

[1] The actual transfer to the School Board had been in October 1874; it was on 5 February 1900 that the premises were transferred to the school managers, thus pre-empting the 1902 Act. It is uncertain whether what had previously been described as 'school premises' actually included the school house; a split of ownership is alluded to in an Elementary School Return of 1903, illustrated later.

select except as hereinbefore mentioned. The School was enlarged by the Board in 1876 and again in 1901 when a piece of the adjoining land was purchased and added to the premises.

The lease was extended to 1934. There is no mention of anything having actually been done in 1934, which may explain the subsequent uncertainties and disagreements about who owned what and who leased what and from whom. This uncertainty was to impact in later years on the school's freedom of expansion. The managers noted in July 1949 that *the headmaster would like the matter* (renewal of the lease) *to be treated as most urgent; it was imperative that there should be more accommodation when the school resumes in September.* The managers and the headmaster wrote to Taunton asking them *to come to terms with the trustees as the negotiations had become unduly prolonged.* It's not known how that issue was resolved, but it was, as there were subsequent extensions over the coming decades.

It's at this point that one mystery can be solved. Subsequent generations of highly paid legal advisers have been unable to track down the original 1844 Trust Deed. I can verily confirm, from the Board's very own minute book, that the Board sent it on 15 March 1875 to Messrs Brittan and Sons of Albion Chambers, off Broad Street in Bristol. A Solicitors' List shows Brittan Harley & Duval as practising in 1943 at 19 Orchard Street in Bristol. The firm mutated, via a convoluted partner route, into the present-day firm of Meade King & Co. of 20-24 Orchard Street. It was with a Mr E. Meade King that the school managers conferred in 1899 regarding the purchase of more land. The Trust Deed might still be festering on a dusty shelf at 20-24 Orchard Street.

OVERCROWDING, FLOODING, AND CEMENT UP TO YOUR KNEES

Welcome to an unguided and somewhat haphazard virtual walk round the school premises through the ages.

Primary education in Bishop Sutton had proved such a hit in its first thirty years that talk turned in the 1870s to whether a replacement building was needed. In late 1874, just after the backdated start date for the 30-year lease in favour of the School Board, Sir Edward Strachey Bart. was en vacances at the Hôtel Louvre et Paix in Marseilles. We know that because the Board wrote to him there on 9 November on what seems to have been the subject of a new school: *Sir Edward, I have today received your letter of the 5th inst[1] to the School Board. Col Strachey* (Edward father) *had before written me an almost similar letter. It seemed to be the feeling of the Board that as the great majority of the children come from Bishop Sutton and a large number from the other side of the present school, it would not be desirable if new schools are built to move them much nearer Stowey than they are at present.* What the previous correspondence said is anyone's guess, but it might be relevant that the Strachey family home at Sutton Court lay closer to Stowey (which had its own school) than to Bishop Sutton. Stowey lies to the east of its larger neighbour so, by 'the other side of the present school', the Board must have meant the western side. The plural word 'schools' was often used to refer to the infant section and the junior section, whereas nowadays we would use the singular.

----

[1] For anyone not versed in Latin abbreviations, 'inst' (short for 'instant' which, OK, isn't actually Latin) means this month. 'Ult' (ultimo) means 'last month', and 'prox' (proximo) means 'next month'. Still encountered on stuffy legal letters from time to time.

Quite what resulted – if anything – from the letter of the sunbathing Sir Edward is unknown, but on 16 November 1874 the Board wrote to the Secretary of the Charity Trustee Office, 14 Queen Square, Bristol, pointing out that *Bishop Sutton School House and Buildings will, in order to satisfy the requirements of the Education Act, require a large outlay and in fact it can scarcely in any way be well fitted for school purposes. It has consequently become a question to the Board whether a fresh site could be obtained … . The Board considers that a portion of the Garden belonging to the Charity Trustees and rented by Mr Sheppard and adjoining the churchyard would, if a site is required and the land could be obtained, be a good one. Could the land be obtained, and on what terms?* This would be part of Tithe Apportionment plot 1479, referred to earlier.

All this talk of a new school, or of extending the existing one, had come about as a result of overcrowding, which was to become a perennial thorn in the flesh of the school managers and the headteachers. We can surmise that the Board perhaps didn't mean a 'fresh site' as such, but rather the acquisition of adjoining land. Be that as it may, in January 1875 the Board resolved *to make enquiries as to a fitting architect to plan and arrange the necessary alterations to the Bishop Sutton School House*. They wrote to Stuart Coleman of Clare Street in Bristol, asking him *to furnish plans for the additional buildings required by the Education Department; these costs, if possible, not to exceed £400.* The architect did as he was asked and the Board put the plans out to tender. Messrs Cowlin & Son of Bristol was the only firm eager for the work, but their quote was staggeringly high. The Board wrote to the Department: *only one tender received, £1,239, more than double in excess of what it was anticipated the work would cost … It is presumed that the near approach of winter has deterred builders from offering tenders*. The Board would postpone seeking any further tenders until the following spring, but reassured the Department that *the interests of the children will in no way suffer during the winter months*.

Keen to get cracking, the Board applied in December 1875 for a loan of £600 from the Public Works Loan Commissioners, 3 Bank Buildings, London EC, payable in one instalment. (Interestingly, when Chew Magna had wanted to build a new school in their village in March 1881, 116 ratepayers protested *against the recent resolution of the School Board to purchase land sufficient to build a complete set of new schools and schoolmaster's house. We are in this matter decidedly opposed to the imposition of any additional burden on the Rates of this Parish*. Victorian Chew Magnans' social conscience wasn't well developed: it was in that village that property owners had campaigned against a public water supply on the grounds that they would have to pay for it.)

Come February 1876, and the Board wrote to Mr Coleman asking for revised plans. They chased ten days later: *I have been daily expecting to hear from you and shall be glad to do so.* The blunt style of writing was typical of its day. The next chaser, a week later, was even blunter: *May I beg to hear from you at once?* The plans did arrive and tenders were to be submitted by midday on Saturday 8 April. Alfred J. Box of Bristol came in at £575, Beavers and Sons of Bedminster at £730, Gait and Son of Ston Easton at £465. And the unsurprising winner was, yes, you guessed it, the men from Ston Easton. For some unexplained reason, the Board agreed to pay them £550. In October 1876 the Board sent £8.15d.0d to solicitors to draw up the mortgage with the Public Works Loan Commissioners. The loan was formalised, repayable over 25 years at £36.8s.0d a year. The Board had originally wanted repayment over 50 years. £200 was paid on account to Gait and Son. Lessons couldn't continue while the works were ongoing, and two rooms were hired from John Gibbs at 5/- a week, with an undertaking to repair any damage done. The

Gibbses are thought to have lived at or near the site subsequently forming The Lodge petrol station.

The extensions caused temporary problems for three children whom headmaster Jones refused to admit *until the new school room would be ready*. It still wasn't ready when classes returned in September 1876 after their summer break, and Mr Jones noted that *the children will be taught for a short time in a dwelling house in the village*. Probably chez Gibbs again. The secretary to the Board was cross. His letter of 12 September 1876 to Gait and Son was to the point:

Gentlemen, I am directed by the Board to express to you their great annoyance at the slow progress you are making with the alterations and additions ... I am to point out to you that if penalties are incurred by you under the contract through delay, the Board will seek to enforce them against you and they will on some ground claim compensation from you for any extra rents incurred by them in the hiring of other premises for school purposes through your not having complied with the terms of the contract. I am, gentlemen, Your Obedient Servant, W. W. White, Clerk.

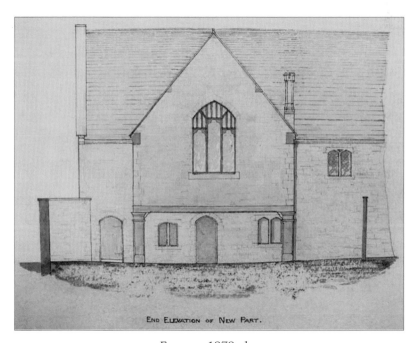

From an 1878 plan

The school was finally ready by 20 February 1877 *when wet from the unfinished playground at the back of the school came into the room.* Flooding had always been a problem and remained so until recent times. The field at the back sloped gently down towards the building, drainage in the area had never been good and the school bore the brunt. Mr Jones damply protested on Friday 2 February 1877 that his school had to be closed *owing to the water from an adjoining field coming into the room*. With a deft addition of occupational detail, headmaster Hill wrote in February 1883 that *a man (mason by trade) was sent by the Board to see the school and to report what could be done to prevent the wet and draughty state of the school and cottage.* In April, perhaps as a result of the mason's investigations, *the workmen have been in the school and on the premises all the week, stopping the wet from roofs, walls and windows. Plumber mending windows and leadwork, replacing lead gutters on the roof, mason cementing walls and carpenter repairing doors etc.* In September 1885 the children all dashed into the yard to be the first to spot a brush poking out of the chimney. Mr J. Langridge was sweeping it for a florin. There was a dispute in January 1886 when the Board decided *to have a valuation made of the work done by Mr Joseph Symes for which he has sent in a bill amounting to £4.10s.0d and that Mr Jonas Weaver of Chew Magna be appointed valuer.* He valued the work at just £2.16s.0d. The Board had already paid £3 to Mr Symes on account, and resolved *that no further sums to be paid.* Mr Symes was presumably allowed to keep the unwarranted four bob for whatever work it was that he'd done. On the morning of Thursday 18 March 1897 Mr Brown complained that *owing to the large room being flooded, there was no school held, but the children met in the afternoon although the floor was damp.*

In May 1886 headmaster Brown complained that *the school is very much overcrowded. Took a class out in the playground for repetition.* This didn't mean it was the second time he'd done it. In June, Her Majesty's inspectors (HMI) said: *My Lords trust that the Board may take the necessary steps for supplying the increased accommodation which appears to be much needed.* On 20 June 1888 Mr Brown commented: *weather being wet and temperature high, found work very trying in overcrowded school; there were 133 children present on Tuesday afternoon and 131 present on Wednesday afternoon.* In September 1888 *all the members of the School Board visited the school to view the premises and consult respecting the required additional accommodation.* Nothing happened. The September 1893 inspection commented that *the ventilation of the schoolroom should be improved and a window blind should be provided for the large window in the south wall ... the main room is not free from draughts and is not well ventilated ... These defects should be remedied with as little delay as possible, or the next Annual Grant will be endangered under Art 85(a) of the Code. A good supply of water should be provided for the School.*

In 1897, the inspectors reported that *the infants' room is habitually used for a larger number of scholars than that for which it is passed by the Department.* This was apparently in flagrant contravention of the last two lines of the same Art. 85(a) as had caught the school out nearly four years earlier. The inspectors droned on: *the average attendance of the infants must not again be allowed to exceed 38.* The 1898 Mixed School report by HMI stated that *on the whole* [the children] *are making as good progress as can be expected considering the overcrowded state of the school. An enlargement is now imperatively needed. I think a new room should be built for the infants and their present room used as a class room for the mixed school.*

A meeting of the Board in September 1898 was enlivened by a communication from the Education Department stating the bleeding obvious: *The Bishop Sutton School was overcrowded.* This had potentially dire consequences and *the clerk was instructed to reply, stating that immediate steps would be taken to carry out* [the Department's] *requirements and to beg that the Grant may not be further withheld (average attendance 113, 123 on books).* The wording suggests that the grant had been partly withheld on a previous occasion. In October 1898 headmaster Wightman wrote: *it is very difficult to obtain perfect order in Standards I and II owing to the crowded state of the classes.* This was echoed by the 1899 HMI report on the infants: *they are making fairly good progress. Their teachers have worked zealously, but their efforts have not been as successful as they would have been if the room were not habitually overcrowded.*

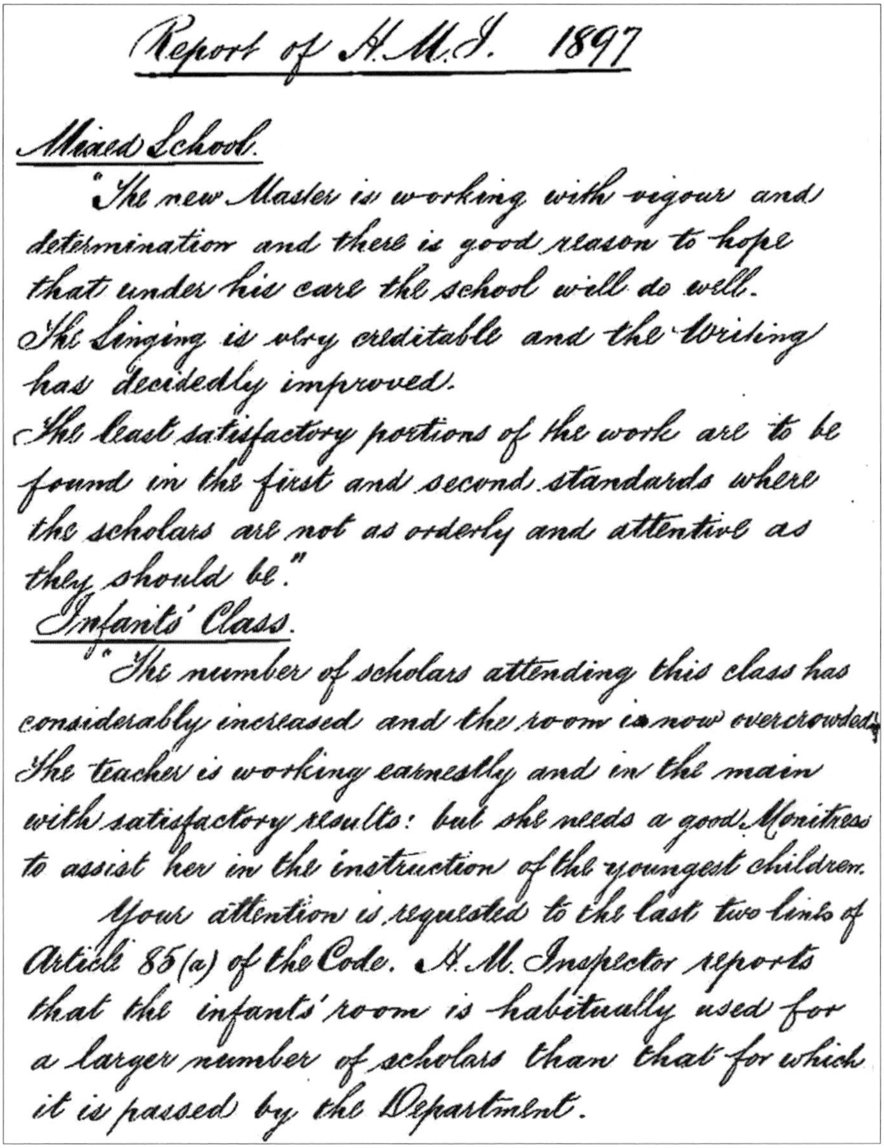

> *Report of H.M.I.   1897*
>
> <u>Mixed School.</u>
>
> "The new Master is working with vigour and determination and there is good reason to hope that under his care the school will do well.
>
> The Singing is very creditable and the Writing has decidedly improved.
>
> The least satisfactory portions of the work are to be found in the first and second standards where the scholars are not as orderly and attentive as they should be."
>
> <u>Infants' Class.</u>
>
> "The number of scholars attending this class has considerably increased and the room is now overcrowded. The teacher is working earnestly and in the main with satisfactory results: but she needs a good Monitress to assist her in the instruction of the youngest children.
>
> Your attention is requested to the last two lines of Article 85 (a) of the Code. H.M. Inspector reports that the infants' room is habitually used for a larger number of scholars than that for which it is passed by the Department.

1897 inspection report highlighting the overcrowding

The Board would need to borrow to fund any extensions, and made tentative enquiries of the Education Department. The Board was sent away with a flea in its ear: the Department replied on 30 January 1899 that this was all very well, but what about *repayment of the £600 expended on the premises out of the loan sanctioned in June 1876?* It's unclear as to how the Board responded, although a fair chunk of the loan must surely already have been repaid. In any event, the Department asked that draft plans be prepared, but warned that *it appears doubtful, however, whether any alterations could make the premises permanently satisfactory, and the Board should consider whether it would not be best to provide an entirely new School. In the absence of plans, My Lords are of course unable to express any opinion as to the best course to pursue. The whole question should be dealt with by the Board without delay, as additional accommodation is urgently required.* What happened for the first few months of 1899 is unclear, but it seems that the Board scurried around looking for some land on which to build. In August 1899 they explained to solicitor Mr Meade King that they had met *Mr Isaac Mapstone[1], owner of the land on the south side … and agreed to purchase ¼ acre for £35. One pound was then paid on account.* The solicitor was to sort out the conveyancing. The Mapstone land was immediately behind the school, extending across the back of the churchyard and adjoining a right of way on the western edge of the school garden.

From an 1899 plan showing the front of the building, facing the main road

Now that they'd almost got the land sorted, the Board wasted no time in instructing architect Maynard Froud of St Stephen's Chambers, Baldwin St., Bristol. The Rev. Galbraith would meet him at Pensford railway station, take him to Bishop Sutton and deliver him back to Pensford. Mr Froud looked over the school and drew up plans. The Board was impressed and the Education Department – now no longer enamoured with the notion (and cost) of a brand new school – passed the plans subject to retention of the south window and the positioning of the infants' cloakroom. In came the tenders: W. G. Bindon £772, E. Colston £490.14s.0d, S. R. Gorvett £640, W. Kingstone £595, Thomas Lewis £569, H. A. Shipp £694 and F. W. Walker £450. Mr Walker's was accepted *subject to completion of the purchase of the land.* In February 1900 the Board invited Mr Meade King along to their meeting and he explained *that the Board were within their building rites* (sic) *as shown by the plans viz 60 ft from Mr Baker's building in course of erection.* The Board *resolved to complete purchase of Mr Isaac Mapstone's land and to pay him 5/- (if demanded) for a quarter's rent of the said land.* Mr Baker[2] eventually offered, in September 1900, to give up his building rights for £5. The Board agreed.

----

[1] The 1871 census listed Isaac Mapstone as licensee of the Butcher's Arms, the 1891 census as a farmer at Fiddlers Green House (Sutton Wick) and the 1901 census as a retired innkeeper living at Stowey Bottom.

[2] Mr Baker must have been an absentee landowner: no Bishop Sutton Baker was listed in either the 1881 or 1891 census.

Mr Baker's ongoing erection seems to have been on his land to the immediate west of the school, and close to the newly constructed Myrtle House (now Copperstacks). A conveyance was drawn up on 8 March 1900 between Herbert John James Andrews ('shorthand writer of Bishop Sutton'), Isaac Mapstone ('farmer of Bishop Sutton') and the Chew Magna School Board. In the tortuous language beloved of lawyers, the Board acquired *all that plot piece or parcel of ground situate at Bishop Sutton in the county of Somerset which said plot piece or parcel of ground contains by admeasurement one quarter of an acre or thereabouts and is more particularly delineated in the plan endorsed on these presents ... assigns the right at all times hereafter by day or by night and for all purposes with or without horses carts carriages or wagons to go pass and repass to and from the land.*

After all the admeasuring, passing and repassing, along came a problem in the shape of Mr Fedden, who was renting Mr Mapstone's land and saw the chance of a small windfall. The Board read *a copy of Mr Fedden's letter claiming 40%* (a copy letter elsewhere referred to 17/-) *interest in the purchase money. Resolved that Mr Meade King be instructed ... to insist on the immediate completion of the purchase of the land and to pay 5/- only to Mr Mapstone, if demanded, by way of compensation for loss of rent during the winter period.* This was all beginning to drag on, and in March 1900 Mr Walker – the builder chosen by the Board – demanded *an extra £15 in consequence of the large increase in prices of building materials since tender accepted. Agreed.* The solicitors' bill of £41.18s.8d and architect's fees of £12 were paid, and *the Public Works Loan Commissioners loaned £598.* That was penny-pinching. The Board had asked for £600.

From an 1899 plan

Maynard Froud was wearing both an architect's and a building manager's hat, and he didn't have it easy. On 7 September 1900 the headmaster complained that *work has been greatly interfered with by the noise of workmen. Oral lessons could not be taken.* On 14 September *schoolroom very dirty owing to new door being made ... the hammering of the workmen has interfered with the lessons.* On 5 November Mr Walker knocked down the toilets, and the Board protested to Mr Froud that *the offices have been taken down without providing temporary ones. The Board are very much annoyed with such proceedings and I am to request you to take steps to have temporary ones erected immediately.*

In February 1901 the Board felt obliged to apologise to the Education Department for *the long delay in carrying out the work … which has been caused by great negligence on the part of the Contractor, who has been severely reprimanded.* Perhaps the headmaster caned him. The Board was losing patience, and in early March the clerk wrote to Mr Froud asking him to think very carefully about whether he might want to employ another builder to complete the works: *Mr Wightman has been over today and says that the cement floor in the (I think) kitchen or scullery is defective and that both he and Mr Walker's man on stepping on it sinks into it over their boots. Water again comes thro' the floor in the New Room. The grate too is faulty; the pit between the offices is full of water coming in thro' the concrete.* In June the Board insisted that Mr Froud meet them *re Mr Walker's continued unsatisfactory and unfinished work and to take steps to have the same completed immediately.*

This was all going to cost, and the clerk applied to the Department of Education for a further £200. The Board resolved that *no further payment be made to Mr Walker.* The architect was told that the school *was flooded during the recent rain and if we get wet weather the same thing would again occur, resulting in the closing of the school.* On 4 September *Mr Froud was requested to inform Mr Walker that unless the work is properly completed by Monday next, then the work would forthwith be taken out of his hands.* The builder didn't comply, and the Board agreed *that Messrs Lovell and Manning be authorised to get the works completed and the yard asphalted.* It's unclear whether that's the Lovell of the Jesse Lovell family or, indeed, whether the work was completed but on 14 October 1901 Mr Wightman finally *received order to take possession of the new infants' room.*

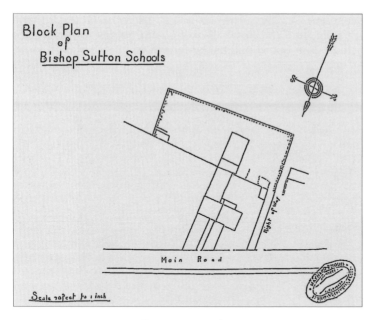

From a 1900 plan

Later that month, *the main room flooded half way across through the yard sloping towards the school,* and Mr Wightman *was obliged to reorganise on that account.* In December: *levelling of playground commenced to stop water coming in.* In March 1902 the headmaster was cross to see that *the whole of yards covered with stones, they cannot be used for play. This work was commenced December 6th.* At a snap inspection in December 1902, HMI wrote that *the girls' play ground cannot be used. This latter should be remedied at once in order that the physical exercise can be properly carried out.*

With frequent plans and re-designs, it's difficult to keep track, but a Somerset County Council Elementary School Return of 28 February 1903 gave a usefully definitive picture:

Date of erection of buildings	1844 and enlarged by the School Board in 1876 and 1901		
In whom ownership vested	Old portion – the Vicar and Churchwarden and overseers of the Parish of Chew Magna and their successors.		
How many rooms are used for instruction?	2 boys / girls		1 infants
Dimensions of main room	38' x 18'		
Dimensions of class rooms	19' x 17'		29' x 20'
Cloakrooms	yes		yes
Dimensions	12' x 4'		20' x 13'
Playgrounds	203 sq yds		487 sq yds
Gymnastic apparatus	-		-
How far are closets and urinals from school buildings?	28' away		
Separate approaches for each sex?	yes		
Water, earth closets or privies?	Earth closets (tank)		
Accommodation recognised by Board of Education	118		60
Number on books on last day of school year	40 boys, 40 girls		51
Average attendance during last school year	35 boys, 38 girls		34
On what date does the school year end?	30 June		
Is Evening Continuation School held in building?	Yes		
Are the school buildings habitually used for Parochial or other purposes?	Used for Sunday School and for parochial purposes incl. occasional election purposes and concerts with the consent of the managers.		
Are the buildings insured:	yes		
(a) in what office?	Royal		
(b) what amount?	£1,200 (under 1 policy: buildings £1,050, furniture desks fixtures etc £150)		
(c) amount of annual premium	18/-		
(d) when paid?	Michaelmas		
(e) to whom paid?	Mr W. W. White, local agent, Chew Magna		
Is there a teacher's dwelling house?	yes		
Is it occupied by the head teacher?	yes		
What is its gross estimated rental according to the parochial valuation list now in force?	£5.15s.0d		

Interesting on several points:

- It was only the 1840s buildings that were owned by the vicar and churchwarden (a letter of April 1905 to the Education Department reaffirmed that the 1844 Trust Deed had *related only to the old portion of the School and Master's*

House). The dimensions quoted in the 1843 application for a grant towards the building of the school suggest that the 'main room' in the above return formed the original extent of the school.

• There were only three classrooms.

• There were two playgrounds (one for the boys and one for the girls): the inspection report of 1902 had referred to the *girls' play ground*, and Clifford Dury was caned twice on the hand in 1906 for *being in girls' play ground*. The map in a 1900 conveyance showed a small 'playground' between the school and the main road. Alongside it to the west was the 'garden'. There was a small 'yard' behind the school.

• There were still separate entrances for boys and girls, as was the Victorian norm and as is still indicated above the doors in many an old school (although not at Bishop Sutton).

• There was an Evening Continuation School

• By 1903, the school was designed to hold 178 children.

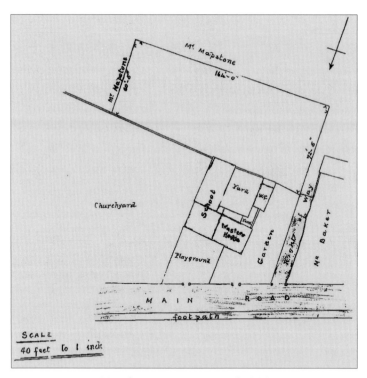

Map from a conveyance of 1900

By late 1904 several necessary repairs had built up, and in the following April plans of work were prepared and presented to contractors for tender. On 3 June 1905 *Mr Flower called re the alterations.* This may well be the Flower building contractors of West Harptree; one of the sons (Henry) was the husband-to-be of monitress (and later pupil teacher) Mabel Carpenter. Mr Flower's tender was accepted and he started without further ado: Mr Wightman wasn't happy with the quality of the work and moaned in the logbook on 19 June 1905 that *rooms were in a filthy state owing to the workmen. No yard can be used.* On 19 July *work is greatly interfered with by work outside*, but by 17 November *the school walls are now fairly dry.* In June 1908 an inspector commented that *the playground is in a very bad state. Its surface is so rough that it is useless for either play or physical exercise.* In May 1908 Mr Wightman wrote that the *boys' yard cannot be used owing to tank and drains being open.* On 24 September 1909 *workmen are tarring the yard*, but on 3 June 1910, *the patches on the play ground are a complete failure as the tar runs.* In April 1911 it was thought prudent *to obtain a load of tarred gravel for the girls' entrance.* The yards were re-tarred in September 1919 and again in August 1926. Sand was used to help the tar to dry, and the occasion was important enough for Mr Wightman to commit to posterity the comment that in October 1926 he *brushed the yard to clear sand from drains.*

From a 1904 plan

But we're running ahead of ourselves. On 4 June 1908 *the main room flooded owing to thunderstorm when rain fell in torrents. Standards I to VI went on with their work outside,* but presumably not until the rain had stopped. On 30 August 1910 the *infants' room flooded as well as part of main. Water coming from cupboard bottoms as spring. 10 am water increasing in main room. Dismissed 10.05.* At ten to nine on 14 December 1911 Mr Wightman *found the floor of infants' room covered with water, apparently arising from a spring under the floor.* The following Monday: *fires day and night dried the room so that it could be used today*. On Friday 22 December 1911 the *infants' room again flooded. Fires kept burning.* The spring was still there at the beginning of the present century when the new hall was built.

The school used local builders wherever possible, but they did have to be kept sweet. In December 1908 the school managers wrote to the Education Department: *Mr Albert E. Harvey of Bishop Sutton has applied to me for payment of his account for £4.5s.2d for work done at the teacher's dwelling house. Please instruct me what reply to give to Mr Harvey, who is badly in want of the money as he is only in a small way of business and has very little to do just now.* No reply. In January 1913 a letter winged its way to the authorities: *The managers beg to draw the attention of the County Education Committee to the unsatisfactory manner in which tenders were invited for repairing and cleaning the school at Bishop Sutton in Aug 1912, tradesmen at Chew Magna (3 miles distant) being asked to tender, while capable tradesmen at Bishop Sutton were ignored, causing much dissatisfaction.* The dissatisfied village tradesmen were Messrs Treasure and Ferris.

School could be a dangerous place. In January 1912 Mr Wightman recorded that *some plaster fell from ceiling of lobby.* In April 1912 *the colouring falls from walls of Main and Infants' Room.* In March 1917 the ceiling in the main room fell. No-one was reported injured. In November 1921 *a mass of ceiling plaster fell in the boys' lobby,* and in October 1929 *school in bad state owing to plaster falling from the interior walls.* In February 1945, *just before school opened this morning, a large patch of plaster fell from the ceiling of the juniors' room. I asked Mr Treasure to give an opinion as to the danger of more falling. He then removed all the plaster from one section of the ceiling. The children meanwhile were accommodated in the infants' room.*

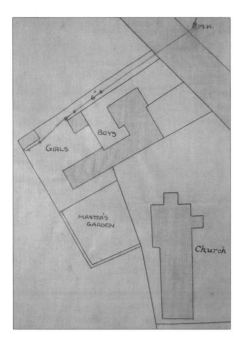

Plan of school relative to church, 1909

In July 1920 the managers asked Clutton RDC to do something about the ditch at the approach to the school, *suggesting the construction of a raised footpath over it so that children may not have to walk thro' water.*

In September 1923 Mr Wightman *refused admission of boy from Stowey owing to overcrowding,* and in 1924 the increasing roll necessitated yet more extensions to the buildings. Plans and specifications were issued in July, and work started straight after Christmas. By 7 January 1925 *all children now use the girls' entrance* and by 29 May Standards I and II were *in the enlarged classroom.* In October 1931 the managers saw fit to note that *when Mr Hutchins, the correspondent, was in the playground on Monday, his attention was drawn to the thick layer of small dust, necessary just after the ground had been newly tarred, but not at all pleasant or desirable now. It is suggested that the playground be swept and it is certain the present situation causes much unnecessary dust in school.* No severe difficulties with rising damp had been reported since 1911 but on Thursday 12 July 1934 *school was closed at 3.15 pm, a very heavy thunderstorm caused the flooding of two rooms to a depth of about 2" and the partial flooding of a third. After the water was brushed out, the children were sent home and the fires were lighted to dry the floors.* No more flooding worthy of logbook mention for another 16 years.

On 3 September 1935 a new term dawned, and Mr Bailey reported that *the yard has been repaired, tarred and sanded, the outside of the school has been painted, a new flag pole has been erected.* Or, as the children's hymn blithely puts it, 'God's in His Heaven, all's right with the world'. On 21 April 1936 the headmaster wrote that *the new children have come today and so the infant room is rather crowded again, Miss Harvey has some brighter children working with the 1st class, and these will be promoted to Standard I in July and so relieve the overcrowding.*

March 1939: *I have asked the managers to remove the railings across the yard*. Not quite soon enough, for a few days later *Denis Mapstone cut his face badly when he fell on the iron support to the railings in the centre of the yard*. A fresh reminder went out to the authorities, but nothing happened until 18 July 1940 when it was time to melt metal for Spitfires: *the railings across the yard were removed today – there are holes left which have to be filled in later*. This was wartime and things moved slowly on the hole front. It was only in May 1941 that the County Architect came *to see the condition of the Yard as I had reported the holes in it*. In April 1942 the managers took matters into their own hands, and *the various repairs* [were] *carried out by Mr Treasure and Mr Elford so that the holes in the yard are now filled in*. In a doesn't-he-know-there's-a-war-on moment on 30 September 1939, the headmaster *reported to the managers the following necessary repairs: the stove pipes, loose blocks in infant floor, leaky stop taps, need of painting in lavatory walls and the need for a new wheelbarrow*. Mr Bailey submitted a further long list of repairs in April 1946 including *leaking overflows, broken windows, window curtain of big room, easing of hoppers, erection of lavatory screen, repair to cloakroom roof, raise desk seats*. For good measure, he *also asked that the interior be redecorated and that a new stove be supplied*. On 6 May 1946: *school reopened after the Easter holiday. None of the repairs asked for have been carried out*. In October 1947 there was a lack of illumination: *on leaving the meeting* [the managers] *remarked on the darkness of the playground, the correspondent was asked to write Taunton to see if it was possible to have some lights installed*. Taunton not only agreed, but also added *a few shillings on account of any additional wiring needed*.

With no major alterations having taken place for many a long year, we now stand at the threshold of an era of prefab buildings, wooden huts, HORSAs and other acronyms. It is not easy to establish which temporary classroom was which, as they went under a variety of different names. Anyway, in May 1947 *work began on the prefab classroom that is to be erected for the senior group*. In September the sonorously named Mr Ding of the County Architect's Department *met Ministry of Works officials here today and took over the new classroom from them*. The following day, *the upper group began its work in the new classroom*. In April 1948 *the H.O.R.S.A. was finally handed over to the County*. A HORSA is a Hutted Operation for Raising School Age, which only goes to show that even in the 1940s they were coming up with ridiculous names. Not to be confused with the Horsa gliders that dropped British troops near Pegasus Bridge in Normandy in the opening hours of D-Day in 1944.

By February 1949 the school was again on the hunt for more accommodation for the junior classroom. Miss Rolfe, County Inspector for Primary Schools, came along for a look-see and recommended that *the Methodist Schoolroom be used as an additional schoolroom*. The managers *agreed to the suggestion, seeing it as the only suitable place in the village*. Things moved quickly and by the beginning of September 1949 *Miss Harvey and Miss Thomas have been taking it in turns to use the Methodist Hall, we have the use of this building as a separate classroom from today*. Mr Bailey observed that *a week's trial with the use of the Methodist Hall indicates that the best use of the room would be made by letting the infants use it nearly always, i.e. it should become their classroom*. And so it came to pass.

The new decade saw new flooding. In February 1950 the managers commented that *there was regular flooding of houses in The Street. Could it be because of an obstruction in the stream under the main road?* Glorious technicolour arrived in July 1957 when the managers asked *that two sets of colours be used when the school is redecorated*. During Mr Price's proprietary perambulation on 13 November 1963 he noticed *that the tall chimney over the roof of the Junior Classroom appeared to be leaning slightly near its top ... telephoned Messrs Battens and chalked the playground so as to keep children away from the possible danger area.* At 8.30 the following morning, Mr Batten *expressed the opinion that there was no immediate danger. The chimney was in need of repair but this could be left until after the Christmas holiday, quite safely.* Mr Price rubbed out his chalk. By 10 January 1964 *all possible danger is now removed.*

The school had weathered the storms of the previous few years without serious mishap, but on 3 June 1958 *heavy rain the previous night entered the boys' cloakroom to such an extent as to necessitate mopping up.* At the end of January 1959 the main road was flooded and the PC *suggested that pavements be lowered to enable the floodwater to percolate into fields and disperse.* Having a funny five minutes on 14 August 1959, Mr Price wrote that *County Council workmen today began the work of asphalting the playground with asphalt.* In November 1964 the ceiling did its party trick again – this time in the canteen – and *Messrs Battens were informed and temporary repairs were carried out until a more opportune time.* A suspended ceiling was fitted during the summer holidays of 1966 in both the main and the lower junior classrooms. In November 1977 Mr Price arrived at school to spot that *portions of kitchen ceiling had, in two places, fallen down during the night. A considerable mess was caused.* [It was] *arranged for meals to be supplied from Timsbury Central Kitchen. The Area Surveyor later came to examine the kitchen and deemed it advisable to renew the whole ceiling and the kitchen would be closed until the work had been completed by Messrs Taviner ... the main classroom* [will be] *used for all meals purposes.*

With one Hutted Operation for Raising School Age having been erected in 1947, the next major hutting event was in March 1967 when Taunton agreed that *a prefab classroom* [is] *to be erected in the playing field.* Work started on the foundations during January 1968, on the classroom itself during February, and the children moved in during March after the County Architect checked that it wouldn't fall down. By September 1970 the floor had worn out – too much pacing up and down by teachers – and Marston Flooring Ltd of Frome leapt to the rescue for £154.18s.0d.

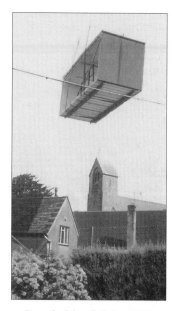

A Victorian relic at the school was done away with in March 1970: the flagstone floors were removed. Perhaps the school celebrated by putting the flags out. No more chilly feet on chilly mornings. In July 1971, *in view of structural changes to be made to the cloakrooms and playground, photographs were taken of them as they are at present to be retained for future reference purposes.* It is a shame the photos have gone missing. The builders, Maggs, worked valiantly through the summer holidays, but by 8 September *although stock cupboards and cloakrooms were ready*

Portakabin aloft in 1968

for use, lavatories and other alterations were far from complete. The oil tank for the central heating was re-sited *from the centre of the yard to a position in the south west corner*, and work continued on the toilet block. There was a hiatus over the winter, but on 5 January 1972 Mr Price spotted that *the workmen are continuing with the work of sanitary improvements, having been away for some weeks.* The morning of 7 January saw *the old toilet block (i.e. the boys')* in the middle of the *playground demolished and the new toilet block for both boys and girls has come into use for the first time.* Later that month, *the old girls' toilets were today converted into storerooms and have gone into immediate use.* Result: bigger playground. In March 1972 Mr Price was told *that the pedestrian access to the school, which had been considered unsafe for children, will now be changed; the contract has gone to G. Tovey, Stanton Drew.* Work began in June 1972: *the path, which takes in part of the School House front garden, will be completed during the coming week.* Further works were undertaken in June: *Mr S. Heal has been asked to carry out the following repairs at the school: Buildings £1,850.65 (incl. £152 contingency), Grounds £107 (incl. £9 contingency), School Meals £907.25 (incl. £25 contingency), Fencing £167 (incl. £17 contingency). The east wall of the kitchen will be demolished and rebuilt.* In July 1972 Mr Price was told *that it is proposed to install fluorescent lighting throughout the school.*

On 6 December 1972 Mr Price documented that *it had been raining heavily for several days and a heavy shower at about 2.30 pm caused flooding in the main classroom to a depth of 2 cm.* (This was the first reference in the logbook to centimetres, although kilos had made an early appearance in 1933 when a man came to look at the school weighing machine.) The headmaster spoilt the effect rather by going on to say that *in addition, water collected at the rear of the cloakroom to a depth of about 6".* Mr Price was a bit of an expert when it came to things damp, and he wrote: *in my opinion, the existing drainage is inadequate to cope with flood water, and the flooding at the rear of the school is because the water is drained only by soakaways.*

Mr Price had contacted Taunton in September 1972, *pointing out the increase in numbers and asking for the provision of another classroom,* suggesting that *the existing classroom could be used as a hall or for PE.* Mr Hendy, the Assistant Education Officer, dared *to hint at a strong possibility that another classroom will be provided in the 1973 Minor Buildings Programme.* This was all well and good, but Mr Price felt that it *would accentuate difficulties during the autumn and spring terms, particularly when the continual use of the cloakrooms is required.* It was decided in November 1972 that *it would not be possible to bring a caravan classroom into the school grounds and that a hutted class would be provided to be ready by September 1973 and sited in the playing field next to the present hutted classroom.* This was to be *a prefabricated Pratten classroom (a wood-clad permanent structure).* After some heated discussions surrounding the heating, the new facility was ready on 15 November 1973, to be used by the 2nd year infants.

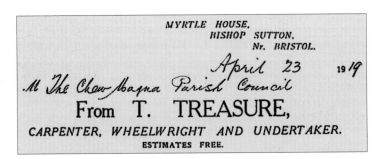

As premises draws to a close, it's nostalgic to observe that what was acceptable in 1977 certainly wouldn't be acceptable now: in November of that year *it was decided to paint the interior of the two junior classrooms and the painters will carry out the*

work while the classes are in progress. But health and safety was nevertheless becoming an issue: the governors noted at their meeting in July 1978, when skateboarding was being discussed, that *the headmaster would not like responsibility, damage could be caused, the playground is too small and not suitable.* With his retirement not far off, Mr Price was understandably not in a mood to take risks.

The logbook closes, as far as premises goes, with further wet. In May 1979 *the Water Board men inform me that water appears to be leaking somewhere underground on the premises. This has been the subject of a previous investigation.* Not one, Mr Price, but numerous, and dating back to the 1800s. The head dutifully *reported the matter to the Area Surveyor's office.*

The children skimmed their knees in the playground and, when they were little, got lost in the buildings, so it's not surprising that there are vivid memories. There were spreading horse chestnut trees by the railings, and it was near those railings that the Treasures had their workshops; Mr Treasure would clean his brushes on the workshop wall. Ken Rapps recalls there being two playgrounds, little for the infants, and big for the others. Jean Veale remembers that the playground had iron railings separating the boys from the girls, divided left to right. Cynthia Holman recalls that Miss Jenkins' classroom had a stove in the middle, with the chimney reaching into the ceiling.

HOT AND COLD

Heating, temperature, fuel and electricity feature strongly enough in the logbooks to warrant a chronological tale all of their own. Temperatures also affected absences, and it's under 'Absence, punishment and royalty' that the observant reader will find further riveting stories of the heat, the cold and the ice.

As with most homes in the village, heating in the school was by open coal fire until relatively recent times. A colliery down the road until the 1920s and mines in nearby villages until much later meant that coal was plentiful, if not necessarily cheap. The first relevant reference in the school records was in March 1875 when the Board approved payment of £1.8s.0d to Bishop Sutton Coal Co. In May 1878 they gave Mr H. Frappell ten shillings for faggots. These were not balls of chopped meat wrapped in part of a sheep. Mr Frappell's bundles of wood might not have been of the desired quality, as in September 1889 the Board wrote to the headmaster: *I am told that Mr Edward Hasell is a very likely man to have some fagots* (sic)*, will you kindly enquire of him if he can supply half hundred (60)* [sic!!] *to do so and send bill to me, 15/- per hundred is about the price.* In July 1888 the Board invited *sealed tenders … for hauling coal to the Chew Magna and Bishop Sutton Schools from Bishop Sutton colliery.* William Faux's was accepted at 1s.8d per ton to Bishop Sutton and 3s.4d a ton to Chew Magna. Ordering the fuel was one of the headmaster's more tedious tasks. Sorting out the fires was equally irksome. Fires needed chimneys. Chimneys smoked. On 31 October 1879 Mr Northam wrote: *no fire in the classroom this week owing to the chimney smoking so badly.* Little eyes were also watering in January 1906 when *chimneys smoking badly, especially in the infants' room.* There was a rare treat on Thursday 18 October 1907 when *smoke and dust came down the infants' room chimney.* An imaginative teacher would have told them it was Father Christmas on a practice run.

Mr Wightman discovered thermometers, and enthused endlessly about the highs and lows. Temperatures – here and in subsequent records – were quoted in

Fahrenheit; the Celsius translations are mine. 23 January 1907, *temperature in school at 9.30 am 34°* (1 C). 24 January 1907, 32° (0 C). The following day, *it has been very cold in the main room in spite of large fires.* By 1 February 1907 it was still only 46° (8 C) at 9.30 am. These temperatures were most unpleasant for the children, many of whom had only one set of clothes. If they arrived at school wet, they'd spend the whole day in damp attire in a room that was barely above freezing. Hardly surprising that mothers kept their offspring at home when the rain was bad or the roads flooded. 22 January 1909: *the main room has been very cold in the mornings – one day only 4° (2 C) above freezing point.* 1909 found the headmaster (and the inspectors) quite angry at being unable to heat the school satisfactorily. HMI had commented in July of that year that *thermometer records kept last winter and spring show the rooms to be insufficiently warmed.* The school managers, nice and comfy in their warm winter overcoats and linen summer suits, could sometimes be quite unreasonable. When they discussed the HMI report, they *begged to say that having never heretofore heard of any complaint in respect of the insufficient heating at Bishop Sutton School and not having before them any thermometric records of the school buildings* blah blah blah. They were possibly more concerned about higher fuel bills than about the children's welfare. The Board wrote to the Education Department: *the question of heating Bishop Sutton School was again considered. The managers, while not acknowledging the necessity or utility of the proposed heating alteration, would prefer that the alteration should be carried out by the County Education Committee themselves.* Mr Wightman was not happy and kept records throughout the autumn and winter of 1909 to 1910. The Celsius figures are mine.

Date	Time	F	C	Headmaster's comments
25.10.09	9 am	47	8	
26.10.09	9 am	48	9	
28.10.09	9 am	49	9	*Fires to be lighted at 7 am*
5.11.09	9.30 am	50	10	
15.11.09	9.15 am	48	9	*Snowing at 9 am*
17.11.09				*Therm. did not reach 56° (13 C) during the day*
22.11.09	9.15 am	37	3	
	4 pm	54	12	
28.1.10	9 am	31	-0.5	*I raised the room to 39° (4 C) but in so doing had bad ventilation.*
25.2.10				*Sent graph of temperatures to managers.*

The fires and stoves were potentially dangerous. In October 1910 Mr Wightman noted that *heat from the stove pipe caused charring of woodwork which is too near.* In March 1911 he *applied to the managers for two fire guards.* It was decided in January 1911 *that coals for Bishop Sutton School be obtained from Messrs Lovells' Colliery at 13/6 per ton delivered.* This was an eightfold increase since 1888. The First World War played havoc with coal production and there were shortages for domestic and educational consumption, even though Bishop Sutton School enjoyed the proximity of a mine. In 1915 the Board told the Education Department in

Taunton that *during the winter months of November, December and January the schools shall reopen at 1.30 pm and close at 3.30 pm*[1] *thus effecting a saving in fuel and light as well as giving children whose homes are distant from the schools a good opportunity of reaching their homes before dark.* March 1917: *had difficulty in obtaining coal.* Partly as a wartime measure and partly due to cost, the managers ordered *that notices be posted in the schools asking the teachers to use every economy in the use of fuel and to avoid as far as possible leaving big fires at the close of school in the afternoon.* Sometimes the weather was unexpectedly benign: on 25 January 1918 *stoves in main room were not lighted this week as the room was warm enough without them.* Whether it would have been warm enough for today's occupants is another matter. On 5 May 1919 Mr Wightman decided that fires were unnecessary, *as the temperature at 9 am was 56°* (13 C). To put it into context, the Government's current (2009) recommended 'comfort' temperatures for offices are between 21 C and 24 C.

The wartime shortages had worried the managers, and in August 1919 they wrote to Taunton: *having in mind the very great difficulties experienced last winter in procuring a regular supply of coal (the school having to close several times) together with the great costs of same, beg the County Education Committee to adopt a system of Hot Water circulation throughout the school, which in their opinion would be far more economical and efficient than either open grates or stoves.* Central heating, eh? The school would have to wait for another 47 years.

National events of 1926 gave cause for concern. On 14 February the chairman of the PC called a Special Meeting and *stated that owing to the industrial crisis caused by the General Strike it may be necessary to make arrangements for the supply of food and other necessaries for the parish,* [and] *in regard to Coal, the Voluntary Emergency Committee wished that any member of the Council to whose notice information was brought that any person was requiring a supply of coal (particularly in cases of illness) notice should be sent to one of the parish representatives who would communicate with HQ at Farrington Gurney.* There were no further references, so it's assumed that the school struggled through, although the strike did affect all local collieries.

Bishop Sutton School by unknown artist

The stoves were not as efficient as they might have been. In February 1936 Mr Bailey commented that *the Senior Room has been rather cold today – the wind blew dust and smoke from both stoves into the room and we could only have one open fire burning.* The spring of 1936 was chilly: on 21 April *fires are still going as the weather is rather cold, inside temp 9.30 was 46°* (8 C) *(with fires lighted).* On 10 January 1938 *it was so dark as to interfere with reading and written*

----
[1] It is not clear at what times the school had previously opened and closed.

work. There had been similar comments previously: the buildings were old, the windows were small and it got dark early in the winter; this often affected lessons. Typical entries were from 19 December 1879 when *the discipline has been rather lax this week, especially in late afternoon, owing to its getting dark before closing time 4.30*, and 27 October 1936: *the afternoon timetable was not followed as the main and infants' rooms were too dark to allow of any reading or written work – singing and oral work alone being possible.* Hey presto, on 15 February 1938 *Mr Goodliffe, North Somerset Electricity Co., came to the school.* He must have reported back favourably, as on 12 May *the electric current was laid on to the school today.* It was still a thing to be treated with respect, and on 23 November 1938 Mr Bailey deemed it worthwhile to write in the logbook: *artificial light necessary during the afternoon.* It was to be some time before the novelty of the switch on the wall wore off. On 25 April 1939: *owing to particularly heavy rain clouds, lights have been used between 2.45 pm and 3.30 pm.* On 31 October 1939: *a very dark morning and it was necessary to use artificial light.* One assumes he'd drawn the wartime blackout curtains first. The school was perhaps lucky to have electricity: although some parts of the village had been connected to the grid in 1936, parish councillors recorded in March 1943 that *the proposal to provide electricity to Bonhill Terrace and Ham Lane was rejected due to cost.* In March 1958 the PC *reported the decision not to go ahead with* [full] *electrification of the parish.*

On 22 January 1940 *temperature recorded during the weekend was 9° (-13 C); the stop tap controlling all water to the building was frozen and burst, this has been repaired today.* The war and the years immediately following brought fuel shortages across the country. Miners were working overtime and yet transport difficulties and, in 1947, plummeting temperatures posed problems galore. Mr Bailey's logbook entries became shorter: his fingers were probably too cold to hold his pen. 25 January: *I was compelled to close the school today as we have no fuel left. The Coal Co. say their lorries will not make the journey from Bath as the roads are too bad.* 29 January: *I again phoned the Coal Co. without result.* (Incidentally, this was the first mention in the logbook of a telephone). 8 February: *a mere ½ cwt of coal delivered today*. That was about 25 kg and would have lasted only a couple of days in the sub-zero temperatures. 14 February 1947 when night-time temperatures were falling to all-time lows: *to save fuel, only two rooms have been used this week.* 24 February: *again, two rooms only have been used as fuel ordered three weeks ago is not yet to hand.* In desperation, Mr Bailey *rang the company on 25 February with regard to closing the school as we had no fuel.* Luckily, *fuel was delivered in the afternoon, and it was not necessary to close.*

Conditions in the children's homes would scarcely have been any better, and several former pupils remember well the winter of 1947 when coal was unobtainable, logs and twigs for kindling were frozen under snow, and families wore their day clothes at night, shivering together in one bed to keep warm. Even into the 1950s the problems persisted. 12 January 1951: *fuel is very short and I have phoned the Fuel Supplier.* 15 January: *owing to the acute shortage of fuel we have used only one room here, other children have worked in the Village Hall and the Methodist Hall.*

The cockles of Mr Bailey's heart were warmed in December 1952 by the news that *a new 'Eagle' stove will be installed in the Junior Room* but, being cautious, he asked *for fire protection on the ventilators where the stove pipes are near wooden vents.* In January 1953 *a new stove has been placed in the Junior Room, asbestos sheets have been placed over the wooden vents.* Asbestos, the new ultra-safe insulation material. The new stoves weren't altogether fit for purpose: on 2 March 1953 *Miss Chivers reported that the temperature of her room was 36° (2 C) at 9 am and on 3 March, 40° (4 C) at 9 am.* The Chief Education Officer (CEO) was peremptorily informed in March 1953 that *an additional coke heater for the 'hut' would have the effect of overheating the heads and not materially affecting the cold feet of those occupying the classroom; [we] recommend either a mat to be provided under each desk or matting to be laid over the floor.* On 18 November 1955 *Miss Chivers' room has been very cold this week, fires are lighted quite early and appear to burn well, yet the temperature of the room remains low. I have asked Miss C to keep a record of temperatures ... Both teachers' and children's feet and legs become chilled.* The headmaster had made tests with a thermometer and found that there were 15 degrees (8 C) between the floor and half way up the wall. As a result, *the classroom hut floor was to be taken up and a new asphalt one laid.* This did little for toe temperature: in December 1956, *on occasion, the children have had to vacate the 'hut' until it was sufficiently warm.* A coke burner was installed in April 1957; this was quite a novelty and Mr Bailey hoped that *it would burn at night and so render the room warm in the morning.* It worked. On 21 February 1957 he wrote: *this was a cold frosty morning with snow on the ground, yet the 'hut' was reasonably warm – the new stove kept burning all night ... The coal house has been emptied and cleaned and will now be used for a PT equipment store, the former store (a smaller one) will be given over to coke storage.*

1957 had started with a serious petrol and heating fuel crisis – leading to rationing – as a result of the Suez Canal dispute which prompted oil embargoes by the Arab nations. On 31 December 1956 Mr Bailey took *a telephone call from the Correspondent Lord Strachie, informing me that the holiday was extended until the 14th because of the petrol shortage. The teaching and meals staff were advised.* The headmaster wrote on 5 February 1957: *three tons coke here and two to the Methodist Hall were delivered today. This is not in accordance with what was ordered, but it was a very wet day and unloading had begun before I was aware of it so I accepted delivery.* In December 1958 the managers unwittingly resurrected an idea first mooted by their forebears in 1919, and told *the CEO that central heating in the place of the present stoves might be more economical as regards fuel and cleaners.* The response in 1919 had been much the same as that from March 1959: *owing to severe restrictions by the Ministry of Education being placed on capital expenditure, the question of central heating in place of stoves could not be considered.* One of the richest countries on Earth couldn't afford to keep its children warm.

Petrol coupon 1957

The 'hut' may have been sorted in 1957 but the rest of the premises had not. In April 1962, *owing to the difficulty of heating the large classroom, it was suggested to the Education Authority that there should be a false ceiling, and the reply received was that it would be very costly. Daily readings of the temperature were taken for a fortnight and sent to the CEO.* Taunton did agree that *an Alicon No. 4 stove should be installed in place of the present open-fire grate,* but nothing was done until July 1965. The 1962-3 winter, which is explored elsewhere, had the expected impact on the school's heating. 29 March 1963 (by which time the appalling conditions had only a couple more days to run): *owing to the freeze-up it had been most difficult to dig up the frozen fuel,* the headmaster proposed that *a shed might be erected to* avoid such an happening (sic) in the future. An estimate of the cost was prepared and forwarded to the CEO. There's no record of any response, but as the 1962-3 conditions haven't reappeared in over 40 years, perhaps a shed wouldn't have been an effective use of taxpayers' money after all. Finally, Central heating (oil fired) was installed in all classrooms during the 1966 summer holidays. It had been rejected in 1959 as too expensive. It wasn't entirely trouble-free. On the morning of 13 September, Mr Price found that rain water was entering the corner of the junior classroom. The County Architect found that the wall had been weakened by a trench dug for the central heating. In November of that year, trouble to the central heating system caused the main classroom to be filled with oil vapour which left a film of oil over the classroom and its contents. Mrs E. Saunders, cleaner, carried out extra duties to clean the affected classroom during the closure. Eighteen months later, three night storage heaters were installed in the temporary classroom ('the one on the field', as the headmaster helpfully elaborated). In April 1968 Mr Price discovered that the central heating system was out of order and it was reported that a large nest had been built in the chimney. The nest was removed.

In October 1970 came a Flanders and Swann 'Gasman cometh' moment. On the 16th: four radiators not functioning correctly. Battens informed. Air lock. Note that by the 1970s, the logbook entries had been whittled down to staccato comments. 5 November: pump broke down. Messrs Bourton of Temple Cloud said pump was burnt out. New one ordered from AT Services, Crewkerne. 9 November: oil and electric heaters placed in school overnight. New pump brought at 10.30 am but couldn't be installed as wiring had been removed by Messrs Bourton and would have to be replaced.

Stringent attempts by the Government in 1972 and '73 to control inflation by pegging back wage increases resulted in miners picketing power stations, ports and coal depots. The situation was not helped by the Yom Kippur War between Israel and Egypt, which prompted oil embargoes to the West. The Government hadn't built up coal stocks and were forced to introduce a series of panic measures, including the declaration of a State of Emergency. On 15 November 1973 Mr Price received a telephone message from the CEO's office that night-storage heaters in both infant classrooms were to be kept in operation despite National Announcements that electric heating was not to be used in schools. Politics had spread to local authorities, many of whom openly flouted government diktats. The country was becoming ungovernable. By February 1974 the Central Electricity Generating Board scheduled nationwide power cuts, turning off electricity for up to nine hours a day, with a daily rota system in operation from 7 am to midnight. A mandatory national maximum 50 mph speed limit was introduced to conserve fuel, and the population was gravely urged to share baths and brush their teeth in the dark. Television shut down at 10.30 every evening. A three-day working week was introduced in factories. Disruption to school and domestic life was considerable. Bishop Sutton School had to work around a lack of electricity and brought candles, car batteries and portable generators into use. Many people, of course, revelled in the excitement as a welcome change to the gloomy shambles that the country had become. But everything eventually returned to normal or, at least, as normal as the strike-ridden 1970s would ever be.

On 8 April 1976 the governors wrote: Saving Power – the school now closes at 3.30 pm and in the summer time 3.45 pm. It must have had the desired results, as on 8 July 1976 they further recorded that all schools have been congratulated on the Saving of Power Scheme. The morning of 4 October 1976 was unexpectedly dark: on turning on the central heating for testing purposes, clouds of thick black smoke were emitted from the chimney. Wrensons Ltd of Bristol repaired the pump.

An unfortunate sequence of events was set in train on the morning of Friday 10 December of that year, when *it was extremely cold in Miss Stuckey's classroom and it appeared that the timing mechanism was faulty. Messrs H. L. Bush of Bath promised attention a.s.a.p.* By the following Monday, *the electrician had not attended to Miss S's classroom, which continues cold, so an electric fire with guard has been used to warm up the room. Anne Tingley, age 5, fell over the electric fire and burnt the back of her left leg on the guard which was, of course, very hot. She was taken to the surgery at Chew Magna where it was treated. It was pronounced to be not a serious burn and she was allowed to return to school. Her mother was informed when she returned home in the evening.* On the Tuesday morning Mr Price took *A. Tingley to the surgery at Chew Magna at 10 am for her to be examined by the nurse in regard to the slight burn she received yesterday. It was pronounced to be healing and drying up very well.* Nothing was said about when Miss Stuckey's radiator was eventually repaired.

PRIVIES, OFFICES AND NUISANCES IN THE YARD

The discerning reader will spot that in all this talk about premises, little has been said about toilets. This was deliberate. The best has been left till last. Toilets, lavatories, cloakrooms, closets, WCs, privies and offices. All these terms were used somewhat interchangeably throughout the records, although 'offices' was the preferred euphemism until well into the 20th century. Those of a sensitive disposition are advised to skip the next few pages. As we've seen, clean water was a scarce commodity in Bishop Sutton, but we'll start secure in the knowledge that children merrily played – quite possibly on their way to school and back – in the stinking brook festering its way down Sutton Hill Road. Perhaps with that in mind, HM inspectors ordered in October 1877 *that an*

Farthing 1912, halfpenny 1934, penny 1902 (actual size)

apparatus for washing hands be procured. The purse-string holders agreed and in November 1877 *a wash basin was fixed up in the lobby.*

The first logbook mention of toilets was at the May 1878 meeting of the School Board. *The schoolmaster from Sutton attended to complain of the inconvenient position of the closets. The Board would meet at school to review.* The Board met and opined that *the average number of girls (some 50) makes it necessary that another seat should be added to the one already in their closets. The time for recreation being only ten minutes does not allow of them all being accommodated with but one seat. The infants (many of whom are not yet 4 years of age) ought to have a lower seat as the present one seems too high.* One can picture the bewhiskered gentlemen squirming in embarrassment at having to discuss little girls' toiletry requirements and practices. In June 1878 Mr E. H. Perrin of Temple Cloud – Kelly's Directory of 1875 listed Edward Hayward Perrin as 'gentry' – wrote to the Board to complain about something of a lavatorial nature. The Board replied: *I beg to acknowledge your letter of the 29th ult and Dr Wilson's Report on the Sanitary*

Conditions of Bishop Sutton School, and in reply I am directed to inform you that the matter has been previously under the consideration of the Board and that measures are now being taken to remove the nuisances complained of. Sadly, we don't know what the nuisances were which so exercised the gentry of Temple Cloud. The Board decided in July 1878 *that Mr John Jury's plans* [for closets] *be accepted at £8.0s.0d.* 'Jury' could well have been 'Dury': the two spellings were often confused.

On 5 April 1878 Mr Northam enthused to his logbook that *on entering the school on Wednesday afternoon, I found a very sickening smell throughout the place, arising from the closets.* His wife had often reported herself sick from the same affliction. In May 1878 *there was a very bad smell coming from the closets and George Harris (age 10 yr 10 mo) had to be sent out, feeling faint and sick.* The accuracy with the lad's age is commendable.

In May 1878 Mr Northam observed *the inconvenience of a good deal of water in the girls' passage to the closets*, so his relief would have been profound in August when *the old closets were removed.* Don't think that we're talking about anything remotely resembling flushing toilets. We're talking about a pan anchored to the floor, with the noisome contents falling into a cesspit. And with swarms of flies (and mosquitoes to nip unwary bottoms) in the warm weather. Sometimes something had to be done about the smell, and in May 1883 the Board paid Mr Treasure £1.2s.0d *for cleaning out closets.* He probably deserved every penny. But the young ladies must have gone and filled them up again, for Her Majesty's inspectors commented in September 1884 *that there is a very bad smell from the girls' offices. Any fault in the construction of the cesspit should be at once remedied.* Hygiene was in its infancy and there was no running water anywhere in the school. Toilet paper? No. You did at school what you did at home and resorted to the squares of old newspaper stuck on a nail in the wall. But ideas did gradually change and in September 1885 the Board accepted *Mr Tovey's tender for erecting wash house in Bishop Sutton School yard for £9.*

Back to the cesspit. It needed to be emptied every so often, and a nasty job it was too. The headmaster kept children at arm's (or nose's) length: on Wednesday 5 May 1886 he *closed school in the afternoon for the rest of the week to allow of the cess pool being cleaned out.* In 1893 the inspectors reported that *the girls' offices are dark and their condition is not sanitary.* They went on: *in addition, the contents of the cesspool are not removed with sufficient frequency.* But civilisation was steadily slithering not only to the farther reaches of the British Empire – whether the locals wanted it or not – but also to the girls' toilets. In September 1893 the Board read the inspectors' report *re the ventilation and girls' offices and resolved to put in a window 4' x 2' in the upper part of the gable of the southern wall to open on centre pivots in the ceiling efficient empty the cesspools when the weather permits and cut holes in the doors of girls' offices for the purpose of admitting light (tender of Mr Colston accepted £2.10s.0d).* Rearrange the words 'the ceiling efficient empty the cesspools' into something that makes sense. But we get the drift.

In the face of complaints from headmaster Brown, the Board authorised Mr Lovell in July 1887 *to provide a necessary supply of water.* A useful coincidence that the chairman of the Board was Mr Lovell. The situation was dire in dry periods: that same month, Mr Brown observed *that rain water all exhausted, employed man with cart to fetch water for cleaning drains etc by order of the Board. A*

Jesse Lovell
Chairman

permanent supply of water is much needed in this school, there is no water fit for drinking on the premises, nor even for the master's household. In April 1888, with Jesse Lovell presumably still not having tapped into his private supply, the Board agreed *that £1 per annum be paid to Noah Gibbs for the supply of water to the Bishop Sutton School and School House,* he being the village's carrier-cum-haulier. That arrangement worked for only a short time, as the Board wrote to Mr Gibbs in February 1891: *I am surprised to hear from Mr Brown that you refuse to supply any more water to the Bishop Sutton School House. I again beg to inform you that the Board have resolved to pay you £3.10s.0d for the same, which amount will be paid you as soon as you have completed your purchase of the property.* This may have been a new house on or near the site which became The Lodge Filling Station, as earlier censuses suggested that the Gibbs family already resided in that location. Mr Gibbs must have agreed, as the Board decided in May 1891 to extend the agreement *by which he engages to supply the school and the Master's House with Spring Water from the pump in his premises for 12 years from January 1st 1891 on condition that he receives at the present date from the Board the sum of £3.10s.0d.*

While the PC was forming well-examining sub committees who went for nature walks in Strawberry Woods, the Board authorised their chairman in July 1900 *to secure a supply of water for the Bishop Sutton School and School House.* Perhaps they meant a piped water supply, as Mr Gibbs had been ferrying water to the school for some years. But a piped supply was clearly a pipe dream and in May 1903 the Board asked *Mr Lovell if he will kindly undertake to allow water to be had from the stand pipe for the use of the Bishop Sutton*

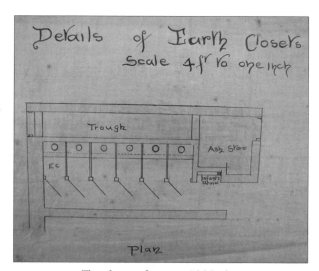

The closets from an 1899 plan

School and School House. The stand pipe was *opposite The Red Lion Hotel.* Hotel? Mr Lovell did so allow, but wanted 2d per week. The Board agreed, but the supply wasn't always reliable: in May 1905 Mr Wightman commented drily that there had been no water all week.

In 1894 the inspectors stated that *the pit* [for the toilets] *must be lined with impervious materials and properly ventilated.* In 1896 they repeated that *the tank of the offices must be cleaned more frequently.* In August 1899 they stated glibly that *the offices are too near the school; the School Board should rebuild them further away.* Possibly in connection with that decree, Mr Wightman noted that *on Monday 19 November 1900 the contractor put up temporary offices.* On 12 December he wrote that *the temporary offices are a nuisance to the school and house.* You'd think he'd be relieved that he and the pupils did at least have somewhere to relieve themselves. This was all part and parcel of the Board v Walker v Froud premises dispute covered earlier.

The dispute gurgled on. In January 1901 the builder *promised to have the offices fit for use the next day, also to remove the open tank.* Two days later he'd done nothing of the sort and the Board intervened. Apart from the inconvenient lack of a proper convenience, the open tank would have rendered today's Health and Safety police apoplectic. By 15 March the school did at least have one toilet operational, which was *being used by boys, girls and infants*. This must have grossly disturbed the head's sense of justice, as he repeated the following week that *boys and girls for some time have had to use the same set of offices*. 14 March 1902: *the WCs smelling very badly*. This was the first use in the logbooks of the term 'WC'. In April 1905 *the tank has been very offensive this week, the wind bringing the stench into the school*. Just what you need on a nice warm day. In March 1906 the managers formed the view that *a Coal and Wash House are essential.* Perhaps the wash house erected in 1885 by Mr Tovey had become derelict.

By 1910 the 20th century had finally caught up with the school, and piped water with water meters had been installed. They occasionally proved unreliable, or perhaps the headmaster just ran out of shillings. That July there was *no flushing of offices owing to water meter.* By July 1917 there was some form of automatic flushing system and the managers asked Mr Wightman *to arrange that water should not be wasted through failure to regulate the automatic flushing.* On 16 February 1917 *offices have not been flushed for 14 days owing to masses of ice in pipes and tanks.* On 1 March 1929, *pans of offices remain frozen so had to use disinfectant.* But, utmost relief, on 7 March Mr Wightman gleefully reported that he was *able to flush offices today.* The long-suffering and Jack-of-all-trades headmaster had his work cut out with these toilets: in February 1929 he was *out of school most of the morning, clearing a choked drain from the offices.* Wary ever since, he *opened and tested all drains* in September 1929. Reopening after Easter in April 1938 was delayed as a result of *difficulty in getting proper fittings; the changing over of the water supply from Bristol to Clutton RDC has not been completed and consequently there is no water in the girls' cloakroom and the hole in the roadway has not been filled in.* The remedy was found by *re-laying pipes under the roadway leading to the yard.*

The amount of water that the school was consuming preyed on Mr Bailey's mind, so in March 1939 he asked Clutton RDC for *a key of the meter chamber, at present one cannot see the dial; I could then regulate the supply according to the meter reading and our requirements.* Certainly not, said Jobsworth of Clutton, but they did agree to read the meter more frequently *in the headmaster's presence.* Clutton also suggested that *perhaps the water tanks for flushing the lavatories are too large.* Mr Bailey's continued pestering resulted in a terse reply in April 1939 to the effect that *they do not regard 25,000 gallons of water used in December quarter as excessive.* That's around 114,000 litres or 10 litres per pupil per day. In May 1939 *the Clutton RDC Water Engineer called to report 3,500 gallons for April*; some 16,000 litres or four litres per pupil per day. The war years didn't bring any logbookworthy problems, although in January 1945 there was *no water owing to fracture of main in the village.* The pipe may have been damaged by the tanks clattering through the village the previous year in the run-up to D-Day.

After the long years of rationed soap and the years of austerity that followed, Mr Bailey's staff were minging and in March 1952 he applied *for the provision of washing facilities for the teachers.* Wishing to keep him sweet, the managers *approached the CEO with the request that a Staff Convenience providing cloakroom facilities for the female members of staff should be made by converting the end cubicle of the girls' block of lavatories.* But no: *the reply received was to the effect that there was necessity for some provision of this nature, but owing to economic measures there were no funds available.* This was not encouraging, and in September 1952 the managers protested to the CEO that *the absence of such an* amenity possibly contributed to teachers endeavouring to obtain appointments elsewhere. Taunton wouldn't relent; *provision would be considered in the next financial estimates, but no undertaking could be given as there was a large number of Sanitary projects to be carried out in the county.* The proposal was finally approved in July 1953 and the lady teachers were inconvenienced no longer. The cold weather of 1 December 1952 meant that *it has not been possible to turn the water on in the lavatories. The cleaner has had to carry water from the school to flush them. There was a reading of 20° last night* (-6.7 C). Occasionally there was a little too much detail: in February 1953 Mr Bailey observed that *the septic tank of the school has been emptied, there was a blockage in the first chamber.*

He asked in March 1955 for *the question of drinking fountains to be raised again.* As an example of 1950s belt-tightening and inefficiency, they were finally approved in July 1957 but not fitted for several months. On the brighter side, Mr Bailey saw fit to note in February 1955 that *all the children have now been given individual towels.* The bitterly cold February of 1956 entailed *periodic flushing by hand as frost necessitates the cutting off of the water.* The children had to wait another few years for anything other than cold water: in July 1961 *the County Architect paid a visit and inspected the sinks for the installation of hot water.* Supply headmistress Miss V. A. Thompson made her mark in July 1961 by writing: *trouble in the girls' lavatories, which appears to be connected with the flushing system.* The 1962-3 winter had a predictable effect and on 29 January *the outside lavatories can only be operated by constant attention being given by Messrs Battens, plumbers.*

The Sixties had arrived. The Beatles, Harold Wilson's white heat of technology, drainpipe trousers, the invention of sex. In December 1963 Bishop Sutton School shared in the general euphoria by having its *drains connected to the main sewer.* Mr Price was alarmed in March 1970 to find that *the sinks in the main classroom were blocked. Messrs Batten were informed and a workman attended and cleared the obstruction which was composed of an accumulation of unidentifiable materials.* The foundations for new toilets were laid in September 1971, with the governors having successfully petitioned for them to be set further back against the wall to free up more playground space. In January 1972 *the old toilet block* (the boys') *in the*

*Churchill crown 1965
(actual size)*

middle of the playground was demolished and the new toilet block for both boys and girls has come into use for the first time. Later that month, *the old girls' toilets were converted into storerooms and have gone into immediate use, and heating and lighting is now installed and in use in the teachers' toilets and the new block.* Beforehand they'd had to take woolly gloves and a torch.

And if there were problems with the school toilets, you could always use those on the rec. Public toilets in Bishop Sutton? Yes. The PC minute book recorded in July 1968 *that the toilets on the village playing field should be repaired at a cost of £90 to £140.* The toilets might not have survived for long after that, as the question of repair was deferred until the meeting to be held in September 1968 and seems never to have been mentioned again.

WHAT WENT INSIDE, OUTSIDE, AND UNRELIABLE ENGLISH FLAGPOLES

It wasn't just the children and teachers and buildings that made up the school. There were the books, the furniture, the flagpole and the telephone. And, of course, the bell.

You'd think it would be one of the more important appurtenances in any well-ordered school. Strange then that it received only fleeting mention. The first was in June 1873 when *one of the monitors, Margaret Harvey, came late to school, reproved her for it, she said the clock had stopped in the night and she did not hear the school bell.* In March 1877 headmaster Jones *had occasion to speak about the unpunctuality of scholars this week due chiefly to want of a bell,* and in October the Board *proposed the school bell be erected at the gable end of the school buildings.* In June 1901 the Board wanted the bell to be put in order and used regularly. And then nothing for nearly 80 years when, in March 1977, Mr Price wrote that *Mr Taviner (a workman) removed the old school bell; the PTA have asked that it be restored to working condition and moved to mark the occasion of the Queen's Jubilee Year.* No-one can remember when (or for whom) the bell had last tolled: almost certainly many decades earlier.

The bell and the washing apparatus: from the logbook of October 1877

By the late 1800s there was a strong improving and educational element in the play of middle-class children, expressed most graphically in the importance attached to books. This was a major distinguishing feature between the spare-time activities of middle-class children and those of their lowlier brethren. The better off were avid readers, while the children of the poor read little or nothing. Schools did what they could: in September 1875 *a new series of reading books were given by order of the School Board for the use of the children here. There are now two complete series in the school.* Text books and exercise books didn't come free until the Assisted Education Act of 1891, and in March 1878 new headmaster James Northam experienced *great difficulty in getting the children to provide themselves with copybooks* (being books illustrating good penmanship, for the copying thereof). *Several children in the 1st, 2nd and 3rd classes have not had one for two months and some have never had one.* April 1880: *children not providing copybooks, there seems to be a determination to resist the demands of the Board.* In June of that year *Mrs Ferris removed her girl on account of the copy books difficulty.* Things hadn't improved markedly by October 1888, when headmaster Brown was moved to write: *there is great difficulty in getting the children to buy exercise and copybooks, many being without them.*

In March 1908 Mr Wightman *commenced a lending library of 60 volumes.* However, a November 1922 inspection observed that *there is no branch of the County Rural Library in this important village school*, so presumably the headmaster's 60 books from 14 years previously had either disappeared or fallen apart. Whether anything was done was unrecorded, but by June 1933 headmaster Bailey wrote: *the Rural Library has been in operation one week* and, in March 1949, *the County Librarian called to discuss with Miss Harvey the increase in the number of borrowers of books and the possibility of increasing the County supply of books.* In February 1952 Mr Bailey noted that *from today the issue of library books to the general public will cease as a branch of the County library has been opened in the Methodist Hall.* March 1956: *an order for library books and a book shelf has been submitted to the LEA with a view to making part of Miss Chivers' room into a reference library.* By 1964 the public library at the Methodist Hall had proved either non-viable or impractical, and in February of that year the PC reported that *the County librarian proposed to introduce a mobile service in place of the existing library service which is permanently established at the Methodist Schoolroom. The Council decided to express concern and request the facilities remain undisturbed.* For how much longer the facilities remained undisturbed isn't clear, but certainly a mobile library service was in operation before long.

Florin (2 shillings):1915, 1936, 1954; 10p 1969 (all actual size)

Even in flinty Victorian times the children had to sit on something and work at something, and to the pupils' glee *the school was closed* (Monday 13 October 1873) *to put up new desks.* In a jobsworth moment, the Rev. Galbraith (Chairman of the School Board) called in March 1886 *to investigate the reason why the master applied for a new black board.* In March 1893 the Board *accepted Mr Treasure's tender for three desks for £3.10s.0d on condition that they be made Pitch Pine sized varnished and fixed for that sum.* The inspectors fulminated in March 1915 that *the desks of the Main Room are unsatisfactory in the following respects: (a) the seats are too low, (b) the vertical distance between the seat and desk top (13") is too great, (c) the horizontal distances (from 3½" to 4") between the seats and the desk tops are excessive, (d) the surface of some of the desks is very rough.* In August 1919 they asked that *chairs and collapsible tables should displace the long desks in the Babies' Room.* 'Babies' was Victorianese for infants. The managers deferred a decision. In January 1926 dual desks arrived. Children could finally sit next to their best friend or be made to sit next to their worst enemy.

Stowey School closed in 1945. Mr Bailey wasted no time in commandeering the equipment, and *brought from Stowey School a cupboard and some stock, new and old, particulars of which are entered in the stock book*, the whereabouts of which is unfortunately a mystery. Bishop Sutton's dual desks from 1926 had served their purpose, and in October 1948 Mr Bailey *made application for six chairs to enable the locker desks from Harptree to be used, also that the County find more modern furniture to replace the dual desks if possible.* By 1950 the children were slouching, and it wasn't necessarily their fault: in February of that year, Mr Bailey reported that *it was necessary that additional furniture be requisitioned as the posture of some of the children was being adversely affected.* This was the age of mend and make do: in October *various desks received from Clandon* (presumably Clandown, near Radstock) *and Compton Martin, some for use and some for dismantling for the wood they contain.* No further logbook entries until September 1979 when *arrangements are in hand for nine trestle-type dining tables and 72 new junior-size chairs to be delivered. Also the replacement of 15 tables with 15 double desks with lift-up lids is in hand.*

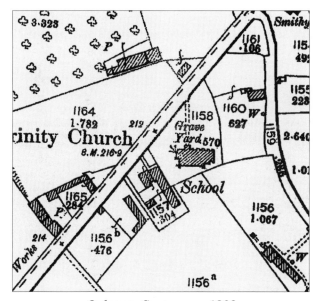

Ordnance Survey map 1903

And then there are those bits and bobs that don't fit anywhere else.

May 1901: *bead counters introduced for infants.* A weighing machine arrived in May 1908. In December 1933 *the Inspector of Weights and Measures inspected* [it] *and found it to be .3 kg overweight, this he corrected.* This was the first appearance in the school logbook of a metric unit. Centimetres had to wait until 1972 for their debut. The children were weighing themselves too energetically and in November 1939 *the brass arm of the weighing machine has been broken off.* With the cupboard and stock having been requisitioned the previous year, Mr Bailey spent Tuesday 2 April 1946 *removing blackboards, easels and odd books from Stowey School.*

On 4 June 1953 *as part of the Coronation Celebration, a television set was installed in the school for the benefit of the children, the cost being met by the local Coronation Committee.* It's not clear whether this was a permanent fixture or merely for temporary enjoyment. In April 1956 *Messrs Dunscombe supplied an Amfon Stylist Sound Projector to school on behalf of the Education Foundation for Visual Aids. The 'Hut' is to be blacked out for this, and a 5 amp point put in.* This was all rousing stuff. In April 1956 *all equipment for the Sound Projector has now been received, the girls have made the blackout curtains for the 'Hut', the electricity point has been installed.* In March 1967 the managers noted that *the County Education Officer was unable to obtain a tv set from the County for use at the school owing to lack of funds; the headmaster organised a most enjoyable concert to raise money to buy one.* Yah boo sucks to Taunton. In June 1972 *the school's PTA resolved to present the infant classroom with television sets. One was installed in the hutted classroom at a cost of £50; the one for the HORSA classroom will be installed in September.* It cost £35. The clerk to the governors added: *the areal* (sic) *being provided free.* The PTA bought video recorders in 1978 and in July 1979 *a demonstration was given of the new Banda duplicator,* again courtesy of the PTA. A generation of children was to get (a) high on the meths smell and (b) their fingers stained on the pinky-purple ink. But as a harbinger of Health and Safety things to come in the following decade and as a slap in the face to PTAs all over the land, Science Advisor Dr Armitage visited in September 1979 and *instructed that all domestic television sets must be withdrawn from use as they were a potential danger.*

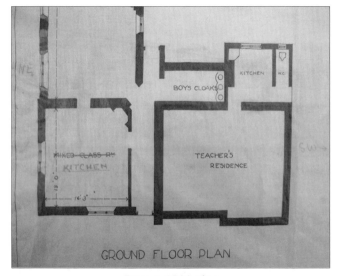

From a 1900 plan

Moving seamlessly from potential dangers to flags, the logbook entry of 31 August 1914 read: *flagpole erected in the playground.* It was saluted on and off for many years until it was replaced in September 1935. Amazingly, given a First World War patriotic fervour that led people to change their names from Nilsen to Nelson and from Marten to Martin, and to kick passing dachshunds, the clerk to the managers wrote to the Education Department in April 1914: *before issuing the specifications* [for the flagpole]*, may I be allowed to insert the word 'foreign' before the words 'fir pole'. This appears to me most important as English-grown fir poles are not nearly as strong and lasting as foreign ones.* In truth, and out of fairness to the clerk, the War To End All Wars didn't start for another four months, but it's a shame to spoil a good story

And now to the telephone. In January 1882, a Bath newspaper reported:

The wonderful performances of applied physical science at the present day have gone far towards annihilating both space and time. Not many days ago, people gathered and were enabled to use the miraculous hearing tubes applied to their own ears and could listen to

words spoken in another place by the aid of conducting wires. If the range of communication by telephone should ever be so far extended as the electric telegraph (i.e. abroad), there would be some embarrassment in the exchange of congratulations of New Year's Day. The night of one country is the yesterday of another and the tomorrow of a third. This instantaneous circulation of New Year's Greetings may prove to be not a simple matter, let Science do whatever it will.

Villagers in Bishop Sutton had to wait some 60 years to apply a publicly provided miraculous hearing tube to their ears. There had been a phone box outside the village post office since 1934 or shortly thereafter: the PC meeting of March of that year instructed the clerk *to communicate with the Postmaster-Surveyor of Bristol to request that a Public Telephone Kiosk be provided for the Village.*

It's not recorded when the telephone came to the School House, but calls were being made and received by 1947. The notion of a phone in the school buildings themselves was first mentioned in September 1955, when an *application has been made to the Bristol Telephone Manager for an extension bell to be placed in the school cloakroom.* Nothing happened, and the next mention wasn't until March 1964 when Mr Price *made a request to the CEO that an extension of the telephone in the School House should be made to the school premises. A reply was received to the effect that this matter would be considered when funds were available and that there were many schools on the waiting list.* Two years later, in July 1966, the CEO *regretted that an extension of the telephone to be made to the school premises could not be considered at present owing to lack of funds.* It's not recorded when the funds were eventually found, but a return sent by the school to Taunton suggests that a phone was finally installed in the school itself around 1969, number Chew Magna 817, amended in 1972 to 2817, lengthened in the 1980s to 332817. All this palaver about having a phone installed seems incredible in these days of walking into a shop, exchanging a few details and notes of the realm and walking out with something small and shiny that'll give you the cricket score and let you communicate by satellite with China.

The school house (to the left of the photo, behind the flagpole) in the late 1950s

THE HEADMASTER'S BATH

Although this book concentrates on the school itself – or, at least tries to – the School House is not without its relevance. Until quite recent times it had been a separate entity despite being physically joined on. It's where the headteacher and family lived and where the logbook was probably written, perhaps in front of the fire in the lounge. The lounge is now the current headteacher's office and the fire is no more, although the rather fine surround remains. One word of caution: the Victorians tended to use the term 'School House' to refer to the actual school as well as the place where the teacher lived. That practice is still commonplace in rural America.

The first relevant mention of the house itself was in March 1878 when headmaster's wife *Mrs Northam was absent from sewing owing to sick head ache brought on, I believe, by the constant bad smells in the cottage and school*. The often unsanitary conditions were frequently spotlighted, and Mrs Northam's afflictions were mentioned more than once.

Until comparatively recently, living in the house was a condition of headship at Bishop Sutton. That said, the Board faced a dilemma in December 1895: *Mr Brown's application for permission to leave the School House and reside elsewhere and to be granted an increase of £10 to his present salary having been considered, it was resolved that permission be given to him to sublet the said House to a tenant to be approved by the Board, but the Board regrets that they do not see their way to an increase in salary*. The entry remained silent on the background to the application. Perhaps the Browns wanted to escape the insalubrious conditions that had afflicted Mrs Northam, or perhaps they didn't want to live over the proverbial shop. The Board's decision wasn't legally very sound and nearly ten years later, in April 1905, the school managers wrote: *Mr Wightman having applied for permission to let the School House now occupied by him and to reside in a house near, it was found on referring to the Trust Deed of 1844 that the House could not be used for any other purpose than as a Master's residence*. So that put paid to Mr W's plans. Aged 34, he was in the School House with his 33-year old wife Florence and their 3-year old daughter Victoria. The 1901 census also listed a 14-year old servant girl. Having been told that he had to stay put, the headmaster asked for more space, only to be told in March 1906 that *the managers do not recommend extra bedroom accommodation.* Perhaps it was by way of compensation that they agreed in January 1908 *that Messrs Lovell and Manning be authorised to fit a new range for the Master's kitchen.*

The official records probed the minutiae of domestic life, and it's a joy to read that in September 1919 the managers told the Education Department *that it is important to have an immediate decision re bath at Bishop Sutton School House as Mr Wightman may loose* (sic) *the opportunity of securing the proposed bath at a very modest sum, which is about to be removed from a house close at hand*. Former pupils recall the headmaster as being of large build, perhaps in the region of 17 stone. Had he outgrown his bath and needed to replace it? We shall probably never know. We shall probably also never know whether he was allowed to take advantage of the bath going begging. But one advantage of having what was effectively a tied cottage – apart from not having far to walk to work – was that the kitchen was kept up to date: in January 1923 *a tender was accepted to supply and fix a 36" Besbar No. 4 Range in the kitchen of the School House*. This may have been partly behind the Education Department's decision in July 1926 that *in view of improvements, rent for School House should be increased from £9 p.a. to £12 p.a.*

An era came to an end in April 1965. Headmaster Price and his family moved out of the School House for a new property on what was then called Lake View Estate (now Parkfield and Hillside Gardens), from where he could still keep a proprietorial eye on the school. He would now need to get up three minutes earlier to get in on time. The Education Authority let the School House to Chew Valley School teacher Mr Jarratt. Goodness knows what sort of wild parties he was holding, but in June 1969 the Architect's Department was asked to undertake repairs to: *front bedroom, replace casement fastener and ease window and replace glass; stair landing, replace broken floor boards; rear bedroom, replace broken window glass; dining room, repair broken window glass; kitchen, replace rotten skirting; larder roof, stop in cracks and give two coats of Aquaseal No. 5.*

In November 1972 Mr Price enquired *as to the possibility of being able to use part of the School House to relieve overcrowding in the school as the present tenant (a Mr Henshawe) is leaving at the end of this term.* The reply a fortnight later: *it would not be possible to use part of the School House to relieve pressure of numbers at the school because of the need to provide housing for teachers.* In July 1974 the governors received a letter *from Mrs Wilson, headmistress of CVS, re the School House, which she would like one of her school staff to rent.* The building was an integral part of the school and it seems rather lax that the *managers were not aware that the School House was empty, but would like to be told by the Education Committee when it was up for re-let, and for Bishop Sutton School to get first chance of the School House for any teaching staff of that school. Mr Price stated that Mr Moore of CVS was wanting a house for a member of his staff who was married with children, and that being the case, the managers thought that as Mrs Wilson's member of staff was a single person, the married teacher from Chew Valley should have it in preference to a single person from Chew Valley.* Didn't Mrs Wilson and Mr Moore talk to each other?

The governors wanted a new tenant to be responsible for the School House garden: *at the moment the garden was not at all tidy, so in future front and rear garden to be kept tidy.* In March 1975 it was noted that *Mr Powell (a teacher at Bishop Sutton) was being married in August and as Mr Marshall the present occupier of the School House was waiting for his house to be finished building at Stanton Drew, Mr Price had made an application on Mr Powell's behalf for the School House should he require this.* And then the aggravation started. This, from the governors' minutes of July 1975: *Mr Price stated that Mr Powell was given to understand that the School House could be rented to him, he was being married on 2 August and had planned to go to the house after he returned from his honeymoon. Heard nothing from the Council so went to see them again, and they told him that there was to be a meeting on 29 July and that they could not tell him anything until after that date. The managers felt that this was not good enough, as in the deeds of the house it stated that if a master from Bishop Sutton School needed the house, then he should be given preference.*

Mr Powell was given his matrimonial home. And that was that as regards the School House. It wasn't incorporated into the school proper until the 1980s.

EXPANSION

More children, fresh ideas about the importance of physical exercise and a very laudable wish to preserve playing areas for future generations rather than allow them to fall into the hands of developers, led the school authorities on several occasions to search for more territory. The land to the rear was the obvious target.

Originally farmed, it was subsequently used partly for allotments and partly (and possibly unofficially) for school gardening. Ownership of one particular section of the land was to prove contentious.

In April 1917, when the villagers were pressing for allotments, the PC despatched councillor Wyatt and the clerk to interview *Mrs Mapstone and her sons in respect of a piece of land at the back of the school, and had arranged to take it at an annual rent of £3.10s.0d per acre for the purpose of letting out as allotments. Rent to be charged would be 7d per perch[1]. Applications received from Alfred Dury, William Edgell, Hugh Dowling, Henry Roper, Alfred Lynes, Alfred Withey, Ernest Reynolds, Ernest Dury, Thomas Sheppard (20 perches each), Robert Chapman (25 perches) and James Marsh (10 perches).*

What comes next has very little to do with the school but everything to do with village argy-bargy. The villagers had wanted allotment land; now they'd got it, they abused it. At its meeting in February 1931, the PC considered *the question of the state of the allotment field … . Mr Wyatt and the clerk who had recently visited the field reported that the unlet lots comprising some one third of the whole were in a deplorable state, the clerk also reported that he had much difficulty in getting the rent from many of the tenants. Unanimously resolved that the tenants be given notice to quit from 29 September 1931.* In March 1932 the councillors *appointed a deputation to wait upon Mrs Mary Mapstone of Regil, the owner of the allotment land, to endeavour to arrange terms and to offer up to £20 to take over the field at once.* This was the same absentee landlord family as from 1917. Oh no, retorted Mrs Mapstone a fortnight later, *£20 is not enough and the Council would anyway have to clear the land up.* The Council asked, in a Stanley Holloway sort of a way, *how much to settle the matter?* No reply. The Council asked what it would cost to clear the land. "£40.16s.0d", said a valuer. The Council was willing to offer £40, but *a further deputation was arranged, which offered £30 to Mrs Mapstone's brother-in-law Mr Mapstone* [who seemed] *favourably disposed to accept but wanted to consult his other brother who was a co-trustee.* Too many Mapstones were starting to spoil the broth, especially when the owner's son Mr H. G. Mapstone called unannounced at the parish clerk's office and rejected the £30 offer.

Agreement was finally reached with the Mapstones in July 1933, the eventual upshot being that Mrs M owed the Council £2.9s.6d against the valuer's fee of one guinea, leaving the valuer to extract £1.8s.6d from the lady from Regil. It then went quiet until July 1937 when the PC suddenly remembered that *Mr G. H. Mapstone hadn't paid the amount due as at 25 March 1933, as £10 rent was due to his mother from the Council.* Quite how that little dispute was resolved wasn't recorded.

In the meantime, the councillors had discovered that John Tibbs of Wicks Green *has the necessary horses and implements* and would undertake the levelling and clearing. Mr Tibbs had a look and said that he couldn't do the work but Mr A. C. Coles of Tonbridge (Chew Magna) could. The Council accepted Mr Coles' quote for £30 and would send valuers to assess the land once it had been cleared. Mr C did his thing, the valuer reported that the land had been properly levelled and left *in plough* [although] *there is a considerable portion of it still very couchy and I am very doubtful if this can be got rid of in one year. I do not know what your Council proposed to do with this land, whether they intend to crop it to corn this fall* (sic)*; if so, doubtless some of the couche[2] could be got out in the next cultivation*

----

[1] A perch (pole or rod) was 5½ square yards.

[2] Elymus repens, and usually spelt 'couch'.

for the corn crop, but there is, as I say, quite a quantity of couche in various parts of the field. Honestly I do not think that one year's cultivation is going to kill all the couche in the field as it was left in such a bad condition.

Never, in the history of potential school playing fields, had so many perches turned so couchy.

The school wasn't the only one to have its beady eyes on the land. In March 1926 the Rev. C. V. Browne asserted to the CEO in Weston-super-Mare that *the parishioners of Bishop's Sutton* (sic) *were anxious to enlarge the churchyard and for this purpose would like to have the piece of garden ground which forms part of the school premises.* What did the managers think? The managers recommended *approaching the owners* (the Mapstones) *of the allotment field adjoining the school premises with a view to selling a piece of their land to the Church authorities.* That didn't work, and after more dillying and dallying it was decided that some of the School House garden should be exchanged for a piece of ground of equal value immediately at the rear of the school premises on terms to be agreed. And that's what seems to have happened.

But as if all that weren't enough, the parish councillors attended their meeting in May 1937 to be read *a letter from Rev. Trene* (sic) *of Bishop Sutton saying that he wished the field back of Church, Ordnance Survey 1156, be reserved as burial ground.* It wasn't to be so reserved. 1156 had originally been a large 4.8 acre plot behind and to the southwestern side of the school[1]. The plot was divided, perhaps around 1880, into plot 1156b (0.476 acres of which subsequently became Copperstacks under a different plot number), 1156 (a 1.067 acre plot adjacent to Church Lane, being the bit that the Rev. Treen wanted but didn't get), and 1156a (over three acres, being all the rest).

Subsequent attempts having come to nothing, by July 1947 the school was again eager to enlarge the playing field. They asked the LEA *to expedite the acquisition of land adjoining the school to provide more playing space, such extention* (sic) *being urgently needed in view of the increase of senior scholars now attending the school.* The Mapstone family still owned the land at the rear, and in July 1948 two parish councillors *kindly consented to take the headmaster to Ridgehill to interview Mr Mapstone with a view to speeding up the negotiations.* Ridgehill is the same place as Regil. No progress was forthcoming and in January 1949 the managers impatiently chased Taunton. They chased again in July. A couple of months later they were told that *subject to the approval of the County Council, field OS 1156a will be acquired as a playing field for the school.* In actual fact, it would only be part of plot 1156a, the southeastern half of which would eventually become the land for the houses to the northwest of Highmead Gardens. It was, everyone thought, all sorted by mid-December 1949 when the County Architect *recommended the erection of chain link fences 8' high along the boundary wall.*

And then it all went pear-shaped. In July 1950 the County announced that the cost of the fencing would be £40, for which the LEA had no cash. Oh and actually, there

----

[1] The plot extended to the east as far as Church Lane, to the south almost as far as the track running southwest from the right-angled bend on Church Lane to what was then a footpath running northwest from the aforementioned track to the main road immediately to the west of what is now Little Mill House – for those interested in such things, that selfsame footpath used to continue across the main road in a northerly direction to join Stitchings Shord Lane; the northern part of it is still a public footpath – and, to the west, to the footpath that led to the track that led to the right-angled bend in Church Lane. Easy peasy.

wouldn't be a field to fence: *the Ministry would not grant the purchase of the 2-acre field owing to the need to effect savings in educational expenditure.* Livid, the managers fired off a missive to the CEO *informing him that the field would in all probability be sold at no distant date* (sic). That stung Taunton into action and in October 1950 the LEA *confirmed that the ground earmarked as a Playing Field will be provisionally reserved for the school.* On the basis of finders keepers, the managers' clerk offered *to provide poles and labour to erect the fence if the County Education Committee would provide the necessary chain link fencing and wire.* And so it came to pass.

But earmarking wasn't the same as buying, and four years later in November 1954 Mr Bailey asked the managers to address *the purchase of the field at the back of the school to extend the playground.* Again nothing happened and after a full twelve months had elapsed, the managers once more asked *the CEO as regards the sale of the adjoining piece of land on which the Education* (sic) *already had a lien.* In February 1956, and possibly not directly involved with the foregoing, Mr Bailey noted that *the Local Authority have been given a year's notice to quit the school garden. I have asked: (1) they purchase the field at the back, and (2) rent part of it for school garden and house garden.* Who gave them notice? The vicar and churchwarden of Chew Magna, in whose name part of the school was almost certainly still vested? Or someone else?

The following might shed some light: The school was told in March 1956 that *owing to the land which comprised a possible playing field and the present school garden being earmarked by the owner, a builder, for development as a building site, correspondence has ensued … in an endeavour to have part of this land for the purposes mentioned.* Taunton admitted to having completely taken their eye off the ball: *letter from CEO stated that the Committee has taken no further action as regards the acquisition of a playing field.* A land swap was proposed: in November 1956 Mr Bailey, who prudently felt by now that if he didn't sort it out himself, then no-one would, asked *if the Authority will release the ground of the churchyard to Mr X[1], and if the alternative land has been arranged.* Taunton wouldn't agree, and told the managers in March 1957 *that Mr X does not wish to leave land for school gardening and that in view of the opening of the New School* (Chew Valley Secondary) *it is proposed to take no further action in this matter.* That appeared to put the kibosh on it all until July 1959 when the managers again enquired *whether any further action had been taken with regard to the acquisition of the land next to the school.* The response: *endeavours had been made to acquire from Mr X an alternative plot of land for a school garden, but the occupier was not prepared to lease any of the land which he had purchased.*

Things on the ground weren't exactly quiet during all this intrigue. In July 1960 *four trees which had been planted 26 years ago by the previous headmaster next to the wall dividing the school yard and the churchyard appeared to be causing damage. The CEO had been informed and it was decided by him that these trees should be cut down. An estimate had been received from Mr D. W. Price of 71 Council Houses, Pensford, agreeing to felling and removing these trees for the sum of £15.*

Back to the possible acquisition of land at the back of the school, where nothing had progressed since the previous lack of progression in 1956. In December 1964 the managers reported that *the County Council are being recommended to acquire 1.326 acres in OS1156a adjoining the school grounds.* This was the large plot which

----
[1] Initial changed.

the Council had earmarked in 1950 and which was now partially required for the planned Highmead and Parkfield Gardens. *A further communication will be sent when conveyance to the Council has been completed.* Perhaps a false dawn, as on 1 April 1965 the school was told that *the land for a school playground has not been acquired by the County Council but it was anticipated that it would be soon.* But all good things come to he who waits, and in July 1966 the managers were cock-a-hoop to get *a letter from the CEO which stated that a plot* (1.006 acres)*, part of parcels 1156a and 1156b, had been bought for £2,750 from Mr X.* Plot 1156b was the plot to the east of where the current Copperstacks stands. These transfers became a thorny issue in July 1967 when the managers thought it wise to enquire about the right of way from the road to the playing field. It was suspected that an access existed along the school's southwestern boundary with Copperstacks. Copious research was undertaken and Mr Price even took himself off to the National Archives in Kew.

The remainder of this little saga is consigned to the footnote below[1], and can safely be skipped.

----

[1] Mr Price discovered that sometime before 1966 a Mr Y (initial changed) had bought the property Bois Pont (previously Myrtle House, now Copperstacks) from Mr Treasure, whose workshops were still there. At the same time as buying land from Mr X for £2,750, Somerset offered £80 to Mr F and possibly his neighbour Mr C for further land at the rear to make up the remainder of the plot that Taunton needed for the school playing field. £80 would have reflected the then value of the garden land. Mr F and his neighbour objected and submitted an application to build a property in their rear gardens which, if successful, would have brought the value of their land up to residential value. Taunton reacted in March 1968 by slapping a compulsory purchase order on parts of Mr F's and Mr C's rear gardens. The authorities had to pay residential value for the compulsory purchase which was, of course, what the two gentlemen had wanted in the beginning. Possibly for the sake of appeasement at a later date, Taunton agreed a drainage easement over its land down to the main road to do away with the septic tank which had existed at the boundary up until that time.

In 1968 the curtilage of Copperstacks (then Bois Pont) extended from the main road up to the school's pedestrian access gate and the old toilet block in the middle of the playground. The strip from there up to the field, which formed part of the 1966 transaction with Mr X, was owned by Taunton. Mr F believed that the boundary of his land was not the wall of the Bois Pont workshop but a point somewhere on the school side thereof. If this was true, then Mr X had not sold to Somerset County Council the entire length of the strip of land from the main road up to the gate into the field. That meant that the plans that everyone had been looking at for all these years were incorrect. It didn't help that Mr F's deeds were in safekeeping in the NatWest's vaults in Bedminster when the bank was inundated in the 1968 floods and the ink ran so badly that no-one could read anything.

Further investigations by solicitors in the 1980s suggested that although the school was designated a County Primary School, there was no concrete evidence that Somerset County Council had ever actually owned the old School House part of the site. That land had been leased to Somerset – subsequently Avon – by trustees of the old School Board. There were pointers to this in the school records: as a result of a dispute involving the provision of electric power to the Church, the managers commented in December 1956 that *the vicar and churchwardens of Chew Magna were the owners of the school property, and not the Somerset County Council.* The longstanding nature of the lease to Somerset County Council almost definitely meant, however, that the Council enjoyed security of tenure via possessory title. The Diocese of Bath and Wells had certainly at some time agreed to Somerset occupying the School House. As regards the disputed strip, it was eventually and pragmatically decided that it was in the joint ownership of the Council and the householders at Copperstacks, and a land-swap was agreed.

Now that the school had acquired all the playing field land for posterity – or until further evidence should come to light – something needed to be actually done with it. It was still waste ground, but in July 1965 the school was told that *the playing field would be put in order when County funds allowed.* The cheque was in the post yet again. Gates were erected at the entrance to the field in July 1967. In December the managers emphasised to Taunton *that it was imperative that the footpath over the waste ground behind the school* (possibly running to the electricity substation on Highmead Gardens) *be made up and the land cleared. It was stated that the dumping of rubbish was making the work of future clearance difficult.* Bishop Sutton being what it was – a village occasionally prone to scruffiness – it was considered sensible to ask Taunton *that a notice forbidding the tipping of rubbish on the plot behind the school be erected.* In September 1968 *Messrs Dando and Dark started the work of clearing and levelling the playing field ... hoped to seed it before the winter.* In olden days, the headmaster would have got the senior boys to do it. Two problems: (a) there weren't any senior boys any more and (b) they might not have been allowed to do it in case they hoed their toes and sued. But it was ready by October, trees were planted with the spade-wielding help of Rural Science Organiser Miss Gibson, and by mid-December 1968 the County had found the money for a packet of grass seed. But nothing's ever straightforward and in March 1969 Mr Price told the managers that *an awful amount of stones had been left on the surface which would have to be removed, also that the field should be flattened and it was understood that this was to be done. The path had now been completed round the permiter* (sic) *of the field.*

Classroom in 1971
The following are thought to be pictured: Claire Young, Ian Tibbles, Kim Heron, Tony Elms, Bobby Dabinet, Jason Hunt, Emma Robbins, Mandy Barter, Kenny Scammell, Jackie Flower, Lisa Marsh, Justine Hacker and Karen Penny.

On Saturday 24 May 1969 Mr Price *noticed that a quantity of soil had been taken from the northwest corner of the school playing field.* Managers' secretary Mrs Stephens went to inspect. It was decided to leave the matter in abeyance for the weekend in the hope that the soil would find its way back again. It didn't, and enquiries on the following Monday revealed that it had been taken by a Mr Z[1] of Parkfield Gardens, *whose property backs onto the playing field.* Mrs Stephens and Mr Price went to have a little afternoon chat. Mr Z *explained that he had mistakenly taken the soil and undertook to return the whole quantity.* By the following morning the field was all shipshape and Bristol fashion again. In July Mr Price reported that *the stones had now been cleared from the field, but it has to be levelled, as the surface is uneven, and until this is right the bill will not be passed for payment.* Whose bill is not known.

The managers wanted *a padlock to be put on the gate so as to keep it locked after school hours so that it could not be used by the general public.* Mr Price did as he was asked, bought a padlock for the gate and fitted it. He had to tell the managers the following day that *unfortunately it has now been stolen.* As a result of the mistaken theft of the soil a few days earlier, Taunton agreed to fence the top part of the field.

The field had been levelled, soil was no longer being borrowed, the grass (couch-free, one assumes) was nice and green, and on 14 July 1970 Mr Price proudly wrote in his logbook that *the School Sports was tonight held for the first time on the school field.* An Infant Climbing Frame was delivered in March 1972 *to be placed in the school field near the hutted classroom.* The following month, *a load of stone chippings was delivered today for surfacing the area around the Infant Climbing Frame.* Nice and soft for the infants to fall onto.

With the land at the back secured and in the school's ownership (give or take an easement or two), it was time to do something about the playground itself, and in March 1971 Taunton *agreed to extend the playground further at the back at a cost of £100.* It was then decided that the School House garden, which had been home to assorted weeds for a very long time, could be put to more profitable use. Mr Price's initial enquiries came to nothing: in November 1972 he was *informed that the cost of extending the playground to include part of the School House garden would be too great for it to be done at the present time.* It was over two years before any headway was made: in April 1974 *part of the School House garden* [was] *levelled and covered with scalpings to make a parking space and increase the play area.* The headmaster refused to give up on his idea of maximising the available space, and told the governors in March 1975 *that the School House garden at the rear of the school was never used by the occupants of the house and was kept tidy by the school groundsman.* The new authority in Avon slapped down any rejuvenation of the area. They were too strapped for cash. The governors reapplied, suggesting *that if we can't have the whole area covered with tarmac, then it could be seeded over with grass seed as a temporary measure.* That came to naught, but when the Education Department's aptly named Mr Carrot paid a visit to the garden in October 1975, he thought Mr Price's proposals rather sound. He must have had a quiet word in the appropriate quarters, as part of the old School House garden was transformed into an extension of the playground.

The copse at the top of the field was home to a family of elm trees. During heavy rain in November 1972, three of them were *found to have been effected* (sic) *and*

----
[1] Initial changed.

were leaning at what I felt to be a dangerous angle. The County Architect's Office was informed. A tree expert pronounced that they would have to be de-topped. Just in time for some of the remaining elms to be smitten by Dutch Elm Disease in April 1974. Nine trees had to go, but the school did enjoy a bonfire from the diseased wood. In November 1975 Mr Price *observed that several trees in the copse in the school playing field appeared to be dead. They could be a source of danger to the children and to neighbouring houses, I reported the matter by telephone.* The tree expert arranged for the remaining elm trees to be felled in November 1976. The playing field was elmless.

WHO'S BEEN USING MY SCHOOL?

Holy Trinity Church was a bit of a Johnny-come-lately in comparison with the primary school, which had predated it by some seven years. Until the Church was ready, the curate conducted divine services in the school room. The relationship between dog collar and blackboard was sometimes a little frosty, but the spats can wait until after a fleeting look at the church itself.

The Chew Magna Vestry Meeting in August 1844 thought it would be a good idea to build a church in Bishop Sutton so that the Anglican faithful wouldn't have to trek to Chew Magna. Several of the builders found digs in the village and quite a few allegedly left in a rush after the topping-out ceremony, inadvertently forgetting to pay their landladies.

The plaque inside the church.
The line under the curtain rail reads
'be set apart and declared free'.

By the 1890s the church was in such a bad state that major alterations and redecoration were needed. It was closed for several weeks, and a room was again set aside in the school for services, marriages and baptisms. In October 1898 the School Board agreed that *the use of the Bishop Sutton School be granted to the Rev. Hill on Wednesday next in connection with the reopening of the Church.* In April 1904 the School Council wrote to the Rev. Hill at Stowey Vicarage: *7s.6d required for the use of the Bishop Sutton School on March 4th for the convenience of a candidate for confirmation.*

A religious census of March 1851 found: *Bishop Sutton (Holy Trinity Chapel of Ease), free sittings 300. Attendances: general congregation 38 [at] morning sittings, afternoon 99, evening 0; Sunday scholars morning 51, afternoon 51, evening 0.* And, for the Methodists: *Minister John Wareham, Wesleyan Chapel, free sittings 100, other sittings 134. General congregation morning 40, afternoon 90, evening 0; no Sunday scholars*. We'll come on to the Sunday School later, although it is untrue that there was no Methodist Sunday School in 1851. No matter, the figures showed just how strong the lure of the church(es) was. Anglican curates with sole responsibility for Bishop Sutton were the Rev. William Holmes Orr from 1869 to 1875 and Rev. Edward Clowes to 1885. The incumbency was then extended to include Stowey: Rev. James Samuel Hill from 1885 to 1924 (almost famous for his 1924 book 'Place Names of Somerset'), Rev. Francis McDonald Etherington to 1926, Rev. Henry Mortlock Treen to 1940, Rev. William John Freeman to 1946, Rev. Robert William Ellis to 1949, Rev. Thomas George O'Freely to 1954, Rev. Arthur Lee to 1957 when he left for Kalamunda in Western Australia, Rev. Ivan Edmund Holt to 1976 and Rev. Barrie Arthur Newton to 1981. The Rev. Holt was an interestingly multi-tasking vicar, who advertised his extra-curricular services in the June 1965 Parish Magazine: *Private tuition in English, French, Latin, Greek, Hebrew, Maths, Scripture, terms moderate, tel. CM 65, recognised by Ministry of Education.* One of his letters to parishioners in the magazine read: *My Dear Friends, never in human history has the world needed more 'the turning upside down' or may it not be the turning right side up … the inhuman and unnecessary daily toll in lives upon our all-too-inadequate roads by a fast growing number of motor cars and motor cycles drives all thinking people to despair not only for the body of man but also for his immortal soul.* Quite so.

Disputes arose from time to time between the spiritual and the pedagogic neighbours, and it wasn't just the cupboard love affair to be gleefully recounted shortly. In March 1970 the *termly managers' meeting was held at the school at 7.30 pm. Mr Brice from CEO and a representative* (Mr Clarke) *from County Legal Department were present to clarify any connections which might exist between the church and the school so as to overcome any misunderstandings which might possibly arise between Church and School* (sic). *Mr Price* (headmaster) *stated that the Church had stated that they could use the one classroom on any day after 6 pm*[1] *and that when once the Parish Council had this classroom and the Church also required the use of a school on the same evening, they did not like it as they couldn't have the usual classroom. Mr Clarke brought with him a very old document*[2], *and it would seem from this that the Board had the classroom from 6 in the morning until 6 at night, except on Saturday, Sunday, Good Friday and Ascension Day. So it would seem from this that the Church could have use of the classroom from 6 pm, but in future, it was decided that the Church and the Parish Council would have to pay for the time of the school, which in the past they had not done. The charge to be: caretaker 6/-, heating 4/-, light 4/-.*

The secretary to the managers certainly had a way with language.

In December 1976 *the Parochial Church Council asked if they could have the use of the school kitchen, also two classrooms for use when the new vicar has the induction service on 10 February 1977. They would also need this for the Bishop of Bath and Wells to change and also for the service of refreshments after the service. The managers recommended that this should be free to the Church and no charge made, and supported this as the relationship between the Church and the school had always been first class.* That was a rather charitable distortion of the facts.

----

[1] A point first made by the school managers in 1905 when they wrote to the Education Department stating as much.

[2] This 'very old document' would have been the Deed of October 1874 transferring the school to the School Board.

Which brings us to the cupboard love thing. The vicar had certain legal privileges as a result of the statutory connection in the early days between the two establishments, although quite why he insisted on exercising proprietary rights to the school when he had cavernous premises of his own is unclear. The first reference to niggardliness was in July 1885 when, *in ref to the accommodation of the Sunday School requisites at Bishop Sutton,* [the Board] *resolved that the doors of the cupboard be divided and that the upper portion comprising the top shelf be placed under the exclusive control of the Rev. Mr Hill*. This petty little quarrel rumbled on for years. In 1891 the Rev. Hill must have written to the Board, who, after putting the vicar's request (whatever it was) to a vote – *4 in favour, Mr Lovell against* – replied as per the letter illustrated below.

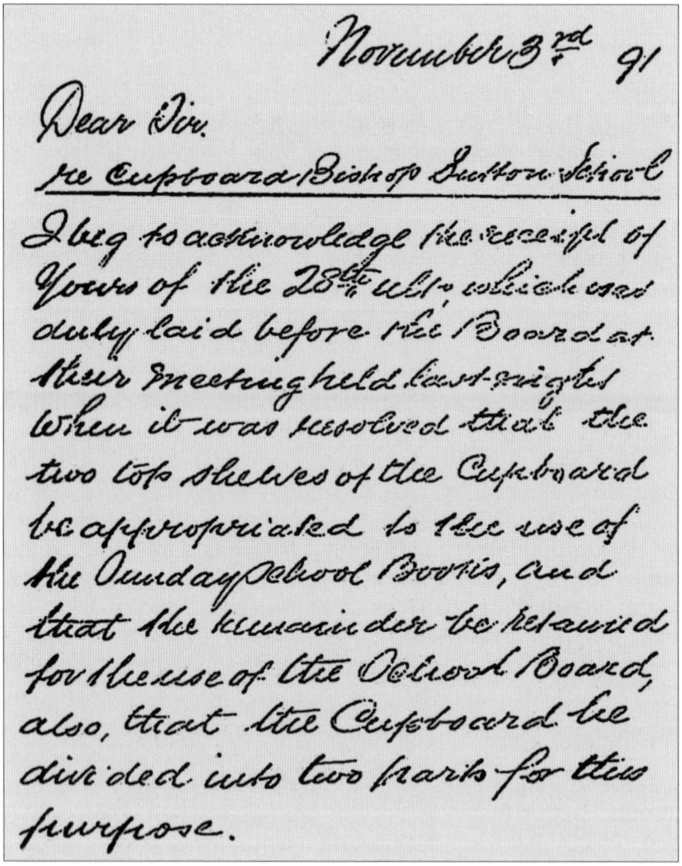

The cupboard didn't feature again, but sins on the Sabbath rekindled the headmasters' gripes. On Monday 13 March 1911 Mr Wightman *found marks on school walls in main room. Evidently done yesterday during Sunday School hours.* On Monday 25 February 1918 he *discovered some writing on inner walls of boys' offices evidently done yesterday by one attending Sunday School.*

Now to more lively pursuits. In March 1927 the County Education Secretary received *a letter from Miss Queenie V. M. Wightman (Hon. Pianist, Treasurer and secretary of Bishop Sutton Folk Dancers), who wishes to recommence country dancing, which she had formerly held in the Village Hall; as now included in the County Sports, I have asked the Education Committee to allow me to use the Infants' Room one evening weekly, weekly charge 2s.3d.* Queenie was the 'Victoria M. Wightman' (aged 10 months) listed in the 1901 census as the only child of headmaster James Wightman.

It wasn't just Sunday School pupils who mistreated the school. On 5 February 1894 the Board *received a written communication from Mr Brown complaining of the disorderly condition of his school after a public meeting held therein on Thursday January 18th* [and] *resolved that the trustees of Bishop Sutton School premises be requested to take measures to prevent a recurrence of same.* Mr Brown's logbook version of the events was that *on Friday morning the older children had to remain in the yard till 9.35 while the room was being rendered fit for their reception.* In November 1955 the CEO *asked that a room should be set aside for Civil Defence Courses to be held weekly until completion of the course.* Quite what happened for the next nine years went unrecorded – although Doug Price's nuclear bunker has already been mentioned – but *instructions in Civil Defence commenced on 27 September 1964 in a classroom on each Thursday, and the course would consist of 20 sessions and take 30 hours.* By 1974 Stowey and Bishop Sutton Women's Institute were using classrooms for their monthly meeting at £1.14 a time. In July 1978 it was the turn of the Adult Education Tailoring Classes: *Mr Price was reluctant to use a primary school for this, as the chairs and the tables were really not suitable.* Unless the tailors had small bottoms. Later that year the school was used by the *Ladies' Forum for wine making and wine and cheese party.*

£1 (green), 1978-88

Children welcomed political elections as they got the day off and the chance to see their dads (and, after 1918, their mums) in school doing something secret with a little pencil and a small piece of paper. The Board agreed in November 1885 *to give such furniture as they have in both school rooms* (Chew Magna and Bishop Sutton) *for the use of the Sheriff on the Polling Day the 8th December of the parliamentary election for North Somerset, and also supply fires for both schools at a cost of 15/- to go to the School Fund.* On 9 April 1949 the managers charged *5/- for heating and lighting of the schoolroom for the County Council election, also the caretaker's fee of 7/6 for preparing the rooms and clearing up after the polls.* All those spoilt ballot papers littering the floor, no doubt. Public riffraff couldn't be trusted: in March 1922 when the school was needed for District Council Elections, Mr Wightman was advised *not to leave any books about and lock all drawers and cupboards.* On 5 June 1975 *the school was closed because of voting in the National Referendum on entry into the European Common Market,* and on 1 May 1979 *Miss Williams called at school this afternoon to collect the key for the Presiding Officer to open the school at 6.30 am for the General Election as it had been decided not to leave the matter for the cleaners.* By the late 1970s the governors had had enough, and when they met in July 1978 they tersely noted: *re use of school for elections, there were three halls available in the village, why not use them?* But in December of that year *Mr Price received Information Bulletin No. 53 from the County dated October 1978 about polling stations, in which it was clearly stated that the Returning Officers have a statutory right to use as a polling station accommodation in a building maintained by an LEA.* Spoilt ballot papers would again litter the floor the morning after.

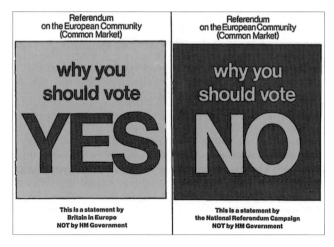

1975: referendum leaflets for and against Britain's continuing membership of the Common Market. 67% of voters said 'yes', 33% said 'no'.

Not only was the school itself in demand, but also the grounds. In December 1969 Mr Price was *asked for permission to use the playing field for a charity match for the Youth Club, the boys would be playing the girls and the proceeds would be given to the Silver Lining Club. Mr Price stated that the field was really only suitable for Junior football,* but the managers gave their permission for the use of once only, but that *the match should not be played on a Sunday, which was the day asked for.* Nothing much was allowed to happen on Sundays in the '60s.

CHAPTER FOUR

HEADS, TEACHERS, STAFF AND THE TALE OF EMMA FERRIS

£45 A YEAR, HOUSE AND COAL, THREE MONTHS' NOTICE EITHER SIDE

Were any of Shakespeare's whining schoolboys with their satchels and shining morning faces in Bishop Sutton, creeping like snails unwillingly to school? Or were any of the headteachers as described in Oliver Goldsmith's 1770 poem 'The Village Schoolmaster'?:

> There, in his noisy mansion, skilled to rule, the village master taught his little school;
> A man severe he was and stern to view, I knew him well and every truant knew;
> Well had the boding tremblers learned to trace the day's disasters in his morning face;
> Full well they laughed, with counterfeited glee, at all his jokes, for many a joke had he:
> Full well the busy whisper, circling round, conveyed the dismal tidings when he frowned;
> Yet he was kind, or, if severe in aught, the love he bore to learning was in fault ...
> While words of learned length and thundering sound amazed the gazing rustics ranged
>   around;
> And still they gazed, and still the wonder grew that one small head could carry all he knew.

We shall see.

Our knowledge of the headteacher(s) for the first thirty years of the school's existence is currently restricted to what was in the censuses. The first one to postdate the building of the school was 1851, which listed Miss Ellen Elizabeth Hassell (25 and born in Newmarket, Cambridgeshire), as schoolmistress at Bishop Sutton National School. Her widowed mother Elizabeth (55 and formerly a grocer) lived with her. It's just about feasible that Miss Hassell was the school's first headteacher. She was listed again (now aged 35) in the 1861 census, but this time with her mother's prior occupation as 'formerly innkeeper'. By the time of the 1871 census, Miss Hassell was living alone. Her mother may have died.

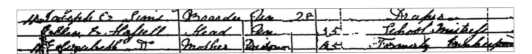

Census 1861 (second line): Ellen Hassel, school mistress

It was under Miss Hassell's headship that the school's first logbook started. The school managers confirmed in 1874 that she was to be *continued at £45 a year, house and coal, three months' notice either side*. For reasons unknown, she tendered her resignation in May 1875. Adverts were placed in the School Board Chronicle (Islington), The Schoolmaster (Fleet Street, London), The Mercury (Bristol), The Times & Mirror (Bristol) and the National Society's Paper (Westminster). Applications were received from as far afield as Maldon (Essex), Dudley, Rochester, Kidderminster, Taunton and Finstown in faraway Orkney. The records didn't say who was invited in for a grilling, but all the interviews were to take place at the same time on the same day. *No travelling or other expenses will be allowed.* The Board found no-one from the first round, but then stumbled across

Mr John Jones, formerly assistant master at King Street and Tower Street Board School in London, currently without work and living at 1 Avon Cottages, Albert Road, Bristol. The 1871 census suggests that he may have been a chemistry teacher, born in 1841 in Lancashire. The managers wanted someone quickly and Mr Jones must have used that to his advantage, as the Board wrote to him: *if [we] fixed the salary of the Master of this School at £80 p.a. would you be disposed to accept?* J.J. was so disposed and the Board appointed him on 16 August 1875, throwing in the School House *free of rates and taxes excluding any share of the grant.*

It's a fair bet that Mr Jones didn't put himself out to be friendly to his young charges. Only a few months after he started, the Board reviewed *the case of the Master of the Bishop's Sutton School having flogged a boy named Edward Harvey* [and resolved] *that the clerk write the Master expressing the opinion of the Board that he had too severely beaten the boy and requesting that in future he would abstain from corporal punishment except in cases where it was absolutely necessary and then not with such severity as in the present instance.* Mr Jones resigned on 14 May 1877. The managers wrote to him on 15 May: *Your resignation ... was considered by the Board at their meeting yesterday and I am directed to inform you that they accept it. Yours truly, W. W. White, Clerk.* All had nevertheless

Advertising for Miss Hassell's replacement

not been what it seemed. The Board wrote to the Education Department in Whitehall on 20 August 1877: [We] *were dissatisfied with Mr Jones' management of the School and finding the number of children attending the School, instead of increasing as it ought to have done, was diminishing, the Board came to the conclusion that it was necessary to change the Master. Instead however of giving Mr Jones notice to leave, the Board gave him the opportunity to resign of which he availed himself.* The inspectors had actually thought rather well of him: Ernest Wix commented that *Mr Jones maintains excellent order and is a careful and accurate teacher.* Mr Wix hadn't asked Edward Harvey's opinion.

So it was back to the advertising. Notices were placed in The Schoolmaster and in The Times and Mirror: *Wanted by the above Board, about the month of August, man and wife as Master and Mistress of the Bishop Sutton Board School. Wife need not be certificated[1]. Average attendance about 80. Joint salary £100 per annum with residence. Applications with testimonials to be sent to me no later than the 7th June next.* There were five aspiring candidates. One, a Mr Symons, hadn't read the rubric properly and the Board had to write to him: *you had better let me know the ages of*

----

[1] A certificated teacher was one who had passed through a training college or, following a period of apprenticeship in a school, had sat for college exams in his or her spare time or, in some instances, had been a successful teacher for at least 12 years despite a lack of qualifications.

yourself and your wife, and say what duties in the school your wife would be prepared to undertake. Invitations were sent to the most promising of the candidates on Tuesday 12 June for a joint interview the following Monday at 6 pm. They were to visit the school *during the afternoon of that day* [and] *inspect the dwelling house. Your best plan of reaching Bishop Sutton is perhaps from the Pensford Station on the North Somerset Railway from which it is about 2 miles distant.* The winners of the talent competition were Mr and Mrs Robinson from Cropton National School near Pickering, North Yorkshire. They were appointed on 18 July but for some reason didn't take up the post. Other applicants withdrew too, and the Board had to readvertise in August.

Bishop Sutton School's Dark Ages were about to begin.

Mr James Northam brandished his 1st Division, 3rd Degree Certificate together with testimonials from his existing school at Minster Lovell near Witney, Oxfordshire. Without being interviewed, he and his teacher-wife Elizabeth were offered £100 a year between them. The Board's letter of appointment was dated 28 August 1877: *the last Master had left, but the Board will make temporary arrangements for carrying on the school until you can commence your duties.* The Minster Lovell Two had not seen Bishop Sutton at that stage and asked to do so. *You can come any day,* said the Board, *at Bishop Sutton you had better ask for either Mr Arter or Mr Cook (both members of the Board).* The Northams couldn't start straightaway. Mr Jones agreed to carry on until they could: *Your application for a testimonial was considered and the Board decided to withhold it for the period.* That was a good inducement to him to stay on for a few months! Mr and Mrs N started on 11 January 1878. The Board would rue the day.

'The Village Pump'

The school records could leave intriguing questions unanswered. What, for example, prompted the Education Department to write to the Board in August 1878 to doubt the Northams' references? The Board retorted that Mr Northam had been selected in consequence of his good testimonials, one of which was from the Rev. H. C. Ripley: *He has been 18 months in charge of Minster Lovell National School. He has been conscientious in the discharge of his duties and painstaking in the instruction of the children. As regards his character he is thoroughly respectable, steady and quiet. Mrs Northam is an efficient sewing mistress and a great favourite with the children.*

A mere fortnight after starting, Mr Northam invited his predecessor Mr Jones round to the School House for a fireside chat. Mr N's logbook entry is illustrated on the next page. Mr Jones clearly would not be added to the Northams' Christmas card list.

Exercised by what he'd heard, and keen to be a new broom, Mr Northam spent the next day examining the different classes. *The Reading was bad throughout. The chief faults were indistinct pronounciation* (sic)*, some words muttered over any how, final letter(s) and syllable disregarded – a drawling tone[1], want of fluency, no attention to stops and a disconnected jerking style of reading. The I Standard in many cases had to spell such words as 'he', 'any', 'many', 'why', 'sung', 'water'.*

----
[1] This 'drawling tone' was criticised by several headteachers.

> *1878*
> *Jan. 25th* Monday—Mr Jones, the late master visited the school, and I complained to him of the little work done during the past 6 months of the school year; especially in Geography, Grammar, and Arithmetic. They have spent most of the time in going over last year's work. The IV standard have only got so far as the manufacture of England. All the V standard has done is learnt four lessons from a little book. In Arithmetic the III standard have only learned to divide by one figure, and several cannot do that.
> IV Standard have only learnt to multiply (money) by two figures, and not a single child has got a single sum right during the past fortnight. The other standards are equally bad. I standard have no notion of notation beyond two figures, & the other standards beyond hundreds. When I called Mr Jones's attention to it, he answered "No, I haven't taken much trouble with them, I used to set the sums on the black board for them to copy off". I asked him if it was right that he had only taught the IV standard to multiply by two figures and allowed them to call off their answers by single digits, and he said "Yes; I haven't taken much trouble with them.

Mr Northam's logbook version of his chat with Mr Jones

He set about remedying matters, aided and abetted by a stern manner, a lively cane and copious and meticulous notes in the logbook. So conscientious was he that he regularly wrote:

> *Nothing of importance has occurred.*

It's time to bring Emma Ferris into the proceedings. Her first appearance was in the 1871 census. Then aged 9, she was living somewhere in the village[1] with her father George (35, a blacksmith), mother Mary Jane (34) and siblings Mary (10), William (7), George (3) and Thomas (3 months). Emma's story actually began in 1876, two years before Mr Northam appeared on the scene. An existing scholar at

----

[1] The 1891 census was more specific: 3 Coalpit Road (near the current Brents Garage).

Bishop Sutton, she was considered by an inspector to be suitable for pupil teachership, and underwent a medical examination. On 1 April of that year, Charles Howell Collins Esq MRCS of Chew Magna certified that *she has been examined by me and appears free from any ailments or constitutional disease.* The Board accordingly wrote to headmaster Jones on Wednesday 27 September 1876: *I shall be glad if you will arrange for Emma Ferris and her father to attend the Board meeting on Monday 9th proximo at 3 o'clock to execute the agreements binding the former as pupil teacher.* Emma's pupil teachership wasn't entirely trouble-free. Mr Jones had written in the log on 9 March 1877 that she was *15 minutes late yesterday and 10 today.* In September 1877 an inspector commented that Emma had *passed* [an exam] *fairly, but should attend to handwriting.* The following January, the new headmaster *was obliged to publicly reprove the pupil teacher and monitress for encouraging the children in rebellions and disorderly conduct, by slily* (sic) *grinning at them when I reproved any of them.*

1877: 'Emma Ferris 15 minutes late yesterday and 10 today'

A few days later, Mr Northam *found the pupil teacher in a deliberate lie respecting her brother, as proved by three first class girls.* He was referring to girls from the first class, not to first-class girls. Emma was allegedly becoming proper awkward and it served the headmaster's subsequent purposes to bring his wife (the sewing mistress) in on the act: on 15 November 1878 *the pupil teacher was very saucy and insolent to Mrs Northam when spoken to by her about hitting the little children, and favouring, concerning which complaints had been received.* Four days later, Emma *was insolent when told to put some coal on the fire.* In a distinct lack of pre-Christmas joy, Mr Northam wrote on 6 December that *the bad behaviour of the pupil teacher continues. She seems to be above her work, and if corrected in any way she openly resents it. I have found her guilty of untruth in three different cases this week.* Determined to strengthen his argument, he told the School Board that Emma *was asked to apologise, but declined … since Monday she has behaved worse than ever, if possible, and has spread a false report that Mrs Northam struck her before the children.* Emma was suspended until after the next Board meeting on Friday 10 January. In a fit of post-Christmas generosity (or perhaps in an appreciation of the likely facts), the Board *accepted the explanation of the pupil teacher's statement, and having excused her behaviour to Mrs Northam, Emma Ferris returned to work on Tuesday.*

All well and good, one would have thought, but on 12 January, two days after the Board meeting, Emma said she wanted to resign, presumably giving a month's notice. Mr Northam ordered her to attend school until excused by the Board. She did, but on 17 January *she was disobedient by refusing to sing with the infants.* On 31 January she continued *to act defiantly.* Emma must have changed her mind about resignation, as Mr Northam wrote on Friday 7 March: *Had no Scripture lesson to-day, spent the time in investigating the cause of a disturbance which occurred on Monday night while instructing the pupil teacher. A number of boys, two of them the pupil teacher's brothers being amongst them, assembled round the school gate and beat up old tins and threw stones at the school. This appears to have been organized by her three brothers, probably by her father's consent, as they agreed beforehand to start from his blacksmith's shop, and her brothers supplied them with tins and William told them, "That's right, you go up to the school, and make a most dreadful noise, and I'll go in the shop".*

What happened between then and 2 June was unreported, but Mr Northam asked the Board on that date that his daughter *be appointed as a pupil teacher in the room of Emma Ferris.* The Board *carried unanimously that the application be declined.* On 6 June 1879 Mr Northam wrote: *Mary Jane Elmes, 10 years, shewed me a black bruise on her arm, which she alleged to have been made by the pupil teacher. The pupil teacher admitted pulling her round by the arm, and two other first class girls heard Mary Elmes say "Oh Emma did hurt my arm".* On 11 June the headmaster followed up Mary Jane's black bruise with: *this evening the Sewing mistress was obliged to order the pupil teacher to leave the room during her private studies for being insolent in word and act, and refusing to go on with her work when told. The mistress had to reprove her for certain improprieties of behaviour, when she knocked her hand on the table, saying "Do you know who you are speaking to, hold your tongue, it is of no business to you what I do out of school hours". The mistress told her to go on with her work, and not to be so impudent, when she stuck in her needle and put her work in her lap beside the table. The mistress then ordered her to leave the room.* It's not clear whether it was Emma or Mrs Northam who wanted to keep their evening activities to themselves but, regardless, this clearly wasn't a meeting of minds.

Things went from bad to worse. On 13 June Mr Northam *wasted considerable time this morning owing to what I believe to be wilfulness on the part of the pupil teacher. There appeared to be a penny mistake in taking the pence* (the school fees). *After she had counted over the money, and I the books* [sic] *three times to no purpose, I found she was pretending to mistake a fourpenny bit[1] for a threepenny bit. The coin was in a good state of preservation.* The next day, Mr Northam changed tack and emphasised that Emma *wasted the time of the infants in the class room by refusing to tell them the words of a*

1836 groat (with hole!) and 1856 threepenny bit, both actual size

school song she had to teach them. And lest the monetary myopia from the previous day go overlooked, Mr Northam spent time on 16 June in meticulously copying the following sum into the logbook *as a specimen of the pupil teacher's*

----

[1] A groat (a silver fourpenny coin) was the same size and weight as a silver threepenny bit, and confusion would have been entirely possible in the dim light of the school.

carelessness at her studies. I believe she blunders to be wilful.

Blundering to be wilful

Blunders to be wilful' would have enriched Emma's CV no end.

The poor girl was totally browbeaten by her supposed mentor and his wife, and left on 4 July 1879. Emma requested a testimonial and the clerk wrote to the Rev. Richard Hill of Timsbury in respect of what was presumably Emma's application to be a pupil teacher there. An extract from the letter is illustrated on the following page.

It would be interesting to know what happened to the young Miss Ferris, as she seems on the face of it to have been a plucky, principled and dedicated prospective teacher. By the time of the 1881 census, she was no longer at the family home but there were the additions of Edward (13, who hadn't been listed ten years earlier), Annie (8) and Agnes (5). The 1891 census showed Emma back with her parents and several of her brothers and sisters, and listed her as 'certificated schoolmistress'. Her experiences clearly hadn't put her off teaching and she was now fully qualified at a school somewhere locally. By the time of the 1901 census, the only Ferris at the original family property was Thomas Ferris, 30 (who was 3 months old in 1871 when Emma was 9) and described as 'shoeing and blacksmith'. In later years, the Ferris smithy was to become Brents Garage.

*The managers' testimonial for Emma Ferris, referring to
a misunderstanding of a 'very trivial nature'*

Hands up for who replaced Emma as temporary monitress. Yes, no other than Rosa Northam. Not listed in the 1881 census, she was perhaps the headmaster's sister. Nepotism was one of Mr Northam's guiding principles: he had persuaded the Board to take his daughter Sarah on in July 1878 to replace Jane Tibbs, whom he'd contrived to dismiss as monitress. The headmaster fell ill at the beginning of February 1881 and his 20-year old daughter Eva stepped into the breach. Her logbook entry of 11 February 1881 read: *I, Eva Northam, having completed my apprenticeship as a pupil teacher, took charge of this school on February 8 on account of my father's illness.* On 18 February she poignantly wrote: *the school was closed on Tuesday as my father died during the night. On this account myself and Sarah Northam were excused.* The census conducted in April of that year listed just Elizabeth (46, born in Kentisbeare, near Cullompton), Eva (20, also from Kentisbeare), Sarah (18, 'monitress', born in Winsham, near Chard) and Carrie (10, 'scholar', born in North Cerney, near Cirencester). Mr Northam's teaching had taken him around a bit.

It could be that he was quite a conscientious old stick after all. Perhaps he just lacked self confidence. He sometimes treated the logbook as his own diary: in an incident (which will crop up again later) involving Mrs Martin of Hollow Brook, he wrote: *Caution – don't depend on children's tales, and to the children always tell the truth.* Sometimes, as in October 1880, it was almost as if he was talking to himself: *G. White showed great obstinacy of temper in the Arithmetic lesson by pretending he could not do division of money. He is preparing for V Standard, and has been doing the same sort of sums all the week. The fact is, according to my believe* (sic)*, that he wants to get off school for work, but he has not passed the Standard. So he wants to draw me into a contest so that I may give him a beating, and then he would make that an excuse for leaving, but I do not intend to beat him, only keep* [him] *in.*

Conscientious or not, he had now died and the Board advertised for a new incumbent. Trouble was, Mrs Northam was ensconced in the School House, no doubt with her daughters in tow. But if she were happy to fly in the face of Victorian propriety and share the small premises with a strange man, then the Board would offer her *£20 a year as Sewing mistress with the joint use of the House* with the master (*to be not under the age of 30*) to be appointed; if not, then she must leave and the Board would *advertise for man and wife as schoolmaster and Sewing mistress, joint salary £100 p.a. with residence*. It seems that Mrs N was happy – perhaps even eager, her being a widow and all – to live under the same roof as a man not under the age of 30, for the Board advertised and received no fewer than 21 applications. Perhaps they too fancied their chances. *Four were chosen* [for interview], said the minute book: *Walter Sewell, J. Warren, J. P. Sargent, Thomas Everest, John Barker.* I make that five. Second class railway fare would be paid both ways if not appointed, only one way for the successful applicant.

The school remained temporarily under the custodianship of young Eva, who had a much lighter touch than her papa. Whole weeks went by when *nothing of importance happened*, a phrase she'd clearly picked up from him. Sister Sarah was still a monitress, and the Board resolved in April 1881 that her wages *be increased by 6d per week, making 2/- a week.* Eva relinquished control on 8 April 1881 when the Board appointed John Barker (certificated master of the 2nd class, born in Albury, Hertfordshire). He would move into the School House, but he was listed in the 1881 census (undertaken on 3 April) as a 'temporary lodger' with Edwin and Mary Fear. They lived with father Charles (an impressive 87), Kate (10), James (4) and Benjamin (7 months) somewhere in the vicinity of Stitchings Shord Lane and Ham Lane.

It took Mr Barker only a week to spot his predecessor's apparent failures: he found *the children on the whole backward in Geography, Standards IV and V weak in Arithmetic, the copy books are also generally untidy.* What's more, Mr Northam's *record-keeping was poor.* Something didn't enamour Mr Barker to the school – perhaps he found Mrs Northam and her daughters insufferable – and on 2 May 1881 he resigned. He'd lasted for four weeks.

The Board readvertised and came up with five applicants. None was suitable but the managers chanced upon Mr Lewis Hawkins (certificated master 2nd class, 1st division) and took him on to start on 6 June 1881 when Mr Barker's period of notice ended. *Salary £80 a year, average attendance about 80, joint use of residence with the widow of the late Master*. Given Mr Northam's recent death and Mr Barker's astonishingly short tenure, it was hardly surprising that Mr Hawkins engaged himself *in endeavouring to put the registers and other books in order, as I found them to be in a confused state.*

That September the Board gave *Sarah Northam monitress a week's notice to leave.* In an apparent fit of pique, her indomitable mother applied to the managers for another daughter to take the place *of her sister as monitress.* It's not clear who that was, as the only other Northam daughter listed in the 1881 census was Carrie, then only 10. There may have been an older sibling living outside the parish. The Board rejected the application, *considering that no stipendiary monitress was required in the school*. The wily Mrs N then seems to have bypassed the Board and brought her dubious charms to bear on the Education Department itself, which wrote to the unsuspecting managers on 2 January 1882 to tell them that Mrs Northam and her daughter Sarah were to be employed *from this day* [as] *acting teachers* at the school at a joint salary of £15.12s.0d.

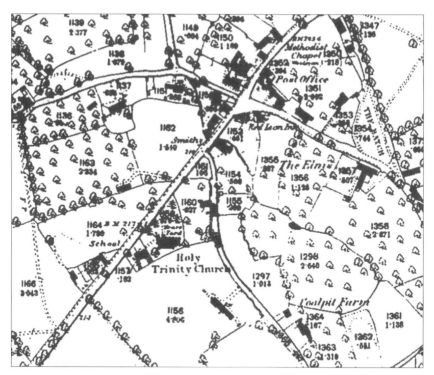

Ordnance Survey map 1885

By the end of January 1882 Mr Hawkins found that *the present staff of the school work very unsatisfactorily. I examined Standards I and II (taught by Mrs Northam) and find a decided backward tendency instead of any signs of improvement.* A conscientious man, he spent much of the following month in examining Mrs Northam's classes himself, and much of the rest of the spring in coaching the children: *I have still devoted much time to the lower Standards. They now do their Arithmetic considerably better. Standard I have commenced simple subtraction and Standard II now divide correctly by numbers 2, 3, 4, 5, 6.* We don't know whether or not he was a kind man, but he tried hard to improve levels of attainment and made no comments in the logbook about punishments. He confessed to being concerned about low attendance and admitted to not working to a strict timetable. Perhaps he just had his mind on other things: on 19 May 1882 he resigned as he'd found a position in India.

With Mr Northam pushing up the daisies, the Board was anxious to move on and resolved on the very day of Mr Hawkins' resignation *that the clerk do at once give Mrs Northam and her daughter Sarah Northam three months' notice to leave the services of the Board.* The Board would provide a testimonial.

Mr Hawkins offered to find a replacement to cover the remaining months of his notice period and beyond, and suggested an Allan Robert Hill. The Board was happy and the fourth headmaster in as many years came along. It's not known whether Bishop Sutton was his first headmastership, but he was a sufferer from verbal diarrhoea: some days he would ramble on for a whole page. He too was unimpressed by the Northam mother-and-daughter team. His first logbook entry – Wednesday 7 June 1882 – included a comment about *attendance poor due to the*

Sunday School Tea, there was no sewing as Mrs Northam and Sarah Northam went to the tea. Sunday School teas, like Sunday School treats, were never on a Sunday: fun on the Sabbath was not encouraged. For the remaining months of the Northams' period of notice, Mr Hill continued to voice his concerns about their absences. 14 July 1882: *Mrs Northam late all the week each from 10.20 to 10.30 and afternoon from 2.25 to 2.40. Absent all day today, working two days this week.* Mother and daughters finally moved out of the School House, but not without one last act of malevolence: on 3 July 1882 *the clerk was instructed to write to Mrs Northam requesting her, as she had left the House, to deliver up the key.*

Hardly surprising that she was regularly away. She'd only gone and established her own school elsewhere in the village. Mr Hill wrote on 29 September 1882: *Charles Frappell, Joseph Frappell and Edward Harvey all gone to Mrs Northam's school.* Something prompted the authorities to get involved: on 6 November 1882 *a letter from the Education Department respecting Mrs Northam's school was read and the matter was ordered to stand over.* On 22 December 1882 Mr Hill wrote: *24 names taken off the register this week, most of these children have not been present since the harvest holidays, but attend Mrs Northam's school. Names have been kept on the books pending steps to be taken by Board.* The competing establishment perhaps wasn't all it was cracked up to be: on 5 January 1883, *Thomas Jones Harvey readmitted from Mrs Northam's school.*

Just what the recalcitrant family was up to is unclear, but in February 1883 *a letter from the Inspector of Nuisances with reference to Mrs Northam's school was read stating that the Sanitary authority saw no reason to interfere.* Sounds very Monty-Pythonesque: an Inspector of Nuisances. The authorities needed to close this pesky lady down, and they enlisted the help of the Attendance Officer to find evidence of her incompetence. He *furnished a report as to Mrs Northam's school showing that at present she had 33 children there.* [The Board] *resolved that in order to test the efficiency of* [her] *school, the following parents Alfred Tibbs, William Dix, Henry Burridge, Thomas Elmes and Edwin Fear be summoned for the non-attendance of their children at the Board School.* The case reached court, and on 21 August 1883 Mr Hill was absent for part of the day *to attend the Magistrates' meeting in Temple Cloud on some test cases of children summoned from Dame's School*[1]. *Children in the 3rd Standard* [were] *examined in Reading, and as they could read the words in the first infant primer, the cases were dismissed as being taught properly.* Two more of Mrs Northam's pupils were examined a week later: *the justices dismissed the summons. The Board resolved to withdraw the four remaining cases.* The court clearly thought that the school managers had overstepped the mark. One up to Mrs Northam.

References to the dame school continued. In March 1883 *Walter Henry Hassell admitted this week from a Dame's School.* In May 1883 *Burridges gone to Dame's School.* In July 1883 the headmaster *admitted four boys and four girls – four of these being infants, the remainder, children who have attended Mrs Northam's school during past year. These I have examined and find (except in Reading which in some cases is improved in quantity) that they have lost what they did know.* So why had parents taken the children away from the Board School? It may be that the

----
[1] 'Dame school' was a term commonly used to describe small private schools, typically run by an elderly woman who limited her instruction to reading, writing and sewing. Fees were around 3d a week and the quality of education was generally iffy. Many dame school headmistresses and teachers were little more than child minders. We unfortunately don't know enough about the dame school in the village to comment authoritatively.

fees were lower elsewhere, or that Mrs Northam had a loyal following despite the apparent evidence against her, or that some parents simply felt that the teaching at the 'official' school was too academic. It may generally have been the weaker scholars who had been attracted to the dame school. In any event, *George Elmes has again returned to Dame's School, but really working a donkey cart for coals*, wrote Mr Hill in September 1883.

Winning a top prize for gall, but presumably realising that the days of her school were numbered, Mrs Northam applied to the Board on 1 October 1883 for *the post of Sewing mistress at Bishop Sutton School.* Her letter probably left the Board members spluttering into their cocoa. The clerk *was directed to inform Mrs Northam that her application could not be entertained, the Board having already filled up the situation.* In January 1884 Mr Hill *admitted four children this week who have just left the Dame's School, they are all very backward,* and in March 1884 headmaster Brown *admitted six children from Dame's School. Every child failed in Reading, Writing and Arithmetic of their last Standard.* And that was the final mention of the dame school. The Northams left Bishop Sutton, apparently without trace.

Back to Allan Robert Hill, whose application for permanent mastership of the school was accepted by the Board on 3 July 1882. But not just Mr Hill. With him came his sister-in-law, Mrs Rice. Joint salary £100 a year with the use of the house. Things didn't go the Board's way. For reasons unknown, Mr Hill soon decided he'd had enough and handed in his notice on 6 August 1883. The managers could hardly have been happy at losing yet another headteacher. Mr Cook and Mr Brown applied, as did a Miss Creighton. The three of them attended an interview and Mr Brown was chosen. Having seen off six heads in eight years, Bishop Sutton School was to see only four in the next 96 years.

The only known picture of Mr Brown

On 22 October 1883, '2nd class certificated' headmaster Ebenezer Brown took charge. The 1891 census listed him as being 33 – so only 25 when he came to Bishop Sutton – born in Bath, married to Mary (27). Their children Lionel (6), Frederic (4) and Dorothy (1) had all been born in Bishop Sutton. Two school monitresses, Annie Field and Lucy Ashman, were boarding with the family. Mr Brown found *order fairly good. Examined all the children, mixing the various Standards to prevent copying ... every child in 2nd Standard failed in Arithmetic.* He adopted a more concise (and much neater) logbook style than his predecessors, had a thing about 'irregular children', and meticulously reported absences to the Attendance Officer. He asked for more monitors so that he could concentrate on the infants, but financial strictures at the Education Department meant that he often had *all the Standards above the first to teach unaided.* This was at a time of average attendance of 85.7. A not uncommon log entry was that of 10 June 1889: *very hard at work all the week, having so many classes to teach.* Or, later that month, *greatly inconvenienced for want of a teacher.*

Mr Brown's approach could be firm. In October 1890 parent Mrs Sarah White wrote to Board member Mr Lovell. He passed her letter to the Board, verbally adding his own accusation that the headmaster was prone to being too energetic with his cane. The Board's clerk copied Mrs White's letter into the minute books: *Sir, I am taking the liberty in writing to inform you of Mr Brown beating my little girl, this is the second time lately he has done it, I took her down to him the first time and told him he could give her as much extra work as he liked and I would see that she did it but I should not allow him to beat her. I told him if he did it again I should go to someone else and he told me he should do it and I could go where I liked. I am, Sir, Yours Obediently, Sarah White.* The Board wrote to the headmaster, copying Mrs White's letter to him and calling for an explanation. Duly summoned to Chew Magna, Mr Brown gave his side of the story and additionally felt it wise to confess *that he had inflicted corporal punishment upon William Perry, Arthur Shepherd, Kate Elmes, Albert Tucker, Edward Harvey and Ella White … approved by the majority of the Board, Mr H Strachey and Mr Lovell dissenting.*

Then it went embarrassingly wrong. The Board accepted Mr Brown's explanation as to why he'd punished Mrs White's daughter, but had taken at face value Mr Lovell's verbal accusation that Mr Brown did tend to overstep the mark. The minutes went on to state: *through inadvertence* [the clerk inserted] *an inaccurate paragraph respecting some general charges made … of excessive punishment by Mr Brown … was inserted in the Public Newspaper report of the last meeting.* What made it worse was that Mr Lovell wouldn't repeat his accusations, so the Board had to withdraw them. Mr Brown didn't sue his employer for libel.

The Board crossed swords with the headmaster again at the end of 1890: *I am instructed to inform you that the members (includ-ing the Chairman)*

'Through inadvertence'

do not approve of your closing the school last Thursday with 47 in attendance.

He really didn't have it easy on the teaching front, did Mr Brown. In September 1892 he again *applied for more help, but the Board has not, as yet, taken any steps to procure same. With only one assistant (who has to teach Needlework in addition to the infants' class), it is very difficult to make much progress, just at this time of the school year when there are so many new rules to be taught to so many different Standards by the same teacher.* An early example of Churchill's 'Never in the history of human conflict ….'. Stress levels may have caused him to be active with his cane: in October 1892 it was reported that *Job Harvey of Bishop Sutton having appeared before the Board and complained of excessive corporal punishment inflicted upon his son Wallace Harvey by the Master Mr Brown, it was resolved that Mr Brown be requested to attend the next meeting of the Board to give his explanation of the case.* Mr Brown said his piece, and the Board agreed that *the punishment on this occasion was not excessive.*

School management wasn't just about authority and discipline. It could also be about being considerate: on the day before the school closed for the Christmas holiday in 1892, *Miss Payne was absent on Friday, the master having given her leave as she had a long railway journey to her home in Cornwall where she will spend the vacation.*

By early 1893 Ebenezer Brown's handwriting was deteriorating. But not enough to prevent him from being granted a rise of £10 a year *upon the following conditions: two monitors be appointed from 25.3.1895 at 1/6 a week each as assistants in the school.* The additional help didn't dilute the head's strictness: in June 1896 *a letter from Job Harvey* (he of the 1892 protest about punishment inflicted on his son Wallace) *complaining of Mr Brown's treatment of his son Herbert having been received and read, the Board regret that this accident has occurred; to prevent a reoccurrence the Board will request Mr Brown to put up notices in the school that no child will be permitted to leave the room till 10 am and 3 pm unless the child be ill in which case a statement to that effect should be made to the teacher, when the child may leave immediately.*

On 18 January 1897 *Mr Brown sent in his resignation to the Board, having obtained a more lucrative post, viz that of master of Chew Stoke.* On 22 March Miss Mary Bowles (later to become Mrs Harvey), a teacher at the school from 1895 to 1902, *presented to the Master on behalf of the Teachers and Scholars a thermometer and aneroid barometer mounted in a very handsome walnut case as a mark of esteem on his leaving Bishop Sutton School where he has worked for the last 13½ years.* Mr Brown went off on 16 April to instigate Chew Stoke's first school logbook, and he stayed there until April 1903.

Bishop Sutton was the place to be for an aspiring headteacher, and no fewer than 72 applications were received. Four candidates were selected*: P. Herbert Arch, J. B. Wightman, G .F. Cleverly, J. W. Thomas. Interviews Saturday next at Chew Magna Schoolhouse at 2.30 pm,* [the applicants were] *to have viewed the Bishop Sutton School prior to attending.*

The Wightman years began. James Bestwick Wightman, born 3 December 1871, had begun his teaching career as a pupil teacher at King Street School in Derby, followed by two years' training in Westminster. He had qualifications in Chemistry, Mathematics, Physiography (physical geography), and Sound, Light and Heat. He would steadfastly see Bishop Sutton school through the First World War, the Twenties and part of the Great Depression. He is the first headmaster of whom there are personal recollections, and is the subject of many a hearty tale. But first to the documented facts: the School Board unanimously appointed him on 12 March 1897 at a salary of £90 a year plus house. His previous post had been as Head Assistant at Clifton Industrial School.

He and his two teachers Miss Bowles and Miss Curnow coped with an average attendance of 100. HM Inspector's 1897 report was reassuring: *the new master is working with vigour and determination, and there is good hope that under his care the school will do well.* The 1901 census listed the family as headed by James Wightman (30, schoolmaster, born in Derby), his wife Florence (29, born in Clifton) and Victoria (10 months, born in Bishop Sutton). They employed a boarder – Elizabeth Price, aged 14, born in Pontypridd – as a 'general servant'.

N.B.—A separate Form is to be filled up for each Teacher in the School except Pupil Teachers, for whom a different form is provided. Additional copies of this form, if required, will be sent on application.

Education Act, 1902.—Enquiry Form No. 5.

SOMERSET COUNTY COUNCIL.

COUNTY EDUCATION COMMITTEE.

Return of Teacher's qualifications, remuneration, etc.

(Chew Magna Bd.) *Bishop Sutton* School.

Full name (surname first) *Wightman, James Bestwick*

Exact Date of Birth ___ *3rd Dec. 1871.*

If formerly a Pupil Teacher (a) in what School *King St. Higher Grade. Derby.*

(b) during what years *1st 1885 - 6 - 4 - 8 to 30 Sep 1889*

(c) position in Scholarship list *352*

If Trained (a) Name of Training College *Westminster*

(b) Period of Training—Give dates *1890 - 91 Two years.*

(c) Final position in Class List—Year _____ Div. I. No. _____ Div. II. No. _____

If not Trained (a) Date of passing Certificate examination _____

(b) Position in Class List—Year — Div. I. No. — Div. II. No. —

Date when Parchment received *Nov 1893*

University degree, if any. (Give date, subjects and class) —

Give full particulars (year, stage, class, etc.) of any Science and Art Certificates, University Certificates, or other Certificates of public examining bodies—

1891 Chemistry Practical. W. 1st Class "D". & Mathematics 2nd Stage 2nd

1890 Theoretical 2nd Physiography. W. 2nd

Sound, Light & Heat. ACP 1903 {Teaching. Geography. Physiology / History. Arithmetic. Chemistry} PASSES

Is the Teacher entitled to superintend Pupil Teachers? *Yes.*

Position in School *Head master*

Date of appointment *12th Mar 1897*

Is appointment under written agreement *No. By Minute.*

What notice is required to terminate the appointment *Three months*

	In 1901.			In 1902.			How and when paid.
Annual Salary :—Fixed	100	0	0	100	0	0	*Cheque. Quarterly*
Increase from Government Grant, if any						+ P.T. grant £2.	
„ „ Special Aid Grant, if any							
„ „ other sources, if any. Specify							

N.B.—ENTER ON A SHEET OF FOOLSCAP AND ATTACH SECURELY TO THIS FORM EXACT COPIES, WITH DATES, OF ANY MINUTES RELATING TO THE APPOINTMENT, ITS DUTIES, REMUNERATION, ETC.

Signed *J. B. Wightman* Teacher.

Read, together with the copies of minutes entered on the attached sheet, and the whole Signed as correct at a duly convened Meeting of the ~~Managers~~ of the _____ School (or the *Chew Magna* School Board)* held on the *23rd* day of February, 1903.

John Iredell Chairman.

W. S. Milton ~~Correspondent or~~ Clerk.*

* Strike out the words that do not apply.

Mr Wightman's details, as submitted to Somerset County Council, 1903

The logbooks under Mr Wightman's regime were short on fascinating facts and long on attendance and lessons. There were nonetheless items to prompt a soupçon of interest. In January 1903 *school closed for a week owing to my absence through the death of my father and the school being short of an assistant*. In June 1907 he was *away in Bristol as witness to give evidence in the case of Clutton Rural DC and J. Lovell & Sons*. I can find no trace of what was being discussed, but Bishop Sutton's benefactor, major employer and entrepreneur may well have brought in 'his' headmaster for support in some action brought against him. In May 1915 Mr Wightman applied for the headship at Chew Magna School, but withdrew. There were occasional poignant entries in the logbook, such as on 24 February 1920 when he *was wired from B'ham to see my brother. Returned same evening*. Three days later, *left at 9 am. Brother dying*. By early 1923 the handwriting was shaky and the entries in the log were typically limited to: *rather cold morning, interest being shown in work*. He soldiered on, however, and his final entry was on 30 June 1931: *My notice of resignation expired today. Appointed 25.3.97*. (The school records had stated 12 March.)

James Wightman is recalled with respect and fondness. Girls certainly had a soft spot for him. Marjorie Reed remembers him as a lovely man if you were in his good books. He would put his arm round her shoulder and listen to her read. She saw Mr Wightman and teacher Miss Harvey (Marjorie's 'aunt', so perhaps she was a bit biased) as 'running the school in perfect harmony'. Eunice Ogborne recalls that she would sit on his knee and that he had one of the first radios in the village. Dick Chapman remembers the headmaster's love of marble-playing: he would send boys to Mrs Dury's shop with a penny for replacements. He was, however, of portly build and found it difficult to get down to ground level, so he tasked boys to bowl for him. His interest in technical things, as evidenced by the radio, is recalled by Ken Rapps, who remembers seeing him at the school gate, passing round a telescope to a crowd of big boys watching the R101[1] airship gliding over what is now the Lake.

Mr Wightman

The 1930 inspection report was glowing: *It is understood that the head teacher is retiring in December next. He has given many years of earnest work to the school under conditions which in themselves have formed a severe handicap, and lately, owing to indifferent health, he has found it increasingly difficult to carry on his duties as efficiently as he would wish*. Indeed, it seemed to several pupils that in his later years at the school, he 'he did very little work indeed'. He was renowned for his involvement in village life: he formed a brass band and played the organ in the church. This skill must have run in the family as his daughter gave piano lessons locally. He did have his sterner side, however, and Evvy Harvey remembers being caned, aged 13, in front of the whole class for kissing a girl. Comment has also been made that Mr Wightman was regularly locked out of the School House by his dominant wife. Now that would have been the talk of the playground.

----

[1] The R101 airship – at 777 ft, the largest in the world – had made her maiden flight in October 1929. She left for India on 4 October 1930 with 54 passengers and crew, watched by a crowd of over 3,000. Ballast had to be dumped to compensate for overloading, there were strong winds and the aft engines broke down. In the early hours of 5 October she went into a dive and crashed at Beauvais, near Paris, bursting into flames. 48 people died. The funeral procession through London was watched by thousands.

> Throat interfered with W.C. flushing for two days.
>
> " 23   Attendance this week 88%. Isolated cases of
>   Mumps, measles and scarlet fever.
>
> " 30   91%. Miss Maggs ill & absent to day.
>
> Feb. 6 Atten. 91%. Work progressing.
>
> " 18   Ash Wed: school closed.
>
> 19th & 20th Master away with tonsilitis
>
> Mar ?   been cold week. Another case of scarlet fever
>
> " 13   Scholarship Exam. Registers tested
>
> " 16   H.M.I. visited the school.
>
> " 19   Was out of school in the afternoon.

Mr Wightman's increasingly shaky writing, 1931

In a brief interregnum, Mr J. W. Sidwell acted as supply for a couple of months, and Reginald James Bailey (known as 'Bill Bailey' behind his back) arrived on 29 October 1931 – previous residence 5 Station Road, Midsomer Norton – for his first headmastership. He saw the school through the part of the Depression missed by Mr Wightman, through the traumas of the Second World War and the austerity years of the early 1950s, right through to 1957 when, as he laconically wrote in the logbook: *The school broke up for the Xmas holiday and so its status as an all age school ends … the managers attended this afternoon and I was presented with a cheque and framed picture.* He left to become an Anglican priest. It's a shame that his logbook entries were so sparse.

Stowey Sutton parish councillors wrote to the headmaster on 9 August 1955 to offer their condolences on the death of his wife. He subsequently married Evvy Harvey's sister.

Recollections are tinted by whether the recollector was a boy or girl: Mr Bailey was softer with the latter than with the former. He was strict (according to Jean Veale), yet very nice (according to Joan Bunney). His generosity and help were praised by everyone. Pauline Heron remembers him treating her really gently when she was 10 and her mother died. May Woodward was in the school netball team and Mr Bailey would take her in his car to tournaments in Taunton.

He would drive the football team to other schools. Dick Chapman and Eunice Ogborne both remember just how many children could be shoe-horned into his car. After he'd taken his son Martin to Clutton to catch the

Mr Bailey

train to grammar school, Mr Bailey would pick children up from Stowey and bring them to Bishop Sutton, wiping the inside car windows with half an onion in the winter to stop them steaming up. He was a keen engineer, and Dick recalls him bringing an old car engine into school for the senior boys to take apart and put back together again. Dick's father had been the first in the village to take a driving test and was introduced by Mr Bailey as 'the first official driver in Bishop Sutton'.

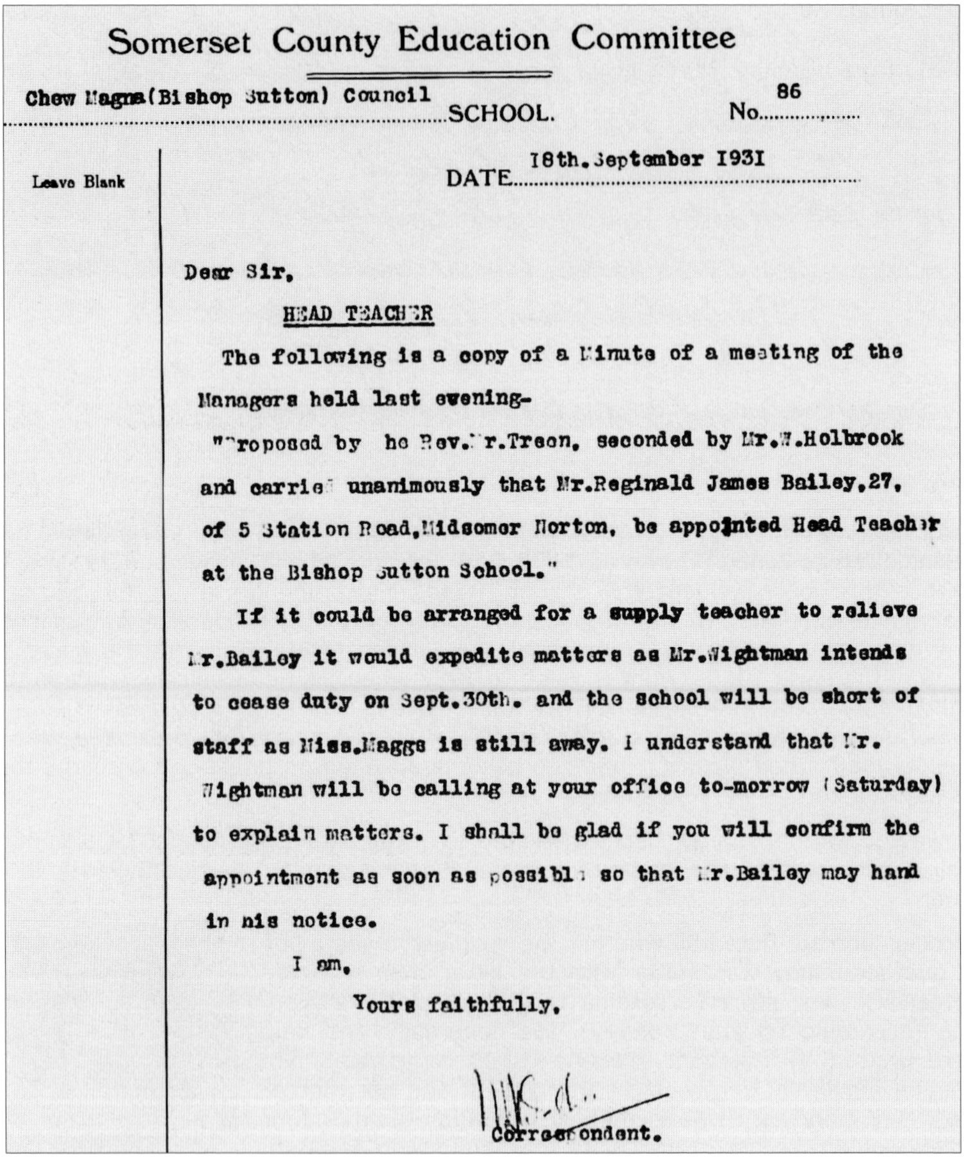

Somerset County Education Committee

Chew Magna(Bishop Sutton) Council
....SCHOOL.   No. 86

Leave Blank

18th. September 1931
DATE...

Dear Sir,

HEAD TEACHER

The following is a copy of a Minute of a meeting of the Managers held last evening–

"Proposed by he Rev. r.Treon, seconded by Mr.W.Holbrook and carrie unanimously that Mr.Reginald James Bailey,27, of 5 Station Road,Midsomer Norton, be appointed Head Teacher at the Bishop Sutton School."

If it could be arranged for a supply teacher to relieve Mr.Bailey it would expedite matters as Mr.Wightman intends to cease duty on Sept.30th. and the school will be short of staff as Miss.Maggs is still away. I understand that Mr. Wightman will be calling at your office to-morrow (Saturday) to explain matters. I shall be glad if you will confirm the appointment as soon as possible so that Mr.Bailey may hand in his notice.

I am,

Yours faithfully,

Correspondent.

Mr Bailey's appointment 1931

He was the frequent butt of practical jokes but was seemingly content to play along with the buffoonery and gain in stature from it. One former pupil recalls that Mr B came into the class one day to find paper pellets on the floor. "I'll go out, and when I come back, I want the culprits in front of my desk", he thundered. He went outside, but was seen peering through the window to make sure that he stayed one step ahead of the game. He wasn't beyond a bit of trickery himself: he would let the unwitting children choose their favourite carol and then make them sing it themselves. Ever practical, he gave shovels to the boys in the harsh 1947 winter and got them to dig paths to the classrooms through the deep snow in the playground. He loved sums and would seize any opportunity to make the children practise: "Five minutes to playtime, let's do some mental arithmetic". The sound of his step would make the class fall quiet before he entered the room. He was also a dab hand with a dap[1]. One former pupil reflects that if it wasn't a dap, it was anything vaguely suitable he could lay his hands on. He kept two canes in the school room, a thick heavy one and a whippy Charlie Chaplin one. Ken Rapps ruefully remembers that either could ensure a fair degree of good behaviour. Reginald Bailey might have been a strict disciplinarian, but Ken points to his kinder side: he would set up a table-tennis table in the small classroom and a quarter-size billiard table for Youth Club meetings. He let boys borrow the school football to practise with on the rec. A keen sportsman, he's remembered by Dick Chapman as playing all sports, organising and joining in.

School	Name	Position	Grade	Commencing Salary	Date of Commencement	Annual increment	Date from which first increment shall commence	Maximum Salary
				£		£		£
CHEW MAGNA BISHOPS SUTTON CL.	Mr. R.J. BAILEY	Head Teacher	II	276	–	12 =9=	1st Sept. 1932	393

The deduction for the current year in respect of the use of the Teacher's dwelling-house will be £.12.

Mr Bailey's commencing salary £276 p.a.

Retirement of the Headmaster	The Chairman mentioned that the present occasion was the last at which the Managers would have the pleasure of Mr.Bailey's presence, as he was leaving at the end of the year to take up training for Holy Orders He said that during the time he had been Correspondent to the School Managers he had realised how much the Headmaster had been concerned for the welfare of the Teaching Staff and the Pupils. Mr.Bailey had put forward a number of proposals and he, the Correspondent, had conveyed them to the Education Committee, and, in most cases, the results had been satisfactory. On behalf of the School Managers the Chairman expressed the hope that Mr.and Mrs.Bailey would have every success in their new life and that in the future they might see them once again in Bishop Sutton.

Worth mentioning here, if only because it doesn't fit neatly anywhere else, is that in his reports to the Education Office, Mr Wightman had always signed: *I am Yours obediently, Jas B. Wightman*. Towards the end of his tenure, when his health was failing, his reports were written by someone else and simply signed by him. Mr Bailey always signed: *Yours sincerely, R. J. Bailey*. Changing times, changing degrees of formality.

----
[1] Sandshoes for Geordies, sannies for Scots, gutties in Belfast, pumps and plimsolls elsewhere.

A new term started at the beginning of January 1958. Most of the older children had gone to the new Chew Magna Secondary Modern School, and Bishop Sutton was to be run by only three members of staff. Three male and two female candidates had been considered for the post of headship, but it fell to a Welshman to be appointed. Supply headmaster Mr J. J. Painting guided the school through the first months of 1958 until Mr Price could start on 21 April. He and his wife Mair made their mark on the village and the school as soon as they arrived from Solihull. Everyone spoke well of them.

The style of logbook entries had been steadily changing over the years, and Mr Price took the changes a step further. There's little tittle-tattle to be gleaned from dry comments about absences and the increasingly bureaucratic administration. Luckily, parish records and pupils' and parents' recollections provide a rich store of information about what became known as the 'Tom Price Years'. The breathless prose of a Parish Magazine article of 1979, the year of Tom's retirement, said most of what there was to say on the factual side, and I'm happy to repeat it:

From the autograph book presented to Mr Price on his retirement

Tom Price was born in 1915 during the First World War in the small village of Alltwen in the Swansea valley. At that time neither of his parents could possibly have foreseen the part he would play in another small mining village in Somerset. Tom went to the local council school until he was 14 and left to take a job in the tinplate and steel industry. During this time his thirst for education and betterment was unquenched and he avidly attended night school and took correspondence courses. At 22 he joined the Bristol Police Force and experienced many hair-raising incidents in the rougher parts of Bristol. Taking time off from his beat-pounding, he met in the Welsh Society, and eventually married, Mair who was teaching in Bristol at that time. At the outbreak of war in 1939 he joined the RAF, trained in South Africa and qualified as a pilot and was appointed to a navigation training school. He rejoined the police force when demobbed, but the urge to better himself had not diminished and he applied for an emergency training course for the teaching profession. He eventually graduated at Llandrindod Wells and obtained his first teaching post in Solihull.

Mair joined him there …. in those days life was hard and teachers' pay very inadequate, but Tom persevered, applying for and obtaining four different teaching posts with promotion each time in the space of nine years. He was eventually appointed as deputy headmaster to a large primary school and made principal of an evening

To Mr. Thomas Price from all his friends and pupils, past and present, on the occasion of his retirement as Headmaster for twentyone years at Bishop Sutton County Primary School.

institute. In 1958 he applied for and obtained the headship of our school and during his term in office the school has expanded from 65 pupils to a peak of 150 with a corresponding increase in staff. Tom has immersed himself in the school activities, academically as well as leisurely. A swimming pool was opened in 1968, new class rooms constructed, including kitchens for school meals, the playing fields enlarged, incorporating a small copse where the children can study nature in the practical sense. Tom realises none of this could have been achieved without the support not only of the PTA but of the whole village, and he is most grateful for all the help that has been given to him during his 21 years as headmaster.

Not only will his name go down in the records of the school, but since the very offset Tom and also Mair have wholeheartedly joined in every village activity. Tom has served on the Parish Council for 18 years, and only this year has retired from the scene. In bygone days he was secretary of the Royal British Legion for five years and in addition to being a playing member and treasurer of the cricket team was in charge of the Sutton Youth cricket team and secretary of the Downey Cup League. He was the leader of the Youth Club and in 1965 formed the popular Men's Forum. No committee seemed complete without Tom, his experience and willingness to help were always available from the instructing of the young to the providing of transport for the elderly at the Silver Lining Club. Tom, like all Welshmen, loves his rugby and although normally a placid man, his emotions run riot at the sight of those famous 15 red jerseys. His father was an excellent violinist – Tom doesn't profess to follow in his footsteps, perhaps rather modestly, but he does love the violin and plays regularly in the Norton Radstock Orchestra.

Although both village and school were generous and unstinting in marking his retirement, his own words in the logbook of 18 July 1979 were typically brief: *A special tea was given at school today to mark my forthcoming retirement. I received a presentation from the children and a concert was held in the Village Hall ... another presentation was made by the Village as a whole.* The Parish Magazine was more fulsome:

On Thursday July 19th the pupils of the school paid tribute to their headmaster. The Village Hall was packed to capacity and, as Mr Wells the MC so aptly remarked, "This is the Tom Price Show". No professional party of performers could possibly have entertained so sincerely and enthusiastically. They included a song dedicated to their headmaster, written by Bridget Martin and Claire Young. After the concert Mr Tom Ogborne thanked Tom for his 21 years of devoted service. Amongst the presentations were a t.v. set, cheque, a framed coloured photograph of the entire school and a book with the autographs of pupils past and present together with their parents. In his reply, Tom stated that the past 21 years were amongst the happiest in his life and if he could turn the clock back he would love to be on that threshold for the second time.

The song was to the tune of Uncle Tom Cobleigh.

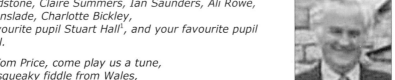

> Tom Price, Tom Price, it's twenty-one years,
> Since you first waved your cane in this school,
> All the village still hear you shouting for miles
> At Dean Goldstone, Claire Summers, Ian Saunders, Ali Rowe,
>   Tony Greenslade, Charlotte Bickley,
> And your favourite pupil Stuart Hall[1], and your favourite pupil
>   Stuart Hall.

Mr Price 1971

> Tom Price, Tom Price, come play us a tune,
> On that old squeaky fiddle from Wales,
> But wait while we stuff cotton wool in our ears,
> With Paul Weekes, Karen Crosse, Desmond Perry, Bernie
>   Scammell, Daniel Bickley, Jill Compton,
> And your favourite pupil Stuart Hall, and your favourite pupil Stuart Hall.

Mr Price 1979

----
[1] Stuart Hall has been described – anonymously – as 'the school rascal'.

Tom Price, Tom Price, come dance us a jig,
With your dainty feet and such elegant style,
Come do the Gay Gordons for us for a while,
With Scott Pearson, Penny Bagust, William Hunt, Libby Young, Oliver Hill, Mandy
*   Bendall,*
And your favourite pupil Stuart Hall, and your favourite pupil Stuart Hall.

Tom Price, Tom Price, please take us to camp,
We'll roll down the Combe, and eat spam every day,
And when the day's finished you can sing us some songs
To John Stevens, Debra Morris, Richard Brent, Tracey Brooks, Simon Holman, Karen
*   Stuckey.*
And your favourite pupil Stuart Hall, and your favourite pupil Stuart Hall.

Tom Price, Tom Price, we're sad you must leave,
We'll miss maths tests, school parties, and scripture and sums,
And we'd all like to thank you for all you have done,
From Eileen Stuckey, Mary Jenkins, Linda Lade, Mair Price, Diane Clarke, Joan Davidge,
*   Cynth Holman,*
And your favourite pupil Stuart Hall, and your favourite pupil Stuart Hall.

The children's presentation to Mr Price on his retirement

Mr Price retired on 31 August 1979.

The recollections of past pupils are legion. Joan Davidge remembers children in a village shop referring to the headmaster as 'Tom Price'. "It's Mr Price to you", he snapped, having overheard them. He considered himself to be 'on patrol' at all times: Joan recalls being on playground duty and glancing at Mr and Mrs Price's house at the back of the school field. Mr P, who had popped home for lunch, was standing in his back garden looking across at the school, checking that the teachers were at their allotted positions. The then school nurse, Bettina Cohn, recalls his sense of humour and his keen interest in his pupils: he would enrol children at Bishop Sutton whom other schools wouldn't accept. He had wanted trees round the school field; the Education Authority wouldn't pay, so Tom did (and, as Bettina wistfully points out, children were allowed to climb trees in those days). Monica Castle (née Hill, at school from 1964 to 1969) can still hear the violin that the headmaster would bring in and play 'as a treat'. For the children, it was anything but. Several former pupils also said that 'he was very Welsh' and therefore sometimes difficult to understand.

Teresa Dowling (née Heron, at school from 1966 to 1973) remembers that Monday mornings were when Mr Price tested the times tables. "Six twos", he'd belt out in stentorian tones and then point to some hapless child. Woe betide the pointee if he or she didn't know the answer. He was always keen to join in with games of conkers. His support of the school football team was unnervingly boisterous. Delvin Dowling was at primary school at Felton and remembers being petrified long before the coach taking him and his team-mates arrived at Bishop Sutton, such was their awe at Mr Price's considerable presence as he stood on the touch-line yelling "Come on Sutton!". Teresa too recalls that presence. She had run home one day after Mrs Jenkins had made her sit at a table of boys. Teresa was in her front room, giving a doctored version of the story to her mother, when they saw the headmaster striding up the drive. "Oh, that's nice", said Mrs Heron, "Mr Price has come to see us". Teresa did not share her mother's joy.

> The school closed today for the Summer Holiday closure.
> 31st August 1979. Today, I retire from my appointment as Headmaster of this school.
> (Signed) Thomas Price.

40 YEARS OF SERVICE TO ANY CAUSE
IS SOMETHING TO BE PROUD OF

In the early 19th century, elementary teaching was often taken up by those too old, too sick or too inefficient to earn an honest crust in any other way. In North Wales in the 1840s, a contemporary claimed gloomily that teachers were drawn *from the lowest class in society which contains individuals competent to read, write and cipher*. The class of schoolmistress was, he mused, composed of persons who had been employed as seamstresses, charwomen and servants of the most humble description. Things had improved considerably by the 1880s. A report of The Commission Appointed to Inquire into the Elementary Education Acts England and Wales 1888 stated: *As a whole, the present body of teachers are a very honourable class, and have a great sense of their duties to the children in regard to the formation of their character and their moral guidance. We are told that nine tenths of the supply of elementary teachers is made up of those who have formerly served as pupil teachers*.

What was it like at Bishop Sutton? As with headteachers, we are reliant on other records to tell us who may have been teaching at the school prior to 1872. The 1851 census listed Elizabeth Phillips, 35, born in Chew Magna (which may have meant Bishop Sutton), as a 'schoolmistress'. She was the widowed daughter of Joseph Collins (60, a widower and agricultural labourer), and lived with him and her brothers George (23) and Charles (16), and what were probably her children, Elizabeth Ann (7) and Mary Maria (5), both born in Tenby, and John (2), born in Chew Magna. The location of this somewhat crowded house in Bishop Sutton was unspecified[1]. Was she helping Miss Hassell at the National School, or was she running a dame school? We shall probably never know. By the time of the 1861 census, Elizabeth was still living with dad but was now described as a 'dress maker'. Come the 1871 census, and an Elizabeth Collins (aged 59) was listed as a 'schoolmistress', born in Clutton. If that's the same Elizabeth as in 1851 – perhaps having reverted to her maiden name – then she's gained a few years in age and has changed her place of birth. To add confusion to mystery, the 1881 census listed, somewhere in 'Sutton', an Eliza (sic) Collins as widow and 'schoolmistress', aged 58 and born in Clutton. Kelly's Directory of 1872 also listed a Mrs Elizabeth Collins as village postmistress.

The 1861 census listed the Applebees, next to (or perhaps opposite) The Red Lion. Anne (15) was described as 'teacher, National School' and the eldest of six children. The head of the family, Charles, was a miner, and his wife Isabella didn't work Also listed in the 1861 census – at an unspecified address – was Martha Pople (53), born in Winford and described as 'schoolmistress'. She lived with her husband Samuel (52), a gardener. In contrast to Anne Applebee, the term 'National School' wasn't used, perhaps suggesting that Martha Pople was operating a dame school somewhere in the village.

The school logbook didn't mention the names of any teachers until September 1875 – three years after it was begun – when the Board appointed Miss Ellen Cook as Sewing mistress at £12 p.a., three months' notice on either side. She soon left, and Mrs Frappell replaced her in November 1875 on the same terms. She stayed the course until October 1877. In September 1882 Miss Maria Creighton was appointed as assistant mistress at £30 a year. She had *served her time at Compton Martin as pupil teacher, passed her 5th year's examinations at Wells April 1880, obtained 2nd class at the scholarship examination at Fishponds July 1880, was assistant mistress at Paulton for 11 months, born 3 September 1862*. A year after she started, the Board promoted her to *Sewing mistress, her salary to remain at £30 p.a. as before, the Board undertaking to make her a present of £5 p.a. if HM Inspector report on the Needlework is satisfactory*. This was probably the same Miss Creighton who, in August 1883, applied in vain for the position of headmistress following headmaster Hill's resignation. She left the school in March 1891.

In the meantime, Hannah Bailey had moved from Marston Sicca, near Stratford upon Avon, on an annual salary of £35. Commencing her duties in January 1886, she didn't have an easy start. She fell ill only a month later and then her father died. Hannah had a few days off, causing headmaster Ebenezer Brown to have *a very hard week's work*. Further illness led to her asking the Board to let her resign. Mr Brown would be in for another spell of hard work. Miss Ellen Paul started in March 1886. She'd been a PT at Weymouth, qualified at Cheltenham Training College, had been mistress at Walsall Wood in the Black Country and gained a post at Clifton National Girls' School. The Board took her on *for four months certain* at £35 a year. Six weeks later, Mr Brown let her leave school on a Thursday morning

----

[1] The 1871 census suggests that it was four buildings away from the post office, then situated on the other side of the road from its current site.

to catch a train to Staffordshire for the weekend. She was absent on the following Monday, *her only reason being that it was raining. Reported case to School Board.* The Board did not renew her contract.

The main road c1910, looking westwards. The school is out of sight on the left behind the church and the trees. The pavement is in much the same position as now; the road has been widened to the left.

Our assumption that the Victorians were not very mobile is not borne out by the teachers at Bishop Sutton, who were a pretty nomadic bunch. Miss Creighton had been reasonably close to hand at Paulton, but Miss Bailey hailed from Warwickshire and Miss Paul from Walsall. Bishop Sutton scholars would have become used to all manner of accents. Which neatly – and superfluously – introduces the apocryphal tale of the Brummie children evacuated to Somerset in 1940. A neighbour asked their mum how they were doing. "Not bad", she replied, "they went, saying 'we am', and come back saying 'we be'".

Louisa Julia Willis did rather better than her predecessor, Ellen Paul. Appointed in August 1886 from Chew Stoke on an annual salary of only £27, she made a good impression: in October 1886 the headmaster wrote: *Miss W carefully prepares her lessons and the children take much more interest in them under her tuition than they did under their former teacher.* Misgivings in January 1887, however, prompted him to report to the Board that *Miss Willis had absented herself from her duties for a week alleging illness as the cause. Resolved that* [she] *be requested for the future to forward a medical certificate to the clerk of the Board.* Perhaps not the most auspicious time for Louisa to be asking for a pay rise, but she did, only to be told to apply again when she had been in her post for six months. She made a careful diary note for two terms hence, and the Board replied: *I beg to inform you that your application for an increase of salary was considered … and it was decided to increase it £2.10s.0d a year.* She must have touched Ebenezer's soft spot, for in December 1888 he gave her *leave of absence to attend a wedding on Tuesday.* For reasons unknown, she left the school in June 1889.

It was now down to Mr Brown, Miss Creighton and a couple of monitors to look after more than a hundred children. By March 1890 the Board had been persuaded to take on extra help in the form of 22-year old Annie Marie Field from Hambrook, Bristol, at £30 a year to teach Standards I and II. By the following year the Board asked her to teach the girls to sew for an extra £5 a year. At the time of the 1891 census she was lodging with the headmaster and his wife Mary at the School House. With Miss Creighton having left in 1891, the Board appointed 19-year old Lucie Ashman of Locksbrook, Bath, and previously a PT at Weston National Girls' School (Bath) from 1886 to 1890. She must have sought guidance from the Board as to accommodation, and the clerk replied: *I think you had better write Mr Brown (Master) respecting lodgings in Bishop Sutton. His address is The School, Bishop Sutton, Pensford, near Bristol. I am about 3 miles from this school, still I shall be pleased to assist you all I can in arranging for your arrival. I think people for Bishop Sutton generally book from Bristol to Clutton on the North Somerset line, but I don't think there is a conveyance running between Bishop Sutton and Clutton Station. If that should cause you any difficulty, then book to Pensford, one station before Clutton. Conveyances run between Chew Magna and Pensford, I could then meet you here and get the Man to take you on to Bishop Sutton.* Mr Brown must have found her a spare bed, for at the time of the 1891 census, she too was lodging at the School House.

This camaraderie didn't last long. Lucie was a sickly soul and wrote to the Board seeking permission to leave. Their response: *I am sorry your health has not been good during your short stay at Bishop Sutton*, but no, she would have to serve her notice and no, she had not been given to understand that she would be teaching the Upper Standards. (She had been given the infants, for which she didn't consider herself competent.) The Board's clerk wrote to Mr Brown, alerting him to the likelihood that Miss Ashman's parents didn't approve of her living in Bishop Sutton. Perhaps the Northams hadn't been exaggerating when they complained about the smells of the School House. More of Lucie later. The final paragraph of the clerk's letter to the headmaster was unusually blunt: *You had better come over tomorrow evening (Tue.). I want to see you.*

The logbooks then produced one of their occasional puzzles. In April 1892 a Miss Lovell *presented the Board with a bill for services given in Bishop Sutton School as teacher from October 12 1891 to March 8 1892 at the rate of 5/- per week.* Was she the monitress Miss Bessie Lovell who started at the school in October 1891? She isn't mentioned anywhere else, so we shall probably never know, but it was a very plucky young lady indeed to present the Board with anything, let alone a bill. In May 1892 Lavinia Payne came up from St Austell where she had been a PT. She was 21 and merited an annual salary of £40. She stayed two years; long enough to *be presented with an album subscribed for by about 40 of the children* when she left in August 1894.

Mr Brown was still struggling with the sheer number of pupils, and in December 1892 the Board agreed that his wife Mary Kate could be employed at £30 a year as an 'additional teacher' in charge of Standards I and II. Thursday 13 July 1893: *she had to leave school in the morning and was absent all the following day, suffering from abscesses on her gums and a swollen face.* Monday 8 January 1894: she was away for a week *by the doctor's orders.* Tuesday 22 January 1895: *Mrs Brown is confined to her room, suffering with a severe cold and by the advice of her doctor has sent in her resignation to the Board as the doctor says she is too delicate to resume her school duties for some considerable time.* In March 1895 Mr Brown wrote to the Board *on behalf of his wife, tendering her resignation as assistant mistress*. The Board accepted.

Bishop Sutton School. The notice reads 'King Edward VII Coronation Year 1902'.
The photo was taken outside what is now the central part of the building, overlooking the
road: the left-hand window is much the same as it is today.

With Miss Payne having gone in August 1894, the Board offered her post to Martha Emma Hunt (24), a PT at Spaxton School near Bridgwater. She offered her resignation the day after starting, but withdrew it two weeks later. She finally left in December 1894, *having obtained another appointment*. Then came Mary Sophia Bowles at £45 a year. She'd been a PT at Winsley School near Bradford-on-Avon. She became Mrs Harvey in September 1901. Unusually, she was not required to leave: the Board wrote to her on 7 June 1901, *in reply to your letter of the 1st inst informing of your intended marriage in August next and asking to be allowed to continue your duties in the Bishop Sutton School after the event, I am directed to say that your services will be retained*. She left in December 1902. Perhaps baby Harvey was on the way. The April 1901 census listed Sophia Bowles (25 and born in Winsley) as 'school mistress', living at Bon Hill (sic) Villa with grocer Fred Lovell (32) and his wife Adeline (28) and their two children.

Incidentally, the 1901 census also listed a Clara Atkins (31), a 'pupil teacher (Art. 68)' and living with her parents George and Sarah at Stowey Bottom. There's no record of her in the Bishop Sutton School records; she may have taught at Stowey. She was getting on a bit for a pupil teacher.

Elizabeth Mary Curnow came from Totterdown, Bristol, in January 1897 and left five months later. There were nine applications for the vacancy, and Olivia Turkington was appointed from St James' Girls' School in distant Whitehaven (Cumbria). She requested a rise the following month, was turned down, and was asked to resign at three months' notice. She was replaced in November 1897 by Alice Maud (or May)

Symes, who had been apprenticed at the British School in Poole. She stuck it out for rather longer than her predecessors, although all the logbook found to say about her was that she was the subject of a complaint by a Mrs Parfrey in November 1900: *on enquiry,* [the Board] *found it to be a trivial matter.* Miss Symes was allowed to go home early on Thursday 18 July 1901 *as her father was dying.* He passed away on Tuesday 23 July and his daughter was given a couple of days off. The 1901 census listed Alice Syms (sic) (21, assistant schoolmistress) as boarding with Albert Harvey (30, stonemason) and his wife Emily (36) at 'Sutton Street' in what appears to have been the first house along the main road after the Church Lane junction, heading westwards.

Another teacher not cut out for Bishop Sutton was 21-year old Ellen Frances Bowles from Holcombe Rogus, near Wellington, Somerset. It was deemed worthy of note that she had *not been a PT.* Appointed in 1902, she was given charge of Standards I and II and Sewing but resigned in September 1903. Eleanor Beynon was formally appointed but decided to go elsewhere and Miss Bowles offered to stay on temporarily for £3.15s.0d a month. She went a few weeks later in the school's expectation that Lilian Braund would be coming at £50 a year *and no bonus.* Quite why she wasn't to get a bonus is unclear, but the words were underlined in the logbook. Miss Braund was appointed to a post in Devizes, so never started.

We might assume that deference and respect a century ago were such that people of good standing such as teachers would be reliable servants. Wrong. They would routinely accept a job and then gaily reject it in favour of another, causing problems for the school and fresh advertising costs for the managers.

FORM E 2, 1903.

SOMERSET COUNTY COUNCIL.

COUNTY EDUCATION COMMITTEE.

RECEIVED 19 OCT. 1903

Application for the post of ___*Assistant*___ *Teacher* in the ___*Bishop Sutton Council*___ School.

Full name (surname first) ___*Brown Mabel Ailsa*___

Exact Date of Birth ___*13th of April 1882.*___

Present address (in full) ___*2 Woodleigh Villas. Canterbury Rd South Farnboro*___

Permanent (or home) *address* (in full) ___*51 Broadway, Frome Somerset.* Hants___

If formerly a Pupil Teacher (*a*) in what School ___*Frome Wesley Girls & Infants School*___

(*b*) during what years ___*1897 1898 1899 1900.*___

(*c*) position in Scholarship list ___*3nd class.*___

Mabel Brown applies for job as assistant teacher at 'Bishop Sutton Council School', 1903

A lack of bonuses was clearly commonplace: Adelaide Gertrude Stevens was appointed in February 1903 on *£50 p.a. and no bonus.* Another nomad, she had originally taught in Rotherham, moved to Blaby (near Leicester) and left Bishop Sutton within two and a half years to take up an appointment in Uxbridge, Middlesex. In came Mabel Ailsa Brown from Farnborough, Hampshire. In response to her question as to where she might live, the managers recommended: *you had* *better write Mr Wightman, headmaster, to secure you suitable lodgings and to advise you how best to get to Bishop Sutton from Bristol. I think you will find Mr Wightman a kind and considerate man to work with.* She resigned ten months later: the managers told the Education Department that in spite of her qualifications, *she had had no previous practical experience whatsoever in teaching in an Elementary School.*

Mabel's place was taken in September 1904 by 21-year old Maude Ethel Lowe from Macclesfield, Cheshire: *assistant teacher, £45 p.a., annual increases £2.10s.0d to max salary £60. For accommodation, she was referred to Mrs* (sic) *Thomas Elmes at Bishop Sutton, or Mr Wightman.* Mr Wightman grumbled on 9 January 1905 that *Miss Lowe, whose notice expires on 13 January, did not return here* [after the Christmas break]. Amy Lelilia (or possibly Letitia) Jones arrived from Drybrook, Gloucestershire, in 1905 but only stayed a few months. Step forward Ellen King from Street Council School, Somerset, appointed in November 1905 to replace Adelaide Stevens. She taught at Bishop Sutton until February 1910. An additional teaching post was created – there were now over 120 children – and Mrs Mary Elizabeth Wheeler from Blaenau Gwent, Glamorgan, was taken on in June 1906. On 10 July Mr Wightman *had occasion to speak to Mrs Wheeler about beating children,* and on 17 July he received complaints that she was *boxing ears.* On 14 September she was *away in South Wales without notification,* was absent the whole of the following week, came back unannounced on 29 September and left for good on 21 December.

There then arrived what would prove to be the first really long-serving teacher, although not without her foibles. Originally from Chepstow and then teaching at Newbury, she was taken on in February 1907 at £50 a year and stayed until July 1939. 21-year old Emily Batt. The logbook said very little about her other than that she had a day off in 1917 *owing to death at her home,* in 1930 as her father had died, on 4 December 1934 when her sister and mother were both ill, and again on the following day because – as Mr Wightman succinctly put it – *her sister is dead.* Miss Batt returned to school 12 days later, had a day off in January 1935 as her mother had died and another one the following week for the funeral. She did nothing wrong (apart from being unfortunate in the relations department), but pre-war finances were such that teachers' jobs were being axed, and the managers reluctantly gave her notice to leave at the end of August 1939. Luckily she found herself a job at Butleigh School near Glastonbury. Surprisingly for someone who had taught for over 30 years at Bishop Sutton, she is scarcely remembered, although Ken Rapps does recall that she lived opposite the drapery.

Teachers and monitress (or PT) in 1910 – the lady on the right may be Miss Batt

In the meantime, Emily Kempton had come from Shepton Mallet in April 1910 as infant teacher, was cautioned in July *to be more careful for making an alteration in the infants' register,* required help in September *as she cannot follow the syllabus or timetable by herself,* and resigned in April 1911. Sarah Dyke from Hilperton near Trowbridge was given the post of uncertificated teacher in June 1911, made two errors in September *in totalling her register* and gave notice in March 1912 *to terminate her engagement as she is going to Canada in June.*
Mr Wightman was either interested in her welfare or glad to see the back of her: he

subsequently added: *sailed 26 June*. She was replaced by the melodiously named Alma Beatrice Yapp (2 Matlock Villas, Portfield Street, Hereford) in June 1912 as uncertificated infant teacher, who left in April 1914 to be replaced by Blanche Maddaford who, having accepted the post, promptly rejected it the following day. Enter stage-left Beatrice Stembridge, previously of Norton-sub-Hamdon School near Yeovil and latterly of 3 York Avenue, Ashley Down, Bristol, who joined in March 1913 and left in April 1914. As a mature 29-year old, she really ought to have shown more dedication. A replacement wasn't easy to find, and in May 1914 Mr Wightman wrote to the Board: *as there is no possibility of obtaining two uncertificated teachers, will you please ask if my daughter may be employed temporarily to help me in the Main Room and with the infants at the rate of £20 a year?* The managers commented in their consequent letter to the Education Department: *The rate seems high as compared with the salaries paid to the monitresses viz £12 p.a. and who have been some years in the school and many years older than Miss Wightman who, I understand, is at best 14 years of age[1]. What reply shall I please give Mr Wightman?* The Department came back: 'take her on, but only as a temporary monitress at 3/- a week' (around £6 per school year). Miss W didn't accept the offer.

Miss Stembridge's eventual replacement – and let's not forget the substantial advertising costs that these positions necessitated, let alone the inconvenience and lack of continuity for the school and the children – was Eva Young who joined in July 1914. Perhaps chastened by the lack of staying power of previous incumbents, Mr Wightman asked her *to make herself proficient in Needlework in school by visiting one or more good schools* before she started. She may have been Bishop Sutton's first teacher with university-style training: she'd spent two years at the Elementary Training Department of Bristol University. She perhaps felt that Needlework was beneath her, as she left in October 1915. Miss Margaret Ellen Tebb had started in June 1914 from Hull, and left in July 1916.

Mabel Carpenter (top left) at West Harptree School, 1896. Elsie Rosa Carpenter (b.31.5.1889, d.16.2.1976) (middle of second row wearing a white smock) married Herbert George Treasure of Bishop Sutton in 1915. Wilfred Harold Carpenter (born 16.5.1892) is in the middle of the front row.

Miss Batt from three paragraphs ago might not have stuck in former pupils' minds, but Mrs Flower (née Carpenter) certainly did and – because children can be cruel – not always for the kindest of reasons. Born on 3 February 1886, her long teaching career began as a monitress at Bishop Sutton. In an appointment that was to have the very best of outcomes for the school, the Board agreed on 7 May 1900 *that Mabel Carpenter be appointed*

----
[1] The April 1901 census had listed a Victoria Wightman as being 10 months old, which would have made her nearly 14 in May 1914.

monitress at Bishop Sutton School to replace Ethel Harvey. On 30 September 1901 the *indentures of apprenticeship of Mabel Edith Carpenter as pupil teacher in the Bishop Sutton School were duly signed and sealed*, and in March 1905 she was given the post of assistant teacher. Mabel resigned on 20 December 1912 and married West Harptree builder Charles Henry Flower ('Harry') in 1913. On 26 November 1915 *former teacher Mrs Mabel Edith Flower taken back on* (at £60 p.a.) *to fill vacancy following Miss Young's resignation; she was a very excellent teacher when on the staff*. Henry Flower had been called up to fight in the Great War and his wife, who had been living at 1 Quaperlake Street in Bruton, may have needed the money or wanted the companionship.

SOMERSET COUNTY COUNCIL.

COUNTY EDUCATION COMMITTEE.

RETURN OF PUPIL TEACHERS.

Full Name (*surname first*) _Carpenter, Mabel Edith_

Exact Date of Birth _3rd Feb 1886_

Home Address _Manor House._
Compton Martin. Nr Bristol

When did the apprenticeship begin. Give exact date _1st July 1901_

When will it terminate. Give exact date _30th June 1904_

When will the Pupil Teacher sit for the King's Scholarship examination ? _Christmas 1904_

What arrangements are made for the instruction of the Pupil Teachers. Give the fullest possible particulars—
Instructed by the Master 8.30 to 9 a.m. Private Study 7.30
also evenings ½ hr. after dismissal in the afternoon.
Needlework taught by Mrs Fo
Friday afternoon for Private Study.

Mabel Edith Carpenter

This is where it becomes sad.

On 12 June 1916 she was granted two days' leave *in order to see her husband at Chatham*. On 13 November 1916 she was *absent; notice just received that her husband was killed in action*. She returned to school on 20 November. She was given an afternoon off in November 1917 *as her brothers were going to the Front*. She was allowed a week off in November 1920 *owing to the death of her mother*, and again in January 1928 *owing to death of her brother*. In September 1928 she had the afternoon off *to bury a relative*. She left in July 1947, having taught at Bishop Sutton for the best part of half a century. Mrs Flower was a much-loved teacher. In a rare betrayal of personal feelings, the school managers wrote on 14 July 1947:

Mrs Flower

[we] *have received with regret the resignation of Mrs Flower, and in view of the very long and faithful service she has rendered the school, and of the undoubted influence and service she must have had on the young life of the village,* [we] *wish to place on record* [our] *appreciation of her work and trust she will enjoy many years of happy retirement.* On 17 November no less a VIP than the Chief Education Officer himself, Mr M. W. Deacon, *came to the school in the presence of the managers and a large body of children and parents and presented Mrs Flower with an electric kettle, electric blanket and treasury notes in token of the villagers' appreciation of her work here since she was appointed monitress in April 1900.* Mr Deacon said that *it gave him a great personal pleasure to come to such an occasion, 40 years of service to any cause was something to be proud of. Mrs Flower had carried out her duties with a sincerity and charm which had won the respect and love of all.*

Her leaving was accompanied by the usual bureaucratic blunder. The vacancy was advertised *as for a qualified assistant for the Upper Junior Class,* whereas the managers had actually asked the Authority *to appoint an additional assistant master qualified to take Rural Science and the keeping of small livestock.* The records are sadly silent on how small the livestock should be. A replacement wasn't readily forthcoming, and Mrs Flower graciously offered to stay on for another month if necessary. On 1 October 1947 *at 10.30 this morning Mrs George from Draycott arrived as a temporary teacher in Mrs Flower's place. As no intimation for her coming had been received, Mrs F was here.*

Bishop Sutton

SERVED EDUCATION IN THE COUNTY

Bishop Sutton has lost one of its best known and most highly respected residents in the death of Mrs. Mabel Flower, which occurred at her home, Wheelgate, on Monday.

She was 78 and was loved in the village and adjoining neighbourhood for her Christian influence and for her willingness at all times to help any worthy cause or anyone in need.

She had lived in Bishop Sutton for the greater part of her life and had been a widow since her husband was killed during the First World War.

PRIMARY SCHOOL

She was a teacher at the local primary school for a long period and she served the local Methodist Church with devotion for the greater part of her life.

She was a Sunday School teacher and trustee for over 40 years and was also the church treasurer for many years. She attended regularly twice on Sundays until her recent brief illness.

Her interest in the general life of the parish was widespread, for she was a member of the local school managers, also a governor of the Chew Valley Secondary Modern School.

Mrs. Flower was a member of the local "Silver Lining" club for the older residents.

BRITISH LEGION

She served the British Legion with devotion and was the Poppy Day organiser in the village for many years.

Everyone in the village will mourn her passing, especially Miss Harvey, with whom she resided for many years.

It was fitting for the funeral service to be held at Bishop Sutton Methodist Church yesterday (Thursday) where many paid their last respects. Interment was at Harptree Cemetery.

Mrs Flower died in March 1964. What do her pupils remember of her?

Marjorie Reed was her niece and had been taught by her at Bishop Sutton School. She explains that her aunt had done a correspondence course for teaching, and wasn't certificated. As a result of the death in France of Mrs Flower's husband, she became a staunch supporter of the British Legion. Dick Chapman recalls that she would become very emotional on Remembrance Day. "Lord Strachie would make an imitation grave, we'd stand for two minutes' silence, and all the children would crane forward to watch her cry. How cruel can children be?" (At this point in our chat, Dick's wife Olive protested that school hadn't taught him good manners.) Dick also recalls that she taught Sewing and Needlework and took children on nature walks. Peter James too recalls the flowers that pupils routinely collected in those days: they would take the pressed specimens into school for Mrs Flower to identify. "A most wonderful person".

Alongside her as a school stalwart was Mildred Kathleen Harvey, remembered with equal fondness. Appointed in July 1916 to replace Miss Tebb, she was born in 1897 and *commenced as uncertificated teacher in the infant room, late of Keynsham Parochial Infant School, passed Oxford Senior.* Apart from her retirement, the logbook referred only to an occasional absence through illness and to a day off in January 1951 to attend her nephew's graduation ceremony at Bristol University. Miss Harvey turned 58 in October 1955 and told Mr Bailey that she wished to retire at the end of the 1956 summer term. The school would not allow this to pass unnoticed. The managers wrote: *owing to Miss Harvey's long service in the teaching of infants it was decided to advertise the fact in local papers, asking old pupils to subscribe to a presentation.* On 26 July 1956 *the main room was crowded this evening when Miss Rees-Mogg JP, Chairman of Clutton RDC, presented Miss M. K. Harvey with a copy of Sir Winston Churchill's 'History of the English Speaking People Vol. 1' and £21 in treasury notes on her retiring after 40 years' service at this school. The Lord Strachie presided. I gave the school's appreciation and Miss Harvey replied by recalling some of the things happening in the school 40 years ago. Miss Gillian Treasure, daughter of the first scholar admitted after Miss Harvey came (Mr Raymond Treasure) presented a large bunch of sweet peas from the garden. Tea was served by the Senior Girls under Miss Chivers' guidance after the company had adjourned to the Yard where there was room for movement.* And, at the end of term, *prior to the close of school for the summer holidays, the managers met at the Infants' Room.* What happened then is illustrated in the logbook extract on the following page. Further testament to the affection in which Miss Harvey was held by several generations of schoolchildren was the fact that *this is the first time the managers have been present at a school assembly or dismissal.*

Miss Harvey had lived for many years with the widowed Mrs Flower at Wheelgate on Church Lane, and on 20 March 1964 the managers wrote *a letter of sympathy to Miss Harvey on the death of Mrs Flower.*

It's the pupils' recollections that paint the best pictures. Marjorie Reed, who looked on Miss Harvey as an 'aunt' (Mrs Flower having been her real aunt) and who was taught by her for a time, explained that Miss Harvey's "eyesight was bad so she was advised to go into teaching". Dick Chapman recalls her being very strict but very fair, a well-liked teacher. Ken Rapps remembers her as being a 'cut above' and Pauline Heron reflects that she would "make you sit there until you got your spellings right". A lovely lady, even though she did 'dollop out the Virol'[1]. One

----
[1] A bone-marrow preparation for children and invalids.

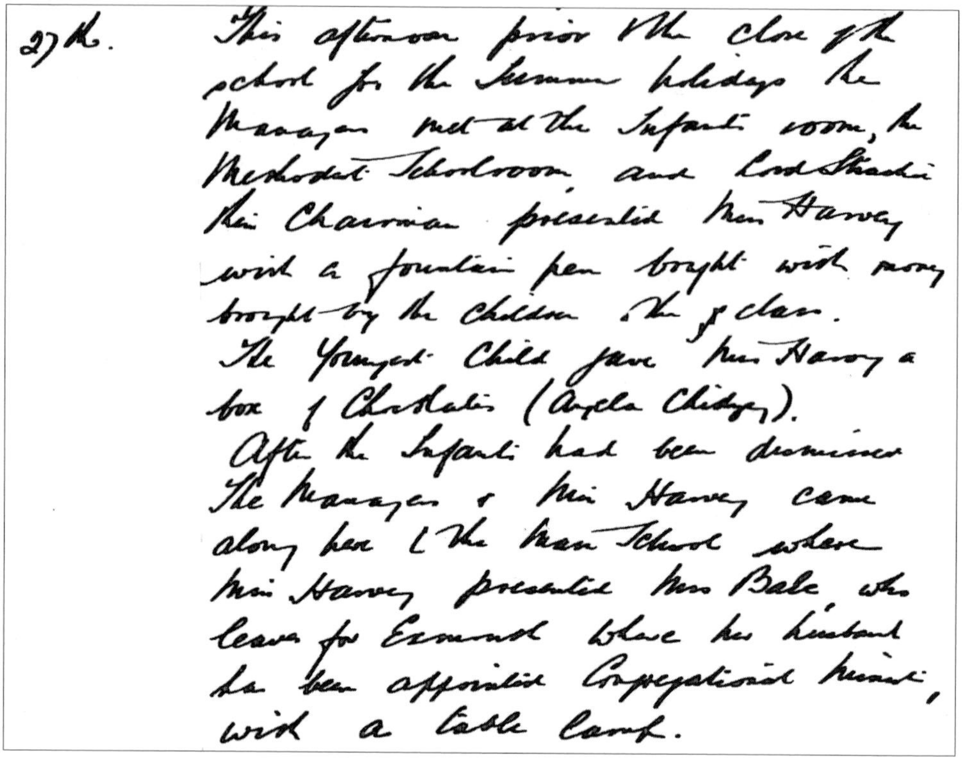

[handwritten log entry in manuscript]

Miss Harvey's retirement

former pupil remembers Mrs Flower and Miss Harvey as the only people she knew as a child who had been on a foreign holiday.

Miss E. Beatrice Maggs was also of the much-respected ilk, and many are the reminiscences of the lady who travelled from 4 North End, Midsomer Norton on her motorbike. Her CV must have stood out, as *31 applications were considered for the vacancy for a certificated teacher*. She started on 10 October 1927, aged 25, and first entered the hall of logbook fame in June 1929 when the County Education Secretary spotted that *the whole month's salary had been claimed from certificated teacher Miss E. B. Maggs, although absent re mother's illness*. The authorities commented cuttingly: *no payment to be made for anything other than own illness*. Her unreliable transport lent her a certain notoriety. In October 1929 she *was late on two mornings owing to motor cycle breakdown* and on 11 September 1931 was *absent through motor cycle accident*. No-one quite knew what to make of this new breed of motorcycling and smoking female teacher: a week later, *the managers approved an increase in salary for Miss Maggs although she was still absent as she had met with an accident on her motor cycle after leaving school on 10.9.31 and her medical certificate is enclosed*.

*Not Miss Harvey's
Virol, but similar*

Then tragedy struck. On 4 September 1937 Mr Bailey wrote: *Miss M absent today, she informed me yesterday she would have to obtain medical advice as her throat was troubling her*. Two days later, *Miss M sent a doctor's certificate for absence due to laryngitis.* On 22 September, *I received news today that Miss Maggs died this morning.* On 29 September *the afternoon session began at 1 pm and closed at 3.15 to allow the staff to attend the funeral of Miss Maggs.* A headstrong product of the Roaring Twenties, she was firm but fair. William Tovey (quoted in 'Bishop Sutton and Stowey Millennium Memories') recalled that 'she had a stick that long, and she'd bring it down and she didn't stop at nothing. She let you have it right left and centre. On the hand, on your behind, across your back. I'd done nothing hardly; couldn't she whack'. She would cane children she spotted scrumping apples.

The school saw a sequence of teachers who couldn't quite match Mrs Flower, Miss Maggs and Miss Harvey for long service, but whose contributions were invaluable all the same. Audrey Smale arrived from Hirwaun near Aberdare in November 1937 and returned to Hirwaun in November 1941. Her leaving prompted one of Mr Bailey's rare subjective logbook comments: *her departure is deeply regretted by us all.* Miss Thomas came from Bristol in July 1941 as a trainee teacher and left a week later to be replaced by Miss Goulding, who was asked by the wartime authorities in September 1943 to reopen Norton Malreward School. Kathleen McDonnel started in September 1944 and went ten months later. Mrs Fitton started in January 1946 and left that summer to take up a post in Chew Magna.

Bettina Cohn and Mair Price recall giving teachers board and lodgings in the 1970s. The two ladies were often eaten out of house and home, as 'school dinners weren't always enough for 20-year olds'. Janet Bradbrook (née Harvey), who lived at Mendip View in Church Lane, recalls that teachers also used to lodge next door with a Mrs James.

The Second World War had played havoc with education. Children had been evacuated hither and thither for varying periods of time and had often gone home again without informing the authorities and without attending school when they got there. There was a dire shortage of teachers: thousands had been displaced by the war and hundreds had been killed. Those still in the profession in 1945 were helped by retired colleagues and supplementaries, but it was estimated that 100,000 volunteers were needed if there was to be any real regeneration in education. The Emergency Training Scheme was introduced, an intensive one-year course aimed primarily at men and women coming out of the Forces. Enhancements were designed to make the job more attractive: starting salaries for older recruits commensurate with age and experience, sabbatical terms, the removal of the frequent marriage bar for women, and general pay rises and maintenance allowances. The first product of the Scheme to come to Bishop Sutton was Megan Jones of Senghenydd, Glamorgan, in December 1946 from Hampton Emergency Training College (ETC) in Middlesex. She went back to Glamorgan in December 1947.

Playground 1948. The three boys are Leslie Bown, John Coles and Jeff Bendall. It's not known who is pinned underneath, or who the onlookers are.

23-year old Barbara Edser, also from an ECT and also a Glamorganite, came in December 1947 to specialise in PT, Art, Craft and Drama, but didn't return after a government course in September 1948. Miss Edser wasn't at the school for long, but is remembered by Janet Bradbrook as having been very popular. It might not have been Miss Edser – it might have been Miss Jones – who hit Pauline Heron on the head with a ruler, but Pauline remembers the ruler. (She also remembers one girl on a nature walk throwing a stick which got caught in a teacher's hairnet.)

In January 1948 the managers asked Taunton *to expedite the appointment of a Woodwork instructor on account of the shortness of staff at the school.* Along came Frederick John in May 1948 from Wrexham ECT. The school's first ever male teacher (as opposed to headmaster), he was appointed as *Handicraft Instructor and to fill in his time with general subjects.* Two other teachers had turned the post down as they couldn't find suitable accommodation in the village. This lack of lodgings was to prove a bugbear for many years to come. It was hoped that by the time Mr John arrived, the school would be properly equipped with a Handicraft Centre, but that was not to be and he had to teach general subjects full-time. He was sent on a three-month Ministry course in London in September 1948 and found a new job at a school in Bath a year later. The managers strove valiantly to find the right man to run the Handicrafts Centre that they eventually managed to set up at the Village Hall. Brian Renshaw arrived late 1948 – initially as a temporary replacement for Mr John – on an annual salary of £322.10s.0d. Within three weeks, he received his call-up papers for the Naval Air Service but was nevertheless given a permanent post as assistant master (Woodwork). He went off to sea the following month, returned 18 months later and then disappeared (at least, as far as the available

records are concerned) in July 1950. Les Bown recalls that Mr Renshaw was new to teaching and understandably concerned not to make careless mistakes. When taking the children on nature walks, he would count them all very carefully at every field gate. A former pupil believes that he left teaching to go into carpentry.

Ten shillings (brown), 1961-71

Having completed her training at Homerton College in Cambridge, Miss Haworth reported for temporary duty in September 1948 as *a qualified assistant mistress* on £361 p.a. For anyone interested in trivia, her car broke down on Monday 10 January 1949 on the way to school, in November 1950 she was away *having to attend a Police Court in Cheshire to give evidence concerning a motor accident she witnessed while on holiday*, and on Monday 23 June 1952 she *was a little late this morning as her car had a puncture on the way*. Motor vehicles and Miss Haworth were clearly an unhappy mix. At the school for nearly four years and featuring in the records solely in connection with car breakdowns and accidents, she left in June 1952.

The school's third male teacher arrived in March 1949 in the shape of 27-year old Ronald Samuel James from Burderop ECT near Swindon, who lodged at Morecambe Farm, Blagdon. The records portrayed the interview process: *the application forms and references were considered by the managers and the candidate was submitted to an oral exam on his attitude to disciplinary action in keeping order in the classroom, his opinion on school meals, sport etc and music. The candidate answered the questions satisfactorily and was most enthusiastic about music.* There was sadly no mention of just what Mr James's opinions were to stodgy semolina or the latest jazz craze. He went on his way in December 1952 but not before he'd impressed himself on Pauline Heron's memory by fighting a boy with a ruler. This was allegedly not an isolated incident. Colin Symes recalls that Mr James would insist on teaching unwilling children the Brother James Air (a.k.a. The Lord's My Shepherd) and playing the piano with his back to the class, where absolute bedlam was reigning. His unerring ability to hit a small child on the head from a fair distance with a piece of chalk was legendary.

36-year old Russell Jones from Mountain Ash, Glamorgan, joined in January 1950 to teach Woodwork, having just completed a course at Loughborough following his initial training at Redland, Bristol. He promptly pronounced himself *dissatisfied with the benches and the Hall,* [and] *felt that he cannot make a success of his task.* He left three weeks later. Colin Symes remembers Mr Jones hurling lumps of wood about the place. He didn't endear himself to his pupils by not resting until every single one of them had learned the names of all the component parts of a plane. 'Propeller' was not one of them.

Hiliary Joyce Thomas came from Llanelli in September 1949 as a nominal replacement for Miss Edser – who'd left a year earlier – but went in February 1950. She was replaced in February 1950 by Miss Edworthy from Bedminster Down, Bristol, at an annual salary of £270. By January 1951 she had become Mrs Lovell and had set up home at Severn Beach. The journey to Bishop Sutton was too long and she resigned at Easter 1951. Mr Ingram from Dilton, Westbury, Wiltshire, was appointed Handicraft master in July 1950; Mr Bailey was perturbed in October of that year to receive a letter from the CEO explaining that Mr Ingram's appointment had been retrospectively cancelled as he had failed in one subject of his final City and Guilds exams. Subject to the managers' consent, however, *he might continue to be employed in a temporary capacity.* The managers consented. But in September 1951 Mr Ingram presented the headmaster with a double challenge: not only did he fail another subject in the exam, but also he was going to Tasmania at Christmas. He meekly asked if he could stay on until a successor had been found. He could and did. With Woodwork remaining untaught for several weeks, the job was offered in February 1952 to Mr Avery of Ottery St Mary, Devon, who wouldn't make a firm decision until he'd found a house, especially as he was *engaged to be married.* The managers gave him a week. He started teaching in March 1952. In January 1953 he intimated *that he may have to leave for domestic reasons* and he duly did, at Christmas.

In December 1951 Mrs Coxhead from Pontefract accepted the post of assistant mistress subject to being able to find digs. Whether she could or not, the Education Authority decided they didn't want her after all and Miss Chivers of Holcombe, near Radstock, started in March 1952 as 'senior mistress'. She was appointed deputy head teacher in May 1956 (with a special allowance of £80 p.a.) and left in 1957 to become the first deputy head of the new Chew Valley Secondary Modern School. Miss Haworth (she of motor vehicle fame) had left in June 1952 and the managers confirmed the appointment of Mrs Bale of Whitchurch, Bristol, who had already been teaching at the school in a temporary capacity. She stayed for over four years and left – on the same day as Miss Harvey – for Exmouth where her husband had been appointed as Congregational minister. She was presented with a table lamp.

In March 1953 *Lord Strachie informed me that the Authority have decided that we need an extra male teacher, and they propose to advertise for one.* Those were the days. If you wanted a male member of staff to counterbalance an overdose of females, you jolly well worded the advert accordingly, and September saw the appointment of David William from Treorchy, Glamorgan as assistant PE master. His temper was allegedly as short as his hair. A few months later he was off on a fortnight's post-National Service training. Six months after that, it was his Reserve Army training and two months later he was called up for 14 days with '2 *Reserve*'. In between all that soldiery, he found time to accept another post in Newport, Monmouthshire, and left in May 1955. Many months went by without the school's adverts for a male teacher being answered.

Future of Teachers	Correspondence with the C.E.O had taken place regarding the future of Teachers when the new School at Chew Magna had been completed. The reply was to the effect that it is the policy of the Education Committee, on the reorganisation of a School, to arrange for any Teachers who are employed full time in the teaching of senior children to be transferred with the children. That the Teachers concerned who are on the permanent staff of the Bishop Sutton County School when the reorganisation of the School is effected will be offered appointments on the staff of the new School. That on the basis of the present establishment of this School there will be one Teacher for Juniors children only, and the Managers should bear in mind, should a vacancy arise, for a Junior Teacher. That as the Managers are unlikely to be able to obtain an Assistant Master for Physical Education post, and one who was qualified to work with fixed apparatus at the New Secondary Modern School, it is advised that they should continue with the services of a Supply Teacher pending the reorganisation of the School.

1957 - transfer of teachers to Chew Valley School

A new teacher was urgently needed to replace Mr Avery, and Mr Berrell started in January 1954. He tendered his resignation in May. As Mr Bailey fatalistically wrote: *we shall require a new Handicraft teacher*. Ronald James's post as assistant master of the 'Junior School' had been unfilled since December 1952 – yes, I know it gets confusing – and the managers appointed Philip Hopp (34) of Cheltenham[1], to start on Thursday 1 July 1954. By the end of playtime that morning he'd been nicknamed 'Hoppalong Cassidy' from the popular radio show of that name, and that's how his former pupils remember him. Having suffered a couple of years of taunting, he found himself another post in April 1957 rather than be transferred to the new Chew Valley School as was usually the fate (welcome or otherwise) of those who taught the older children at local primaries. Ivor Cotton from The Wrangle in Compton Martin replaced Mr Berrell as Handicraft master in January 1955. The length of his tenure at the school was not recorded, although by the mid-'50s logbook entries were generally short on those facts that would help someone write abut the school fifty years later.

With Mrs Bale having departed in 1956 with her lamp tucked underneath her arm, the managers appointed Miss B. Dillon from Nottingham. Aged 26, she was no novice, but the move to the damper West Country did nothing for her health. She was away with a cold, had flu, was advised to take a week off, phoned in sick, or couldn't phone in sick but didn't come in anyway and *gave formal notice to terminate her employment* in July 1958. The children and staff had a collection and

----
[1] Mr Bailey wryly noted that *the length of time which has elapsed since* [Mr James] *went and before* [Mr Hopp's] *appointment was made was that the post was advertised as a Music teacher*.

she *was presented with a cheque from the children, staff and well-wishers.* Miss Harvey had retired in July 1956. It was never going to be easy to replace her as infant teacher, arguably one of the most influential jobs at the school. Miss Brigg from Bradford, Yorkshire, was quickly appointed. She also quickly resigned, in July 1957.

But then to a new era of infant teachery. Having interviewed three candidates for the post of infants' mistress, the managers selected Eileen Stuckey from Hinton Blewett. She started in January 1958. Little was recorded about her – although, as observed before, this was the age of distinctly spartan logbook and minute book entries – until October 1970 when she was promoted to deputy head. She retired in 1980, and is very fondly remembered. School nurse Bettina Cohn recalls that Miss Stuckey had wanted a baby to be brought in to be bathed. Bettina, adopting a strictly professional view, didn't see it as a particularly wise move – the school was draughty – and brought in a doll instead. Some children went home and told their mothers they weren't doing it right. Someone commented that Miss Stuckey, a lay reader at the Chapel, was "hot on religion", but the comment that best encapsulated how pupils felt about her is that she "gave them a sense of security and set them on a path to success". Monica Castle recalls her as being sweet, "the loveliest lady".

Miss M. A. E. Wilson of Brighton was appointed in April 1959, after three earlier sets of interviews without a suitable candidate being found, to take charge of the Lower Juniors. She stayed in post for nearly six years, during which time she married a Mr Fletcher. Miss Webber stepped into Mrs Fletcher's shoes in August 1964 but left for Cheddar in July 1966. *The managers received this information with regret.* Miss Durrant was appointed in 1968, but the records were silent as to how long she stayed. Mrs Jenkins started the same year but, again, there's no indication of when she left. Teresa Dowling remembers her smacking both girls and boys (but only if

£1 (green), 1960-77

they deserved it) and pulling a girl's hair for not sitting up straight. In January 1970 Mr Price's wife Mair *began her duties as 0.4 temporary teacher and is in charge of a section of the infants' class.* By July 1970 she had been asked to join the permanent staff and in December 1972 the *managers decided that they would like Mrs Price to be a full-time teacher.* In August 1973 she took charge of the Upper Juniors. She left on 21 December 1979, warmly regarded by her pupils and by the wider village community; Welsh to the core like her husband and remembered by many for her comforting lilting voice. Teresa Dowling recalls that Wednesday afternoons were Project Afternoons, and Mrs Price would come in with a basket full of bits and bobs for crafts.

Mrs Holland *took up her duties with the second year infants' class* in September 1970. She left at the end of December as she was expecting a baby, and there was a large farewell party. *She was presented with a pan set and a cheque.* Miss Hopkins *was chosen at interview for the post of assistant mistress from September 1970*, and that's all we seem to know about her.

Mr Price told the governors in March 1972 *that he would like a male teacher, another lady would be of no advantage, he would like the new teacher to be interested in games and swimming.* Luckily for Mr Price, the Sex Discrimination Act was still some three years away. The search was on. Four male candidates were interviewed and in May 1972 Mr R. E. S. Callicott accepted the post of *assistant master in charge of Upper Juniors* as from August. He left in December 1973 for promotion in Bristol, had a farewell party and *was presented with a gift token.* Miss Marilyn Coates was given the post of 'infant mistress' in January 1974. Mr Callicott's numerical replacement was Mrs J. Martin. Mid-May 1974 the governors appointed Mr D. H. Powell to replace her as a 'Scale I assistant'. Mr Price wrote on 26 July 1977: *David Powell terminated his employment at this school today. He is being transferred to Nailsea Junior School under the deployment scheme[1] after having volunteered to do so.*

By the mid-'70s, many staffing decisions were being taken out of the governors' and headteacher's hands. In September 1977, for example, Mr Price *received notification that Mrs J. Baker of Chew Magna was appointed a part-time teacher in charge of Upper Juniors for one morning per week.* In December 1978 *Miss L. Lucas of Keynsham was appointed for a fixed contract of two terms as temporary replacement for Mrs Townhill who leaves at end this term.* The fact that this was the first we've heard of Mrs Townhill just goes to show how little information the logbooks were imparting by this time.

TEACHER'S HELPERS

Below headteachers and teachers on the pedagogical scale came monitors, pupil teachers (PTs), supply staff, clerical assistants and supernumeraries. They all had their place in the smooth running of the school. In pre-First World War days, they were firmly encouraged to know that place.

In 1846 the Committee of the Privy Council inaugurated an independent PT system whereby in schools approved by an HM inspector, 13-year olds could be apprenticed to a teacher for five years. They would combine daily teaching with private study and after-school tuition from the head. At the end of each year of apprenticeship, the PT took an exam conducted by the inspectors and, if successful, earned an annual salary ranging from £10 for first year candidates to £20 for those in the final year. At the end of the apprenticeship they could sit for a Queen's Scholarship exam to gain entry to a training college or remain in school as unqualified assistants, perhaps studying in their spare time for a teacher's certificate. From 1847 they could take a qualifying exam as an 'acting teacher' while holding down a job in a school. Many teachers chose this option, but by 1914 only 32% of all the women employed in elementary schools were trained at a college, against 27% who were untrained (i.e. hadn't been to college) but certificated, with the rest neither trained nor certificated.

Once pupil teachers had progressed to trainee teachers – if indeed they did – their future success often seemed to depend less on knowledge and more on moral qualities, neatness and plainness of dress. Teachers with a college background were not always welcomed. In 1887 a government commissioner in Todmorden, Lancashire, was told that such teachers *come from poor houses, half educated; they*

----
[1] A scheme that applied widely in the public sector, whereby volunteers could move to another location where there were staff shortages. They received a nominal payment for doing so and it enhanced their career prospects.

know a little, but they do not know enough to show how little they know. A girl goes up to a training college and she comes back exceedingly conceited so that you cannot manage her.

A rare local reference to the exams was on Saturday 30 June 1877 when *the PT attended at Radstock the annual examination of HM Inspector.* In June 1891 PT Lucie Ashman had wanted to leave the school without serving her notice. This put her in a difficult position as she also wanted to sit her exams. The Board wrote to her: [we have] *granted you leave of absence to attend the Queen's Scholarship Examination on the 8th, 9th, 10th July next provided that you supply a substitute who shall be approved by the Board.* Lucie found someone, and the Board wrote: [We] *approve of your substitute and will allow you to attend the Scholarship Examination.* They made it clear that they expected her to return to school afterwards. She didn't. The Board wasn't being especially anti-Lucie: you were only allowed time off for your teaching exam if you produced an acceptable substitute teacher for the period in question.

The importance of Santa's little helpers to Victorian schools is evident from the figures. In 1870 there were over 12,000 certificated teachers in England and Wales, against 16,000 PTs and 1,200 supplementary teachers. By 1880, there were over 31,000 certificated teachers, against 32,000 PTs and 7,600 supplementaries. As regards the supplementary teachers, the only requirement was that they – they were nearly always female – must be at least 18, have been vaccinated against smallpox and be recognised by HM Inspectors as *employed during the whole of the school hours in the general instruction of the scholars and in teaching Needlework.*

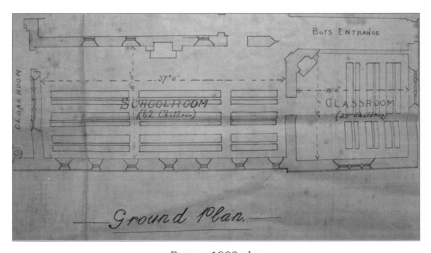

From a 1900 plan

Untrained child monitors and monitresses often provided the headteacher's only teaching assistance. A monitor – paid an average of two guineas a year in 1904 – had a short light cane (a 'pointer') as a badge of office for pointing to the letters of the alphabet on a big wall card but equally useful for banging on desks. Or on children's bottoms. Monitresses wore ankle-length skirts and a small black or coloured apron, as opposed to the shorter skirts and white pinafores worn by the pupils. Monitors were simply expected to dress more smartly than the male pupils. As uniform, or the lack of it, didn't feature in the logbooks, it's worth mentioning here that Ken Rapps recalls that there was nothing particularly formal in the 1930s for the boys: shirt, tie, short trousers, but no cap or blazer. The girls too were expected to dress smartly.

Monitors and PTs were mentioned in the Bishop Sutton logbooks from the very beginning until they vanished from the scene around 1919, although 'pupil teachers' were mentioned in passing in an inspection report from 1974. Monitress Margaret Harvey had the privilege of being the first to have her name in logbook print or, more accurately, in averagely neat handwriting: don't believe that the Victorians always scribed in flawlessly flowing copperplate. She got her name in lights in November 1872 for coming in late. Later that month, headmistress Hassell observed that *one monitress, Ellen Wyatt,* [was] *kept at home by her mother in the morning after leave was refused. Standard I had no teacher in consequence.* The monitors were effectively teachers on the cheap, and heads didn't always hold them in high regard: on 24 January 1873 *one of the monitors, Elizabeth Harvey, came to school late this morning (again) and has been very careless and inattentive with her class lately.* These young prospective teachers were nevertheless indispensible and the Board recorded in November 1874 that *the three present monitors should be continued as weekly servants at a rise of 6d per week each.* Sometimes the monitorship was a makeweight pending other employment: in November 1875 *G. Appleby, one of the two monitors, has this week discontinued to teach in school. His father intends to give him another trade.* The problems – perceived or genuine – posed by Emma Ferris from some pages back were preceded by those posed by an unnamed PT in February 1875: the Board heard from Miss Hassell that *the PT had several times encouraged the children to disobedience and rebellion.*

Farthing 1851, halfpenny 1855, penny 1854 (all actual size)

School Board members didn't expect to be challenged – or, quite possibly, spoken to at all – by uppity young monitors or PTs, and could be stern. In July 1878 they *refused the notice from Jane Tibbs, monitress, requiring a rise from 1/- to 2/- per week. Proposed, seconded and carried unanimously that Mr Northam's daughter be elected to fill the place of Jane Tibbs at 1/6 pw.* The Board wrote to Jane: *Madam, I am directed to inform you that your services as Monitress at Bishop Sutton School will not be required after the 5th inst. Yours obediently, Geo. Booth, Clerk.* Sometimes there was poaching from other schools: in August 1882 the Board advertised *in The Schoolmaster and Bristol papers for a transfer PT for the Bishop Sutton School.* There were no replies.

Monitors were commonly taken on in the expectation that they would progress. In October 1884 the Board expressed the wish that *a monitor will be engaged with a view to his becoming PT eventually.* George Tibbs came along on a trial basis *to see if he will be a suitable candidate for probation at next exam.* He manifestly wasn't, and in February of the following year headmaster Brown wrote: *I find the boy*

George Tibbs of very little use as monitor – he takes no interest and puts no energy into the work. In March: *George Tibbs not liking teaching and possessing no energy, I have a lad named Thomas Victor Ferris on trial in his place*. This may be the Victor Ferris who was 'readmitted' on 9 February 1885 at age 14, *having previously left to go to work*. With a truly Dickensian sense of social hierarchy, Mr Brown wrote in January 1886: *Thomas Victor Ferris leaves this school Friday 22nd … he has conducted himself well during his engagement, thoroughly satisfying his master*.

In November 1887 William Sheppard was working as a monitor at 3/- a week. In January 1889 the Board wrote to the Education Department in Whitehall: *I beg to inform you that William J. Sheppard was on the 7th September 1888 duly articled as a PT at the Bishop Sutton Board School. The engagement dates from 1st July 1888 and ends on the last day of June 1892*. In June 1889 an inspector reported that William *has passed an unsatisfactory exam. Should he fail to the same extent next year, the Grant will have to be reduced. HM Inspector recommends that he should take the 1st year's paper again and that his engagement should be extended one year*. The Board's clerk wrote to Mr Brown, explaining that he would confer *with Mr Sheppard and his son to ascertain if both are willing to comply with the Inspector's recommendation, and would try to arrange a personal interview with them as soon as possible. Until the matter is decided, I think you had better give him his last year's work to do again*. The lad was a minor and his father therefore had to take decisions for him. The Board advised Whitehall the following month that Master Sheppard had declined to comply and had resigned.

As we have seen, the monitors didn't always progress as hoped. In September 1896 *Frank Harvey, who has been a paid monitor in this school for the last year, left having obtained a situation as clerk*. Note that he was a paid monitor, suggesting that some were unpaid. Once Frank left, the Board authorised Mr Brown *to engage a temporary monitor at 1/6 per week*. That was still the going rate over two years later: in January 1899 *Mr Wightman reports that he had secured the services of Ethel Harvey as monitress, salary 1/6 p.w.* She applied in December 1899 for an increase. Reply: *Your application for an increase in salary was unsuccessful*. Lily Parfrey and Nelly Steele were taken on as *PT candidate monitors* in October 1906. In July 1908 the Board resolved that *in the opinion of the managers, Lily Parfrey if retained for another year would be likely to pass an exam in qualifying for pupil teachership, and also she shows promise of making a good teacher*.

The last logbook entries relating to monitors and pupil teachers were in April 1918, when the managers recommended Emily May Harvey for appointment as PT, and in April 1919 when Ella Daunton was taken on in the same role. The School Admission Register shows that Emily was born in June 1904 and started at the school in April 1908; Ella was born in November 1905 and started in November 1908.

Supply teachers were a different kettle of instructor and didn't make a logbook appearance until March 1935 when Miss M. D. Bailey covered for Miss Harvey's and Miss Batt's absences. There was a comment the following year that despite Mrs Flower's recurring illnesses, *no supply is available*. But after 1936 the supply of supply teachers seemed inexhaustible, often to the extent that the head was the only permanent member of staff at the school. The situation was fraught during the war years, when Mr Bailey mildly protested at regular intervals *that the authorities cannot send a supply teacher*. The pre-war situation slowly resumed, however, and until the late 1970s a supply teacher was generally just a phone call away, even if the permanent teacher would only be off for a couple of hours.

Invariably welcome, there was the odd occasion when supply teachers weren't. One stand-in, in October 1947, was Mrs George from Draycott, who is recalled by one former pupil as 'walloping Selwyn Griffiths on his bad ear'. Supply teachers were clearly not immune from the percussive impulses often felt by their permanent colleagues. Mrs George was described by another villager as 'a bit of an ogre'.

Miss I. G. Wright, a supply teacher in the late 1950s, taught Maths. Eric Price remembers her fondness for times-tables. He had opened his school report – addressed to his parents – on his way home. Miss W caught and suitably chastised him and sealed the report in another envelope, writing on it that Eric had been rude enough to open the first one. She would 'rattle out "nine eights" and if you didn't know the answer, you stayed behind'. But she did have her softer side. A group of Eric's friends was given detention on his birthday. He told her about his party and she asked how many of the children were going. "All of them", he lied, and she set all of them free.

School football team 1931-32
Back row (left to right): Don Harris, Jack Tovey, Jim Harvey.
Middle row: Ted Small, Howard Tibbs, Vernon Tovey(?), Harry(?) Harvey,
Bob Lyons.
Front row: Alan James, George Dury, Hew Walker, Don James (?)

It was usually down to the head and his teachers to handle administration and clerical tasks, but as bureaucracy and form-filling gathered pace, Education Authorities began to pay for assistance. In June 1958 Miss June Hammond was taken on as clerical assistant *in addition to her duties as supervisory assistant.* Miss E. Harvey arrived in June 1962 – Teresa Dowling recalls that she lived in Plum Tree Cottage on Church Lane. Miss Harvey was followed in February 1974 by Joan Davidge and Diane Clark. Joan recalls being paid 22½p an hour, not only for dinner duties but also for helping with the children's reading. Cynthia Holman recalls that in the pre-computer days of 1978 when she started as a school secretary and did all the administration, she worked 14 hours a week; the school was allowed 32½ hours of ancillary staff but Tom Price split those hours between Cynthia and two assistant teachers. Teresa remembers that on Monday mornings the children would line up and give the supervisory assistant their dinner money and their Savings Bank pennies.

EMPTY THE CESSPITS, SWEEP THE WALLS, CLEAN THE WINDOWS

Although the early logbooks suggested that it was the headteacher who performed all the housekeeping duties – a suggestion not altogether unconnected with the fact that it was the headteacher who wrote the logbooks – cleaners, caretakers and, later, groundsmen, were employed. The first reference was in June 1878 when the Board wrote to a Mr Kennard in Bishop Sutton: *Dear Sir, please supply Mrs Edgell with 1 large sweeping brush, 1 small ditto, 2 black lead brushes, 1 small one for putting it on, 1 packet of black lead, 1 mop and handle*. No cleaner should be without a small ditto. The 1872 Kelly's Directory had listed Joseph Weston Kennard as a wholesale family grocer and dealer. By the 1889 edition he had the additional string to his bow of a 'musical instrument dealer'.

After a series of caretakers, the Board took Miss Emma White on in September 1900 *at £8 p.a. plus 15/- per year for firewood*, increased to £10 p.a. in 1902. Her 'Caretaker's Duties' read as follows:

Daily: Offices (toilets) *to be swept out, rooms, passages, cloakrooms. Every day after school closes, to dust thoroughly every morning before school opens, to cover cesspits with ashes every evening, to see all bowls are left clean, to see playgrounds are tidy, to have fires burning at 8 am in Winter. Weekly: In addition to the above, to scrub seats and floors of offices, blacklead firegrates, tidy playgrounds. Monthly: In addition, to empty and clean cesspits of offices, to clean all windows (both inside and out), dust maps, wash desks. Holidays: to scrub all floors of rooms, passages etc, to empty and clean cesspits, to sweep walls, clean windows, to whitelime inside of offices, find all materials etc required for use in your duties as caretaker. 15/- per year will be allowed you to provide firewood for use in the schools.*

In February 1906 Mr Wightman wrote, *I find the school is cleaned very often by one of the girls*. Perhaps she was moonlighting for the cleaner. In November 1912 *the old 'Conscience Clause' was taken down for cleaning and is missing*. It stated that parents could remove their children from religious instruction, and the headmaster had to apply for a new one. In July 1917 he *was informed that Mr J. C. Hurle, Chairman of the County Education Committee, was sorry to say he found the Bishop Sutton School dirty*. To add insult to Mr Wightman's inevitable injury, this was in *great contrast to Chew Magna School*. The headmaster *was requested to pay greater attention in future to the instructions to managers and to see that the caretaker performed her duties*. Hardly the time for Miss White to be applying for a rise. The clerk wrote to her: *I have to inform you that the County Education Chairman recently inspected the Bishop Sutton School premises and reported that he found them … apparently uncared for, and that until your work is better done, then I cannot possibly recommend an increase. I trust that you will see to it that there shall be no further cause on your part for a second complaint. All the copper pipes and brass taps in the offices must be scoured and kept bright in future.* Miss White resigned in August 1917 and it wasn't until October that a replacement came along in the form of Mrs E. Harvey, at £12 p.a.

In addition to the role spec advised to Miss W in 1900, Mrs H had to see that the drains were clear, dust the ledges, examine the ventilators, clean the map rollers with a damp cloth, wash towels and dusters at the weekend ready for the Monday morning, and sweep the yards and roadways. Within a year she *reluctantly resigned for domestic reasons,* and in October 1918 Mrs S. Chapman (*wife of soldier on active service in France*) was taken on *at £15 p.a. plus 15/- for firewood.* She wasn't in the job long and Mr Wightman complained in March 1919 that her replacement, Mrs Kate Tovey, was responsible *for fires not burning at 9.15.* This was not an isolated oversight: a few days later, *cleaner did not come. Had to light fires myself.* The managers resolved in April *that her services be dispensed with.* They gave the job to Mrs A. G. Williams at £15 p.a., which they quickly increased to £26. But six days after this hefty rise came into effect, Mrs W resigned and it took three months to find someone else: word must have spread quickly throughout the village that the cleaner's job at the school bain't be all that it were cracked up to be. In August they found Mrs A. Dix at £20 p.a. The £26 that Mrs Williams had been paid was clearly considered too generous. The reduced pay didn't stop Mrs D from lasting the course – she didn't retire until 1936 – although she did manage to break three panes of glass in April 1920 (*done whilst cleaning*). All seemed to go well for eleven years, but in October 1931 she complained to supply headmaster Mr Sidwell *of lack of dusters and a poor brush.* A cleaner won't get far with a poor brush. The said Mr Sidwell *discovered a full supply of new school cleaning materials in an outhouse belonging to the schoolmaster's house. I have put the necessary replacements ready for use.* In November 1931 Mrs D *mistakenly destroyed the Royal Wall Atlas (The World).*

It's not clear what happened between November 1931 and December 1941 when Mrs E. Saunders first brandished her mop. She went part-time in February 1950 at £86.13s.4d a year. The logbook ignored cleaning until March 1960 when something prompted a letter from the CEO *pointing out that Mr Saunders was covered for industrial injury and consequently he could clean the school windows, but should an accident occur the Somerset County Council would not make up the wages earned by Mr Saunders in his normal employment. It was agreed to employ a firm of local window cleaners.* Whether this Mr Saunders was the husband of Mrs E. Saunders is not recorded, but Mrs E. Saunders didn't retire until 31 August 1977. There couldn't have been a single nook and cranny in the school that hadn't received the undivided attention of her duster. Mrs Joy Collett was appointed cleaner-in-charge.

> (*a*) **Daily Duties of Caretaking and Cleaning Staff.**
> (i) **Offices.**
> The importance of adequate attention to offices cannot be too strongly emphasised and it is important from an educational as well as a hygienic viewpoint that they should be maintained in the highest possible state of cleanliness. They should be examined daily and if necessary should be cleaned and thoroughly flushed. Pail closets should be emptied every day. A reasonable supply of toilet paper should always be available and may when necessary be purchased locally. A separate statement of instructions for working earth closets of the "Swanmore" type is available on application to the **Chief Education Officer** or the **Divisional Education Officer** as appropriate.
> **Hand basins should be cleaned daily.**

Cleaner's duties 1954

The first mention of a groundsman was in July 1969 when an advert was placed in the Post Office window for someone to work for 12 hours a week. The outcome of this high-profile recruitment campaign wasn't recorded, but the logbook did say in May 1979 – nearly ten years later – that *Mr L. J. Smith of School House began his part-time duties as School Groundsman*. He didn't have far to get to work.

A full list of heads, teachers and staff at the school from 1870 to 1979 can be found in Appendix 2.

LIVING WAGE, ROSY HUES AND LONG WEEKENDS

What were conditions of employment actually like in schools? How did teachers hone their art and what guidelines did they follow? How much did they earn?

Mrs Isabella Beeton (1836 to 1865, she of 'The Book of Household Management') considered in the 1850s that a yearly income of £150 justified the employment of a maid, and that a man earning £500 a year could afford a cook. A man with £1,000 a year could stretch not only to the cook, but also to a manservant and two housemaids. Office clerks earned around £150 a year at that time. The headmaster of a good public school got at least £1,000 and top lawyers were raking in over £15,000 p.a. in the 1880s, equivalent to over £700,000 in 2009. This made teachers' salaries look paltry. In 1870 a certificated female received around £58 a year and her male counterpart £90. Although the job was unattractive to most educated men, it was more worthwhile for women than the usual avenues open to them such as dressmaking, cleaning or cooking. Women's lower rates of pay were tempting for hard-pressed School Boards with limited cash at their disposal. But overall, and despite the drawbacks, teaching in the early days of Bishop Sutton School did afford men and women of relatively humble backgrounds the chance to be part of a respectable profession with modest prestige. Far more modest than teachers would wish. Successive governments have tried to remedy the position, and many teachers would argue that successive governments have failed.

In 1914 the average teacher's salary was still only £1.17s.6d a week or less than £100 a year, but nevertheless about 60% higher than an agricultural labourer's. The salary may not have been generous, but the First World War was about to bankrupt the country and economies had to be found. On 5 March 1923 the school logbook stated: *2% reduction agreed by staff*. That proved insufficient to balance the Education Authorities' books, and further cuts were needed. On 20 October 1931 Mr Bailey – who had only been in his job for a fortnight – *received and returned completed form of acknowledgement of receipt of copy of the resolution of the Somerset County Council relating to the cut* (of some 5%) *in the salaries of teachers, a copy of which was given to each member of staff*.

In Coronation Year 1953, a teacher's average weekly earnings were £16.9s.7d, a train driver's £8.8s.6d, a nurse's £7.17s.8d and a farm worker's £5.13s.0d[1].

Teachers and monitors were paid quarterly in the late 1800s, and the system for putting them in funds was rather convoluted. A letter from June 1877 from the School Board clerk to the headmaster was typical: *I enclose the following accounts: your own £20, Mrs Frappell* (the Sewing mistress) *£3, W. Edgell* (presumably a monitor or pupil teacher) *£1.16s.0d, total £24.16s.0d, and a cheque for £24.16s.0d. Please pay the bills and send me receipts*. The individuals presumably had to raise an invoice and give it to the headmaster, who passed it to the Board for verification. The Board then sent the headmaster a covering cheque or warrant which he then encashed at the post office[2] or bank in Chew Magna. He then distributed the cash

----

[1] Figures taken from government statistics.

[2] The post office in Bishop Sutton couldn't encash postal orders or warrants until the 1890s.

and got a receipt which he sent to the Board, who annotated their records.

In November 1902 the school managers *resolved that a certain proportionate sum of the annual grant, to be hereafter fixed, be annually distributed amongst the whole of the teaching staff in such proportions as the Board of Education decide upon after the annual reports have been duly considered.* Bonuses aren't a modern invention. The managers agreed in October 1903 *that one third of the total grant be set aside for the purpose of a bonus to the teaching staff and that it be divided pro rata according to salaries and according to the time spent in teaching.* A managers' minute book entry of November 1903 read: *bonus rescinded with a view to rearranging the bonus system as regards the female teachers.*

NATIONAL UNION OF TEACHERS.

OBJECTS OF THE UNION.

I. To unite together, by means of Local Associations, Public School Teachers throughout the kingdom, in order to provide a machinery by which teachers may give expression to their opinions when occasion requires, and may take united action in any matter affecting their interests.

II. To afford to the Education Department, to School Boards, and to other Educational Bodies, the benefit of the collective experience and advice of Teachers on practical educational questions.

III. To improve the general education of the country by seeking to raise the qualifications and status of Public School Teachers, and by opening out a career to the best qualified Members of the profession.

IV. To watch the working of the Education Act ; to promote the insertion of such new Articles in the Code of Regulations as may from time to time be found necessary in the interests of Public Education ; and to secure the removal of such regulations as are detrimental to the cause of educational progress.

V. To establish a Scheme, whereby retiring allowances may be secured to aged and incapacitated Teachers, and to seek the removal of such restrictions from the existing pension Minutes (1884) as were not contained in the Minutes of 1846 and 1851-61.

VI. To establish Provident, Benevolent, and Annuity Funds in connection with the Union, for the benefit of the Scholastic Profession.

VII. To establish and support in connection with the Union an Orphanage and Orphan Fund for the Children of Teachers.

VIII. To secure the representation of the profession in Parliament.

IX. To raise teaching to the dignity of a Profession by means of a Public Register of duly qualified Teachers for every class of Schools ; by the appointment of a Representative Educational Council and the creation of a Ministry of Science and Education.

J. H. YOXALL, *General Secretary.*
C. JAMES, *Assistant Secretary.*

The National Union of Teachers, 1870

The National Union of Elementary Teachers, founded in 1870 (and dropping the 'Elementary' in 1889), surveyed teachers in 1891 and found that for one in three it was a condition of their employment that they undertake out-of-school activities such as playing the organ or training the choir. Not till 1903 did such impositions end. There's no record of their having ever applied in Bishop Sutton, yet when headmaster Lewis Hawkins was taken on in 1881, the Board did propose to him *the post of organist at the Church at a salary of £15 a year payable by the Vicar and Churchwarden*. He didn't take the Board up on its offer.

There were only two local references to a teachers' association. On 7 July 1884 the School Board minute book noted that *The Chew Valley Teachers' Association* met at Chew Magna Infants' School – this was the first time the 'Chew Valley' was mentioned, in any context, as a separate geographic area – and on 25 November 1969 *the school was closed for the morning session because of full staff withdrawal of labour in support of NUT policy. The managers and Authority were informed. No school meals were served and the school was reopened at 1.30 pm.*

Lest anyone think that it's only modern-day teachers who suffer from stress: George Howe, headmaster of Market Rasen Methodist School in Lincolnshire from 1876 to 1905, wrote in his logbook in 1883[1]: *I observe from the papers that a Master has committed suicide through overstrain and I can truthfully say that I and all the teachers of this neighbourhood are daily suffering from this same pressure. Teachers are expected to perform miracles, but my doctor tells me nothing will do me good but complete rest. Query: how can a teacher obtain rest?* The following year he added gloomily: *When I first entered my pupil teachership, teaching had its rosy hues, but alas they have all vanished.* Edmund Sargent, former secretary of the London Pupil Teachers' Association, griped in 1887 that most PTs had little interest in general reading or cultural activities, as *all knowledge was valued according to its bearing on exams.*

What we refer to now as 'teaching practice' didn't feature in the logbooks until 1926 when Somerset Education Council explained that *Mr S. W. Noakes [was] to attend on 13-17 December as a portion of his training … no doubt the head teacher, with the approval of the managers, will give what assistance he can to Mr Noakes during his period of training. There is, of course, no payment attached to the services of this teacher, which is merely to be regarded as part of his training.* Perhaps it didn't work out too well, as there were no further entries until May 1947, when *two students from Redland Emergency Training College came to begin three weeks' teaching practice.* Nothing then until September 1954 when *Miss Hudson and Miss Stacey and two tutors from the Fishponds Training College are here today with some six students of the College. They will come for five successive Thursdays and take one class in the Upper Juniors.* To a Bishop Sutton lad or lass, Fishponds may have seemed quite exotic. But not as exotic as the Far East, whence, on 29 September 1954, *Mr C. H. Cheng, Senior Lecturer of Northcote Training College of Hong Kong, visited this school. It is a very nice school.* Mr Bailey's usual powers of description hadn't deserted him. The entry was written by Mr Cheng.

In May 1957 *four Sudanese students visited the school today, they are women who have had experience of teaching in the Sudan, with them was Miss White who is going to Tanganyika to teach. Unfortunately, the infrequency of the local bus service caused them to curtail their visit somewhat.* Bad enough trying to get a bus to Bristol. But to Khartoum? In May 1957 *a student from the Fishponds Training College here for a month, proposes to go to Uganda after training.* In May 1971 *the school was visited by a party from Seamills Junior School, Bristol, who wished to look at a rural school.* It's not mentioned whether the governors arranged for a

----
[1] From the Royal Commission on the Working of the Elementary Act, 1887.

tractor to be parked outside for effect.

The training (or 'professional development') of the school's own teachers could give parents and their offspring the chance of a long weekend break. The practice started intermittently as long ago as 1890: *on Friday 17 October, school closed to enable the master and one assistant to attend the Drawing Exam at Fishponds Training College*. In May 1906 Mr Wightman *spent the day in Knowle (Bristol) School making notes of good points*. In January 1928 *Miss Batt spent Wednesday morning at South St. School in Bedminster and the afternoon at Barton Hill School, Bristol*. In May of that year *Mrs Flower and Miss Harvey spent the day at Hanham Rd Council Infants' School studying methods*. But it wasn't until Friday 20 April 1934 that regular 'teacher-training' weekends arrived: *School closed today to allow staff to attend Refresher Course at Bristol, all members of staff attended*. This long weekend was an annual event – apart from 1943 and 1944 – until at least 1957, the venue varying between Bristol, Weston-super-Mare, Frome, Bath and Taunton. There was scarcely any mention of what the teachers thought of these excursions or how good the Danish pastries and coffee were, but the April 1940 course was clearly considered a profitable use of the teachers' time: *many ideas put forward by lecturers have been discussed and the teachers have been invited to use what seems to them to be good*. Monday 10 February 1936 brought a day out in Mr Bailey's car for him, Miss Batt, Miss Harvey and Mrs Flower *for a lecture by Dr Montessori*. In February 1965 the teachers attended a half-day course *to discuss mathematical development in primary schools*. In June 1976 Mr Price *was absent during the morning to attend a Maths Course at St. Matthias Training College*, but perhaps wished he wasn't: *on my return to school, I found that there had been a leakage of water in the boys' toilet*.

1959: school trip to Windsor with Mr Price

The first use of the phrase 'in-service training' wasn't until January 1978 when *the school was closed, teaching staff in-service training. The day was spent at Fosseway and Hilltop Special Schools*. On 9 March 1979 *the school was closed to enable all teaching staff to attend in-service training day on the new Literacy and Mathematics Record Cards at St. Andrews Primary School, Congresbury*.

HE COULD NOT FIND A HOUSE TO BUY WHICH WAS WITHIN HIS MEANS

Readers who have got over the exciting vision of Literacy and Mathematics record cards will recall that a common problem besetting teachers or prospective teachers was a lack of housing. It wasn't just teachers, of course, who were so beset, and it shouldn't be assumed that the problems were restricted to Bishop Sutton.

The story locally starts – as far as the records are concerned – at the PC meeting of January 1919 when *a communication was received from the Clutton RDC re the Housing Scheme. After considerable discussion, resolved that the questions submitted by the Council should be answered as follows: (1) Number of houses required 20 or 30, for which two fields* [might be available] *in Bishop Sutton owned by Messrs Lovell & Sons and Messrs Lyde & Sons, (2) that the houses should have three rooms up with kitchen parlour and scullery with fixed bath downstairs, (3) that the rent should be from 5/- to 10/- per week according to the district and the wage earner.*

In July 1926, by which time the council houses had been built on Bonhill Road and round the corner on the main road, the PC Housing Committee raised the question of further accommodation. It was decided that the 30 new houses proposed for Bishop Sutton should be of the 'parlour type' with rent of no more than 5/- p.w. and should be built *upon the piece of land owned by the Oakhill Brewery Co. in the occupation of Mr Tudor Harvey*, who was landlord at The Butcher's Arms.

The October 1932 PC meeting heard that *Clutton RDC had received several applications for houses at Bishop Sutton*. The councillors pondered whether more housing was really needed, *taking into consideration that the Bishop Sutton Colliery has been closed down with no prospect of it being reopened and also that no new industry is contemplated in the near future.* Clearly not in tune with the parishioners' feelings: in April 1933 *a petition was received from a number of the inhabitants of Bishop Sutton asking for increased housing facilities.* The PC did what PCs do in the face of potential contention: they formed a sub committee to kick it all into the long grass, although in December of that year the Sanitary Inspector did come along to discuss the requirements and was *informed that there were no houses in Bishop Sutton scheduled for demolition and only two for necessary repair. Unlikely that new houses would be sanctioned under the Housing Act.* In July 1934, Murphy's Law being what it is, *Clutton RDC notify that 12 new houses have been approved for Bishop Sutton.* The Council suggested the following sites: *Mrs M. Mapstone's land at Church Lane* (presumably the old allotment field behind the school) *and Mr Lovell's land in Wick's* (sic) *Road adjoining colliery.*

Nothing was done until 1950, when the January meeting of the PC (by now Stowey Sutton) noted in respect of the *Wick Rd Housing Site that* [there would be] *28 houses, two thirds of the total would be distributed between miners and farm labourers, not necessarily of this parish.* And that's when the brickbats started flying. At a public meeting in April 1951, *Mr Matthews expressed no confidence in the Parish Council. Mrs Chidzey enquired how and when was the Wick Rd site chosen and Mrs Higby felt that the new site would create a slum area.* At an Extraordinary Meeting of the Council in May 1951, *the representative* (unnamed) *discountenanced a parishioner's statement that the new site would create a slum area, replying that it was usually the residents themselves which created a slum area, not the houses.* On a similar topic, the 1959 Annual Parish Meeting *opposed the erection of a shelter for workmen, women and children by The Butcher's Arms* [because of] *the use which it would receive without the strictest control being maintained by the police.*

Looking along the main road towards the crossroads, c1920. Southlea is on the left

The last mention of problems afflicting teaching staff was in late 1955 when *Mr Foster, who had been appointed as an assistant master PT, had asked leave to withdraw as he could not find a house to buy which was within his means.* By the end of the 1960s Highmead and Parkfield were built and inhabited. Little to do with new houses or with teachers' problems, but the following is of mild interest. The PC meeting of August 1956 heard that closure orders had been *served on Pit Cottages at Wick Road, and a demolition order re the cottages in The Street / Church Lane* (between The Red Lion and the Church Lane junction). *Re the latter, the property owners had appealed as the present structure could be retained for store buildings. As Church Lane was scheduled for development, the Council were asked not to support the appeal.* The cottages along The Street were pulled down, leaving just the lower part of the wall fronting the main road, but the building at the bottom of Church Lane was reprieved. In May 1970 the councillors were told that *demolition of Rowland Cottages, Sutton Hill Road is in hand.* In March 1959 the PC agreed that the council houses in Bishop Sutton should be numbered 1-66 in order to assist the postman and that those called 'Wick Road' and 'The Crescent' should be renamed 'Woodcroft'.

Shilling: 1887, 1929, 1940, 1957; 5p: 1970 (all actual size)

CHAPTER FIVE

CHILDREN, LESSONS AND INTERFERING PARENTS

HOW MANY, HOW OLD, AND HOW NAMED?

The number of pupils between the early 1840s and the first logbook entry some 30 years later is uncertain, although census records suggest that even as far back as 1851, most Bishop Sutton children between the ages of 5-ish and 11-ish were officially 'scholars', even if their parents didn't send them as regularly as they ought.

The opening entry in the school's first logbook (Friday 1 November 1872) set the pattern for presence and absence: *One girl has been admitted into the school this week, one girl has been absent from sickness, and two girls on leave. Wednesday being a wet day, the school was more thinly attended than on any other day of the week*. In January 1876 *three girls were admitted last week from Widcombe. They had never been in an organised school before*. What was meant by 'organised'?

It's clear that during the last three decades of the 19th century at least, parents and teachers turned a partially blind eye to haphazard attendance. A combination of logbooks, minute books and Education Authority records shows that the number of children at school at any one time often fell woefully below what it should have been, and the headmaster's frustration was evident: on 26 October 1882 *attendances are low, average only 69 out of 122, although 45 names were sent in to Attendance Officer last week, and 60 week before, it makes no difference*. Registers were taken before the morning session and again after the lunch break. They were meticulously checked by school managers until the 1920s, when it was decided that the managers had better things to do. Attendance could vary considerably between morning and afternoon, and from one day to the next. This, from 1882: *Thursday 9 June am 93, pm 85; Monday 23 June am 96, pm 100*. Children often appeared only fleetingly on the school roll, and the entry of 19 October 1885 was typical: *took names of five boys and three girls off books, they having left the parish*. In January 1905 Mr Wightman admitted *three Dokes, father a gipsy. They had never been to school before*. Clearly true travelling gipsies, for on 27 January they *left the district*. The 1870 Education Act didn't fundamentally change the as-and-when nature of attendance: in March 1876 *two new scholars admitted, one about 5 years old, the other about 11, both unable to say the alphabet*. In April that year, *two boys admitted together with two girls this morning, the boys have not been to school for some time and are unable to read monosyllables though 8 and 11 years of age respectively*. Sometimes children returned from the fire to the frying pan: in February 1885 the headmaster *readmitted Victor Ferris age 14, having previously left to go to work.*

What about the very young? School had its uses for mothers who worked, wanted to be alone or couldn't cope. In February 1885 Mr Brown took in *Bertram Grist age 3*, in March *Mary Perry age 3*, in April *Clara Dury and Elizabeth Harvey, both age 3, and Edward Tibbs age 3*. This under-age admittance contributed towards the need for premises extensions, and in April 1890 *the infants now have the classroom for themselves alone*. This was to be only a stop-gap measure, and the Board decided in June 1890 that *until further notice the schoolmaster be directed to refuse admittance to children under 5 years of age*. Eight years later, this policy was unpopular and in September 1898 Mr Wightman wrote: *I have had much trouble with parents since the holidays because I will not admit babies of 3*. In October 1922 the overcrowding led the Education Department to ask him for the names and addresses of all children on the register not resident in Bishop Sutton or Sutton Wick. What they did with the information wasn't recorded.

Five decades on, and the under-5s were still presenting difficulties. Financial restraints prompted the new county of Avon to decide that as from September 1977 no child was to be admitted until the term after their fifth birthday. One governor at Bishop Sutton *felt very strongly about the position of the statutory school age of 5, and felt that he would rather a cut be made here than on books and other facilities, but it was proposed and seconded that a letter should be sent to the county to deplore the fact that Avon should not withdraw the resources and facilities for the rising 5s*. Some schools neatly side-stepped the issue by operating a pre-school or nursery. This didn't always engender neighbourly headteacherly love. Zera Wilson, then headmistress of Chew Stoke School, recalled that *one of the local headmasters considered that the children in Chew Stoke had an unfair advantage because I ran a playgroup in school. I did point out that he could run a playgroup too if he was able to comply with the Social Services Regulations, also that his parents could join the Playgroup Leaders' courses I ran. He threatened to have my playgroup closed down, but was unsuccessful*.

The school c1910

At Bishop Sutton in March 1897, *a large number of infants have been admitted this year, many of them being babies who know nothing at all*. The classroom of their own in 1890 was merely a fond memory by 1927, when *a curtain is needed to separate Standard I and infants during some lessons*. In 1949 the infants were moved to the Methodist Hall, where the 5-year olds were at one end and the 6-year olds at the other. May Woodward recalls them taking a numbered or lettered cushion to doze on in the afternoon, and one former pupil from the 1950s remembers trays of sand to trace letters in. Another remembers the infant classroom doubling as the village library; one lady used to come in with a wire-haired terrier.

One rich vein running through the logbook until well into the 20th century was the 'country cousin' attitude adopted towards Stowey School. In March 1884 headmaster Brown *admitted a very troublesome boy named George Burridge this week truanting on Tuesday and Wednesday and cursed me when I charged him with his fault. I locked him in school for dinner time but he escaped through the window.* A week later: *the boy Burridge has not put in an appearance since, and on enquiry I find he goes to school at Stowey.* The proximity of the two establishments was either convenient or inconvenient, depending on which side of his bed the Bishop Sutton headmaster got out of that day; it was a nuisance having to accept children from Stowey but, equally, useful to be able to palm them off there. From 1927 the older Stowey children had to come to Bishop Sutton at the age of around 12 in any event, but until then, pupils seemed to move between the two schools for a pastime: in September 1881 headmaster Hawkins *admitted six scholars who had been attending Stowey School.* In August 1895 Mr Brown *admitted four fresh scholars from Stowey School, they are all very backward for their respective ages.* In February 1902 *Evelyn Edgell, a very dull girl, has gone to Stowey School. No reason given.* Perhaps too dull even for Stowey, she returned to Bishop Sutton the following month. In December 1924 Mr Wightman *admitted Nash from Stowey School. At request of Stowey Correspondent and the County Secretary, J. Betteridge admitted. These children are all very backward but appear to be fairly intelligent.*

Stowey headmistress Mrs Smith was concerned for her pupils' welfare at the 'big school' and in April 1936 she visited Mr Bailey *to see the conditions into which Stowey children enter when they come here as seniors.* On Tuesday 6 November 1945, the remaining *ten children were admitted here from Stowey School.* It had closed for good; a sad day, especially as Stowey School had opened its doors some seven years before its larger neighbour in Bishop Sutton.

Older children started arriving during the '30s and '40s from other surrounding schools that had lost their all-age status. In September 1945, for example, *14 senior children formerly attending West Harptree School have been transferred here.* Bureaucracy caused problems. In January 1947, *seven children from Ubley are attending here*, but by February, *of the eight children from Ubley School, five have returned but three arrived here today as they live in Compton Martin and the 'bus passes their homes. I have referred the matter of their future attendance to the LEA.* In July 1947 *it was proposed to transfer six children from Ubley as from 1 September.* Five arrived on 1 October: *they will travel on the school bus at present serving Compton Martin and Harptree.* In September 1948 came *the transfer of the 16 East Harptree Parochial School seniors.*

By August 1955 there were 150 pupils at Bishop Sutton, and Mr Bailey noted in August that *no children have come to us from Ubley or East Harptree as this school is now very crowded.* Matters hadn't been satisfactorily resolved by the following July, when Mr Bailey remarked that *cards* [have been] *received from East Harptree for the children due to come here in September, but there is some doubt among the head teachers as to who, if anyone, comes. I have written to the CEO to ask.*

The logbooks were generally silent on pupil numbers between 1886 and 1905. Average attendance figures from 1906 to 1972 were quoted in various records and returns submitted to the County including, for example, the pithy 'Somerset Co. Council List of Elementary Schools shewing the numerical power of Teaching Staff based on Article 12(a) of the Elementary Schools Code 1906'. From 1973 onwards it was back to the very hit-and-miss school logbooks. The tables in Appendix 3 show, for comparison's sake, some statistics for Bishop Sutton, Stowey, Chew Magna and Chew Stoke. By way of context: in 1906 when Bishop Sutton had an average attendance of 117 and Stowey 28, West Harptree had 57 pupils, East Harptree 90, Chelwood 37, Chew Stoke 87, Litton 34, Stanton Drew 69 and Norton Malreward 32. In 1906 the largest elementary school in Somerset was Midsomer Norton West Mixed with 353 pupils (which would have included the over-12s) and the smallest was Oare with 10 (on Exmoor; it was in Oare Church that Lorna Doone was shot at her wedding by her half-brother Carver in R. D. Blackmore's novel 'Lorna Doone, A Romance of Exmoor'). By 1945 the largest was Bishopsworth (which still fell under Somerset) with 294 and the smallest East Lydford (near Castle Cary) with a mere 8.

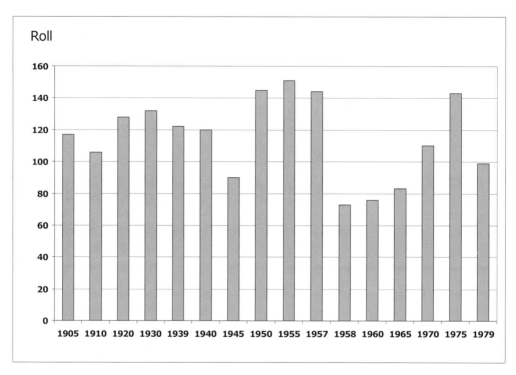

Number of children on roll at Bishop Sutton School, 1905 to 1979

In graph form, the ups and downs of the Bishop Sutton School roll are, well, graphic. The numbers fell dramatically in 1958 following the removal of the older children to Chew Valley School, but took only 20 years to recover before dropping back again. At the time of writing in 2009, there are some 140 children at the school.

In July 1936 – to take one year at random – Mr Bailey taught 40 children in Standards VI and VII, Miss Maggs 25 in Standards IV and V, Mrs Flower 30 in Standards II and III, and Miss Batt 19 in Standard I, leaving Miss Harvey with 29 infants. Standards I and II formed the Lower Juniors, Standards III and IV the Upper Juniors, and Standards V, VI and VII the Seniors (spread across three classes).

Budgets were constantly being squeezed. Mr Bailey was less than pleased to be told in May 1939 – presaging the wartime lack of supply teachers – *that the LEA have decided to reduce the staff by one uncertificated teacher. I have pointed out that this will seriously handicap the school, as in September we have an extra Standard of 14-15 year old children and further it will be difficult to run distinct juniors and seniors divisions with one teacher less*. But the decision had been made and Miss Batt had to go. In September 1943 *the County Authority asked Miss Goulding to leave to reopen Norton Malreward School*[1]. Mr Bailey went on to say that *this leaves certificated headmaster and two uncertificated assistants. Unfortunately this also means practically the end of specialisation except for Needlework*.

By the autumn term of 1957, with Bishop Sutton's days as an all-age school numbered, the staffing position looked thus: Mr Bailey with 24 children (8 girls, 16 boys) in Form 4; Mr Dibble (supply) with 17 children (8 girls, 8 boys) in Form 3; Miss Chivers with 40 children (18 girls, 22 boys) in Forms 1 and 2; Mrs Davies (supply) with 25 children (12 girls, 13 boys) in Juniors 3 and 4; Miss Dillon with 25 children (13 girls, 12 boys) in Juniors 1 and 2, and Miss Martin (Supply) with 21 infants (11 girls, 10 boys). Mr Cotton had no forms but responsibility for Handicraft and Art. The already redundant word 'Standard' had been replaced, at least in the headmaster's mind, by the word 'Form'.

Bishop Sutton opened as a 'true primary school' on 6 January 1958. Mr Price's first logbook entry on 20 April – he having been unavailable until then – read: *the Spring Term commences and I have taken up my appointment as Head of this School. There are now 82 children on roll*. He taught 27 in the Upper Juniors, Miss Dillon had 27 in the Lower Juniors and Miss Stuckey 28 infants. This picture remained more or less unchanged until the late 1960s when the roll had increased to over 100, with Mr Price teaching 52 in the Upper Juniors. The age profile changed over the years: by 1969 the largest class was the infants with 43, *and only 33 in the Upper Juniors*. By 1972 the increasing birth rate of the late Sixties was being felt and numbers went up to 148. Mr Price wrote in September of that year that *space prohibits the formation of another class, but a group of 12 children from Lower Juniors has been formed and these are being taught in the large classroom by the headmaster and Mrs Price*. Mr Price had taken a back seat from teaching by 1974 although liked to keep his hand in now and again.

Numbers steadily fell (through some ups and downs) to 110 in January 1979 and only 88 in September of that year. *This is a considerable drop on September 1978 figures. Staffing ratio is Head plus 3*, said Mr Price at the end of the summer term, perhaps with an I'm-glad-I'm-retiring look on his pen. Not since 1966 had the roll been so low. Why? There were fewer births, and increasing car ownership permitted greater competition from other schools such as Chew Magna's Catholic Sacred Heart School and Chew Stoke's Church of England Primary School.

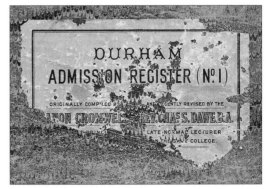

The school's Admission Register 1906. 'Durham' is the style, not the name of the school!

----

[1] Numbers for Norton Malreward, one of the smallest schools in Somerset, ranged from a peak of 36 in 1907, falling steadily to an average of 15 by the early 1930s. The school closed in 1938 with 11 pupils. The authorities reopened it in 1943, possibly due to wartime petrol shortages making it difficult to transport the village children to other schools. It closed for good in 1945.

Skipping back to the late 1800s and early 1900s, we know that children were transferred to Bishop Sutton from other schools, partly as a result of their parents moving into the village in search of jobs. One column in the School Admission Register of 1906 to 1935 – the only volume surviving – was for noting any previous school attended. Of the 728 children admitted during those years, at least 408 had no previous school and were therefore either born in Chew Magna parish (which included Bishop Sutton) or moved here before the age of around 5. The remaining 320 came from across the country, but with the majority from local villages and a fair few from South Wales, reflecting the need for miners to travel further afield to find work or, in some case, to expand their experience. For anyone who likes lists and numbers, Appendix 4 shows where the children hailed from. The figures illustrate not only the link between Bishop Sutton and Bristol, but also the relative lack of any traditional link between Bishop Sutton and Bath. Only one child had come from a school in London. There had been a dramatic change over some 70 years: the 1861 census listed very few children under the age of 12 as having been born outside Chew Magna parish.

Part of the index of the School Admission Register. The number quoted was merely sequential. The names were crossed through when the child left the school.

That's where they came from. What were they called? The 'Highways Accounts Book 1844-1846' listed the men too poor to be able to pay rates and therefore made to work on the roads. Some of those men – the following are those from Bishop Sutton Tything – may well have been fathers of the first children at the school: Applebee, Andrews, Baker, Batten, Bendle, Brown, Binding, Burwell, Chiswell, Chivers, Clements, Clothier, Coles, Collins, Cook, Dagger, Dodson, Dury, Eason, Fanks, Filer, Foot, Gibbs, Halett, Harris, Harvey, Hassell, Hoskings, Hynam, Jones, Lane, Layker, Luckman, Lyppiate, Melluish, Perry, Robbins, Sage, Sheldron, Stallard, Sweet,

Tombes, Travis, Vecke, Webb, White, Withey, and Whore. 'Whore' may have been a misspelling.

The most common Bishop Sutton surnames at the time of the 1841 census were Filer and Harvey. By 1871 the Harveys were reigning supreme. Of the 728 children listed in the school's Admission Register (1906 to 1935), 271 had one of 20 surnames shared by eight or more children: Chapman (10), Chidzey (10), Clark (15), Coles (22), Dury (25), Edgell (10), Harris (15), Harvey (31), Hill (8), James (12), Lyons (11), Marsh (10), Moody (8), Perry (12), Small (9), Stevens (8), Tibbs (14), Tovey (17), Walker (16), Wyatt (8). Amazingly, there were only three Smiths. No 'foreign' names and hardly any of obvious Welsh, Scots or Irish origin.

The 1871 census of the village listed Christian names that would appear strange today (although perhaps not as strange as Brooklyn or Poppy Honey): the three virtues Charity, Mercy and Temperance were well represented, as were biblical characters such as Isaac and Jonas. There were a fair few Fannys and Hepzibahs; one boy born in 1857 was christened Inkerman, presumably after the Crimean War battle of 5 November 1854 where British and French soldiers practised their bayoneting skills on the Imperial Russian Army[1]. The period spanned by the Admission Register was one of huge social change from the overt patriotism of the Edwardian era and the Great War to the influence exerted by Hollywood stars. The top fifteen boys' names from 1906 to 1935 were William (26), Arthur (18), George (15), John (13), Frederick (10), Reginald (9), Alfred and Cyril (9 each), James, Edward, Ernest, Maurice, Stanley and Thomas (8 each) and Walter (7). For the girls: Gladys (14), Doris, Kathleen (12 each), Edith, Lily, May (10 each), Margaret, Phyllis, Violet, Lilian (9 each), Elsie, Hilda, Olive (8 each), Mabel and Alice (7 each). No Kylies and not even a hint of a Jade.

SERRIED RANKS AND OBJECT LESSONS

Rural schools had their challenges. *It is a very hard matter to cultivate the intelligence of our children*, wrote the despondent head of Holberton School in Devon in the 1890s. *There is no foundation to work upon, they have seen nothing; to talk of railways, manufacture, telegraphs or ordinary Arts of Civilisation is to make sure of not being understood at the very commencement.*

That makes you stop and think.

Our image of Victorian and Edwardian schools is of serried ranks of scholars being cajoled by means of regular punishment into learning their lessons off by heart in front of a scary master or mistress. Teachers aimed to strengthen children's character and prepare them for adult life by instilling habits of hard work, orderliness and perseverance. The Government's 'Payment by Results' system made it imperative (for the school) that the scholars passed exams. It reinforced in teachers the need to cram facts into children's brains, best done by making them learn by repetition. This made it difficult for children to tell stories in their own words; they would use stilted phrases, the meaning of which they often didn't understand. The exams emphasised Arithmetic and English to the exclusion of almost everything else, although History and Geography were added to the curriculum in the 1860s. The lessons depended to some extent on what sex you

----

[1] This was a month before the Battle of Balaclava, when British troops realised that they had been poorly equipped for the cold weather and resorted to cutting holes in their woolly socks and pulling them over their heads, thereby giving the English-speaking world a new hat.

were: boys were expected to leave school to work on the land or join the Forces and were taught practical 'manly' skills. Girls' futures would be built around home and family, so they learnt sewing and basic cookery.

By the 1920s methods of teaching the very young were beginning to change. Maria Montessori was encouraging imagination through play and manual dexterity: grammar was taught using coloured cards, and practical skills such as tying shoe laces were introduced. Children worked in small groups. There were experiments – not in Bishop Sutton – with 'free schools' such as Summerhill in Dorset, set up by Mr A. S. Neill in 1924, with no punishments and few rules. Love, closeness and personal responsibility would, it was thought, subdue indiscipline among children and enable them to develop naturally. Mr Neill was accused of anarchy and irresponsibility, but some of his ideas did gradually gain momentum in education circles. It wasn't until after the Second World War that progressive theories came to influence the state education system. Primary schools became increasingly child-centred, with opportunities for self-expression and creativity. There was a more relaxed atmosphere, fewer rigid rules and far less corporal punishment. For the first time, it was formally recognised that educational achievement was closely linked to home background and parental interest, and so parental involvement was actively encouraged.

But back in the Victorian day at Bishop Sutton, it was all properly regulated, without any of this namby-pamby progressive-theory wufty-tuftiness. In March 1873 Miss Hassell *sent a new time table to the Inspector, the Rev. H. B. Barry, for his approval*. In March 1876 headmaster John Jones *received five packets of register cards to register the school and home work of the older scholars*. In October 1882 *the first class* (presumably the juniors, as the infants were usually described as 'infants' or 'babies') *were studying Object Lessons, use of verbs in sentences, how cases of nouns and pronouns depend upon it; the second class, 'adjectives'; the third Standard, 'chief rivers of Scotland'; the first class* (presumably headmaster Hill is now talking about the older children), *'Indo-China'; the second class, 'general definitions'; the fifth class, 'simple proportion by principle of unity or first principles'*. Nothing too taxing, then.

Which brings us neatly to Object Lessons[1], a staple of the primary school curriculum and much loved by Victorian educationalists. They were a method of teaching children everything there was to know about a chosen thing, and a programme was

----

[1] An object lesson on an apple, for example, would encompass the following, depending on children's abilities and age. *Parts: core, pips, peel, pulp, juice, stalk, surface, inside, outside. Qualities: spherical, bright, odorous, coloured, opaque, natural, vegetable, juicy, hard, nice, solid, pleasant. The pips are brown on the outside when ripe, white in the inside, pointed oval, hard, bright. The core is membranaceous, stiff, yellow, hard, semi-transparent. Remarks on words: spher-ical is derived from sphere, teacher to give instances of similar terminations; children: cylindr-ical, crit-ical, con-ical. Odor-ous is derived from Latin odor (scent), teacher to give instances of similar terminations; children: nutrit-ous* (sic)*, indigen-ous. Veget-able is derived from Latin veget-are (to grow as a plant); teacher to name other words derived from this; children: to vegetate, vegetation. Juicy is derived from juice; teacher to give some other instances in which the names of qualities are derived from those of substances in a similar manner; children: stone, ston-y, milk, milk-y, water, water-y. Semi-transparent is derived from semi, Latin trans (through) and parens (ap-pear-ing); teacher: what is the meaning of semi; children: half.*

suggested and approved for the forthcoming year by HM Inspector and by the local clergy. In Bishop Sutton in the 1880s, object lessons ranged from Pig to Square to Red to Slate to Spring to Mining to Beekeeping. 18 May 1883: *object lesson to infants given by assistant on the Elephant and Camel*. This wasn't the name of a pub. 25 May 1883: *object lessons in Currants, Horse, Wheat, Cow, Rice, Salt, Cork, Acorns, Sugar*. For the 1891-92 school year the lessons were categorised as to 'forms' (e.g. Circles), 'objects' (e.g. Table, Squirrel), 'morals' (e.g. Honesty). The need to prepare for life after school was reflected in the object lessons: under 'Employment' in the 1890s, for example, children would learn about hay and harvests, shearing sheep and milking cows. Some of the lessons were obscure: 'Lac[1] and Cochineal Insects' made an appearance in 1897.

Coalmining in the Somerset Coalfield, a series of three booklets ('Source', 'Teacher's Guide' and 'Activity'), produced in the early 1970s for the County of Avon. The picture on the front of all three booklets is of Greyfield Colliery (closed 1909), near Clutton.

Object lessons disappeared as a teaching method around the turn of the century. The February 1903 *Elementary School Return to Somerset County Council* – which lamentably seems to have been the only one to survive – listed the curriculum as comprising Reading, Writing, Numbers, *lessons on common things and varied occupations*, Physical Exercise, Physical Training (boys), English, Arithmetic, Drawing (boys), Needlework (girls), Geography, History, Singing, Cottage Gardening (boys). Physical Exercise and Physical Training were regarded as distinct entities, although the difference wasn't explained. Little was documented about the minutiae of the lessons, but in March 1908 Mr Wightman noted that the infants were *practising writing with pens* and, in January 1914, *infants now using pen and ink*. This was presumably when slates were withdrawn in Bishop Sutton. Zera Wilson believes that they were abolished at Chew Stoke School in 1905, although a former Chew Stoke scholar recalls having used them there as late as 1920.

Before embarking on the individual subjects, it's worth bearing in mind headmaster Hill's comment from June 1882: *the girls are far behind the boys in nearly all their subjects and more irregular*, and Mr Wightman's from July 1908: *I have today called the special attention of the teachers to the importance of leading children to think for themselves as I find too much 'telling' in the lessons.*

VULGAR FRACTIONS AND HALF CROWNS

Generations of schoolchildren will testify that maths is a tricky subject, not helped by the intricacies of pre-decimal money and of imperial weights and measures. In October 1876 headmaster Jones *taught the III Standard long division in simple rules*

----

[1] For those of an inquisitive bent, lac is a resinous substance secreted by certain insects and used in the manufacture of shellac. Cochineal is a Mexican homopterous insect or the crimson substance obtained from the crushed bodies thereof and used for colouring food and for dyeing.

and began money addition sums. The IV Standard are learning Practice and Bills of Parcels. A wariness of arithmetic was rife among parents too. On Friday 24 May 1878 headmaster Northam wrote, taking care to replicate the mother's actual words, *Mrs Hazel called to say that "her boys were not to learn the nasty mess of sums, and other mess of things they got to learn. Because they didn't do no good, they only muddled their heads". All she wanted "was for them to be learned reading and writing".* In June 1882 new (and very conscientious) headmaster Alan Hill *gave lessons from the blackboard to the IV Standard in Arithmetic, they not having learnt at all the tables of weights and measures yet, also to the II and III Standards in the same subject, individually to the few in the V and VI Standard. Each day took one class for 40 minute lesson after school hours.*

In January 1882 Standard III was taught *on complex money such as guineas, crowns, half guineas, half crowns added up and made into simple long division* ('simple long division': a contradiction in terms, if ever there was one). In November 1885 the headmaster *taught IV Standard addition and subtraction of decimals, V Standard subtraction of vulgar fractions, IV Standard reduction of avoirdupois weight*. In February 1885 Mr Brown *paid particular attention to IV Standard Arithmetic. This Standard is mainly composed of girls of about 12 who are often kept at home.*

Half crown: 1887, 1940, 1967 (all actual size)

Surprisingly there were few references again to maths until comparatively recent times, although one wonderful find in the dusty depths of a drawer in the school was an anonymous teacher's (possibly student teacher's) exercise book from 1957-58 in which he or she made notes about how things were (or should be) done. Under 'Arithmetic', for example, was written: *Aims: to cultivate a habit of attention and concentration; to develop a power of reasoning and self-reliance; to stimulate children to solve their own problems; to give children the means to tackle everyday arithmetical problems. Standard I* (note that the term 'Standard' was still in use)*: count to 100 by 1,2,5,10; tables 2,3,4,5,6,10; terms 'couple, pair, dozen, score'; addition, subtraction, multiplication and division of tens and units; the value of coins; shopping; meaning of ½ and ¼; measuring in feet and inches; Standard II: numbers to 1,000; tables 12 x 12; pence to 10/-, ½d, ¼d, ¾d; four rules*[1] *in money, shopping, change; four rules in weights, lb and oz; four rules in capacity, pints, quarts, gallons; four rules in length, yards, feet, inches. The clock, practical work, measuring in ½" to 1';* *making squares and rectangles.* That would have kept them busy until their elevenses. This was all followed by a mini personal diary: *Standard I, it is obvious that I shall not be able to progress with the formal work until the younger children can set their work down properly.*

----
[1] Division, multiplication, addition, subtraction.

ARITHMETICAL TABLES

Numeration Table
Units ....(1).................1
Tens....(.)....(.)............ 12
Hundredy,.........................123
Thousands .....(.).............1234
Tens of Thousands,.......12,345
Hundreds of Thousands.....123,456
Millions 1,234,567
Tens of Millions 12,345,678
C. of Millions 123,456,789

Sterling Money Table
4 Farthings ....1 penny d.
12 Pence ....1 shilling s.
2 Shillings ......1 florin
2 Shillings & sixpence 1 Halfcrown
5 Shillings ....1 crown cr.
10 Shillings ....1 half sov.
20 Shillings, 1 sov. or 1 pound £
21 Shillings ....1 guinea

Arithmetical Signs
+ Plus ; sign of addition
− Minus : sign of subtraction
× Sign of multiplication
÷ Sign of division
⊔ Sign of equality
: :: : Sign of proportion
√ Sign of the square root
³√ Sign of the cube root
° Degree, ' minute, " second
∴ Therefore

Troy Weight
For Gold, Silver, and Jewels.
24 Grains....1 pennyweight, dwt.
20 Pennyweights...1 ounce ......oz.
12 Ounces .... 1 pound .....lb.

Apothecaries' Weight
For Mixing Medicines.
20 Grains.........1 scruple ......scr.
3 Scruples ......1 dram ....dr.
8 Drams.........1 ounce ....oz.
12 Ounces ......1 pound ....lb.

Avoirdupois Weight
For all Goods except Gold, Silver and Jewels.
16 Drams 1 ounce ....oz.
16 Ounces 1 pound........... lb.
14 Pounds 1 stone ....st.
28 Pounds 1 quarter ....qr.
4 Quarters 1 hundredweight cwt.
20 Cwt...... 1 ton ....tn.

Hay and Straw Weight
36 lb. Straw.................1 truss
56 lb. Old Hay ....1 truss
60 lb. New Hay ....1 truss
36 trusses ....1 load

Long or Lineal Measure
12 Lines ....1 inch ....in.
12 Inches ....1 foot ....ft.
3 Feet .... 1 yard ......yd.
2 Yards ....1 fathom .....f.
5½ Yards.........1 Pole
40 Poles ....1 furlong ...fur.
8 Furlongs or 1760 yds. 1 mile

Cloth Measure
2¼ Inches ...1 nail
4 Nails ....1 quarter of a yard
4 Quarters....1 yard

Solid or Cubic Measure
1728 cubic inches...1 cubic foot
27 cubic feet......1 cubic yard
24¾ cubic feet ...1 solid perch mason's work
12¾ cubic feet ...1 solid perch brickwork

Imperial Heaped Measure (Lbs. Avoird. of Water)
8 Gallons 1 bushel ....− 80
3 Bushels 1 sack ....− 240
12 Sacks.....1 children...−2880

Imperial Dry Measure
Avoird. of Water—lb. oz.
2 Glasses ...1 noggin ·· 0 5
4 Noggins 1 pint ....·· 1 4
2 Pints ....1 quart ...·· 2 8
4 Quarts ....1 gallon....·· 10 0
2 Gallons ...1 peck ....·· 20 0
4 Pecks..... 1 bushel ·· 80 0
8 Bushels ...1 quarter..·· 640 0

Square Measure
144 Square inches 1 square ft.
9 Square feet ....1 square yd.
30¼ Square yards 1 square pole
40 Square poles....1 rood
4 Roods.............1 acre

Table of Motion
60" Seconds..........1 minute
60' Minutes ....1 degree
30° Degrees ....1 sign
12 Signs, or 360°..the circle of the earth

Table of Time
60 Seconds.........1 minute
60 Minutes ....1 hour
24 Hours ....1 day
7 Days ....1 week
4 Weeks ....1 month
365 Days ....1 year
366 Days ....1 leap year
52 Weeks ....1 year
12 Calendar or 13 Lunar Months } 1 year

Days in the Month
Thirty days hath September,
April, June, and November,
All the rest have thirty-one,
Excepting February alone,
Which has but twenty-eight days clear,
And twenty-nine in each leap yr.

MULTIPLICATION TABLE

2 Times	3 Times	4 Times	5 Times	6 Times	7 Times	8 Times	9 Times	10 Times	11 Times	12 Times
1 are 2	1 are 3	1 are 4	1 are 5	1 are 6	1 are 7	1 are 8	1 are 9	1 are 10	1 are 11	1 are 12
2 - 4	2 - 6	2 - 8	2 - 10	2 - 12	2 - 14	2 - 16	2 - 18	2 - 20	2 - 22	2 - 24
3 - 6	3 - 9	3 - 12	3 - 15	3 - 18	3 - 21	3 - 24	3 - 27	3 - 30	3 - 33	3 - 36
4 - 8	4 - 12	4 - 16	4 - 20	4 - 24	4 - 28	4 - 32	4 - 36	4 - 40	4 - 44	4 - 48
5 - 10	5 - 15	5 - 20	5 - 25	5 - 30	5 - 35	5 - 40	5 - 45	5 - 50	5 - 55	5 - 60
6 - 12	6 - 18	6 - 24	6 - 30	6 - 36	6 - 42	6 - 48	6 - 54	6 - 60	6 - 66	6 - 72
7 - 14	7 - 21	7 - 28	7 - 35	7 - 42	7 - 49	7 - 56	7 - 63	7 - 70	7 - 77	7 - 84
8 - 16	8 - 24	8 - 32	8 - 40	8 - 48	8 - 56	8 - 64	8 - 72	8 - 80	8 - 88	8 - 96
9 - 18	9 - 27	9 - 36	9 - 45	9 - 54	9 - 63	9 - 72	9 - 81	9 - 90	9 - 99	9 - 108
10 - 20	10 - 30	10 - 40	10 - 50	10 - 60	10 - 70	10 - 80	10 - 90	10 - 100	10 - 110	10 - 120
11 - 22	11 - 33	11 - 44	11 - 55	11 - 66	11 - 77	11 - 88	11 - 99	11 - 110	11 - 121	11 - 132
12 - 24	12 - 36	12 - 48	12 - 60	12 - 72	12 - 84	12 - 96	12 - 108	12 - 120	12 - 132	12 - 144

Back cover of the author's primary school exercise book, 1962

DRAMA, LITERATURE AND THE FLICKS AT KNOWLE

The regular references in the logbook after 1924 to pupils attending plays suggest that there had been little theatrical work before then. In December of that year, however, *elder scholars attended play The Merchant of Venice, previously prepared in school.* On 13 May 1936 *the children of Standard 7 having read Pickwick Papers, an experiment was carried out by allowing them to listen to the BBC Literature programme this afternoon.* This was one of the first mentions of the children listening to the radio at school. From the late 1940s onwards, trips to the theatre were a regular occurrence. In January 1947 it was a Bristol Old Vic Co. performance of Treasure Island at the Theatre Royal, and in February 1950 thirty children went there to see As You Like It. Performances were sometimes closer to hand: in May 1965 *the Juniors visited Chew Magna School to see a play performed by the South Western School Drama Society.* On the afternoon of 14 February 1967 *the whole of the school went to East Harptree Theatre to see plays acted by the Theatre Centre Ltd.* This particular outing was repeated each year until at least 1970.

And there was the cinema. In September 1954 *senior children went to the Odeon in Bristol to see the film of Romeo and Juliet which was being shown at a special children's performance at 9 am.* An early start for children that day. One Wednesday afternoon a year later, *70 senior children attended the Odeon Cinema Bristol and saw the colour film Romeo and Juliet.* The use of the word 'colour' is a salutary reminder that many films were still in black and white. On Tuesday 19 December 1977 *the junior children were taken to the Gaiety Cinema[1] this morning to attend a special showing of the film When the North Wind Blows.*

DRAWING AND ART

The occasional mentions in the logbooks of drawing and art are apt to raise a smile. On Wednesday 10 October 1906 *drawing was not taken as many of the boys were wet.* On 23 November of that year, Mr Wightman *drew the attention of teachers to the importance of drawing from real objects, submitting a carrot done by elder boys as an example.* Let's hear it for the exemplary carrot. According to the anonymous teacher's exercise book of 1957-58, *Art leads to an appreciation of beauty of line and colour ... very small and timid work done.*

Anne Saunders (at school from 1943 to 1954) recalls the Brooke Bond tea drawing competition: she drew leaves and won savings stamps as prizes.

ENGLISH: CALLING 'YOU' A TRANSITIVE VERB

For many children, English and Grammar were almost as unpopular as maths, especially given the Victorians' penchant for learning by rote. In February 1876 [Oliver] *Goldsmith's Deserted Village* [was] *approved by HMI for recitation this week.* This 1770 ode had 432 lines. The logbook does not say whether HMI expected the scholars to be familiar with all of them. In January 1877 the managers received a letter dated 8 December 1876 from the London School Board *with reference to altering and reforming the present mode of spelling.* The managers *did not think it desirable to join the London School Board in any representation to the*

----

[1] The Gaiety Cinema was a Bristol social landmark. On the corner of Crossways Road and Wells Road in Knowle, it was the last family-owned cinema in the city and was showing films from 1933 to 2000. It's been estimated that some eight million people passed through its doors.

Education Department. They had their doubts about the wisdom of changing their title to the Choo Magna Skool Bord, or similar[1].

A card posted in Hay on Wye in 1908. The message reads, 'Pity cannot come up for fair. What do you think of this for Night School?'

In April 1878 Mr Northam commented that *the 3rd class Reading is very bad. The children mutter and pronounce their words very badly, thus many mistakes seem to escape the teacher's attention ... Several of the IV and V Standard girls showed great obstinacy of temper in the Grammar lesson, by pretended ignorance. Thus after I had just told them that 'is' is always a verb, they would call it a pronoun*. This revelation was lost on Emily Harris who, on the following day, *showed the same obstinate spirit in the Grammar lesson, calling 'you' a transitive verb after I had just said it was a pronoun*. Parents were not always supportive: in May 1880 many *are opposed to their children learning Geography and Grammar, hence the children will sometimes be contrary about it*. And not just those called Mary Mary. Sometimes the teachers introduced a spot of variation: on 13 April 1881, *1st class took dictation instead of transcription*. Two days into his headship, in June 1882, Mr Hill noted that *Reading appears to be rather in a drawling style, it may be the fault of the locality*. It's not recorded where Mr Hill hailed from, but drawling speech in Bishop Sutton? Surely not. Headmasters had a thing about local speech patterns: in January 1887, Mr Brown (who hailed from Bath) paid *great attention to expression, a difficult thing to acquire in this school*.

One cannot fail to be impressed (or baffled) by the technical language utilised in the

----

[1] There is no indication from the logbook that Bishop Sutton School was one of several throughout the country - including this author's – which experimented in the 1960s with the Initial Teaching Alphabet (ITA) introduced by the Simplified Spelling Society. Like most such proposed spelling reforms, it quickly died a death, although a street name written in the ITA can still be seen by the Abbey in Bath, carved into the stone.

pursuit of English excellence. In June 1882 Mr Hill *gave lesson to V and VI Standards on simple sentence, the subject and predicate, with enlargements.* He was a devil for detail, was Mr H. In October of that year: *have tried for some time past to correct the prevailing errors of placing Capital letters (sic) in the wrong place and leaving them out, where required.* This was an age when criticism was more frequent than praise, but in November 1881 *the V and VI Standards did their analysis fairly well, George Tibbs and Ed Treasure having no mistakes in a complex sentence of two principal and four subordinate clauses.* This may be the same George Tibbs who, three years later, proved woefully inadequate as a pupil teacher.

Lest ye remain unconvinced of the emphasis placed on grammar, in February 1883 Mr Hill *gave Grammar lessons to 1st and 2nd class on the verb, the former principally on regular and irregular, transitive and intransitive, the latter, the verb generally. As some weakness was shown in the parsing*[1] *for home lessons on Wednesday, one lesson was devoted and afterwards the table given for home lesson of the classification of the English Personal Pronouns.* In June 1883 the headmaster *recapitated the rules of syntax (19) to 1st class with practice in syntactical parsing.* Hands up, all those who can't quite remember all nineteen of the rules of syntax. In February 1886 the IV Standard were treated to *lessons on Latin prefixes.* You can just picture the boys and girls merrily skipping home afterwards, their little faces all aglow, eager to try out their new-found knowledge on their unsuspecting mums and dads.

The thoughts of the anonymous teacher from 1957-58 are shown to the right. He or she went on to explain that the appropriate topics for Standard I (the first post-infant class) were: *Name and address, letter-writing, telling the story of a picture, autobiography.* For Standard 2: *the description of toys, a game, an animal, a person; dialogue, narrative, letters to accept and decline invitations, thanks, apologies. Children should join script to form a cursive form during their first year, but with an emphasis of flow and control. The simple italic principals (sic) to be introduced during first year and developed in Standard 2. Ink to be used directly it is felt a child is ready. The importance of punctuation was to be emphasised: full stop, question mark, commas. The informal discussion of the Infant Room should continue. Poems or passages should be carefully chosen to give practice in ennouciation (sic). There should be dramatisations of poems or* stories to increase the awareness of the beauty of correctly spoken English.

English

Aims:

Free, fluent expression in speech and writing
To form habit of reading for pleasure.
To give children the means whereby they can gather useful information from books.
To help them to write richly & fully.
To help appreciation of good literature & poetry.

Every child to keep a Diary

The school may sometimes have cast its eyes to the farthest horizon. On

----

[1] For anyone who needs a quick refresher: a transitive verb has an object, an intransitive verb doesn't. Parsing is the art of categorising the constituent parts of a sentence, e.g. temporal clauses, adjectives, conjunctions etc.

11 November 1935 *a letter was received from a school in Madison, Wisconsin, USA. It was written by 4th grade children, 9 years of age, a reply will be sent from the corresponding class here.* It's unlikely that the Wisconsin teachers stuck a pin in a map and came up with Bishop Sutton. Perhaps a family had emigrated to Wisconsin from the village years before. There are no further references; no-one here (or in Madison, if my approaches to newspapers there are anything to go by) remembers anything, and there's no knowing whether the promised reply was ever sent.

On 29 July 1955 the managers recorded that *a school magazine from material collected from the children of the school had been published and the managers had each received a copy. They desire to place on record their appreciation of a work which was most interesting and which must have taken much time in its presentation.* I have not managed to find a copy of said magazine.

GARDENING, JAM MAKING AND POULTRY KEEPING

It seems strange nowadays that gardening played such an important role in the life of the school until well into the 20th century. But it did. For the boys. The girls were inside, sewing. Not only were there formal gardening lessons, but older boys who had finished their written work might be sent out to spend an hour or so in the master's cabbage patch. As they could leave at 14 or earlier and would generally have little use for academic subjects, the view was taken that they might as well be doing something practical.

The first horticultural mention in the logbooks was in February 1901, when *the ground was prepared for cottage gardening.* In April 1902 *the garden was commenced in front.* Only boys of a certain age were entrusted with horticultural intricacies: Mr Wightman specifically commented in May 1902 that *potatoes planted by six boys over 12.* It would be useful to know exactly what *The Scheme of Teaching Gardening* was, as suggested by the County Education Committee, but the managers unanimously resolved in April 1912 *that it be carried out at Bishop Sutton.* This schemed planting was all well and good, but the school was running out of garden. After some negotiations

Bishop Sutton Council School.

Report on the Work

AND CONDUCT OF

Douglas Mellish

................................*December*............ 1933

Subject	Marks	Max.	Remarks
English	40	40	Excellent.
Arithmetic	24	30	Vg.
Art	28	30	Vg.
Geography	27	30	Vg.
History	24	30	Good worker
Gardening	24	30	Excellent.
~~Nature Study~~		30	
Science	17	50	Vg
~~Cookery~~		30	
Hygiene	10	10	Excellent.
Games and Ph'cal training	17	20	Good.
Handwork	24	30	Excellent. Careful
Total	245	270	= 91½ ?.

No. in Class 18

Position 1.

Attendance Vg

Class Teacher *Bailey*

Conduct *Excellent.* Head Teacher *Bailey*

Takes great interest in work. Prin & Paulton

Douglas Mellish's report, 1910.
Top of the class!

with the PC, Mr Wightman proudly announced in March 1923 that *he had obtained 20 perches* (some 600 square yards) *of land*. With no time to lose if they were to benefit from the warmer weather, *the boys commenced clearing land for school gardens* on the very same day. By the beginning of May the boys were working *in the gardens on Wednesday and Friday afternoons*, and on 18 May *gardening boys were in the gardens from 11 am*. All this fresh air was so invigorating that Mr W himself got in on the act and on 17 July *spent three hours in gardens*.

By December 1923 *another piece of garden has been obtained for school and has been roughly dug this week*. It's difficult to ascertain from the plans where all these bits of new garden were, but a perch here and a rod there would make all the difference. On 25 January 1924, *boys spent three hours in new garden clearing the ground*. Possibly of snow. In March 1924 the boys were being given *more than ordinary time to gardening owing to fine weather*. In September 1925 *extra time given to Senior boys for weeding and cropping*. All this toil bore fruit or, at least, savoys and sprouts, those being the gardening boys' produce during November 1925. With the autumn crops in the larder, it was time to look to the 1926 harvest, and on 31 March *Gardening Class has done practical work in Garden sowing small seeds*. In March 1932 yet more land was *taken over for school gardens*. The following February *Mr Snellgrove, County Inspector, called at the school and suggested that application be made for fruit stocks for the school garden for grafting in 1934*. No note was made of any outcome, but in March 1936 *Standard VI children were allocated one part of the garden where they could have small individual plots for study of the life cycle of plants*. Ah, so it wasn't just physical graft; there was an element of academic study involved. But later that month, the graft had started again: *the senior boys have spent a part of the last three days in the garden as the weather has been suitable for digging*. Sun's out, lads; down with your pens and out with your hoes. March 1939 saw the manure delivered for the garden. Along came the war with its food rationing and Digging for Victory; waste ground suitable for vegetables was being compulsorily acquired all over the country, and at the end of September 1939 *the boys began to break up the new ground to add to the garden – this was previously waste*. By the end of November *proposals for taking over more land in the allotment field were sent to the managers*, and mid-January 1940 *notice has been received that 40 perches* (¼ acre) *of extra land may be taken out for gardening*. This new ground *needed manuring badly*. Or perhaps well. September 1940 *saw much work being done in the garden this week – the potato crop in the new garden is very poor*.

Two and a bit months into the war and the logbook solemnly announced in November 1939: *it is proposed to begin poultry keeping*. There was no further mention and the fortunes (or otherwise) of the Poultry Keeping Club can only be guessed at. But Friday 2 July 1943 was a red-letter day for Bishop Sutton School Bunny Lovers. Mr Bailey wrote: *Mr Snellgrove called, he inspected both the garden, and the rabbits of the Rabbit Club*. Before they could go into a wartime Woolton pie, no doubt. With the war won, the children's efforts turned to jam: on 5 July 1951 *currants were picked in the school garden for jam making tomorrow*. Where that particular batch of jam was made wasn't explained but on 13 July 1951, *7 lb of jam received from the Pensford* [Cookery] *Centre*.

What do former pupils remember? Remarkably little. Sheila Walker recalls that the boys were taught how to grow vegetables while the girls were taught how to sew. Dick Chapman recalls that the senior boys had a plot in the garden and if you were lucky, you were allowed to take the produce home.

Salad days soon faded. In February 1956 *the Local Authority have been given a year's notice to quit the school garden.* We've already seen that the owner, a builder, had earmarked the land for a building site. Regardless of that disquieting news, on 23 April 1956 *normal work according to the time table has been suspended to allow boys to work in the school garden to get the plots ready for sowing.* But an era had come to an end, and in January 1957 *the wall between the school and the former school garden has been repaired and the entry to the school garden closed.*

Joan Challenger's report, 1952. Top of the class!

GEOGRAPHY:
VILLAGE CHILDREN DO NOT TRAVEL TO ANY GREAT EXTENT

Chambers' 'Geographical Readers of the Continents (Asia)', printed in 1901, stated: *No other nation but the British has ever held sway over a dependency so wide in extent, so dense in population. Over those countless numbers of people, Britain has established a system of rule that has spread the blessings of peace, security and justice throughout the length and breadth of the land.* That referred to India, the Jewel of the Empire, but it could have been any of the other innumerable countries, territories and rocky outcrops that were tinted red on the globe. Geography, like History, was imbued with a sense of Britain's place in the world. What else mattered unless in a context of subjectively demonstrating how much better and more fortunate we were than upstart foreigners? The two subjects tended only to examine the Empire, to places deemed to be of economic or military importance to Britain, or to places where the British had fought valiant battles against spear-wielding natives. Pretty much until the First World War, Geography involved memorising lists of capes, mountains and oceans which then had to be pointed out on a map. One inspector observed sourly that it wasn't uncommon *to find a child able to indicate readily the exact position on a map of Flamborough Head or Ardnamurchan Point, and at the same time fail to give satisfactory proof that it understands the meaning of a map*[1].

Geography and History were recognised as separate curriculum subjects under the Government's Payment by Results regime in 1867, but the first reference in the school logbook wasn't until May 1880 when, as we have already seen, headmaster Northam observed that *many of the parents are opposed to their children learning Geography*. There was therefore probably an underwhelming reaction to the news in September 1881 *that the Geography readers arrived this week*. The pupils were treated a year later to *the Northern and Midland counties of England from maps with III Standard; principal islands, seas, peninsulas, capes and coast line of Asia from maps to 1st class*. That November gave the fascinated 1st class geographers of Bishop Sutton a deep insight into Baluchistan which, for the benefit of any reader whose memory is a bit fuzzy, is a mountainous desert area falling partly in Pakistan, partly in Iran and partly in Afghanistan. That part of the world was tricky: Mr Northam had already written in October 1879 about the difficulty two boys had had with Hindustan, Ceylon and Bab-el-Mandeb[2]. The latter are the straits at the southeastern end of the Red Sea. 'Oh yes, of course they are', I hear you mutter. This was all of questionable use to Chew Valley children, but not to be put off by any sense of pragmatism, headmaster Hawkins spent much of December 1881 giving *lessons to Standard II on the names of the chief countries in Europe, cities, mountains, rivers and lakes. This Standard is backward and dull throughout*. A somewhat sweeping statement. Out of fairness, he was hindered by his tools: *I find the maps very old and unsuited to the requirements of the Code*. And then a huge leap forward to 1951 when *the County Education Service Film Unit gave one historical Local Government and four Geography (Woollen Trade etc) and Malaya films*.

----
[1] From an 1875-76 report 'Schools Supported by the School Board of London'.

[2] Further details of this heinous misdemeanour are explored under 'Spare the Rod and wet your pants'.

The anonymous teacher from 1957-58 said of Geography: *this subject should aim to develop an interest in peoples of other lands. Climatic differances* (sic) *should be discussed. A journey round the world which starts from the children's homes in Bishop Sutton and discussions on relative time and distances should be included as well as actual facts given about each country visited en route. Village children do not travel to any great extent and find it difficult to visualise distance.* Subjective but fair in a 1950s devoid of foreign holidays and television travelogues.

Former pupils' memories of the subject seem to be restricted to Ken Rapps' recollection of being sent to Mr Treasure's workshop next door to the school with sixpence to buy putty to make a contour map.

HISTORY: THE GREATEST EMPIRE THE WORLD HAS EVER SEEN

The importance of the Empire in the Victorian and Edwardian psyche is hard to exaggerate, and it showed in the teaching of History just as much as Geography. The Empire was everywhere from Camp Coffee with its Indian bearer on the label, to toy soldiers with 'Empire Made' on their base. Textbooks were influenced by imperialistic messages ranging from the benevolent and paternalistic to the xenophobic and jingoistic. Pupils came to share in the pride and the sense of racial superiority exemplified by books such as Thomas Nelson's 'Highroads of History' series, published from 1907. One of the books opened with a eulogy on the flag:

No Briton can help being proud of the Union Jack. It flies over the greatest empire the world has ever known; and wherever it flies there is to be found at least justice and fair dealing for everyman. Men have fought to make it glorious and have died to shield it from dishonour. Every British boy and girl will desire not merely to keep the flag unsullied but to blazon it still further with the record of noble deeds nobly done.

Teachers brought up on Sir John Seeley's 1883 imperialistic work 'The Expansion of England' – and often avid fans of Rudyard Kipling – would preach patriotism with a fervour that bordered on the religious, although what the average Bishop

Patriotism in children's books

Suttonian actually got from the Empire (apart from the banana) is hard to assess. But what the average Bishop Suttonian knew was that it was theirs and they were proud of it. There were powerful reminders of the Empire (subsequently called the Commonwealth) and of the aftermath of the Second World War until well into the 1950s and beyond. Millions of people would tune in on Sundays to hear the wireless announcer say in theatrical tones: "The time in Britain is twelve noon, in Germany it's one o'clock, but home and away it's time for Two-Way Family Favourites", where soothing ballads and invigorating Elvis were interlaid by the vexing news of insurgencies in Malaya, Kenya or Cyprus. Children were still happily collecting labels from Robertson's jam jars to exchange for golliwog badges, and choosing their skipping rope playmates with "Eeny meeny miney mo, catch a nigger by his toe", and schools were teaching uplifting songs such as 'De Camptown ladies sing dis song, doo-dah, doo-dah'.

History in the early days was pretty much restricted to elevating tales of British derring-do, with occasional reference to what the Romans did for us. In August 1898 Mr Wightman noted that *History lesson for Standards I to III include The Ancient Briton, Julius Caesar's Visit* (that's one way of describing an invasion!), *Druids, Caractacus, Boadicea, Roman Walls and Roads, Introduction of Christianity, the Norsemen, Alfred the Great, Canute, Harold, Norman Conquest.* There were then few specific mentions to History until October 1950, when it was brought closer to home: *a class of 30 children went to Messrs Hollands Pottery at Clevedon in connection with their History classes.* Such visits became a regular feature of the curriculum. In October 1962 Mr Price *visited Stowey Church with the Upper Juniors for two periods in the afternoon for Social History lesson.* In April 1964 he took them *on a visit to Stanton Drew to examine the Stone Circles as part of their History work.*

The anonymous teacher from 1957-58 said of History: *as with Geography, children find great difficulty in being 'aware' of time. Therefore it should be realised that an interest can be developed only through the familiar. Connections should be found – e.g. music, pottery, mines, clothes and many other present-day interests to form links between the children's lives and the differences which would be experienced through the ages.*

The rest, as they say, is History.

SCIENCE AND STALLIONS

If the logbooks are anything to go by, Science wasn't taught as a separate subject – or possibly at all – until 1933. In February of that year *Mr Snellgrove, County Inspector, called at the school and suggested that application be made for a Science Apparatus.* There were few further science-related notes until October 1951 when Mr Bailey *sent in a requisition for furniture to make a special practice room.* To the joy of potential pyromaniacs, calor gas was fitted to the science benches in September 1952 and – just in case – a fire extinguisher was eventually delivered in July 1956. But it wasn't until September that *Mr Hopp has filled the fire extinguisher which is now ready for emergency.* In December 1957, *acting upon a telephone call from the County Office, I have today allowed boys to dismantle the Calor gas fittings here. These are not required at the Secondary Modern School and are to go to Dulverton.* In February 1974, *60 of the upper junior children were taken to visit the Science Fair at the*

*Punch cartoon 1937: "I'm not sure, Sir, but I **believe** I've split the atom."*

Bristol University with two other members of staff, and in October 1979 *Mrs Mary Horne, Scientific Services, visited to discuss science activities in relation to Stowey Quarry*.

And that was that as regards Science, although there are two vaguely science-related reminiscences: Les Bown had a book on shire horses. He passed it round the class and by the time it came back to him all the mares had been turned into stallions. Colin Symes, who lived next door to a butcher's in West Harptree, would bring in cows' eyes for lessons on animals.

SCRIPTURE AND ASSEMBLIES, HYMNS AND BLESSINGS

Victorian schools presented the Bible as fact. No other religions were afforded lesson space. Pupils learnt stories from the Old and New Testaments, were expected to know the Lord's Prayer ('Our Father, which art in heaven …') and the Ten Commandments by heart and to have more than a nodding acquaintance with the Book of Common Prayer, one version of which included the exhortation *to submit myself to all my governors, teachers, spiritual pastors and masters, to order myself lowly and reverently to all who are set over me*. Although the Conscience Clause from the 1870 Education Act had entitled parents to withdraw their children from Religious Instruction, few exercised the right. Despite the emphasis on religion, Scripture was rarely mentioned in the logbook as a separate subject, and the only note of note was from the anonymous teacher's 1950s notebook: *Scripture, introduction to the School Service Book … I want my children to appreciate their Assembly with the School. Writing out and learning the first school prayer, writing our own Harvest Prayer. St Matthew the man, the birth of Christ written to prove Jesus was the Messiah. Choice of psalms, God our Father, His gifts*. There is no reference anywhere else to a school prayer and no-one can remember one.

May Woodward recalls that the day always started with assembly and ended with grace. Monica Castle and Teresa Dowling fondly remember the morning assemblies in the late 1960s under Mr Price's leadership, when Miss Stuckey and Mrs Price would take it in turns to play the piano. There were usually two hymns, always The Lord's Prayer, and there was a (fake) cake with candles whenever it was someone's birthday. Grace was always said before school dinner: 'Dear Lord for what we are about to receive make us truly thankful, amen', eyes down, tuck in. Cynthia Holman believes there was still a daily religious assembly in the late 1970s. The hymns would have included such favourites as Daisies are our Silver, Buttercups our Gold, and Jesus Friend of Little Children. Plus All Things Bright and Beautiful; by the 1950s the verse 'The rich man in his castle, The poor man at his gate, He made them, high or lowly, And ordered their estate' was generally omitted. The world had moved on. The hymn sung at the beginning of term, when children arrived all ruthlessly scrubbed and with cruel haircuts, may well have been the traditional 'Lord behold us with Thy blessing, once again assembled here …'. At the end of term it was probably part II of the same hymn: 'Lord dismiss us with Thy blessing, Thanks for mercies past receive …'. Well, that was what we sang at my primary school.

SEWING, COOKING AND SPECIALLY INTERESTED GIRLS; WOODWORK AND BOYS

The logbooks implied that sewing was the be-all and end-all for girls. In truth, it pretty much was, certainly until the First World War and to only a slightly lesser extent for many years thereafter. Society ladies took a benevolent interest in the subject and formed a roster on which the Board could call, as per a letter from November 1877 to Miss Cook of Bishop Sutton: *Madam, I beg to inform you that your name has been added to the list of Ladies appointed by the Board to superintend the Young Children in Needlework and the supply of the necessary sewing materials in the Board Schools.*

The Board wrote in December 1884: *with reference to an enquiry respecting the Sewing in the absence of Miss Creighton,* [we] *are of opinion that Arithmetic may be substituted on the afternoons during which the Sewing has hitherto been carried on.* What bliss: no Needlework, sums instead. The Board had a certain pecuniary interest in sewing: they resolved in May 1895 *that in future, samples of sewing materials be submitted to the Board before being ordered.* Someone had doubtless been buying something inappropriate. In March 1933 inspectors *suggested that application be made for a sewing machine for Senior Girls.* A 1937 inspection report stated: *in spite of the cramped conditions under which Needlework is taught, the Senior Girls turn out practical garments, many of which are stitched by machine. The older girls use the machine regularly, but as there is only one, they must frequently wait their turn to use it. Space can possibly be found for a temporary needlework table so that specially interested girls could cut out more easily.* June 1952: *an ironing board has been received for the use of the Needlework class, an electric iron was received last week.* Until then, the girls had presumably been dashing away with a 'flat' (or 'sad') smoothing iron while they were stealing hearts away.

NEEDLEWORK.

N.B.—The material used, whether in the exercises performed before the Inspector or in the garments shown to him, should not be so fine as to strain the eyesight of the children.

GIRLS' AND INFANTS' DEPARTMENTS.

BELOW STANDARD I.

Needle drill.—Position drill.
Strips (18 inches by 2 inches) in simple hemming with coloured cotton, in the following order, viz.:—1. Black. 2. Red. 3. Blue.
Knitting-pin drill.
A strip knitted (15 inches by 3 inches) in cotton or wool.

STANDARD I.

1. Hemming, seaming, felling. Any garment or other useful article, which can be completed by the above stitches, *e.g.*, a child's pinafore, pillow-case, or pockethandkerchief. In small mixed country schools, strips (18 in. by 2 in.) of hemming, &c. may be shown, at the discretion of the managers, in place of a garment.
2. Knitting. 2 needles, plain, *e.g.*, a strip on which to teach darning in upper Standards, or a comforter.

STANDARD II.

1. The work of the previous Standard with greater skill. Any garment or other useful article as above.
2. Knitting. 2 needles, plain and purled, *e.g.*, muffatees.

Needlework instructions 1890s

Cooking as a subject – strictly for the girls – made a logbook appearance in February 1913 when *girls went to Cookery Centre on Thursday afternoon for the first time.* The whereabouts of this facility wasn't mentioned; a logbook entry ten years later stated that *Cookery commenced today at the room opposite the school.* This would have been the tin Scout Hut. In June 1918, possibly on the back of wartime economy measures, the school wrote to the Education Department under the heading 'Food Preservation Demonstration': *Your letter on this subject has been duly considered both by the managers and by the Women's Friendly Association* [who] *recently held a demonstration in conjunction with cookery, and as the fruit prospects of the district are so very bad they are of opinion that the kind offer of a demonstration next month had best be deferred for another season.*

By January 1926 it was at the Village Hall that the Cookery saucepans were bubbling over. They were still bubbling in January 1937, but *the plant from Felton has not arrived.* Equipment, not herbs. By early 1939 Cookery classes were held at Blagdon. We know this, as on 4 February of that year *a telegram received at 10 am this morning from Blagdon saying that Cookery for tomorrow is cancelled.* Quite what happened during the war years is unclear, but it's unlikely that precious petrol would have been used to ferry girls outside Bishop Sutton to practise on rationed food. In January 1948 *Cookery classes resumed at Blagdon, 13 girls from here are gone* (sic). It wasn't long before the classes moved to Pensford: in June 1949 Mr Bailey deemed it noteworthy that *two classes of girls attend the housecraft centre at Pensford on one day each week.* There may have then been a move back to Bishop Sutton, for on 31 October 1952 Mr Bailey *went across to the Domestic Science Centre this afternoon on the invitation of the children to see the Hallowe'en Fare they had made.*

Former pupils remember that girls would go to Pensford by coach for Cookery, originally all day, then half a day. They would bring biscuits back in a tin. When they weren't cooking, they were scrumping apples under the railway viaduct. One teacher used to bring her washing in for the girls to do. She was very strict, and would make them scrub off their nail varnish.

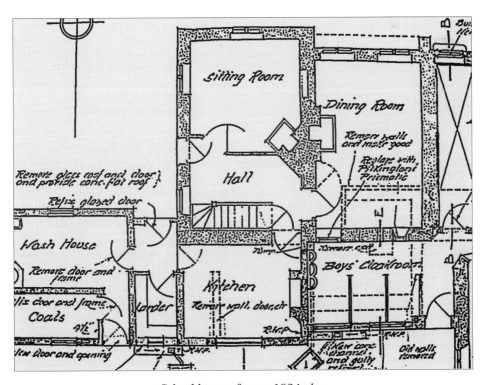

School house, from a 1924 plan

The terminology in the logbook makes for difficulty in knowing where Sewing ended and Handicraft or Handiwork began, but in July 1928 *Standards II and III did some good handiwork, making flowers in paper form from the actual flowers*. Origami comes to a Chew Valley school near you. This was the era of make do and mend, and the managers tried valiantly to instil sewing prowess: in September 1951 they agreed that *Mr* (sic) *Penrose should hold a dressmaking class on 4 October and continue such classes on Thursday evenings*. In March 1953 Sewing mistress Miss Chivers *went off to Dillington House this afternoon to attend a Needlework course for one week*. Dillington House (near Ilminster) was still there in 2009, 'inspiring people in business and the public sector since 1950' (according to its website). Sewing or Needlework was still important enough by the late 1950s to warrant the attention of the anonymous teacher: *Aims of Needlework: to offer an outlet for constructive ability; to provide scope for individuality; to lay foundations for a useful accomplishment*.

Woodwork doesn't seem to have been practised much – if at all – before the Second World War, but it hit the logbooks with a vengeance thereafter and was a frequent bane of the managers' and headmaster's life. It was difficult (a) to find a suitable venue with the right equipment, and (b) to find Woodwork teachers, not least because so many men were being called up for their National Service, were still serving in the Forces, or simply found the pay unattractive. The lads were missing out: the girls had been sewing and crafting for generations, but the boys were out cabbaging. In June 1948 *tools and benches received for the Woodwork class. The benches are in need of much repair and a request has been submitted to the LEA that we be allowed to purchase locally the timber required to repair them*. Make do and mend. By June 1948 *one fixed woodwork bench received from Queen Camel Centre* (near Yeovil). They had the benches, but finding a teacher to do something with them was a different matter. In April 1948 *Mr Clarke, appointed to the post of Woodwork instructor, had written declining as he could not find accommodation. Mr Simmonds expressed strong disapproval of Mr Clarke's actions in not taking up the post*. A bit harsh. Mr Simmonds probably had somewhere to live. *The managers decided to ask Mr Bert Marshall if he would accept the post, but realising the difficult position with regard to accommodation, they adjourned the meeting for a fortnight while Mr Marshall tried to find accommodation*. He couldn't, and Mr Frederick John was appointed in May 1948.

Chew Magna boys had been coming to Bishop Sutton for some time for their Woodwork lessons, but the lack of efficient communication between the two schools could lead to problems: on 27 March 1950 *Mr John is away and I had to send the Chew Magna Woodwork class back to Chew Magna when they arrived*. Trying to work out who could dovetail their joints on which day was a challenge, and Mr Bailey suggested in January 1951 *that all classes should be mornings only, and that Chew Magna should have Monday and Tuesday, Pensford on Wednesday and Bishop Sutton Thursday and Friday*. The Woodwork Centre became the proud possessor of a new grindstone in September 1952.

Mr Avery, who'd been woodworking since Mr John left, expressed a wish to leave by Christmas 1953. The managers reported in October that *Mr Brennan offered post as Assistant Master Woodwork but withdrew his application as he was not satisfied with the amenities of the Village Hall for carrying out Woodwork, and the difficulty of obtaining suitable accommodation for him and his family*. It was the old problem of digs again. Philip 'Hoppalong Cassidy' Hopp was eventually found. Things on the wood front wound down as the opening of Chew Valley School approached, but in December 1956 *a power lathe was delivered to the Woodwork room – the Hall – from Messrs Tysack*. On 17 October 1957 *Mr Cotton spent the afternoon at the new secondary school at Writhlington, where he saw the equipment and fitting of the metal work shop.* Woodwork and any Metalwork came to an end. In December 1957 *Mr Cotton and his class today carried the Woodwork equipment to the new school.*

Joan Bunney recalls the Woodwork lessons at the Village Hall. Being a mere girl, she was naturally not allowed to take part, but she does remember the boys locking the teacher out once. Colin Symes remembers that the woodworking tables were stacked up on the right-hand side. Les Bown recalls making rosewood pipes in Woodwork; the older boys would take them to Brents Forge to get a light and would puff away merrily.

In July 1975 Mr Price was *given a kiln from Chew Valley School; he would need some help financially to put this kiln in, so that it could be used for the children to be fitted where the coal bunkers are.* He received the necessary financial assistance.

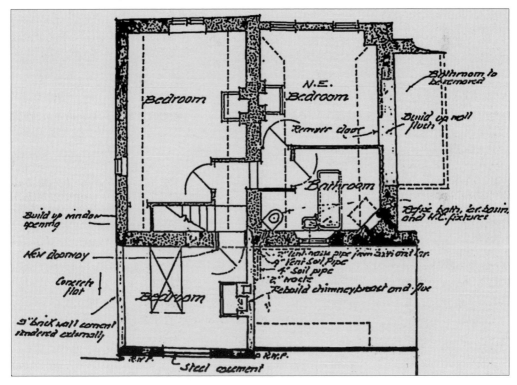

School house, from a 1924 plan

In a practice dating back to the very early days, the school sold many of the crafts produced by the pupils. In February 1882 *the School Board received from Elizabeth Northam 2s.4d for garments sold to children.* The Record of Sales book, started in November 1935 and ended in April 1966, meticulously listed what was made and how much it was sold for. In 1942, 140 articles fetched £5.5s.9d plus garden produce at 8 shillings. 1948 was down to a miserly £1.15s.0d from only 13 bits and bobs. 1955 enriched the coffers by a very healthy £19.2s.10½d from 69 articles, but 1957 was epic: 108 items sold at £29.4s.9d. By the 1960s, however, there were no senior children to make senior things: only £1.13s.7d from 17 items in 1962. From 1948, if not earlier, monies were passed to the County Treasurer.

The range of items was comprehensive. Taking three years at random: 1937's offerings included knitted hats at 5d and 8d, pinafores at 6d and 7d, a felt pochette at 6d, a tea cosy cover at 6d, peg bags at 2d, dish cloths at 1d, a nightdress at 1/6, a case to put it in at 6d and a pair of knickers at 4/6. In 1941 potatoes and carrots were sold to evacuee families from the school garden for £1 (presumably not per potato and carrot), together with 1 cwt of potatoes at 7/-. There were wartime belts at 2d and 6d, nightdresses at 1/7 and 6/9 – why would one nightdress cost more than four times that of another? – a pair of rompers at 6d and Mrs Flower bought overalls for 1/6. 1954 saw handkerchieves at 4d, cases to put them in at 1/-, chairbacks at 2/9, blouses at 4/-, 4/4½d and 5/-, and stools (*made by boys*) at 5/-. The girls did a runner for 3/3. There were coal gloves, blotters, a d'oyley case, calendars, hot water bottle cosies, pixie hoods, a hussif[1], a duchess set, an appliqué picture and balsa wood models. The Record of Sales book faithfully recorded the changing fashions. A dirndl first made an appearance in July 1950 when two were made and sold to B. Bendall and V. Sainsbury at 5/- each, and nine in 1951 at prices ranging from 2/6 to 6/6. None was made after 1952; the dirndl was passé.

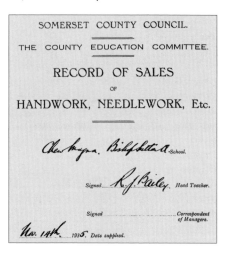

DATE.	ARTICLE SOLD.	NUMBER SOLD.	PRICE RECEIVED PER ARTICLE	TO WHOM SOLD.	TOTAL AMOUNT RECEIVED.	
					NEEDLEWORK	HANDWORK.
July 1964.	Skirt	1	4 -	Carolyine Raynon		
	Ball	1	9	"		
	Tray Cloth	1	9	"	5	6
	Apron	1	9	Hazel Walker		
	Needlecase	1	6	"		
	Cushion Cover.	1	9	"	2	0
	Tray Cloth	1	9	Janet Flower		9
	Apron	1.	9	Rossalyn Baxter		
	Tray Cloth	1	9	"	1	6

School Sales Book, July 1964

Our anonymous teacher wrote: *Handwork: to develop manual skills leading to accurate work, to foster self-reliance and perseverance by production of well-made articles, to encourage resourcefullness (sic) and iniative (sic), to lead to appreciation of work well done.* Spelling was not a strength.

----
[1] A sewing kit for those of a non-military bent

Song and dance: handy Norsemen and Making Music

Singing was hugely important. It's sad that so many of the Victorian songs have been lost.

It all started, as far as the logbooks were concerned, in October 1872 when *Miss Orr (daughter of Rev. K. H. Orr) came to teach Singing.* In 1881 headmaster Hawkins taught the children Home Dear Home, and Hark the Village Bells are Pealing. Happy England and Pretty Bird were added to the repertoire in 1881. In June 1882 Alan Hill *practised them* (sic) (i.e. the infants) *with North Wind doth Blow[1] and Where, How, Why and When?* Mr Hill wrote with grudging praise: *five out of eight songs were sung pretty well by some as Music has not been taught, the rest require more practice, and all require a great deal of modulation.* By the winter term of 1883 the children had progressed (*except sounding the chords and finding the starting note from the tonics*) to O Who Will O'er the Downs, Too Late for the Train, and The Handy Norseman. No self-sufficient rural community should be without its handy Norseman. The method of teaching may well have taken all the fun out of the Friday afternoon sing-songs: Mr Hill wrote in June 1883 that the lessons consisted of *names of notes, various notes which may be used (with rests) to make bars of (or 4/4 time, bars, dots, repeats, slurs etc).* This attention to detail paid off, as ten days later *the Rev. E. Clowes visited the school and made the following report in the visitor's book: 'Visited school at 4.45 and heard the children sing by Hullah's system[2], and was much pleased at the progress made'.* The visitor's book has sadly not survived.

In July 1883 came The Busy Little Mother (*with actions* – dashing away with the aforementioned smoothing iron?), and How to Spend Sixpence. For the exams in June 1884 the infants had to sing Who Has Left the Room? Perhaps the examiner, in despair. The older scholars joined in with No! No! No!, and What is Home Without a Mother? (another of those Victorian tear-jerkers). October 1884 would doubtless have gladdened political hearts: the children were *taught a round entitled Labour's Strong and Many Children*. 1885's portfolio (which hasn't passed the test of time) included The Slave's Dream, Polls Welcome Robinson Crusoe – which sounds like a newspaper headline on election day – and The Little Disaster. Time to re-read the chapter on toilets? Songs set for the June 1886 infants' exam included Little Boy Blue and Little Tommy's Toilet. In July 1886 *all the children* (even the girls?) *taught new song When I'm a Man.* In November 1886 Mr Brown *taught new song Rule Britannia[3].* Singing was always a reliable substitute if other subjects became too taxing. Mid-June 1909, for example, *very warm in school this week, consequently the last lesson has been Singing.*

Singing was always more melodic with accompaniment, but the pupils went without for many a tuneless year. In March 1907 Mr Wightman *banked £8 towards a school piano*; by February 1908 they were still a bit short so they gave a concert *in aid of a piano for use in school*. All this was a bit premature, as the clerk wrote to the

----

[1] The north wind doth blow, And we shall have snow, And what will poor robin do then? Poor thing! He'll sit in a barn, And keep himself warm, And hide his head under his wing. Poor thing!

[2] A popular Victorian system for sight singing devised by John Pyke Hullah (1812 to 1884).

[3] New to the schoolchildren, that is; the music was written by the English composer Thomas Augustine Arne (1710 to 1778) and the words by the Scottish poet James Thompson (1700 to 1748).

Education Department in October 1908: *before the managers decide for or against the introduction of a piano into the school, they would like to know how much your Committee would contribute towards it*. The committee raided its coffers, the school broke into its piggy bank, and by the following January the managers agreed to *the purchase of a piano*. Those selfsame ivories were perhaps still being tickled in July 1949 when *the piano required a thorough overall* (sic), *it was suggested that a new one would be a great asset to the school seeing as there was on the staff two very good musicians*. The new piano arrived in October. In December 1946 Mr Bailey applied *for the instruments to start a percussion band*, and a recorder group started in October 1979.

The meaning of 'Westbury' in this 1951 photo is unclear.
Top row (left to right): ?, Wendy Hudson, Mary Tossell, Sheila Daniels, Daphne Dimmock,
Anita Blanning, Eunice Compton, Ariel Smith, Janet Tovey, Jean Hill.
Front row: John Tike, Leslie Bown, Alan Walker, Barry Huggins, George Weedon,
Ivan Maggs, Heather Dury, Pearl Smith, June Gregory, Beryl Bendall, Isloyn Griffiths,
Basil Boyd, Selwyn Griffiths, Cecil Currell, Colin Parfitt.

Apart from a Music Competition in Bath, *which kept the children away* in April 1913, the logbooks didn't mention any outside musical participation until May 1950 when *the Upper Juniors attended a concert at Keynsham Grammar School. They played a percussion item*. In May 1951 *a representative from the school attended a meeting at Radstock of the joint schools' Singing Together Committee; it has been decided to enter the school for the April Singing*. Singing Together was still going strong in

1974 when the headmaster *took a party of Upper Juniors to CVS to take part*, and for each year thereafter until 1977 when Mr Price and his wife Mair were co-organisers. In May 1961 the Upper Juniors sang two songs *in the Making Music Festival at Wellsway Modern Secondary School at Keynsham.* The then term was either 'secondary modern school' or 'modern secondary school', and it was only later that the former drove out the latter. In May 1962 the headmaster *took the Upper Juniors to CV Modern School* (now he's started missing a word out) *to take part in the annual Making Music Festival*. This took place until at least the late '60s. In March 1967 *Miss Stuckey and I took a party of children to Bath to compete in the recorder section of the Mid-Somerset Festival. They took 3rd place*. 1969 saw them at Fosseway School in Bath, where they brought home 2nd prize.

Our anonymous teacher from the late 1950s wrote of Music: *history, music written treble and bass, middle C, time names ta-aa, ta. Hand of Happiness by Schubert, John Barleycorn, Rosie's New Skirt, Bobby Shaftoe and Go Tell Aunt Nancy*.

By 1926 – and possibly much earlier - competitive country dancing had joined music as a cultural activity, and in April of that year there were *many children in the Folk Dancing Classes*. On a December afternoon in 1961 *Miss Wilson took the Upper Juniors to Wellsway Modern Secondary School Keynsham to take part in the Country Dance Festival*. This was an annual event until 1968, but wasn't mentioned again until 13 July 1977 when *a combined Chew Valley Country Dancing Festival was held on the field. Many of the area schools attended and the afternoon went well*. Several former pupils remember the competitions. Ken Rapps remembers hating them.

In March 1949 Mr Bailey *received one portable gramophone supplied to the LEA sent direct from the maker HMV*. This may feasibly have still been in use in March 1971 when *a rep from the Fire Brigade called to inspect the hutted classroom. He pointed out that the lead for the record player was a little worn and I replaced the worn part*.

Health: the sniggery bits

Along with conventional lessons came those other aspects of children's lives that the authorities deemed worthy of incorporation into the curriculum. Such as health education. It was to be a long time before sex was deemed a suitable topic, but 'Hygiene' was moderately acceptable and an occasionally convenient euphemism. The first mention of anything vaguely related was in November 1936 when *the Health and Cleanliness County Cinema Van gave a showing of pictures bearing on Cleanliness this afternoon*. By 1949 the whole 'Health' thing had been given a certain structure: in March, Mr Bailey *was away attending a course of lectures organised by the Central Committee for Health Education at the Bristol University*.

Eventually, times started to be a-changing. It was 1970. Desmond Morris' Naked Ape had been on the shelves for a couple of years. On 16 July *the PTA held their AGM and Mr Price told them he would show the Sex Education Film subject to discussions with parents, and the County were anxious that parents should be asked about this*. The County and the governors were nervous. But two years later, Dr Comfort's Joy of Sex brought hairy naked people onto bedside cabinets all over the country and proved a bodice-ripping success, so with sex on the agenda and Mrs Whitehouse getting very uppity about it, it was decided that something should again be said to the children. In November 1972 *two BBC film strips concerning Sex Education were shown at a PTA meeting. By popular demand, they were shown again the following evening*. 'Strips' was perhaps not the most apt of words. Having mastered sex, attention was turned in 1974 to other vices and in November *a meeting of the PTA was held at the school at 8 pm, at which Miss A. Gibson, Avon Area Health Authority, showed films and talked about Smoking*.

PRIVATE LESSONS

Sometimes the pupils allowed themselves – or were browbeaten by ambitious parents – to be taught in the evenings. Sometimes the teachers were perhaps compelled to teach in the evenings to make ends meet. Pupil teachers were obliged to take after-school lessons from the head in any event: in March 1879 *the PT received no private lessons this evening, the school being used for a missionary lecture*. An 1894 inspection of *Chew Magna Bishop Sutton Evening School*[1] – which suggests that evening lessons were important enough to merit their own inspection – observed that the *attendance has fallen off, only five pupils being in attendance on the evening of the Inspection*. That same report noted that the headmaster was teaching Geography at evening school *with the aid of a lantern*. Damning with faint praise, the inspector commented *that it has been fairly successful*.

LARGE BUNS, PLENTY OF TEA, AND TRIPS TO WINDSOR CASTLE

The logbooks – especially in earlier times – tended not to distinguish between those treats, outings and similar diversions organised by the school, those organised by the great and the good or by local associations, and those flowing from membership of one of the two Sunday Schools in the village.

But first, some church background. Charles Wesley often preached in Pensford, and people would have walked the four miles from Bishop Sutton to hear the famous evangelist. The fact that cultured society was not wholly against the moral revolution propounded by early Methodism may have been a factor behind the building of the first Methodist Chapel in Bishop Sutton in 1778. In September 1782, when Wesley was 79, he wrote in his journal: *I preached at Chew Magna, at Sutton, Stoke and Clutton*. That must be true, as it says over the Chapel door in Bishop Sutton: *Charles Wesley preached here 17 September 1782*. It was at this chapel that Sunday School in the village began in 1820.

By the early 1830s Methodism in Bishop Sutton was very strong and 117 children attended a Sunday School run by a Mr Gilbert. The doctor in Chew Magna told Sir Edward Strachey around that time that the problems of 'careless parents, unkempt bairns and neglected homes' in the village had been transformed: 'when I saw the great change I never enquired after the cause, I knew the parents had been to the little Chapel'. In 1866 Mr Treasure became chief officer at the Sunday School. Helped by Mrs T, he provided the first school treat – consisting of 'a large bun and plenty of tea' – and gave awards for regular attendance and good

----
[1] 'Chew Magna Bishop Sutton School' was indeed the formal title of the school until 1958.

conduct. He went to Bristol one day to collect some prizes but, memory failing him, came back without them. To save the children from disappointment, he returned to Bristol on foot and walked back with the big bundle of books on his shoulders. One year he provided every family in Bishop Sutton and Newtown with a copy of the New Testament.

At some point, the Chapel was extended out towards the road, as can still be seen from the different colour and shape of the stones in the side walls. The congregation soon outgrew even the enlarged building, and in 1911 fundraising started for a new Chapel alongside. Appeals, collections, bazaars and concerts produced the then colossal sum of £950. The new Chapel opened in 1916 – although the plaque on the wall says *New Wesleyan Church AD 1914* – and the old Chapel became the Sunday School. To add further confusion, the foundation stone of the new Chapel is inscribed *For the Sunday School, Charles Tucker, Superintendent*. In the early 1920s Henry Strachie painted a memorial inside the Chapel to the six men from the village who died in the Great War, depicted as angels and modelled on local people.

'Bishop Sutton Wesleyan Sunday School 4th Annual Outing to Weston-super-Mare, [Tuesday] *1 July 1919*'

By the 1920s an average of 60 attended the morning Sunday School at the Chapel, and 120 in the afternoon. Children would sometimes take their tea with them in the afternoon – to be eaten at a friend's house later on – and then be collected when their parents came to the Chapel for the evening service. The big treat was the Sunday School Anniversary, usually at the end of April. Best clothes all round, and for the girls a straw hat or Easter bonnet. There would invariably be an outing, a tea, and the presentation of inspiring prizes (generally books) for regular attendance. The outings, which often involved the whole family, were the highlight of the year. Entitlement was based on regular attendance at Sunday School and the payment each week of a few coppers, all recorded in a little book. Until the First World War, a farm cart would take the excursionists to a field for sports and a picnic tea, but by the 1920s it was the chara to Weston. For many locals, this was their one chance for a whole year to sit on a beach, and their only trip as a family. If their luck was in, the sea was less than half a mile from the Front. Eunice Ogborne recalls Sunday School outings there on three double-decker buses.

Until the 1920s – and perhaps later – there was a Band of Hope service, where participants were encouraged to sign a pledge not to drink alcohol. On Monday 8 June 1896 there had been a day off school *for the Band of Hope Treat*. A Wesley Senior Guild was started in the village in 1924 and a Wesley Junior Guild in 1928.

Until the late 1950s at least, the Church of England Sunday School operated in competition with that run by the Methodists (Wesleyans). Ken Rapps suggests that which Sunday School you went to depended largely on whose Christmas party came first. The Methodists had their own hall. The C of E, ominously, didn't. This was a sizeable bone of unchristian contention, but suffice it to say here that the Church of England Sunday School usually met at the primary school, where it staked proprietorial rights. The Methodists usually won the Sunday School Popularity Stakes because (a) they didn't meet in the very school where the children had to spend so much time during the week, and (b) they appear to have organised more trips and treats. It's certainly the Methodist Sunday School that most people remember, and it's invariably their treats and outings that are the ones mentioned in the logbooks.

Ken Rapps recalls that the Church of England Sunday School was held in the central classroom of the primary school and that the Rev. Treen officiated. He was 'no good on discipline' and the children rejoiced not in the spiritual upliftings occasioned by the vicar's ministrations, but in playing him up. They placed lighted matches in the ink wells for the pong and twanged pins in the hinges of desk lids for the ping. The vicar is remembered as driving a Bullnose Morris: a sturdy car, but not one designed to pull away with half a dozen young ruffians hanging on to the back bumper. The earnest gentleman was a student of Egyptology and hieroglyphics, and Ken recalls that trying to drum up interest amongst the children was like flogging a dead horse.

Time to go back to the logbooks. Sunday School outings are intermingled with other treats. The following is in roughly chronological order.

On the evening of Friday 26 January 1872 *the Annual School Treat was given to the children, when they had a tea and saw an amusing Magic Lantern entertainment*. On Wednesday 22 August 1883 *there was a Sunday School Treat of the non-conformists taking place in the afternoon. The attendance was small, viz 30*. On Friday 19 July 1878 *there was a holiday in the afternoon on account of a public tea by the Dissenters* (Nonconformists). On Friday 5 December 1889 Mr Brown *gave half a holiday on Friday afternoon, there being a Free Tea given to all the children in the parish*. The teas and treats were often at the 'Big House': school was *not opened Tuesday afternoon 19 September 1893, Mrs Strachey having given a treat to all the children of the parish at Sutton Court*. The Stracheys were always generous to the pupils. On Wednesday 18 July 1894 *a half holiday was given on the occasion of a Sunday School Treat to which 90% of the children were going*.

The treats and teas seem to have waned after the 1890s, to be replaced by excursions, invariably arranged by the Sunday Schools but normally taking place on weekdays. On Monday 28 June 1909 Mr Wightman wrote: *over 100 children gone to Weston. Registers ordered to be marked, 37 present in the morning*. Monday 26 June 1911: *owing to an outing to Weston-super-Mare only 53 present in the morning and nearly the same in the afternoon*. Friday 17 September 1920: *attendance suffered through motor outings*. Wednesday 20 July 1921: *many away owing to an outing to Weston-super-Mare*. That bracing resort could get a little samey, especially if the tide was out and the mud was in, and on Wednesday 5 July 1922 *only about 30 children went to Weston, school was open as usual and registers were marked. Notice was given for closure but I ascertained that only the elder ones were going*. The last logbook record of Sunday School outings was on Wednesday 24 July 1946, when *attendance in the afternoon was affected by a Sunday School outing to Weymouth*. Perhaps Sunday School outings thereafter took place on Sundays, it no longer being quite so verboten to have fun on the Sabbath.

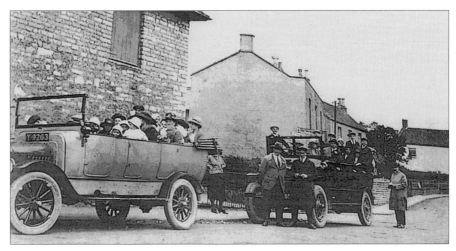

An outing ready to set off from the junction of Ham Lane and The Street

By 1930 outings were being organised by Bishop Sutton School itself. On Wednesday 15 May of that year *school closed for the day to allow party to make educational excursion to Windsor Castle and Runnymede*. June 1934: *44 children went on Educational Tour to Stonehenge, New Forest and Southampton Docks (incl. trip over RMS Berengaria[1]). School closed*. Friday 21 June 1935: *school closed, 28 scholars made Educational Excursion to London*. It was in the 1930s that Jean Veale remembers the children being taken to see the trains at Swindon, where it rained all day. She also recalls that they went on a boat at Southsea. The younger children were not generally subjected to long journeys on slow and smelly buses; they went to Bristol Zoo. The school closed on Friday 23 June 1939 *to allow 39 children to go to London; the children were taken over the Houses of Parliament, Westminster Abbey and the Zoo while a motor bus tour took them past many important places*. No visits seem to have taken place during the war years, partly because of fuel rationing, partly because air raids on large cities made them places best avoided, and partly because it may have been difficult preventing the evacuees and local children fighting on the back seat of the bus. On the first post-war trip, on Ascension Day in May 1948, *a party of 30 children went to Windsor and Eton, were shown over the Castle and went to Runnymede by river*. In June 1949 Mr Bailey and

----

[1] The Berengaria was built as the Imperator for the Hamburg-Amerika Line, making her maiden voyage from Cuxhaven to New York in June 1913. Seized by the US Navy in May 1919 as a troop transport, she was handed over to London in February 1920 as reparation for the sinking of the Lusitania and sold to the Cunard Line. She became their flagship and was renamed 'Berengaria'. In March 1938 she caught fire in New York harbour and was sold for scrap that November.

Miss Howarth *took 20 children to London on an educational journey covering the Houses of Parliament, where we were conducted round by the member[1], Westminster Abbey, Buckingham Palace, the Tower and Madame Tussauds*.

Excursions then came thick and fast. On Thursday 20 March 1950 *Miss Thomas and junior class spent the afternoon at Bristol Zoo; they have been studying farm and other animals and have also visited Mr Wyatt's farm*. In May of that year Mr Bailey and Mrs Howarth *took a party of 28 children on an educational tour of Portsmouth dockyard and harbour and of HMS Victory*. One former pupil recalls being shown the engines on a ferry. In November 1950 *a party of 24 children went to Laverton's Cloth Mills at Westbury*. They enjoyed it so much that the trip was repeated the following summer. On Wednesday 27 June 1951 *a party of 60 children went to the Festival of Britain Exhibition on the South Bank; to release the teachers for this, the school was closed*. One former pupil recalls that the trip started at Clutton Station, but Handicraft master Mr Ingram avoided the train fare by cycling all the way to London from Bishop Sutton on his racing bike with wheel rims made of bamboo.

It was ship-spotting time again in July 1951 when Mr Bailey *took 30 children to the aircraft carrier Campania[2] at Avonmouth. We went at 9 am and returned at 11.45*. The traffic at Bedminster Down and on the Portway was clearly more benign in those days.

On Sunday 30 March 1952 *Mr Avery took a group of 30 senior boys to the Schoolboys' Own Exhibition in Bristol*. In July 50 children *went to the Gold Museum at Blaise Castle; Miss Chivers gave the children much information about the various trees in the grounds*. To finish off a hectic year, on Monday 27 October *forms 1 and 2 went to visit the Radstock Co-op Bakery and Dairy*. In July 1953 it was London Airport and Windsor. One pupil recalls that some of the children paid to go up in turns in a small plane which flew over water tanks. Messrs Hopp and Cotton *took the Upper Juniors and Lower Senior Group to the Roman Baths* in July 1955, and in March 1956 *a party of senior scholars have gone for a conducted tour of Bristol telephone exchange*. Later that year, *form 2 went to Sutton Hill to see a lime kiln in use. They were able to see one under construction*. No-one seems to knows just where on Sutton Hill these lime kilns were.

The school was closed on Friday 15 June 1956 when a party of 60 went to Southampton and the Isle of Wight. Those not given the opportunity of being sick on the Solent went in October *to the Waterworks Station at Stowey where water is pumped for Bristol, west Gloucester and Bath*. June 1957 was the River Dart: by train from Bristol to Totnes, by river to Dartmouth and Kingswear and then back by train. June 1959 was Windsor Castle again, but in January 1960 there was a rare winter visit: *during the morning the junior children visited the Trout Hatchery at Ubley to see the trout spawning being carried out*. 1960 was London (*36 children travelled, accompanied by 6 adults*), 1961 Southampton and Winchester for the junior children, and 1962 *spending the morning at the Science Museum, proceeding*

---

[1] Labour's Walter J. Farthing (retired 1950), MP for Frome, in which constituency Bishop Sutton then lay. (Information supplied courtesy of the Parliamentary Archives.)

[2] The Campania was an escort carrier built at Harland & Wolff in Belfast, launched in 1943 and commissioned in March 1944. After a distinguished wartime record, she was laid up at Gareloch in 1946. Loaned to the Festival of Britain Organisation in 1950 for use as a mobile exhibition ship, the ship then carried equipment for the atom-bomb trials on Monte Bello Island off the northwest coast of Australia in October 1952. She was broken up at Blyth in November 1955.

up the Thames to the Cutty Sark in the afternoon. June 1963 was the school journey to Cardiff. Visits were paid to St Fagans Folk Museum and the Empire Pool. The journey to Cardiff was by boat from Weston-super-Mare and the return by train via the Severn Tunnel. That particular trip proved so popular that it was repeated in 1968, 1971 and 1975.

July 1964 was assorted history in Bath, June 1965 and July 1969 the Amphitheatre and lead mines at Charterhouse, the Cheddar Gorge and Caves, Glastonbury Tor, Wells Cathedral and Swimming Baths, and in 1966 the Bristol Docks, Brandon Hill, Bristol Museum and Art Gallery and the Zoo. Something novel in September 1966: the junior children were ... taken by coach to pay a visit to the newly built Severn Bridge. We left at 9.30 am and had returned by 12 noon. In December the Upper Juniors visited the Bristol Waterworks installation at Chew Stoke, where they were shown a film, and Barrow Gurney where the various processes were examined. July 1967 was Berkeley Castle, Blaise Castle Folk Museum and the Wild Life Trust at Westbury-on-Trym. June 1972 was wild life and Blaise Castle again, with Cabot Tower thrown in.

Not an outing as such, but on Friday 5 November 1971 a fireworks display was given on the school fields from 7-8 pm with refreshments included. The PTA felt that this was the safest way for the traditional event to be carried out. I agreed after ensuring that adequate safeguards were adhered to. This was the first and only logbook mention of fireworks. Tuesday 3 July 1979 found the infants at the Bird Sanctuary at Rode. They were supervised by their teachers and supported by parents. On the Friday of that week there was an entertainment to the children by Bobby the Clown.

No outings were recorded for 1970, 1973, 1974, 1976 or 1978.

Bristol Zoo with Mr Price in 1958

Joan Davidge (school secretary and assistant in the 1970s) recalls that the trips to Weston sometimes incorporated the aviary on the A38 near Cross, and that it was always Brents coaches of Bishop Sutton who provided the transport for school excursions. May Woodward remembers the away days to Weston, Clevedon and the

Houses of Parliament. She believes that the parents had to pay the costs; there are unfortunately no remaining records of how much they were.

School trip to Cheddar 1948. Mr Bailey is on the left.

CHARTERHOUSE, GOBLIN COMBE AND ACCIDENTAL DISLOCATION OF LEFT ELBOW

The Activities Weeks that are now rather taken for granted didn't materialise until the early 1970s. On 1 May 1972 Mr Price *was away from school today and shall be in Charterhouse Outdoor Centre for the* week. When he came back, he noted in the logbook, with some relief, that *he was accompanied by the 15 children. All in order.* He added: *this is the first time the school has been away to camp.* The week was shared with the children of Chew Stoke school, where headmistress Zera Wilson explained it all in rather more detail in her logbook: *I took 15 children to Charterhouse camping. We shared the camp with Bishop Sutton School. Activities included pot-holing, orienteering, a nature trail and visits to the lead mines, Cheddar Gorge, Gough's Caves and Jacob's Ladder, Priddy, Ebor Gorge and Wookey Hole and Roman amphitheatre.*

On Wednesday 8 October 1975 Mr Price took himself off for the morning with Paul Martin, headmaster of Paulton School, *to pay a visit to old Batcombe School to investigate the possibility of its being used for Outdoor Centre purposes by this school.* It wasn't suitable. The following week, Mr P popped out *for an hour to pay a visit to Goblin Combe Camp for camping purposes.* The new LEA in the new county of Avon preferred Goblin Combe (near Bristol Airport, Avon) to Charterhouse (Somerset) and in 1976 Mr Price and Mr Powell *took 20 children to stay there, the time to be spent in Field Studies and outdoor activities.* The same in July 1977. Charterhouse wasn't totally ignored, however, and in May 1978 Mr Price took his wife and the *4th years and some of the 3rd year juniors to Charterhouse to spend the day in Field Study Activities in that area.* 20 June 1978 found Mr Price *out during the afternoon to buy supplies for next week's school camp at Goblin Combe.* Bars of Kendal Mint Cake from Stuckey's, perhaps. But he rued the day that he went to the Combe in June 1979: *with Mrs L. Lade, Infant Teacher, I took the Upper Juniors to stay at Goblin Combe for a 4-night stay. During our afternoon exercise, I accidentally fell and dislocated my left elbow which necessitated my being taken to the Bristol Royal Infirmary where it was treated. I continued to visit the camp in a supervisory capacity, having arranged for additional help for Mrs Lade.*

Teresa Dowling recalls one occasion at Charterhouse when the girls went into the boys' tents. Mr Price was so cross that he punished them by making them all walk the mile or so down to Velvet Bottom.

DULLNESS, IMBECILITY, BACKWARDNESS

'One teacher used to say we were hard to teach in Harptree because we were born on the wrong side of the hill and were dull because of all the lead in the water'. So recalled a former pupil of East Harptree School. Whether there was anything in the water – such as it was – in Bishop Sutton to cause children here to be what was generally termed 'backward' isn't known, but there have always been children who, for whatever reason, have found learning difficult. One of the most far-reaching changes in education since the mid-1900s has been in the treatment of 'backward' and disabled children who would once have been put away in an institution or 'special school', their parents often marginalised as a bad or non-competent influence.

What did the logbooks have to say about the situation locally? Prepare yourselves for a shock, but do bear in mind that the term 'backward' embraced the whole spectrum from 'further behind in their studies than they should be' (as, for example, in 1924 when Mr Wightman admitted two children from Stowey School who were *very backward but appear to be fairly intelligent*) to dyslexia to actual mental or physical handicap. But the whole spectrum was tarred with the same unfeeling brush. Several names in the following paragraphs have been abbreviated for sensitivity.

In June 1883 headmaster Allan Hill observed: *lessons have been prolonged an hour mornings and afternoons each day, some children being exceedingly dull and almost imbecile.* In October 1886 Ebenezer Brown wrote: *the Satchell children who were admitted last week are fearfully backward, not knowing their letters although 8 and 9 years old respectively.* So aghast was Mr Brown that he despatched the Attendance Officer to the Satchell household. The officer *prevailed on the parents to send three more children to school, these with the two already admitted make five* (he was no dullard when it came to maths, was Mr Brown), *aged from 6 to 12. All of them put in the infants' class, not being able to read words of one syllable. The eldest girl (12) has only been to school a month in her life.* One can imagine the feelings of the older children on being made to sit with the infants. Mr Brown observed in May 1888 that *as many children who have been absent for several weeks through illness are very dull, work is very hard.* In 1904 Mr Wightman noted that R.S. and N.N. *are certified as defective children.* In March 1931 he damned a whole class with faint praise: *I found work had progressed. I found better expressions of intelligence.*

Evidence of formal assessment first came in 1937 when *Miss Rawlings, Educational Psychologist, gave a reading test to children between the* [dates of birth] *2.8.29 to 1.8.30; she also tested six other children for backwardness and suggested that four were of a lower mental age, while two were 'retarded'.* This was most inconvenient, as the infants' room was used and examinations in the school could not be continued as all children had to work in the other two rooms. In February 1938 *the name of S.T. was removed from the register by order of the County Authority as he is mentally unfit to attend school.* Difficulties were still apparent in more recent times. Dr Willcox visited the school on several occasions during 1950 and examined children with IQs ranging from 45 to 79. One pragmatic response was to bring in peripatetic teachers, a practice which began in March 1961 when the CEO *offered the services of a teacher for backward children to commence with the summer term. Agreed – three sessions per week.* By July of that year, Mr Price noted *that the special training was having satisfactory results.* Peripatetic teachers have helped children with learning difficulties to the present day. In March 1952 Miss Blythen, the County Psychologist, came to see P.J. who had been *referred to the LEA after she had strayed from home the night following the school pantomime. The headmaster took the opportunity too of asking the psychologist to see R.M., who was best treated almost as a baby.*

Distressing though much of this may sound to today's observer, it's worth reflecting that some of these children were only at Bishop Sutton School – renowned for its caring attitude - because they had been rejected elsewhere.

SPORTS: GET THOSE ARMS UP, AND JUGS OF COLD WATER

There was a growing emphasis in Victorian times on team games, which The Board of Education's 1912 'Suggestions for the Consideration of Teachers and Others Concerned in the work of Public Elementary Schools' recommended to teachers as a way of creating *an esprit de corps and a readiness to endure fatigue or submit to discipline, and to subordinate one's own powers and wishes to a common end.* Such wholesome virtues were moreover seen as invaluable in times of war and were encouraged for that very reason. Physical Exercise or Physical Training – often called 'drill', 'squad drill' or simply 'exercise' – made frequent appearances in the logbook. Bishop Sutton School took it all very seriously, and sometimes in public: in August 1877 *Mr G. Arter and another gentleman were in school this morning and saw the children exercised.* Mr Arter was the chairman of the Board. Headmaster Jones clearly didn't know the name of his companion.

Alfresco PE and PT were weather-dependent. Late May 1899: *drill time was shortened this week owing to the intense heat.* Early July: *very hot week, no drill done in the yard.* Harry Potter was ninety years or so in the future, but in January 1904: *wands for drill used for the first time.* It was decided in 1927 that *Standards 4 to 7 boys and girls will drill separately.* Until then, they'd presumably all vaulted together. It wasn't only the children who got to jump up and down: in January 1934 *all members of the staff enrolled in Physical Training Class given by Miss Smith and Capt Fitzgerald at Midsomer Norton.* The latter, a local PE and Drill Inspector, had acquired some renown for devising special exercises for those with posture or foot difficulties, and paid regular visits to local schools. In March 1949 *Mr Ray Warren of the Bristol Rovers FC gave one hour's coaching to the senior boys,* and again in November 1951. Getting hold of one of Bristol Rovers' legends was a real coup. Warren had joined the club in 1934, starred in 69 league matches before being called up to serve in the Tank Corps, and was one of the few players to appear for a major club both before and after the war. Rovers awarded him a second benefit match (against Cardiff City) on 8 March 1947. Rovers won 1-0, but the match was remembered most vividly for the appalling weather conditions: the club asked for 200 volunteers to clear snow from the terraces. This being the age of austerity, they would need to bring their own shovels.

In November 1953 agility equipment was erected in the school yard and *the tool shed was moved to make room for this.* November 1956 saw the arrival of two large landing mats from The Stephenson Arcade Ltd, and in September 1957 the LEA's Miss Maconochie *suggested asking Tratman and Lowther of Bristol for an estimate for the repair of the infant scrambling net.* In June of the following year she visited *in connection with the climbing apparatus removed from the Methodist Hall and its installation in the playground.* This was probably the climbing frames that Monica Castle recalls: although they would be considered hopelessly dangerous today, she can't remember anyone falling off, getting hurt and suing the school. Civil Defence

BRISTOL ROVERS FOOTBALL CLUB, LTD.
Official Programme **3d.**

THE CAPTAIN: " WE'VE HAD A MIGHTY ROUGH TRIP, BOYS, BUT IT LOOKS AS THOUGH THE GOOD OLD SHIP IS COMING IN TO SMOOTHER WATERS NOW."

Ray Warren

being all the rage during the Cold War period, Mr Price remarked in October 1959 that *the County PE organiser visited the school to discuss the possibility of placing a commando net in the playground.* In December 1969 *new goalposts supplied and fitted in the school playing field by Messrs Batten.* They seem to have survived until November 1976 when *one set of goal posts had been damaged, presumably by the recent high winds. New posts will be obtained a.s.a.p.* In July 1978 the headmaster asked for *better PE access to be provided* [for equipment], *pointing out that the old coke storage spaces could easily be converted for this purpose.* The authorities refused, saying there was no money available.

There were no references at all to cricket, so perhaps it wasn't played at the school. Tennis didn't make a logbook appearance until July 1954, when Somerset Education Authority was asked *to authorise the covering of two of the windows for Padder Tennis at a cost of £4.18s.0d. This was refused as it was not the policy of the Committee to provide wire screens for classroom windows.* Padder Tennis, or Short Tennis, is ordinary tennis but played on a smaller court. Whether there was any 'ordinary' tennis is not recorded, but there were courts opposite the school.

The records don't state whether the children wore different clothes for PE, or whether the girls simply followed the time-honoured practice of tucking their skirts into their navy-blue knickers, but in February 1938 the headmaster *received the shoes for PT as supplied by the Authority.* The children weren't allowed to take them home, they had to be put somewhere, and in May 1938 *Miss Peake called to discuss provision for the storing of the shoes.* The Authority had started something they couldn't control: in November 1938 the school *made application for extra pairs of shoes for PT as so many children have outgrown those they were supplied with at first and we are unable to fit them up.* The war intervened, clothing coupons were introduced and daps weren't provided again until 1948 when, in November, *112 pairs of gym shoes received from the Co-op Society in Bristol; it has been possible to equip all children for PT.* There was no mention of whether the school benefited from the divi. Football apparel too had fallen foul of the war, but the same month saw *Coupon Equivalent Documents for football jerseys received from LEA (48 coupons).*

It was swimming that attracted more logbook space than any other activity. The teachers could hardly take their young charges to Stratford Mill for a dip in the pond – which is what the children did off their own bat in hot weather – but organised swimming arrived in 1949: in March, *Capt Glazebrook came to school. I asked him about facilities for swimming and he advised application at an early date.* In May, the managers agreed to Mr Bailey's *request that swimming should be included in the curriculum for the coming season,* and the following month he received *telephoned permission for the swimming classes to begin.* On the allotted day *the 1st class went to the Jubilee Baths at Knowle, Bristol. 14 boys attended.* This became a regular occurrence and in July 1951, *three children were awarded Swimming Certificates by the Bristol Corporation.* The Jubilee Baths at Knowle were the school's preferred venue, but time was tight with around 40 children leaving school at 11.30 for a session from 12 to 12.30, returning about 1.15. Les Bown recalls the baths without much fondness. He only managed to get one year's swimming in, as 'they stopped it in the second year, and by the third year I had to leave'. Joan Bunney recalls that anyone sitting shivering on the side had a jug of cold water thrown over them. That would gladden the hearts of today's litigants. If anyone forgot their costume or trunks, they were made to swim in their underwear.

Mine was red. What colour was yours?

It was high time that the school got its own facilities. In February 1968 the managers were told that *at a recent meeting of parents, the matter of a swimming pool was mentioned; the parents were 100% in favour. The Parents' Association had looked into the matter and the pool could cost approx. £850 and it was decided to see if a loan was available, and the balance to be raised by donations etc.* The parents lost no time, and at the end of March the Education Authority confirmed that *a grant of £170 would be made.* The managers asked for a loan of £650 *for as long a period as possible.* Fund-raising kicked off with a Spring Fête in May 1968 which brought in £150. Work began on the foundations on 20 May: *voluntary labour was provided by the parents.* Eleven days later the ground was ready, and on 12 June Messrs Dando and Dark started the *'erection'* of the pool – a strange word to use for something that went in the ground – and on 14 June it was *being filled with water from adjacent tap.* Swimming began on Tuesday 18 June 1968 – it perhaps having taken that long to fill the pool – and *all the classes gave swimming demonstrations* at the Parents' Open Day on 17 July. From inception to doggie paddle in only four months: a testimony to the dedication, enthusiasm and hard work of the parents. The managers noted that *Mr Price would like to express his thanks for all the help the parents had given in connection with this.*

Within a month of opening, the juniors were enjoying three sessions a week and the infants two. Swimming replaced all other summer PE. There were inevitably a few teething problems and Swimco had to sort out *some swellings and leaks at several joints in the marine boarding,* but it was all going, well, swimmingly and Mr B. M. Long, Chief PE Organiser for Somerset, brought his ribbon-cutting scissors along at 3 pm on 10 September 1968. *Many parents attended and refreshments were provided in the main classroom.* Fundraising continued: £5.12s.6d at the school sports in June, '£5 or £6' at a pre-Christmas dance (perhaps too much Tizer was consumed to allow for accurate counting), a total of £431 by July 1969 and a further £79.16s.0d at the PTA Spring Fayre in May 1970. The loan had been repaid within two years. Mr Price was very proud of his new facility, and in March 1969 contentedly went off *to attend a course at King Alfred's School in Burnham-on-Sea on the maintenance of swimming pool equipment*. The water was regularly tested by the qualified authorities, and was always declared fit apart from occasional cloudiness, put down to alkalinity and chlorination. In May 1971 a new changing room *was provided through parents' voluntary efforts*. One slight drawback was that the pool was unheated, and at the beginning of June 1972 the headmaster noted that *very little swimming has been carried out during the present summer due to the unusually cold unsuitable weather*.

The school in the 1970s. Note the swimming pool top-right.

There were squabbles, perhaps fuelled by envy. In February 1972 the governors *brought up the matter of the pool in connection with the school holidays. The pool was closed during part of the school holidays* (presumably the previous summer) *because of the use of the pool by children from other schools, and Mr Price was away, so the pool was closed. What would happen if this sort of thing I again this year, and why should Bishop Sutton School children suffer because of this?* I hasten to emphasise that the clerk's note is copied here verbatim. In April 1973 Mr Price told the governors *that the swimming pool would only be used during the school holidays, unless he felt that the parents could cope with it. It should only be used for children of the Bishop Sutton School, the children in the school, children leaving to go to Chew Valley School, and the children coming into the school from September. Mr Price stated that the pool could only be used because the parents were good enough to give up their time to look after the children in the school*. Glad we managed to sort that one out.

The baths at Wells were frequented alongside the Bishop Sutton pool: in July 1971 Mr Price was *out of school until 10 am having taken a party of eight children to undergo the Intermediate Swimming Test at Wells Swimming Pool. All were successful*. By March 1975 the school pool was becoming rather small for the demands being placed on it and the governors found that the recently opened pool at Paulton was available for an hour a week in school time: *this was a better pool than the one at Bishop Sutton, and would allow the children much more scope*. True, but unfair: the pool at Paulton was built with taxpayers' money, the one at the school with voluntary contributions and parents' honest toil. Anyway, it was realised in December 1975 that there was *no money available for travelling to the pool* (at Paulton)*, so this matter has been dropped, as it would cost approx £10 per week*. By 1979 a budget had been found for children to be bussed to Keynsham to use the pool there. The school pool – remembered with fondness by my own children - was closed in the late 1990s as a result of Health and Safety regulations requiring that a qualified life-saver be in constant attendance when the pool was in use. This proved impractical and too expensive.

Inter-schools competitions didn't feature until September 1923, when the school was closed in the afternoon for the Bishop Sutton team to enter the Blagdon and District School Sports at Blagdon, gaining ten prizes and winning the Challenge Shield for six months. The competition alternated between different local venues: 1924 at West Harptree, 1925 back to Blagdon (where Bishop Sutton obtained nine 1st prizes, two 2nd's and three 3rd's) and 1926 at East Harptree. In July 1927 *L. Prime qualified for the Championship Sports at Stamford Bridge*. This was a huge feather in Bishop Sutton's cap, not to mention L. Prime's. In June 1935 the Junior School Sports were at Midsomer Norton: *some 40 scholars took part and obtained three 1st, four 2nd and three 3rd-class certificates*. On 31 October 1935 *school closed at 3.40 pm owing to the dull weather* – no electricity in those days – *it was very dark in all rooms* and, worst of all, *a Girls' Netball Team match with Timsbury had to be postponed*. It was played a fortnight later: *the match was lost 20-2*.

In June 1938 the Area Sports came to Stowey, where *seven schools competed, a full team from this school took part*. The last pre-war venue was Bishopsworth in 1939, and Bishop Suttons success in taking eight first prizes, 13 seconds and five thirds must have gone to Mr Bailey's head: that evening he committed to his logbook the fact that *at the Area Sports were schools from the Area*. The competitions resumed in 1946 at Pensford, and that year a Bishop Sutton School team also *represented the area for some events in the County Athletics meeting at Glastonbury*. On the weekend of 18 June 1949 *four scholars from this school were in the Area team* (of the Inter-County Athletics meeting) *and were placed as follows: Pat Winstanley 1st prize in the age race, 2nd prize in the hurdles; Shirley Cook 2nd in the age race; Dennis Chubb 4th for the half-mile*. In 1956 Bishop Sutton's Julie Stock represented the area at the County Senior Athletic Meeting in Taunton, and 36 children went to the County Area Sports at Keynsham to win three 1st prizes, three 2nd and five 3rd. A sad day dawned in November 1957 when *St Benedicts School* (Charlton Lane, Midsomer Norton) *visited us today for netball and football, this will be the last time, ending a series of inter-schools matches which began in 1932*. Primary-only status came in 1958 and the school prepared in May of that year for *participation in Area Sports at Keynsham; a representative team has been chosen and will be accompanied by a party of spectators, a coach has been hired*. If the logbook is to be believed, however, Bishop Sutton School's new status may have been too high a hurdle for inter-schools competitions, the only subsequent mention being in June 1960 when *a large party from the school went to Broadlands Secondary Modern School to take part in the Area Sports*.

Rounders didn't feature in the logbooks until July 1975 when Mr Price *accompanied Mrs Jenkins with a Rounders Team to CVS to participate in a competition*. There were annual six-a-side football tournaments against Chew Valley School, and in

April 1974 Mr Price *took a party of 12 boys who competed.* Either two teams, or a lot of substitutes. Did they all go in one car? Probably not. It is unlikely that Mr Price followed his two predecessors' successes in the Cramming Small Children Into a Small Car competition. Eunice Ogborne recalls that Mr Bailey used to shoe-horn seven children into his two-seater (with dickey seat) to Midsomer Norton for tournaments. Eunice was the biggest, so she sat in the front.

What did our anonymous 1950s teacher have to say about competitive sport? *I was away with influenza. The children each wrote me a letter. Home match against Chew Magna. Both teams had over 50% absentee* (sic) *and lost their games which lacked spirit.*

Netball in the late 1970s

All this area and county malarkey was great for those who excelled at sports, but the lack of a playing field at the school made it difficult to organise anything for the majority of the children who were content simply to sack-race against their classmates or have one leg tied to that of their best friend. But then, in October 1931, Mr Bailey *received a letter from the Miners' Welfare giving permission for their recreation field*[1] *to be used for the school children's football only.* A welcome gift for the headmaster, whose tenure at Bishop Sutton had only started that month. Things suddenly looked more promising on the school sports front. The first specific mention of an annual school sports day wasn't until Tuesday 17 May 1949 (when it was held *in the Welfare Field*), although it is known that the children egged-and-spooned prior to then. On Wednesday 23 July 1958 *the school children and staff went to the Recreation Ground at 3 pm to take part in the First Annual Sports* (since becoming a primary-only school). On Saturday 25 May 1968 an experiment was

----
[1] In 1931 the Recreation Field (or Ground) was still owned by the Miners' Welfare Organisation.

tried: *the school sports were held at the Rec Ground at 7.30 pm. It was the first time for it to be held in the evening, and it proved quite successful.* On the evening of 17 July 1970 *the sports were held for the first time on the school field. It was very well attended and successful.* The evening experiment only lasted until 1972, when the PTA *voted for the annual school sports* (on Thursday 13 July) *to be held in the afternoon and not in the evening.* It's in the afternoons that they've stayed.

School Sports Day on the rec 1948
From left to right: David King,
Heather Perkins, Ann Saunders, Audrey Bendall, Sonya Tovey,
Queenie Leonard, Daphne Small, Glenys Chubb

Away in a Manger dressed up as a donkey

Until Queen Victoria's Albert introduced his funny German ideas, an English Christmas consisted of a mince pie and a couple of days of sombre religious reflection. Charles Dickens did some fine-tuning, and we've had twee cards with glittery robins and snowy pillar boxes ever since. Relentless Americanisation added the commercial frenzy we know today. In late Victorian times, pillars of the local community would visit schools and graciously give pupils tea and gifts of fruit and small toys. Such events, rewarding though they were, also neatly bolstered the class structure of contemporary English society, as the children were expected to acknowledge with suitable meekness the benevolence of their social superiors. The rich man in his castle and the poor man at his gate showed them the way in the carol in which Good King Wenslas Last Looked Out or, as adults churlishly insist, Good King Wenceslas Looked Out.

The first festive reference in the logbook was on Christmas Eve 1884 when *Mr Lovell at 12 o'clock distributed cake and oranges to the children, the costs of which were defrayed by an entertainment given by the children on the evening of 12 December.*

Festivities continued on into the new year and on the evening of Wednesday 2 January *Mrs Strachey of Sutton Court gave the children a Magic Lantern treat, Christmas Tree Cake and oranges for all the children present*. Not much else found its way into the records until the annual School Christmas parties came along in 1935, although the school had doubtless been merrily yuling on a regular basis long before that.

It wasn't easy finding premises for do's. Tuesday 17 December 1935: *annual School Party in the Hall – this is rather early in the week as other events in the village prevent having the Hall later*. Christmas 1939 was enlivened by the *traditional tea and oranges, the juniors were all given a present, and the infants a present from the Christmas tree (given by Lord Strachie)*. The parties and concerts continued during the war years – although the oranges often fell foul of German U-boats – and it wasn't unusual for the jollity to be extended, as on 9 January 1941 when *a show of films was given to the schoolchildren as part of the Christmas entertainment*. 1942 was a lean year: *the Children's Annual Treat, tea and pictures took place today. Funds were obtained by a sale of toys etc given by friends*. On Wednesday 22 December 1943 *the annual School Treat was given today; all schoolchildren, children under 5 and evacuees were entertained to tea and a conjuror's show*. Mr Bailey probably didn't intend to suggest that the evacuees were a race apart.

Although rarely mentioned in the logbooks, there was an annual nativity play given by the infants, where parents could cry when they sang Away in a Manger and where at least one child could be a donkey. The panto, generally spread across two nights, took various forms. Oh yes it did. The logbooks were quiet on the specifics, but former pupils recall that shows often alternated – at least by the mid-1950s – between songs from the shows and the more traditional Christmas fare. One success was clearly the December 1949 production (oh yes it was): *the Village Hall was very crowded this evening for the Annual School Concert, which this year took the form of a pantomime 'Babes in the Wood'. Every child in the school had some part to play*. It replaced the 1948 party-cum-panto which had been postponed to Tuesday 1 March 1949 due to measles, the compensation for which was a special tea after the annual sports day on 17 May. Much the same in 1950 when *the junior party has had to be postponed until after the holidays as so many of the younger children are still away with chickenpox*. In 1952 the seniors had *a Social Dance with refreshments, competitions, prizes etc*, but a new twist came in 1954 when *the Upper Juniors and Lower Seniors gave puppet and marionette shows to the rest of the school*. The proceeds from shows were ploughed back into school funds or for Christmas treats. For some unknown reason, 1963 was barren: Mr Price reported to the managers' meeting in December that there *would be no concert this year*. Apart from occasional mishaps, the concert or panto had always been held in December. Oh yes it had. But as an experiment, 1973 saw it on Tuesday 3 April when *it was held in the Village Hall at 7.15 pm. It was very well attended, the Hall being full to capacity*. Perhaps the parents wanted to ingratiate themselves with Her Majesty's Inspector Miss Kellett, who was also there.

May Woodward remembers from the late 1930s that her younger brother was the Christmas pudding in a panto at the Village Hall one year with a sprig of holly on his head. Dick Chapman recalls one school play in the early 1930s when he played Father Christmas. He had to go off the stage with his beard and come back on without it. One former pupil recalls that children would star in different roles, running off one side of the stage and round the room back to the other side where they appeared in fresh garb. Colin Symes recalls that the school Christmas parties were in the Village Hall, often with music by Maurice Symes' band (Colin's father). Teresa Dowling explains that the Christmas parties for the younger children were in the main hall, but the games were in the junior classroom in the old building. They played Squeal Piggy Squeal and Blind Man's Buff amongst other party favourites.

Christmas panto 1952

Sorry to shatter an illusion, but the gifts for the children for the various merriments were not made in Santa's grotto at County Education HQ. On Thursday 14 November 1974 headmaster Price *was out of school during the morning on a visit to Bristol to buy Xmas gifts for the forthcoming party and some sheet music from the Arcade*.

Carol services didn't generally gain a mention until the late '50s, but the logbook entry of 18 December 1958 probably reflected subsequent custom: *an end of term Xmas carol service was held in the main classroom at 11 am today. Parents were invited, and the service was well attended*. The school managers and their chairman would all be there, trying not to look self-conscious on little chairs in the front row. By 1960 there was additionally a morning Combined Schools Carol Service at a suitably large local church, involving the Upper Juniors and the headmaster. That year it was in Keynsham, in other years at Wells Cathedral, Chew Magna or, in 1966, 'Chew Valley School'. That was the first time that the simple term 'Chew Valley School' was used, as opposed to 'Chew Valley Secondary Modern School' or a variation thereof. The children would return late morning to Bishop Sutton for their party in the afternoon.

Logbook entries relating to the 1969 evening carol service in the Village Hall gave an insight into finances: *it was well attended and £4.13s.9d was collected. After payment of £1.5s.0d, the remaining balance of £3.8s.9d was given as a contribution to a charity to help children suffering from mental handicap*. In 1974 the annual service – held in Holy Trinity Church – raised £9.35.

WHAT HAS THE SCHOOL EVER DONE FOR ME?

It was calculated that across the country, only around one in twenty children in the 1920s won their way to secondary education. And in Bishop Sutton there was little tradition of either secondary education or the scholarships to get you there. But expectations were rising and business started demanding qualifications for its office staff. Nevertheless, Bishop Sutton children who were not deemed 'clever' enough or, more commonly, those whose parents didn't have the money or the aspiration to send their children elsewhere, remained at school in the village until they could legally leave. Until 1957, that is, when Chew Valley Secondary Modern School was built, which took the children from the age of 11.

The first notable reference in the logbook to further education was in June 1920 when *Elsie Harris and Lily Daunton passed the exam for scholarships at Secondary School. Two boys and three girls sat at Chew Magna for the Labour Certificate*. This was a basic test of competency – introduced under the Employment of Children Act 1903 – in Reading, Arithmetic and General Knowledge and children needed it in order to get a 'good' job.

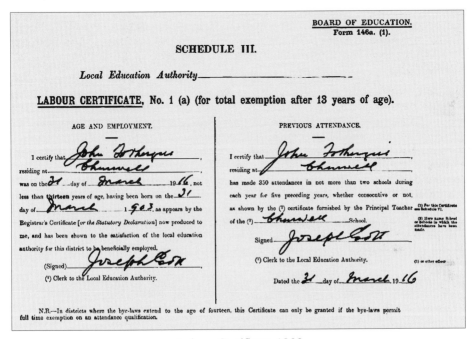

Labour Certificate 1903

In July 1921 Mr Wightman proudly reported that *K. Harvey and A. Peters had gained free scholarships at the Colston Girls' School and F. Hughes to Midsomer Norton Secondary*. Sometimes the Forces played their part: in September 1925 *Sidney Moody obtained a nautical scholarship to the training ship Mercury*[1]. In March 1925 the 'Free Place Examinations' took place at the school and lasted most of the day. One invigilator was village postmaster George Holbrook. In July 1926 *Yvonne Treasure and Millicent Moody passed part II of the Scholarship Exam and are awarded scholarships for Midsomer Norton County School*. In the 1930s, Special Place Examinations generally did away with specific exams set by individual schools. In 1938 *ten children took the Special Place Examination*. In July 1940 *Christine Treasure and Nigel Harvey passed the second part of the Special Place Examination*

----

[1] The Mercury, a barque previously named 'Illova', was built in 1885 by London philanthropist Charles Hoare and was moored at Hamble. It closed in July 1968 after training over 5,000 boys.

and have been awarded places at the Merrywood Secondary School, Bristol[1]. Exams continued during the war years, and in March 1942 Mr Bailey wrote: *Scholarship examination. Ten Somerset candidates, three Bristol and one B'ham set. The Ministry of Information gave a talkie film shown to the children in the afternoon.* Whether that was solace for having sat the exam or to keep the other children quiet is not clear.

The 1944 Education Act raised the leaving age to 15. The intention was that all children in England and Wales would leave primary school at 11, having been selected on the basis of the 11-Plus exam to attend either a grammar school to follow an academic curriculum, or a secondary modern with a practical bias. In the Chew Valley, however, the arrangements were rather different. There were only two all-age schools: Chew Magna (for children from Chew Stoke, Winford, Regil and Dundry primaries) and Bishop Sutton for those from the Harptrees, Compton Martin, Ubley and Blagdon. The Chew Valley was the last area in Somerset to get a new secondary modern.

In July 1945 notification was received that *Roger Harvey, Peter James and Elizabeth Tibbs have passed part 1 of the County Entrance to Secondary Grammar Schools exam.* In September 1946 *all four of the girls (Barbara Weedon, Jennifer Hunt, Gloria Whittingham and Jill Dun) who passed part 1 of the Special Place exams were successful in the 2nd part and have left school.* It wasn't just the secondaries and grammars in the immediate vicinity that appealed to the aspiring child or parent: in September 1947 *John Chidzey who passed part 1 of the Scholarship Exam has now been accepted for the Crewkerne Grammar School.* In February 1952 *John Matthews and Rachael Small were interviewed in the Bristol University Council Chamber in connection with the 13+ review of pupils – their mothers were present at the interviews.* Best frocks for the mums, no doubt. In February 1953 *14 children sat for the exam for allocation to Grammar Schools.* 14 children required five invigilators: Mrs Flower, Miss D. Harvey, The Lord Strachie, the Rev. Dr O'Bealy and Mr Simmonds. They caused logistical problems, these exams: *there was some reorganisation of classes and time tables to allow the candidates to have a room to themselves.*

Mr Bailey was proud to see his scholars succeed. A particular red-letter day was in 1952 when, on 17 September, he wrote a congratulatory letter to Peter James and proudly committed to his logbook: *Peter James, a former pupil of this school, has been awarded a County Scholarship tenable at Bristol University.* On 20 July 1955 he was prouder still: *Peter James has gained a 1st Class Honours BSc degree at Bristol University.*

The headmaster was caring and conscientious and did his utmost to ensure that his pupils did as well as they possibly could. On 26 April 1956 he went *to Keynsham to meet the panel considering my appeal that J.P.[2] be interviewed for the allocation of a Grammar School place.* He heard on 30 April *that the appeal has not been successful.* In June 1960 he was informed *that Margaret Wood had been allocated to Keynsham Grammar School. Neil Paulley had also been allocated a place at the same school but had been accepted at Bristol Grammar School.*

----

[1] Merrywood opened in Knowle West in December 1908, catered for 500 scholars of both sexes, and closed in 2001.

[2] Name abbreviated for sensitivity.

The integrity of exams was (and is) taken very seriously. In 1958 the managers observed that *in consequence of certain exam questions and their answers having been in the newspapers, it was considered necessary for those who had sat for the exam on 28 January to do so again on 18 February*. Bet that went down well.

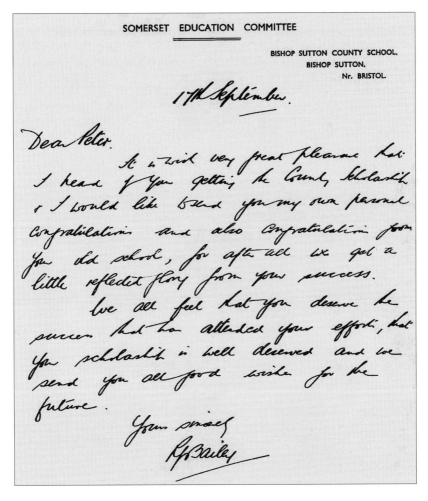

1952 letter of congratulations to Peter James. 'For after all we get a little reflected glory from your successes'.

In January 1942 Sheila Walker sat for the scholarship exam that would enable her to go to grammar school. She couldn't bear the thought of not passing, and on a snowy wartime morning before going to school for the exam she psyched herself up by walking round and round her garden singing 'There'll always be an England'. A few weeks later came the magical day when she arrived at school to be told that she had been successful. Another boy – John – had also passed, and he gave her a lift on the crossbar of his bike back through the village to tell their parents. Sheila's father happened to be home, so both mum and dad were there to hear the good news. They were over the moon, and a few days later she was rewarded with a new bicycle. Sheila went to Merrywood Grammar School in September 1942. Her mother, by then confined to her bed – she passed away shortly afterwards – had given her a half crown for the bus fare and any extras she might have to pay for. She was devastated when the bus conductress made out she had only handed over a florin, so Sheila was immediately robbed of sixpence. When she left Bishop Sutton School, her friend Christine gave her a letter incorporating a drawing of a burning school. Merrywood later suffered from a serious fire.

Ken Rapps recalls the sighs of relief – perhaps not always genuine – if you failed your 11-Plus, as there were far fewer exams at secondary moderns than at grammars. Peter James recalls that in his day, Somerset Council generally wouldn't pay for children to go to a grammar school in Bristol as it was outside their area, so for most of those lucky enough to pass the 11-Plus, it was Wells or Midsomer Norton. Furthermore, the County would only pay for a limited number of siblings in large families to go to grammar school. Children could consequently find themselves in jobs beneath their intellectual capability simply because of the way in which the financial system operated.

Mid-1930s, with Mr Bailey
Back row (left to right): Trevor Lyons, Vernon Tovey, Cyril Noakes, Reg Bass, Jim Harvey, Donald James, Henry Walker.
Third row: James Gay, Don Harris, Jack Tovey, Ted Small, Gordon Ashford, Leslie Harvey, Cyril Chidzey.
Second row: John Kingston, Annie Walker, Betty Dagger, Amy Marsh, Eunice Montgomery, Phyllis Bayley, Phyllis Kingscott, Den Edgell;
Front row: Barbara Cole, Thora Bowditch, Dolly Walker.

It was all well and good – well, wellish and goodish – for those who went on to another educational establishment, but what about those who stayed at Bishop Sutton? What did the school do to prepare them for the day they'd have to leave and earn a living, in so far as there were many choices in an area traditionally based around the farm, the pit, or the family business? It was especially difficult for girls.

Put bluntly, they would marry and have children, society didn't expect married women to work, and any money that the family had spare for education would usually go to clever sons in preference to clever daughters. If the girls were lucky, they were sent to commercial schools where they could learn stimulating things like shorthand and typing and comptometry. Or to Fry's chocolate factory at Keynsham, which paid well and provided transport. Money was always a big draw. And even into the 1930s there were girls who went into domestic service. Exceptionally rare was the girl from the Valley who went to university.

Employment opportunities didn't feature in the logbook until March 1926, when Mr Wightman wrote: *a mixed class of 10 began a course in Daily Work lasting two weeks – one week at the Village Hall and following week at a farm*. In April 1934 the children brought in their three-legged stools for a *Practical Dairying Class at the Memorial Hall, 10 children attending*. Nothing then until July 1946, when Mr Bailey *took a party of 16 senior boys down the Pensford Mine*. And brought all 16 back up again. T'trip down t'pit was then an annual occurrence until May 1956. Colin Symes recalls that boys would be taken in their final year to Bromley colliery, Pensford having already closed. Colin was scared stiff. July 1950 found the senior class *at Messrs Frys at Somerdale to spend 2½ hours going over the factory*. In October 1952 it was only the girls who got the chance to sample the chocolate.

Authorities at national level got in on the act too: in November 1946 *Miss Hartill of the Ministry of National Service called to interview leavers, there was only one lad to be interviewed*. In September 1951 *careers films were shown by the Central Office of Information, operator for the Ministry of National Service*. In March 1949 *Miss Walker of the Ministry of Labour interviewed four leavers today, the fifth was absent*. In October 1951 *Mr Lee of the Ministry of Employment Youth Section gave a careers talk; there are six boys and six girls leaving at Xmas*[1]. In February 1954 *Miss Manners of the Youth Employment Committee interviewed the Easter leavers, four girls and one boy*. After 1957 the challenge of preparing pupils for their first pay packet fell to CVS.

Teresa Dowling recalls that when children left Bishop Sutton School, they were presented with a bible.

HER FATHER AND MOTHER MADE USE OF THE MOST THREATENING LANGUAGE

The past 150 years have seen a major shift in the relationship between children and parents from formality, authoritarianism and distance to informality, libertarianism and hugs. Victorian and Edwardian children referred to their parents as mother and father, which gradually gave way by the 1930s to mum and dad. To school managers and teachers, parents were a double-edged sword. Their help (and, sometimes, influence) were invaluable, and they did have their uses when it came to raising money. They could, however, be a real pain. The logbooks showed both edges of this sword. They also showed that pushy parents storming into school to demand explanations or seek retribution is not a modern phenomenon.

In December 1872 *Alfred Harvey, being kept after school hours to do a sum, was taken out of school by his mother after she had been told it could not be allowed*.

----
[1] You had the right to leave at the end of the term during which you'd reached the school-leaving age.

Who was the village busybody who had Mrs H believe that the headmistress had no right to keep Master H in? Detention was often a sore point. During 23 October 1882, *several kept back for neglect of their lessons, some do not even attempt to do them at all, day after day, and do not try when kept in, saying "their parents will not have them kept in as punishment"*. Parents sometimes disapproved of the lessons, especially those they either didn't understand or didn't see as necessary for a life of farm labouring, servanting or mining. Schooling still cost a penny a week, and parents felt that this gave them the right to demand a say in what was taught. One subject to find particular disapproval was Sums. In January 1873 *the parents of Elizabeth Elmes (Standard II) and Phoebe Treasure (Standard I) have threatened to remove them from the school as they consider the Arithmetic of those Standards too difficult for children of 7 and 8 years of age*. The week beginning 18 March 1878 didn't get off to a good start on the maths front either. Kate Coles' parents had allegedly told her not to do a particular sum. Not any old sum, but £63.13s.5½d divided by 3. For further details of this distasteful saga, you are respectfully referred to the sub-chapter on sparing rods and wetting your pants. On Monday 10 June 1878 – it possibly having taken her that long to get over the ignominy of being made to stand around the classroom for several days – *Kate Coles exhibited another fit of sulkiness for which she received two touches of the cane, neither of which amounted to a blow. In the evening her father and mother came round and made use of the most insulting and threatening language, freely mixed with oaths*. And we've already seen how Mrs Hazel belaboured headmaster Northam in May 1878 on the grounds that sums were messy things that muddled boys' heads.

The next noteworthy incident was noteworthy both for its descriptive qualities and for showing how the headmaster used his logbooks as a personal guide to self improvement. On the morning of Friday 14 June 1878 *Mrs Martin of Hollow Brook came to the school to know why her boy Fred had to "stand on the stool all the morning on Wednesday and hold a slate over his head the whole time", stating that her own children had told her so, and Albert Hyman (10 yr and 4 mo) had told her the same thing this morning. I answered now these children shall tell you what it was, and giving a slate to a 1st class girl, I said now you tell and show Mrs Martin what Fred had to do. She thus became satisfied that all he had to do was to stand on a stool and do some writing. Caution – don't depend on children's tales, and to the children always tell the truth*. In November 1878 in an incident involving Kate Coles (again), Mr Northam reminded himself of his previous caution.

It wasn't just Sums. The headmaster wrote in May 1880 of the opposition of many parents to Geography and Grammar: like sums, they were of little benefit if you were unlikely to have much money, travel further afield than Farrington Gurney, or write a letter. It wasn't only lessons that bothered parents. In April 1874 Mrs Lupp removed Mark Thomas and Walter from school *because Mark had been sent home to have his head cleaned*. In March 1879 Eliza Drury's mother *made a great complaint against the pupil teacher hitting Eliza about the head*. Sometimes – just sometimes – the parents themselves asked for their children to be chastised: On Friday 18 May 1883 Mr Hill *punished Seth Hyman by request of parent for playing the truant on Monday afternoon and Tuesday*. The following week, young Seth was *brought to school by his mother for truanting again this week, viz Monday, Tuesday afternoon and Wednesday. I punished him and he was kept in school all day till 6 pm, his mother sending him dry bread to eat*. That was thoughtful of her. But it didn't work: on Thursday 31 May she dragged Seth back to school again by his ear, *having been absent twice Monday morning truanting*.

On 5 April 1978 *Mrs X[1] called this morning to complain that A (her son) had been refused permission to go to the toilet by a teacher. He was suffering from nerves and was under the doctor. She did not wish him to sit by Maggie Y and could not understand why no-one wanted to play with him. I pointed out that A had only been to school for six days since before Christmas and that the school could not be blamed for his troubles. I told her that he was perfectly happy by Maggie Y. There was no truth in the toilet story.* Perhaps not, but on 11 April *Mrs X called at 9 am to ask if the Education Welfare Officer could call to see her. She said that A was away from school as he was suffering from nerves having been frightened by Maggie Z on his way home from school yesterday.* Perhaps the poor lad just had a thing against girls called Maggie. Almost a year later, *Mr P spoke to me, on behalf of a group of parents, concerning the unclean smelly state in which A came to school. The children in his class had complained to their parents.* Boy A was subsequently given a place elsewhere.

Joan Davidge remembers combing a boy's hair before a school panto. His mother came in to complain that Joan had interfered with him. Sheila Walker (a pupil from 1936 to 1942) reflects that 'every child walked to school. The children from Stowey walked a mile each way, and the children from Knowle Hill two miles each way. I cannot remember any mother ever taking a child to school. School was considered to be the teacher's domain, and there was certainly no parent-teacher consultation'.

Parents mean Open Days. The first one may have been in March 1934: *Some 30 parents attended. Talks on the health of children and the work of Bath Advisory Committee for Juvenile Employment were given by Miss Lamb and Miss Bridle.* It's not clear whether that was the start of a trend to allow parents across the hallowed threshold, but it wasn't mentioned again until 1952 when, on 23 July, *all parents were invited to come to the school, quite a number of them came along and as a result our Open Day was very satisfactory.* On 31 July 1954 *normal work was carried on except that needlework, woodwork and paint work articles were on display. Nearly 100 parents took the opportunity to come along and talk with the teachers. 32 lb of jam was made in the DS Centre from fruit from the school garden. This was sold to children at cost price.* Jam quickly lost its appeal, and in 1956 *a number of puppet shows, an infant play and a physical training display by the senior girls* were used as an inducement. By 1959 the school was open in the evenings as well as during the day. This proved so popular that in 1960 times had to be restricted to 2.30 to 4, and 7 to 8. By 1978 the usual routine was an afternoon or evening at the school, with a concert by the infants and a Country Dance Display by the juniors.

On 15 December 1967 the managers *recorded that a PTA had been formed.* Whilst this may initially have been viewed with some scepticism, both managers and teachers very quickly came to rely on the Parent Teacher Association as a source of support, funds and publicity. A pattern for ensuing years was set in September 1969 when *the PTA opened their season* (which makes it sound like a debutantes' ball) *at 8 pm with a wine and cheese party. It was reasonably well attended.* In other words, there was something good on the box that night. By June 1972 fundraising was in full gear: the PTA raised £90 at the July School Fête and by December they had contributed enough to buy the school three television sets. In April 1973 they donated a cassette recorder, in April 1978 a video recorder and, in July of the following year, a duplicating machine. PTA fundraising didn't just introduce technical

----
[1] All the names and initials in this paragraph have been changed.

gizmos to the school, but also different experiences for the children. In November 1974 *a talk and film show was given by Mr Edwards of The Royal Mission to Deep Sea Fishermen. It was very well worth while. A play was performed in the main classroom for the whole school in the afternoon. It was called 'Miss Jones and the Magic Journey' and was performed by Avon Theatre Group. All expenses were paid for by the PTA.* The PTA's involvement with the swimming pool is highlighted elsewhere.

And finally on the parent-related front: the man with the big camera was an annual visitor to the school from the 1890s and yet, amazingly, the only reference in the logbook was as recently as November 1976 when *the school photographer visited the school during the morning.* Parents, grandparents and doting aunties and uncles love cluttering the mantelpiece with photos of the younger members of their family. One day they will learn, for the benefit of future historians, how useful it is if they write a date on the back.

1971
Back row (left to right): Mr Price, Teresa Wookey, Rosalind Harvey, Rose Mary Veale,
Joanna Phippen, Gary Beams, Mark Fryer, ? Flower, Wayne Compton;
Second row: Beverly Penny, Teresa Heron, Alison Harvey, Katy Gibbons, Susan Small,
Carl Gerrick, Gerry Oakley, John Reynolds, Robert Veale;
Front row: Yvonne Tovey, Katherine Owen, Caroline Stevens, Ross Tibbles,
Stuart Harvey, ?, Sue Roper, Karen Woodward, Sarah Wookey, Deborah David.

THE SCHOOL REOPENS ON JANUARY 6TH
AS A TRUE PRIMARY SCHOOL

Chew Valley School celebrated its 50th anniversary in 2008. Bishop Sutton School is part of that history. Plans had been drawn up many years before but had to be shelved during the war, and it wasn't until 1956 that construction eventually began. Mr J. C. Wright was appointed headmaster in November 1957, and the doors opened for 292 pupils – 'students' was a much later term – at the beginning of the

1958 January term, with the official ceremony on 23 March 1958. The proposed name was to have been Chew Magna School until it was pointed out that most of the site was in the parish of Chew Stoke. 'Chew Valley' seemed a tactful compromise.

Chew Valley School shortly after opening in 1958

CVS itself believes that the year of its conception was 1939 when the site was acquired, but we may know better. The entry of 20 February 1931 in Chew Magna PC minute book: *a letter was received from the Somerset County Council stating that it was proposed to erect a Senior Elementary School for the parishes of Chew Magna, Chew Stoke and Winford at Chew Magna to accommodate some 240 senior scholars*. A February 1935 HMI report for Bishop Sutton had stated: *It will be a good thing when the Seniors (almost 50) can be transferred elsewhere*. On 1 September 1938 the PC discussed *the senior school site* [and decided] *that no action be taken by this Council to obtain the necessary signatures in protest to the erection of the New School. If no objection is received from any ratepayer by Oct. 1st, then the Parish Council would then write and protest to the 'Educational Authorities' their objection, not to the school, but to the proposed site*. There was no mention of where the proposed site was, but as the present site was bought in 1939, we're probably looking at the same place.

Back to the PC minutes, this time for the newly formed joint parish of Stowey Sutton: in December 1953 *a letter from the East Harptree PC was read by the Chairman. The clerk was instructed to* [state that] *the Parish Council are agreed in principle that the building of a new Secondary Modern School is long overdue, but we wish to emphasise that this statement is not to be taken as a criticism of the existing schools in this area*. There seemed no pressing desire on the part of local PCs to see their primary schools reduced in size by the transfer of senior children elsewhere. In July 1955 a letter from the CEO prompted the Bishop Sutton managers to worry *that difficulties might arise at the school if the 11-year old children in all the contributory schools who were allocated to the Secondary Modern school are transferred in the normal way to Bishop Sutton. Having regard to the circumstances, it was decided that, subject to the concurrence of the Ubley and East Harptree schools, the children of 11 to 12 yrs of age should be retained in those schools for the time being*. Stowey Sutton PC received formal notification in August 1955 of *the proposals of the County Council to erect a school at Chew Magna*. The notification was simply *read out for information*, the time for objections or further consideration having passed.

Bishop Sutton School was to change for ever, and thoughts turned to logistics. In January 1957, a representative *from the County office called to list the furniture etc that will go to the New School when it is ready*. Bishop Sutton was about to lose some kit. With the day fast approaching, with children apprehensive about being the first generation to leave the village en masse, and with parents bothered about the cost of the uniform, *Mr Wright, the Head of the new Secondary Modern School at Chew Magna addressed a meeting of parents here at the school this evening* (14 November 1957); *the meeting was quite well attended*.

And thus came to an end the first long chapter in the history of Bishop Sutton School. On Friday 20 December 1957 Mr Bailey wrote in his logbook for the last time. The headmaster of Bishop Sutton Primary School wasn't available for the new term, and it was down to supply head Mr J. J. Painting to write the logbook entry on 6 January 1958. Mr Price arrived at the end of the Easter term.

Before ten years had elapsed, more changes were mooted. In December 1965 Mr Price *attended a conference at which it was stated that by 1971 there would be three comprehensive schools at Keynsham*. That came to nothing, but in March 1968 he *told the managers that Chew Valley School should be comprehensive by September, and that the school children would automatically go there unless it was especially asked for by a parent for the child to go elsewhere*. CVS had opened as a secondary modern for those who had failed their 11-Plus, but was now to become a Comprehensive for everyone.

Last logbook entry as an 'all age' school, and the first as a primary school

CHAPTER SIX

ADMINISTRATION, INSPECTIONS, TRANSPORT AND SCHOOL DINNERS

WE NEED TWO BIG SAFE BOXES

The 1870 Education Act introduced the concept of locally elected School Boards, and that's our starting point. We know virtually nothing about the management of the school at Bishop Sutton for the first 30 years of its existence, but there would doubtless have been a body of men representing the vicar and churchwardens of Chew Magna, in whose name the school was vested.

The Board decided the overall direction of the school, and its members would visit periodically to check the register and generally make sure the headteacher wasn't stepping out of line. Until the 1950s, they were painstaking in their reporting of the topics discussed at their regular meetings.

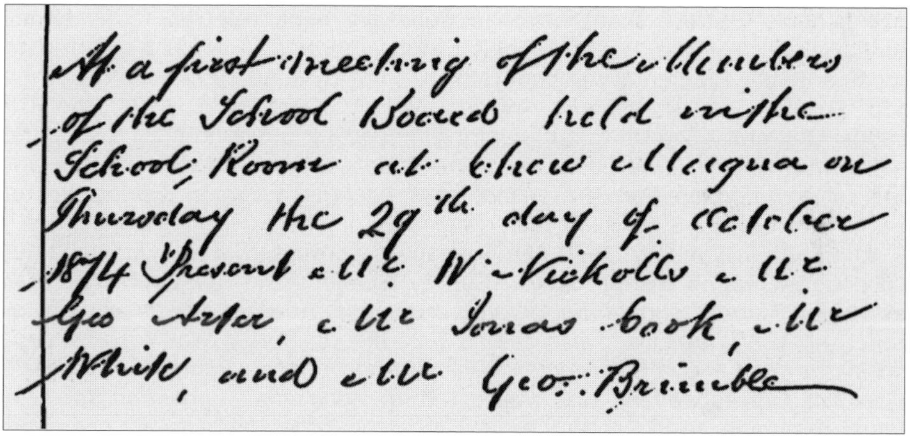

At a first meeting of the Members of the School Board held in the School Room at Chew Magna on Thursday the 29th day of October 1874 Present Mr W Nicholls Mr Geo Arter, Mr Jonas Cook, Mr White, and Mr Geo: Brimble

The opening entry of the School Board's 1874 minute book

The entry illustrated above went on to say: *proposed and carried unanimously that the Public and the Press be excluded from the meetings*. Although that decision was rescinded in November 1881, only rarely were Mr and Mrs Public present, and then only by invitation or command. Straightaway the Board advertised in the Bristol Times and Mirror, The Press and The Post for a clerk at £20 p.a. They needed someone reliable and had to advertise three times before they gave the job to Mr W. White. Most meetings were held at the School Room at Chew Magna, although some were at Mr Cook's house at The Elms, Sutton Hill Road; the 1871 census listed Mr Cook (56) as 'manager of colliery' and living with his wife Eliza (46) and their children Joseph (22), Eliza (sic) (20), Lamborne (12), James (13) and India (10).

The clerk would write innumerable letters on the Board's behalf, all messily – and often illegibly – copied onto very flimsy numbered sheets in the School Board Letters Books, first using the letterpress process[1] and then, by 1886, carbon paper. Six thick volumes spanned the years 1874 to 1926. A few intervening ones (and any subsequent ones) are missing. The Minute Books of the meetings of the Board (and the subsequent school managers and governors) cover the period 1874[2] to 1929 and from 1948 to 1975. Any from 1930 to 1947 have disappeared. I have not read those from 1976 onwards.

Having got cracking in the early 1870s, it wasn't long before the managers were up to their knees in paperwork, and in February 1878 they decided to procure:

Two safe boxes into which were put: Education Acts and manuals thereto, Census of children, Letter Book, Minute Book, Petty Cash Book, Cash Book, Ledger, Postage Book, Abstract Book, register of mortgages, insurance policies, blank notices of meetings of the Board, note paper, envelopes, foolscap paper, blotting paper, receipts, Copy Trust Deed for Bishop Sutton School, Poor Book records, various deeds and documents.

Two gert big safe boxes, then.

The Education Act 1902 had abolished Boards in favour of statutory Local Education Authorities and School Councils. An early decision locally was that the 'Chew Magna and Bishop Sutton Elementary Schools' should be rechristened the 'Chew Magna Council Schools'. Before then they had generally been referred to as either the 'National Schools' or the 'Board Schools'. Kelly's Directory of 1923 referred to our school as a 'Public Elementary School (Mixed)', but by June 1932 preferred the term 'Bishop Sutton Council School'. Incidentally, in September 1931 the County Education Secretary wrote to an aspiring applicant for a job at Bishop Sutton School: *I have to state that under the Committee's scheme for the reorganisation of schools, it is proposed that the school shall become a Junior School.* No further reference can be found to this radical suggestion. There was a bizarre spell from 1949 to 1958: in January 1949 the managers spotted that the official title was actually 'Chew Magna Bishop Sutton County School'. The managers *felt that the words 'Chew Magna' should be deleted from the title as it was confusing and answered no useful purpose, also seeing that Bishop Sutton was to be a separate parish in the near future[3], it would be more appropriate without the words 'Chew Magna'.* The correspondent *was instructed to send the suggestion to Taunton.* Someone remembered in September 1952 that no letter had actually been sent, so the managers' secretary was told to sharpen his pencil and be quick about it. There were further bouts of amnesia, and the matter wasn't mentioned again until December 1958 when *the Ministry of Education agreed*. Chew Magna Bishop Sutton County School was no more.

Back to the minute books. They contained, inter alia, turgid details of triennial elections for the members of the Board. Worthy gentlemen of the community – it would be many a long year before ladies were invited to take part – came and went;

----
[1] A dampened sheet of thin semi-transparent tissue paper was laid against the inked side of the original document and then placed in a handpress. The two sheets were squeezed together, producing a mirror image of the original text on the tissue, which was then glued, back to front, into the Copy Letters Book.

[2] The Board had been established a year or two earlier.

[3] Stowey Sutton Parish Council was formed in 1949.

Mr Lovell was invariably included, as were assorted Lords Strachey / Strachie[1] and, of course, the vicar. In the 1970s, the Education Authorities replaced the term 'school managers' with 'governors', although it was years before it caught on.

Dissent in 1928: Mr Wyatt resigns from the 'so-called School Managers' as they 'are treated as school children by a certain body which is above them and who get a decent salary for their work .... What is the use of myself arriving in all weathers a distance of three miles'?

Although businesslike and formal in a starchy Victorian wing-collar sort of a way, the managers did have their human side: in January 1882 they *resolved unanimously that the Board, at its first meeting after the sudden death of Mrs Arter, desires to sympathise most kindly with the Treasurer* (Mr Arter) *under his bereavement.* Being

----
[1] On 21 July 1967 after many years of loyal, friendly and well-connected service as secretary and sometime chairman, *The Lord Strachie told the meeting of his intention to resign in favour of a younger person.* He was 85.

pillars of the community, the members were sometimes asked to become involved in matters only peripherally affecting the school. In August 1883 they agreed *that the Petition for Sunday closing of Public Houses now presented be signed by the Chairman on behalf of the Board*. A similar request arose in March 1885 with *an application from the Central Association for Stopping the Sale of Intoxicating Liquors on Sunday,* [which] *requested the Board to sign a petition to Parliament*. Ten years later, in May 1894, the business in hand again turned to alcohol. It was *proposed by Mr Collins and seconded by Mr H. Strachey that the Board disapproved of the headmaster Mr Stampe* (of Chew Magna School) *continuing to hold the office of Traveller to a Brewery and Spirit business, and request him to consider whether he ought not in deference to their wishes resign the said office*. Mr Stampe was subsequently persuaded to do so although, as he moaned in a letter to the Board, *it means a loss of income which I can ill afford*. The Board was not sympathetic.

Minute book entries steadily became shorter. They had been meticulously handwritten until 1949. From then until 1969, separate sheets of paper were meticulously and neatly typed – with no mistakes – and glued into the book. From 1970, sheets littered with typos and misspelt words were simply stuck in, using sellotape of less-than-archival quality.

One gubernatorial responsibility was to interview prospective teachers, many of whom no doubt found it a scary experience. The records rarely saw things from the candidates' point of view, so thank you for the recollections of Cynthia Holman, who was taken on as school secretary in 1978. The governors sat in horseshoe fashion, with her on a chair in the middle. She reckons she only got the job as she was good with figures. The process was probably no less daunting a generation earlier: the managers noted in March 1953 that *a communication had been received from the CEO suggesting that his inspectors should interview students at training colleges and make appointments to fill vacancies. This would enable schools to receive teachers with the highest teaching marks, and was a better way than by advertisement and interview. The managers agreed to this procedure*. The idea then fell into abeyance, to be resurrected in 1974 when the governors objected.

So that was the local management. What about the more distant county-level management? And distant it was too: former teachers and administrators have commented that Taunton rarely bothered much with the northernmost reaches of their Somerset empire, and local managers and headteachers were left much to their own devices.

In July 1903, Mr Wightman wrote: *the school today comes under the control of the Somerset Education Committee*. On 1 April 1974 Mr Price wrote: *today the school ceased to be under the control of the Somerset Local Education Authority and entered the county of Avon as provided by the Local Government Act. The school will, in future, be administered by the newly created Avon LEA which has its main offices in Bristol*. His opinions were not recorded, but it's fair to say that most local people were unenthusiastic. Bishop Sutton would fall within the Wansdyke[1] division of the new county.

----
[1] The original Wansdyke had been a system of defences constructed by Southerners in 400 AD to keep the Northern riff-raff out. It stretched from Savernake Forest (near Marlborough) to Maes Knoll (near Norton Malreward), and possibly on to Portishead. Parts of it can still be seen near Stanton Prior. The name is thought to derive from Woden, who moonlighted as God of Tribal Boundaries alongside his day job as Scandinavian God of War. The logo on Wansdyke Council's vehicles was meant to represent the earthwork.

The hands-off approach generally adopted by far-off Taunton found no favour with nearby Bristol, and the new county wasted no time in coming up with new ideas which didn't always go down well locally. In July 1974 the governors *read letters received from Saltford Primary School re correspondence to managers and appointment of head teachers. Mr Price is supposed to service the meetings instead of the correspondent. The managers were all of the opinion that they would rather keep the old way of interviewing staff and not the new way of Education Committee just sending staff, they were also afraid of losing the local touch.* In other words, the headmaster was expected to take the minutes rather than the secretary, and Avon would simply send new teachers along, thus avoiding the risk of local governors employing someone not to the county's liking. The governors didn't concur. And, of course, there was the inevitable new stationery: in July 1975 Mr Price was *away from school during the afternoon to attend a conference at Clutton School to discuss with a Treasury Department official the various forms which are to be brought into use.* He probably just couldn't wait to get home to his wife Mair's bara brith.

'The Square', Bishop Sutton, 1950s

I'M NOT PAYING FOR HALF A WEEK'S SCHOOLING

When the school was built in 1842, the application form for a National Society grant referred to overheads being met by subscriptions from three or four individuals amounting to some £25 a year. The managers decided in 1873 to continue to conduct Chew Magna and Bishop Sutton Schools under the voluntary principle rather than under the School Board system and compulsory rate. That decision was rescinded in 1875 and the Board resolved to accept money from the rates and government grants. From then until the very early years of the 20th century, the school derived its income – apart from relatively trifling sums raised from the sale of goods – from four main sources: fees (nicknamed 'school pence'), grants, the Poor Laws, and local charities.

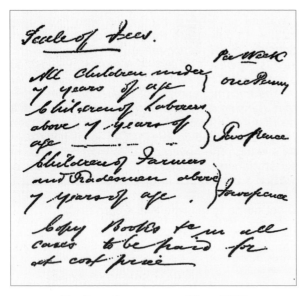

The Board's summary of fees 1875

Taking school pence first. The Rev. Ommaney's 1842 application had stated that the weekly fee would be 1d per child. The 1870 Education Act had empowered School Boards to charge a weekly fee not exceeding 9d and to pay the fees of the poorest children. It's therefore reasonable to assume that fees were much the same at Bishop Sutton pre-Act as post-Act. One of the local Board's earliest decisions, in July 1875, was *that the following scale of fees for Bishop Sutton School be adopted, viz all children under 7 years of age 1d per week, children of farmers and tradesmen above that age 4d per week, and children of labourers above that age 2d per week, and the copy books etc in all cases to be paid for at cost price.*

The school records brought home not only how difficult it could be in a village where money was hard to come by, but also how much administrative work was involved for the head. No Excel spreadsheets in those days. 7 February 1876: *received 8/- from Mr George Ferris for school fees due 25 December 1875.* 2 June 1876: *received this week the sum of 8s.2d from Mr George Ferris, being the school fees for the past three months for his children.* 16 October 1876: *received from Mr Arter 1s.4d for school fees for F. Cousins.* These people paid on an as-and-when basis and could be trusted to do so. The majority would have paid weekly or even daily, meaning that the headteacher had tottering piles of copper and silver to count, safeguard and hand over to the School Board. In September 1876, for instance, the clerk wrote: *Please let me know <u>at once</u> the amount of your school fee and for books &c for quarter ending 29th instant, and as soon as you can, pay the money to Mr Arter* (the Board chairman). January 1877: *paid to the treasurer £5.16s.7d for school fees taken during past quarter, and 2s.3d for books etc.*

The rules regarding payment of school fees weren't applied as rigidly as one might expect, given the Victorian ethos of paying your own way in life. The Board would sometimes soften a bit in the face of parents' pleas: in February 1882 *Mrs Burridge of Bishop Sutton attended, and the Board decided to remit the school fees for her children named Susan and Henry, ditto Mrs Jones for her children Margaret and Charles.* Sometimes the Board would soften a lot: in March 1888 it was agreed *that the school fees for Mark Filer's children be remitted for a month and that the missing school fees be forgiven.* In May 1890, *agreed that as Mark Barwell of Bishop Sutton is suffering from the effects of an accident to his eyesight, the school fees for the following children under his care be remitted for one month from the present date, viz Ernest, Herbert, Edwin and Arthur Radford.* In June 1890 the Board deferred *the arrears of school fees of Mark Filer's children on the understanding that they attend regularly in future and that their school fees are regularly paid.* They didn't and they weren't. Letters from the Board had been dropping onto the doormats of errant parents for some months, as illustrated below.

It was potentially risky to entrust shiny school-pence pennies to youngsters: in August 1882 headmaster Hill *punished several children for spending their school money before coming to school*. And parents could be uncooperative. On that same day *Mrs Dix complained of her girl Elizabeth being sent home for her school fees since children were dismissed, declaring that "she was not going to pay for half a week's schooling"*. But then along came the Assisted Education Act 1891 that put paid to it all. The Board unanimously resolved that *on and after 1 September 1891 [it] agrees to the acceptance of the Fee Grant of 10/- a year for each child over 3 and under 15 years of age in average attendance with the conditions of the Elementary Education Act 1891 re fees, and that the Board Schools of Chew Magna and Bishop Sutton be free, also that no charge be made for books and stationery on and after 1.9.91*. Mr Brown wrote in his logbook: *at a special meeting of the Board, free education was adopted on and after September 1st. Books are also to be supplied gratis in future*. The impact was immediate and considerable. Within a week, the headmaster was reporting: *average attendance 74.2. NO school fees have been collected this week, and the percentage of attendance has improved*. (The capital letters are Mr Brown's.) Attendance improved by some 10%. School pence had gone. The school's sole outside income was now from grants and from monies still being paid by the Guardians of the Poor or by charities.

February 4th 90.

Sir,
I am directed to inform you, that the Board decline to remit the School Fees of your Children attending the Bishop Sutton School. All arrears of School Fees must be paid.

Yours faithly.
W. E. Multon

Mr Harvey

1890: Dear Mr Harvey, You must pay your children's school fees.

Grants were paid on a payment-by-results basis from 1862 under the Government's notorious Revised Code. There was an annual exam in the three Rs, and schools had to achieve satisfactory levels of average attendance. Religious Instruction was obligatory, although it didn't earn any financial reward. Girls had to learn Needlework. From 1867 additional specific grants were offered for English Grammar, Geography and History. From 1875, grants were earned by the proficiency of the whole group rather than of individual pupils. By way of recompense for the abolition of school pence, the 1891 Act introduced government grants based on the school roll.

Chew Magna School Board.
Bishop Sutton School.

SCHOOL FEES ACCOUNT.

Local records incorporated few specific breakdowns of the capitation grant other than the ten shillings per child per year in 1891 mentioned above, but the school's Cash Book – unfortunately only one has survived, covering a very short period –

gave a brief indication of how the school had been funded in earlier times. For the school year 1876-77, the grant was £48.1s.0d and school fees £24.10s.1d. The figures for 1877-78 were £52.5s.0d and £26.1s.1d, for 1878-79 £42.17s.8d and £27.13s.0d, and for 1879-80 £56.16s.0d and £32.17s.9d. Whether or not the Board decided to charge full school pence was irrelevant as far as the grant was concerned. Chew Stoke School's logbook referred in 1897 to a Government grant of 15/- per year per infant and £1.0s.6d for the older children.

A letter from October 1875 from the Board's clerk to its chairman Mr Geo. Arter sheds some light on how the grant was physically paid: *I have a cheque for the grant for the Bishop Sutton School but as it is in peculiar form and requires some filling in, I retain it until I see you.* By peculiar, he meant 'specific', rather than 'strange'. Payment-by-Results grants were finally abolished in 1904 to be replaced by straightforward capitation.

The cash records[1] were treated very seriously indeed. In February 1876 Mr Jones wrote: *the school was closed yesterday as I had to go to the Clutton Union to attend*

'Award of Merit for Attendance' (not Bishop Sutton)

at the auditing of the books of the School Board. Sums involved were often large, and it was no longer considered wise to have so much cash lying around. In September 1891 the Board *resolved that the payment of accounts by the cheque system in accordance with the instructions of the Education Department be adopted and that Alfred Deedes of Messrs Stuckeys Banking Company Bristol[2] be appointed treasurer and that the clerk be instructed to obtain cheque book containing 500 forms.* A thick cheque book!

The third element in the equation in the early days was monies from the Poor Law fund. The historic relationship between schools and the Guardians of the Poor was evidenced by the printed preface in the school's Cash Book of 1876: *Order of the Poor Law Board dated July 6 1871.* For those interested in such things, the book was published by *Shaw and Sons, Fetters Lane, London, Printers and Publishers of the Books and Forms of the Local Government Board, Factory Inspectors, Commissioners in Lunacy, County Courts, Friendly Societies, Savings Banks &c.* With all those customers, they must have made a good profit, must Shaw and Sons. Now based in Kent, they have been publishers, printers and stationers since 1750, currently supplying office stationery, legal forms and forms on disk. They weren't supplying forms on disk in 1876.

In September 1875 headmaster Jones *received from Mr J. Cook, one of the School Board members, the sum of 8s.8d on account of children paid for by the Poor Law*

----

[1] Purely for the record: the school had been numbered 12731 in the Ministry's books in 1872. The managers were advised in December 1958 that the official Ministry of Education number for the school was to be 2004. Somerset County Education Authority Treasurer's accounting number for the school was 22. Enthralling stuff.

[2] Stuckey's – a West Country bank – amalgamated with Parr's Bank in 1909, which amalgamated with London County & Westminster Bank in 1918, which became the Westminster Bank in 1923, which merged with the National Provincial Bank in 1969 to become the National Westminster Bank, which shed most of its letters to become the NatWest, and was acquired by the Royal Bank of Scotland in 2000.

Guardians. In November of that year Relieving Officer Mr Pike gave the Board 7s.10d *on account of children paid for by the Clutton Union*. It was the Relieving officer who implemented the Poor Law system; he would visit homes, assess the level of need and liaise with the authorities. In connection with the children of pauper families *brought into the school by the School Attendance Officer*, the Board directed headmaster Northam in May 1879 *to refuse them admittance and notify the same to the School Attendance Officer so that he may see the parents and instruct them to apply to the Board of Guardians for payment of the fees*. Charity didn't necessarily begin at school, it began at the offices of the Board of Guardians under the Poor Relief schemes. There would have been a sense of shame for most children whose parents couldn't afford to pay. For a few it would have been an excuse to wander the streets. In May 1879 *several children were sent home this morning for non payment of fees*. In April 1880, *sent back Julia and Fred Martin, Susan and Henry Burridge, Charles and Jessie Veale for non-payment of fees*. Just to add a touch of authority to the sending back, Mr Northam added: *according to order of the School Board*. In April 1881 *many children absent through not having made application to Guardians for payment for school fees*. The Board noted in February 1888 that with *Arthur Peters, James Edgell, Ernest Harvey, Edward Harvey and Jeremiah Harvey being paupers, the Clutton Board of Guardians will be asked to pay their school fees*.

In November 1876 the headmaster helpfully explained where the Poor Law money actually came from: a sum of 11s.2d *from Mr Pike on account of the children's fees was paid out of the rates*. Like all things council, things could go wrong. In July 1893 the Board resolved that *in consequence of there being no funds out of which to pay officers' and teachers' salaries due on 24th inst., the clerk be instructed to write to the Overseers of the Parish of Chew Magna requiring immediate payment of the balance of the precept due on 21 March last and the whole of the precept due on 10 January, or legal proceedings will be at once taken to enforce payment*. The overseers eventually coughed up: by the time the councillors met in September 1893 they had received *precept due 21 March £20 and precept due 24 June £70*.

From Bishop Sutton's 'School Fees Account' book 1889

Before moving on, it's worth looking briefly at the more general situation of those with no money. In the 1800s very poor families could apply to the parish for outdoor relief, being financial assistance to paupers living in their own homes. When assessing need, the Boards of Guardians (a group of local ratepayers who administered the workhouse and dealt with financial affairs) expected children regarded as being of working age to find a job before aid was given to their parents. Many orphans were put into workhouses, where they posed a particular challenge to the guardians, who didn't want them to become a long-term burden on the ratepayers or fall under the influence of unsavoury inmates. And that's not to say that the overseers themselves were always savoury. One solution was to segregate the orphans from the older workhouse population and provide a teacher. Another, much cheaper, solution was to send the little blighters out to work. Many girls thus became household servants working for little more than room and board for families who couldn't afford more professional help. Although few youngsters from workhouses ever managed to obtain positions leading to better jobs, some children were sent to ordinary schools, as may routinely have been the case at Bishop Sutton. It was these children whose fees were paid by the Poor Law Guardians.

August 1882: school's logbook entry of monies received

The Poor Law Amendment Act of 1834 had grouped together all the parishes in the district into a Poor Law Union with one centralised purpose-built workhouse. The Act abolished out-relief (or outdoor relief) for the able-bodied. Clutton Union Workhouse (which covered Bishop Sutton) was built in 1837 and incorporated an infirmary and school. It was renamed 'Cambrook House Institution' in 1919. The 1891 census revealed 144 inmates and five staff. An inspector's report in 1909 stated that there were beds for 172 inmates and that all were occupied. The residents were a motley crew: short-termers who were destitute as a result of being out of work through sickness or injury or lay-off, unmarried mothers, the feeble-minded and those too old to work. The workhouse also provided food and temporary accommodation for vagrants and itinerants, of which no fewer than 545 passed through the doors in the first six months of 1913. By the end of the Great War, some German prisoners of war were living in the workhouse and working in the gardens.

The workhouse was obliged to keep registers of births and deaths. There was no cemetery and the dead were usually taken for burial to the parish to which they belonged. A Workhouse Master's Report and Journal entry for June 1842 stated that *the Committee are of opinion that it is not necessary to have a hearse to take Martha Ford's child to High Littleton Church, it being only about 5 weeks old and could be carried by a woman*. The Guardians eventually relented and allowed the body *to be taken by two women*. Place of birth was not listed in the register, so it's not certain who were Bishop Sutton people, but local surnames from The Medical Officer's Record of Examination of Children (Clutton Union 1914-17) included *Jonas Filer, aged 7, good health except nasal catarrh, 53 lb; Evelyn Filer, aged 6, improving, 45 lb, abdomen enlarged, to see dentist*. Presumably not to have the enlarged abdomen treated.

From the Clutton Poor House register

Nothing to do with Bishop Sutton School, but nevertheless fascinating in a ghoulish sort of a way, were the workhouse conditions as per the following random entries from the 'Workhouse Punishment Book, Clutton Union 1851-1898': *John Chiswell, William Nash, Frederick Giles for not breaking 3 bushels* (about 5 cubic yards) *of stone each from 1 till 6 pm, no cheese for supper; John Chiswell for using obscene language, locked him up 8 hours on bread and water; Ruth Sage insulting the matron, locked up from ½ past 6 pm to 6 next morning; Ruth Sage not picking 1½ lb of okum[1] in 5 hours, no bacon for dinner; Caroline Cox and Charlotte James*

----

[1] Okum – usually spelt 'oakum' – was the loose fibre obtained from unravelling old rope, and was often used for sealing the joins between planks on sailing ships. It was often impractical to provide work that was genuinely useful, so by the 1850s – and long after the use of iron in the building of ships had made oakum almost unsaleable – prison and workhouse inmates were frequently kept occupied in pointless tasks. Hence the expression 'money for old rope'.

*for sleeping during divine service, no cheese for dinner; Sarah Minty, acting
indecently, no cheese for dinner; Caroline Davis, Martha Dury, stealing potatoes and
cooking them in a bowl in the laundry, locked up for 3 hours*[1].

Responsibility for Poor Law Unions rested with the Poor Law Commission until 1847,
when it was succeeded by the Poor Law Board. In 1871 the Local Government Board
assumed control and in 1919 the Ministry of Health took over. The last meeting of
the local guardians was in March 1930, three days before the nationwide dissolution
of all 643 Poor Law Unions. The Frome Area Guardians Committee then took over
locally under the control of Somerset County Council. The facility finally shut its
doors in June 1967.

Closely connected with the Poor Laws, although largely without their stigma, were
the charities, from which local children could, did and do benefit. The key ones
relevant to Bishop Sutton were the Tegg Charity, the Richard Jones Charity and the
Bread Charity. Several others, including the Selby Charity – in 1772 *James Selby
gent of Bristol gave £100 to the vicar and churchwardens of Chew Magna parish, the
interest to be distributed yearly amongst the poor of Bishop Sutton tything* – had
lapsed over the years or been incorporated into others. Some are still in existence.
In most instances, 'Chew Magna' includes Bishop Sutton. The following gives a
flavour:

In 1684 John Tegg of Stowey bequeathed his two paddocks at Moreton, once two
successors had died, *for the education of the poor children of Chew Magna, for ever;
to be disposed of by Mr John Atheale and Mr Thomas Sherborne*, both of Bishop
Sutton. In 1875 the income fell to the School Board to administer, and the rental
monies came to Bishop Sutton School. By 1922 the half acre of land involved was
bringing in £15 a year. John Tegg of Stowey may have discussed his affairs with
Richard Jones, also of Stowey, for when the latter died in the late 1680s, his
trustees spent £1,600 on an estate near Langport and £400 on houses in Newton
St Loe and Stanton Drew, the net rental monies for which were to be used, inter
alia, for the relief of the poor in Stowey and Chew Magna. Kelly's Directories of the
early 1900s explained that the Jones Charity monies were distributed at the
discretion of the owner of Stowey House.

The Bread Charity dates from the death in 1804 of William Abraham, who
bequeathed *£100 5% stock, the dividends arising from the said stock … every year
for ever, to pay the same to the vicar and churchwardens to be laid out in bread and
given to the second poor* (of Chew Magna). The 'second poor' were those who didn't
qualify for Poor House relief. In April 1951 the Charity's income was £18.4s.9d
against expenditure of £5.6s.6d at Montgomery's bakers in Bishop Sutton. By 1956
the balance in hand was £11.9s.3½d, and bread tickets were still being distributed.
In 1963 the idea was mooted of broadening the terms so that financial help could be
awarded to any needy parishioner. There was no enthusiasm and it was re-
confirmed in 1971 that the Charity was restricted to giving out bread, restrictive
though that had become. In 1974 no distribution was made *because of the high cost
of bread*, despite a balance of £50.33. The Charity was eventually wound up in 1988
and amalgamated with other local charities to become the Chew Magna Combined
Charity.

It wasn't just charity in, but also charity out. Local children were generous to those
less fortunate than themselves. The managers proudly noted in March 1960 that *the
pupils had amongst themselves raised £9.13s.2d for Barnardo's Homes, £9 from*

----
[1] The examples are actually from 1851 to 1859, entries thereafter being few and far between.

Job-a-Bob[1] (sic) and £1.16s.0d by a concert staged entirely by themselves. On 5 February 1976 representatives of the news media, i.e. Evening Post, HTV and Radio Bristol, called at school during the day in connection with the painted cards to be painted by the children for issue to members of the Silver Lining Club and others, to display in their windows should they be in need of assistance because of illness or other incapacity. The matters were announced in the press, radio and t.v. subsequently. Bishop Sutton pupils became regular guests of the elderly: in July 1977 they entertained the Silver Lining Club at the Village Hall and on 14 December 1978 the Upper Juniors gave a Christmas Concert to the Silver Lining Club this evening.

From the school's Statement of Account 1902

Back to money in and money out. Details of income and expenditure were haphazardly available from the Bishop Sutton Board School Estimate of Expenditure on Maintenance for 1902 and 1903. This, for example: *Received: annual grant £112.12d.0d, fee grant £56.12s.6d, Teggs Charity £11, rates £320.4s.6d. Outgoings: salaries – Wightman (with School House) £100, Gertrude Adelaide Stevens £50, Ellen Frances Bowles £35, Edith Mabel Carpenter PT £15.12s.0d, Dora Annie Bendall monitress £3.18s.0d – books and stationery £13.16s.10d, apparatus and furniture £14.4s.6d, repairs £258.4s.3d, rent £4.13s.10d.* One annual expense was insurance: much later than the above period, but in November 1953 the managers took out *a policy of insurance to cover them against death, bodily injury to persons and damage to property should any such occur whilst the school premises were being legitimately used after school hours. Limit of indemnity £5,000, premium 5/-.*

----
[1] The correct title of the national annual Boy Scout escapade was 'Bob a Job', which started in the late 1940s. Scouts would knock on doors and offer their services for one shilling (a bob), although they did prefer to be paid rather more than that. The monies went towards Scout funds. The recipients of the service were given a sticker for their front door to deter other job seekers from pestering them. The hugely successful and enjoyable activity petered out in the 1970s.

satisfied with the teaching. Advantage has
been taken of the recent wide extension
of free education to call the attention
of school managers to the facilities offered
by the Post Office to school savings' banks
The circular, dated 12th October, 1891, on thrift.
has now been included in these revised instructions under Appendix V. The memorandum on

School Savings Bank memo from the early 1890s

To round off the money side of things: savings. In far-off pre-credit-card days, thrift was a virtue and was encouraged by government, society and, by extension, the school. Many parents, accustomed to sending their children to school with a penny a week, continued to do so after the 1891 Act had made elementary education free. In January 1893 headmaster Brown accordingly *opened a Penny Savings Bank in the school by means of Shilling Stamp Deposit Forms from the Post Office*. This was

probably a forerunner of a scheme from the 1950s, remembered by numerous former pupils who were given a long strip of twelve penny-sized perforated paper pockets. When the strip was full, it was exchanged for two sixpenny Savings Stamps with their picture of Princess Anne. Prince Charles graced the 2/6 denomination. When the Savings stamps amounted to a whole £10 – if they ever did – they were exchanged for a £10 National Savings certificate.

In October 1936 Mr Bailey *was away from school with permission of the managers to attend the West Regional Conference of the Savings Association*. In March 1941 he was *given £5 by a person (who wishes to remain anonymous); from this each child who is a member of the Savings Association has been given two 6d stamps. Each child not a member has had two stamps placed to his or her credit as an incentive to join the scheme. This applies to local children and leaves 3/- balance for the next three entrants*. Note that evacuees were excluded. The importance attached to savings was such that for several years from autumn 1951, films were shown by the National Savings Mobile Unit. In September of that year *the programme included Switzerland, Squirrels, Training of Dogs and the Syrian Desert*. Sometimes, as in February 1952, the great and the good would come and sit at the back: *National Savings pictures were shown to the children today. Lord Strachie, Chairman of the managers and of the Clutton District Savings Association was present*. In September 1976 *the District National Savings Organisation called to discuss various aspects of the movement*. By the late 1970s, the scheme seems to have lapsed.

BEWHISKERED GENTLEMEN, VIRILE HYMNS AND MUNCH'S THE SCREAM

Until very recent times –it may still be there – there was a harrowing poster in the staff room at Bishop Sutton School of Edvard Munch's 'The Scream' above the word OFSTED[1]. Today's teachers may consider the poster apt, but their Victorian forebears would have considered it even apter. They had more than enough inspections and exams to fret over. There were exams arranged by the headteacher to check on progress: these didn't frighten the headteacher, although the findings might. Annual visits from inspectors appointed by Bath and Wells Diocese underlined the importance of Religious Education, but these gentlemen also rarely frightened the headteacher and were often positively nice to the children.

	Standards of Examination in the		
	Standard I.	Standard II.	Standard III.
•Reading - - -	To read a short paragraph from a book not confined to words of one syllable.	To read a short paragraph from an elementary reading book.	To read a passage from a more advanced reading book, or from stories from English history.
†Writing - - -	Copy in manuscript characters a line of print, and write from dictation not more than ten easy words, commencing with capital letters. Copy books (large or half text hand) to be shown.	A passage of not more than six lines, from the same book, slowly read once, and then dictated word by word. Copy books (large and half text hand) to be shown.	Six lines from one of the reading books of the Standard, slowly read once and then dictated. Copy books (capitals and figures, large and small hand) to be shown.
††Arithmetic - - The work of girls will be judged more leniently than that of boys, and, as a rule, the sums set will be easier.	Notation and numeration up to 1,000. Simple addition and subtraction of numbers of not more than three figures. In addition not more than five lines to be given. The multiplication table to 6 times 12.	Notation and numeration up to 100,000. The four simple rules· to short division. The multiplication table and the pence table to 12s.	The former rules, with long division. Addition and subtraction of money.

'Standards of Examination' in the 1890s: note the patronising comment bottom-left regarding Arithmetic: 'The work of girls will be judged more leniently than that of boys, and, as a rule, the sums set will be easier'. .

Worse, far worse, could be the annual visits by Her (or His) Majesty's Inspectors (HMI), which represented an ordeal for heads, teachers and pupils alike. A sense of deep foreboding would precede a visit by HMI, who controlled not only the school grant prior to the abolition of the Payment by Results system in 1904, but also the headmaster's sanity. Let M. K. Ashby, in his 'Joseph Ashby of Tysoe 1859-1919', tell a typical tale:

Joseph Ashby, who attended [Tysoe School, near Warwick] in the 1860s, remembered that he and the other children would listen anxiously for the sound of the dog cart which heralded the arrival of the inspector and his assistant. In would come two gentlemen with a deportment of high authority and with rich voices. Each would sit at a desk and children would be called in turn to one or other. The master hovered round. The children would see him start with vexation as a good pupil stuck at a word in the reading book he had been using all the year, or sat frozen with the sum in front of him. One year the atmosphere so affected the lower Standards that, one after another as they were brought to the Inspector, the boys howled and

----

[1] The Office for Standards in Education, a government body set up in 1993 to inspect and assess the educational standards of schools and colleges in England and Wales.

the girls whimpered. It took hours to get through them.

Inspectors' reputations preceded them. In 1911 the Chief Inspector of Schools described teachers of infants and juniors as *uncultivated and imperfectly educated people who are for the most part creatures of tradition and routine.*

Back to the logbooks. In November 1872, when Miss Hassell examined Standard I in Arithmetic, she *found five of the children very backward.* In March 1873 she again *examined Standard I and found them very backward in every subject, some of them appear to be incapable of learning.* And the vicar would drop by: on 29 October 1873 the Rev. Ommaney felt that *instruction is somewhat impeded by the want of parallel desks which will, I hope, be soon supplied.* When he moved on, the Rev. Clowes took his place and had a fun day on Thursday 18 October when *he tested the register and inspected the drains.* In November 1875 HMI coldly observed that although *the children passed a creditable examination in all subjects, it would be well if the form IX could be ready by the time of the Inspector's visit and if some representation either of the School Board or managers could find it convenient to be present at the Inspection. The school portfolio should also be ready for the Inspector.* No doubt a snap visit about which the School Board had known nothing.

The Board followed the inspections very carefully and very nervously. They wrote to the Education Department in Whitehall in May 1876: *I shall be obliged by your furnishing me with a list of the children presented last year for examination, shewing those who passed and those who did not.* The Board wanted to be fully prepared for the next visit, and wrote accordingly to Mr Jones on 19 July. The letter is illustrated. The inspectors arrived. Mr Nickolls (chairman of the School Board) and Mr Cook (a Board member) hovered menacingly and almost certainly sycophantically. The school was examined by Mr Rowland Hamilton HMI, and his assistant. There were 81 passes out of 99; 35 were presented in the Standards and 26 were presented in the infants. That didn't sound too bad. In September the Board wrote to the headmaster: *Herewith I send you the Report on your school. Please copy it in the log book by the first time I am at Sutton. I will call and sign it.*

Forewarning of an inspection in 1876. The postscript reads: 'Please send me the receipt for what Mr Arter paid you a few days ago'.

It was bad enough that the headteacher had to suffer the slings and arrows of outrageous inspectors, without having to write their reports out personally and in laborious longhand for the chairman of the Board and the chief inspector to sign. Not until much later was he allowed to delegate the chore to a secretary.

The 1877 inspection report found *the discipline good and the examination in the upper Standards creditable, especially in Arithmetic, but the work of Standard I, especially the Reading, was indifferent; a washing place is needed.* The inspector in September 1884 noted sniffily that *there is a very bad smell from the girls' offices.*

Inspection report 1882

If it wasn't HMI poring over the children's knowledge, it was the diocese. If it wasn't the diocese, it was the headmaster. And if it wasn't him, it was the School Board. On 20 January 1878 the bewhiskered members noted that *the children come very unpunctual to school, Mr Arter spoke of the necessity of coming on time and said he was pleased to see a very great improvement in the children's cleanliness within the last fortnight.* Perhaps the Board had installed the washing place recommended by an inspector the previous year. By August 1878 a Board inspection observed that *the school seems to have been neglected, and the master, who has only been appointed six months, has had to contend with bad attendance.* What the inspector didn't say was that the children had also had to contend for six months with the master. All was not lost, as the Board did find *signs of careful teaching in the school, the Reading was very fair, and the discipline is good.* There is always a proviso: *the rooms should be cleaned more often and a proper coal-shed built.* By September 1881 the Board generously opined that *considering the disadvantage of sickness and a double change of master, the result of the examination was decidedly creditable, especially in Arithmetic, and the children who are in very fair order answered with considerable spirit and intelligence in the class subjects.* The proviso this time was that *the infant girls should learn to knit.*

No more School Board inspections after 1882, at least according to the logbook, but HMI and the diocese continued to make their presence felt. On 22 December 1882 *school was dismissed by the Rev. E. Clowes, who distributed the prizes earnt* (sic) *by children at the diocesan examination to the number of 30*. The men with dog collars tended to test the children only on Scripture and associated subjects; they were usually easier to please – often putting poor oral work down to the shyness of the pupils – and the children were generally presented with a little something. In March 1887 *the Diocesan Inspector visited the school in the morning and asked for half a day holiday in the afternoon for the children who had pleased him by their answers*. The clergy did occasionally have their firmer side: in June 1883 the vicar *witnessed the military drill* [and was] *glad to see that the children generally were much more in hand, and that Mr Hill had proceeded so well in gaining control over them*. Amazing what a lively thwacking with the school bible can do. In October 1883 diocesan inspector Mr Mitchell enthused: *these children show a very ready and complete knowledge of all their work. The infants have been carefully taught and answer well, as called upon. The same may be said of the other two groups. The scholars take an evident interest in their work. The written papers do them credit. Repetition of Scriptures with the two upper classes is a little deficient in accuracy*. Perhaps the children didn't know their Malachi from their Micah.

The authorities would advise the school of the programme of exams for the ensuing year. In June 1876, for example, headmaster Jones *received the examination schedule for this school from the Education Department in order to have a copy of it in school*. In January 1886 headmaster Brown *received notice of Scripture Exam from Diocesan Inspector for the 30th inst., affixed same to school door*. Sometimes there was a debate about the timing of the exams. After he'd nailed the notices up, Mr Brown went on to say: *Scripture exams formerly took place in the autumn, the last in November. The managers have altered the time to spring, considering it better for the children, hence the reason of another exam so near the last. After this coming Inspection is over, Scripture examinations will take place annually about April*.

In June 1886 the inspector observed of the infants that *more care is needed in teaching writing, and the children appeared to have little idea of the relative sizes of the letters. The object lesson was fair, but the children should not be allowed to answer out of turn or simultaneously*. That good old Victorian adage of only speak when you're spoken to. The inspectors could be real miseries at times: in June 1886 they protested that the infants *should not be allowed to reckon on their fingers*. June 1887: *Reading was very monotonous and indistinct. Spelling was very fair, but Writing needs considerable improvement. The Grant for English has been recommended with hesitation. No Grant can be recommended for Geography. Considering that there is no classroom, and that the school is very crowded, I do not think it possible for more than one class subject to be taught successfully*. The premises problems couldn't be laid at the door of the headmaster.

The inspectors were wont to dot a capricious number of i's and cross a pedantic number of t's. In September 1893 they reported of the infant class: *if reasonable care had been taken to meet the requirements of Art 98(b)(3), it would be possible this year to recommend payment of the intermediate variable grant. The register must be tested on behalf of the Board at least once a quarter at irregular intervals as required by para 6 of Appx II of Instructions to HM Inspectors*. And they could be quite cutting at times, these officious officials: in June 1894 they carped that *the introduction of two new class subjects* (no mention of what they were) *throughout the school was a hazardous experience and, as might have been expected, the scholars had not acquired a large amount of useful information. Unless they show much more knowledge next year, they will not pass again.* Sometimes the children only had themselves to blame. The 1895 report commented ominously *that the best results can scarcely be expected until the children attend school with greater regularity.*

> **General rules relating to inspection.** 3. My Lords would again remind you that all hurry or undue haste on the day of examination is incompatible with the proper discharge of your main duty:—that of ascertaining, verifying, and reporting the facts on which the parliamentary grant is administered. An early attendance at the school is absolutely indispensable, not only on account of the greater length of time available for work, but in the interests of the children, who are far more capable of sustained exertion in the early part of the day. It is especially necessary to avoid the attempt to do two things at once, e.g., giving out dictation or sums while hearing the reading of another class; retaining children in school in the dinner hour, and thereby not allowing sufficient time for the meal; prolonging the examination to a late hour in the afternoon ; and embarrassing young scholars by want of clearness in dictation or in asking questions. As far as possible it should be arranged that during your visit of inspection no class shall be left unemployed. Infants should not be detained beyond the ordinary hour for dismissal ; and other children whom it is proposed to examine later should be relieved by a short interval for recreation before that time.

HM Inspection guidelines from the late 1890s: 'It is especially necessary to avoid the attempt to do two things at once ...'

> Report for year ending June 30th 1900
>
> **Mixed School** "The scholars are in good order, but their progress is interfered with by the overcrowded state of the school. It is hoped that the new classroom will soon be built, but on the occasion of my last visit little progress had been made and the work was apparently stopped.
>
> The teachers work hard, and on the whole the children show a satisfactory knowledge of the elementary subjects. The girls in the upper standards do not answer at all well in either History or Geography. Singing, Drawing and Needlework have been carefully taught.
>
> The ceiling of the mainroom needs repair."

Inspection 1900: 'the girls in the upper standards do not answer at all well in either History or Geography'.

The diocesan inspectors' generosity of spirit didn't wane with the passing of time. In February 1897 Mr Mitchell wrote: *all present except two sick babies. The exam shews that the school has throughout been taught conscientiously and efficiently. Considering that all were in their places (the very little ones excepted), the answering was even and satisfactory*. Mr Richard T. Curry wrote in June 1899: *the infants must be supplied with thimbles when sewing*. Too many little fingers being punctured by too many blunt ends of needles. In May 1901 Mr I. G. Marshall gushed: *the infants are very bright and eager and I had some very original answers. The elder children did very well indeed and I feel sure they are being taught in the best possible way. The tone of the school is excellent and great care has been given to the singing*. These diocesan reports heartened Mr Wightman in readiness for governmental ones. The 1902 HMI observed that *the section of the school which receives most of the master's personal care has made considerable progress, but the two lower classes are very deficient in attainments and attention, and constitute a grave defect in the efficiency of the school. The teaching of Needlework leaves much to be desired*.

Diocesan inspector Mr R. N. Edwards was a real sweetie. In February 1904 he found the infants to be *a most pleasing class, children bright, intelligent and well taught, especially pleased with the singing. Elder children: an excellent tone in this school. The children did very well in their Scripture exam*. He was still in his job in June 1918: *I am pleased again to report so well upon this school, the whole tone is so excellent. 43 infants examined and I have seldom found an infant class so good and the work so even, I mark all the subjects 'excellent'*. What a lovely man. The 1912 HMI wasn't so glowing: *Class 2 appear to have quite forgotten their Geography. Needlework appears to be well taught, specimen work has been reduced to a minimum, and the time is mainly spent in making and repairing garments*. Every so often everything seemed to come as a bit of a shock to the poor unsuspecting head. How else can Mr Wightman's logbook entry from April 1917 be explained?: *exams seem to have taken place during the Easter holidays*.

Today's media can accuse heads of sending difficult children home to avoid their bringing the whole school down at inspections. A new phenomenon? This, from the Board's minute book of 5 May 1897: *the Attendance Officer having reported that Mr Brown had sent Lilian Ferris home on the day of the inspection, resolved that the clerk be instructed to write to Mr Brown asking him for an explanation*.

There was an inspectorial interlude during the war, and not until September 1919 was Mr Wightman's peace and quiet disturbed again, this time in the form of Mr G. H. Grimrod Esq. The bone-chillingly Dickensian name faithfully recorded in the head's transcription was belied by the not-at-all bad report:

Seven years have elapsed since the last report was sent. The same headmaster is in charge now as then, but there have been several changes in the subordinate staff. The present teachers are earnest and industrious and are doing much good work. The school has advanced since last reported upon. The work is in several respects better and the order has improved and the children show more interest in their work. The most pronounced improvement is in the accuracy and intelligence of the Arithmetic ... the girls greatly outnumber the boys, are in the main good readers, the boys read fairly ... the infants are in kindly and capable hands ... the children recite fairly well, but their singing is harsh. The babies are kept interested and employed, but they appear to spend the bulk of their time in the not very comfortable gallery.

Unusual for a diocesan inspector to get out of bed the wrong side, but the one who visited the school in May 1922 did. *Standards I and II: this group was rather weak in the Old Testament and there is always a danger of the children learning a great deal of detail in some of the OT narratives without grasping the fuller meaning of what such narratives should teach in their own individual lives. A good set of religious pictures is highly desirable*. But all was sunny again when Mr Thompson came from Bath and Wells in July 1925: *I found a little company* [of infants] *anxious to tell me all they knew, and a happy little lot they appeared to be*. In 1927 co-diocesan Mr Merrick wrote: *another excellent feature throughout was the attention given to private prayers; this is indeed commendable*. In July 1934 the Rev. Maclean noted that *the hymns chosen are virile and with good tunes*. Nothing like a virile hymn to liven up an end-of-term summer day in Bishop Sutton.

HMI Mr Johnson's report of November 1922 was daunting:

Attention is invited to the following points where improvement is desirable: (1) Uncontrolled answering in oral lessons, which has become habitual with a few older boys in the first class, is a serious hindrance to the progress of the younger and the slower thinking children and should be repressed. (2) The older girls (Standard VII) have become self-conscious and diffident and do not do their teacher credit as they might in oral work ... (4) In the study of History, the children need some general chronological framework for the arrangement of events to enable them to trace their connection with each other ... (6) There is no branch of the County Rural Library in this important Village school. Girls: hitherto it has been possible to admit only nine girls from this school to the Cookery Centre (less than half the number eligible). Boys: no practical instruction of any kind is provided for the older boys.

The library recommendation fell on deaf (or finance-constrained) ears. It had to wait until June 1933.

By the 1940s, the general tone of inspection reports was more relaxed and reassuring. In April 1944, for example, Miss Grant – the first time an 'inspectress' was mentioned – wrote: *earnest sincere work is being done by all members of this school. The headmaster and his three women assistants cooperate wholeheartedly in the children's interests. The use of broadcast lessons has been one of the factors of this beneficial development. The entrants' class provides a pleasant introduction to school life*. In 1951 Miss Grant came to a managers' meeting and told them that *better buildings would be most desirable, but no funds are available. Education of older children was sound and satisfactory despite the many difficulties such as reduced teaching staff, inadequate accommodation etc.*

By 1961 logbook entries were short and sweet and said little about inspections; the findings and observations may have been committed to other records which have not surfaced. The headmaster's comment in his logbook in January 1961, for example, was simply: *Mr Coles, HMI, came to school at 10.30 am and left at 12 noon. He returned at 1.30 pm and left at 3.25 pm. During his stay he visited each classroom*. Successive years' entries were no more forthcoming.

The last noteworthy report was in June 1973 when the school was inspected *by Miss G. Kellett and Mr Monkman ... They spent the whole day carrying out a full Inspection of the school in all its aspects. This is in connection with a survey of all schools in the Chew Valley. They gave me an excellent report, congratulating the staff and me in achieving very satisfactory standards in all aspects of education*. The eventual combined report of January 1974 (Inspection Report of Chew Valley Schools, A Survey of Primary Education in the Chew Area of Somerset') covered the following schools, the numbers in brackets being the roll: Felton (159), Bishop Sutton (145), Pensford (120), Winford (111), Dundry (79), Chew Stoke (71), East Harptree (70), Chew Magna (69), Stanton Drew (62), West Harptree (46) and Ubley (39). Bishop Sutton was the second largest in the area, but with four full-time staff and one pupil teacher – Felton had three full-time and two pupil teachers – was perhaps the most expensive to run. All eleven schools had been built pre-1903, despite Somerset Education Authority's *vigorous policy of replacing pre-1903 primary schools at the rate of 14 or so a year ... and those in the Chew Valley have not yet appeared high enough on the priority list to obtain a place in the programme.* The report went on to note that it was *desirable that schools should have a sewing machine.* In those pre-National Curriculum days, *with the exception of fixed points on the timetable, staff are free to plan the time to suit the needs of their classes.* The wide-ranging document made the following (selected) comments, which do not necessarily relate solely to Bishop Sutton:

Department of Education and Science
Elizabeth House York Road London SE1
Telegrams Aristides London Telex 23171
Telephone 01-928 9222 ext **2767**

T. Price, Esq.,   Your reference
Headmaster,   Our reference S. 437/7/09
Bishop Sutton County Primary School   D.S.46/73
Bishop Sutton   Date 21 JAN 1974

A Survey of Primary Education in the Chew Area of Somerset

Sir

I am directed by the Secretary of State to enclose .ohe (1)..Copy.. ~~copies~~ of a report by HM Inspectors.

- *The increasing number of children under 5 who are admitted, some being just 4 on entry, gives some cause for concern when conditions are not satisfactory for them; too often these young children are expected to fit in with the activities planned for the older ones.*

- *Unless the teaching of French can be put on a sound basis with sufficient time to provide continuity of treatment and the opportunity to range more widely than simple oral exercises, it should not be attempted.*

- *The rich resources of the Valley offer excellent opportunities for biological, historical and geographical studies; the many activities include the interviewing of village personalities ... visits to churches, farms, airports, historic remains, the Mendips and surrounding countryside.*

- *There is interesting and stimulating work with a range of materials such as clay, paint, fabric and waste materials in two and occasionally three-dimensional forms. Much more use might be made of fabrics, printing, dyeing and embroidery. Needlecraft can be a subject in its own right for boys as well as girls if it is used, for example, in making collage, puppets and costume dolls.*

- *Assemblies are carefully planned and children are encouraged to take an active part, writing prayers and playing recorders.*

- *The rural situation of these schools has by no means isolated them from the community outside the parishes.*

- *There is good humour in the schools, despite the challenges offered by the limitations of the premises.*

Sovereign 1916,
half sovereign 1901
(actual size)

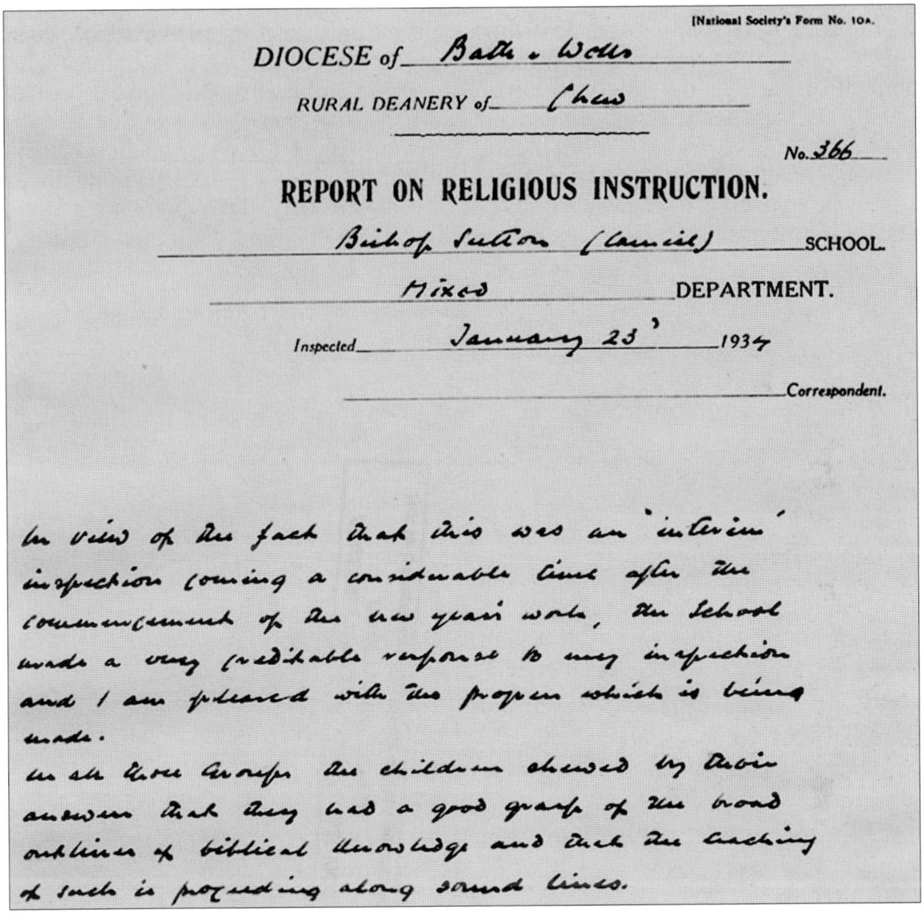

[National Society's Form No. 10A.]

DIOCESE of _Bath & Wells_

RURAL DEANERY of_ _Chew_

No._366_

REPORT ON RELIGIOUS INSTRUCTION.

Bishop Sutton (Council) _____SCHOOL._

Mixed _____DEPARTMENT._

Inspected_ _January 23,_ _1934_

_____Correspondent._

In view of the fact that this was an 'interim' inspection (coming a considerable time after the commencement of the new year's work, the school made a very creditable response to my inspection and I am pleased with the progress which is being made.

In all three groups the children shewed by their answers that they had a good grasp of the broad outlines of biblical knowledge and that the teaching of such is proceeding along sound lines.

1934 diocesan report: 'the children shewed by their answers that they had a good grasp of the broad outlines of biblical knowledge'.

You've all done very well

In February 1876 the managers wrote to headmaster Jones: _the Board has decided to award some prizes to children attending the Board Schools and I am directed to send you a paper shewing the way in which children will be entitled to such prizes, which I now do. You will intimate the fact at once to the children and do what is necessary on your part to carry out the intentions of the Board._ Whether awards were given prior to 1876 for good behaviour, good attendance and good work isn't known. As will be seen, eligibility for a little something wasn't always clear cut.

Prize giving was a formal business and the school would be full of starchy Victorian ladies in flowery Victorian headwear. In August 1878, for instance, the Board sent an invitation (_Mrs Filer will distribute the Prizes in the Bishop Sutton School on Friday the 9th inst. at 11 o'clock_) to numerous local (and not so local) worthy burghers including Mrs Dowling, Mrs Arnold, Mrs Adlam of the Manor House, Mrs Bush of The Castle, Mrs Crothers of Highfield, Mrs Hale of Harford House,

Mrs Collins of The Beeches, Mesdames Brimble and Shorland of Chew Hill (all in Chew Magna) and Mrs Nicholls of 18 Royal Crescent, Weymouth. The worthy of Bishop Sutton itself comprised Mrs Arter, Miss Cook, and Mrs Beard. Mr Northam was also invited, but it would have been churlish not to. He was the headmaster. In October of the previous year the Board had written to headmaster Jones, requesting him *to furnish me with a written statement procured from the 'Log Book' shewing what Ladies have visited the Bishop Sutton School since the 8th February 1875 and the dates of their respective attendance.* The Board either wanted to make sure that no-one was missed off the 1878 invitation list, or the members were having a sweepstake amongst themselves as to whose wife had visited the most often.

In August 1878, in an example of bureaucracy and complexity gone barking mad, the Board *unanimously carried the prize scheme proposed to be adopted:*

1. *Three different coloured cards value 10, 40 and 80 marks respectively to be used;*
2. *A register to be kept by the teacher of each division recording any bad marks;*
3. *Marks to be counted up at the end of every 4 weeks and cards given out and changed according to the number of marks recorded;*
4. *Any child losing his card loses all claim to the marks which might have belonged to him;*
5. *Cards should be such colors (sic) as dark blue, red, dark green, as they will be easily soiled;*
6. *Bad marks to be given for lateness, want of cleanliness, bad conduct etc.*

   (a) *Every child making 350 attendances and passing in two subjects in any Standard – 1/6;*
   (b) *350 and three subjects – 2/-;*
   (c) *400 and two subjects – 2/-;*
   (d) *400 and three subjects – 2/6.*
   (e) *Each infant with 250 attendances and attending on day of exam – 6d.*

The prizes to consist of suitable books of the value stated.

Given the stretching targets, the entry of 6 September 1886 (*re resolution 5.8.78 re Prize Scheme*) comes as no great surprise: *only one boy and one girl earning the greatest number of good conduct marks – prize value 2/6. Only one boy and one girl making the highest number of attendances during the year – prize value 2/6.* Half a crown wasn't to be sniffed at in 1886, although the winners would doubtless have preferred a shiny silver coin to a book of that value.

The Queen Victoria Medal (actual size), issued by the London School Board to J. Crossing 'For punctual attendance during the school year AD 1901'. There is no reason to assume that good attendance was not similarly rewarded at Bishop Sutton.

In September 1884 Mrs Dendy *gave eight boxes of toys to the infant girls who were present at the last government Inspection.* 30 November 1886: *Lady Strachey and some other ladies attended the school and distributed prizes to the children at 12 o'clock.* 'Some other ladies' was assuredly headmasterese for 'unidentified haughty females with improbable hats wandering imperiously round my school'. Later that year, *the Ladies' Committee awarded prizes to the girls who presented the best needlework in each Standard.* The Board could be a curmudgeonly bunch: in September

1891 *they resolved that scholars who pass in all three subjects be presented with a certificate to that effect*. That was nice. But *cost of certificates not to exceed 3d*.

Good attendance was the pinnacle of Victorian virtue. In January 1901 the Board noted *with satisfaction that five children did not miss an attendance during the year ended Xmas 1900: Arthur Harvey, Fred Harvey, George Tovey, Wilfred Tovey, Mabel Tovey*. Irrespective of the preponderance of Harveys and Toveys at the school, that was pretty impressive. The Board wanted *the names of the children to be exhibited in the School*. Pour encourager les autres, no doubt. In July 1924 the Chew Magna Horticultural Society *awarded the following prizes: Drawing 1st prize, Needlework two 2nd prizes, Knitting 1st prize, two 2nd, one 3rd, Darning 1st prize, School Gardens 1st and 2nd prize, School Sports Team three 1st prizes.* The logbook is disappointingly quiet on quite why the Chew Magna Horticultural Society was awarding prizes for knitting in Bishop Sutton.

BEHIND THE BIKE SHEDS, SCHOOL TRANSPORT, BUSES AND TRAINS

All this lessoning and inspecting and prize giving was all well and good, but how did the children get to school?

The first local reference to LEA-provided school transport was in respect of push bikes. Yes, push bikes. In 1870 James Stanley had constructed the first penny-farthing, and low-framed Rover 'safety bicycles' with both wheels the same size had hit the road in 1880. Belfast vet John Boyd Dunlop invented the pneumatic tyre in 1888, and once the freewheel system was perfected a couple of years later, bicycling became popular with both sexes. It was one of the few outdoor pursuits that women could share on equal terms with men. Mr Brent and Mr Harvey had begun stocking safety bicycles in Bishop Sutton in the early 1900s. But provided by the LEA? Yes. It was 1930, and it was Chew Stoke.

In January of that year, Chew Stoke was designated an elementary school (as opposed to the all-age school that it had hitherto been) and the older children were to go to Chew Magna. Somerset County Council provided any pupils living two miles away or more with a new cycle, or paid them a shilling a week to use their own. The practice spread to Bishop Sutton when it started taking older children from local schools that had lost their all-age status, and headmaster Bailey reported in January 1948 *that some shelter for cycles was advisable in view of the number of cycles arriving daily*. No fun for the older children not to have bike sheds to lurk behind. Not only were those children living more than two miles away eager to claim their free bikes or a bob a week in lieu, but cycles were also becoming the favoured means of getting to school, even for those living nearer.

The request for cycle sheds came to nothing, and in May 1951 the school pressed again, *as boys cycled from other schools and there was no place away from the weather where they could be stored*. This implied, wrongly, that it was only boys who cycled. The reply was to the effect that no storage space was provided for cycles for scholars who resided less than three miles from the school. This was silly, as the authority would provide bikes for those living two miles away. Mr Bailey retorted that the 20 to 30 boys concerned had been transferred from other schools and had previously been conveyed by a coach provided by Somerset but now withdrawn. The weather wasn't doing the bikes any good and he wanted the matter to be reconsidered. It wasn't. In July 1951 *the CEO stood by his decision*. In September 1955 Mr Bailey noted that *three boys from West Harptree have been told they can no longer ride on the coach but must either walk or cycle to school*. This

further increased the number of bikes at the school and the managers again asked
the CEO *to authorise the provision of a bicycle shelter*. Again, the CEO refused. The
Authority had no money.

Cycling brought its risks. A 1952 incident involving Tony
Tucker and some holed stockings will be spotlighted later.
Zera Wilson at Chew Stoke School explained in September
1953 that *a bicycle was provided for Raymond Marshall
who was to have a week's practice on it before proceeding
with it to Bishop Sutton*. Perhaps the authorities had been
mindful of the stockings. In July 1954 *a police constable,
on the request of the headmaster, attended at the school
and made an inspection of the pupils' bicycles and at the
same time gave advice to their owners*. Cycling Proficiency
tests had been introduced by the Royal Society for the
Prevention of Accidents in 1947, but the first mention at
Bishop Sutton wasn't until 1975 when, on 8 July, *Sergeant
Harris came this morning. All 25 children passed*. In July 1976 *a presentation of
Cycling Proficiency certificates took place; Mrs L. Organ, Wansdyke Road Safety
officer, presented certificates to the successful candidates who were all successful
with one exception*. There were to be no more cycling-related references in the
logbook.

*The author's Cycling
Proficiency badge*

*Punch cartoon 1969: "Turn her round and head for
the amusement arcade".*

By the 1940s, when few parents had cars, the main means of transporting far-flung
children to and from Bishop Sutton had become the coach, the times of the public
buses being unsuited to school hours. The first logbook mention was in March 1947
– by which time senior children from villages along the A368 were being transferred
to Bishop Sutton – when the CEO asked the managers to appoint *a supervisor to
travel on the bus bringing the scholars from Compton Martin and West Harptree. It
was agreed that as the bus came from Blagdon, the matter be referred to Blagdon*

County School. No-one had been found by July, and the CEO asked the managers *to approach the bus company*. Quite what came of that buck-passing isn't clear, but in November *Mrs Fear from Ubley came in on the school bus today as she is the 'Guide and Steward' in charge of the children*. In May 1949 *Mrs Payne of West Harptree began her duties as guide on the bus from East Harptree*, but in March 1950 the CEO told Mr Bailey to tell her *that her service would not be required after April 29th*. We know not whether the children were insufficiently naughty, whether Mrs Payne had been naughty, whether the Authority was yet again lacking in cash, or whether the bus no longer ran. The latter seems unlikely. In April Mr Bailey wrote that *14 of the children from West Harptree are away as they are not allowed to ride on the bus*. Two days later, *there are still nine children away for want of a coach*. In October the CEO protested *that the contractor conveying pupils complained that his vehicle was overcrowded if both adults (Mrs Fear and Mr James) were carried. The correspondent has replied that, after enquiries, he would inform the managers that the complaint was a frivolous one*.

Photo from 1946, taken in the playground at the side of the school.
Back row (left to right): John Matthews, Michael Dew, John Cole, Rhona Marsh,
Rachael Small,
Pauline Dowling, Geoff Bendall, Bernard Hunt, Maurice Redman.
Front row: John Challenger, George Chidzey, Janet Harvey, Mavis Walker, Margot Brown,
Maureen Edgell (or possibly Janet Chubb), Ann Lennard.

Nothing to do with Bishop Sutton, but correspondence in the Copy Letters Book from 1924 is worthy of note. The managers had written to the Education Department in Weston-super-Mare to say that *Mr Chater is unquestionably the better man for the purpose as he is a bona fide motor car proprietor of great experience and has various motor vehicles and two assistants, whereas Mr Sampson is a general haulier with one small motor trolly* (sic) *which he occasionally converts into a private car for the conveyance of small outing parties*. The two gentlemen had presumably tendered for school transport for Chew Magna School.

In the same way as everyone remembers their school, so everyone tends to remember how they got there and back. Wendy Childs (née Gooderham, at school from 1952 to 1956) caught the bus from West Harptree operated by Brents. The coach from Ubley was run by Herbie Coles under the supervision of Mrs Fear. The Maid of Mendip. That was Herbie's company, not his (or Mrs F's) nickname. Joan Bunney recalls that many children had bikes. Her father would always be repainting hers and she never knew what colour it would be when she woke up in the morning. He also extended his foible to wheelbarrows. Joan remembers too that people would sometimes hire cars to move children and objects from one school to another. Geoff Brent explains that his brother Michael drove on the original school run from Compton Martin in 1950. Their family's first coach was a 1939 Bedford 25-seater bought from Wems in Weston-super-Mare, followed by a 1940s 27-seater. The Bishop Sutton School contract was with Brents, but the LEA's was with Blagdon Lionesse, and the County would often play one company off against the other. Geoff would take dry pupils to the Jubilee Baths in Knowle and bring wet pupils back. He recalls that the worst behaved children were generally those from the 'jumped-up families'. Colin Symes lived at West Harptree in the late 1940s and was bused to Bishop Sutton for a couple of years. He then had to cycle, as he lived within three miles and was no longer eligible for school transport. The bus came from Blagdon and was operated under the name of Blagdon Lionesse by proprietor 'Twister' Lyons.

A brief diversion to look at non-school transport in Bishop Sutton.

In the 1800s, the carriers and hauliers travelling to and from Bristol would take passengers for an appropriate fee. By the early 1900s, people increasingly needed to travel for work, shopping or (occasionally) leisure, but transport in the Valley remained a challenge. It was too far and too hilly to cycle easily to the nearby towns, cars were rare, and buses represented the only viable possibility for several decades. The Bristol Tramway Company began running vehicles to and from Bishop Sutton in 1923 with service number 38 and a fare of 1/3 single and 2/- return, starting and finishing at Prince Street in Bristol. In the early days it was known as the Sleeper Service: the driver bringing the last bus out had lodgings in the village so that he could take his bus back in the mornings. The route to Bristol was via Chew Magna and Whitchurch; Dundry Hill being too much for the engine. That said, there was a regular service at one time from Bishop Sutton to Hinton Blewett up Sutton Hill Road! A service from Bath to Weston-super-Mare started in 1928, with stops in Bishop Sutton.

The PC soon expressed an interest in the buses. In July 1927 they wrote *to the secretary of the Bristol Tramways and Carriage Co. pointing out the inconvenience caused to passengers being unable to obtain accommodation in the last bus from Bristol, and had received the following reply from the Company: Dear Sir, I beg to acknowledge receipt of your letter of the 26 June and quite appreciate the inconvenience frequently caused to long distance passengers by their being crowded out of omnibuses by short distance riders. The Company are, however, unable to exclude these people, being public vehicles plying for hire, we are unable to pick and choose our passengers. Yours Faithfully, Traffic Superintendent.*

Evvy Harvey remembers that Mr Gibbs ran a horse bus to Bristol – probably earlier than 1927 – and when they reached Hursley Hill, the passengers had to get off and walk a few hundred yards because the horse couldn't manage the weight. The frequency of the motor bus service to and from the village depends on who you talk to and what period you're talking about: one pupil at the school in the late '30s recalls that the buses only ever ran in the early mornings and late afternoons. Dick Chapman remembers that there were eight a day, and always busy. Colin Symes believes that there were two buses a day to and from Fry's in Keynsham. The drivers were always helpful and polite, although woe betide you if you had nothing smaller than a ten bob note. The same driver would usually operate for a week at a time and if regular passengers weren't at the stop he would ask after their health and, if necessary, wait for them. If you went to a late picture show in Bristol, you'd miss the last bus home. Joan Bunney recalls that poorly children would be sat on the open steps next to the driver, who would keep at least half an eye on them to make sure they didn't fall out when the bus went round a corner.

'BUS BURNT OUT AT BISHOP SUTTON.—Wreckage of a motor 'bus gutted by fire, yesterday, as the driver was starting it up. Inset, Mr. Noah Gibbs, the owner and driver.

Noah Gibbs and his burnt-out bus in the 1920s

As seen earlier, public transport did occasionally merit a mention in the logbook. In May 1957 *four Sudanese students visited the school ... the infrequency of the local bus service caused them to curtail their visit somewhat.*

It's a tantalising thought that Bishop Sutton and neighbouring villages along the A368 came very close to having their own railway. It might not have survived the Beeching cuts of the early 1960s, but it would have made travel easier for a lot of people for a very long time. In 1885 the Great Western Railway formed The Chew Valley Tramway Company and applied to Parliament to extend the North Somerset Railway from Blagdon to Pensford and so help the coal mines of Bishop Sutton and Bromley. There were to be stations at Compton Martin, West Harptree and Bishop Sutton. The application was rejected, but rumours abounded in late 1904 of a replacement scheme, and in April 1905 the PC minuted that *in consideration of the numerous*

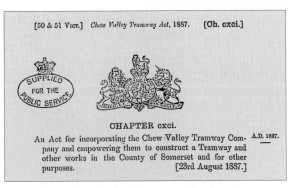

[50 & 51 Vict.]   *Chew Valley Tramway Act,* 1887.   [Oh. cxci.]

CHAPTER cxci.

An Act for incorporating the Chew Valley Tramway Com- A.D. 1887. pany and empowering them to construct a Tramway and other works in the County of Somerset and for other purposes.   [23rd August 1887.]

Chew Valley Tramway Act 1887

advantages which they feel sure will result to all classes of this community by the construction of suitable railways in this district, this Council hereby record with great satisfaction upon learning that such a line is proposed to be made running through this parish, uniting the Blagdon Railway with the Pensford Station GWR. In June 1905 the councillors assented *to the carrying out of the Blagdon and Pensford Light Railway on condition that proper and adequate accommodation be provided for the public in respect of the various public footpaths in the parish which will be crossed by the railway.* Not to be caught napping, in April 1905 the *Parish Meeting of Stowey approved of the proposed light railway between Blagdon and Pensford.*

BISHOP SUTTON

LIGHT RAILWAY.

PLANS AND SECTIONS.

MAY 1917.

Alas, it was not to be. Well, not then anyway. But in May 1917 it was all looking a little more likely. The Bishop Sutton Light Railway Commission was formed, and plans were drawn up by William Foxlee of 53 Victoria Street, Westminster. Numerous people would have been affected: at the colliery end of the village, Jesse Lovell and Sons (*owners of Colliery buildings, works, engine house, yard office, spoil heaps, telephone wires and poles, three cottages, gardens and pigsty, numerous fields and orchards*) and, moving eastwards, the Trustees of Bristol Municipal Charities (*orchard, field, pond, footpath*), Chew Magna PC and Clutton RDC (*footpaths*), the Rev. William Hunt, Emily King, Trustees of the late Eliza Bush, Wm Candy Lyde, University of Cambridge, Octavia Hassell, Mary Jane Board (all a field apiece), Anne Maria Jackson (*orchard*), Fred Lovell (*house, gardens and outbuildings occupied by Tom Edward Moody, Bonhill House*), Sarah Amy King (*field, rough slope and stream*), Rt Hon. the Lord Strachie (*fields*) and, last but not least, Somerset County Council who owned the '*Bath Road*'.

Bishop Sutton's intended railway station

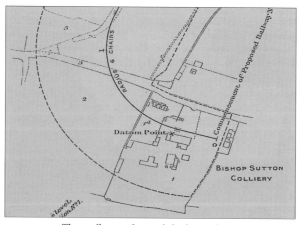

The railway that might have been

It came to naught. 'Little Bonhill' cottage on the left down Bonhill Road is the sole reminder of what might have been. It was built as Bishop Sutton's railway station.

TAPIOCA, COCOA AND CANTEENS

The jump from railways to school catering is rather jerky, but it's nevertheless time to examine custard with the skin on, strange cake pudding and apricotty fried eggs. We'll see that the French were organising school canteens in the 1880s but that we were a bit behind. The French can hang their heads in shame, however, in the face of the British pinta.

A few English schools had started to give simple free meals to the very poorest pupils in the late 1800s, but Bishop Sutton wasn't amongst them. The Education (Provision of Meals) Act 1906 permitted (but didn't compel) LEAs to provide meals for elementary schoolchildren. Almost all declined to do so, perhaps following the lead set in Oxford where, in 1910, the Schools Medical Officer declared that school meals would do little good and might cause much harm: *the two lessons they* (i.e. parents and children) *must learn are to be self-reliant and to take a pride in themselves*. In 1914 the Government provided money to cover half the cost of meals but reduced the grants almost immediately because of the cost of the war. Even by 1939 only half of all LEAs were providing free school meals, feeding just 160,000 children a day. French enfants had been relishing ragoût and crème brûlée for some fifty years before their English counterparts were heaving over soggy cabbage and lumpy semolina.

And the school logbook? The first dinner-related entry was on Monday 12 June 1882 when *Mr Arter called to inform me that Thomas, Elizabeth and Robert Saunders were playing in the streets … they were kept without dinner, but ran away in the afternoon from school*. No further mention until mid-November 1912: *a wet week, many children are staying to dinner*. In June 1918, Mr Wightman *spoke to teachers re being present during dinner time*. Perhaps they'd been enjoying a warm summer's day with a quick fag in the churchyard. It's difficult to know what the actual position was as regards school meals, as the word 'dinner' was often used for both 'dinner time' and 'the meal that was being eaten'. There does seem to have been some provision for eating at lunchtime, but most children simply went home. In September 1925 the school managers wrote to the local Education Office in Weston-super-Mare: *The Head Teacher informs me that about 15 to 20 children remain on the school premises for their midday meal, many of them being children of the Village, why they don't go to their homes seems strange*. Perhaps there was no-one at home or perhaps they just wanted to stay and eat what must have been their mums' packed lunch with their friends. Mr Wightman's further findings were that *14 children remain on wet days: six from Nine Elms (Widcombe) 1¼ miles from the school, two from Knowle Hill (1 mile) and five from Hollow Brook (under 1 mile)*.

Wartime conditions made it imperative that children were properly fed, and a policy of nutritionally balanced school dinners was introduced for all pupils, providing 40% of daily protein and 33% of daily energy needs. The Government covered 70% of the cost, rising in 1941 to 95%, and families paid 5d per meal unless entitled to free dinners. But it wasn't until January 1943 that representatives from the LEA started their *preparation for the school providing proper meals* at Bishop Sutton, and in July *work began in connection with the 'School Dinner'; workmen are putting washing-up facilities in the store adjoining the School House*. The inverted commas were the headmaster's: dinners were clearly a novel thing. Monday 20 September 1943 saw the great day arrive: *36 children partook of the School Dinners supplied by the Temple Cloud Cookery Depot for the first time today*. The Temple Cloud Cookery Depot had originally been the Temple Cloud Workhouse. Sadly the log omitted to record what the children ate, but on 29 September Mr Bailey asked the Cookery Depot manager *if the meals can be hotter – they are only lukewarm by 12.45*. By the following autumn, things were improving: a new water heater was installed in September 1944 together with a hot cupboard for plates. (When the schoolmaster's house was incorporated into the main school buildings in the early 1980s, the old domestic kitchen was sometimes used for small groups of children to practise cookery.)

Bishop Sutton, probably in the 1920s: there is no phone box outside the post office, and the monkey puzzle tree is still in its infancy.

There were always administrative problems, and newfangled technology didn't help. On Friday 11 May 1945 *many of the dinner children are away, 15 out of 62; owing to telephone congestion I was unable to get through to the kitchen to stop the food being prepared*. By September 1945, the meals were being sent *from Churchill rather than Temple Cloud as formerly*. By May 1946, 64 children, six staff, and helpers were eating from a school roll of around 100. In June 1946 Mr Bailey *met Miss Hall and Mrs Hodder, County Meals Organiser; I pointed out the crowded conditions and difficulties under which the Seniors sat down to dinner and it was suggested that a hut could be obtained as a dining hall*. On 3 February 1947 – a bitterly cold month – *the dinner consisted of soup (of which there was little), a small sandwich and a tart for each child. I informed the kitchen supervisor that insufficient was sent*. On 5 March, *Churchill kitchen phoned this morning to say they could not supply dinner. Children living near were sent home, and dinner obtained for the remainder, an expense of 7s.3d was incurred – forwarded to the LEA*. The weather remained bleak, and two days later: *poor attendance, six children to dinner, four brought own, two supplied by HM* (whatever or whoever that was – surely not 'His Majesty'), *only three children came in on the 'bus*. Mr Bailey was informed *that no dinners will be sent out next Monday, Tuesday or Wednesday*.

It was recommended in October 1948 that *Mrs A. Coles of Weeks' Rd* (sic) *Bishop Sutton should be appointed as additional canteen help at a wage of 2s.0½d a school day plus a free meal and a retaining fee of 6s.5½d a week during the school holidays.* She would work alongside the two existing ladies. The number of children now eating school dinners had outgrown the available facilities, and in November 1948 *the dinner equipment* [was] *taken along to the Village Hall and dinner will be taken there in future.* It's unlikely that they sat on the floor, but it wasn't until January 1949 that *two tables and seven forms were received as part of the dinner equipment.* It was all very well having meals there (and it did mean that children could walk off the spotted dick on the trek back to school), but no-one had considered the impact on the Hall's electricity bill. In May 1949 the head *advised the County that we used 9 units of current per day for 66 days last term at the Village Hall for meals*, and in September *a separate meter was installed at the Village Hall for the County's electrical equipment.* Whether Mr Bailey had to stockpile shillings is not recorded.

In January 1951 he applied *for 86 forks and 100 knives to replace the very poor types that were supplied when we began school meals*, but it was to be nearly six months before *new cutlery was delivered to replace the wartime issue of very poor quality.* Perhaps eager to try out the new implements, the Area Dinner Organiser came in June and *had dinner here; she says she will try and obtain a steriliser for our knives and forks and suggests that we should have some potato portioners for serving potatoes.* No well-equipped kitchen should be without its potato portioners. In September 1952 the school took delivery of *three drums of Izal cleaner for the canteen.* The lure of the new and nicely disinfected cutlery was irresistible and in May 1953 *Miss Dugdale Bradley* (a name straight from the Monty Python cast list)*, the Meals Organiser, came and saw our meal and advised that: (1) the helpers have their meal after serving the children, (2) they wear caps, (3) we have an additional knife box and fresh covering for the serving table.* As from February 1954, noted Mr Bailey, *our meals will come from the Keynsham Cookery Department.* By February 1952 the number of meals being taken was *free 7, paid 100, teachers 3, helpers 3.* In March 1953 it fell *by about 20 since the price was raised – 80 is now the average number.* The logbook didn't say what the pre- and post-increase prices were; the Government had funded 100% of the cost in its cradle-to-grave blitz of 1947 (up from 95% in 1941) but introduced a charge of 6d per meal in 1950, rising to 1/- in 1957. By September 1955 *a Milk and Meals return shows 77 meals for payment, 4 free, 8 adult, 130 milk, there being 137 children present out of 151.*

School Meals	The Correspondent reported that he had brought to the notice of the C.E.O the frequent serving of "Cake Pudding" at School meals, and that this food did not seem to be appreciated by the children. A reply was received that the Supervisor of the Central Kitchen sends out less of "Cake Pudding" than usual. A menu of four weeks dinners was sent to the Headmaster and this shewed that "Cake Pudding" would be served five times.

Although many people recall – or think they do – school meals as being uniformly 'ugh', the logbooks don't reflect that notion. Well, not very often. In July 1956, however, the managers discussed *'cake pudding'.* Further spellbinding details appear above. Anyone know what cake pudding is?

In 1957 the children were still eating at the Village Hall, and the question arose as to whether meals could be served at the school again once the older pupils went to Chew Valley. In September *Miss Dugdale-Bradley* (who had acquired a hyphen during the past four years)*, meals organiser, called to see the possibility of our* *having meals here after Xmas. I recommend that the big room be the dining hall and that the small classroom with the 'lean-to' roof be the scullery. An alternative is to use the 'hut' for dining which will not be as convenient.* Things moved slowly, but in February 1959 *Mr Teague of the County Architect's Department and Mrs Binks of the Schools' Meals Service called and proposed to establish a self-contained canteen at school, and the purpose of the visit was to discuss the siting of the kitchen.* The managers *proposed that the classroom adjoining the School House should be the kitchen and that meals should be served through the doors leading into the small classroom and the large one next to it.* The architects reconsidered, the CEO procrastinated, and then said 'no'. The managers stuck to their guns: they wanted *the small classroom to be retained as such and used as a dining hall; it was anticipated that there would be an increase in child population as more and more houses were built.* Democracy ruled, so the managers' views were ignored. Conversion work took nearly a year, but on Tuesday 24 April 1961 *dinners were served in the main classroom today; the use of the Village Hall having been terminated. Until the kitchen is in operation, the meals will be brought from Keynsham Central Kitchen as heretofore.*

The Big Day arrived. On 16 May *the school's kitchen came into operation – meals were cooked on the premises for the first time.* In December the managers appointed Mrs Parfitt as cook-in-charge and Mrs Kate Small (who had joined the Dinner Service in April 1945) as *general assistant subject to her passing a medical examination.* On 11 October 1962 *Mrs C. L. Parfitt reported that the school's kitchen oven was giving occasional electric shocks. I reported the matter to Weston-super-Mare and afterwards rang Taunton in an endeavour to obtain prompt attention.* The following day *an electrician repaired the electric fault in the kitchen, and the oven is now functioning correctly.* Mrs Parfitt got over the shock of the shocks, but in December she resigned and Mrs Small took over as cook-in-charge. Mrs Small's saucepans simmered away merrily until she retired in 1975. On 7 June 1976, *Mrs Johnson offered post as cook.* On 18 November, Mr Price arrived at school to find that *portions of kitchen ceiling had, in two places, fallen down during the night. A considerable mess was caused.* While the ceiling was being put back, *meals and utensils will be supplied from Timsbury Central Kitchen and the main classroom used for all meals purposes.*

Industrial action by school meals employees hit the kitchen on 22 January 1979 *and no meals were provided today. Children brought packed lunches or went home.* On 2 July of that year *Mrs T. Beames was interviewed for the post of school cook and accepted. Mrs L. Johnson, the present cook, will take a similar post in Broadlands Secondary School Keynsham in September.* On 8 October 1979 *Mrs Beames starts a one-month course at Redland College. Meals being transported from Timsbury.*

In 1967 the Government stopped funding school meals and passed the full financial buck to LEAs. The price promptly shot up to 1s.6d (7½p), and convenience foods with cheaper ingredients of less nutritional value started to appear on menus. In 1969 the price rose to 1s.9d (almost 9p), but across the UK almost 5.5 million children were still having a daily school meal. The figure for Bishop Sutton School is unknown. In the inflation-ridden '70s, the price rose steeply: to 12p in 1971, 15p in 1975 and 25p in 1977. Lower nutritional content hadn't led to sufficient savings, and in 1978 the Government announced plans to halve the £380 million annual spend by further reducing quality and using yet more packaged foods. The price of a meal went up to 30p. By 1979, according to the school logbook, it was 35p.

Kate Small recalled that the crockery had to be carried across the playground to the School House scullery and the washing-up done there. The Catholic tradition of fish on Fridays doesn't seem to have extended to Bishop Sutton, and Colin Symes says that there was always meat stew on Fridays: "gorgeous". With a fine memory for detail, Joan Davidge can still taste Mrs Small's sponge cakes: with half an apricot on top surrounded by cream, they looked like a poached egg. Teachers dished out cod liver oil. Monica Castle insists that the meals were always excellent, although custard with the skin on and milk puddings did feature strongly. No veggie alternatives or funny foreign muck. May Woodward particularly recalls Eiffel Tower lemonade crystals (i.e. crystals, lemonade for the making of), although it's unlikely that these were on the school meals menu.

Teresa Dowling can still smell the 'wonderful' food, which included today's no-go areas of tongue and calves' hearts. There was a downside, however: one particular teacher would make you eat the food whether or not you liked it or not and whether or not it made you sick. If necessary, sawdust was brought in to cover the regurgitated diced carrot on the floor. Eric Price reflects that when the infants' classroom was at the Methodist Hall, the young ones had to walk all the way alongside a very busy main road to the Village Hall for lunch and then back again; he remembers the food arriving there in metal containers.

The schoolchildren c1934, possibly dressed for a pageant.
Boys (left to right): Leslie Lyons, Jim Rapps, Ken Perry, Brian Travis, Jim Gill,
Owen Owens,
'Chum' King, Sid Ogborne, Dick Dury, Dennis Noakes, James Gay, Percy Adams,
? Gay,
Jim Harris, Ken Rapps, Bob Walker;
Girls: Audrey Perry, Mildred Clark, Ruth Curry, Marion Harris, Eunice James,
Gladys Yates, Vera Edgell, Jean Montgomery, Peggy Bowditch, Betty Mellish,
Sadie Lyons, Gwen Stokes, Mildred Marsh.

Before moving on it would be wrong not to highlight the red-letter day of 30 September 1957. Mr Bailey excitedly noted that the County had delivered *6 tea cloths and 12 dust cloths*. Bet the teachers were talking about their windfall for months to come.

Finally, to milk and cocoa. In 1924 the Government let LEAs provide children with free milk. Many LEAs opted out, and there's no indication that Somerset opted in.

The school logbook did record in December 1930, however, *that children staying to dinner appear to be regular with their cups of cocoa*. The headmaster was presumably not referring to the drink's laxative qualities but to the frequency with which the children partook. The cocoa was provided by the Education Authority. The logbook didn't say how the cocoa got to school, what the funding arrangements were, or – if the cocoa was in powder form – how the school obtained the milk. When did free milk officially start in Bishop Sutton? It seems to have been on 22 October 1934, as that's when Mr Bailey wrote in his logbook that 57 children received milk and that *this number promises to increase when the children who have whooping cough return*. There is evidence from other schools that this may have been the starting date across the Chew Valley. The school milk at Bishop Sutton came, at least in the early years, from Hucker's Dairy in Chew Stoke. In January 1937, Mr Bailey *received notice that Milk Grant is now for one bottle only and each child (i.e. on the free list)*. The meaning of his words is uncertain. The war brought a more regimented approach, and in December 1939 Mr Bailey recorded that *in order to continue a supply of cocoa in playtime, the school has been registered as a catering establishment under the Food Control [Order] – registration certificate was received today. There are 38 children who take their bottle of milk made up as cocoa*. What we don't know is whether the milk (and/or cocoa) at Bishop Sutton was free before 1946 when the School Milk Act gave one-third of a pint of milk daily and gratis to every pupil under 18.

As a cost-cutting exercise, the Government withdrew free milk from secondary schools in 1967. It was taken away from primary schools in 1971 for all schoolchildren over the age of 7 by 'Margaret Thatcher, milk snatcher' (as per the chants and posters of the resultant student demos up and down the country), the then Secretary of State for Education. She had argued that the Government was spending £7 million a year on school books but £14 million a year on school milk. There were to be no more greasy marks on milk monitors' jumpers from carrying heavy metal crates from the playground into school and back again.

There are fond memories of that little bottle. Dick Chapman recalls the winter mornings when the milk had been left to freeze outside in the crate since the float delivered it in the wee small hours: 'you had your bottle and a straw but the bluetits had often got there first and pecked through the silver top. If you got a column of ice, you'd suck that first, then drink the milk'. Teresa Dowling remembers not so much the milk in the winter, but rather the milk in the summer: after being left on the window sill all morning, it was disgustingly warm and beginning to smell. She also recalls that the children would sometimes drink their milk at the churchyard wall, where there were families of slowworms which the boys would delight in throwing at the girls.

R5I4 TOP SUTTON		
COLLECTIONS		
A.M		P.M
I	7.15	2	3.0 NOT SAT

Enamel plate from the old letter box
at Top Sutton

CHAPTER SEVEN

ABSENCE, ROYALTY, WEATHER AND PUNISHMENT

PLANT YOUR BEANS ON SUTTON DAY, STAY AWAY ON ASCENSION DAY

In the early days of the logbooks, holidays could be granted at the drop of a hat and were sometimes not announced until the last minute. It wasn't until the last minute that it was known when the weather would be good for the harvest. Schools – at least in rural areas – generally arranged spring, summer and autumn breaks around the peak times of agricultural work. Otherwise, as was made abundantly clear in the records, children would simply be kept at home.

Holidays weren't always as they are now. February half term wasn't introduced at Bishop Sutton until 1947[1], and there was no break in October until 1924. A Whitsun[2] break (as opposed to just Whit Monday) in late May or early June didn't feature until 1905; the centuries-old religious festival was abandoned (in the educational sense) in 1970 in favour of the prosaic 'Spring Bank Holiday'[3]. The main summer was described as 'harvest holiday' until 1883, but 'midsummer holiday' then steadily came into vogue.

When shops start selling Christmas cards in September, one of the more mindless observations of our times must be 'Christmas has crept up very suddenly this year'. But it caught the newly formed School Board unawares in 1874. At their meeting on 14 December, the clerk wrote: *a fortnight's Christmas holiday is to be allowed commencing on 23rd instant*. Not much notice there. Other religious and religious-ish festivals (in addition to Christmas, Easter and Whitsun) regularly brought the children a day or half day off school. Harvest Festival wasn't one of them: on only one occasion did it lead to the children being granted time off: on the afternoon of Wednesday 23 September 1885 *school was closed, the Harvest Festival being held in the village*.

It was Ascension Day[4] that gave rise to the most contention over the years. Everything started off happily. On 23 May 1873 *the children had a half holiday on*

----

[1] Possibly only as a result of the fearsome winter that year, as it wasn't granted in 1948 or 1949; it became a permanent feature from 1950 onwards.

[2] The Bank Holiday Act of 1871 added Boxing Day, Easter Monday, Whit Monday and August Bank Holiday Monday to the existing national days off on Sundays, Good Friday and Christmas Day.

[3] Nothing to do with Bishop Sutton School as such, but the jury is still out on whether the weather would have been better had the Government stuck to the old moveable Whitsun feast. The hottest Whit Monday was in 1944 (29 May) when the temperature reached nearly 33 C (91 F) in parts of England, and the coldest was 1891 (18 May) when most of the south of the country was buried under snow. Worth bearing in mind when there's torrential rain on the next secular Spring Bank Holiday Monday.

[4] Ascension Day celebrates Jesus' ascension to heaven after he was resurrected on Easter Day. It falls 40 days after Easter, and is always on a Thursday.

Ascension Day. But there are hints of a veiled gripe behind Miss Hassell's logbook entry of twelve months later: *Thursday 22 May being Ascension Day, the Vicar of this parish claimed the school for use as 'Sunday School', consequently a holiday was given*. The school also closed on Thursday 15 May 1890, *the churchwarden having a right to the use of the premises on that day (Ascension Day)*. This was all getting a bit much, and on 4 March 1895 the Board *resolved that the holidays on Ash Wednesday[1] and Ascension Thursday be for the future discontinued*. The resolution clearly foundered as logbook entries remained thick, fast and annual for another seven decades. In 1939 it was the fault of a legal technicality: *the school closed today, Ascension Day, according to the rule in the transfer deeds*. In 1951 *the school closed for Ascension Wednesday as has been the custom since it was built*. Mr Bailey must have been confused, as Ascension Day is always on a Thursday. In 1958 and 1959 it was *long established custom* that was to blame for Ascension Day closure. The custom was tolerated for several years more but was questioned again in April 1965: *why was the school closed on Ash Wednesday and Ascension Day and, as there was no known reason for this, the Correspondent was instructed to make enquiries of the CEO*. Any response wasn't recorded, but the habit of closure on those two feast days seems to have died out by the late 1960s.

Apart from the usual national holidays, the pupils were routinely given at least half a day off for (in no particular order) Empire Day, County Council elections, Parliamentary elections, Local Authority elections, School Board or School Council elections, 'Club Days', a royal birth, sundry Sunday School outings, or the wedding or funeral of a local bigwig. The managers or vicar would additionally grant a half day off now and then if the children had been very good. By the 1940s a stipulated number of days' school attendance was introduced. On 12 June 1946, for example, *school reopened after the Whitsun hols. It is unusual to open on a Thursday, but it was necessary this year to get the number of attendances (210 days) required by the LEA*.

We'll start with 'Club Days'. It's a puzzle to know where one club ended (e.g. Clothing Club) and another started (e.g. Sutton Club), but most of them featured in the school logbooks in one way or another over the years. They may all have had a common ancestor in the self-help benefit clubs founded throughout the country from the 1700s onwards to alleviate distress caused by death, sickness and joblessness. The increasing demands of changing employment conditions and rising population had made it more difficult for the system of Parish Poor Relief to cope. This in turn lent greater importance to the clubs. Many of the local ones met at The Red Lion and it was The Red Lion Social Club that would eventually carry the banner for many of the village associations. Club Days were invariably in May or November, the significance of those two months dating back to medieval cattle fairs. The number of clubs dwindled over the years as a result of amalgamation or falling membership.

Let their story be told through typical logbook entries. Headmistress Hassell wrote on Friday 22 November 1872: *school very thinly attended from the parents going to Chew Magna to the Clothing Clubs[2]*. Tuesday 6 May 1873: *the children had a half holiday in consequence of the Village Club. Many of them were absent on the*

----
[1] The first day of Lent in the Christian calendar, and the day after Shrove Tuesday (Pancake Day). It falls 46 days before Easter.

[2] Villagers handed so much per week to the Club treasurer towards clothes or shoes; when enough money stood against their name in his books, they bought the desired item from the Club.

following day also. The Village Club also rejoiced under the name of 'Bishop's Sutton Club' or simply 'Sutton Club', and had its main festive day (including a 'Feast' in Victorian times) on the first Tuesday in May, with sideshows and a parade through the village led by a brass band; there was a smaller follow-up celebration in November. Both occasions prompted at least half a day off school. The Club seems to have quietly disappeared in the 1950s, perhaps to be revived by The Red Lion Social Club in the 1970s.

Thursday 20 November 1873: *the school was very thinly attended in consequence of the children going to Chew Magna to get their clothes out of the Clothing Club*. The birth of a Clothing Club (or Benefit Club) in Bishop Sutton itself can be dated to the beginning of May 1876, when headmaster Jones wrote: *attendance this week is considerably below the average owing to the arrival of a Benefit Club of the village*. There was a Clothing Club here until at least the late 1930s. Dick Chapman recalls that in the '20s and '30s you paid in your 6d a week at the Methodist Hall. On Tuesday 1 May 1877 and again on Wednesday 1 May 1878, a half day's holiday was granted for *the anniversary of the local Sick Club*. On Monday 3 May 1880 Mr Northam *gave notice that tomorrow this school will open at 8.45 and be carried on till 1.10, omitting the Religious Instruction on account of the anniversary of the Village Club*. Friday 9 May 1884: *average for the week 77. This low average is owing to Sutton Club Day. Opened school on that day in the morning, only 27 were present, so by order of Board gave half holiday*.

c1910
Headmaster Mr Wightman is on the left, near the window. Teacher Miss Batt may be the lady on the extreme right. The only pupil whose name is known is Samuel Treasure, sixth from the right on the second row, the tall boy in the starched white collar.

Some of the goings-on on Sutton Day can be gleaned from Mr Brown's helpful note of 1886, when he *gave a day's holiday on Tuesday May 4th, that day being the day on which the Bishop Sutton Friendly Society take their annual 'walk*[1]. *Owing to the attractions of swings, roundabouts and other amusements, the usual accompaniments to the 'Club Day', the average for the week is only 72.7.*

The caption reads 'New Wesleyan Chapel, Bishop Sutton, opened 10th June 1916'. In the foreground, Bonhill Road leads off to the right.

The last logbook entry relating to Bishop Sutton clubs or societies was on Tuesday 5 May 1914: *school closed today, anniversary of Village Friendly Society*. After 1914, either the headmaster didn't report the occasions when the school was closed or, more likely, the events took place at a weekend. In 1977 the Parish Magazine advertised that the village parade *would start at The Red Lion 5.30 pm, arriving at Woodcroft, where Tom Price will officially open the new bus shelter (the second shelter financed by The Red Lion Social Club). Parade then to return to The Red Lion forecourt where various produce stalls, amusements and competitions will keep going until dusk. Everyone to dress in Victorian dress if possible*. The crowning glory of the headmaster's career: opening the new bus shelter.

Bishop Sutton Club Day went down in local folklore as being the day by which gardeners should have planted their beans. Some authorities would have it that they should be planted on Sutton Day itself.

Labour prime minister James Callaghan introduced a May Day public holiday in

----

[1] This may have been a simple procession, or possibly the traditional 'beating the bounds', a custom which had existed in parishes across Britain and much of Europe for well over a thousand years. Local people would walk round the perimeter of their farm or parish, pausing as they passed certain trees, walls and hedges that denoted the extent of the boundary to beat them ritually with sticks and to pray.

1978, *the first holiday to be granted on this day by the Government*, as Mr Price explained. Unusually, that year's holiday did fall on the first day of the month. The new bank holiday revived the old Bishop Sutton tradition of May Day celebrations, which had seemingly died a death several years before. On Monday 7 May 1979 the school *was closed for May Day, the children performed a May Pole dance at The Red Lion Square as it was Village Club Day*. Had the long-defunct Club Day been resurrected?

Eric Price recalls that the Village Fête was held in the field behind the Methodist Chapel before moving in later years to the rec. A marquee housed the accompanying Flower Show with its vegetables and fruit. Each year, the British Legion arranged a fair with roundabouts, swings and dodgems. The fair people would came on the Wednesday or Thursday from Mark (near Highbridge) to start setting up and they packed up on the Sunday. Eric's father Doug used to repair the fairground lorries. Isobel Hill recalls 'Coles's Fair' on land beyond Brents. A circus came intermittently to a field where Rushgrove Gardens are now. There was a gymkhana by the Village Hall. Joan Davidge remembers that on May Day the children would march along the main road and assemble on The Red Lion car park dressed in Edwardian costume. Pauline Heron still has the brass ends of the poles holding the banners that were paraded through the village on Sutton Day. Joan Bunney recalls the Miss Bishop Sutton Carnival Queen element of the Sutton Day celebrations; one year at the preliminary contest at Midsomer Norton, she and her friends put up her cousin Ray as queen, dressed in a wig and dress. It was the way he walked that gave him away. His fellow competitors, being female and not wishing to be outclassed, called the police and wouldn't let Ray back into the hall.

If there were any risk of running out of local festive days, children would take advantage of those from elsewhere: Friday 5 June 1874: *a very thin school during the whole week, clubs in the neighbouring villages have caused it*. The Chew Magna Show closed the school for the morning of Friday 22 July 1921; the number of children who inadvertently forgot to come back in the afternoon is not mentioned. June 1949: *many children are away today having gone to the Bath & West Show*.

The idea grew in the closing years of the Victorian era that a day was needed for formal reflection on the glories of the British Empire. The Earl of Meath shared this sentiment, and in 1903 founded the Empire Day Movement. By the following year he had persuaded many LEAs to adopt 24 May (Queen Victoria's birthday) as an appropriate day for waving flags and singing rousing songs. The Empire was at the height of its power and influence and nobody questioned the rightness of our position in the world. Well, nobody in Britain anyway. It wasn't until 1916 that Somerset Education Committee actually decreed that Empire Day be observed, but for once the Chew Valley got in first. In April 1905 the local school managers wrote to Mrs Frances Shaw (The Grange, Chew Magna), Hon. Sec. of the North Somerset Branch of the Victoria League, asking her to draw up a programme of events. To give the children something to hoist and salute, the managers applied *to the Somerset County Education Committee for the grant of two Union Jacks* (one for Chew Magna and one for Bishop Sutton), and told the Committee that they would be having their celebrations on 24 May. But it wasn't to be all hoist and no work. The managers instructed *that the children attend school on Empire Day when the Rev. J. Galbraith will address them on the Empire and the Flag at 11 am*. They did get the afternoon off. Mr Strachey added a few more details in the managers' minute book: *I came to the school to witness the celebration of Empire Day. The children sang appropriate songs after a lecture on patriotism and the National Flag given by Mr Wightman. On leaving the school, all the children saluted the flag*. In 1909, the children *spent the morning in singing, history of Empire and march past the flag*. They would probably have been given red, white and blue rosettes to wear.

The school had pangs of patriotic angst in 1923: Empire Day fell during the Whitsun holidays and there was the possibility that the children would forget to salute the flag at home. The managers sought the advice of the Education Department, who decreed that *Empire Day can be observed on any day after Whitsuntide but not before*. The managers decided that *it was to be observed on the King's birthday, 4 June. Mr Atchley has promised to provide the gramophone for the Record of the King's Speech*. On the actual day, a Monday, *HM's speech was listened to, and a programme was carried out before the managers and parents. A holiday was given in the afternoon*. On Monday 25 May 1936 Mr Bailey wrote: *radio broadcast to schools used as Empire Day commemoration 11 to 11.30*. In 1946: *the flag was flown today, Empire Day. Mention of this was made in the morning assembly and the special BBC Empire Broadcast was heard by the seniors*. In 1949: *the flag was flown and suitable hymns etc used in the morning assembly with reference to Empire Day, likewise each class engaged in some activity in this connection*. 24 May 1955: *the children told briefly the reason for observing the day*. By this time, the Empire (by now called 'Commonwealth') was of dwindling importance. There were no further references in the logbook.

A rather tatty poster for a British Legion Church Parade in the 1920s.
Starting from Stowey Church at 2.45 pm, there would be an open-air service at 3.30 'in a field kindly lent by Mr Lovell', a Dedication Service at Holy Trinity led by The Rev. F M Etherington, and finally a Social at the Village Hall (admission 9d at the door).
The name of the 'Bishop Sutton Band Conductor' is just legible: Mr J. B. Wightman, the school headmaster.

The only mention of Trafalgar Day (21 October) was in 1931, when *the flag was run up and the National Anthem sung. Trafalgar, and Nelson's famous signal[1], were alluded to in a short address*.

----
[1] Traditionally, 'England expects that every man will do his duty'. The actual wording is subject to historical debate.

HAYMAKING IS A GREAT INDUCEMENT TO ABSENCE; BROKEN HOOTERS

There were reasons aplenty for children to be away from school legitimately. There were even more reasons for them to be away illegitimately. As Miss Hassell dolefully wrote on 10 July 1873: *haymaking is a great inducement to absence*. Not looking a gift horse in the mouth, she gave an object lesson on Haymaking the following week.

Children, especially boys, were co-breadwinners in most families and they were often off doing agricultural things: mid-October 1872, *the school has been thinly attended in the afternoons of this week in consequence of the children being employed to assist their parents in picking up potatoes*. They not only got them off the ground, but they put them in too: mid-April 1873, *the boys have attended very badly this week being employed in helping to plant potatoes*. Many of them were still at it a fortnight later, *which has made the attendance very low, the upper classes have been almost emptied, only one or two boys being present*. On 2 May 1873 William Harvey and John Harvey were away *keeping sheep*. And not as pets. Harvesting didn't always coincide neatly with school holidays, and when school reopened in September 1873, *attendance very poor in consequence of the continuing wet weather having prevented the harvest being gathered in, the children are many of them still gleaning*[1]. No sooner was the harvest in, than it was time to look to the fruit crops. 10 October 1873: *the children attend very badly, many of them are apple picking*. This continued for the rest of the month, and on 31st *the attendance is still very bad, nearly half the children are employed in picking up apples*. Some were still going strong on 7 November, but most had drifted back by mid-month. If it wasn't gleaning, it was gardening. At the end of June 1876, *several children are now at home in order to help at the gardens – these are normally those in the 2nd and higher Standards*. In July 1879 attendance was small *owing to operations in the hay fields*.

Work was often a convenient excuse, as on 1 October 1880: *the low average continues. Some are employed in getting up potatoes, but more are wasting their time in the street*. In February 1887 the Board wrote to Mr Pike, Relieving Officer at Pensford: *I am directed by the Board to inform you that a child named Elizabeth Withey, daughter of William Withey of Ham Lane, Bishop Sutton, is in the service of Mr Henry Rich of Littleton, Chew Stoke, who is not exempt from attending school, she having only passed the 2nd Standard*. What Mr Pike did with the information was not recorded. The 1881 census listed Elizabeth as having been 6 years old, which would have made her 11 or 12 in 1887.

By the 1890s, agricultural absences were either too commonplace to merit a mention, or becoming rarer, and it wasn't until 1894 that haymaking was mentioned again: *being in full operation, has badly affected the attendance during the week*. But in 1897 they were at it afresh, taking an end-of-July day off *picking apples, potatoes and blackberries*. Children were still being kept away with the connivance of employers. In September 1893 the Board wrote sternly to Mr James Bird. The letter is shown on the next page.

----
[1] Gathering the useful remnants of the crops from the fields after harvesting.

In March 1896 it was Mr Manning's turn to receive a stern letter. See picture below. The 1891 census had listed Elizabeth Gray (2, Top Sutton) as a widowed needlewoman. She had five sons, of whom Frank would be 11 or 12 in 1896 and William 15 or 16, so the letter probably concerned Frank. Samuel Manning was a farmer on Ham Lane.

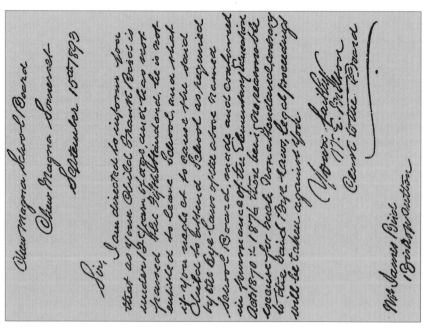

Letters to Mr Bird (1893) and Mr Manning (1896) threatening prosecution for allowing under-age children to be employed

In 1898 HM Chief Inspector Howard summarised the position nationally: *So long as certain farming operations can be performed by children, it appears that employers and parents will continue to break the law, magistrates will be slow to convict, school attendance committees will not press cases against employers and parents, managers will not furnish names of offenders for fear of making the school unpopular and teachers will not make enemies by furnishing information*. In May 1900 the Board warned *Mr John Chancellor that he is rendering himself liable to a prosecution if he employs John Chiswell or any other child under school age during school hours*. In June 1920 *Maud Harvey* [was] *allowed to leave for home employment*. In June 1921 Mr Wightman noted that *G. Harvey, M. Tibbs, E. Harvey passed the Labour Exam in Standard 6 and were allowed to leave*. The last agricultural-based entry in the logbook was as late as 3 July 1951 when *attendance is very bad in the top class through boys working, chiefly haymaking*.

If it wasn't work, it was leisure. It's not just in recent times that parents sneak their children out of school when the sun shines or there are cheap tickets to be had. On 17 July 1896 *Minnie, Arthur and Lilian Lovell absent all week being at Weston-super-Mare for their holiday*. Headmaster Brown complained in July 1897 that *the attendance has been very poor this week, several families having left for holidays*. Friday 1 September 1911: *attendance poor as many have not returned from holidays* (which ended on Monday 28 August). The same in 1913 when *several children extended their holidays and have not yet returned*. 23 July 1951 (four days before the holidays officially started): *attendance poor this morning as some children have gone on holiday*. On Monday 6 June 1955, 88 children out of 150 on the roll hadn't returned following the previous week's Whitsun holiday. They couldn't all have been stuck on the Exeter Bypass in their dads' Ford Pops.

Weddings, funerals, birthdays and the like were good reasons to bunk off. On 24 January 1879 Miss Arter, daughter of the School Board chairman, celebrated her 21st and the children were given a day off. They were given another day off on 30 July in honour of her wedding. On Friday 11 March 1881 nearly two thirds of the children went to a funeral. There is no obvious explanation for a day's holiday in March 1897 after headmaster Brown announced his resignation: perhaps the pupils just needed time to dry their tears. On Wednesday 9 September 1908 there was *a holiday in the afternoon, as a large proportion of the children were going to Miss Hill's wedding*. She wasn't a teacher but was presumably someone big in the village. On Wednesday 10 September 1913, *owing to a wedding at the Chapel the attendance was very poor in the afternoon*.

The most innovative excuses are left until last. Tuesday 21 May 1907: *bad attendance this afternoon owing to a Sham Fight in the neighbourhood*. Monday 22 May 1916[1]: *several late probably owing to alteration to summer time*. In the absence of alarm clocks in most households in 1921, people used substitute methods of being woken, and on 19 June *there has been some late coming today due to the variation of the hooter at the Colliery*. Three months later: *some late coming, probably owing to the Colliery hooter not being correct*. Finally, on Thursday 19 January 1939, *six boys are away beating*. That would be pheasants.

Today's concerns about absenteeism were applicable ninety years ago. In frustration at the ease with which children could be away, Mr Wightman wrote in October 1913: *some long periods of absence appear to be granted to a few children* and, in June 1920, *attendance shows many cases where absence could have been avoided*.

----
[1] The year in which the clocks started going backwards and forwards.

YET ANOTHER ROYAL VISIT TO BRISTOL

In June 1887 headmaster Brown wrote: *the School Board gave a day's holiday on Wednesday 15th inst., that day being selected for celebrating the Queen's Jubilee in this parish. Each child had a good tea and a medal paid for by public subscription.* The village celebrated loyally for the next few days, and Her redoubtable Majesty would not have been amused to hear that *the Jubilee rejoicings have attracted many children from school and lowered the averages.* A decade later, she was still busily reigning and the Board closed the school *on Monday 18 June and Tuesday 19 June 1897 to commemorate HM's Diamond Jubilee.* Two years later, on 15 November 1899, she graced Bristol with her imperial and imperious presence and walking stick. Bishop Sutton children had a day off to go and see her. How they got there isn't recorded.

With all that jubilating while she was alive, it's surprising that her death on 22 January 1901 warranted nary a logbook mention. But the Board did close the school on 20 June 1902 *in honour of the coronation of His Majesty Edward VII,* Victoria's bearded and somewhat dissolute son and heir. The new king should have been coronated on 26 June 1902 but went down with appendicitis. Westminster Abbey was re-booked for 9 August, so the school's celebrations were a bit hasty. Not to worry, Bishop Sutton schoolchildren had another day off on 16 September *owing to Coronation Festivities.* On 9 July 1908, the school was closed *owing to His Majesty the King's visit to Bristol.* On 23 June 1909, *HRH The Prince of Wales* (the future George V) *passed slowly by the scholars as they stood to attention in the road.*

Edward VII himself passed away in 1910. His son George V was next in line and on 16 June 1911 the school was closed for a day so that he could be crowned. Papa and Grandmama had set the tone, and George and his lady wife (Princess Victoria Mary of Teck, better known as Queen Mary) came to Bristol for the day on 28 June 1912, giving the children another holiday. The couple were so impressed that they came again on 9 June 1925: *school closed on the occasion of the visit of the King and Queen to Bristol.* On 15 March 1935 the vice chairman of Chew Magna PC convened a public meeting *at Bishop Sutton to make arrangements for celebrating the Silver Jubilee of their Majesties the King and Queen.* Headmaster Bailey wrote that the school was closed on 6 May 1935 *on the ocasion* (sic) *of His Majestie's* (sic) *Silver Jubilee.* Two unbefitting orthographical misdemeanours in the same sentence.

On 24 June 1923 *school closed on the occasion of the Marriage of HRH The Duke of York*, the happy couple being Prince Albert Frederick Arthur George, second son of King George V and Queen Mary, and The Honourable Elizabeth Angela Marguerite Bowes-Lyon. They went on to become the parents of the present queen. The managers shut the school on the afternoon of Friday 28 November 1934 for the Royal Wedding of Prince

George (Duke of Kent[1]) and Princess Marina (to be Duchess of Kent). HRH Henry The Duke of Gloucester (third son of George V) married Lady Alice Christabel Montagu Douglas Scott – hands up, those who didn't know that – on 6 November 1935. There's no mention of any visit to Bristol, but the children did get the day off for the wedding. On 15 November Mr Bailey wrote ruefully (or perhaps in a spirit of elation): *today concludes the 4th consecutive week in which single holidays have broken into the school work.* They would have been the General Election of 14 November, the Royal Wedding above and two other days which weren't explained.

On 21 January 1936, George V died. *The Flag was flown at half mast, the death of the King was mentioned in the Morning Assembly, when I made a short address fitting to the occasion, and the hymns 'Let Saints on Earth' and 'My God, my Father make me strong' were sung. Psalm 23 was read for the Bible reading.* On 22 January 1936 *all children assembled in the main room today at 9.55 to hear the reading of the Proclamation at St James Palace announcing the succession of King Edward VIII. Miss Batt lent her wireless set and reception was very good. The National Anthem was sung and today the Flag flew at the mast head.* This was the first logbook mention of a radio on school premises. The school was closed for George V's funeral on Tuesday 28 January. Edward VIII's abdication broadcast to the nation was

on 12 December 1936, but Miss Batt left her wireless at home. Mr Bailey wrote on Monday 14 December 1936: *the National Anthem was sung at Morning Assembly in honour of the King's birthday. In the Assembly on Friday* [11th December], *I outlined the position to the children by saying that King Edward VIII had renounced the throne and that his brother would succeed him.* The birthday that the school was honouring was that of Edward's brother George, who had stepped into the breach. The country now had an unexpected and inexperienced king, a shy man who would give the monarchy a new popularity and stand by Churchill's side in marshalling his people through World War II. He and his wife Elizabeth won enormous admiration by refusing to seek safe haven abroad and by visiting bombed cities (including Bristol and Bath) after major air raids.

Sheila Walker remembers the abdication crisis. She was only 5 but can still hear the children chanting in the school playground 'Mrs Simpson stole our King'. For the coronation celebrations for George VI she can still picture the children all assembled at Stowey in fancy dress. The long procession led by a band walked a mile to the rec at Bishop Sutton. Sheila carried a rifle and was dressed in a Grenadier Guard's scarlet uniform. A clown had been hired to add to the entertainment and wobbled his way from Stowey on a huge ball. Bishop Sutton School either didn't take part in the celebrations – which is unlikely – or

Mr Bailey didn't write anything in the logbook. We have to look to Stowey PC, which minuted a right royal bean feast there: *Coronation tea 24 loaves 8/-, 7 lb butter 8/2, 3 lb ham 4/6, 30 dozen fancies £1.10s.0d (i.e. a penny each), 4 lb slab cake 4/-. Following commodities promised: coronation cake, ginger cake, two sponge cakes, small cakes, 4 lb slab cake, 5 lb butter, 3 lb ham, milk. Coronation cups would be presented to children before tea, to be used at it. Five coronation mugs, value 1/10½ remained surplus, one to be presented to each*

----
[1] Killed in an air crash in 1942

child born in Stowey during 1937.

On 20 November 1947, Bishop Sutton School *was closed on the occasion of the Marriage of HRH Princess Elizabeth and Lieutenant Philip Mountbatten, Duke of Edinburgh*. Prince Charles was born on 14 November 1948, and on the following morning *the flag was flown and the National Anthem sung to mark the occasion of the birth of the Royal Baby*. Note the headmaster's reverential use of capital letters.

In 1949 the joint parish of Stowey Sutton was formed. One of the councillors' first momentous quandaries was how to commemorate the Festival of Britain, the event that drew millions to the South Bank in London to ooh and aah at the Skylon tower, and prompted parties, commemorative stamps and lots of tea towels and ashtrays. On 28 May 1951 the Council discussed the possibility of *holding a local event to celebrate the Festival of Britain. The item was not met with any enthusiasm and a vote to its rejection was carried*. Bah humbug. Bishop Sutton School did, of course, send some of its older children to the Skylon where they met one of their teachers who'd cycled there on his bamboo bicycle.

The flag was flown on the occasion of the King's birthday on 7 June 1951, but his death on 6 February 1952 went unnoted in the school logbook.

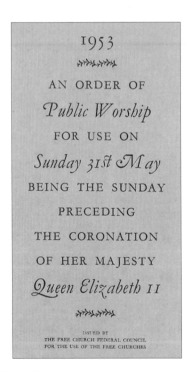

The PC set to and worked out how best to greet its new young queen. According to the minutes of 22 May 1953, *the Coronation Fund stood at £154. Arrangements to provide 250 teas on Coronation Day were in hand: 170 children would receive Coronation mugs, and 103 pensioners a gift, two members of HM Forces serving*

overseas would receive a postal order for 2 guineas. What did the schoolchildren do, apart from festoon the place with red, white and blue bunting and try to remember that the opening words of the National Anthem – for the first time in over 50 years – were no longer 'God save our gracious King'? On 4 June 1953 Mr Bailey wrote: *as part of the Coronation Celebration, a television set was installed in the school for the benefit of the children, the cost being met by the local Coronation Committee.* Eric Price remembers the celebratory bonfire on the slag heap at the back of the Old Pit Garage. A television set was brought into the Methodist Sunday School Hall and was a highlight of the village festivities.

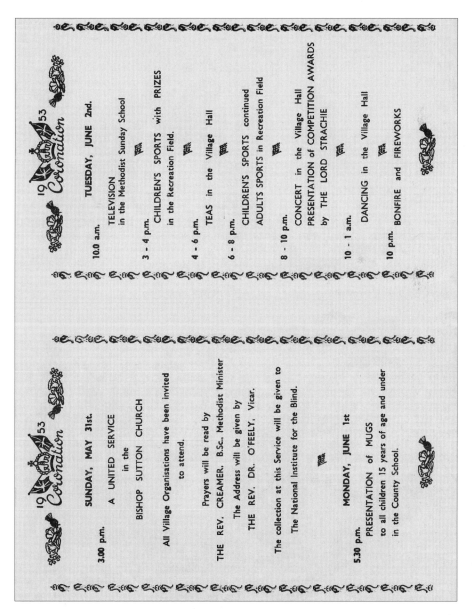

Bishop Sutton Coronation programme 1953

The school was closed on 6 May 1960 – a *holiday being granted for Princess*

Margaret's wedding (to Anthony Armstrong-Jones) – but the rapid succession of royal happenings of the pre-war years was a thing of the past and there was no more waving of little paper Union Jacks until 12 June 1970, when *the Lower Juniors and infants went to Farrington Gurney to see Prince Charles, who is paying a brief visit on his way to Bath*. On Monday 20 November 1972 *the school was closed on the occasion of Her Majesty's Silver Wedding Anniversary, in common with all schools throughout the country*. On Wednesday 14 November 1973 *the whole school was closed on the occasion of Princess Anne's wedding to Capt. Mark Phillips*.

The nation hung out the flags for the Queen's Silver Jubilee in 1977. People really did get very excited. Apart from the very few curmudgeons who wanted no part in it. The punk rock group The Sex Pistols did quite well with their anti-monarchist hit single sarcastically entitled 'God Save the Queen', but there was no outward sign of rampant republicanism in Bishop Sutton. The school logbook and PC minutes show that most villagers were intent on showing their loyalty to their monarch by having a thoroughly jolly time. The village's preparations started in December 1976 when parish councillors decided to form a Silver Jubilee Committee. The Council *would advance a loan (if required) for the purchase of mugs etc*. In April 1977 the loan of £150 was converted into an outright grant. The school's preparations started in March 1977 when *Mr Taviner removed the old school bell; the PTA have asked that it be restored to working condition and moved to mark the occasion of the Queen's Jubilee*. On Friday 3 March 1977 *a special tea party was given in the school yard by the PTA to commemorate the Queen's Silver Jubilee. A souvenir present was given to each child*.

In July 1977 the PC discovered that there was £509 left in the Village Silver Jubilee Fund, *and after providing evening entertainment for senior members of the parish and making a contribution to the National Fund, still £400-£450 left. Committee suggests a clock*. Deliberations continued for a whole year. In July 1978 it was decided *to give some funds to youth projects in Somerset*, and by the following April *mugs and crowns had been given to all the village children*[1].

The huge effort put in by members of the Jubilee Committee was richly applauded in the Stowey Sutton Parish Magazine, which gushed:

Well, it's over! The months of planning and preparation by the Jubilee Committee for our celebrations were put to the test over the holiday, and judging from the wonderful response from the Parish it is fair to say that a good time was had by all. Our festivities got off to a very glamorous start by the choosing of our Jubilee Queen at the Youth Club Disco. What an incredibly difficult task our two Judges, Miss Sarah Pitt of Radio Bristol and Mr Ken Rees of HTV, had! Our nine contestants all looked lovely, and it was a difficult decision indeed to select the three finalists. However, Debbie David, Rosalind Harvey and Susan Roper were chosen to go forward to the Jubilee Dance for the crowning. Mr W. Kellaway performed the crowning ceremony most ably and with a roll of drums and a round of applause Rosalind Harvey was declared our Queen and duly crowned. Rosalind, who is 16 years old, was born in Bishop Sutton, went to the Primary School, was a Girl Guide and is now a Ranger … She looked lovely in her crimson cloak, jewelled crown and Jubilee sash … The Village Hall was ablaze with red, white and blue.

----

[1] Although outside the scope of this book, it's worthy of note that in December 1981 the PC suggested that *monies remaining in the fund* [could be given] *for a cup for the Primary School*. Trouble was, the school didn't want one: the headmaster *did not think that the provision of another cup for the primary school was acceptable; he suggested various alternatives and it was decided to donate the remaining money towards the cost of a new maypole*. The fate of the Jubilee maypole is not known.

ORGANISERS OF THE STOWEY – BISHOP SUTTON
SILVER JUBILEE CELEBRATIONS

JUBILEE DANCE . . . . Mrs. C. Hillman–(Young Wives)
Mrs. J. Hawley–(Playgroup)

JUBILEE QUEEN CONTEST . . . . Mr. Bill Pittman–(Youth Club)

THANKSGIVING SERVICE   The Rev. Barrie Newton–(Church of England)
The Rev. Kenneth Britton–(Methodist)

EXHIBITIONS
Village Hall . . . . Mrs. W. Duck, Mrs. I. Marden–(W.I.)
Mrs. Joyce Small–(Silver Lining Club)

Refreshments . . . . Mrs. C. Pittman–(British Legion Ladies)

Primary School . . . . Mr. Tom Price

OPEN SPORTS . . . . Dr. G. Sharpe, Mr. D. Powell

TUG OF WAR . . . . Mr. J. Ashby–(British Legion)

CHILDREN'S FANCY DRESS . . . . Mr. T. Ogbourne

BARBEQUE . . . . Mr. R. Street–(Red Lion Social Club)

BONFIRE . . . . Mr. L. Collett–(Cricket Club)

CHAIRMAN OF COMMITTEE Mrs. D. E. S. Shellard. Tel.: Chew Magna 2648
SECRETARY . . . . Mrs. R. Metcalfe. Tel.: Chew Magna 2851
TREASURER . . . . Mr. L. Hammond. Tel.: Chew Magna 2673

LUCKY
PROGRAMME   357
DRAW No.

Designed and produced by A. R. Brace. Tel.: C.M. 2906

The school's Jubilee tea party in 1977

POST OFFICE STORES

C. J. & W. G. PITTMAN

Your MACE Grocers

*

Wish the Queen, her family and you all

A Silver Jubilee to remember

You are welcome at —

The Croft

HEALTH, BEAUTY
GIFTS & CRAFTS

+

Judy Bristow

Wick Road, Bishop Sutton

Carolyn and Peter Bickley
welcome you at
SHELL LODGE
FILLING STATION

For Petrol,
Shrubs, Conifers, Plants
and many other garden requirements

OLD PIT GARAGE

(L. C. H. MANNI)

BISHOP SUTTON

AA   BRISTOL   RAC

Telephone: Chew Magna 2582

24 Hour Breakdown & Repair Service

Something Special —

THE SILVER JUBILEE

for your "Something Special "

Visit

Audrey Stuckey & Edna Pittman

At THE DRAPERY

PROGRAMME

SATURDAY 4th JUNE

Grand Jubilee Dance

at the VILLAGE HALL

8 p.m. to ~2 o'clock

Dancing to the "Riverside Showband"

Supper and Licensed Bar

SPECIAL EVENT–THE CROWNING OF OUR JUBILEE QUEEN

SUNDAY 5th JUNE

OPEN AIR THANKSGIVING SERVICE

10.15 a.m.   Procession with Band of local Youth Groups and Congregation from the Red Lion Car Park to the Playing Field.

10.30 a.m.   Thanksgiving Service on the Playing Field. (In Church if wet)

TUESDAY 7th JUNE

2.00 p.m.   Exhibition in the Village Hall of floral art and Jubilee mementos. Refreshments. Open Painting Exhibition in the Primary School—all day.

2.00 p.m.   Procession of JUBILEE QUEEN and Attendants on decorated float followed by children in Fancy Dress.

2.30 p.m.   Judging of Fancy Dress.

3.00 p.m.   OPEN SPORTS on Playing Field.   "Knobbly Knees" Contest.   Tug-of-War Contest. Teas.   Ice Creams.

Distribution of Jubilee Gifts will take place during the day in the Village Hall.

Presentation of prizes by JUBILEE QUEEN.

8.00 p.m.   BONFIRE and BARBEQUE with Licensed Bar on the Playing Field.

See back page of this programme for your lucky number in the Jubilee Draw ! !

F. E. BRENT & SONS

FORGE GARAGE

BISHOP SUTTON,

REPAIRS & SERVICE
COACHES FOR HIRE

Telephone: Chew Magna 2569

Lawrence J. Potter

Wholesale and Retail Butcher

*

Bishop Sutton, BRISTOL, Avon
BS18 4XD

Telephone: Chew Magna 2235 (Wholesale)
2337 (Retail)

COME TO

THE CHEW VALLEY SOFT
FRUIT CENTRE

(D. and M. Mellish)

GREENACRES, BONHILL
BISHOP SUTTON

(Tel.: Chew Magna 2567)

All our produce is of the highest quality
—hand picked and selected

G. C. Stuckey

NEWSAGENT & GROCER

Local Newspaper Deliveries

Toys, Greeting Cards
High Class Provisions

THE STORES
BISHOP SUTTON
Tel. Chew Magna 2268

Wedding Cakes a Speciality

N. E. TIBBS

Baker and Confectioner

BISHOP SUTTON   Chew Magna 2695

Cream Cakes and Pastries
Hovis and Wholemeal Bread

" God Bless the Queen
Long may she reign "

Bishop Sutton Silver Jubilee programme 1977

After two weeks of sunny weather, our spirits were dampened on the Sunday morning by the rain and wind, and all hopes of an open air Thanksgiving Service had to be abandoned. However, undaunted, the procession led by a 12-piece band and followed by Girl Guides, Brownies, Scouts and Cubs went ahead, and a packed congregation in Holy Trinity Church heard the Rev. Barrie Newton and the Rev. Kenneth Britton conduct the special Jubilee Service. As Tuesday approached, the weather was again in everyone's minds, but despite this the Village took on an air of gaiety as bunting and flags flew from houses and across roads. The Primary School was open again for another viewing of the Exhibition of paintings by the children and some adults. At 1.40 pm the excitement started as the procession of decorated Traders' Vehicles left Sutton Wick and moved through Bishop Sutton, led by the Jubilee Queen in her robes and seated on a beautifully decorated float, prepared by Mr Bill Pitman and members of the Youth Club. Following along behind the floats came the children in their dozens in every type of Fancy Dress, having previously assembled in the Primary School. The sun at long last appeared when everyone collected at the Playing Field, and the afternoon's entertainment began. The Primary School children put on a display of country dancing. A fascinating exhibition of Jubilee Souvenirs, mementos and photographs organised by the WI was set out in the Village Hall, and up on the stage the children lined up to receive their Jubilee Mugs and Crowns.

Away in the corner of the Village Hall – with never a break and never a grumble – that incredible band of British Legion Ladies ... dressed in Jubilee hats and aprons, served us tea, homemade scones and cream and cakes – in all serving over 500 teas! By 8 o'clock the smell of barbecued steaks, hamburgers, sausages and chickens was wafting over the Village as the members of The Red Lion Social Club got under way with the cooking, and here kindness and generosity prevailed, for Mr Lawrence Potter ... supplied and gave the meat for the occasion, and Montgomery's the Bakers gave all the bread rolls. To warm us up, the Cricket Club had built an enormous bonfire, and to entertain us there was a disco. So ended our Jubilee Celebrations, and we feel sure even Her Majesty would have approved!

Snow, snow and more rain

The British love their weather. 'Twas ever thus, and the climate was a favourite topic in the school logbooks. Snow, which closed the school for days at a time, could be fun. Water generally couldn't, and flooding and poor roads were such that heavy rain frequently prevented children in outlying areas from getting in. By 'outlying', we're talking no further than Ham Lane or Bonhill. Teachers could usually cope when conditions were bad: the absence of transport forced them to live locally, their legs were longer than children's and they could therefore wade through deeper snow or water and, unlike so many of their pupils a hundred years ago, could afford boots. An absence of sturdy footwear kept many a child at home. In October 1914, the head *sent home F. Satchell for boots*. Had he simply forgotten them, or had he really come to school barefoot? After about 1900, either the climate improved or parents could afford more (and more waterproof) shoes or at least cut-down wellies. Or perhaps the weather was simply passé as a logbook topic. The following extracts depict the major or more typical incidents, in roughly chronological order.

20 December 1872: *the weather this week having been very bad, the attendance has not been so good, some children not being able to get through the water on the roads*. 30 January 1873: *the weather having been very wet this week, many children have been unable to attend*. On the following day: *the weather being very cold, with snow, some of the girls who live at a distance were unable to attend*. The boys were generally taller (or more foolhardy) and presumably battled their way through. The roads were so bad that it didn't take much for them to become impassable: on 24 July 1874 *very thin school this afternoon in consequence of a thunderstorm*. Heavy rain coinciding with the end of the holidays was a recipe for chaos: on 3 September 1877 *school reopened this morning with 27 present only owing probably to the heavy rain* (out of 107 on the books that week).

Snow was not only a regular occurrence – as, indeed, it was in most parts of the country until the 1970s – but also there was an awful lot of it. On 18 December 1874 *those who live at a distance have been unable to attend from a fall of snow*; by 23 December *the weather has been so severe this week that more than half of the children have been absent*. Tuesday 20 January 1880: *there was a deep fall of snow, and still deeper during the night*. The school remained shut for the rest of the week. And if it wasn't rain or snow, it was the wind: on 15 October 1877 there were only 38 present out of around 100 possibles, *a great many being kept at home to pick up the firewood brought down by last night's gale*. 18 June 1880: *owing to lightening* (sic)*, there was no sewing. I considered it dangerous for them to hold their needles*. It's best not to shelter under trees during a thunderstorm, but to sew?

The logbooks weren't always consistent, and it wasn't every bout of bad weather that merited a mention. 1881, for instance, was billed as the worst of the century, with the lowest ever recorded temperatures in the West Country and a snowstorm lasting 33 hours from 8 am on Tuesday 18 January. Snow in railway cuttings and narrow valleys was up to 30 feet (9 m) deep. Nary a mention in the school logbook. Perhaps Bishop Sutton just missed it.

On Thursday 7 December 1882, *weather was so bad and snow so deep that the school was closed today, only 48 present*. 1 March 1886: *snow storms throughout the week, several infants unable to attend in consequence. Upper classes attended well*. All this talk of snow, yet rarely were we told just how much. But on Tuesday 11 January 1887 *the most heavy snowstorms of this winter occurred, snow settling to a depth of 18"* (46 cm)*, the roads being impassable. Closed school until Thursday afternoon, when only 79 children were* present. On Monday 14 February: *an exceptionally severe snow storm rendered it quite impossible for the children to attend, therefore closed school for the rest of the week. Reopened on Monday 21st, only 60 present. The roads in some places are still impassable and the weather continues to be severely cold in the extreme. Average attendance for the week only 61.2*. On Friday 8 February 1889 *a heavy snow storm prevented many infants from attending school all the week*. Recognising an opportunity when he saw it, Mr Brown gave an object lesson on Snow the following Monday. If it wasn't one thing, it was the other. Sometimes both: Friday 8 March 1889, *school closed all the week owing to heavy snow storm followed by flood*. On the morning of Monday 5 January 1891, Mr Brown *reopened school in very severe weather. Ground covered with deep snow. Average attendance for week only 49.9, average of infants only 7.6*. By the following Monday, *weather still very bad and roads almost impassable for little children*. At the beginning of March, *very heavy falls of snow rendered the roads almost impassable, which necessitated the closing of the school for the rest of the week*. Bishop Sutton missed the worst of the phenomenal blizzards that pasted areas further to the west, and thus forfeited a mention in the snappily titled book 'The Blizzard in the West, A Record and Story of the Disastrous Storm which Raged Through Devon and Cornwall and West Somerset on the Night of March 9th 1891'.

An aside. Bad though those these winters were, they were as nothing compared with what had befallen the West Country in 1683. The snow was deeper than a man, and people were dropping like flies. Ubley's parish records observed that those trying to cross the Mendips *did travell till they could travell no longer, and then lye doune and dye*.

In June 1897 in Bishop Sutton the mercury was at the opposite end of the scale: on the 4th and 26th *drill was not taken in the open air as the heat was so great*. On 21 July 1899 *the heat has been very great this week which, together with the overcrowded state of the school, has interfered with the progress*. This heat didn't foreshadow a mild winter, and on 14 February 1900 *the roads were impassable owing to snow, and children did not come. A thaw set in, and by 1 pm the following day the road was flooded and children could not get here. The drainage in the yard was choked and the school flooded. The main road was 1' (30 cm) deep in water. I had to send some children in carts*. On 4 October that year, *through heavy rain and the watercourses being blocked, the schoolroom was flooded during the dinnertime. It was impossible to have the children in school.* 15 May 1901: *children spent 10 minutes in the playground for fresh air. Too rough for play.* Presumably it was windy. 3 August 1906: *a very heavy shower occurred about 9 am, many children were sent home wet.* 8 July 1908: *severe thunderstorms with torrents of rain at 1.45 pm. I sent three children home as they were wet through.* No waterproof jackets for children in those days and, in any event, most parents could only afford one set of clothes. If those got wet, then children would have to sit in them all day with little chance of drying them properly overnight. Moreover, children weren't chaperoned to school as they are now, so weren't steered away from tantalisingly deep water and thick snow.

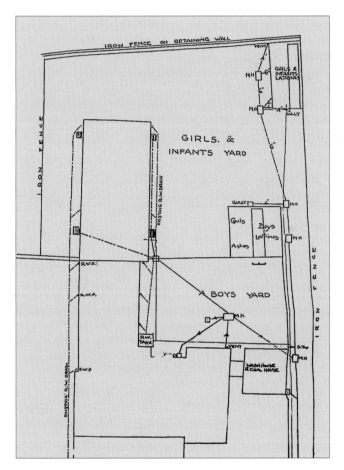

From a 1906 plan

31 July 1908: *no play allowed owing to the intense heat.* There was a challenge of a different sort on 3 December of that year: *dull weather, mental vigour has required much keeping up.* 7 July 1911: *very hot and children lacking in energy.* At the end of 27 July 1911, it was *very hot during the week; having no shade, did not allow playtime,* and on 8 September 1911 *there was no drill or play owing to the intense heat. 84° (29 C) at 11 am in shade, and between two doors.* A commendable level of detail. On the night of 12-13 January 1920: *during the gale, two windows were*

damaged and water entered the main room. On 17 June 1920: *terrific thunderstorm at 3 pm – torrents of water. Drains not capable of carrying water away. Work had to be suspended at 3.10 pm, and many children had to remain until 5 pm. Main room was flooded.* 19 July 1921: *extremely hot, children were fatigued.* 11 July 1927: *terrific thunderstorm with torrential rain. All rooms at 2.45 had water over floors to a depth of 2½"* (6 cm), *cleaned at 5 pm and fires were burning all night. First part of morning, Standards III to VII had lessons in the playground. Fires continued all day.* Gales in 1928 again damaged the roof and windows, and November 1929 saw *rainfall totalling 8.63"* (22 cm), *being four times the average for November.* Headmaster Bailey was a stickler for detail, and he was notably sticklerish on 15 November 1935: *attendance today was so far below normal as to make it necessary to record the reasons, these are (1) the outlying areas of the village are flooded to a depth sufficient to prevent children attending, (2) there are several children who got very wet during yesterday's holiday (General Election polling station) and are away in consequence.* The high winds of 14 December 1936 smashed glass panels in doors.

The war brought its own anxieties, so it's hardly surprising that there was only one meteorological reference throughout those years: on 29 January 1940 *attendance this morning has dropped to 50% as the roads are so slippy* (sic). But then came the winter of 1947 which, along with that of 1962-3, will not be forgotten in a hurry by those who lived through it. Still suffering badly from the after-effects of conflict, Britain was brought to its knees by its cruellest weather for two centuries. From late January 1947 to mid-March, many places had snow virtually every day, with drifts of up to 23 ft (7 m) driven by winds of more than 100 mph. These were the most violent snowstorms recorded in the UK. Most roads were blocked and public transport virtually ground to a standstill. Coal couldn't be moved from the mines, and fuel for heating ran out. By the end of February the Government limited electricity to five hours a day, and gas – not that there was any in Bishop Sutton – was down to a quarter of its usual pressure. Traffic lights – also not a feature of the local landscape – were switched off to save electricity. There was pack ice in the English Channel. Food supplies were running desperately short: a fifth of the national livestock perished, and winter crops were frozen into the ground. Bread was rationed for the first time ever. Although Bishop Sutton was as badly affected as most other areas, the logbook's only two entries are from 4 February (*Dr Barker Asst SMPO was here today as she was unable to come yesterday as the roads were blocked*) and 6 March (*when heavy snow has blocked roads and attendance this morning is 42, i.e. 45.1%*). Colin Symes recalls that the snow was so deep and crisp and even solid that you could walk over walls.

1954 was also a winter for thick woollies: on 28 January *road conditions are still bad owing to frozen snow, our min. and max. thermometer registered 10°* (-12 C) *last night, i.e. 22° of frost. The dinner van was late yesterday. All football and netball matches have been cancelled.* Note that the dinner van was merely late; in those days drivers simply[1] fixed chains over the tyres and ploughed steadily through the snow. On Friday 14 January 1955 *snow fell during the night and was very deep this morning, consequently the attendance today was bad, 42%. Miss Chivers was unable to get here.* On the following Monday, *the difficult road conditions have again made the attendance poor.*

Bishop Sutton and its school might have suffered from occasional flooding, but it was little more than an inconvenience. Elsewhere, lives were lost, and in September

----
[1] This is unfair: it was actually very tricky.

1952 the PC recorded that the village had collected £33.13s.6d for the Lynmouth Flood Disaster Appeal, *plus £7 from a subsequent dance.* The East Anglia floods of March 1953 claimed over 300 lives and Bishop Sutton raised £38.12s.6d for the Disaster Fund. Somerset was spared, but that month the councillors read *a letter from L. Dagger* (re '*Ham Lane inundations*') *re the intraversability in the lane during wet weather.* Intraversability has always been a challenge in an inundated Ham Lane. Colin Symes recalls that Moreton was also perpetually soggy and that Ben Bridge[1] was frequently flooded.

School year 1956-57
Back row (left to right): Margaret Dury, Angela Perry, Pam Woodward, Andrew Parfitt, Martin Tibbs, Margaret Wood, John Marsh.
Middle row: Ian Tovey, Diana Harvey, Jane Lyons, Janice Spencer, Carol Bassett, Susanne Montgomery, Jean Gallop, Pamela Walker, Shirley Perry.
Front row: Neil Paulley, Alan Buttifant, Frankie Gallop, Alan Small, Ray Matthews, Christopher Small, Ivor Elms, Alan Elms, Michael Chidzey.

The Great Bishop Sutton Floods were on 26 November 1956. Mr Price described *flooding to a depth of 2' (61 cm) outside the gate when it was time for the children to go home; some reached the road via the churchyard, some through Mr Treasure's, the coach and cars were filled by using the PT forms to walk on; the junior room was flooded to a depth of 2" (5 cm). I learned that the coach had to make a very wide detour to reach Harptree and was consequently very late.* Things weren't much better the next day, when *the attendance was very poor as a result of the flooding and the landslides which accompanied it.*

And then came the 1962-3 winter. At the time of writing, this was the last Really Big One. The start of the new term was officially delayed from Monday 7 January to

----
[1] At Heron's Green, a hundred yards to the east of the present road from West Harptree to Chew Stoke; Ben Bridge is still partly visible when the water level of the Lake is low.

Thursday 10th *because of heavy snowfalls and severe wintry conditions. The yard is covered with approx 3' (90 cm) of snow, and difficulty is being experienced with frozen cisterns in the outside lavatories.* It's a wonder anyone could get to them to find out. By Tuesday 15th *attendance has improved greatly, although the weather continues to be very cold and the conditions difficult.* Tuesday 29 January: *the wintry conditions continue and the outside lavatories can only be operated by constant attention being given by Messrs Battens, plumbers. There is, however, a good level of attendance in spite of the severe weather.* Not until Easter did the snow in Bishop Sutton finally melt. The March 1963 Annual Parish Meeting minuted that *the District Councillor's acknowledgment of the hard work and efforts of staff and men who endeavoured to clear the snow from the main roads was not shared by the parishioners present* [who] *felt that the leadership and supervision had been non-existent.*

The winter had indeed been awesome. The coldest on record – even colder than 1881 – the thermometer in most parts of the country fell below freezing just before Christmas 1962 and remained stuck below freezing – and often a long way below – until well into March. A blizzard over the South West at the very end of December brought snowdrifts 18 ft (6 m) deep. Night-time temperatures at the beginning of January fell to -10 C (14 F), enough to paralyse most of Devon, Dorset and Somerset, with train and road services grinding to an icy halt. The weather gods had more tricks up their sleeve. The snows returned with a vengeance in the third week of January. To compound the difficulties, there was freezing fog, and pack ice on the Severn. Chew Valley Lake froze solid, but the authorities still did their utmost to prevent ice-skating. By the end of January the temperatures did slowly start to rise. But only until early February, when a further 3 ft (nearly 1 m) of snow pitched[1] across the West Country and lasted until early March, when the thaw suddenly set in and the floods came. Thick snow had lain on the ground virtually everywhere for nearly ten weeks. Colin Symes recalls that the road to Bath was blocked for six weeks, although it was cleared more quickly in the direction of Churchill. Joan Davidge remembers that Hinton Blewett was cut off for three weeks.

There was a two-year respite until 1965. It was almost a case of déjà vu, so Mr Price probably felt that nothing would be served by commenting. The WI's Bishop Sutton Village Scrapbook of 1965 recorded that *on Friday 5 March, Mr Lyons of Montgomery's Bakery drove part way to the cut-off village of East Harptree and walked right to the top of Mendip to deliver bread. At places, the loaves had to be left at some prearranged spot for customers to collects. Snow drifts were impassable.*

As a contemporaneous newspaper report put it:

A sudden blizzard struck the West last night. Within an hour there was road chaos, and the picture became grimmer every minute … roads were blocked and villages cut off. From all over the area came reports of crashes, roads jammed with slithering cars, power and telephone breakdowns … After the blizzard, the great freeze-up. In the worst March weather for more than 10 years, traffic chaos hit Britain yesterday, leaving the West Country almost cut off. More than 60,000 square miles of southern England, Wales and South West England were closed to motorists.

The next milestone in a decade of decidedly nasty weather was the North Somerset floods of Wednesday 10 July 1968. Bishop Sutton was on the very edge of the chaos. There were no deaths here, but nearby villages were less fortunate. Heavy rain had fallen for most of that day and became torrential by the evening,

----
[1] Ask a West Countryman

accompanied by thunder and lightning. Several places had more than 5″ (13 cm) of rain in less than 24 hours. By early next day, almost every river, stream, drain and gully in the area had burst. Telephone communications were knocked out and emergency services were severely hampered, with roads blocked by trees and floodwater and bridges washed away. People were trapped in Pensford, Chew Magna, Chew Stoke and Keynsham. Rescue centres were set up. The police warned at 6.30 am that the dam at Chew Valley Lake might not hold. If that gave way, a massive tidal wave would career down the valley with truly tragic consequences. Mass evacuation of low-lying areas was considered but, with most roads impassable, the logistics would have been almost insurmountable. The dam held.

Chew Valley Floods 1968; plaque at Woollard Bridge

Seven people lost their lives, hundreds more suffered a terrifying ordeal, bridges that had stood for centuries were washed away or severely damaged, and countless houses and shops were engulfed. The school logbook remained silent, but the Parish Council minuted on 16 July that *the Youth Club was asked to carry out a house-to-house collection for the North Somerset Flood Relief Appeal. £21 raised.* That doesn't sound much, especially in light of the monies collected in 1952 and 1953 for the admittedly more devastating floods further afield.

Bad winters were a regular occurrence into the Seventies. On 6 January 1970 *severe icy conditions were in evidence this morning and the yard was a sheet of ice, making it unsafe for playground use.* The South West was cut off from the rest of the country by the blizzards of February 1978, and the Education Office announced that *all schools in Avon were to be closed because of the heavy snowfall.* Two days later, to the chagrin of the children, Mr Price wrote: *weather conditions having been improved* (sic)*, the school was opened today.* On 23 January 1979, *heavy snow having fallen during the night, I decided to close the school for the day as three of the staff were unable to come.* On the following day, *school reopens, although much snow remains and very cold.* By the late Seventies, the authorities had become more willing to close schools. Children were no longer expected to dig their way through, and teachers were living further away and didn't fit chains to their tyres.

But 1979 was not to be a re-run of '47 or '63 or '78. Let alone a re-run of most Victorian winters. It would be a long time before Eric Price would be able to take his mum's tea tray onto the sledging field behind Church Lane again.

PLAYING TRUANT, DONKEY CARTS, AND FELONIOUS THEFT OF MADEIRA CAKE

It was truancy that prompted the knock on the door. The 1870 Education Act had empowered School Boards to introduce bye-laws making it compulsory for children aged between 5 and 12 to be at school. Attendance Officers could be appointed to check on truants. The Chew Magna School Board bided their time until June 1878 when they asked if *Mr Treasure would undertake the office of School Attendance Officer for Bishop Sutton*. This didn't mean that children had got off scot-free before June 1878: in October 1877 *the Govers were punished for truancy* and in March 1878 *several boys have been truanting this week playing at marbles - punished*. The outcome of the Board's discussions with Mr Treasure (who lived next door to the school and was therefore a convenient candidate) wasn't recorded but may have been unsatisfactory, for the first actual mention of an Attendance Officer wasn't until 28 October 1879 when *Mr Veale attended school at 2.45 to make enquiries about*

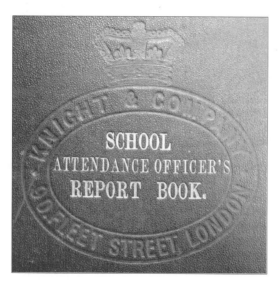

several irregular scholars. In May 1881 the Board told *the masters of both schools* (Chew Magna and Bishop Sutton) *to furnish the School Attendance Officer fortnightly with the names of all children who had made less than 15 attendances in that period*.

The first recorded prosecutions were in June 1881, when *the School Attendance Officer reported that William Dix and James Fear were convicted and fined 1/- and 1/- costs on each case for not sending George Dix and Christopher Fear to school*. April 1883: *32 names were sent to the School Board Officer for being absent six times over the past fortnight. 14 names have been taken off the register for continuous absence*. Alfred Withey was deregistered in May 1883: *he was absent nine weeks, being about the streets with donkey carts etc*. It was in the headmaster's financial interests to maximise attendance – more pupils, more grant – but there may have been altruistic educational reasons behind his report to the Board in April 1884 of *cases of children who are not attending any school and who are between 3 and 5 years of age. Have drawn the Board's attention to the great drawback there is in receiving children of 6 and 7 who have never been to school*. In November 1884 *the parents of Sydney Austin and Albert Harris fined by magistrates 1/- and costs for neglecting to send them to school*. This was to no avail: a fortnight later Mr Brown noted that *all the Austins have been absent since the magistrates fined the parents*. In October 1885 he *sent another long list of irregulars to Attendance Officer, and also a list of the 12 worst cases in my monthly report to the Board*. The administration and form-filling must have been a nightmare. In November 1886 Mr Brown observed that William Derrick, Ellen Dury, and George and Charles Saunders were summoned *for irregularity of attendance, fined by magistrates 2/- in each case*. George and

Charles were subsequently *sent to Industrial School*[1].

Sweet irony: in March 1885, with *the Attendance Officer Mr Veale not having attended before the Board*, the Board directed their clerk *to ask him for an explanation of his non-attendance*. By December, *has sent no report or explanation of his absence*; he resigned that day and forfeited his salary from 24 September. So out with Mr Veale and, in April 1886, in with Henry John Radford. In October 1891 he ignominiously followed his predecessor in the direction of the early bath: the Board would dispense with his services if *he does not send in his resignation by 12 noon tomorrow. ... Not received, therefore dismissed. Mr George Price appointed at £10 p.a.*

Children's attendance wasn't improving, and in September 1891 the Board instructed *that a weekly list of all absentees on each day the schools are open be given by the masters of Chew Magna and Bishop Sutton Schools to the Attendance Officer and that he be instructed to visit weekly instead of fortnightly each case so reported.* The Board wrote to those parents whose children didn't attend: *I am instructed to inform you that unless [name of child] is sent regularly to school, the Board will take legal action against you without further Notice.*

1890: the Board threatens legal proceedings against Ellen Filer's parents

The School Attendance Officers' Report Books for Chew Magna School Board from 1891 to 1895 afford a fascinating and often harrowing insight into the social circumstances of the time, into the vernacular language of the time, and into the innovative excuses that parents came up with for keeping their offspring at home. The phraseology used in the books points to the Attendance Officer's wish to record verbatim what he was told at the child's doorstep. The volumes are thick, and the short period covered by each one is an indication of just how busy the

----

[1] Established under the Industrial Schools Act 1857 to facilitate better provision for the care and education of vagrant, destitute and disorderly children who, it was thought, were in danger of becoming criminals. The courts decided which Industrial School the child was sent to – Bath was the favoured choice for Bishop Sutton children – and, once sentenced, the child would usually stay there until the age of 16, although suitable boys could join the army or work in the mines from 14. Mr Wightman had been the Head Assistant at Clifton Industrial School before coming to Bishop Sutton. The occasional references in the school logbook to 'Industrial School' related exclusively to 'disorderly' children who, a few generations later, would probably have been sent to a borstal (a corrective training school for offenders aged 15 to 21) or Approved School. In more recent times, they are likely to have stayed at a mainstream secondary school under careful supervision.

officer was. The same names cropped up time and time again. The following extracts – Bishop Sutton addresses only – are typical and I make no apology for transcribing so many of them. Everyone will find a favourite quote. Mine's that of Mrs Roynon.

> *Mother said she had no Boots for them and she sent her eldest Boy to Timsbury for Boots and they had none their size*

Jane Brock, widow, Ernest 11 yr 11 mo, Edward 8 yr 7 mo, mother said they could summons her or do what you like, they could have her few things what few she had; cautioned that prosecution would follow if not more regular attendance. A year later Mrs Brock said that her sons had no boots, and they didn't have the right size at Timsbury: cautioned with prosecution.

Mrs Isaac Smart, charwoman, Isaac 11 yr 8 mo, mother says she must have him some times as her other son is down in Wells Asylum and they can summons her if they like; cautioned with prosecution.

Austin Maggs, labourer, Florence 9 yr 0 mo, William 7 yr 0 mo, father says that the child got a very bad sore head and the boy won't go to school without his sister; excused. Two years later: Austin Maggs, Denny, Florence 11, William 9, Annie 7, Florence had influenza part the time, excuse of no boots and wet weather last week, water was out in the lanes, none could go.

George Roynon, labourer, Knowle Hill, child [unnamed] 7 yr 4 mo, mother told me that she could not get the boy to school because his teacher did call him a bunch of rags and the children did make fun of him; to be cautioned.

> *Mother told me that she could not get her Boy to School because his teacher did call him a Bunch of rags and the children did make fun of him.*

James Frape, shoemaker, Fred 10 yr 2 mo, Herbert 6 yr 9 mo, father said he had ecxema (sic) very bad all over him, promised to send them more regular.

William Coles, labourer, Sutton Wick, George 8 yr 0 mo, mother said he had been minding sheep for Farmer Morgan during the holidays and they wanted him another week, but will go to school regular now.

R. Montgomery, landlord Red Lion, Walter Daunton 8, Lilian Daunton 6, ringworm in head very bad.

Rawlins, labourer, Denny, George 9, Edith 8, have had whooping cough all the winter and got no boots – very bad off, mother promised to send them more regular; to be cautioned.

> *Fell out of a cart and hurted her arm very much*

White, Ella 12, fell out of a cart and hurted her arm very much.

Edgell, labourer, William 9, father ill, the mother says she has no boots for him so cannot send him till she gets some and in such wet weather; to be cautioned.

The little Satchells[1] were serial truanters. In September 1891: *James Satchell, labourer, Hollow Brook, Florence 8 yr 6 mo, Jane 10 yr 9 mo, Arthur 6 yr 6 mo, mother told me that she sent them as regularly as she could, but some times it was so wet she could not send them as they got wet and cold and had to sit in their wet clothes all the day; no action.* A couple of weeks later: *mother told me it was raining one day and two days they were picking up potatoes for their father; attending at present.* The following month: *mother has been ill with pleurisy, wanted Jane to go to the doctor two or three times a week, promised to send them more regular; to be summonsed.* The following year: *mother says she cannot always send them, sometimes they have no boots, sometimes very wet weather, very poor and bad off for clothes etc; the chairman to call on J. Satchell.* A fortnight later: *James Satchel has attended better lately, last week had to buy them some boots so had no food to give them some days so would not send them regular last week.*

'Mother said she had no clothes for John and it had been so wet lately that they had to come back wet through.'

The Cranes weren't far behind, and not just geographically. *Thos Crane labourer, Hollow Brook, Elizabeth 6 yr 8 mo, mother said she could not send her by herself, she goes with the Satchells when they go.* A week later: *mother said they were in debt.* Two weeks after that: *mother said she should use her own mind when she sent her; clerk to write, threatening prosecution.*

The books gave details of the outcomes of court appearances: *James Satchell, summoned May 17 1892 in case of Florence Satchell also of Arthur Satchell, fined 2/- in each case, first offence. Thomas Crane fined 4/- re Eliz. Crane as they did not appear, first offence. Jane Brock (re Ernest Brock), case adjourned till 31.5.92, fined 2/-, first offence. James Satchell summoned Dec. 20 1892 (second offence), fined 2/- per child. Thos Crane summoned Dec. 20 1892 (second offence), fined 4/-.* To put these fines into perspective, average manual wages in the early 1890s were some 30 shillings a week.

'Mother said her father did not earn enough to maintain family – so she was obliged to go out to work – & keep the child at home to mind the baby.'

These Report Books are an historical treasure trove. Boots that could only be bought in Timsbury, flooded roads, children only going to school if the neighbours went,

----
[1] The 1901 census listed the Satchell Family as comprising James (42, a labourer), his wife Matilda (39) and their eight children aged from 1 to 20. Money would have been tight.

mothers defiantly telling the authorities that they could sue till they were blue in the face but they still couldn't pay, ringworm in the head. Bishop Sutton was not the place to be if you were poor. Out of fairness, neither was anywhere else.

Back to the logbook. Village politics made an occasional and intriguing guest appearance. In 1892 the School Board was becoming exasperated by the frequent refusals of *Mr E. Strachey of Sutton Court to sign summonses issued by the Board in cases of irregular attendance of children at the schools.* In October the clerk wrote to none other than The Right Hon. H. H. Asquith Q.C. M.P., Home Secretary. I have taken a pair of sharp scissors to the verbose letter:

Sir, I have been directed … very respectfully to represent to the Home Secretary the inconvenience experienced by the Board in taking legal procedures under the Elementary Education Acts by the refusal for several years past of Mr Edward Strachey J.P., Sutton Court … to sign summonses duly ordered by the Board against parents for the non-attendance of their children at school and very respectfully to ask for your intervention. … Mr Strachey is the only acting Justice of the Peace resident near the centre of the School District, [which] is a rural one, and there is no other Justice resident nearer than five miles. … The Court of Petty Sessions, which sits every fortnight, is five miles distant. Upon an occasion arising for the Order of a prosecution as above stated, the Board is compelled either to wait for the next Petty Sessions for the signing of a summons – a delay which most probably involves additional delay later on, or else to send its School Attendance Officer six or more miles away to look for a Justice, the chances being that [one] will not be found at home when the Officer calls. … By this means, considerable delay, embarrassment and expense have been incurred in the administration of the Board, and injury done to the interests of its Schools. … Prosecutions have [never] been entered upon indiscreetly, or upon insufficient or questionable grounds … [and] I venture respectfully to submit that … it might reasonably be expected to be the duty of the Magistrate … to issue the Summons without his being himself possessed at the time of any detailed knowledge of the merits of the case, the responsibility for which rests on the Board which has not heretofore been accused of anything like vexatious proceedings. … On the last occasion of his refusal, Mr Strachey gave as the reason that his brother, being a member of the Board and therefore a prosecutor, he (Mr Strachey) could not act. … Mr Strachey had habitually or frequently refused to sign such summonses ordered by this Board long before his brother became a Member of it. Allow me, Sir, here to apologize if a mistake has been made in addressing this appeal to you as Home Secretary. I have the Honour to be, Sir, Your Very obedient Servant, J. Galbraith, Member of Chew Magna School Board.

The Home Secretary doesn't appear to have replied.

Sometimes the Board just lost patience with feckless parents. In February 1896 it resolved *that a letter be sent to parents of children not making 80% of attendances: Your --- has only attended the Board School --- times out of ---. You are therefore requested to attend a Board meeting at the Chew Magna Board School on Monday --- to explain the reason of your child's absence. In case of non-attendance, a summons will be issued.* There was a postscript: *In case of illness, a medical certificate will be required.*

This strategy didn't always work and, furthermore, magistrates couldn't be trusted to come up with a decision favourable to the school if parents were taken to court. In December 1896 the Board resorted to writing to the Department of Education to seek their advice. Editorial scissors have again been wielded.

Sir, … The Board [wishes] to draw the attention of the Education Department to the difficulty they are experiencing in obtaining convictions against parents summoned before the Justices of the Peace for Temple Cloud for the irregular attendance of their children at school. On October 13th last several parents were summoned for this offence. In one case, where the child had attended 31 times out of 40 for the month ended September 25th, the magistrates considered that the case ought not to have been brought before them and that the attendance was splendid, and dismissed it with costs against the Board. In another case the parent was summoned for a like offence and was fined, but during October the same irregular attendance on the part of two children was continued and, on November 10th, the parent was again summoned for their irregular attendance. ... The magistrates considered sufficient time had not been allowed to see if their attendance improved, and dismissed the summons with costs against the Board. It must be plain that the efforts of the Board should be directed to make the attendances regular and continuous and that this spasmodic mode of fining renders these efforts practically useless and, further, that the principle of giving costs against the Board, which have to be paid ... by the ratepayer, is an absurdity, especially when the fine is laid on because the Board is trying to do its duty. I might say that my Board never resort to summoning parents for irregular attendances until other means have been taken. ... [The Board] now feel that as their efforts ... are anything but supported by the magistrates, it is almost useless to prosecute, or to pay an officer who is employed in visiting the parents and warning them against the consequences of this neglect of the children's education. The parents are now indifferent to that, and set the magist-rates against the Board. This letter is written in the hope that the Education Department will assist the Board in its efforts to do its duty. I have the honour to be, Sir, Your obed. Servant, W. E. Milton, Clerk.

There seems to have been no reply from the Education Department.

Being an Attendance Officer wasn't exactly a piece of cake. In March 1897 the Board requested Mr Masters of Portbridge Hill, Chew Magna, *not to interfere with the Attendance Officer in the exercise of his official duties*. They were a dangerous bunch in Chew Magna: the Board observed in

The Board resolves to interview the parents of absent children

October of the same year *that the Attendance Officer Mr Brookman had been assaulted in the exercise of his official duties by William Vowles of Chew Magna. [The Board] recommends that he be summonsed*. These interferences and attacks weren't in Bishop Sutton, but it would have been remiss to let them pass unnoted. In a trying-to-sound-educated moment in February 1898, the Board decided not to accede to Mr Brookman's application for an increase of salary, as the members *are of opinion that his duties are less harduous* (sic) *than formerly*. But they did agree in June 1899 that *he be paid 2/6 for each attendance at Temple Cloud Police Court*.

There were then surprisingly few references to truancy for half a century until March 1952, when *Mr Avery reported at lunch time that three Chew Magna boys had failed to return to work after the break period this morning. I have advised their headmaster*. In June of that year Mr Bailey asked the Attendance Officer *to investigate the reason for the non-attendance of Sonya Tovey, Janet Jeffries and Georgina Billing who are home 'minding house' because of illness or absence of their respective parents*. Nothing then until December 1956 when, for a 100% lack of absence, Mr Bailey *asked for Perfect Attendance certificates for Rita Carpenter and Julia Stock*.

Another long interval till 1974 when, on 17 June, *Y*[1], *who has been away for a week without reason many times during the present term, was absent again today. I informed Mr Hird, County Welfare Officer*. Mr Hird discovered that *Y had been playing truant. He would deal with the matter*. On 24 June 1974 *Mrs X telephoned to say that Mrs Z (Y's mother) was having difficulty with Y in making him come to school. She asked if I could help in any way. I called at the house and brought him to school in my car. He came without protest or difficulty. He appeared to be quite happy in school and quite contented when he is here. The difficulty is getting him to leave home in the mornings. His mother is unable to compel him to come. I questioned him and he said that there is nothing about school that makes him unhappy*. 1 July 1974: *Y continues to attend school regularly now. However, on 10 June I was informed that Y and A had left the school during the mid-day break. I searched the village for them but could not find them*. One returned a couple of days later, the other didn't. The Education Officer reported that *Y could not be traced*.

When glancing idly through the Kilmersdon Petty Sessions (1909 to 1911) books for details of punishments meted out to miscreant children's miscreant parents, lots of juicy information came to light and it would be unfair not to share it before moving on to sparing rods and spoiling children. The court sessions – sitting at the Court House in Kilmersdon or Victoria Hall in Radstock – would sometimes have included Bishop Sutton, but the book doesn't list addresses. The following is a selection of cases brought and the fines levied.

Three children aged 14 to 16 playing football in street in Midsomer Norton 2/6; Concealing the birth of a child at Midsomer Norton, committed to trial; Damaging grass at Midsomer Norton, pay costs; Using obscene language at Radstock, 5/- or 7 days; Driving heavy locomotive on highway at Radstock at greater speed than 2 mph, pay costs; Failure to attend camp of 4th Battalion Somerset Light Infantry £1; Riding a bicycle at 9.40 pm at Holcombe, not having a lighted lamp attached, 2/6 plus costs; Riding a bicycle furiously at Radstock 5/- incl. costs; Allowing a dog to be in the highway at Chilcompton not wearing a collar with owner's name and address inscribed thereon, 5/-; Attempting to commit suicide by taking poison at Midsomer Norton, discharged on entering into surety for £5 for six months to be of good behaviour; Application for [an 11 year old boy] to be sent to an Industrial School not being under parental control, father to pay 1/- per week; Employing a young person in a factory at Midsomer Norton without a certificate of a certifying surgeon of fitness, £1 plus costs; Boys 14 and 13 dismissed for letting off fireworks in street at Radstock; Boys 10 and 11 feloniously stealing one Madeira cake value 6d at Kilmersdon, dismissed, fathers having chastised them.

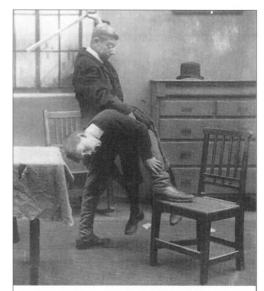

I LOVE DADDY, DEAR OLD DADDY AND I KNOW THAT HE LOVES ME.

----
[1] All initials in this paragraph have been changed.

The best are left until last:

Stanislas Loviguss driving a motor car at a dangerous speed in Silver Street in Midsomer Norton, dismissed with a strong caution; Owner of and in possession of two pieces of cheese exposed for sale in the market at Radstock unfit for the food of man and condemned as such, dismissed by majority of bench; Stealing two cabbages value 2d growing in allotments at Kilmersdon, 5/- or 7 days' gaol; Selling an unsound piece of bacon in the market at Radstock, £1; Failure to attend musketry drills during 1910, 10/-; Travelling on the GWR Railway at Radstock without a ticket, 10/- or 14 days; Feloniously stealing a live pullet value 4/- at Midsomer Norton, £1 or 14 days.

The Temple Cloud Court Register 1925 to 1930 does contain specific references to Bishop Sutton misdemeanours and, arrestingly, includes the name of the felon-nicking officer. Most of these felons weren't children, but the Register nevertheless gives a great insight into local behaviours:

George Montgomery (miner, 28) fined 10/-, having been spotted by PC12 Pope riding a bicycle with no light at 8.10 pm; Arthur Edward Wyatt (Sutton Farm, 21) driving motor car without a light on the extreme right or offside, 2/6 (PC 267 Gill); Ivor Harvey (miner, 23) cycling without a light, 5/- (PC 267 Gill); Mark Dix (miner, 50) carrying a gun without a licence, 5/- (PC 12 Pope); Noah Gibbs (carrier, 50), driving a motor bus without a light on the extreme offside, 5/- (PC 267 Gill); Leslie Stewart George (Sutton Wick, 22[1]) driving a motor cycle without two independent brakes, 5/- (PC 294 Curtis); Frederick Tom Cole (South View, Stichenham Lane, haulier, 21), driving a motor lorry at night without a red rear light, 2/6 (PC 267 Gill); George Hicks (labourer, 45), brought to court by PC 12 Pope for not sending his child to school, 5/-.

A Bath newspaper report of 1882 had absolutely nothing to do with punishment in schools, but it's humorous for all that, and a good way of rounding off on a lighter note:

The extraordinary case of Henry Witcombe, a 31-year old cook and confectioner living at 2 Prior Park Road: "Soon after midnight he came out of Corn Street with his wife and two or three children making a noise with a concertina and refusing to desist". Clerk: "Upon what charge did you arrest him?" Police Inspector: "Being disorderly. He was playing no tune at all. I don't think he could play one". It was at this potentially embarrassing point that the Chief Constable himself intervened: "I wish to withdraw the case".

SPARE THE ROD AND WET YOUR PANTS

It is unnecessarily heartrending to judge yesterday's standards and behaviours against those we expect today. It's all too easy to read the school's old Punishment Book and logbook entries and assume that educational methods were intolerably cruel. They weren't, not by yesterday's standards.

When the first pupils were trooping through the door of the new Bishop Sutton School, the English statute books still listed over two hundred crimes punishable by death. Apart from the obvious candidates of murder, sodomy and trivial breaches of the game laws, it was also a capital offence to impersonate a Chelsea Pensioner or to damage Westminster Bridge. Out of every 20 criminals hanged in the early 1800s, it's estimated that 18 were under the age of 21. The days of breaking on the wheel, hanging alive in chains and whipping to death were gone – although perhaps not universally lamented – but ideas were changing. That said, good old-fashioned gibbeting wasn't abolished until 1834 or the pillory – useful for recycling rotten

----
[1] Strange: two years earlier, in October 1926, when 'Leslie Stewart George of Sutton Wick' was nabbed for driving a motor cycle with side car without any lights and was fined 10/-, he was 36.

tomatoes and smelly eggs – until 1837.

The harsh responses that society nevertheless still expected for infractions of society's rules naturally influenced the punishments inflicted on children. To be thrown into this particular pot was the Victorian reluctance to accept that children could suffer from mental deficiency. Every child could do the work if only he (and she) tried hard enough, and he (and she) was made to try hard by threat of punishment. Fingermarks and ink blots were punishable by cane. Crossings out were strictly taboo. For those who rebelled against the authority of the teachers, there was the ultimate sanction of the Industrial School.

In one instance, children became so incensed at what they viewed as unreasonable discipline that they barricaded their school. In the autumn of 1911 thousands of dockers and miners were on strike, and children took a lead from their fathers. They first downed their slates at Bigyn School in Llanelli and the dispute spread to hundreds of schools across Britain[1]. In Hull, throngs of children paraded through the streets with banners demanding an end to caning. In Montrose, the little strikers wanted better heating, shorter hours, no homework, holidays during potato-picking, free pencils and the abolition of the Attendance Officer. Muted disquiet may have reached Bishop Sutton, but not to the extent that banner-waving scholars paraded along Cabbage Stump Lane.

ANTI-CANE STRIKE.

Schoolboys at Llanelly Demand Shorter Hours and No Punishment.

A strike of infants against the exactions and sternness of nurses is brought within the limits of probability by recent events in South Wales, where they carry labour upheavals to undreamed of limits of immaturity.

The "last word" in strikes at Llanelly is a strike of schoolchildren, which still continues with "unabated vigour and bitterness on both sides."

"It's all very well," a *Daily Mirror* representative was told by one little strike leader, overseeing his pickets outside a school, yesterday. "Our fathers strike—why should not we?"

"But your fathers work twelve hours a day and you only work about four and a half," it was suggested.

"Yes; but our fathers get paid for their work; we don't. Besides which, our fathers pay for us to go to school, and the teachers cane us. That comes to the same as our fathers paying to have us caned, and we won't have it!"

"Now, then!" came a sharp voice from close by, addressing the hero. "Why aren't you in school? In you get."

And in he "got," crestfallen, and in went his followers, sheepishly enough.

A few minutes later the strikers were lined up in the school yard, receiving each in his turn "six on the hand" for being late for school.

From outside came the sounds of tumult, and a "demonstration" of well over a hundred schoolboys came in sight. They were going round visiting the different schools to fetch out "blacklegs."

According to a statement by the headmaster of Bigyn, the "strike" began on Tuesday morning last, during his absence owing to indisposition. Several of the boys, for no definite reason, according to the headmaster, left the playground and did not return to school.

The "strikers," however, obtained recognition on their return to school in the afternoon, when the headmaster, who had also returned, caned every one of them.

----
[1] As a small aside, Britain's longest strike ever was a school strike. In 1914 pupils boycotted Burston School in Norfolk in support of two teachers who had been dismissed. Another school for the strikers was quickly established in the village, but the strike wasn't formally called off until 1939, by which time the children originally involved were all middle-aged.

Moving closer to home, a story from the early 1900s from the Other Side of the Hill[1] – recounted in 'A Century of Childhood' by Steve Humphries, Joanna Mack and Robert Perks – showed how things could get out of hand when mothers complained to teachers about the severity of the punishment. Ada Iles remembered about Edwardian Bristol:

The mothers used to come up and play merry hell with the teachers for caning us. Another thing mother'd go mad about was when we weren't allowed to go to the toilet and we ended up wetting ourselves. Our Aunt Sally'd be up there all the time 'cause she was poor, but she never used to lay a finger on her girls, never. Once she came up and pulled the teacher's hairpins out. Then she caught hold of her hair and started to drag her out of the classroom and into the playground. Of course, we kids were enjoying every minute of it, shouting and cheering "Go on, have her". And the kids in the other classes saw what was happening and they pushed their teachers aside and ran out to join us. It was a proper riot. We were all shouting and screaming. Anyway, they got us back in eventually, and Aunt Sally got summoned, fined five pounds for that.

Although corporal punishment had begun to die out in primary schools by the 1960s, the cane was still widespread in secondary schools well into the 1970s, and in Scotland use of the tawse (a leather strap with one end cut into thongs) was rampant. In 1977, 80% of secondary schools still resorted to corporal punishment. It was finally made illegal in state schools in England and Wales in 1987 after a long campaign by pressure groups such as S.T.O.P.P. (The Society of Teachers Opposed to Physical Punishment). This would all have been utterly incomprehensible to Victorian teachers. It would have been even more utterly incomprehensible to Victorian parents that their great great grandchildren could end up in court for smacking their own children.

Bishop Sutton was not immune from what was happening elsewhere, and the logbooks show that punishment could be brutal. Some observations bring a lump to the throat. Some bring a sense of pure delight at the resourcefulness of the children. And, occasionally, of the teachers. Alongside the logbooks and minute books, it's the School Punishment Book that gives the best insight into just how naughty (or unlucky) some children could be. It details the punishments, which generally varied from 'one on hand' (i.e. 'one stroke of the cane on the hand') to 'two on back' (of the hand) to 'one on buttocks', but the norm was either one or two strokes on the palm of

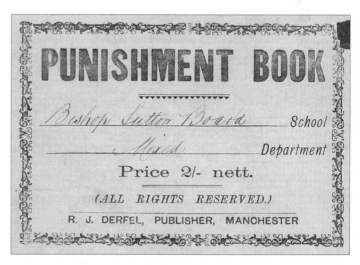

the hand. The only book surviving – and, perhaps, the only one that existed – spans the period from July 1900 to April 1953, but most of the pages are unused and

----
[1] Bishop Suttonians will understand.

there are long gaps between dates, as if the headmaster – for it was he who completed the entries – meant to fill it in later, but didn't. Some months were lavishly punished (13 occurrences during February 1907, for example), but there were whole years with nothing at all. The logbooks themselves were rather more fulsome but, again, with some periods when physical reprimands were de rigueur and others when children either went unpunished or, far more likely, no record was made. In July 1878 – predating the Punishment Book by 22 years – the School Board had *carried unanimously that the master be instructed to report to the Board every case in which it may be found necessary to inflict corporal punishment on any of the pupils under his care.* If the logbooks are anything to go by, this was an instruction honoured more in the breach than in the observance.

The 'What For' column in the Punishment Book provides an authoritative example of just how troublesome (or imaginative) the children could be. In no order of priority: talking, idleness, throwing ink in boy's eye, throwing water, throwing sand, throwing a bible, impudence, filthy talk, inattention, sulkiness, fooling, going home, being in possession of a school rubber, stealing from garden, temper, destroying leaf of two books, making noise with desk.

Someone had to be the first to have their punishment committed to logbook posterity. The honour went to Francis Cousin in February 1878, when Mr Northam gave him *several strokes with the cane for great obstinacy, the school has been very noisy this week owing to many children having bad colds.* What a wonderful non sequitur. Let it not be assumed that it was only boys who were caned. Girls were hit too, although perhaps not with the same severity or frequency. On the morning of 8 March 1878, *Mary-Ann Harvey was guilty of wilful disobedience to the pupil teacher and received two strokes on the hand with the cane.*

Lack of understanding – or downright bloodymindedness – didn't help a child's cause. *On Monday morning* (18 March 1878) *Kate Coles pretended she could not do a figure of the following sum: £63.13s.5½d divided by 3, and had to stand in the corner till late Tuesday morning when she did it all but the remainder, but she still pretended she could not put down that* (sic) *and so had to stand in the corner the whole of the school time till 11 o'clock on Thursday when she did it without assistance. She told the other girls that she knew how to do it but would not, and that her parents told her not to do it.*

The headmaster's phraseology somewhat masks the stark reality of what happened. On Monday morning Kate couldn't do the sum. She spent the rest of that morning, the whole of that afternoon, most of Tuesday morning, Tuesday afternoon, Wednesday morning, Wednesday afternoon, and a couple of hours on Thursday morning, standing in the corner. She was 9 years 7 months old. Mind you, she could be a bit of a one, could Kate. In May 1879 she *was saucy and impudent in word and act on two different occasions this afternoon, and received two slight taps with the cane for it.* One can picture sauciness and impudence in word, but in act? Interesting to conjecture just how slight 'slight' might have been. This unfortunate girl was clearly not teacher's pet: in April 1880 *she showed great obstinacy and sulkiness of temper during the Geography lesson, whereby I was hindered for about 20 minutes. She received several strokes with the cane.*

1878 was a tough year in the annals of the school. 25 March: *Edward Ferris and Hugh Dowling had to write their names 300 times for trying to cheat one* (sic) *in their sums, by passing their slates behind their backs.* In April 1878 headmaster Northam expressed the view that *the children have a bad habit of turning contrary when they are found fault with. Hugh Dowling pretended not to know the words in* the singing lesson today. 12 April: *Emily Harris (V Standard) stayed in till 6 pm, being seized with a fit of sulkiness, because told that her sum was wrong. She pretended she could not divide by 4.* 1879 didn't start much better. 11 January: *gave several 1st class boys four strokes each with the cane for climbing about on different parts at the back, after I had cautioned them on the same day at 12 am respecting lawless behaviour.* Well, what can you expect for climbing on different parts at the back? And how about this, from 3 October of that year: *Fred Treasure and George White were guilty of great obstinacy this morning, on having to stop in and finish learning their home lesson, making the most wilful mistakes, such as calling Hindostan 'Hindocan', Ceylon 'Cinle' and Babel-man-deb 'Bably-ma-beb'.* Shocking. Dyslexia, or similar, clearly didn't exist in 1879. The headmaster was on a roll. A week later *Ellen White showed great sulkiness of temper this morning. In doing her sum she pretended she could not tell a figure 10 from a 2, and marked a ½d thus: $^2/_1$, 2, $^2/_2$, having marked it correctly three times on the same sum just before.* Tricky things, ha'pennies.

A page from the school's Punishment Book

Geography may not have been the children's favourite subject, especially if it led them anywhere near Bab-el-mandeb, and in May 1880 *Victor Ferris showed great obstinacy of temper. He had to learn as a home lesson a list of the southern counties of England. Being unable to say his lesson, I placed him before a map of England and told him to read the names on the map. After having read all except Kent, he pretended he could not see the name. He received two strokes of the cane.*

Perhaps Master Ferris was just short-sighted; it was to be many decades before John Lennon NHS glasses came along. Mr Northam deemed it necessary in July 1880 *to address the whole school on the sin of disobedience.* His successor Lewis Hawkins restricted his comments regarding punishment to a laconic 'had to report an unruly boy' ilk, although he did observe in June 1881 that *many of the children are addicted to coming late and this I intend to do my utmost to prevent.* Possibly not by way of a fatherly arm round the shoulder. Allan Robert Hill took over in 1882 and clearly worked to the axiom that new canes thwack clean. Only days into his job, he noted: *order was very lax, disobedience and general inattention ... I have been obliged to punish several the first few days, order today better, more punished, a few kept behind to finish their work for idleness.* Carelessness was a major threat to Victorian propriety: on 1 December 1882 he kept *the whole school till 5 o'clock today for careless singing during music lessons.*

In July 1882 *Walter and George Bird punished for playing the truant again on Tuesday, being absent on Monday afternoon. Thomas, Jessie and Robert Saunders played the truant on Monday afternoon and all the day Tuesday; punished them by standing on form all day and kept in from dinner. John, Sarah and Louisa Cox caught in the act of truanting and brought to school at 10 o'clock after registers were made up, stood on the form with the three Saunders. All these children it appears are constantly doing this.*

Little boys fight. Always have, always will. In February 1883, *Thomas Harvey and Mark Wyatt punished for fighting in playground.* Having practised on Thomas and Mark, Mr Hill immediately turned to Levi Harvey and George Bird, *who showed great obstinacy and pretended ignorance during the blackboard lesson and laughed at the other children when I spoke to them, for which I punished them.* In March 1883 he *kept the Tuckers without dinner for playing truant, punished the next day for jumping over the wall and running away.* As there were no school dinners at that time, the Tuckers must have been kept sandwichless or simply kept in at dinner time.

Mr Brown being admonished by the Board for 'excessive corporate punishment inflicted upon little girls'.

Under new headmaster Ebenezer Brown, things went quiet on the punishment front until 1890. Perhaps he was a meek individual who believed that the word was mightier than the sword. Yeah, right. We've already seen that the School Board sometimes expressed concern about the strength of Mr Brown's cane-wielding arm, so perhaps he had just been forgetful when it came to detailing his castigations. In any event, he was persuaded to start keeping records. In October 1890 *Herbert Radford was reported as being very disorderly. Kept him in on Thursday and Friday as a punishment. Friday morning Annie White had done no writing after 20 minutes of the lesson had passed, although warned by her teacher, gave her one stroke on the hand with the cane.* In May 1891 the Board noted that Mr Brown *had inflicted corporal punishment on Isaac Smart for bad conduct in school. Approved by the Board, but the Board cannot sanction the expulsion of the boy.* In November 1893 Mr Brown *cautioned the whole school about marking on doors (freehand copies).* Quite what that means is anyone's guess. Sometimes his judgment was sound: in March 1896 the Board wrote to *Joseph Dury respecting his son Leonard who has been punished by Mr Brown for insubordination. Mr Brown's action approved by the Board.*

In July 1900 *Albert Withey was punished for rudeness to a little girl in front of whole school.* Edward Satchell suffered *two on the back* in February 1903. But he really deserved it, for *he was a lazy bad boy.* He evidently hadn't learnt his lesson from the previous June, when he got *two on the back* for being 'stupid'. William Coles' mistake on the last day of term in December 1908 was to *interfere and be impudent to roadmen.* Being impudent to roadmen was worryingly prevalent in the village, and children were regularly caned for it. Geoff Bush got four on his backside in September 1913 for the multi-crime of being *a bad boy, lazy, inattentive and disobedient* (perhaps one stroke for each). Joseph Peddle too perpetrated serial sinning in 1913: *impudent manner, constantly warned, laziness, late coming, talking, laughing.* Four on the bottom. The Attendance Book suggests that Joseph was 7 years old.

1922 was a year laden with misdemeanours. Frank Harvey got *two slight behind* (Mr Wightman's shorthand for 'being invited to bend over and have his backside gently caned twice') in April for *being impudent after being spoken to for conversation with girls (second lunch).* The 'second lunch' gives a nice touch of authenticity. In August, *J. Peddle* (aged 12) *tore leaf of Reading Book Pitmans Geography* and almost certainly got soundly reprimanded therefor. There was more reprimanding to be done in December 1925 when *M. James took two leaves (corners) of Reader Alex (Intermediate) through carelessness.* Mr Wightman deserved a pat on the back for his level of detail. In June 1936 Ronald ('Pussy' to his friends) Williams *refused to take punishment of one on buttocks* and got landed with *three on buttocks.* He was a particular unfavourite of Mr Bailey's: from 1933 to 1936 the Punishment Book recorded eight canings inflicted on him, varying from one on the hand to three on the backside, encompassing swearing on school premises to *hitting boy in the eye with duster after cleaning.* Kenneth Perry was caned twice on the behind in June 1937 for attempting to avoid his just deserts (i.e. *refusing to hold out hands*). There was little of relevance then for nearly 13 years until Mr Bailey wrote in March 1950: *Mr Jones reported to me at 12 o'clock that Michael Winstanley had run out of the Woodwork class and apparently gone home. It appears that he threw a piece of wood across the room, Mr Jones punished him and later he was found to be missing.* The fate of the wood was not recorded.

'Inappropriate behaviour' was an issue. Bishop Sutton was a mixed school of boys and girls up to the age of around 14. Joint honours for being the first to be had up for inexpedient demeanour went to Walter Harvey and Charles Harvey in 1883 who were *punished for indecent behaviour.* Albert Collier was caned twice in July 1900 for *talking to girl and laughing.* Wilfred Bendall was caned twice on the hand in May 1906 for *climbing in offices* (toilets) *and spitting on a girl.* He was also caned once on the hand in July 1908 for *very doubtful behaviour.* The mind boggles. The following February brought chastisement to J. Hynam for the selfsame abomination.

Alec Hillburn was the bane of Mr Wightman's life in 1909: he was caned four times that year (three of which were in May) for *being a hardened bad boy ... interfering with girl in street ... talking and playing ... stealing from garden*. Master A. Dury was caned in July 1909 for *being in company of Hillburn*. In November 1937, A. Curtis was caned once on each hand for *interfering with a girl and taking her apples away*. This must have been Prank of the Month, as a couple of weeks later Sidney Ogborne was caned on each hand for exactly the same thing. The name(s) of the girl(s) and the number of apples were not documented. Cyril Easton enlivened a dull November day in 1937 by *interfering with a girl in the street*. As late as 1951 B.M.[1] was caned once on each hand for *chasing girls in girls' cloaks after warning*. One assumes that he was chasing girls in their toilets, rather than chasing them at random while dressed in girls' clothing. It wasn't all one-sided: Gladys Chidzey (aged 11) was caned on the hand in 1920 for *talking to boys*.

It would be invidious to single out individuals. But you would expect no less. Of serial wrong-doers, the Punishment Book listed the following as each having been corporally punished more than five times: William Coles (between 1906 and 1909), P. Dowling (1902 to 1909), Ewart Dury (1906 to 1909), George Harris (1900 to 1901), Edward Harvey (1902 to 1909), Frank Harvey (1920 to 1922), Percy Harvey (1920 to 1922), W. Mail (1906 to 1909), Edward Satchell (1902 to 1909), Ernest Sollis (1908 to 1909), J. Travis (1908 to 1909) and Ronald 'Pussy' Williams (1933 to

1936). But prizes have to go to Clifford Dury (15 entries from 1906 to 1909 embracing 20 canings) and to runner-up Ernest Noakes (13 entries between 1908 and 1909). The only girl recorded as having been caned on more than one occasion was Gertrude Sollis (on a Wednesday and on the following Friday in September 1909), both times once on the hand, and both times for *talking and cheating*.

The school in 2009, seen from the road

What the records didn't record were those little incidents – some of them commonplace until at least the 1970s – involving the teachers' sports of chalk throwing or board-rubber hurling. These merry activities would be frowned upon nowadays and may even be illegal. There is also no record of dunce's caps being used at Bishop Sutton, or of the public shame that often befell left-handed[2] children, such as having their left hand tied behind their back and being forced to write with their right hand, a practice followed in many schools until well into the 1930s. Teachers – not necessarily here – occasionally devised ingenious punishments such as a pinprick on the tongue for chattering in class, or

----

[1] Name abbreviated to protect the guilty.

[2] Scammish' in North Somerset dialect.

on the finger for fidgeting. For children caught sulking with their head down, a darning needle pushed up through their clothes with the point under the chin generally stopped the sulks.

Not surprisingly, punishments feature strongly in pupils' recollections. May Woodward recalls that lines[1] were common, even though it meant a teacher staying behind to supervise. They were dished out even if children arrived late because of water on the roads; they were told they should have left home earlier. She suggests that discipline was firm but generally fair; everything had to be done properly. Ronald 'Pussy' Williams is remembered by Dick Chapman as being routinely caned by Mr Bailey, with no malice borne. That's by Pussy, not Bailey. One mother (not Dick's) attacked Mr Bailey one day and pulled his hair. Sadly, the logbooks don't mention the affray. Dick only admits to having been caned once – and the event didn't make it into the Punishment Book – but was well aware that if you flinched and withdrew your hand, Mr Bailey would whip the cane up and whack your hand from underneath. Hiding his canes up the chimney was considered uproariously funny (by the boys); once retrieved, the headmaster would use the sooty implements with some vigour on the pranksters. Jean Veale recalls her horror that the whole class was forced to watch culprits receive their punishment. Monica Castle reflects ruefully that she was sent out to the playground for being naughty. Mr Price came out to have a firm but fair word with her as she shivered.

Court records from 1882 in Bath tell a glum little tale:

Frederick Helps (defendant), headmaster of Weymouth House School, was summoned for having unlawfully assaulted and beaten George Nash (complainant), a lad of 12 or 13. The complainant alleged that the defendant first hung a small board bearing the words 'BAD BOY' round his neck in front, and then a larger board on his back. The boy resisted until the string cut his neck. Then the defendant knelt on him and hurt him. The defending counsel said that this case was "the paltriest and most contemptible ever brought". All sorts of people spoke of the headmaster's humanity. The magistrates dismissed the case and fined the complainant five shillings costs. They also suggested it might be a good idea to use leather instead of string in future.

Which is balanced by a lovely story by Joyce Storey, who was born in Bristol in 1918 and attended Two Mile Hill School (Kingswood) in the 1920s, recounted in 'A Century of Childhood':

The teacher wrote the word ABUNDANCE in copperplate handwriting on the blackboard and we had to copy down what she had written. I loved this flowery writing. To me it was exciting and romantic. I had long since finished and was idly sitting watching the others scribbling laboriously away. The word ABUNDANCE conjured up to me A BUN DANCE and I began to draw three happy little buns complete with currants and blue bows dancing a jig. 'Tra-la-la' came a little caption out of their mouths. The paper was soon passed round and a whole series of sniggers and loud giggles followed. Then there was a voice like thunder, "Well?" The teacher extended my stroke of genius at arm's length and after a cursory glance at it, tore it to shreds. "Come out here and fetch the cane", she commanded. The burning humiliation was that you not only had to fetch your torture, you had to return it to its place afterwards. Not a foot scraped the floor, or desk banged, or a cough broke the silence as the cane was raised high in the air and then brought down hard: three strokes on each hand. I nursed my smarting palms beneath my armpits as she drew herself up to her full height and told the whole class that I was a disruptive influence, a state of affairs that could not and would not be allowed to go on.

Thwacking children with a cane is nowadays considered barbaric, sadistic,

----
[1] Writing the same sentence or phrase (e.g. 'I must not chatter in class') out a specified number of times, typically 50 or 100 or, in extreme cases, 1000.

perverted. Former canees don't seem to think it did them any lasting damage whatsoever. Did they mend their ways as a result of being caned? Doubtful.

Now to the part you've been crossing your legs for: lavatorial mistimings. The problems all started – so far as the logbooks were concerned – in January 1878 when Mr Northam, a mere week into his headship, *caned three boys for committing a nuisance in the front yard in the presence of the girls, instead of going to the urinary, and that after I had cautioned them on the same morning.* By 'committing a nuisance', he wasn't referring to dropping toffee wrappers. It continued the following year: in February 1879 Mr Northam *cautioned the boys about making messes about the school gate instead of going to the urinal.* Such conduct was possibly not surprising, given that the nearest lavatorial facilities to many a house in Bishop Sutton were behind the nearest nettle-free hedge. A few days later the headmaster found that *the boys go into the girls' closets instead of their own, and have notice that I should cane any boy I found in offending again.* The fair sex too weren't beyond a splash of lavatorial transgression. On a Thursday afternoon in February 1878, the master punished *Ellen Dando (aged 11) for committing a nuisance just outside the door leading to the closet, and Emily Harris (12) for trying to screen her.* In the same sentence, he wrote: *the bad colds continue.* Hardly surprising, if they were in the habit of dropping their drawers in the cold winter air. In June of that year, *Daniel Smart (aged 8 yrs 2 months) messed in the corner of the girls' passage during the dinner hour instead of going to the urinary, and I ordered him to take a bucket of water and flannel and wash it up, and gave him one rap on the hand with the cane.*

And now for the real tear-jerker. On Friday 22 October 1880 *Alfred Hyman received two strokes with the cane for messing in the room instead of asking to go out.* Alfred was aged 5 years and 3 months.

Lavatorial misdemeanours then disappeared from the logbook. Is it suspicious that it was only Mr Northam who wrote about them?

Holy Trinity Church c1950

CHAPTER EIGHT

PLAYTIME

SEEN AND NOT HEARD, AND KICK WHITE HORSE

The logbooks stretched from the Victorian and Edwardian 'seen but not heard' to the comparative liberalism of the 1960s. The old approach of cultivating emotional control and manliness by initiating children into the adult world at a young age became less fashionable. By the 1920s children were allowed to be children. It wasn't until the 1960s that the harsh forces of marketing started turning them into young adults.

Until well into the 20th century, families were generally large and houses cramped, with children often sharing a bed with siblings. Apart from organised outings, the concept of leisure time was unfamiliar to most working people until after the First World War. Until the 1938 Holidays With Pay Act, few workers had paid leave and were entitled only to the statutory bank holidays. Those employed on the land toiled for more or less all the hours that God sent.

A hundred years ago, girls played with rag dolls and boys played with hoops; radios hadn't been invented, few people read a newspaper and the world outside the immediate Chew Valley was remote. But change was afoot. Meccano had been invented by Frank Hornby in 1901 and came to be seen alongside clockwork trains (introduced by Hornby in 1920) as an essential toy for developing the imagination and practical skills of boys. By the '30s there were few middle-class toy cupboards without a train set. The better ones sold for a whopping £3 in the mid-Twenties, but Woolworths were selling scaled-down versions for 7s.6d. It was partly the increasing affordability of toys – and most of the simpler ones (such as Dinky vehicles) were much cheaper than train sets – that started the trend of mass present-giving at Christmas and birthdays. This was accelerated by the introduction of 'educational' games such as Bayko (1930s), Lego (1950s) and Duplo (1960s), and not-so-educational such as Scalextric (1950s), and Action Man and Barbie (1960s). Many toys encouraged home-based indoor play as opposed to the traditional outdoor pursuits that had previously dominated children's leisure time.

A new childhood custom started between the two world wars: pocket money. Known as the Friday (or Saturday) penny, it was usually ritually handed over to coincide with dad's own pay packet. It was the arrival of pocket money that led to the rise in popularity of comics which, for the first time, gave children (and especially boys) something they could adopt as their own. There were Boy's Own Paper (published from 1879 to 1966, but reaching its peak from the 1920s), Rainbow (1914 to 1956), The Hotspur (1933 to 1981), The Dandy (from 1937), The Beano (from 1938) and Film Fun (1920 to 1962). Much as adults might have railed against the gory illustrations, 'zap kerplunk' language and death by exclamation mark, comics did encourage children to read. Young teenagers developed a strange addiction to Frank Richard's über-fat Billy Bunter at Greyfriars School. Anthony Buckeridge's Jennings and Darbishire exploits at

Linbury Court School extended the trend into the 1960s, countered by the earthy mischief of Richmal Compton's[1] William and his band of Outlaws. There were fewer comics for girls, but they all reinforced the stereotypical yearning to become an air stewardess or nurse or ballet dancer or model. Pre-World War II magazines Girls' Home, Girls' Friend and Girls' Reader made way for Bunty, Judy and Jackie in the 1960s. The heroines naturally expected to give up their job when they married the boy of their dreams.

But the writing had long been on the wall for the simple, innocent times. Hollywood had crossed the Atlantic. Young teenagers quickly idolised stars such as Tyrone Power and Margaret Sullavan and tried to emulate their style. Films such as The Wizard of Oz gave children a new fantasy insight into a technicolour world. The 1920s had seen the birth of radio, which brought its own heroes and heroines and marketing thrusts. Wonderfood, the makers of the 'family' drink Ovaltine, were the first to use the wireless to influence children's play for commercial purposes. The Ovaltiney Concert Party was aired in 1934 on Radio Luxemburg and from it grew the League of Ovaltineys, a nationwide band of 5 to 14-year olds who were sworn to drink Ovaltine loyally every night. By collecting wrappers from Ovaltine tins they could send for a badge and a deciphering kit. By 1938 there were over a million Ovaltineys huddled round their parents' radios noting down the secret messages which, when decoded, would tell them about games they could play in the house or in the garden. Membership was largely restricted to wealthier parents, as poorer ones could afford neither a radio nor Ovaltine. The song was doubtless sung, however, by rich and poor alike:

> We are the Ovaltineys, little girls and boys,
> Make your request, we'll not refuse you,
> We are here just to amuse you!
> Would you like a song or story? Will you share our games?
> At games and sports we're all so keen,
> No happier children can be seen,
> Because we all drink Ovaltine,
> We're happy girls and boys.

The restrictions of the early '40s and the austerity of the post-war years constrained the toy and entertainment industries until the mid-Fifties, although one sign of future trends was the hugely popular radio programme Dick Barton Special Agent who, in 1948, was estimated as having two thirds of boys in Britain – and a fair few girls – tuned in each winter evening. Originally conceived for adults, concerns about its moral influence on youngsters led to questions being asked in the House of Commons. Dick's smoking, drinking and womanising were toned down. Radio's monopoly of home entertainment remained virtually unchallenged until well into the '50s. The BBC's

Listen with mother

---
[1] 1890 to 1969. Her first book was 'Just William' (1922), and she went on to write another 38, the last being 'William the Lawless', published in 1970.

Children's Hour on Saturday mornings became compulsory listening. Running from 1954 to 1967, its long-time presenter Uncle Mac (Derek McCulloch) played record requests from children of all ages. It was renamed 'Junior Choice' with the launch of Radio 2 in 1967 but, by then, children's levels of sophistication were such that they no longer wanted Nellie the Elephant (Mandy Miller, 1956) or The Man from Laramie (Jimmy Young, 1955). The genre died.

In 1956 the first mass craze for children engineered for commercial purposes took off: Davy Crockett, King of the Wild Frontier. The success was built around the Disney film, and was backed by a countrywide launch of buckskin outfits, racoon skin caps – of which 10 million were sold in Britain alone – and even Davy Crockett nougat bars. There were numerous parodies, including:

> Born on a table top in Joe's café,
> The dirtiest place in the USA,
> Fell in love with Doris Day,
> Thought he could sing like Johnnie Ray.
> Davy, Davy Crockett,
> King of the Teddy Boys.

The years leading up to the late Sixties were still largely the world depicted by the Ladybird Books and by Enid Blyton. A world that was safe and simple and bright, where Peter and Jane visited shops, farms, the seaside, smiled at policemen and admired firemen and miners for their honest toil. A world where Noddy could go to bed with Big Ears without being put on a police register. And a world where everyone knew their place: Peter liked going to the library to learn about ships and planes, Jane liked reading about houses and nurses, Mummy dusted and washed up and waited for Daddy to come home from work to sit in front of the fire and read his paper, his slippers on and enjoying his pipe. The educational Look and Learn children's magazine (1962 to 1982) quickly proved a hit in aspirational families. Even the Eagle's Dan Dare, pilot of the future, was pretty aspirational. The concept of 'dumbing down' had yet to be devised.

When television came along – first BBC, and then ITV and its adverts in 1955 – the impact on children's culture and play was massive and immediate. Children's fads –

such as hula hoops in the late Fifties – were inspired by what was on the box. By 1960 most homes had a set, often rented, and children's programmes such as Crackerjack with Peter Glaze and Leslie Crowther, Blue Peter, Watch with Mother, The Adventures of Robin Hood, and Lassie were watched by viewers who, ten years previously, had been playing football or dressing dolls with their friends, reading or listening to the radio. Boys hero-worshipped Roy Rogers (the Lone Ranger), Gene Autry (owner of Champion, the Wonder Horse), and Batman. As early as 1958, it was reported that the average child in the UK was spending two hours a day in front of the telly. This new habit pushed back bedtimes, despite early television closing down from 6 to 7 pm to form a rigid demarcation between children's and adults' viewing and to let parents put their children to bed. By the mid-1960s children were warily watching scary episodes of Dr Who from behind the settee, or staying up for adult programmes which, by now, had acquired an air of social realism: Dixon of Dock Green meets Softly Softly.

The 1960s was a decade of two halves, even for children. It started with Ford Populars, steam trains and My Old Man's a Dustman; rationing was a relatively recent memory, and 'make do and mend' and dowdy clothes were still the order of the day. The decade ended with the Ford Capri, steam was dead, Lucy was in the Sky with Diamonds and tights were replacing stockings. There was hard Izal toilet paper, Harold Wilson's Pound in Your Pocket and 'I'm Backing Britain', the Crazy World of Arthur Brown, Green Shield stamps, Vesta Prawn Curry and Alf Garnett. Free love and men on the moon. The Beatles were greeted by crowds of screaming hysterical girls wherever they went. Television played the largest role in bringing the new world into the living room, and advertising provided ever more opportunities to target the child market.

More or less until the First World War, toddlers had worn white – white clothes could be boiled – and children were togged up like smaller versions of their parents. For many decades after that, girls wore dresses or skirts and blouses, never ever trousers. Boys had shirts and pullovers like their dads, and wore short trousers until they left school. 'Middle-class' boys were rarely seen without a tie. But steadily increasing prosperity (and advertising) quickly brought change. A fashion industry grew up for youngsters. Man-made synthetic fabrics had arrived in the late 1940s and, with them, mass-produced ready-to-wear clothing with bright and exciting new designs. Ladybird was one of the first large companies to recognise the importance of children's spending power and powers of persuasion, and as early as 1948 was selling the first child's T-shirt. A generation of consumer-conscious youngsters was becoming critically concerned about its looks. Beauty contests for young girls became popular, the most famous being the Miss Pears competition inaugurated in 1958. By the late Sixties, music and fashion industries had  begun to see children as important purchasers of their often highly sexualised products, and teenagers had more money to spend on their appearance. Styles of dress and a love of raucous noise brought conflict with parents and teachers. Even in primary schools, girls would wear increasingly short skirts, and bans on transistor radios were a forerunner of today's bans on mobile phones.

Groups such as the Bay City Rollers and The Monkees were emerging, aimed directly at the teeny and weeny-bopper market. Within a few years, both old and young were jigging around to Abba, although heaven forbid at the same time. Fashion advertising was directed at younger and younger children, and even toddlers began to reject the hand-me-downs that had been commonplace only a generation before. For the first time for several decades, clothes designers started to scale down adult fashions rather than create specific children's lines.

The new youth culture accorded little allegiance to the old childhood pursuits of train spotting, stamp collecting, pinning butterflies (dead) onto cardboard or filling the kitchen with soggy papier mâché.

That was a pretty harsh look at commercialisation and consumerism. Was it really like that? Well, yes and no. It's fatuous to state casually that out-of-school childhood hours during the period covered by this book were carefree. They were perhaps less regimented than they sometimes are now, and children certainly had more freedom to roam. Provided they stayed clear of the bull. Strangers were not automatically seen as a potential danger: the media didn't dwell on the lurid, and parents would often remain blissfully unaware of possible risks. With little or no technology, pastimes were less complex. Environmental responsibility was viewed differently: meadows were denuded of wild flowers brought home by the armful to grace mantelpieces, and birds' eggs were collected without a thought that it might not be wholly fair on the birds. Perceptions of safety were different: children cycled everywhere at a time when three times as many people as now were being killed on the roads; during the war they would scour the fields for shrapnel and stray ammunition that might still be mortally dangerous.

The Chew Valley remained pretty unworldly until the middle of the 20th century. There was limited contact with the wider world away from family and close neighbours. Mothers generally stayed at home to care for their children. The church provided much of the social activity and was where many families spent considerable time: Sunday matins, afternoon Sunday School and then evensong. Many boys sang in the choir. Most village families would have had a few toys, but cooking pots, lids and spoons were additionally pressed into service as musical instruments, and a wooden clothes horse and an old blanket would become a wigwam.

Bishop Sutton Holy Trinity Church choir 1965. The names on the back of the original photo read: V. Hughes, R. Carter, B. Leask, Susan Leask, Janet Carter, D. Marden, S. Leask, P. Marden, D. Sage

Until the late 1940s, schools' going-home time was later than it is now, but children had a longer break at lunchtime. The 'Rules to be observed by the Parents of Children attending the National School' (undated, but probably from the 1870s) included the stipulation that the *School hours are from 9 to 12 and 2 to 5 in the summer; and from 9 to 12 and 2 to 4 in the* winter. The only two relevant entries in the school logbook were from November 1878 (*objection having been made to the* [afternoon] *school beginning at 1.30, the summer time was resumed*) and December 1938 (*several requests have been received from parents of children who live at a distance that the children be allowed to leave school a little earlier during the next month. Such children will be allowed to leave at 3.45 pm instead of 4 pm*). By the early 1950s, the hours had settled down more or less to what they are now.

Once school was over and the chores done, children's time was their own. If there was any time left. For a couple of decades after the war, the chores could be extensive: taking cows to the field on the way to school and bringing them back to the farm after school for milking, making the beds, cleaning the boots, helping with the weekly wash or looking after younger brothers and sisters. One former pupil remembers getting a ha'penny a day for housework and errands, and then spending half an hour at the sweet shop window calculating how far she could make the money stretch. In pre-electricity days, the children would help fill the lamps: many people in the Chew Valley, where homes were lit by oil or paraffin lamps – or rush lamps[1] in really poor houses – would normally get up when it got light and go to bed not long after it got dark.

----
[1] Made from the inner core of a water reed, dried and soaked in lard. It would burn (very dirtily) for up to an hour, spitting and furiously dripping fat all over the table.

DAME *(seeing the signpost)*. "Stop, Jenkins – stop! I think it would be safer to turn back. They may have catapults or something dangerous."

(The sign above the wall reads 'To Motorists: CAUTION SCHOOL'.)

Inevitably, the school records were not hugely enlightening about what children got up to outside school – unless it brought them into conflict with teachers – but there are recollections galore. Marjorie Reed, growing up in the village in the 1920s, perhaps sums it up best: 'Playtime was any field, any lane. Mums packed picnics so that children could spend all day in the fields. Who would be the first to spot an oxlip daisy? Playing in the stream at the back of the house. Climbing trees. Playing hopscotch or marbles or Cry Mr Wolf'. There was little reason for children to stay indoors, where it was often cramped and airless, so they scrumped for apples and were chased out of orchards, they collected sticks for the fire and searched the river for birds or water rats. They made rope swings on trees, collected conkers, built go-karts, strung daisy chains and scraped the pith out of sticks to make pop guns. They spun tops and bought marbles for a penny from a village shop or smashed lemonade bottles to extract the glass stopper to save themselves the penny. Swimming at Stratford Mill was hugely popular. It had the closest useable water – albeit very cold – and children had free run of the pond behind the mill wheel. Les Bown tells the story of Jean Tibbs rescuing him from the millpond by his hair; there was a clay bank in a V-shape, and he went back the next day to see just how lucky he'd been. Joan Bunney remembers swimming in the River Chew

Ken Rapps recalls lighting fires and making dens by streams. Whenever he smells sulphuric acid, he's reminded of the charging of accumulators. His family had a radio at Highland Villas (on The Batch); a hole was drilled in a window sash for the wire that connected the radio to the mast just along the lane, which acted as a communal aerial. There was tobogganing in the winter. Ken's cousin James hosted riotous parties with flagons of cider; they held fire-raising parties on Knowle Tump, catching fire to the gorse, and on a clear night you could see the lads' silhouettes. Children played pitch and toss for pennies; older ones of a daredevil bent played tippit at The Colliers' Arms for threepenny bits. Six players round a table, the one in the middle was the rusher. You passed a coin to each other under the table and then clenched your fists over the table. The rusher had to guess who had the 3d. "It was better if there were girls there", says one ex-player. Jean Veale recalls skipping in the road until the Lovells' Sentinel lorry came along. Marjorie Reed recalls that the Treasure family next door to the school made swings and roundabouts in sections and then put them together. There were two swings, a roundabout and a pavilion on the rec. In the 1920s, and possibly for much longer, there was also a children's swing in the trees behind the Chapel.

There are memories of John, who had a car accident on the road past the Lake shortly after it was opened, and never walked again. Ken ('Pickles') Ware, whose father was a shoe repairer, would dry crumbly peas, soak them in Camp Coffee, put them through his mum's mangle, wrap them in cabbage leaves and smoke them. His mother wasn't pleased. Paul from Stowey Bottom died when his tractor overturned. One former pupil remembers that you had to be a member of either Sue Weaver's gang or Glenys Chubb's gang. During the war years some of the older pupils would carol-sing in the passageway at The Butcher's Arms. The Church choir – then about 30-strong – would sometimes lend support, although 'most of them were too old to go out'. Seen through the eyes of a 7-year old, that meant anyone over the age of 40.

Claimed He Saw 'Flying Saucer'

That, while working on a local farm, he saw a "flying saucer," is claimed by Peter James, 16, of Council Houses, Bishop Sutton.

He says it was a round, silvery object, travelling across the sky at a tremendous speed.

He told a reporter: "I was astonished when I saw the disc speeding from east to west, nearly overhead, shining against the blue sky.

"I called out to a friend, but it was gone in a few seconds, and ne was too late. It seemed to disappear behind a cloud bank."

Peter said he was convinced it was not an aeroplane or a balloon —it was travelling too fast.

Picking wild flowers was particularly popular, even amongst boys, and Eric Price was awarded a book for finding more varieties than anyone else. His parents' house was filled with bluebells and primroses. He'd go bird-nesting, his prize possession being a swan's egg from a nest at the Lake. Peter James found a rare marsh orchid at Elwell Wood above Top Sutton. On a separate occasion, he saw a flying saucer. The story quickly got round the village, reached the pub, and then the reporters appeared. Peter now thinks it may have been the vortex from a Bristol Brabazon aeroplane. There were competitions at fêtes and the like for catching the largest number of white butterflies[1]. Using a well-tried tennis-racket method, one girl captured 600. She counted them carefully and presented them in a large jar with '600' painted on the side. The judges didn't count them but she won five shillings anyway. Talking of 'white', that used to be the colour of dog poo: probably the calcium from butchers' bones. There was a pond near today's Toad Hall[2] along the main road, with great crested newts. There were, in fact, newts (great, crested, and otherwise) in ponds all round the village.

----
[1] Cabbage Whites ate cabbage, and were therefore considered a pest, albeit a pretty one.

[2] Toad Hall was not named for the wildlife there, but in commemoration of the toad who hopped onto the doorstep when Teresa and Delvin Dowling moved in.

Les Bown remembers playing cricket in Church Lane with a five-gallon oil drum as the wicket. The bat was supplied by Geoff Filer, whose friends pitied him for having a mother who, if punishment were needed, would hold him up by the hair on the nape of his neck. Dick Chapman, for whom spotting orchids was a touch twee, would play Kick White Horse which, at its simplest, entailed knocking on a door and running away. Dick and his pals perfected the art at the cottages fronting the road between The Red Lion and Church Lane and demolished in the 1950s. One of the doors was at the front – the others were at the back – with a step down from the main road. The boys would make a large snowball, prop it against the door, knock the knocker and run away. Fast. When the door was opened, the snowball rolled into the hall. What a jolly jape. If that got too boring, you'd play Pin a Button: fix a length of cotton to someone's window frame with a drawing pin, thread a button onto one end, hold the other end and hide round the corner. Gently pull the cotton, making the button go tap-tap-tap against the window. The occupant would come out to investigate, not see anyone and then go back in again. Repeat as necessary.

The pit (or pit site, depending on your age) was universally popular. Eric Price recalls the cycle speedway in the early 1950s on the slag heap before the trees grew. Colin Symes picked blackberries on the Mendips for the Robertsons jam factory at Brislington. When he wasn't blackberrying, he was with older boys 'borrowing' munitions from the wartime Home Guard. When they weren't illicitly borrowing munitions, they were licitly being helped to make Boy Scout Rousers, which emitted loud bangs used to simulate bombs and gunfire. All for the war effort, of course. A former pupil from the 1950s, clearly wary of the ghost of Mr Bailey,

anonymously remembers that someone would extract carbide from batteries, bring it to school in Tate and Lyle sugar tins, put it in the ink wells and watch it fizz. Alternatively they'd leave it in the tins, take it to Church Lane, add water, ram the lid on tight, make a tiny hole in it and set fire to the escaping gas. Without necessarily retiring the recommended number of yards. It was the era of the constabulary cuff round the ears if you were caught misdemeanouring. Police were rarely seen in the village, so it was a risk worth taking. Those of a less hooliganistic bent would go hipping and hawing and bring the fruit into school. There were deadly nightshade berries to be picked and fed to the neighbour's cat, and the white juice of dandelions to be licked to see if it really did make you want to wee. There were cuts to be made in your arm to draw blood, whereupon you'd hold your cut against that in your friend's arm in the hope that blood would transfer from one to the other, thus making you 'blood brothers' (or sisters). You perfected ice slides alongside Mr Treasure's railings which separated the school playground from the house next door, and Sheila Walker remembers skating on the ice in the fields opposite the school. One former pupil recalls that she and her friends had wonderful Christmases in the 1920s. There wasn't much in their stockings: only a few sweets, an orange, an apple, nuts, a shiny penny and perhaps a small toy. It was magic.

Perhaps 'carefree' is, after all, the right word.

Children will be children and will always find ways of alarming adults. In April 1978 the PC *discussed the problem of children skateboarding. It was felt that the craze was dying out and one could only warn the children of the dangers.*

Now's as opportune a time as any for a brief excursion into speech and customs, as researched in Iona and Peter Opie's fascinating book 'The Lore and Language of Schoolchildren'. Somerset rituals – practised hereabouts – included not speaking to someone of the opposite sex on St Valentine's Day before it struck 12 o'clock, as that would bring bad luck. On May Day, young girls would get up with the dawn to wash their faces in the dew ('Kissing the Dew'). If you saw a white horse you would spit over your left shoulder, or cross your fingers and spit over them, or avoid looking at the horse's tail. If you saw an ambulance, you'd hold your collar till you saw a dog. If you were foolhardy enough to walk under a ladder, you'd cross your fingers and keep them crossed until you'd seen five dogs. Door-knocking and running away was called 'Knock up Ginger', 'Not Out Ginger', 'Shoeing a White Horse' or, as played by Dick Chapman, 'Kick White Horse'. Many games involved tag or truce; truce in these yer parts was generally 'cree'.

Apart from school sports, older children had ample opportunity for playing in village teams. By the 1920s, football was the winter favourite for the boys, with cricket or tennis in the summer. At one time, there were three football teams in the village (including the famous Walker boys), competing to different standards. Dick Chapman recalls that in the 1940s the first team was in the first division of the Bristol Suburban league and played as far away as Winterbourne and Thornbury, paying half a crown a match for the privilege. The youngsters forming the second team were the Colts, playing in red and white. In earlier times they had been organised by headmaster Mr Wightman and colliery manager Mr Moody. Bishop Sutton might not always have been the most righteous of places, but its behaviour at matches in the '30s and '40s was nevertheless nowhere near as bad as that of some of the nearby villages, especially Peasedown or Coleford. Peter James, amongst others, recalls that for away matches, Bishop Sutton always took a coach full of spectators. Not so much for the cheering on, as for the fisticuffs that followed the match.

For a time the local cricket club played on one of George Mellish's fields at Ham Lane; there was another pitch opposite the council houses at Bonhill. By the late 1940s, cricket was being played at the Miners' Welfare Ground, a.k.a. the rec. In February 1968 the school managers considered the Bishop Sutton Cricket Club's request for help *financially with the upkeep of the playing field to keep the ground in good order so that it was possible for the children of the school to use it. Resolved to give £5*. There were public tennis courts opposite the church.

Closely associated with village sports and the recreation ground were the Village Hall and the British Legion Hall. The former was more or less where the present Hall is, but was only half the size, nowhere near as grand and was made largely of tin. The latter was behind The Red Lion, housed a skittle alley, and was dismantled in the 1990s. The Village Hall has an uplifting background: during the Great War, Miss Workman (of Clifton), Miss Gertrude Ward and Miss Theophilia Yeatman[1] (both of The Redlands, Bishop Sutton) organised clubs in Rouen for the entertainment of the troops. With the war safely won, the PC gave the ladies £450 to build a Village Hall. They bought a site forming part of a plot known as Stocklands from J. Lovell and Sons for £20. When the Hall was ready, a committee was formed consisting, inter alia, of the Rt Hon. Lord Strachie, Gertrude Ward, Henry Dagger, William Saunders and the Rev. Thomas O'Freely. The Hall quickly made its mark with social evenings with dances and card games, and on Friday evenings in the 1930s a husband-and-wife team put on regular film shows, bringing in a portable projection

----
[1] Her name was given to a new road at the Cappard's Farm development.

booth and hand-cranked projector. Bus seats were set out. The audience's annoyance at the regular snapping of the reel was mollified by the fish and chips after everyone had rushed out to avoid having to stand for the National Anthem. Candle grease was spread over the floor for dances. Joan Bunney recalls wistfully that Wednesday nights in the Forties were 'pictures nights' courtesy of a cinema van.

c1992
The old Village Hall, left, was at the eastern end of the current
Village Hall car park. The 'Elf' petrol sign is outside Brent's Garage.

The Village Hall was important to the children, not only for out-of-school activities and as a venue for concerts, but also for meals until the school got its own canteen during the Second World War. Using the Hall involved the school in expense, and in October 1949 the managers asked Somerset Education Committee to *contribute to the cost of cementing the ground outside the entrance to the Hall which, in wet weather, becomes waterlogged, thereby being detrimental to the boys and girls who attend there for woodworking classes and for meals.* Taunton eventually *agreed to contribute 50% of the costs*. The increasing age of the Hall led to its deterioration and, as ever, no-one wanted to shoulder responsibility for doing anything about it. In December 1967 the PC expressed *grave concern about* [the Hall's] *future. A public meeting was to be held to see whether the parishioners still wanted the facility*. There's no subsequent mention of such a gathering, but at the Council meeting in January 1969 the possibility was mooted *of a 1/3d rate to get Hall up together*. In February 1970 it was unanimously agreed *that the Parish Council recommend to the Parish Meeting that a supplementary rate of 4d be levied to complete essential work on the Village Hall*.

SCOUTING, GUIDING AND YOUTH CLUBBING

In 1908 Robert Baden-Powell asserted that 'we must all be bricks in the wall of that great edifice, the British Empire', so he formed the Boy Scouts. The Girl Guides' Association followed in 1910; its handbook was 'How Girls Can Help to Build Up the Empire'.

Bishop Sutton wasn't far behind, at least with the Scouts. A troop was put together on 28 January 1911 by Sir Henry Strachie, who went on to become a national commissioner and receive Scouting's highest honour, the Badge of the Silver Wolf. The Scouts initially met twice a week at his home Stowey Mead in the summer and, in the winter, at the Scout Hut (also inexplicably called 'The Coffee Pot', or simply 'The Pot') opposite the school. The hut was set out with wood and had a vaulting horse. It caught fire one day at the beginning of the Second World War, and Evvy Harvey and Roy Perry are reputed to have put the blaze out with Home Guard fire extinguishers. There was a camp each Easter at Harptree Coombe and each August at Berrow (just north of Burnham-on-Sea), the Scouts being taken there in the back of an open lorry. In later years they would go to join other troops at Priddy, where Dick Chapman confesses to having let the guy ropes down. Sir Henry acted as benefactor to the poorer boys, providing them with uniforms and shoes, and took the Scouts for trips in his car. He is remembered not only for being the perfect gentleman, but also for his accomplished paintings, some of which can be seen in Stowey Church. His preferred subject was naked boys. This didn't seem strange in those days.

Bishop Sutton Boy Scouts 1912

There is little in the school records about the local Girl Guides, but we do know that they were formed in Bishop Sutton before 1927, meeting in the Scout Hut. Sheila Walker remembers joining in the late 1930s, but the war put paid to any camping. Pauline Heron started a Brownie pack around 1964, and Marie Pearson later took over. The Cub Pack was in Stanton Drew.

When schoolchildren weren't Scouting or Guiding, they may well have been Youth-Clubbing. The school logbook recorded in May 1941 that *Mr P. Gibbs called with regard to the Youth Service in the Village. A meeting of local people decided some weeks ago that nothing could be done here (a) without financial help, and (b) unless competent instructors were provided. It has now been arranged that the Youth of the Village shall be shown Ministry of Information films and invited to form a club.* Quite what became of that exciting suggestion wasn't recorded, but several former pupils do recall that children from nearby villages would meet at the Youth Club.

In the absence of any further school records, we're reliant on a local newspaper report from March 1965:

All over Somerset there are complaints about dances and other social events being ruined by vandalism, yet one village in the Chew Valley is an oasis of virtue by comparison. There has been no vandalism in Bishop

THE YOUTH CLUB SAVED HALL FOR THE VILLAGE

Sutton since the local youth club was formed, and there has been no vandalism in the club itself. The Village Hall, one of the largest in the district, was the despair of its management committee. Because it was cold and shabby, local organisations took their functions down the street to the Methodist Schoolroom, or to the little hall run by the British Legion. There were practically no lettings and therefore little revenue. So there was no money for improvements, or even for ordinary maintenance. Even when Lord Strachie came from his nearby home at Stowey Court and made a rousing appeal at a crowded parish meeting, there was little or no response. It was soon after that, however, that the Youth Club quietly moved in. They made pelmets and curtains for 20 windows; they made and installed stage curtains; they fitted up stage and decorative lighting; they constructed and equipped a coffee bar, they redecorated the Hall in attractive pastel shades. They organised special events to raise the money to pay for the materials. They won sufficient confidence among Somerset Youth organisers to secure them a county grant of £40.

THE LAKE, THE QUEEN AND THREE MIDGOLOGISTS

Chew Valley Lake might have little to do with the school itself, but that hasn't stopped it from assuming an ever-increasing importance since it was first mooted in the 1930s. The Lake led to the disappearance of farms and cottages (mostly in the hamlet of Moreton, from where some children had come to school in Bishop Sutton), over 10,000 trees and 70 miles of hedges. 1,200 acres of land were flooded and dozens of people displaced, many of whose families had farmed in the area for centuries. The Lake changed the communication networks of the Valley: in earlier times, main thoroughfares had been chiefly between Bishop Sutton and West Harptree, between West Harptree and Chew Stoke, and between Chew Stoke and Chew Magna. Pre-Lake maps show how twisty the lanes were; in bad weather they were distinctly not good. There was no easy road from Bishop Sutton to Chew Stoke.

The reservoirs at Litton and Blagdon had proved insufficient for the growing needs of the local population and of Bristol. Bore holes sunk in 1934 determined the geological character of the Valley, and an artificial weir proved that the River Chew could produce the ten million gallons a day that would make a reservoir worthwhile. The war put paid to any further work, and it wasn't until 1946 that the Lord Mayor of Bristol cut the first sod. The construction contract went to Messrs A. F. Farr of Westbury, Wiltshire. The lanes criss-crossing the Lake area were closed. The present road over the dam and round the north-east corner of the Lake was built to connect Chew Stoke with Bishop Sutton. The old Herriotts Bridge was straightened – thereby removing a dangerous bend in the road – and Stratford Mill was dismantled and re-erected at Blaise Castle in Bristol. Some properties originally scheduled for demolition weren't needed and are still occupied: Twycross, cottages at Stitching Shord Farm, Wick Farm, Manor Farm. On the other hand, Spring Farm at Sutton Wick probably could have been saved but wasn't. Protests about the building of the Lake were remarkably muted by today's standards. No Swampies in those days. Any criticism seems to have been restricted to the fact that Bristol Waterworks was possibly acquiring more land than was actually needed, and at a cheap price. Many farmers were tenants rather than owners and their compensation was based on two years' rent.

The dam on the new Wally Court Road, under construction in the early 1950s. The two lighter areas bottom-right of the picture are Bushythorn Road and Bilbie Road in Chew Stoke.

By 1956 when the Lake was opened – although it wasn't completely full until February 1958 – 3½ miles of new roads had been built, and 27 million gallons of fresh water a day were flowing through Woodford Mill. That was rather more than the mill had originally been designed for and it had to be pulled down. From across the Lake area, thousands of bits of artefacts and a rather nice pair of bronze tweezers found their way into various museums. Bishop Sutton suddenly had on its doorstep one of the largest reservoirs in the country and an internationally important haven for water birds. The clearance of the trees and hedges changed the local climate and made the Valley more windswept and significantly colder. Along with the microclimate came the midges and flies, about which more later. Of more pressing importance for the locals was the Official Opening. As soon as it became known that Her Majesty would be happy to pop along on Thursday 12 April 1956 with her ribbon-cutting scissors, everyone went into frenzied overdrive. Houses along the route were painted, welcoming parties were organised, PCs dug out any notes they might have on the protocol for meeting royalty, and primroses were replanted from lanes round Bishop Sutton to the bank near the dam. And moved back again afterwards.

The school had begun to get its act together in late 1955. The managers were told that *seats in the covered stand were available for one teacher and 19 children, and in the uncovered enclosure for three teachers and 60 children.* Headmaster Mr Bailey wasn't having any of that: he insisted on an arrangement *which would take all children from 15 yrs of age to 9. All other children would be able to stand on the pavement opposite the school.* Letters to-ed and fro-ed, and his proposals were eventually approved. The chairman of the PC persuaded the Palace in March 1956 to arrange for *the royal car* [to go] *slowly past the school so that those children not going to Chew Magna can see the Queen.* So all the children would get to experience the royal wave from one vantage point or another. On the actual day, their excitement was at bursting point. Mr Bailey wrote in the logbook: *12.4.56 Visit of HM The Queen. The normal routine of the school was not followed today. In the afternoon, 80 children and five staff went to Chew Stoke to the inaugural ceremony of the new reservoir. 20 of*

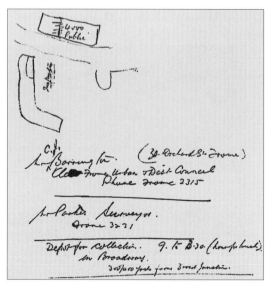

Mr Bailey's notes in preparation for the Royal Visit – the 'U' at the top is the small tower set back from the road, with the viewing stands alongside and opposite.

these remained for tea, the remainder and those left here were entertained to tea in the Methodist Hall. The children remaining here lined the road opposite the school and saw HM pass at 4.20. The flag was flown and decorations put up to mark the occasion.

Her Majesty arrives

The children had a day off, the Queen and Prince Philip and assorted county high sheriffs and people with expensive outfits had a whale of a time, councillors got back to their day-to-day business of footpaths, roads and pavements, and the Lake slowly filled up. The PC minuted prosaically: *bunting had been loaned from Norton Radstock UDC for the visit of HM, and had been returned after the memorable event.* Some of the after-effects of the occasion were predictable: eighteen months later, the PC voiced their *disappointment that the hedges hadn't been sheared since the Queen's visit.*

Copy 26/6/56

To Her Majesty The Queen,
    Madam.

It is the unanimous will of ~~every person in~~
this Parish, as ~~expressed~~ most enthusiastically
at the annual Parish Council meeting, for me to
convey to your Majesty & your Husband
The Duke of Edinburgh, their grateful thanks
for making possible the most happy day
everyone had on the occasion of your
recent visit & passage through this village
to inaugurate Chew Valley Lake.
    It is the first time on record
that a reigning Sovereign has visited us
& we are indeed proud, & our love &
loyalty, that we tried to show you that day,
is most firmly established.
    I have the honour to remain, Madam,
your Majesty's most humble & obedient
                                        servant.
                    Albert Ward
        Chairman, Chew Magna Parish Council

Chew Magna Parish Council's draft thank-you letter to the Queen

The Lake before it was full

Which brings us to the midges. Swarms of them were attracted by the Lake's fresh water, they were begetting in biblical numbers and taking to the skies on balmy evenings. Of which there were many, even after the onset of a cooler microclimate. It wasn't long before they were truly rampant, even to the extent that motorists were complaining to the police that their windscreen wipers couldn't cope with the goo of a thousand squashed insects. The tale of how Stowey Sutton PC tried valiantly to deal with the problem is so good that it just has to be included here, despite being utterly devoid of any scholarly content.

In July 1956, only weeks after the Queen's visit, the councillors received *further complaints regarding swarms of knats* (sic) *and mosquitoes at Bishop Sutton. The clerk was requested to write to the Sanitary Inspector to inform him of the position and enquire whether there is any potential danger arising from their unwelcome appearance*. By mid-November there had been no response, and the pest continued despite the colder weather. The Council anxiously noted that *treatment of the Lake by any insecticides is likely to be toxic to human beings*. By January 1957 advice was sought *from Mitcham and Morden RDC* (in Surrey) *who were spraying*. One

BUCKINGHAM PALACE

30th May 1956.

Dear Sir,

I am commanded by The Queen to write in reply to your letter of the 26th May.

Her Majesty has learnt with great pleasure of the message which you were asked to convey to her on behalf of those present at the Annual Meeting of the Chew Magna Parish Council.

Her Majesty was delighted to learn that her passage through Chew Magna had given so much pleasure to all concerned.

Yours truly,

The Chairman,
Chew Magna Parish Council.

The Queen's letter of thanks for a lovely passage through Chew Magna

assumes they had a lake of their own and weren't spraying the Chew Valley from Mitcham and Morden. By July *the problem was such that the inhabitants of Bishop Sutton complained bitterly that a nuisance was evident. Bristol Waterworks suggested ways and means of destroying the insects. They would install lights at strategic points around the Lake to see whether the insects could be attracted from the village.* Attentive readers will recall that the absence of streetlamps meant that Bishop Sutton was a haven of dark.

This was all getting absolutely nowhere, so at the end of September 1958 the PC *set up a small sub committee of three councillors, which would regularly report the habits of the midge and submit these reports to Bristol Waterworks*. The three intrepid midgologists – names unknown – tip-toed along the lanes with their magnifying glasses, spiral notebooks and sharp pencils.

In January 1959 the Council glumly noted that *Bristol Waterworks' one-year research showed that 'the midge appeared to have established itself for years to come'*. Oh joy. The Council *agreed that the problem was a national one and individual action was necessary*, and instructed its clerk to write *to the British Nylon Spinners and acquaint them of our difficulties and enquire whether they could provide a material which would keep the insects out of the houses*. In the meantime, the three midgologists continued to prowl the area.

British Nylon Spinners couldn't help – so Bishop Suttonians were spared the exotic thrill of going to bed behind mosquito nets – and bigger guns had to be brought in. In May 1959 the PC wrote to Time Incorporated in California. The Cold War being at its height, Time Inc. possibly had more pressing things to investigate than some midges at a lake – an insignificant puddle by American standards – in a far-off country about which they knew little, and by September the Council had received no response. But by this time, there had been a long hot summer in Somerset and most of the midges had embarrassingly disappeared. The Council needn't have troubled our transatlantic cousins after all. The three midgologists were about to be called off when, out of the Californian sunshine, came a letter from the Los Angeles Department of Health, from whom Time Inc. had sought advice. It was solemnly read out to the Councillors, who sat on the edge of their seats, ears agog.

> Midge problem, Bishop Sutton. Correspondence from British Nylon Spinners and M/s Small & Tidmas were read. The Clerk reported that he had also written to Time Incorporated for further information regarding experiments carried out in Los Angeles to abate the mosquito nuisances.
>
> It was unanimously agreed that the Clerk should continue to follow up the lines of enquiry.

The Parish Council writes to Time Inc. in 1959

They were to be disappointed: *The opinion held by the Department was that the experiment* (in Los Angeles) *was not too successful because the Gambusia Affinis fish*[1] *penetrates very shallow water. The entomologist was referring the Parish Council's letter to the Bureau of Vector Control, State Health Dept. Berkeley, California for additional information. They require the exact species of midge involved.* To add to what had now become a rather farcical situation, *Cllr Lord Strachie stated that from experience he found the swarms of midge were evident when winds were in an easterly direction.* Whichever direction the midges had been attacking Bishop Sutton from, they had largely vanished. The Council decided not to send the three fearless midgologists back out again into the danker corners of the Chew Valley armed only with a small net and an empty matchbox to find some specimens for the Bureau of Vector Control. The midge, gnat or knat just melted away as the ecosystems developed. Well, more or less. You can still see columns of them in the vicinity of the Lake on warm evenings, but they don't blacken the clothes on the washing lines of Bishop Sutton any more.

Children who were at the school at the time remember only that the midges were a

----

[1] Or mosquito fish, which preys on midge larvae.

blinkin' nuisance. But flies aside, former pupils do recall the building and the opening of the Lake. Colin Symes recalls the huge earth-moving equipment being gingerly manoeuvred along the narrow lanes. Joan Bunney remembers crawling through the waste pipes with her friends. She also remembers one boy coming to school one morning and announcing (either proudly, or in tears; Joan can't remember which), 'they're going to flood our house'. No-one believed him. Les Bown figured that as he was just about to start National Service and might have to die for his Queen, he'd better go and see her.

And that seems to have summed up the position. A huge enterprise – the fifth largest artificial lake in the United Kingdom[1] - which just sort of appeared. It quickly turned into a tourist destination with its own challenges as well as jobs in the tea shop. The PC recorded in February 1961 *re weekend traffic: it was unanimously agreed that the Police be made aware of the situation (re people going to the Lake) and asked to place portable direction signs at Twycross Corner in order to dissuade motorists from entering Ham Lane.*

Bishop Sutton, c1930, possibly taken from the top of the slag heap behind the pit. Mountain Ash Farm on the main road is the upper house at the extreme left. The cluster of buildings bottom-left includes Montgomery's bakery; the large house in the centre is where the Brent family lived. The church is in the background.

---

[1]

    1   Rutland Water in, yes, Rutland
    2   Kielder Water in Northumberland
    3   Pitsford Water in Northamptonshire
    4   Grafham Water in Cambridgeshire (ex-Huntingdonshire)

CHAPTER NINE

DIRTINESS, ILLNESS, ACCIDENTS AND SAFETY

BREEDING RATS AND FLIES

Before we're overcome by the warm glow of childhoods past, it shouldn't be forgotten that there was another side to the children's village. For want of a better word, 'unwholesome'. Some of the Dickensian unwholesomeness affected the children, some didn't. In the 1870s, the Rev. Francis Kilvert was curate of Clyro, near Hay-on-Wye in Herefordshire, and wrote his 'Journal of a Country Curate'. There's little reason to assume that life for some people in Bishop Sutton at that time was not dissimilar from what he described in Clyro:

In one of the bedrooms was a dark hovel hole almost underground. Here an old man of 82 lay dying next to a fair-haired little girl of 4 years old. In another the bedroom was a low and crazy loft in the roof which was so dark that it was impossible to discern the features of the occupants. A small and filthy child knelt or crouched in the ashes of the hearth before a black grate and cold cinders. No-one else was in the house and the rain splashed in the court and on the roof and the wind whistled through the tiles. Almost all the glass was smashed out of the bedroom or rather bed loft window, and there was only a dirty cloth hanging out before the ruin of the window to keep the wind away.

As regards Bishop Sutton, the records point to varying degrees of scruffiness, hardship and insalubrity. In June 1887, for instance, the parish councillors were treated to Mrs Dendy's complaint surrounding a dead dog, as illustrated.

In Neil Bentham's 'A History of Blagdon 1914-2002', Ikie Smart recounted that his family used to live in Bishop Sutton. This would have been in the 1920s:

We lived in a farm cottage. There were five of us children then, and father had the cottage on condition that he worked on the farm. But he wanted his Saturdays off so that he could go on going to the market (he had a stall at Bristol market). Well that went on for quite some time, and then the farmer said "I want you all the time". Father didn't want to give up this job on the market in Bristol, he said he couldn't do

Complaint was made by Mr Dendy that some person whose name is known to Mrs Frey, of Bishop Sutton has caused a nuisance at Bishop Sutton by throwing the Carcase of a large dog in the stream which supplies her cottage and other, with water for dietetic and domestic purpose, and the Council request the Sanitary Authority to investigate the matter as they consider that the person causing the nuisance should be prosecuted

James Andrews

Unorthodox disposal of a dead dog

it. So he lost the job, and we were put out on the side of the road, all of the family, with our few bits of furniture and all. That's what the farmers could do in those days … so we were left standing on the side of the road, and if it hadn't been for another old farmer there, who gave us a little place to go for a while, we should have been left standing there, with nowhere to go. That's how it was in them days.

'Hard Times', 1885, by Sir Hubert von Herkomer (1849-
1914), inspired by his meeting with a group of itinerant
workers near Bushey in Hertfordshire.

In June 1934 the PC *noted that there was a great deal of refuse being deposited in the roadside at Bishop Sutton and that it was desirous that a system of collections of refuse should be adopted*. In September 1949 the scourge of the distasteful ditch – first commented on fifty years previously – exercised the councillors again. They *heard that the open ditch from Top Sutton proceeding through the Village to the corner of Stitching Shord Lane was stated to be in a very unhealthy condition and was regarded as a public nuisance*. This picturesque aspect of the village is recalled by several former pupils; its sheer vileness made it a magnet for children. By the following month, *the Sanitary Inspector was serving notice on each owner of property in which the stream passed to clean out their portion of the ditch. Cllr Coles stated that certain residents disposed of excretia* (sic) *direct into the ditch, to which Cllr Strachie remarked this action was a contravention of regulations*. People were not noticeably law-abiding when it came to disposing of excreta at a time when there were still few lavatories worthy of the name, and regulations had no effect. Little was done, and by July 1950 the Council informed the authorities *that the brook was again filled with green slime; the smell was fearful. Cllr Saunders successfully moved* – not a wise choice of word, given the circumstances – *that the Sanitary Inspector should be asked to seal the cover of the well which was situated at the side of the road, and in consequence was proving to be a nuisance and a danger to children who remove the tin covering and play in the precincts of the well*. In March 1951 Cllr Bowditch reported *that a small child had fallen into the brook and but for the quick rescue by the child's parent, a serious state of affairs may have resulted*. Peter James recalls that Sutton Brook stank to high heaven and children happily paddled in it. It was eventually enclosed in a pipe. That resolved one dilemma, but unpleasantness was still breaking out all over.

The headmaster voiced his concern in March 1960 *that an open ditch containing sewage had been dug against the wall surrounding the school garden; this lay within 20 yards of the infants' classroom and was a source of possible danger; it was traced to the overflow of a septic tank provided for some residential buildings*. The abattoir (on the main road) and the pigs were also causing passers-by to hold hankies to their noses. In July 1955 the managers complained of *the smell caused by refuse being discharged from the slaughterhouse, and the large number of flies presumably caused by the same nuisance*. In October 1962 the Council decided *that because of the nuisance caused from pig keeping, and due to the nauseating smells emanating from the sties, the District Council should be asked to investigate a bye-law restricting the keeping of pigs in the residential parts of the Village. The motion was carried without dissent.* Taking a pragmatic but doubtless legally unsound (and certainly ungrammatical) stance, *the Chairman felt that at planning permission stage the pigs and their sties ought not to be any closer to the neighbour's house than to the owners of the pigs own home. The meeting agreed.* Sixteen months later, in February 1964, *the Sanitary Inspector carried out an investigation and was surprised at the number of pigs kept in the area.* In July the Council reported: *re nuisance of smells, the owner of the abattoir challenges the PC's assertion that parishioners had objected to the smells from the processing of fat.*

A local newspaper reported in April 1965 Mr Luxford's annoyance at the smells pervading his house. The article went on to relate the story told to the court: *A stream which is an open sewer runs through our garden. There is always a terrible smell – the smell of pigs and slaughtering, of fatty cooking and boiling bones. I came to live in the country because I wanted to be able to breathe some decent air after being all day in the city".*

After several years' agonising, the PC finally applied in 1961 to enter the Best Kept Village competition. Tellingly, Bishop Sutton did badly. On hearing the results in October 1962, the Council commented: *the generalisation arising from the Report was not accepted by the Parish Council, it was the Council's opinion that a lot of individual effort was displayed by residents.* In 1966 the councillors decided that discretion was the better part of valour. The village would not re-enter.

The house in a bad odour

Western Daily Press Reporter

Mr. Clifford Luxford's house in Bishop Sutton is the centre of a small sandwich, a valuation court was told yesterday.

On one side of the course is a large slaughterhouse. On the other— a piggery.

"They both breed rats and flies," Mr. Luxford told the court at Temple Cloud, Somerset: "The smell is so intense it gets right into the house.

The entrance to the 'Cappard's Farm' slaughterhouse shortly before the site was redeveloped in the 1990s. The road into the new estate is more or less where the gates are. The bungalow is no more. The butcher's shop was about 50 yards to the left of the gates; the building still stands.

Parish councillors were told in November 1965 that *open lagoons in Ham Lane are still in existence near the pumping station, which presented a danger to children.* Bristol Waterworks indicated that they would fill in the lagoons a.s.a.p. Spoilsports. Happy-go-lucky youngsters used to enjoy playing there. In September 1968 the PC heard that *buildings opposite the post office* [are] *infested with rats and being used at night by vagrants*, and in the 1970s the Parish Magazine drew attention to the derelict vans and trailer left on the piece of spare ground below Rose Cottage, Sutton Hill Road. Dick Chapman commented that Top Sutton was rough in the 1930s, with big families: 'you wouldn't want to live there if you could help it'. A few hundred yards down the road, there was a small reservoir over the wall at the sunken lawn next to Southlea. It stank. The ditch alongside was always full of blood from the abattoir, and people would collect bucketfuls for their sweet peas. Monica Castle, a pony lover, still shudders when she thinks of the hundred or so horses tethered in a field at the bend on Bonhill Road, awaiting their fate at the slaughterhouse, one of few in the country to have a licence to kill horses.

Nothing to do with the horses, but one former pupil recalls that the lights on girls' bikes were regularly stolen. Nothing to do with the lights, but children would be dared to go along Compton Lane, which ran from Knowle Tump to the back of the Lake. Why? There were fleas along Compton Lane.

SUSPECTED MURDER : SOMERSETSHIRE.—A farmer named George Elms was found dead by the side of the road, a short distance from the village of Bishop's Sutton, about nine miles from Bristol on Tuesday last, by some colliers who were proceeding to their work. It appeared from an examination of the body of the deceased that there were two wounds in the head and one in the face, and a quantity of blood was found in the middle of the road, some yards from the body. The deceased lay with his face in a drain by the side of the road, his hands being doubled up under his head as if to protect it. He was on his knees, and by the side of him was a mark as if he had fallen and endeavoured to get up again, but was unable to do so. His hat, which was a round one, similar to those worn by the countrymen of the neighbourhood, was lying two or three yards off. It was picked up, and on examining it a large r. ··k of blood was found in the inside of the rim, which probably came from a wound upon his forehead, and which appeared to be the result of a blow given on the outside of the hat. There were also some marks, as of coal, on the hat and on his coat. A remarkable circumstance was noticed, and that was, that a portion of his coat was covered with the white mud of the road, as if he had first fallen on it, and the other with the dark mud of the ditch in which he was found lying. The body being found as early as five in the morning, by a number of colliers, and the ground being wet, it was impossible to discover either the trace of footmarks or the appearance of a struggle. Evidence was given before the coroner to show that

Murder most foul in Bishop Sutton, 1853 (part 1)
'A farmer named George Elms was found dead by the side of the road'

on the evening previous to the discovery of his dead body he was drinking at a beerhouse, in Bishop's Sutton, with Hassall, a farmer, and Hopkins, a carpenter. They all left together, Elms being quite sober, and he going in one direction and Hopkins and Hassall in another. Mrs. Vanne and her daughter, who lived on the road which Elms had to traverse on his way home, deposed that they were awoke by the rumbling of a cart about an hour after they went to bed (ten o'clock), and shortly afterwards heard two men coming along the road. The witnesses heard a strange voice say; "Are you going home, farmer?" and immediately heard Elms's voice, which they knew well, reply, "Yes, I am." The strange voice then said, "I am going along the road, and I will go with you." The strange voice then said that "he understood Mr. Stallard, of Chew, was going about a farm," and farmer Elms replied, "Yes, I have been down to Chew to-night, and I have had a glass." They then went on, and the witnesses heard no more. Pools and spots of blood were found at the distance of eight or nine feet from the body. A cart laden with coal, with the shafts propped up, was placed near the road, about fifteen yards from the spot where the body was found, but all the witnesses examined stated that it was impossible the deceased could have run against it and so injured himself, unless he had gone off the road and stooped considerably, and that if he had done so he must have fallen over a heap of stones before he had touched the cart. Besides, the blood was 12 or 14 yards from the cart. Half-a-crown and a knife were found in the deceased's pockets. The inquiry was adjourned.

Murder most foul in Bishop Sutton, 1853 (part 2)

IMPETIGO, SCARLATINA
AND A GREAT CREEPER CRAWLING DOWN HER FROCK

Cholera was a constant threat in the early 1800s, and beyond. This, from the High Littleton vestry book of 3 October 1832:

At a meeting held this day to arrange precaution against the cholera, which is unhappily now in the adjoining parish of Paulton, it is resolved that the following measures be adopted without delay by the Overseers (of the Poor House): 4 pairs of blankets to be purchased; 6 bed cases and bolsters, and more if necessary, to be filled with straw or chaff; all the poor who have not been given a change of body linen (i.e. underwear) in the past year to be given some … Lime, vitriol or vinegar to be used for cleaning filthy and infected houses. Resolved that in the event of cholera appearing in this parish, lime to be placed near the houses which are affected and pitch or tar to be burned to create smoke to purify the air … The bed, bedding and clothes of anyone dying from cholera to be immediately burnt; the burial to be as soon as possible, the body to be taken to the grave in a cart or bier and the grave to be dug at least 8 feet deep.

Even closer to home, the Chew Magna Vestry meeting of 2 August 1849 decided *to take into consideration a Notice received from the Board of Guardians for the adoption of certain measures as may appear desirable to prevent as far as practicable the introduction of Cholera into this Parish.*

2c

CAUTIONARY NOTICE!!

Some cases of Cholera having appeared at the Union Workhouse, to which the disease is at present confined, the Local Board of Health desire to impress on the Public that the progress and fatal effects of this disease may be controlled to a very great extent indeed, by prompt preventive measures, and the Board call upon the inhabitants to co-operate with them in their endeavours to avert the threatened destruction of human life.

Cholera comes to Taunton in the 1840s

WELLS BOARD
OF
HEALTH.

THE MEDICAL COMMITTEE,
OF THE ABOVE INSTITUTION,

Established in this City, for the preservation of the Public Health,

RECOMMEND

To the Inhabitants the following precautions as conducive to that end:--- viz---

1.—That every House, or Tenement, more particularly the sleeping rooms, should be purified by the free admission of air into them at all convenient hours, and the removal of all *soiled* linen, and other offensive articles.
2.—That the Walls of each room be whitewashed, and the Floors, Doors, &c. well scoured, and Cleansed.
3.—That the greatest attention be paid to cleanliness of person and apparel.
4.—That Flannel be worn next the skin, either in the shape of a belt round the waist or as an underwaistcoat.
5.—Abstinence from all excesses or irregularities of living ; more especially drinking ; it having been remarked that the first victims of pestilential disorders, have been habitual drunkards.
6.—Avoiding all unnecessary exposure to night air.
7.—That all drains, gutters, sewers. cess-pools, &c. &c. be cleansed out, and kept *constantly clear from obstructions.*

How the authorities in Wells hoped to combat the disease

When the school was opened in the Bishop's Sutton Tything of Chew Magna, medical assistance was scanty and expensive, and sanitary and hygiene conditions were not of the best. Families were generally left to their own devices and, if all else failed, to rest and prayer. Minor ailments were treated with grandma's remedies such as sage and vinegar for a sore throat, or inhaling the smell of tar to help bronchial problems. Colds were fed and fevers were starved. Until well into the pre-antibiotics and pre-immunisations 20th century, life was risky. It wasn't just the birth and death bits that were dodgy, but all the bits in between, and especially the childhood bits. In 1900, 163 babies in every 1,000 died before their first birthday. One toddler in four didn't live to see their sixth birthday. The overall situation was worse in cities than in rural areas such as Somerset, but nowhere was it encouraging.

Measles, mumps, whooping cough, scarlet fever and flu could have the school closed for weeks on end. Tuberculosis (TB), diphtheria and scarlet fever could lead to serious disability, or be fatal. Many diseases were 'notifiable'[1], and the Medical Officer would step in to give advice. It wasn't unusual for children to be sent to school by parents – perhaps because there was no-one to care for them at home – and sent back again by the headteacher.

Improved health went hand in hand with improved welfare and better food, but there was a long way to go. In 1913 the Chief Medical Officer estimated that of the six million elementary school children in England and Wales, 10% suffered from a serious vision defect, 5% from defective hearing, 3% from suppurating ears, another 3% from adenoids, 10% from general bodily dirtiness, 2% from TB, 1% from heart diseases and 1% from ringworm. The figure for ringworm would have been higher in rural areas: it was usually caught from milking cows.

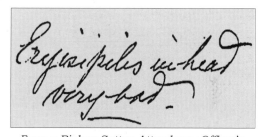

From a Bishop Sutton Attendance Officer's report, 1891.
'Eryisipilis in head very bad'.
Properly spelt 'erysipelas', and also known as 'St Anthony's Fire', it is an acute bacterial infection of the skin.

Most of these illnesses and ailments feature somewhere in the Bishop Sutton School logbooks. Although the records might imply that parents kept their offspring at home as soon as there were crops to be gathered in, it was sickness that represented the major cause of absenteeism. Poverty was never far behind, and poverty often brought with it dirtiness, especially as clean water wasn't easy to come by.

Gatherings were quite popular. Not of the Methodist or Temperance variety, but those that afflicted the body's extremities and resulted in the formation of pus; things so horrible that they're no longer mentioned in polite society, but were often the topic of the day in the logbooks. Broken chilblains were the talk of the staff room.

----
[1] The long list of diseases which must be notified to the Local Authority under the Public Health (Infectious Diseases) Regulations 1988 includes diphtheria, measles, mumps, rubella, scarlet fever and whooping cough, alongside more exotic afflictions such as anthrax, plague and leprosy,

Let the logbooks dish the dirt. And the illnesses. Heaven only knows what went on in the first thirty years of the school's existence, but it couldn't have been any better than the 1870s, which were plagued by rashes, itches[1] and carelessness. Not to mention coughs, colds, mumps, scalds, chickenpox and broken bones. Pride of place for the first recorded poorly pupil went to William Ferris who, on 6 February 1873, was absent for a whole week from a gathered foot. Later that month, by which time William's foot had probably degathered, *attendance has been very bad all week in consideration of much sickness in the Village*, and by October *nearly half the children were away*. August 1873: *John Gibbs and Elizabeth Ann Edgell have been absent in consequence of having no shoes*. Boiling water was notoriously dangerous. In July 1873 Alice Willey had *scalded her leg and couldn't come to* school, and in March of that year John Henry Tibbs scalded his foot. Nasty things sometimes afflicted teachers, which could work to the scholars' advantage: in July 1873 *the girls have not had any sewing, their mistress having been unable to prepare it for them through gatherings on her hands*. Nice.

Punch cartoon 1913: "Please, Teacher, Mother says can Albert David sit by 'isself this mornin', 'cos 'e's got a touch o' the measles?"

The Victorians knew that oxygen was good for you. The local variety simply wasn't good enough for pupil Alfred Appleby who, in April 1874, *went to Keynsham for a change of air*. The oxygen wasn't improved by the pigs and the ditch at Top Sutton. 1875 started with a prevalence of sickness in the village: on Friday 15 January two thirds were away, William Gibbs had died the previous Saturday and wouldn't be able to attend school, Ada White on the Wednesday, and the headmistress didn't expect poor Alice Willey to recover from whatever it was she'd gone down with. Sometimes all this illness was annoying rather than tragic. In February 1878 Mr Northam complained that *the work has been much hindered by constant*

----

[1] 'Itch' was the term commonly given to any severe skin disorder.

coughing. On the morning of Wednesday 13 March 1878 Mr Northam sent Fred Lovell home with his siblings James, Ernest and Ellen – no kowtowing there, despite the Lovells not generally being a family to cross with impunity – as Fred and James had *what I considered to be itch*. He sent Walter Bird home in the afternoon with ringworm.

1878 was a good year for creepy crawlies. During the morning of Wednesday 11 September Mr Northam spotted a creeper on Ellen White's head. This prompted a hunt and at *12 midday* (a stickler for detail, was Mr N) he *found five creepers on Alma Noke's head*. The offending children were ordered home to get their heads cleaned. Their parents had the temerity to send them back to school on Thursday, but at 2.30 that afternoon, Alma was peremptorily despatched again to have three creepers removed. The Scripture lesson on 4 October was disturbed by the discovery of two creepers on the head of Elizabeth Withey, who was sent home. On the following day she was sent home again *at 12.10 to be thoroughly cleaned*. No wonder children were so slim: it was all that walking to and from school to be de-creepered. But the worst was yet to come.

On Friday 29 November 1878 the master *sent home Elizabeth Withey with a great creeper crawling down the middle of the body of her frock*. The attention to detail is again admirable. The Withey family didn't have the knowledge or the wherewithal to conquer the infestation and on Friday 28 February 1879, *11 creepers (eleven!!) were seen on Elizabeth Withey at 11.50 and as she has frequently been complained of to no purpose, I gave her one stroke across the hand with the cane*. Nothing like visiting the sins of the parents upon the children. Things didn't improve much. *Mary Harvey hosted four creepers in May 1879*, and *Margaret Jones and Susan Burridge, having been warned several times against dirtiness, received two strokes on the hand for extremely dirty skin*. In April 1880 the aforementioned Elizabeth Withey was again reproved for being all creepered up and, to add insult to injury, *was punished afterwards being perverse in the arithmetic lesson*. Perhaps she was miscounting creepers. In July

The secretary to the Board using a rather blotchy pen to advise headmaster Brown to liaise with Mr Lovell as regards closing the school because of a measles outbreak.

of that year, Mr Northam blanched to see *three or four creepers on Maria Harvey's head about 10 am, about 11 am I saw three others, and at 12 am two others.*

Creepers seemingly made it onto the endangered wildlife list after 1880. They were replaced by a profusion of other adversities. In November 1880 the village endured the double shame of an infectious outbreak and of being called a hamlet: the Board wrote *to the Medical Officer of Health of the Clutton Union directing his attention to a reported outbreak of scarlatina in the hamlet of Bishop Sutton, and recommending him to have an interview with the schoolmaster of that place on the subject.* In July 1881 attendance was the lowest for a year *owing to the measels* (sic). This infuriated Mr Northam: *it is the more inconvenient too on account of the near approach of HM Inspector's visit for the annual examination.* In August 1881 new headmaster Mr Hawkins told the Board that *measles had been very prevalent in the village and that he himself had suffered from them.* In May 1886 Mr Brown *was very ill (suffering from eczema brought on, according to doctor, by overwork and a cold) during the holidays.* Being a man, he was *able to resume work though feeling very unwell.*

Diseases spread like wildfire, and all children from a family were generally excluded from school if one child went down with something catching. In January 1888 measles and scarlatina (synonymous with scarlet fever) kept 34 children away *all the week owing to one or other of these complaints being in the household.* Mr Lovell, Chairman of the Board, braved a visit to the school and intimated that it *will be closed for a period unless some improvement in the health of the children shows itself.* A stern warning indeed, but lessons continued unabated when the Medical Officer of Health for the District, Dr Wilson, called

Please don't inspect our school: the children had only just got over scarlatina when they went down with measles.

by and *considered it unnecessary to close the school as, in his opinion, nearly all who were likely to catch the infection were ill, or had been ill, and he anticipated very few, if any, further cases.* A couple of months later he ate his words, and closed the school from 9 April to 7 May. This would affect the school's performance at the imminent inspection, and the Board requested Her Majesty's Inspector in Bath, H. B. Barry Esq., to defer his visit. He prudently kept his distance.

In January 1890 *the influenza epidemic has at last attacked the children – phew*, it finally got here – *and nearly three fourths of them have suffered with it*. These prolonged illnesses and intermittent closures did nothing for the children's education or the teachers' nerves, and the logbooks were festooned with plaintive comments such as *very hard at work trying to retrieve lost time*, or *the bad attendance has retarded progress very much*, or *children earnestly at work, but many of them have forgotten a great deal*. In March 1898 the Attendance Officer reported that Mark Filer's daughter Plenty was away from school with scarlet fever; the Board thought it best to instruct him *not to send his other children to school for a month*. Measles closed the whole school for four weeks in early 1899. Illness was sometimes viewed almost as a malevolent spirit (*12 children are forbidden to attend school at all as fever has visited their homes*), or as a medieval plague (*children from infected houses have not been allowed to attend*). In September 1907 teacher Miss Carpenter was certified as suffering from cheiropompholyx[1].

As always with unscripted records, there were wry non sequiturs: *Beatrice Clapp has chickenpox and Alfred Harvey has gone to Wales to live* (1890), and *case of chicken pox reported to me, the yard has been covered with gravel* (1898). Also in that year, *A. Withey absent with chickenpox, D. Hill with disease of the brain*.

Matter-of-fact entries can bring a lump to the throat: *A. Travis died this morning. She was at school yesterday*. That was October 1892. The family wasn't listed in the 1891 census, so were perhaps newcomers to the village; we don't know how old the poor girl was. Some children were ill enough to be kept away for protracted periods. In June 1897 the mother of Ethel Padfield, who had *been away for some time*, told Mr Wightman that Ethel was going to hospital. She came home briefly but was readmitted by April of the following year, *having been ill for 12 months at Weston-super-Mare*. One assumes that Weston represented the hope for her recovery and was not the reason for her sickness. In April 1927 the Medical Officer ordered Stanley Adams (aged 7) to attend school for half the day. Although he had officially been admitted to school two years earlier, he *only attended a few times owing to heart and lung trouble*, and died in January 1931.

It shouldn't be assumed that Victorian headmasters only caned and ranted. Mr Wightman had his caring side: in November 1897 *J. Harvey, who returned after three weeks' absence, was obliged to be taken home again at 9.45 am. His attendance was cancelled. I left school for a few minutes this afternoon in order to see him*.

On 22 March 1901, *children are coughing all day, six deaths in the village during the last fortnight*. The fatal illness was unspecified, but the headmaster told the Board that he'd placed chloride of lime in various parts of the school to try to counteract it. In April 1907 he reported that *the very low attendance (around 70%) is through the epidemic of Hooping Cough* (sic), so the managers shut the school for five weeks. Measles brought an extended Easter holiday in 1909, and whooping cough prompted a month's closure in June 1912. Dr Savage ordered four weeks' closure in January 1914 for measles. There was no school for a fortnight in September 1915 due to mumps, and measles prompted an early Christmas holiday in the same year. In April 1922, with overall attendance at only 81%, *two large families, Marsh and Chidzey, still excluded for mumps*. In early 1923, mumps kept the children away for

---

[1] A blister-like pattern of eczema affecting the skins of the hands.

four weeks. In April 1929 the headmaster sent Miss Batt to the doc *owing to indirect contact with Small Pox* (sic); the doctor advised re-vaccination and she remained uninfected.

Given the anti-Teutonic feeling engendered by the First World War, the school managers must have been embarrassed in February 1916 to have to report to the authorities the first case of German measles. The influenza sweeping Europe, which was to prove more deadly than the Great War, reached the Chew Valley. 5 February 1917: *attendance falls to 76%, influenza kept many away*. On 16 February Mr Wightman himself succumbed, but survived. It seemingly went quiet until September 1918, when several children were away: *very poor attendance through influenza and heavy rain*. Things were looking up by November, *as the 'flu cases* (the first time the abbreviated word made an appearance) *are well isolated, being on the outskirts of the village*, but the spring of 1919 brought another onslaught. Overall, however, the village had escaped the worst, and the logbook didn't record any deaths amongst the children. Church records may tell a different story. Flu didn't go away, of course, and prompted a fortnight's closure in January 1927, another four weeks in early 1933 and a week in early 1937.

Death was unfortunately a common occurrence.
From Kent in 1908: 'Dear Mother, Hope you are all well. Thick fog here today. W'm better. School closed for illness. 4 dead. Mr B coming to dinner...'

The 'Rules to be observed by the Parents of Children attending the National School' (undated, but probably from the 1870s) had stated: *The children must be sent to school clean and neat in person and dress*. The children might have been sent to school, but they were frequently neither clean nor neat, and the steady increase in household income in the early years of the 20th century didn't immediately raise villagers' hygiene standards to any noticeable extent. In January 1917 Mr Wightman *sent home J. Bates as he was filthy*. In June 1920 Ivy Harvey was sent home *owing to filthy head*, and in November 1921 two Chidzey children *were excluded for verminous condition*. In December 1931 *Mollie Prime was excluded for ringworm on the back of the hand*. This was unusual enough by now, at least on the back of the hand, for the headmaster to have to notify *the Medical Officer of Health and the County Medical Officer*. As late as 1935, five girls were excluded for *verminous heads*, but in the face of  more effective health advice and support, cleanliness – or rather the lack of it – was steadily laid to rest.

Mass illness became more infrequent by the 1950s, although measles and mumps were still potent forces. 1948's Annual Concert and Treat, for example, was postponed as a result of a measles outbreak, and on 3 October 1950 over 20% of the children were away with the virus. Of 158 children on the roll in December 1954, 117 were away with flu. In July 1963 Mr Price *excluded Wendy Tonkin and Cynthia Bassett with suspected German measles*. In 1968 Andrew Filer was excluded *with suspected whooping cough*, D. Ashby, Peter Scamell, Richard Sage and L. Jenkins with suspected impetigo, and Karen Perry and Denise Simmons with suspected German measles. There were no reports of illness again until 1978, when *two children were sent home feeling unwell*. They didn't blame the broken kitchen steriliser, which was away for repairs at the time, but *this could be the onset of 'Red Flu' which was prevalent elsewhere*.

To end on an unexpected note: Julia Padfield was absent with nettle rash in July 1887.

KNOCK-KNEE AND TREADLE-OPERATED DRILLS

During the last two decades of the 19th century, it became increasingly clear to politicians that medical standards in Britain were not keeping pace with advances made by some European neighbours. By the 1880s medical inspections were being routinely carried out in schools across France (where the doctors were presumably telling the children that une pomme par jour kept the médecin at bay), where properly organised school canteens had also been set up (where they perhaps sold the pommes). The Germans established their first school doctor in Frankfurt am Main in 1883, copied in 1885 in Lausanne by the Swiss. England's first school medical officer wasn't appointed until 1890, when authorities in London roped someone in on a part-time basis. Bradford (Yorkshire) followed in 1893, but not until 1907 was an obligation placed on LEAs to provide medical inspections. None of these government initiatives made it into the school logbook until 1926[1] when, in March, *five children attended at Harptree for eyesight*. In December 1933 *the district nurse showed class teacher exercises to cure* [Francis Tovey] *of knock knee*. Enough to send a modern class teacher loco in loco parentis. By the mid-1930s the Medical Officer was a regular visitor at the school. In March 1941 *Dr Cuthbert (Senior Medical Officer) inoculated 64 children under the new Immunisation Against Diphtheria scheme*, and in November 1942 the headmaster *addressed a letter to parents of all children not immunised asking them to reconsider the matter*. In May 1945 Dr Yates celebrated Victory in Europe by giving *a third injection to 65 children*.

Mass radiography arrived in Bishop Sutton in June 1951, around the time that shoe shops were introducing small x-ray machines to measure foot size. Anyone over a certain age will remember these with some fondness, as they could brighten up an otherwise tedious trip to the High Street. The machines were subsequently linked to the risk of cancer and were hastily withdrawn. But back to mass radiography: notices thereof were sent to the school in June 1951 and distributed to the teachers. A couple of weeks later, Mr James and Mrs Ingram went to Bristol to learn more about it. The next mention was nevertheless not until November 1956, when *the teachers submitted themselves to radiography and the headmaster reported that they had all been granted bills of good health*.

Polio, still a major threat with an awful legacy of children across the country having

----
[1] School dental inspections at Bishop Sutton began in March 1915.

to wear straightening irons on their weak legs, was being vaccinated against by the mid-1950s. It was in the same decade that vaccination of schoolchildren against TB began under the BCG scheme. Try to remember, for the 'Medical' round of the next pub quiz, that BCG stands for 'Bacillus Calmette-Guérin'[1]. By 1967 children were being routinely checked for deafness. Eye-testing had probably been carried out regularly since its first logbook mention in 1926, and was certainly in place when Bettina Cohn was working in the village from 1970 to 1980 as the health visitor responsible for instilling good health in school. She recalls that the main problems were head lice and the boys' inability to take their ties off unaided. Eyes were tested in Mr Price's office, or outside if the weather was good. Bettina had pictures of animals alongside a conventional chart. If young children couldn't recognise a kangaroo, they were asked to turn a letter E in the direction shown on a board. Children made health posters to go up in the school. Nurse Cohn had a list of topics that should be studied. One possibility was footwear: 'children wore silly shoes'. She would also weigh the children: 'no problem with obesity in those days'.

A district nursing service for things more minor than people would have wished to trouble (and pay) the doctor for had operated in the village from 1927, when Kelly's Directory listed a Lilian Grace Burfoot. Nurse Rose Jean Searle followed in the 1930s, and Dick Chapman remembers her as 'cruel and nasty; rode a motorbike and smoked'. He also recalls that Sutton Club money was given to Dr Roper for medical treatment[2]. One nurse at that time lived at Bonhill Council Houses and delivered babies. Her services cost about 6d a week, but her repertoire wasn't restricted to baby-delivering. Ken Rapps has very mixed memories of doctors in the Valley in the 1940s: Dr Brew had told Ken's family there was nothing to worry about when Ken (then aged 14) started retching up black bile, but Ken's father's doctor, Dr Hughes, diagnosed peritonitis. Ken was rushed to Bristol General Hospital in a hired car and recalls being in agony. It was under Dr Brew that peritonitis had killed Ken's mother. Joan Bunney remembers the school nit nurse in the early 1950s as being like a witch, with a black coat and big bag: 'like Mary Poppins, but not pretty'. Joan always had nits. Her words, not mine. Pauline Heron recalls from the 1950s that the doctor held his surgery at Chapel Cottage.

The Chief Medical Officer's estimate from 1913 – the one that discovered that 10% of children were dirty – had included the observation that fully half of elementary school pupils in England and Wales suffered from injurious decay of the teeth. This was a sure reflection of the poor regard in which the British held their gnashers. Tommies fighting in the trenches commonly envied the Germans their teeth. The often disgusting nature of British mouths was remarked upon not only by GIs fighting alongside British troops in the Second World War, but also by medical officers in German prisoner-of-war camps where British soldiers were incarcerated. Until quite recent times, a common 21st birthday present was to be given the money to have all your teeth out. It had never quite dawned on us Brits that if we insist on eating so many sweets, we do need to buy toothpaste.

----

[1] Léon Calmette (1863 to 1933) was a French physician and bacteriologist working alongside Alphonse Guérin.

[2] The system operated in much the same way as Clothing Clubs. Villagers would hand so much per week to the Club treasurer; when sufficient money stood against their name in his books (or when their creditworthiness was considered good), they could withdraw (or borrow) money to pay the doctor.

The school from the churchyard, 2009

The first recorded visit to the school by a dentist was as early as March 1915. Many children may have been curious: a toothbrush was an object of wonder. Many may have been scared: toothache was a known agony and the dentist's treadle-operated drill only slightly less frightening than the devil you know. It was a nuisance for the teachers too, as the dentist *had the use of the classroom during the morning*. One thing for the children to look forward to was that the dentist's visit did sometimes mean the abandonment of lessons: on 22 October 1917, *dentist visited the school. School closed today*. June 1921: *no school Monday or Tuesday morning owing to dentist*. The headmaster himself wasn't risking having any pupils hear his own stifled groans: on 28 May 1923 he *was absent being obliged to visit dentist in Bristol*. Mr Wightman was forewarned in February 1925 as to the dental necessities: *a jug of water, basin for hand-washing etc, fire or stove for heating water, small table, a few chairs, arrange for fire to be lit and the space in front of the table to be cleared of all obstructions*. Sufficient room would be needed to hold down the struggling children. By January 1927 the dentist moved out of a classroom into the Scout Hut on the opposite side of the road, perhaps so that the screams couldn't be heard in the school. The County Education Secretary had asked Scoutmaster Strachie whether the Hut might be available at four shilling a day. Yes, he replied, but it would be five shillings a day and *in addition, you will have to arrange with Mrs W. Dury, The Batch, Bishop Sutton to pay her for the fire etc. Also the room must be left in time for its use by the Girl Guides on the 18th at 6.30. You will have to make your arrangements with Mrs Dury tomorrow as you have left it rather late. I am yours respectfully, H. Strachie*.

There seems to have been a formal dental practice somewhere in the village at that time: Kelly's Directory lists a George Francis Allen as dentist in 1927, attending from Bristol on Fridays from 10 to 4, but there are no further references. By May 1935 the school dentist was at work with 76 children. It's not known what the work involved. In April 1938 *Miss Gayford of the Dental Board gave a lecture to the senior children on Teeth – their Construction and Care*.

It's not clear how the school dental service was financed, but in March 1939 Mr Bailey noted that *dental forms sent in: 76 paid, 4 applied for fee remission, 2 lapsed*. By 1942 something prompted the school dentist to set up shop in the British Legion Hall at the back of The Red Lion: perhaps the thought that he could pop next door for a half of watered down wartime ale should the children become too troublesome. By February 1946 *the dentist is here* (i.e. at the school) *working; he would not work in the Legion Hall as there was no waiting room there*. By January 1949, Mrs E. James was operating a dental clinic in Church Lane, which may have temporarily superseded the school service. Les Bown recalls that Mrs James's was the third house on the left going up – 'you followed the trail of blood up the road' – but by the following year *the dentist was at work in the Methodist Room; under a new system the parents are sent appointment cards and are responsible for getting their children to the dentist, Mr Vigar*. The National Health Service had been born.

SOMERSET COUNTY COUNCIL.

W. G. SAVAGE, M.D.,
County Medical Officer of Health.
Chief School Medical Officer.

TELEPHONE No. 1300
(2 lines).

Health Department,

BOULEVARD,

WESTON-SUPER-MARE.

20. 3. 35.

DEAR SIR,

DENTAL TREATMENT.

The School Dentist will be visiting Bishops Sutton on 5, 8 and 9,

and I shall be glad if you will arrange for rooms at   the Scouts' Room

–   –   to be ready ~~on this~~ each day by 8.45   a.m.

The Dentist will require a jug of water, basin for hand washing, fire or stove in room (so that the water can be heated), small table, and a few chairs. Will you please arrange for the space in front of the window to be cleared of all obstructions. In cold weather a fire or stove will be required in the waiting room as well as in the treatment room.

The dentist comes to the Scout Hut in 1935.
Note the deleted 's' in 'Bishops Sutton'.

By 1964 a mobile surgery was back at the school, where it caused the staff some annoyance: on 1 September *it will be stationed in the school yard until Mr Smedley, school dentist, has carried out treatment for children at this school*. It wasn't until 19 November that the surgery was driven away. In later years too, the unit spent a disproportionate amount of time taking up precious playground space. In 1974 surveyor Mr Yeates *called re the provision of water and electrical points for future visits by the mobile dentist's caravan near the teachers' toilet*. The last mention of school dentistry was in March 1976, when the governors reported that the *Dental*

Surgeon Van was in the yard to do dental check ups, this was for the whole of the school.

Many a former pupil recalls with a shudder the dentist treadling away in his van.

Farthing 1955, halfpenny 1967, penny 1967
(all actual size)

DISLOCATIONS, DANGEROUS TICKLING AND HOLED STOCKINGS

It wasn't only illness and dirt that kept children from their lessons. There were accidents.

The first to make it into the school logbooks didn't injure children, but would have repercussions for them and their families. At the end of March 1889: *accident at coalpit, which will probably soon be closed. Several children have left the parish, and more will soon leave as there is no work for many of their fathers.* The colliery was not to close for another 40 years.

The first recorded mishap involving pupils wasn't until February 1922, when Mr Wightman *was out of school until 10 am helping to get one of infants ready for hospital (broken thigh).* The fact that he was almost certainly the only member of staff – and one of the few villagers – with a car meant that his services were frequently called upon. In July 1933 *there was an accident in school.* Mr Bailey recounted it rather nicely: *Barbara Stokes, age 10, was running across the yard this morning (at 8.50 am) and ran into the railing, put out her hands to check herself and hurt her left wrist; owing to a slight swelling, I sent her to the District Nurse who attended her and advised sending her to the doctor, reporting that one of the wrist bones was dislocated. I took the child home and explained to the parent, who took her to Dr Vaughan in Temple Cloud; he confirmed the nurse's statement.* The episode must have preyed on the headmaster's mind, for he was usually a man of very few logbook words.

In September 1933, William Hill spoiled the exercise *Astride Jumping with Arms Sideways Raising* – a concise title for an exercise – by slipping, falling and hurting his arm. He was taken home, and his mother was advised to let the doctor see him. Dr Brew subsequently found the arm to be broken. In February 1945 Selwyn Griffiths, aged 8, *cut his hand on the ledge of the window of the School House kitchen. As his mother was not at home, I took him to the doctor who treated and dressed the wound.* In January 1947 *John Winstanley fell on his shoulder and it is feared his collar bone is broken. Mrs Flower rendered first aid and as the school 'bus came almost immediately, I phoned his mother and he was allowed to go home.*

Dr Brew – he of Ken Rapps' bile mentioned earlier – came in for several mentions. In November 1948, *Michael Reeves, while packing up the tables and forms at the Village Hall after dinner today, sustained an injury to his right hand by a table falling on it. I found that the doctor, i.e. Dr Brew of Chew Magna, was likely to be at the Ring O'Bells, Compton Martin for lunch*. Miss Harvey was assigned to take Michael to said pub. Mr Bailey didn't report whether the doctor was pleased to be dragged away from his lunchtime pint, or whether the landlord baulked at having underage children in his premises. In any event, *Dr Brew gave him a note for an x-ray at Bristol tomorrow, and Miss Harvey then saw him home*. The assumption must be that the headmaster was still referring to Michael Reeves rather than Dr Brew. It all turned out well, and the logbook for the following week recorded that Michael went back to school with a dislocated knuckle bone in his hand which had been *'put right'*.

In November 1950, *Jane Winstanley's mother phoned me to send Jane home as her brother had met with a motor cycle accident. Today I learn the boy has died*. In the impassive way of logbooks: *this probably explains why Jane left the cookery class and went home this morning*.

Wednesday 8 October 1952 no doubt started as a normal autumn day for two children happily cycling in from somewhere beyond Widcombe. But then: *one, Tony Tucker, attempted to overtake Pam Bridges. There was a car coming in the opposite direction and Tony, cutting in front of Pamela, knocked her from her cycle, her chin was grazed, her frock and stocking holed and her bicycle damaged. Tony's cycle was undamaged*. Holing a stocking was no trivial matter. Eighteen months later, Master Tucker was still a boisterous child. In September 1954 he hurt the small finger of his right hand *when playing in the classroom*. His trip to the Bristol Royal Infirmary, the x-ray, the involvement of the fracture clinic and a broken finger all made for a full report to the CEO.

They were made of tough stuff in those days. Ill or not, injured or not, children were expected to be absent for as short a time as possible. In July 1947, 10-year old George Weedon ran into a wall and cut his chin. Mr Bailey rang his dad, *who came and took him to the doctor; after having one stitch inserted, the boy came back to school*, no doubt regaling his pals with 'orrible tales of torture at the surgery. What with June White impaling her foot on a running shoe spike in June 1949, Rex Chapman's finger being hit by a ball during a football match in March 1950 (necessitating a trip to Dr Pearson at West Harptree), Ivan Maggs cutting his foot at the baths in July 1951, and 5-year old Alan Gibbs cutting his forehead on the edge of a table in March 1952 (stitched by the aforementioned West Harptree doctor, and prompting a report to the Education Authority), a teacher's life was never dull. In November 1952 Pamela Tucker (she of the holed stocking the previous month) *had the point of a needle break off in her finger during the Needlework lesson*. Off she went to West Harptree, where Dr Pearson did the necessary. Another report to the authorities. Form-filling had become rife, and one suspects that the report to HQ was often more bothersome (for staff) than the injury. In May 1952, *14-year old Janet Tovey met with an accident when jumping in the Rec. Field*. The decision was taken to transport her straight to the Bristol Royal Infirmary, where she was kept in as a result of a broken fibula. *A full report was sent to the authority*. Margaret Wood's fall in July 1960 *while on monitorial duties* (sounds very Gilbert and Sullivan) resulted in her banging her head against a milk crate. She was taken to the doctor with a one-inch cut above her right eye, but dutifully returned to school at 2 o'clock. That same month, Mr Price took Christopher Harris to the doctor after *hitting his head on the ground*. Dr Brew pronounced it to be *of a slight nature*, so Christopher was taken back to school pronto.

The school in 2009

Two episodes from 1958 are worth repeating verbatim, if only to show how demanding the teachers' role as custodians could be, especially in the days when there were few telephones in private houses. *During the dinner hour Jean Gallett hurt her left hand at home; her mother sent her to school early for First Aid.* Note that the school was the first port of call. *I phoned the district nurse, who was out, and left a message for her to call and see the child. I was away from school for about an hour this afternoon; Jean Gallett, whom I had left in Miss Dillon's charge, appeared about to faint so I was sent for. After seeing her mother, I took her to Dr Hughes at Chew Magna for attention.* A large slice out of Mr Price's day. Later that same year, *Pamela Higbey, 7 years, complained of persistent toothache and the Principal Dental Officer was informed with a view to arranging treatment.* Nowadays that would have been the parents' job. Teresa Dowling recalls that teachers in the 1970s would go to children's homes to fetch asthma inhalers and do all manner of things they're discouraged from doing nowadays.

Accidents were sometimes unfortunately timed. In February 1961, *Marilyn Lyons collided with a child in the playground. She broke the other child's glasses and received a cut on her own forehead above her right eye. This bled profusely and her condition was such that I took her home for medical treatment after giving her First Aid. She missed her afternoon papers (for the Supplementary Allocation Exam) and the Chief Education Officer was informed accordingly.* All's fair in schools and tests, however, and she *completed the Allocation Exam on 14 March.*

It wasn't only children who could be a little careless. On Wednesday 14 June 1972, Miss Harvey *collided accidentally with some playing children whilst on duty in the playground at 1 pm today. She fell awkwardly and twisted her ankle, but stated she was otherwise all right and was able to carry on.* But all was not as it seemed. By the Friday, *her ankle appears to be swollen*. By the following Monday, *I was informed that Miss E. Harvey would not be reporting for duty. Later I received a medical note certifying that she was suffering from a fractured ankle.* When she came back the following Monday, *her left leg is in plaster, but she was able to perform her work.* The moral of the story is that grown-ups should not collide accidentally with children. A moral from 1973 is not to leave stuff lying around. In November 8½-year old Kevin Pritchard *fell in the yard and hit his head against a wheelbarrow. He received a cut 3″ long on the left hand side of the chest. He was taken to the surgery at Chew Magna and five stitches were inserted in the wound by Dr Walker. There being no-one at home, he was brought back to school. He appeared to be quite well in himself. I later telephoned his father and explained what had happened. The area in which the boy was playing was out of bounds and he had already been told by Miss E. Harvey, supervisor, not to play there.*

The headmaster wasn't above teaching grandmothers how to suck proverbial eggs: in 1976 Tony Ferris was taken home after spraining his ankle. Mr Price *advised his grandmother to bathe it with cold water.* Cold water was a valuable commodity in that memorably drought-ridden summer, but the heat didn't dull the head's powers of description: *Justine Harker fell in the main classroom during the school meal period. Apparently she had tickled Sally Orchard who had retaliated by tickling her in return. Justine doubled up and then fell forward, hitting her mouth against the floor and breaking her tooth. She was taken to the Dental Hospital where she received treatment.*

Then came the incident of the heater. On Friday 10 December *it was extremely cold in Miss Stuckey's classroom and it appeared that the timing mechanism* (of the heating) *was faulty. I informed the contractors, who promised attention a.s.a.p.* By Monday, *the electrician had not attended to Miss S's classroom, which continues cold in the morning. An electric fire with guard has been used to warm up the room in the morning. Anne Tingley, aged 5, fell over the electric fire during the morning and burnt the back of her left leg on the guard which was, of course, very hot. She was taken to the surgery at Chew Magna where it was treated. It was pronounced to be not a serious burn and she was allowed to return to school. Her mother was informed when she returned home in the evening.* On the following day Mr Price, unfailingly attentive where children's welfare was concerned, took Anne *to the surgery at Chew Magna at 10 am for her to be examined by the nurse in regard to the slight burn she received yesterday. It was pronounced to be healing and drying up very well.* And it never entered anyone's head to prosecute someone. In December of that year, *J. Bartlett slipped on the icy yard surface at 8.40 am* – this was in the days before schools were closed at the threat of a snowflake – *and was slightly concussed. His mother was informed and she took him home. He returned at playtime having fully recovered.*

The last logbook reference to any mishap was, perhaps fittingly, the headmaster's about himself. On 25 June 1979 he *accidentally fell and dislocated my left elbow while he was with the children at Goblin Combe.*

LOOK RIGHT, LOOK LEFT, LOOK RIGHT AGAIN

As regards road safety, it all started to go wrong in the 18th century, and a potted history brings a brief respite from the logbook.

Church overseers were responsible for the roads in their neighbourhood and appointed a waywarden to see they were kept in good order. Local owners of horses and wagons were required to haul stones from Stowey Quarry and dump them in various convenient places to be broken up to fill in the ruts caused by farm carts. The Bristol Turnpike Trust was established under Acts of Parliament in the early 1700s, and built a road from Bristol to Wells over Dundry, passing through Chew Stoke to the Blue Bowl and then skirting West Harptree to the west to join with the new road over the Mendips[1]. One of the Turnpike trustees was none other than John McAdam of tarmac(adam) fame. He came up with the idea of digging out the road bed, partly filling it with large stones to form a camber, and then placing egg-sized stones on top. These were compressed by the traffic, thus improving watertightness and drainage. The road had been macadamised. A tar coating was added and, lo and behold, the road had been tarmacadamised.

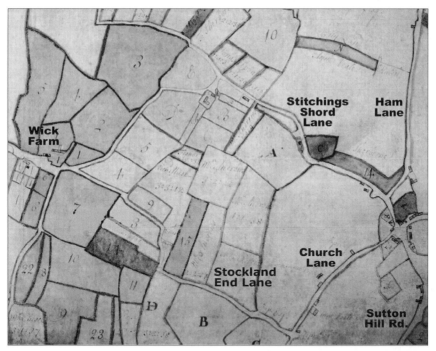

Map by Baber from the mid-1700s. Modern names have been superimposed to assist in orientation. There appears to be no evidence of a direct thoroughfare east to west.

The West Harptree Turnpike Trust was formed under an Act of 1793 with a view to creating and maintaining a road from Churchill through Rickford, Blagdon, Compton Martin, West Harptree and Bishop Sutton (crossing the main Bristol to Wells road

---
[1] Passing the Castle of Comfort Inn and Hunter's Lodge Inn, and then down into Wells through Upper Milton.

west of Chelwood), and on to Marksbury where it would meet the Bath Turnpike Trust road (today's A39). When completed around 1810, the road had carved a much improved route between the numerous lanes in the Bishop Sutton area and particularly near Stowey.

Horses, mules or oxen pulling a coach, gig or wagon were charged 3d to use the new road, passengers an extra halfpenny. Cows, asses, hogs, calves or sheep were a farthing. Tolls for carriages favoured wide wheel rims as they helped to flatten the surface. There was no charge for the Royal Mail, troops going to war, farmers going to market or the dead going to funerals. The tolls could take a fair chunk out of a week's wages, and devious pedestrians became adept at dodging along lanes and paths. Travellers approaching Bishop Sutton from West Harptree had to rummage for their loose change at the toll house and gate at the junction of Wick Road and the lane to Chew Park House. In 1871 the toll collector was 19-year old Mrs Emma Gibbs, and she possibly had the job until 1876 when the West Harptree Turnpike Trust ceased its activities and passed responsibility for the road to the local authority.

The following random entries from The Highways Accounts Book 1844 to 1846 relate to work done on the roads locally. Such work was enormously fascinating to children who, as we know, were inclined to interfere with the roadmen.

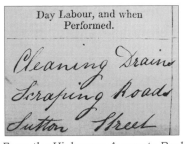

May, cleaning drains, breaking stones in Sutton Street, Wm Perry, 5 days at 1/-. July, pecking ruts and breaking stone, Sutton Weeks (sic), *John Veale, 6 days at 1/4. August, pecking ruts and breaking stones at Twycross and Bonhill, John Veale, 5 days at 1/4, breaking stones*

From the Highways Accounts Book

and spreding (sic) *at Sutton Hill, 6 days at 1/4. March 1845, opening gouts[1] in Sutton Hill, James Filer, 1 day at 1/-; John Hassell, halling* (hauling) *12 yds of stone from Elwell* (a spring near Stowey Quarry) *to Ham and Bonhill.*

The wages and costs of materials were funded from the rates. At the back of the book were detailed the 'Surveyor's Receipts': for example, *received by a rate at 6d in the pound £65.2s.2d, by a rate at 3d in the pound £33.4s.3½d, total £98.6s.5½d; amount paid out £74.7s.5½d, leaving £23.19s.0d in hand.* The men working on the roads were described as being *in poverty and unable to pay the same* (i.e. their council rates).

Those were the roads. How safe were they?

Even when the school was first built, the road through the village would have been busy with horses and carts. By the 1920s it was very busy, and not just with horses and carts. Villagers recall the days before the Avonmouth Bridge on the M5 was completed in 1975, when it was difficult to cross the A368 at weekends and on bank holidays for the sheer volume of traffic. Geoff Brent remembers that by 10 o'clock on summer Sunday mornings in the 1950s, his family's garage was serving petrol to London motorists on their way to the coast, and again late afternoon when they were heading back home. As soon as the Avonmouth Bridge was opened and the M5 joined up, petrol sales dropped by £300 a week, and this at a time when fuel cost about 3/- a gallon (3½p a litre). More traffic nowadays than ever before in the village? Not exactly.

----
[1] Channels cut through the earth of a roadside verge.

The first relevant logbook entry was in September 1910, when Mr Wightman *wrote the Motor Union[1] re notice boards on either side of the school*. The headmaster was clearly concerned enough about the dangers to his pupils that he wanted warnings put up. They weren't. By October 1915, however, it seems that signs near schools were being introduced more widely, as the school managers wrote to the Education Department: *Your comment respecting the erection of 'Motor Notices' near the school has been duly considered, and in reply I beg to say that* [we] *are unanimously of opinion that they are not necessary*. The headmaster's wishes were clearly not shared by the managers. In October 1913 the Parish Council drew the attention of the District Council *to the state of the footpath at the side of the main street at Bishop Sutton and to suggest that it be asphalted*. In September 1916, *children specially warned re motor traffic*. They were cautioned again in December 1919 and then regularly thereafter. And it wasn't just the speed of the vehicles passing the school that was worrying. In a rare touch of environmental awareness, the PC noted in October 1919 that *the inspectors had written to the owners of traction engines respecting the complaint of pollution in Bishop Sutton*. But speed remained the main concern. In March 1921 a parishioner complained about *the excessive speed which motor vehicles pass through Bishop Sutton,* and suggested that *the County Council place some notices at the entrances to the village*.

Everyone remembers learning about a 4 mph limit and the man with his red flag. That's not entirely correct. It was only in the open countryside that you could drive as recklessly fast as 4 mph. It was 2 mph in cities, towns and villages. These limits were in force from 1865 to 1896, when both were increased to 14 mph and, in 1903, to 20 mph. There might not have been many cars about, but they weren't quite as slow as people might think. The Autocar magazine reported in 1901 that *the better motor cars were capable of reaching respectable speeds with very few involuntary stops*. By 1914, when William Morris was producing his Bullnose Morris Oxford, which cost £165 and could do 50 mph, 132,000 cars had been registered in the UK. Average annual wages were then around £100. In 1930 all speed limits for cars and motorcycles were abolished. In other words, you could legally travel as fast as you considered safe on the only straight stretch of road between Chelwood and Churchill, only feet away from the school entrance. By 1932 a new Austin 7 could be bought for less than £120 at a time when average wages were some £200. Irresponsible driving did nothing for the accident rate, and in 1934 the Government imposed a general 30 mph limit in built-up areas, but usually only where there were

SAFETY RULES

1 DON'T run across the road without first looking both ways!

2 DON'T pass in front of, or behind, a standing vehicle without first looking both ways!

3 DON'T play at being 'last across' on any road or street!

4 DON'T follow a rolling ball into the road or street while there is traffic about!

5 DON'T run behind or hang on to the back of a vehicle, or climb on to it!

6 DON'T forget to walk on the footpath if there is one!

7 ALWAYS guide younger Children across the road.

Printed on the back of a primary school exercise book, c1960

----

[1] An early motoring organisation which merged with the AA in 1911 and was partly responsible for the erection of road signs.

streetlights. There weren't any in Bishop Sutton. Ipso facto, no speed limit. (Outside restricted areas with 30 or 40 mph signs, there was no upper speed limit till 1965, when 70 mph was imposed. This wasn't reduced to 60 mph on non-motorway roads until a few years later.) The driving test was introduced on 1 June 1935 and cost 7/6, the same price as a dog licence. The first person to pass the test in Britain was a Mr Beene.

In 1930 there were 2.3 million motor vehicles in the UK, and over 7,000 people were killed in accidents. Cars were sharing the badly maintained and narrow winding roads with large lorries with dubious brakes, horse-drawn carts, stray dogs and unpredictable children, bicycles, and the remaining (and still quite common) steam traction engines. In 1941, with the number of cars down to some 1.5 million as a result of petrol rationing and drivers away fighting, the blackout contributed to an increase in road deaths to over 9,000. By 1972 there were 17 million vehicles and an annual death toll of nearly 8,000. By 2007, with over 31 million vehicles, there were fewer than 3,000 deaths. Contrary to popular belief, today's roads are safer than they've been for the best part of a hundred years. But regardless of the statistics, the perception of danger and risk was less well honed than it is now, and children invariably walked to school by themselves more or less from their first day. Older children would cycle – without helmets – on roads that we now view as scary.

'You dragged this man a hundred yards'. 'But only at 30 miles an hour.'

Following various traffic censuses over a number of years, the 1930 Bristol and Bath Regional Planning Scheme proposed a new road to bypass West Harptree. The nearest monitoring point to Bishop Sutton (on the A368 near Sutton Court) recorded 167 movements a day in 1922, 401 in 1925 and 524 in 1928. That was a lot of vehicles, their drivers itching (or having already itched) to get to the nice straight bit by the school to put their foot down and overtake that lumbering lorry or farm cart. A more ambitious proposal had been to provide better access to the coalfields at Midsomer Norton and Radstock by building a bypass to the south of West Harptree, as well as a road upstream of the Litton reservoirs and along Hollowmarsh

Lane to Farrington Gurney. Both schemes would have affected Bishop Sutton, but neither scheme materialised

Back to speed limits. In September 1935 the PC wrote *to the Commissioner of Transport requesting them to introduce a 30 mph limit to motor traffic through the villages of Chew Magna and Bishop Sutton*. There's no indication of when the speed limit was actually introduced, but the traffic was heavy enough and fast enough in March 1936 to warrant Mr Bailey's speaking *specifically to the infants today as to walking on the pavements going home from school*. In March 1945 the councillors asked for *a 'SLOW' sign to be placed on either side of the entrance to the school. Clutton RDC refused*. In July 1946 Mr Bailey *attended a 'Safety Week' conference at Keynsham, when the safety of school children on the road was discussed*. The problem of speed persisted. By February 1950 a 30 mph limit was in force by the school, but the Council *had no joy in extending* [it] *to Bonhill and to Sutton Wick – proposed that the whole question be placed before the Minister of Transport*. In January 1952 the authorities told the PC that they would not designate the A368 as a trunk road – which would have entailed a general widening – and that *an extension of the road's width in certain places may be the only alteration*. Pauline Heron recalls that the reason for Lyndhurst (on the main road near the junction with Hillside Gardens) being built so far back was because the road was due to be widened. That didn't happen apart from outside the post office. Some lanes nearly lost their rural character, however: in January 1957 the councillors reported *an intention to widen Bonhill Lane and Ham Lane*.

*1950s
road sign*

Dogged persistence eventually paid off, and in June 1957 *the Ministry of Transport agreed to extend the 30 mph sign 730 yards from the Church towards Weston-super-Mare*. This took the limit as far as the last Woodcroft bungalow and about 100 yards short of where the 40 mph limit now starts. There was no noticeable improvement, and in April 1962 the managers reported that *owing to the density and rapid pace of motor vehicles passing the school, thereby endangering the children when arriving and departing from the school premises, the correspondent was instructed to bring this matter before the CEO and to ask him to treat it as a matter of urgency*. Nothing materialised. In January 1963 Councillor (and headmaster) Price asked – in connection with wintry conditions – *that urgent action be taken to clear the pavement opposite the school, as the children were using the centre of the main road to get to school. Men in the village who were unemployed could be utilised*. The unemployed men of the village were not so utilised. Efforts to reduce traffic speed through the village failed and were abandoned. In February 1964 the headmaster arranged for *a Road Safety Film Show in the main classroom by members of the local Police Force*. In July of that year the PC *unanimously agreed that the speed of vehicles through Bishop Sutton exceeded 40-50 mph and was becoming an hazard* (sic) *due to drivers overtaking at dangerous corners. It was decided to report the matter to the Road Safety Committee and suggest the introduction of double white lines*. Over two years later, in December 1966, the councillors were told that *the Road Safety Committee was not in favour of introducing double white lines on roads other than trunk roads*[1]. In the meantime, the police were regularly showing Safety First films in the main classroom.

----
[1] The Committee was referring to the very road that the authorities had refused to designate as a trunk road 14 years earlier!

The managers had begun to seek other ways to improve safety, and were informed in March 1965 that *Somerset Education Department had made provision for a footpath from Church Lane to the school*. Making provision for a path was not the same as actually providing one, and in 2009 there still isn't one. A contemporary article from a local newspaper, referring to the proposed path, stated: *because of housing development, scores of under-11 schoolchildren at Bishop Sutton may have to walk to school along a busy main road, members of Clutton RDC Housing Committee were told. They have been walking to school across a field which is part of an area being developed for housing* (being Highmead and Parkfield). *Stowey Sutton PC wanted an arrangement between the education and planning authorities for there to be a right of way through the estate to the rear of the school*. Pauline Heron recalls that at one time you could walk from the back of the school through allotments to Church Lane, although the practice was frowned upon. On 14 December 1966 the managers appointed George Montgomery *as School Crossing Patrol from 8.15 to 9.30 and from 3.30 to 4.00; a new traffic sign had been received and had been taken into use by the school crossing patrol*. In February of the following year, *Cllr T. Price was disturbed that the pedestrians' rights were obviously not recognised either by the authorities or by motorists*. Yet again he brought the dangers to the attention of the children.

The A368 was very narrow between the post office and Hateley's shop opposite. The resultant queues in both directions were the topic of heated transport caff debates from Cornwall to Caithness. In April 1966 Mr Price resolved *that in order to increase the visibility of motorists, this PC wants steps to be taken to widen the road alongside Hateley's. Carried without dissent*. By the end of November, councillors learned that *plans are afoot to improve the width of the road opposite the PO and convert the property to a number of shops*. By February 1967 Councillor Mrs Hanny *reported that planning permission had been made to develop the land, the dwelling house remained at present, some of the buildings to be adapted for shops with flats above*.

Narrow stretch between the post office and Hateley's shop in the 1960s

From an undated newspaper report of a PC meeting from the mid-1960s:

During a discussion of the alleged dangers of the bottleneck at the post office, "members suddenly discovered that the place was actually the safest piece of road in the village!" No-one could remember a serious accident happening there. The chairman, Mr D. G. Price, said the safety record was obviously due to the care taken by drivers in what they considered a dangerous place. Mrs A. R. Hanny said that heavy lorries still went on the pavement to pass each other, but she was told that there was no record of a pedestrian having been hurt there. It was decided to ask the highway authority to keep the bottleneck on its list of pending improvements.

Less than a year later, there was an accident outside the post office. In July 1967 Mrs Hanny consequently suggested *that some further warning to motorists to reduce speed should be given. The clerk would write to the RDC requesting that*

"SLOW" be written on the road at each end of the approach to the bottleneck. This seemingly simple expedient had first been proposed in 1945. The County Council again rejected the idea: you couldn't go round painting words *on a trunk road*. Not until July 1969 did the County Council finally purchase Hateley's property, and in September of that year councillors noted that *the improvement of the bottleneck at the PO was now on priority 'A' list. It was proposed that a one-way system was to operate at Ham Lane and Bonhill Lane*. Nothing ever came of the one-way idea, and it was to be two years before the main road was widened outside the post office.

Bishop Sutton School, July 1971
Back row (left to right): Claire Young, Mark Jordan, ?, Miss Stuckey, Susan Harvey,
Lynn Perry, Joanne Thompson
Middle row: Emma Robbins, Lisa Marsh, Kim Heron, Jonathan Tovey, Karen Penny,
Mark Ashby, Jackie Tingley, Tony Elms, Doug Dabinet.
Front row: Nigel Saunders, Bridget Martin, Matthew Todd, Justine Hacker,
Michael David, Richard Hall, Robert Filer, Mandy Barter, Jackie Flower,
Iain Tibbles, Bobby Dabinet, Lyn Pearson

Back to the school, and in March 1968 the CEO wrote to the managers asking *that the fitness of the school crossing patrol be considered in regard to the efficiency of carrying out the work.* The managers replied, echoing the headmaster's opinion that *Mr Montgomery's physical ability was unchanged since his appointment.* By this time, car ownership in the village had grown considerably, and Mr Price protested to the Annual Parish Meeting in March 1969 that *the children were being forced to walk in the road because of the cars parked on the pavement* (opposite the school) … *.This was felt to be a matter for the police.* Mr Price also drew his fellow councillors' attention to *the excessive speed of traffic through the village.* By May 1970 it was again *brought to the managers' notice that cars cause a nuisance with parking at the entrance to the school. Mr Price suggested that a letter be written to all parents asking them not to park outside of the school.* The help of the pupils was enlisted, and in October 1970 Mr Price proudly announced that *Dawn Tovey had won a cup for the essay she had written on Road Safety – this was for the whole of the Clutton Area, and she holds this cup for one year.* In March 1971 he noted that *the entrance for the school crossing was still quite dangerous, and the CEO had agreed to put a* *pathway across the School House front lawn and put a barrier across the pavement.* It took a mere 14 months to get the work done: in July 1972 *the new path was now in use for the children to use, and every child now leaves through this new way.*

In April 1971 the PC was told *that work at Hateley's* (compulsorily purchased nearly two years previously) *would start as soon as money was available. There was a probability that when road improvements were carried out at this spot, the speed limit would be raised to 40 mph. There was opposition to this move from the Council, the managers of the Primary School and the pre-school Play Group. A house-to-house campaign was proposed.* The managers protested in the strongest possible terms *that in the view of the narrowness of the road outside of the school, the speed limit should remain at 30.* To no avail; it was increased to 40.

Parking outside the school for picking children up and dropping them off was still a problem in early 1974; indeed, Mr Price *had sent repeated letters about this.* He

Retirement of Mr Montgomery and his lollipop in 1974

asked Keynsham police *if they would make a No Parking area outside of the school in view of the increase in the speed limit to 40 mph.* For once, the authorities listened, and by the beginning of April *zig-zag lines had been marked on the surface and the position has much improved.* Over the next few years, Road Safety films continued to be shown, and Road Safety Officer 'Uncle Ben' and Sergeant Harris came along in April 1976 to warn of the dangers.

The date when the speed limit was brought back down to its current 30 is no doubt buried somewhere in PC minutes.

Having first been raised in 1968, the health of the school crossing patrol again cropped up in November 1973. In view of his age – believed to be 70-plus - was George Montgomery really up to the job? The CEO asked Mr Price *to keep an eye on Mr M.* In December 1974 George voluntarily decided that after so many years of conscientiously and smilingly ensuring the safety of children and their parents, it was time to lay down his lollipop. *There was a presentation of a cheque for £18.15 from contributions from parents and staff.* Mr W. Saunders took up his appointment as Mr M's replacement on the first day of the January term.

CHAPTER TEN

WARTIME AND OTHER NASTIES

PLUCKING RABBITS

Wars fought during the first sixty years of the logbook's existence rarely made it into the school records. Not so with the Second World War, where children felt personally involved in a way not experienced before unless a close relative had been killed. Bombs fell on the village, sweets were rationed, fathers were called up and most mothers had to take jobs. On the plus side, there were plenty of planes overhead to become experts on, there were bits of delightfully sharp and potentially fatal shrapnel in the fields to collect, greens were in short supply, and you never knew when lessons might be interrupted by the air raid sirens. Needless to say, adults saw the war rather differently.

But we're running ahead of ourselves. A skirmish in 1882 hadn't featured in the school logbook but perhaps should have done. The British fleet bombarded Alexandria, and our marines occupied Suez. That put paid to Arabi Pasha's insurrection at Tel-el-Kebir against European influence, and Britain assumed sole protectorate of Egypt. This was clearly a Good Thing (unless you were Egyptian), the celebrations ran long into the night (if you were British), and National Thanksgiving Services were held on Sunday 24 September. Rector Canon Brooke told the congregation in Bath Abbey: "It is the dictate of common sense to believe that no English government could be guilt of the crime of engaging in a war which they did not honestly believe to be practically unavoidable". Exactly.

The Boer War (1899 to 1902) was the first conflict to attract the school's attention in Bishop Sutton. On Thursday 1 March 1900, Mr Wightman reported *a holiday in the afternoon in honour of the relief of Mafeking*. On 5 June of that year, Lord Roberts captured Pretoria. The bush telegraph quickly got the news to the headmaster who, on the following day, wrote: *a holiday in the afternoon in honour of the British occupation of Pretoria*. No holiday was granted in honour of more than 20,000 women and children who died in the British concentration camps, or in honour of Lord Kitchener's scorched earth policy.

What did you do in the War, Daddy?

The War To End All Wars passed almost unnoticed as far as the school records were concerned. The school was closed on the afternoon of Tuesday 6 November 1917 *for children to pick up chestnuts*; on 21 December, *5 cwt of chestnuts sent off today* (just over 250 kilos). They were fed to horses at the front. In her 'History of Chew Stoke School', Zera Wilson refers to a chestnut appeal from the Ministry of Munitions. The war had Bishop Sutton Colliery working overtime, and in January 1918 the *school rooms got very dirty owing to the mud caused by the extraordinary coal traffic*. All those traction engines churning up the unmade road in front of the school.

Gurney or Gournay Court.
The top card is c1905; addressed to Norton St Philip, the
undated message on the reverse reads, 'Dear Mother, I came
here alright Wednesday and I am getting on splendidly, with
love to all from Ethel'. Ethel had perhaps been employed as a
maid at the Court.
The bottom photo possibly dates from World War I and shows a
nurse (or matron) and male staff, who may have previously been
patients at what had become a military hospital.

On 1 October 1918 the school managers made preparations to have *the School Flag hoisted on Peace Day.* Six weeks later, on Monday the eleventh day of the eleventh month: *the children, on hearing of peace, assembled in the yard, hoisted and saluted the flag and sang the National Anthem. After a prayer of thanksgiving, the school was dismissed.* On 14 February 1919, *school closed this afternoon to enable the Master and Mrs Flower to attend Goulnay[1] Court Military Hospital to receive Diplomas of Honourable Service from the British Red Cross Society.* Through the good offices of the Red Cross, war widow Mrs Flower had dedicated much of her free

----
[1] In West Harptree; often spelt 'Gournay', 'Gourney' or 'Gurney'.

time to helping wounded and convalescing soldiers, and she would have received the award with enormous pride. Monday 21 July 1919: *Peace celebrations in Village, school closed*. A memorable time must have been had by all, as on Tuesday, *very poor attendance this morning*.

The memorial behind the altar in the Methodist Chapel reads: *To the Glory of God and in faithful memory of six men of Bishop Sutton who gave their lives to their country during the Great War, they thus shared in the sacrifice which assured the honour, safety and freedom of England and of the Empire ... William James Mail* (6th Somerset Light Infantry, died of wounds in France 1917), *Arthur Henry* Chapman (died of wounds in Flanders 1917), *William Herbert Padfield* (6th Batt. Australian Army, killed in action

Monument to Arthur Harvey in Holy Trinity Church, Bishop Sutton

in Flanders 1917), *William James Hill* (1st 7th Middlesex Regiment, died of wounds in France 1917), *James John Harvey* (16th Devons, killed in action in France 1918), *Arthur Harvey* (1st Coldstream Guards, in action at Mons and in the retreat of 1914, died in England 1917). The only School Admission Register that can be found was started in 1906, too late to have included any of these men, but some or all of them had probably been scholars at Bishop Sutton. Arthur Henry Chapman's namesake died in the Second World War.

Peace only lasted 20 years. As it became clearer through the late 1930s that Nazi Germany was posing an increasing threat to Britain, the Government began its preparations. Bombs were expected to start falling as soon as any war was declared, and plans were drawn up for the enforced evacuation of children and some mothers to more rural areas. Education Offices sent adhesive tape to schools to stick across windows to avoid splintering glass, and everyone was issued with a gas mask. Many former pupils remember trying the masks on, sitting in class wearing them and hoping the inside wouldn't mist up too much. For children with runny noses the experience was particularly unpleasant. It was almost as unpleasant for those sitting next to them. The masks were taken to assembly in the morning, to lessons and to the playground, and were kicked, thrown about and generally abused.

Prime Minister Neville Chamberlain's joyful waving of his 'Peace for our time' bit of paper at London airport in September 1938, following his gemütlich little chat with Adolf Hitler over the Sudetenland crisis, proved naively optimistic. A year later, at 11 am on Sunday 3 September 1939, families gathered round their wireless sets to hear the Prime Minister announce in tones that frightened grown-ups – let alone small children – that "this country is at war with Germany".

If the Great War had featured only sporadically in the school records, its sequel was afforded copious column space, and a combination of the logbooks and villagers' recollections paints a vivid picture of what life was like for pupils in Bishop Sutton. The headmaster's first war-related comment had been from June 1939, when he received circulars *with regard to evacuation of children in emergency, and ARP* (Air Raid Precautions). Sandbags were delivered, to be placed two feet in front of doors to deflect blast, and villagers set to and dug shelters. Sheila Walker's father and some of the neighbours dug theirs in a high bank near their house on The Batch. Dick Chapman recalls that there was one at the top of the allotments behind the school, entered down a shallow flight of steps. There's no mention of it in the logbook, so perhaps it didn't actually belong to the school.

On the Monday, the day after war was declared, Bishop Sutton children went to school as usual, but were sent home again *owing to the Evacuation of London children, as the school is to be used as a receiving centre* (for London and Kingston on Thames). The pupils stayed away for a week, helping their mums to fix black-out curtains to all the windows, scanning the skies for the Luftwaffe, and strutting round with a stick that was meant to look like a rifle and practising how to say Handy Hock[1] in case they captured a Nazi invader at the bottom of their garden. They all trooped back to school on Monday the 11th but were sent home yet again; the managers having instructed Mr Bailey *not to reopen until definite instructions were received*. The headmaster noted that *there were no unaccompanied evacuee youngsters in Bishop Sutton, only some children with their mothers*. On Friday 15th, he summoned the village children back to school *as a consequence of a letter from County Hall in Taunton*. Within the past week, he noted, there had been *two children who came with their mother under the Evacuation Scheme, and four others who came to live in the village a few days prior to the Evacuation*.

On 22 December 1939 Mr Bailey recorded that *the senior girls have knitted ten scarves, five pairs of mittens and two pairs of socks for The Comfort of Serving Men Fund to date*. Not bad, given that the conflict had only been going for 13 weeks! The so-called Phoney War (i.e. nothing much seemed to be happening) didn't prevent a speedy onset of shortages, not helped by a cold winter. School was closed on 31 January 1940 *as a result of coal and coke* – presumably the lack of it – and stayed shut for five days.

Across the country, authorities had been faced – sometimes without warning – with swarms of bewildered and tearful youngsters arriving on station platforms often a hundred or more miles from home, a luggage label round their neck, a few pennies in their pocket, clutching a ticket and clinging on to a sibling's or friend's hand, not knowing where they were or what would happen to them. The administrative tangle of the LEA system was shown at its greatest disadvantage, not helped in the Chew Valley by the fact that the Education Office in Taunton was a long way away. Anxieties were shared by evacuee headteachers whose schools might have been split up and scattered over two or more counties. It wouldn't be long before the tabloid press were regaling their gullible readership with tales of drunken urban

----

[1] The time-honoured English version of 'Hände hoch' (hands up).

mothers and scabby, lousy, thieving children who didn't know what a cow was. In the early 21st century, when parents fuss about strangers offering sweets, or the icy surface of the playground, or the perceived risks of a school trip, it's a sobering thought that those parents' own parents or grandparents were often packed onto a train at a crowded station, not knowing where they were going or whether they would ever see their mums and dads again. And there were no mobile phones.

In Bishop Sutton, things didn't turn out anywhere near as badly as feared, and the evacuee children were generally met with a reassuring welcome, a nice warm cuppa and a loving substitute family who treated them kindly and bought them paper and stamps so that they could write home. Many a local family maintained close contact with 'their' evacuees for decades after the war. It is nevertheless possible that some children – doubtless the tiniest minority – were treated as little more than slaves. Many evacuees had drifted home by Christmas 1939 during the Phoney War, but reappeared in greater numbers when air raids began in earnest. Going home didn't always mean going back to their desks: in January 1940 it was reported that nearly 30% of the nation's children were receiving no schooling at all.

In June 1940, in a typical wartime snafu[1], Somerset Education Authority advised

Mr Bailey that no evacuees were to be sent here. That conflicted with the advice from the previous September, and several evacuee families were already ensconced in the village, some having come of their own volition.

The Phoney War came to an abrupt end. On Friday 12 July 1940 Mr Bailey wrote – clearly in ignorance of wartime censorship requirements – that *attendance was very poor today, there were 58 present this morning and 61 this afternoon, probable cause is that bombs fell during the night between Stowey and Bishop Sutton and it has been a very wet day*. Which was worse, the lack of sleep, the exhilaration of a near miss, or the rain? The bomb on Stowey Crossroads slightly damaged two cottages, caused the ceilings of the Strachie residence to come down, left a large

----
[1] Situation Normal, All F***ed Up.

hole in the road[1], and was talked about excitedly for years to come. A small device landed close to Bishop Sutton School, but failed to explode and was made safe by the Bomb Disposal Squad. Amazingly, it didn't warrant a mention in the logbook. Another bomb fell behind the Old Pit Garage; it too failed to go off, and as late as the 1970s there were people who maintained that it must still be there.

When the sirens went, Jean Veale would hide under the family's round table. Hardly the most robust of shelters, as it had castors and kept moving around. Her sister Eunice remembers coming out of Chapel one evening and seeing the red sky over Bristol where a raid was in full swing. She was too scared to go to bed. Sheila Walker and her family had fitted wooden benches in their shelter in the bank at The Batch, bringing in lanterns and games. They felt safe as they listened to the thuds from the direction of Bristol or Bath. Until there was a spell of heavy rain and the whole thing collapsed, so they took to sleeping under the kitchen table. The village's proximity to Bristol and Bath and Weston-super-Mare (and with the Air Transport Auxiliary Service only eight miles away at Whitchurch Airport) meant that the skies were often full of planes, and children quickly learned to distinguish the sounds and silhouettes of British and German aircraft. The Village Hall was commandeered for the manufacture of clothing under the management of a Mr Goldberg, who had come from London together with his workforce of thirty men and women and their machines. One day the large stove in the middle of the Hall caught fire, sending fumes everywhere and prompting a hasty exit, but work began again after a short break for clearing up. Sheila Walker recalls that as her father had helped to arrange the contract – he was secretary of the Hall – one of the first things the Goldbergs made was a beautiful blue coat for her mother.

Various near misses led to the implementation of safety measures at the school. The headmaster wrote on 3 September 1940 that *one room and one cloakroom has been made splinterproof by wire netting, one room has had cellophane pasted on the windows*. If sheer terror was to send children running to the toilet, at least they'd have some protection while they sat and quivered. On 7 September 1940 *the number of children has dropped considerably – roll is now 103 – many have left the district owing to the bombing of the village during the holiday*. 'Bombing of the village' was more than a slight exaggeration, but the contingency planners had certainly not envisaged evacuation <u>from</u> Bishop Sutton. Despite the Education Authority's advice from June 1940 that there would be no further evacuees, 15 arrived from London during October of that year and several of them attended school. The war didn't stop exams, although in December 1940 *it was not possible to carry out the usual examination programme, owing to the prevalence of mumps and the number of extra children who have come either from Bristol or London recently*. First Messerschmidts, now mumps. (In March 1941, special arrangements were made for exams: *three evacuees from London sat for the London County Council Junior Scholarship*.)

Evacuation created an industry of its own. On 27 September 1940, the Ministry of Health at 3 Woodland Road, Tyndalls Park, Bristol wrote to local authorities. Headed 'Unorganised Evacuation from London', the letter read:

Owing to air attacks on London, a number of refugees are arriving daily in this Region … (1) All women who arrive in the Region from London with children and who cannot find accommodation should be billeted … Women without children who are normally in employment

----

[1] In the 1970s, when the elm trees were felled along the drive to Stowey Mead, they were found to be riddled with 1940 shrapnel.

should be urged to return to their work. (2) Men ... should not be billeted, but should be instructed to return to their work.

This advice was supplemented by The Ministry of Health's Circular 2178 of October 1940:

Under present conditions the Government are anxious to encourage the removal of women and children from London and they remain convinced that the policy of dispersal on which their evacuation plans were based is sound. The experience of last year showed that it is very difficult to persuade mothers to settle down in strange surroundings in the country owing to the break up of their normal lives and interests. It is therefore of the first importance to do everything possible to help these women ... and at the same time to minimize as far as possible the inconvenience to householders.

Weekly billeting allowances were paid: 10/6 for each unaccompanied child to the age of 14 (8/6 if more than one), 12/6 each to age 16, and 15/- for those over 16. Householders received 5/- for taking in mothers of children aged 14-plus and 3/- for mothers of younger children.

INFORMATION ON

BED-WETTING

FOR HOUSEHOLDERS
taking
UNACCOMPANIED CHILDREN

Issued by THE WOMEN'S VOLUNTARY SERVICES
FOR CIVIL DEFENCE

REMEMBER THE IMPORTANCE OF:

Regularity in the day time. Sit out the child on waking in the early morning and after his mid-day rest, also before and after each meal.

Habit forming at night. Before you go to bed, gently rouse the child so that he is sufficiently awake to form the habit of using his chamber. If this upsets the child he may be lifted without being wakened.

Giving plenty of fluid and nourishing food during the day, but nothing after 5 p.m.

BE PATIENT!

As part of a pack issued by the Women's Voluntary Services (WVS) for Civil Defence, and given to householders taking in evacuees, was the leaflet 'Information on Bedwetting':

Protect your mattress – you should get mackintosh sheeting through your billeting officer or the WVS. You should have a yard square and stitch it to any cotton material. The cotton ends tuck under the mattress to prevent the child from kicking the mackintosh out of position. Or, cover the mattress with brown paper, then several layers of newspaper, then brown paper. In older children in whom the anxiety not to have a wet bed is clearly playing the chief part in bringing it about, and who are really keen to work with you to cure the habit, it is often possible to stop all bed-wetting by giving them an alarum (sic) clock and teaching themselves to wake themselves up a sufficient number of times to keep themselves dry. You should avoid: fizzy drinks such as ginger beer, acid foods such as vinegar, pickles or plums, salt foods late in the day such as bacon, kippers or finnan haddock. All of these are thirst-producing. Remember that these children may have come from overcrowded houses and they may now be feeling lonely at night. Town children will have been accustomed to a water closet and if billeted in a rural area with an outside dry lavatory may be unwilling to use this unless it is explained to them.

There would be a lot of explaining to be done about Bishop Sutton privies!

After Sheila Walker's mother died when Sheila was only 11, there was just her and her father in their house on The Batch. They took Mrs McCarthy (or McCartney) in from the East End of London together with her son Tom, who passed his 11–Plus at Bishop Sutton. Tom didn't understand country life and, having seen the fate that befell chickens, tried to pluck a rabbit. Ken Rapps remembers the friendships that developed between village children and those from London. Ann Saunders remembers that it was her father who took the evacuees round the village: if he didn't like them, they'd go to the bottom of the priority list for lodgings. Evacuee Fred Cook managed to tame two jackdaws: he'd bring them to school and they'd fly back to the cottage behind the drapery where they were billeted. Peter James recalls the Blissetts (or Bassetts or Brassetts or Brassicks) being lodged with the Marsh family at the end house at what is now Rose Cottage. The Marshes themselves moved into a council house at Bonhill, leaving the evacuees to fend for themselves. Peter James went to school with the Bingleys, who had been evacuated from London and who emigrated to New Zealand after the war. I'm told that Acker Bilk's stepbrother Billy was billeted in Bishop Sutton, despite having only come from Pensford. There were dark rumours that Billy had wanted to move out, and the host family saw it as an opportunity to earn a few extra bob.

January 1941 saw further excitement. On Friday 17th, attendance was *very low as there was much activity in the air last night and some incendiaries and HE* (high explosive) *bombs fell around the village. This morning only 72 out of 152 children were present.* The rest were probably out collecting shrapnel and looking for bits of cow. In that same month, six local children were admitted to school together with ten evacuees and two returning children whose parents perhaps considered Bishop Sutton not too bad a place to see the war out.

Bishop Sutton's most memorable wartime event – if the logbook is to be believed – was on Sunday 16 March 1941. On the following day there were *only 73 children present (i.e. 48.9%), this is due to air raids last night lasting from 8.45 pm until 4.15 am, bombs fell in the village and caused much minor damage to houses – two patches of ceiling have fallen in the Junior room of the school.* Sheila Walker was taken to a friend's grandmother's in Ubley that night after incendiaries dropped in a field near their house. The military authorities felt it wise to position guns at Chew Park Farm. Anti-aircraft balloons were tethered to lorries and moved around the area, and a searchlight was installed on top of the slag heap at the old colliery.

Hitler enticing Mother to take her children back to the cities

On Sunday 10 August 1941, during the summer holidays, *the school* [was] *closed for lessons* [but] *remained open with Miss Harvey and Mrs Flower in charge for the attendance of such children as wished to come. 8 came.* On Monday 11 August, *as there were only 10 children present … the school was closed,* not to reopen until term began as scheduled in September. The splinterproofing measures of September 1940 were no longer considered sufficient, and on 2 September 1941 *a load of bricks was tipped in the yard this morning to be used to build anti-blast walls in place of sandbags.* Contractors built walls in front of both doors a fortnight later. The blast walls weren't removed until 31 May 1947.

Blast wall (right, with slit) built 1941, still there when this photo was taken in 1947.
Top row (left to right): Terry James, Colin Parfit, John Cook, Ralph Hill, Paul Sheppard,
George Weedon, Leslie Bown;
Middle row: Marlene Coles, Shirley Chapple, Ann Saunders, Heather Perkins,
Janet Tovey, Joan Challenger;
Front row: Heather Dury, Daphne Small, Audrey Bendall, Queenie Lennard,
Jennifer Bingley, Beryl Bendall, Sue Weaver, Glenys Chubb, Joan Marsh

On Monday 13 April 1942, *school reopened after the Easter holidays with 97 Somerset children and 21 evacuees.* By January 1943 there were *95 Somerset children and only 14 evacuees.* Despite the number of evacuee children who had passed through the school since 1939, it had never been felt necessary to implement the shift system common elsewhere, whereby local children would attend lessons in the morning and evacuees in the afternoon, or vice versa.

Former pupils all recall the rationing, but there were advantages to living in the countryside. Townspeople had few opportunities for supplementing the meagre fare that was available officially, but farmers and their friends had more freedom. They had first call on eggs and dairy produce, and poultry and game were never far away. There was generally a lamb or calf that could be slaughtered when required, and there were rabbits in the fields. Anyone with pigs was allowed to retain one animal in exchange for their bacon ration entitlement and was supposed to send any further pigs to the Ministry; a regulation better honoured in the breach than the observance. There was no queueing at the village shops for a sliver of whale-meat steak or a piece of snoek[1]. Rabbit skins were saved, and every few weeks a man would come round and exchange them for a few pence or for a piece of china he carried in his van. Like their counterparts across the country, local children collected anything that could be of value or recycled for the war effort: newspaper, scrap metal, glass. Les Bown remembers that the railings were cut down outside Wren Cottage and Dury's shop – but not outside Oak House and the Chapel – to build planes[2]. Les managed to impale himself one day on the ironwork by the Chapel, so would have benefited considerably had the spikes been removed to go towards a Spitfire.

The war didn't feature in the records again until 13 May 1944: *the end of Salute the Soldier Week - the school has contributed £263.5s.0d to the village total*. That was a huge sum, equivalent to many thousands of pounds now. Most evacuees had drifted back to London and Bristol between 1942 and '43 and were not seen again, although the onslaught of the V1 and V2 rockets in the South East did prompt a few to return to Bishop Sutton in July 1944. Monday 29 January 1945 was the first day back to school after a week of closure *re no fuel* (no doubt a combination of the weather, wartime shortages and transport difficulties), and only 14 children turned up out of 99 on the roll.

The war comes to Bishop Sutton:
American tank outside the Red Lion

For days during the run up to D-Day in June 1944, American military convoys trundled through the village. Colin Symes reminisces that the soldiers would toss chewing gum to the children cheering on the pavements and waving little Union Jacks and carefully crafted Stars and Stripes. Sheila Walker remembers that her tender age of 13 didn't stop the GIs from offering her cigarettes. Jean Veale remembers the wartime dances at the Legion Hall. Her uncle, Noah Gibbs, let her and her friends borrow his big Ford 8. She would pick up soldiers based at Chew Stoke and Norton Malreward – some of whom manned the searchlight and anti-aircraft gun above Stowey – and at the Air Force unit at Chew Park Farm and take them to dances at Ubley. Jean's mother wouldn't have soldiers in the house who drank.

----

[1] A South African marine fish, which was tinned and introduced to a suspicious British population who almost uniformly found it stomach-churningly disgusting.

[2] The railings still remaining (in 2009) by the Chapel seem to the originals, as do those at Oak House and some of those between the churchyard and the front of the school.

Many people remember that the Luftwaffe would machine-gun down the beam of the searchlight at the old pit. When a local ARP team was formed, Ken Rapps cycled round the countryside to see where bombs had fallen, and was tasked to extinguish incendiaries that had dropped in fields. Pauline Heron remembers that the German prisoners of war working on a local farm were invited to tea at her parents' house. Joan Bunney remembers that the poor would sell their clothing coupons to richer neighbours. And all the while, the older ladies of the village knitted away to provide comforts for the British soldiers: khaki or Air-Force-blue socks, scarves, balaclavas, gloves and mittens. The younger ones dreamt of comforts for the handsome, overpaid, over-sexed and over-here chocolates-and-nylons-brandishing American GIs.

The long and wearisome war was finally won, and on Tuesday 8 May 1945 *nearly all the children assembled for Victory in Europe Day, and a Thanksgiving Service was held. The children were then given sweets and sent home. During the day many of them helped build a bonfire which was fired at 10.15 pm.* On Saturday 1 September 1945 *the children of Bishop Sutton, Stowey and Knowle Hill were given a tea and entertainment as a Victory in Japan celebration. The school was closed for two days' holiday.* It was closed again on Monday 24 September for Clutton Rural District's Victory Holiday. The logbook noted that Bishop Sutton School contributed an astonishing £219 to the RDC's Savings Thanksgiving Week in 1945.

Local parishioners Richard Andow, Arthur Henry Chapman, Donald Ewart Dury and William John Perry were killed in action, and Ernest Henry Broadbent Usher and Alfred George Walker died while on service. Arthur Henry Chapman, whose namesake had been killed in the First World War, was born in 1920 and was a pupil at Bishop Sutton School from 1926 to 1934; Donald Dury (born 1923) attended from 1928 to 1937; William Perry (1928) from 1933 to 1940, and Alfred Walker (1917) from 1921 to 1930.

> TO THE GLORY OF GOD
> AND IN MEMORY OF
> Richard Andow
> Arthur Henry Chapman
> Donald Ewart Dury
> William John Perry
> KILLED IN ACTION
> and
> Ernest Henry Broadbent Usher
> Alfred George Walker
> WHO DIED WHILE ON SERVICE
> 1939 — 1945
> THIS WINDOW IS GIVEN BY
> GRATEFUL PARISHIONERS

In February 1947 the chairman of the Church Window Committee, headmaster Reginald Bailey, wrote to selected parishioners:

In order that the names of these men shall be ever remembered in their village, a committee has been formed to raise funds for a permanent memorial. This memorial will take the form of two stained glass windows – one in Bishop Sutton Church and one in the Chapel. The windows will show 'The Good Shepherd', they will be carried out by William Morris Ltd of Westminster; the names will appear in a cartouch[1] at the foot of the picture. It is hoped that a water colour of the design will soon be on view, probably in the Post Office. The Committee are confident that for such a purpose as this you will be <u>very</u> generous, the total cost is £200. The envelope enclosed will be collected in the near future, will you please collect from all your household and have your envelope ready for collection ... (signed) R. J. Bailey, Chairman, W. J. Simmonds, Hon. Treas., Doris Harvey (Miss), Hon. Sec.

----
[1] An inscribed ornamental tablet or panel.

The war changed national mindsets. Crouching in a damp shelter with 50 terrified children or trudging from house to house to keep track of evacuees, teachers across the country found themselves with a new sense of vocation and gained an insight into the meaning of social service. They were becoming welfare officers. The never-ending salvage collections and fundraising in aid of War Weapons Week or Spitfire Week or Battleship Week or Salute the Soldier Week led schools to harness children's enthusiasm for collecting things. Everybody was encouraged to do their bit, and children didn't need much encouraging. Education was becoming what it had rarely been before: a dynamic social affair.

As an aside, and not necessarily directly related to Bishop Sutton, random entries in the Temple Cloud Court Register from February 1941 to February 1943 give the lie to the notion that everyone was putting their shoulder to the wheel for the sake of eventual victory in time of dire national threat:

Holy Trinity Church,
Bishop Sutton c1950

Driving animals without lights 5/-[1], soldier absent without leave 15/-, slaughtering 3 pigs without a licence £50, failure to bury the carcass (sic) of one cow £1, detaining a racing pigeon (Defence Regulations) £5, Aliens Order served on Moszka Liebel Gumpel 5/-, causing unnecessary suffering to a rabbit 10/-, carrying passenger on a bicycle 5/-, failure to produce an i.d. card 10/-, being in possession of War Department property £5, permitting a bull to be kept at large in a field £1, permitting swill to be fed to animals without necessary boiling £3.3s.0d, obtaining rationed food 12/-, using motor fuel for a purpose other than that for which coupons were granted £2.2s.0d, larceny of marmalade £2.

Larceny of marmalade and the serving of an Aliens Order on Moszka Liebel Gumpel are particularly noteworthy.

Later conflicts such as Korea, Malaya, Aden and Cyprus did not make it into the school or village records.

Remembrance Day – generally known as 'Armistice Day' until after the Second World War – was first mentioned in the school records on 11 November 1930, when *children assembled on the Square at 10.55 am to hear the service at the Cenotaph broadcast. 11.15 lessons recommenced.* In 1942 the ceremony was accompanied by the sale of poppies organised by the British Legion, raising £2.16s.0d. The format varied over the years, but usual practice was to gather in the playground to listen to a speech or a BBC broadcast and honour those who had fallen. The unthinking heartlessness of some of the children in pushing to the front to watch one of their teachers cry is recalled by several former pupils. In 1950 *the Assembly Prayers this morning were amplified, special hymns sung to form a School Remembrance Service, and I addressed the children on the reasons we observe Armistice Day and*

----
[1] To put the fines into perspective, average weekly wages in the 1940s were around £6.

why we participated in the Village gathering. There was no further mention until 1956, when *suitable hymns were chosen this morning according to the Remembrance Day observances.* There appear to have been no formal acts of remembrance after 1957 when the older children went to Chew Valley School.

PRACTISING HANGING

In truth, a practice hanging was an isolated incident, but unsavoury things did go on at the school from time to time: there were thefts, attacks, fires. This is the unsavoury section.

In February 1877 *Mr G. Arter* (chairman of the School Board) *was at school to address the boys about breaking fences.* He was presumably telling them off, not telling them how. If they weren't breaking fences, they were breaking each other: in April 1883 headmaster Hill *cautioned George Bird and Frank Tucker for throwing stones at one another. This is a frequent occurrence twice this week. I have strapped up boys' heads owing to it. Farnham Veale had a fearful cut in the back of his head.* Difficult not to be impressed by a name like Farnham Veale.

In September 1883 Mr Hill *punished Thomas Harvey (9) for severe ill treatment to Frances Weaver. When I rescued her,* [she] *was black in the face, said he was practising hanging.*

Dark and dastardly deeds did come to pass on Thursday 7 January 1886. *A concert was held in the school room* [in the] *evening and arrangements were made for a ball to succeed the concert. The concert passed off quietly, but the dancers were attacked by a mob who broke 20 panes of glass in the school rooms and in consequence school was closed Friday 8th till the windows were repaired.* Monday 11 January: *windows not being repaired, could not open school until Wednesday 13th. Attendance very bad, parents refusing to send their children for part of the week.* Hardly surprising, if they might be set upon by an unruly mob rampaging its way from The Red Lion to The Butcher's Arms. *The attack on the school windows took place about 10.30 pm. The matter is under Police investigation, and a reward of £5 is offered for information that will lead to the arrest of those who broke the windows.* With no further reference to the incident, and with nothing in Court records, it seems that no-one was apprehended. Nothing of a similar nature happened again.

In February 1898 the Board resolved that *in reference to the pane of glass broken by Sarah Bendall in the door of the Bishop Sutton Schoolroom, Mr Bendall be required to pay half the loss of restoring the same.* There was little else to report by way of malicious or consequential breakages until June 1949, when *a lavatory pan was broken by a brick from the top of the wall being dropped through by a child climbing.* That same month, Mr Bailey *informed the secretary to the Village Hall Committee that damage was done to a dinner form on Wednesday evening, this is the second time I have reported similar damage and I have requested him to ask the 'Picture People' to refrain from using school forms.* Who were the Picture People?

Public perception of vandalism – in Bishop Sutton at least – was worse than the reality. Having received some paperwork from the LEA on the subject of child delinquency, the PC minuted in January 1950 the headmaster's suggestion *that the clerk should inform the Authority of the exceedingly small percentage of child delinquency existing in this parish, and consequently it would be as well not to advertise any slogans or posters before children, otherwise the tendency would probably invite them to erring ways, this action should therefore be avoided at all costs*. At their meeting in July of that year, the PC asked for *a sign post at the crossroads at Bishop Sutton; it was emphasised that the arms of the sign should be high enough to deter children from climbing the post*[1].

Whilst there was the isolated incident of petty burglary at the school (or, perhaps a spot of opportunism: *several stones were pulled from the boundary wall* one November evening in 1898), the first mention of actual theft was in November 1900 when *a coat was taken by someone from the pegs*. In June 1903 *some plants were missed from the infants' room this morning*. Incidents were nevertheless so rare that when they did occur, every detail was carefully committed to posterity. This, on Thursday 31 January 1974:

At approx 11 pm, Mr Hibditch, the present occupant of the School House, called at my house to tell me that the Main School Door was open and that the spring had been locked back. I immediately went to the school with him and found that the door was as he stated. I made a thorough search of the premises and got the definite impression that someone, possibly an older child, had entered the school, for various cleaning articles were scattered over the main cloakroom floor, the kitchen door was open and someone had used its lavatory and not flushed it. I could not find that anything was missing at the time. The separate classroom had not been entered. I searched for any intruder and locked the premises. [On the following day, Mr Price] went to the school early to see the cleaner Mrs Saunders. She assured me that the school had been properly locked at about 6.30 pm the previous night. She too felt certain that someone had entered the school, for she had left her cleaning materials on the window sill in the classroom. Later, when teachers and kitchen staff had arrived, it was found that a drawer and cupboards in the lower junior classroom and kitchen had been disturbed and that a Europhon transistor radio had been taken from a cupboard in the main classroom. From the kitchen a partly used large tin of coffee had been taken. Other than this, nothing appears to have been stolen, although there were signs of a search having been made in various places. The police at Keynsham were informed, and Deputy Constable Christopher came to the school to make enquiries. I furnished him with all the necessary information. It was still not possible to say where entry had been made, for there were no definite signs of any force being used. I felt that one window in particular could have been used, although entry or egress could only have been made by someone of small build.

Mrs Saunders had been at the school since 1941, so it's most unlikely that had forgotten to lock the door. County Supply mended and strengthened the windows and replaced the radio, and nothing further was heard about the forced entry. No children were observed tottering about the village, high on caffeine.

In March 1979 Mr Price was told about damage caused *to the front offside door of Miss L. Lucas' car which was parked in the teachers' car park. Inquiries revealed that it had been accidentally caused by about six boys of 7-9 years whilst playing in the out-of-bounds area during the mid-day break whilst supervisor's attention was elsewhere*. Repairs would cost £35, and Mr Price asked Avon Education Department whether insurance cover was available. This was the first time that a teachers' car park was mentioned. Whether the school's insurance paid out was not recorded.

Back to public perception, and enter the mid-1950s. Lonnie Donegan was about to skiffle, Bill Haley's Comets were rocking round the clock, the teddy boys and their menacing quiffs were, well, menacing, and the corner by the pub was frightening old ladies. In August 1955 the PC *moved that the Police be asked to move the congregation of youths from the pavement opposite The Red Lion Inn on Sunday evenings in order to obviate the accident risk to parishioners who are forced to walk into the main road traffic to by-pass the collection of 20-30 youths*. By the early

----

[1] At the time of writing in 2009, most of the sign appears to be the original from, one assumes, 1950 or earlier.

'70s, there were challenges of an altogether more alarming nature. In May of that year the PC were told that *children had been reported to have entered Hateley's property and had access to pills left there.*

It was fire that most the worried school authorities, especially in a rural area without a handy fire engine. The first reported incident was in September 1908, when Mr Wightman *found part of the ash house had been burned.* Nothing then till January 1913 when *a fire was noticed near one of the stoves.* When reporting the incident to the Education Department, the managers referred to it as a *slight fire,* but nevertheless one that was worth a claim on the insurance. In March 1931 the PC received *a letter from E. H. Godwin Esq. of Blagdon: 'Dear Sir, it is my ambition to provide and equip an adequate fire brigade at Blagdon to operate within a six-mile radius. The object of this letter is to enquire if your parish has ample fire protection service, if not when my ideal has been realised can any good purpose be served by offering the services of such in Blagdon?'* After considerable debate, a reply was sent to Mr Godwin: *no fire extinguishing apparatus operates in this parish and the absence of a water supply would be a formidable obstacle.* A pragmatic decision: no water in the area, so no point in trying to put fires out. It was to be several years before a fire station was built at Chew Magna.

The Laurels c1910, opposite the present Village Hall. Mont's Lane runs alongside the left-hand cottage. The terrace has either been demolished, or substantially altered to form the row that is there now.

Despite the school's reliance on open fires, the next recorded mishap wasn't until 14 January 1958, when *at about 2 pm Miss Stuckey drew my attention to smoke coming from the roof of the main schoolroom. After evacuating the children, I telephoned the fire brigade and, later, the chairman of the managers. The fire brigade arrived shortly afterwards and dealt with the fire. The east end of the roof will have to be replaced.* The following day *Mr Kemp of the Architect's Department called with a local builder to obtain an estimate of the cost of repairing the fire damage. The damaged room has been vacated and the top class now occupy the small room adjoining*. Repairs were completed by the beginning of March. Two months later, potential disaster struck again. On 14 March *a fire broke out in the Science Room … The fire brigade was called and the conflagration was put out. The fire originated at the foot of the valley gutter and spread to the full length of the ridge, burning rafters and the foot of the valley board. The cause of the fire was a split flue pipe*. Although fire drills must have been practised for years, the first mention in the logbook was in September 1967, and only again in February and December 1972.

No more fires, but remiss not to mention the rodents. In October 1919 the PC *read a circular from Capt E. H. Gurnly respecting forming a committee to carry out the orders for Rat Week. Mr Wightman was appointed to carry out these duties*. Was this our Mr Wightman, headmaster from 1897 to 1931?

To end on a reflective note. The editor of an undated (but almost certainly from the very late 1960s, early '70s) Bishop Sutton Parish Magazine wrote: *One of our readers has forwarded us the following poem he read in a Parish Magazine. We are so often at fault and so quick to put the blame for today's happenings on other people's shoulders – perhaps the following might make us think again*:

> *We read in the papers and hear on the air*
> *Of killing and stealing and crime everywhere*
> *We sigh and we say as we notice the trend,*
> *"This generation! Where will it all end?"*
>
> *But can we be sure that it's their fault alone*
> *That maybe a part of it isn't our own?*
> *Too much money to spend, too much idle time*
> *Too many movies of passion and crime.*
>
> *Too many books not quite fit to read*
> *Too much evil in what they hear said.*
> *Too many children encouraged to roam*
> *By too many parents who don't stay at home.*
>
> *Kids don't make movies, they don't write books*
> *That paint a gay picture of gangsters and crooks.*
> *They don't make liquor, they don't build bars,*
> *They don't make the laws and they don't buy the cars.*
>
> *They don't make the drugs that idle the brain,*
> *It's all done by older folks greedy for gain*
> *And in how many cases we find that it's true*
> *That that label 'Delinquent' fits older folks too!*

£1 (brown), 1923-27

CHAPTER ELEVEN

TRIPE AT STOWEY

For the first hundred years of Bishop Sutton School's existence, its nearest educational neighbour – apart from any nearby dame or infants' school – was Stowey School. Stowey could be the village that time forgot: little changed, at first glance, in five hundred years.

By the 1800s, Bishop Sutton had become more populous than Stowey which, according to directories, had only 188 inhabitants in 1841, 151 in 1851 and 144 in 1921. Until 1949 it formed its own parish. Stowey had once been an important centre for the production of ochre crushed at the local mill (north of Stowey Crossroads and thus some distance from the village) and used as a pigment for sheep marking. C & J Greenwood's 'Somerset Delineated' of 1822 ignored Bishop Sutton but described Stowey as *a parish in the hamlet of Chew, containing 31 inhabited houses and 45 families, 30 of whom are employed in agriculture.* Kelly's Directory of 1861 listed various village charities and Sunday Schools (plural). Lord of the Manor and principal landowner was Sir Edward Strachey Bart. His residence, Sutton Court, was geographically viewed as being part of Stowey. For those fascinated by such things, Stowey's wall-mounted letter box – which is still there – was cleared at 2.35 pm on weekdays only. The shop was at Rose Cottage.

Stowey c1905

There was a National School. The plaque above the door reads: *Stowey School erected at the expense of Mrs James Clark, Lord Mount Sandford and the Revd. Robert Harkness, Vicar of Stowey, A.D. 1837.* The school predated Bishop Sutton's by some five years. Average attendance as per Kelly's Directory of 1897 was 60. The Bishop Sutton School logbook regularly hinted at the opinions of successive headteachers that Stowey School was somehow inferior to Bishop Sutton. There is no objective evidence that this was so. Yet Stowey did get through its mistresses with disconcerting frequency. I have found no records of who the head was in 1837, but by 1866 Kelly's Directory listed Miss Evelyn Tovey. Miss Susan Evans had taken over by 1872, Miss Julia Gleed by 1875, Miss Jane Avery by 1883, Mrs L. H. Gunton by 1889, Miss Hawkins by 1894, Miss Martha Hunt by 1897, Miss Katherine J. Roberts by 1906, Miss Amy Young by 1914, Miss T. H. Clarke by 1919 and Miss Bertha Laurence by 1923. Mrs Smith was in charge by 1936. Until very recent years, Bishop Sutton's only female headteacher was Miss Hassell who ruled the roost from 1851 (and possibly earlier) until 1875.

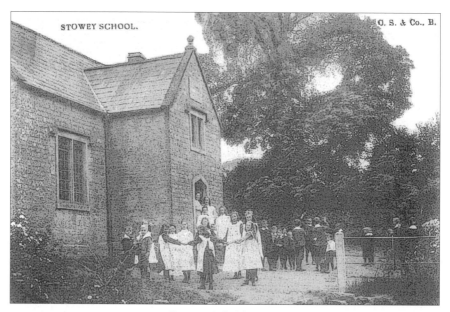

Stowey School c1905

Stowey's last headmistress was Mrs Marjorie Reed, who started there in 1943 as Miss Marjorie Treasure, having moved from Blagdon School. She promised the schoolchildren that they could come to her wedding and sit in the front pew for the service. The vicar only allowed her one day off, although her husband had two days. She left on Tuesday 6 November 1945 as she was expecting a baby, and the authorities in Taunton used the happy event as an excuse to close the school. By then there were only 15 children, although the numbers had fluctuated considerably over the years. Marjorie has wonderful reminiscences but, before sharing them, a quick look at the administrative situation before she arrived. The following notes are from the Stowey PC minute books: in December 1884 *Mr Strachey offered to give the school to the parish and to do so free of legal expenses. Agreed.* By 1926, there were financial difficulties, and a Council meeting was called in July of that year to consider *the future carrying on of the school, as both the Government and County Inspectors had insisted on various alterations being carried out and the school managers being without the necessary money to meet the same.* One suggestion: *the Lord Strachie* (sic – the family had changed the spelling since 1884) *be authorised to negociate* (sic) *with the County Council on leasing the school to the County Council.* At a meeting in October 1926 the school managers reluctantly conceded that they had little choice other than to relinquish ownership: *the County Council would be willing to take over the school at a nominal rent and continue it as a junior school, the older children being sent to Bishop Sutton. The chairman*

*explained the educational advantages of such an arrangement. At the present time,
the headmistress has too many Standards to teach at once to be able to do so
efficiently. Unanimously agreed to lease the parish school to Somerset County
Council.*

Bishop Sutton headmaster Mr Wightman recorded on 14 January 1927: *eleven over-
11 years admitted from Stowey.* William Tovey, born in Stowey in 1915, recalls that
'at 11 we moved on to Bishop Sutton School from Stowey School. Down among the
big boys, the bullies'.

*Postcard of Stowey School pageant,
and the message on the reverse, dated 1905*

What does Marjorie Reed remember? Her school was open from 8.30 to 3.30, and
there were lots of steps to the door. The only water came from unreliable standpipes
at the front or in buckets from the well. There were no proper toilets, merely earth
closets. The school could be divided into two sections, one with a tortoise stove
where the children could be kept warm during lessons, and the other for all sorts of
activities including 'Music and Movement' (a BBC children's radio programme). The

only props for school plays were dual desks: the children had marvellous imaginations. There was no work in the village other than farming: most people lived in tied cottages, and tenants often switched allegiance between different farms. The largest 'income' for the school was if a farmer arrived with five children. The only pupils to come from any distance were the son of the housekeeper at Sutton Court and a child from the Brookside area near Stowey Mill.

The head's sole assistance was from local villagers and their wives. The Challengers ('a lovely family') were such villagers; Mrs 'Plenty' Challenger cleaned, and her husband sorted out the toilets. Marjorie Reed could do pretty much as she liked. She only had one inspection while she was there: 'the inspector was such a nice man'. He was amazed that she could manage on her own. Opposite the school was a yucca plant which only flowered once every seven years and did the honours by bursting into bloom at the very time of the inspection. There were no discipline problems and only one difficult child. The headmistress would put the two oldest boys in charge of the playground.

By the early 1940s school dinners were being provided almost everywhere. But not at Stowey. Some children went home for lunch, some brought sandwiches. Towards the end of the war, however, an 'avalanche of people' arrived with pre-cooked food, about which Mrs Reed had been told nothing. She had no ready source of water and no phone to seek advice, but the authorities were insistent. She engaged Mrs Challenger to help out for the lunch hour. Taunton sent crockery and a calor gas cooker. One of the first meals was tripe, which the children refused to eat. One day, a 5-year old evacuee boy was brought in by his mother. Mid-morning on the following day, his little sister walked through the door. Very pleased with herself, she nestled down next to her big brother and everyone kept an eye on her. Her mother discovered her missing and rushed in a panic to the school, praying that she might be there. County Office in Taunton confirmed that as the girl was 4, she could stay.

Another plaque above the door of the old school reads: *On ceasing to be a school,* [the building] *was presented to the Boy Scouts Association by Edward 2nd Baron Strachie and reopened on September 1st 1951 as the Henry Strachey* (sic) *Memorial Hall.* It is now a private residence called The Old School House. Stowey School was no more.

Crown (five shillings) 1887, 1935
(actual size)

THE END

Children's laughter – and occasional tears and fears – has echoed around Bishop Sutton School for nearly 170 years. One of the oldest primary school buildings in Somerset, the premises have been hacked around, bits have been added on and the school grounds are substantially more extensive than they were in the 1840s. Teachers and headteachers have come and gone, most of them missed by their pupils, but several not. Lessons have moved on from Haymaking, and electronic wizardry has made its appearance. Children are no longer caned for wetting themselves. The school – and the village - has survived wars and bureaucracy, flooding, snow and heat waves. The ghosts of the feared Mr Northam and the respected Mr Price may still haunt the old School House – I hasten to add that there's no evidence that they do! – and there may still be the undiscovered writing slate or quill pen or one of Mr Bailey's canes hidden in some recess.

Will the school still be here in 170 years' time? Will technology have moved on to the extent that children will learn in front of real-time screens at home? Society has played the major part in ensuring the success, resilience and endurance of the school to date. It will be society that decides how the next century of education in Bishop Sutton will look.

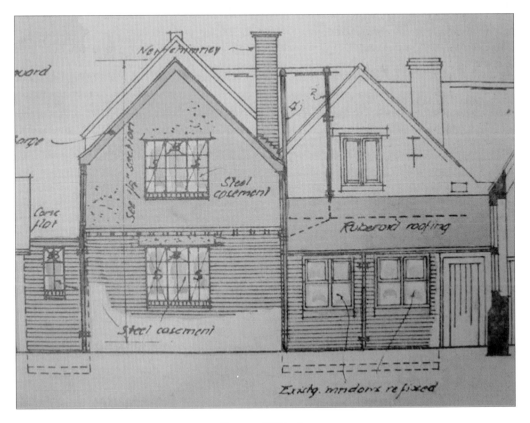

From a 1924 plan

Bishop Sutton. C of School.
3. 10 1930

Gentlemen.

The attendances for the past quarter were:—

	On Reg	Average.	Percentage
July	136	129	89
August	137	117	85
September	133	124	93.

In July there were 2 isolated cases of Scarlet Fever necessitating the absence of 4 ch This caused a drop in the attendance

" August consisted of one day when several leavers were absent

The Scripture Exam was held in July, when an excellent report was obtained.

The School did well in the Blagdon & Area Sports when it gained second place and won the Girls' Trophy Five children were chosen from the School to represent the Area in individual events at the County Sports

I am
Yours obediently
Jas. B. Wightman.

The headmaster's report to the Education Authority, 1930

DATE.	ARTICLE SOLD.	NUMBER SOLD.	PRICE RECEIVED PER ARTICLE		TO WHOM SOLD.
August. 1941	Nightdress	1	6	9	Pat Dury.
	"	1	6	9	F. Assael
	1 Pair Rompers	1		6	S. Nelman
	Nightdress	1		10½	J. Marsh
	Dress.	1	3	0	K Perry
	"	1	2	4½	V. Elsden
	Nightdress	1	1	6	A Dury
	Pinafore	1		6	A. Hill
	"	1	1	0	C. Saunders

Received from Mrs Bailey.
August 15th '41 £1-3-3.
Howard Lovern

From the school's Sales Book 1941

APPENDIX 1

TIMELINE

	School and village	Britain and the world
1842	Building of school commences.	Mines and Collieries Act, children aged 8-13 can work max 6½ hours a day. Brunel builds world's first underwater tunnel, under River Thames between Rotherhithe and Wapping. Queen Victoria is first monarch to take the train, from Windsor to Paddington. First operation performed under anaesthesia.
1843	Rev. Ommaney applies for a grant for a National School.	Nelson's Column erected in Trafalgar Square. News of the World first published. First Christmas cards go on sale. Prince Albert launches Brunel's SS Great Britain.
1844	School opens.	YMCA founded. Samuel Morse sends first public telegram.
1845	Travis Pit sunk near Rushgrove Gardens.	Irish potato famine. Edward Lear's Book of Nonsense published.
1846		Ether first demonstrated as a general anaesthetic. Antoine Sax invents the saxophone.
1847	Jesse Lovell born.	Factory Act passed, children under 18 (and all women) banned from working more than 58 hours a week. Charlotte Brontë publishes Jane Eyre and Emily Brontë Wuthering Heights.
1848	Holy Trinity Church built.	WH Smith opens its first bookshop. Karl Marx and Friedrich Engels write Communist Manifesto. Revolutions in Germany, France and Italy.
1849		Harrods store opens in London.
1850		Robert Bunsen invents the Bunsen burner.
1851		The Great Exhibition opens in London.
1852		Roget's Thesaurus published. David Livingstone discovers Victoria Falls.
1853	Post office opens.	Compulsory smallpox vaccinations introduced in England.
1854		Britain joins the Crimean War; Charge of the Light Brigade; Florence Nightingale arrives in Scutari.
1855	Old Pit Colliery (Church Lane) closes.	First vulcanised rubber football.
1856		Crimean War ends. Louis Pasteur invents pasteurisation.
1857		George Pullman invents sleeping car for trains.
1858		First message by transatlantic telegraph cable.
1859		Big Ben in London becomes operational. Charles Darwin publishes The Origin of Species. Isambard Kingdom Brunel dies.
1860		Mines Act, no children under 12 underground unless they can read and write.
1861		Queen Victoria's husband Prince Albert dies. American Civil War starts.
1862		Government introduces 'Payment by Result' system in schools.
1863	Scoutmaster, painter Henry Strachie born.	First underground railway opens in London, between Paddington and Farringdon Street.
1864		Clifton Suspension Bridge opens.
1865		Lewis Carroll publishes Alice's Adventures in Wonderland.
1866	Travis Pit closes.	J. Osterhoudt patents a tin can with key opener. Alfred Nobel invents dynamite.
1867		Last convict ship sails for Australia.

	School and village	Britain and the world
1868		Fenian bomber Michael Barrett is last person to be publicly hanged in UK. Benjamin Disraeli becomes PM in February, William Gladstone in December.
1869		Suez Canal opens. Unmarried women ratepayers given the vote in local elections.
1870		Education Act, elementary schools for all under age of 11. British Red Cross established. Married Women's Property Act: wives may own property in own right. France declares war on Prussia.
1871		Rugby Football Union established. Charles Darwin publishes The Descent of Man. David Livingstone meets Henry Stanley.
1872	Logbook starts 14 Oct. Miss Hassell headmistress.	Sale of spirits to children under 13 banned. Ballot Act introduces secret ballots in the UK. Licensing Act limits pub opening hours.
1873	School Board formed.	Prince of Wales opens racecourse at Bristol.
1874	School Board minute book starts.	Factory Act: no children to be employed under 9 unless part-time. Winston Churchill born.
1875	Mr Jones headmaster.	Matthew Webb swims the English Channel.
1876	Premises extensions.	Custer's Last Stand at the Battle of Little Bighorn. Alexander Graham Bell patents the telephone.
1877	School bell installed, together with 'apparatus for washing hands'.	First Test cricket match: England v Australia. First lawn tennis tournament at Wimbledon. Avonmouth Docks opened.
1878	Mr Northam hmr. Attendance Officer employed.	Thomas Edison patents the phonograph (gramophone). More than 600 people die when the pleasure boat Princess Alice sinks in Thames.
1879		Thomas Edison tests the first practical electric light bulb. Bristol telephone exchange opened.
1880	Snow closes school for a week.	Education Act: school compulsory to age 10. Britain's first phone book published, listing just 255 subscribers.
1881	Mr Northam dies, Mr Barker hmr for 4 weeks, Mr Hawkins takes over.	Postal orders introduced. Billy the Kid shot dead. Snowdrifts up to 30 ft deep in West Country.
1882	Mr Hill headmaster. Edward ('Young Lord') Strachie born.	Charles Darwin dies.
1883	Mr Brown headmaster.	Black Arabs FC (now Bristol Rovers) founded. Krakatoa erupts.
1884		Greenwich fixed as prime meridian.
1885	Wash house built in yard.	Age of Consent raised from 13 to 16. Professional football legalised.
1886		Sale of beer to children under 13 banned. Coca Cola invented.
1887		Daimler builds first motor car. Exeter's Theatre Royal burns down, 186 die. Queen Victoria's Golden Jubilee.
1888	Noah Gibbs supplies water to school.	Football League formed. Jack the Ripper murders. Pneumatic tyre invented.
1889	Heavy snow closes school several times.	NSPCC formed, Eiffel Tower opens, Adolf Hitler born, Nintendo formed to make playing cards.
1890		Forth Bridge opens. First county championship cricket match: Yorks beat Glos. Van Gogh commits suicide. New Scotland Yard opens.
1891	No more fees for education and books.	Education Act abolishes school pence. Thomas Edison patents radio.
1892		Rudolf Diesel invents the diesel engine.

	School and village	Britain and the world
1893	Penny Savings Bank introduced in school.	Education Act: school compulsory to age of 11. Independent Labour Party formed by Keir Hardie – became the Labour Party in 1906.
1894		Blackpool Tower and Tower Bridge open. Married women ratepayers can vote in local elections. Bristol South End Football Club formed, becomes Bristol City in 1897.
1895		G. Marconi's first wireless message. W. Röntgen discovers x-rays. Oscar Wilde jailed for 'gross indecency'.
1896		Gold discovered in Klondike. A motor car driver in Kent is fined for speeding at over 2 mph. Queen Victoria becomes longest reigning monarch. First modern Olympics, Athens.
1897	Mr Wightman hmr.	US Gold Rush. Queen Victoria's Diamond Jubilee.
1898		Marie and Pierre Curie discover radium.
1899		Boer War starts. Scott Joplin composes Maple Leaf Rag.
1900	Additional land bought at rear. Premises extensions started.	Children can leave school at 12 provided they have passed a Labour Exam.
1901	J. Lovell provides standpipe for water for school. WCs built in middle of yard. New room for infants.	Queen Victoria dies, Edward VII becomes king. First Nobel prizes. British build world's first concentration camps, in South Africa.
1902	School Board replaced by Somerset Educ. Authy and school mgrs.	Boer War ends. Beatrix Potter writes Peter Rabbit. Thomas Edison invents the battery.
1903		Orville and Wilbur Wright fly first heavier-than-air plane.
1904		US army rejects Wrights' machine as 'of no military value'. J.M. Barrie's Peter Pan opens in London. Britain & France sign Entente Cordiale. Empire Day founded. Government's 'Payment by Results' system for schools finally ends.
1905	Premises extensions. First Whit half term.	First suffragettes go to prison.
1906		Bristol City are Division 2 champions.
1907		Anglo-Russian Entente agreed. Bristol City runners up in Division 1.
1908	J. Lovell buys pit. Weighing machine at school. Village lending library starts at school.	William Grace retires after 54,211 runs and 2,808 wickets. Robert Baden-Powell forms Boy Scouts.
1909	School piano bought.	Old-age State pensions introduced: 5/- single people, 7/6 couples. Louis Bleriot flies English Channel. Bristol City FA Cup runners-up.
1910	Water meter installed.	Edward VIII dies, George V becomes king. First public air flights, on Durdham Down, Bristol. Florence Nightingale dies. Girl Guides formed. Dr Crippen hanged.
1911	Boy Scouts troop formed in village.	Amundsen beats Robert Scott to the South Pole.
1912		Titanic sinks, 1490 people die. Barbour clothing company founded.
1913	Cookery lessons start for girls.	Suffragette Emily Davison killed under King's horse in the Derby. Panama Canal opens. Scott and his party found dead in the Antarctic.
1914	Ink introduced, writing slates withdrawn, flagpole erected.	World War I starts.
1915	School dentist starts.	Lusitania torpedoed, 1195 killed.
1916	Children warned about traffic. New Methodist Hall built.	GPO Easter Rising in Dublin. Allies introduce tanks in Battle of the Somme.

	School and village	**Britain and the world**
1917		Russian Revolution, tsar and family exiled.
1918		First World War ends. Tsar and family murdered. School leaving age raised to 14. Voting age down to 21 for men; women of 30 given vote.
1919	Last pupil teacher employed.	Ernest Rutherford splits the atom.
1920	School badly flooded.	League of Nations formed.
1921		First birth control clinic in London. Frederick Banting and Charles Best discover insulin.
1922		George V proclaims Irish Free State. BBC established. Tutankhamun's tomb discovered.
1923	First Dist. School Sports. Garden extended. Bus service from Bristol to village. Barclays Bank opens and closes.	First FA Cup Final at Wembley: Bolton Wanderers 2, West Ham 0. Stanley Baldwin becomes prime minister.
1924	October half term introduced. Lovell family sells Colliery.	Lenin dies. Labour in power for the first time. Logie Baird invents television.
1925	Boys' separate entrance closed.	Stalin takes over in Soviet Union.
1926	First mention of school eyesight tests.	General Strike. Queen Elizabeth II born.
1927	No more mixed PE lessons for older children. Over-11s come from Stowey.	Malcolm Campbell's Bluebird sets world land speed record. Charles Lindbergh flies Atlantic solo. First talkie film: Al Jolson's The Jazz Singer.
1928	School damaged by gales.	Thomas Hardy dies (b.1840). Mickey Mouse makes debut in Steamboat Willie. Women of 21 given the vote. Amelia Earhart first woman to fly Atlantic solo. Dr A. Fleming discovers penicillin.
1929	Colliery closes.	St Valentine's Day massacre in Chicago. Wall St. Crash.
1930		Amy Johnson flies solo to Australia.
1931	Mr Bailey hmr. School football starts on rec.	Empire State Building opens.
1932	Further land acquired for school garden.	Mersey Tunnel opens.
1933	Sewing machine bought. School library starts.	Hitler becomes chancellor of Germany. First bore holes drilled to assess feasibility of reservoir in Chew Valley.
1934	School badly flooded. First Open Day for parents. LEA provides free milk at school.	Percy Shaw invents cats' eyes.
1935	School badly flooded.	First Penguin book published, 'Ariel' by A. Maurois. Driving test introduced in UK. World land speed record broken by Malcolm Campbell on Bonneville Salt Flats: 301 mph in Bluebird - speed was not surpassed until 1950.
1936	Edward ('Old Lord') Strachie dies. Electricity in village.	George V dies, Edward VIII crowned, abdicates, replaced by George VI. Jarrow Hunger March. Civil War in Spain. First t.v. broadcast. Crystal Palace in London burns down.
1937		Frank Whittle invents jet engine. Neville Chamberlain PM.
1938	Electricity in school. LEA provides PE shoes.	Hitler annexes Austria and invades Sudetenland.
1939	First evacuee children at school.	Land for Chew Valley School purchased. World War II starts.

	School and village	Britain and the world
1940	Railings dividing playground removed. Further land acquired for school garden. Henry Strachie dies.	Battle of Britain. First Bristol blitz. Germany starts its campaign of invasion across Europe. Dunkirk evacuation. Churchill becomes prime minister. Battle of Britain. Rationing starts.
1941		Japan attacks Pearl Harbor. USA enters war. German battleship Bismarck sunk.
1942		Baedeker blitz on Bath. First US troops in Britain.
1943	First school meals.	Italy surrenders.
1944		Education Act, free secondary schools established, 11-Plus introduced. D-Day.
1945	Lovell family sells mill. Stowey School closes. Senior children come from W. Harptree Schl.	Ship 'Wilhelm Gustloff' torpedoed in Baltic, killing some 9,000 German refugees. Atomic bombs on Hiroshima and Nagasaki. World War Two ends. Labour landslide at General Election, Clement Atlee becomes PM.
1946	Old Pit Garage established.	Construction starts at Chew Valley Lake. United Nations meets. T.V. licences introduced (£2 incl. radio).
1947	Severe winter. Senior children come from Ubley School.	School leaving age raised to 15. Coal industry nationalized. Indian independence.
1948	First prefab HORSA. Woodwork starts. Senior children come from E. Harptree. First male teacher (Mr John).	Railways nationalized in UK. NHS established. First immigration from Commonwealth. Olympic Games in London. Gandhi assassinated. Berlin blockade.
1949	Electric lights in playground. Infants move to Methodist Hall. First use in logbook of biro (one day only!). LEA provides gramophone.	Joint parish of Stowey-Sutton formed. NATO formed. Clothes rationing ends.
1950	February half term introduced.	First Formula 1 Grand Prix at Silverstone. Korean War.
1951		'O' and 'A' Levels introduced. Festival of Britain.
1952		George VI dies, Elizabeth II becomes Queen. London smog kills 4000. Everest conquered. Over 30 die in North Devon floods.
1953	Television set in school for Coronation.	Queen Elizabeth II crowned. Over 300 die in East Anglia floods. Structure of DNA discovered.
1954		R. Bannister runs first 4-minute mile. Food rationing ends.
1955	Children each given a towel. Civil Defence classes at school. Application for phone.	Bill Haley sings Rock Around the Clock. Ruth Ellis last woman to be hanged in Britain.
1956	Severe flooding at school. Fire extinguisher installed.	Chew Valley Lake opened. Suez crisis.
1957	Drinking fountains installed. Garden closed. First polio jabs. Two-colour paint at school. All-age status ends.	Soviet Sputnik orbits earth.

	School and village	**Britain and the world**
1958	Mr Price headmaster. First supervisory assistant employed.	Treaty of Rome establishes Common Market (EU). Munich air disaster. De Havilland is first jet airliner to cross Atlantic. Campaign for Nuclear Disarmament (CND) formed. Race Riots in Notting Hill. Chew Valley School opens.
1959	Playground asphalted.	Soviet spaceship Luna II hits moon.
1960		Silicon chip developed.
1961	Hot water installed. Best Kept Village competition – loses and doesn't re-enter.	Contraceptive pill available in Britain. Berlin Wall built. Russians send Yuri Gagarin into space.
1962	(Dec.) Severe winter starts	Cuban missile crisis. Marilyn Monroe dies.
1963	(Jan. to March) Severe winter continues, 90 cm of snow in yard.	President Kennedy assassinated. De Gaulle vetoes British EU entry. Rail network axed after Lord Beeching's report. Great Train Robbery. Beatles' first UK no. 1:' From Me to You'. Profumo affair. Alec Douglas-Home becomes PM.
1964	School connected to main drains.	Mods and Rockers clash at Clacton. BBC2 starts. Beatles at Bristol's Colston Hall. Nelson Mandela sentenced to life in prison. Radio Caroline starts. Last hanging in Britain (Peter Allen, Gwynne Evans). Harold Wilson becomes PM.
1965	Highmead and Parkfield estates completed, Orchard Close built. Lakeside Gdns renamed Hillside Gdns. Headmaster and family vacate School House.	Labour Government accelerates expansion of comprehensive schools. Death penalty abolished. Winston Churchill dies. Introduction of Certificate of Secondary Education (CSE). Vietnam War starts. Post Office Tower (highest building in Britain) opens.
1966	Central heating installed. Land bought for playing field. Lollipop man employed.	First credit card introduced. England wins World Cup, beating Germany 4:2. Aberfan disaster, 114 children and 28 adults die.
1967	PTA formed.	Plowden Report, fundamental review of primary education. Francis Chichester completes circumnavigation. Abortion legalised in UK. Concorde unveiled. Donald Campbell dies trying to beat world water speed record. UK first European country to start colour TV broadcasts.
1968	Prefab classroom built. Swimming pool opens. Tibbs' Bakery closes.	Enoch Powell's 'Rivers of Blood' speech. Kray Twins arrested. Last steam train passenger service in UK. Martin Luther King assassinated. Severe Chew Valley flooding.
1969	School employs groundsman.	Beatles' last public performance. Concorde's maiden flight. Voting age down from 21 to 18. British troops in Ulster. Monty Python's Flying Circus starts on BBC. First man on the moon. Prince Charles becomes Prince of Wales.
1970	Flagstone floors removed. Sinks put in classrooms. Playing field opened. First sex education film shown. Village Hall renovated.	First jumbo jet. First Glastonbury Festival. Whit Monday replaced by Spring Bank Holiday. Edward Heath becomes PM. SS Great Britain towed back to Bristol from the Falklands.
1971	Playground enlarged. First PTA firework display.	Decimal currency introduced in Britain.
1972	Fluorescent lighting installed; toilets moved from middle of yard to rear. Flooding in schl. First school camp.	Bloody Sunday in Northern Ireland. Ugandan Asians expelled by Idi Amin. Miners strike.

School and village	Britain and the world
1973	Prefab Pratten classroom. Edward ('Young Lord') Strachie dies. PTA donates cassette recorder.	School leaving age raised to 16. Britain joins EU.
1974	Avon Educ. Authority takes over from Somerset. Playground extended.	IRA bombs explode in Bristol and Bath. 3-day week to save energy. Harold Wilson becomes PM. Watergate scandal.
1975		Avonmouth Bridge opens, joining up M5. EU referendum: 67% vote to stay in.
1976	Elm trees felled in school copse.	Hinkley Point B Power Station opens. Harold Wilson resigns and James Callaghan takes over. Hottest driest summer for 250 years.
1977		Queen's Silver Jubilee. Concorde's maiden flight to New York. Elvis Presley (42) and Charlie Chaplin (88) die.
1978	Headmaster bans skateboarding. PTA donates video recorder. Heavy snow.	Anna Ford becomes first British female newsreader. Bristol's Louise Brown becomes world's first test-tube baby. First May Day Bank Holiday in UK.
1979	PTA buys photocopier for school.	Industrial unrest, Winter of Discontent. Lord Mountbatten killed by IRA bomb. Margaret Thatcher becomes the first female PM.

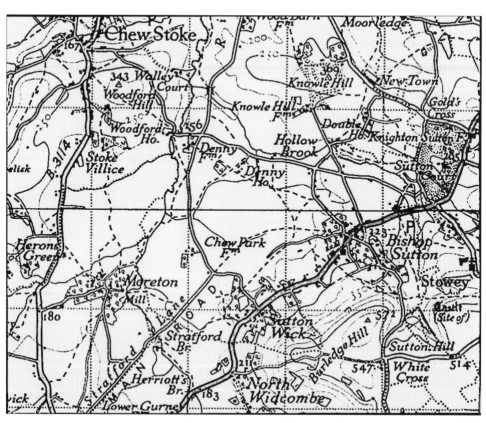

Ordnance Survey 1946

STAFF AT SCHOOL 1870 TO 1979

The list includes only those individuals mentioned in logbooks or other records. A question mark (?) denotes an unknown first name or missing date. 'PT' is pupil teacher.

		From	To	
Appleby, Mr G.	PT	?	1875	
Ashman, Miss Lucy	assistant teacher	1891	1891	
Avery, Mr ?	Handicraft, Sciences	1952	1953	
Bailey, Miss Hannah	assistant teacher	1886	1886	
Bailey, Miss M. D.	supply	1935	1935	
Bailey, Reginald James	headmaster	1931	1957	
Baker, Mrs J.	part-time teacher	1977	?	
Bale, Mrs ?	supply, became teacher	1952	1956	
Barker, John	headmaster	1881	1881	
Batt, Miss Emily	assistant teacher	1907	1939	
Beames, Mrs T.	cook	1979	2001	
Bendall, Miss Dora Annie	monitress	1903	?	
Berrell, Mr ?	Handicraft teacher	1954	1954	
Beynon, Miss Eleanor	assistant teacher	1903	1904	
Bowles, Miss Ellen Frances	teacher	1902	1903	
Bowles, Miss Mary Sophia (to be Mrs Harvey)	assistant teacher	1895	1902	
Braund, Miss Lilian	teacher	1903	1903	
Brigg, Miss Brenda	infant teacher	1956	1957	
Brown, Ebenezer	headmaster	1883	1897	
Brown, Miss Mabel Ailsa	assistant teacher	1903	1904	
Brown, Mrs Mary Kate	teacher	1893	1895	wife of Ebenezer
Burgess, Miss Marjorie	monitress	1906	?	
Callicott, Mr R. E. S.	probationary assistant teacher	1972	1973	
Carpenter, Miss Mabel (to be Mrs Flower)	monitress, teacher	1900	1947	left from 20.12.1912 to 26.11.1915
Chapman, Mrs S.	caretaker	1918	1919	
Chivers, Miss ?	Sewing teacher, deputy hmr.	1952	1957	
Coates, Miss Marilyn (to be Mrs Townhill)	infant teacher	1974	?	
Collett, Mrs Joy	cleaner in charge	1977	?	
Connell, Mrs ?	supply teacher	1978	1978	
Cook, Miss Ellen	Sewing mistress	1875	1875	
Cotton, Ivor	Handicraft teacher	1955	?	
Court, Mrs D.	temporary teacher	1967	?	
Creighton, Miss Maria	infant teacher	1882	1891	
Curnow, Miss Eliz. Mary	assistant teacher	1897	1897	
Daunton, Miss Ella	PT	1919	?	
Davidge, Mrs Joan	dinner duties, became supervisory assistant	1973	1981	
Davies, Mrs Monica	supply teacher	1957	?	

		Start	Leave	
Deer, Miss Nesta	supply teacher	1937	?	
Dibble, Mr V. J.	supply teacher	1957	?	
Dillon, Miss B.	teacher	1956	1958	
Dix, Mrs A.	caretaker	1919	1941	
Durrant, Miss B.	teacher	1966	?	
Dyke, Miss Sarah	infant teacher	1911	1912	left for Canada
Edser, Miss Barbara M.	teacher	1948	1949	
Edworthy, Miss ? (Mrs Lovell from 3.1.50)	assistant teacher	1950	1951	
Ferris, Miss Emma Jane	PT, monitress, teacher	1874	1879	
Ferris, Thomas Victor	monitor	1885	1886	
Field, Miss Annie Marie	assistant teacher	1890	1893	
Fitton, Mrs ?	teacher	1946	1946	
Fletcher, Mrs M. E. A. (née Wilson)	teacher	1959	1964	
Flower, Mrs Mabel (née Carpenter)	monitress, teacher	1900	1947	
Frappell, Mrs ?	Sewing teacher	1875	1877	
George, Mrs ?	temporary teacher	1947	1947	
Gilling, Mrs ?	supply teacher	1937	?	
Goulding, Miss ?	trainee teacher	1941	1943	
Grey, Miss ?	peripatetic teacher	1963	?	
Hammond, Mrs June	supervisory assistant	1958	1962	
Hare, Mrs ?	supply teacher	1953	?	
Harries, Miss ?	temporary teacher	1960	?	
Harris, Mrs S. R.	peripatetic teacher	1974	?	
Harvey, Frank	monitor	1895	1896	
Harvey, Miss Elizabeth	monitress	1873	?	
Harvey, Mrs E.	caretaker	1917	1918	
Harvey, Miss Elsie	supervisory assistant	1962	1972+	
Harvey, Miss Emily May	PT	1918	?	
Harvey, Miss Emma	monitress	1872	?	
Harvey, Miss Ethel	monitress	1899	1900	
Harvey, Miss Margaret	monitress	1872	?	
Harvey, Miss Mildred Kathleen	assistant teacher	1916	1956	
Harvey, Mrs Maria Sophia (née Bowles)	assistant teacher	1895	1902	
Hassell, Miss Ellen Eliz.	headmistress	<1872	1875	
Hawkins, Lewis S.	headmaster	1881	1882	left for India
Haworth, Miss ?	supply, became teacher	1948	1952	
Hazell, Mrs ?	supernumerary cleaner	1979	?	
Higly, Mrs ?	general assistant, dinners	1968	?	
Hill, Allan Robert	headmaster	1882	1883	
Holland, Mrs R.	infant teacher	1970	1973	
Hopkins, Miss ?	assistant teacher	1970	?	
Hopp, Philip	assistant teacher	1954	1957	
Hopps, Mrs ?	temporary teacher	various 1954-56		
Hunt, Miss Martha Emma	assistant teacher	1894	1894	
Ingram, Mr ?	handicraft teacher	1950	1951	left for Tasmania

		Start	Leave	
James, Ronald Samuel	assistant teacher	1949	1952	
Jenkins, Mrs ?	assistant teacher	1968	?	
Jewell, Mr C. B.	supply	1953	?	
John, Frederick	Handicraft teacher	1948	1949	
Johnson, Mrs ?	cook	1976	1979	
Jones, John	headmaster	1875	1878	
Jones, Miss Amy Lelilia (or Letitia)	supplementary teacher	1905	1906	
Jones, Miss Megan	teacher	1946	1947	
Jones, Russell James	assistant teacher	1949	1950	
Kempton, Miss Emily	assistant infant teacher	1910	1911	
King, Miss Ellen	assistant infant teacher	1905	1910	
Lovell Mrs ? (née Edworthy)	assistant teacher	1950	1951	
Lovell, Miss Bessie	monitress	1891	1892	
Low, Mrs M.	temporary teacher	1965	?	
Lowe, Miss Maude Ethel	assistant teacher	1904	1905	
Lucas, Miss L.	infant teacher	1976	1978	
Lyons, Mrs A. R.	temporary lollipop man	1965	1965	
Maggs, Miss E. Beatrice	teacher	1927	1937	died 22.9.37
Martin, Miss J.	supply teacher	1957	?	
Martin, Mrs J.	temporary teacher	1974	1974	
McDonnel, Miss Kathleen	teacher	1944	1945	
Montgomery, George	lollipop man	1966	1974	
Newman, Miss Norah	teacher	1914	?	
Nicholl / Nicol, Miss ?	supply teacher	1950	1952	
Northam, James	headmaster	1878	1881	died 18.2.81
Northam, Miss Eva	temporary teacher	1881	1881	daughter of above
Northam, Miss Rosa	temporary monitress	1879	1879	relative of above
Northam, Miss Sarah	monitress	1880	1882	daughter of above
Northam, Mrs Elizabeth	Sewing teacher	1878	1882	left to run own school
Nott, Miss ?	supply teacher	1953	?	
Painting, Mr J. J.	supply headmaster	various 1958-63		
Parfit, Mr D.	supply teacher	1949	1949	
Parfitt, Mrs C. L.	cook in charge	1960	1966	
Parfrey, Miss Lily	PT	1906	?	
Parfrey, Miss Sylvia	monitress, PT, teacher	<1911	1916	
Paul, Miss Ellen	assistant teacher	1886	1886	
Payne, Miss Lavinia	assistant teacher	1892	1894	
Pierce, Mr ?	peripatetic teacher	1963	?	
Platt, Mrs L.	temporary teacher	1967	1967	
Plummer, Mrs ?	dinner service	?	1945	
Powell, David H.	teacher	1974	1977	
Price, Tom	headmaster	1958	1979	

		Start	Leave	
Price, Mrs Mair	temp. teacher, teacher 1972	1959	1979	
Renshaw, Brian H.	handicraft teacher	1948	1950	
Rice, Miss Edith	Sewing teacher	1882	?	sister-in-law of A. Hill
Saunders, Mrs E.	cleaner	1941	1977	
Saunders, Mr W.	lollipop man	1975	?	
Saunders, Mr ?	caretaker	<1960	?	
Sheldon, Miss Josephine	monitress	1874	?	
Sheppard, Mr W.	monitor	1887	1890	
Sidwell, Mr J W.	supply headmaster	1931	1931	
Smale, Miss Audrey	teacher	1937	1941	
Small, Mrs K.	dinner service	1942	1974	
Smith, Mr L J.	groundsman	1979	?	
Steadman, Mrs J.	supply headmistress	1968	1968	
Steele, Miss Nellie	PT / monitress	1902	1906	
Stembridge, Mrs Beatrice	assistant teacher	1913	1914	
Stevens, Miss Adelaide Gertrude	assistant infant teacher	1903	1905	
Stuckey, Miss Eileen	infant teacher, dep. head 1970	1958	1980	
Sydenham, Albert	monitor	1879	1882	
Symes, Miss Alice Maud	assistant teacher	1898	1902	
Tebb, Miss Margaret Ellen	assistant teacher	1898	1902	
Thomas, Miss ?	trainee teacher	1941	1941	
Thomas, Miss Hiliary	teacher	1949	1950	
Thompson, Miss ?	supply teacher	1963	1963	
Tibbs, George	PT / monitor	1885	?	
Tibbs, Miss Jane	monitress	?	1878	
Tibbs, Charles	monitor	?	1895	
Toomer, Mr ?	peripatetic teacher	1961	?	
Tovey, Mrs Kate	caretaker	1919	1919	
Townhill Mrs Marilyn (née Coates)	infant teacher	1974	?	supply 1978
Turkington, Miss Olivia	assistant teacher	1897	1897	
Webber, Miss N.	teacher	1964	1966	
Wheeler, Miss Mary Eliz.	infant teacher	1906	1906	
White, Miss Emma	caretaker	1900	1917	
Wightman, James Bestwick	headmaster	1897	1931	
William, David	assistant PE teacher	1953	1955	
Williams, Mrs A. G.	caretaker	1919	1919	
Willis, Miss Louisa Julia	assistant teacher	1886	1889	
Wilson, Miss M E A (to be Mrs Fletcher)	teacher	1959	1964	
Withers, Miss ?	peripatetic teacher	1971	?	
Withey, George	caretaker	1893	1900	
Wright, Miss I. G.	supply teacher	1957	?	

		Start	Leave
Wyatt, Miss Ellen	teacher	1872	1874
Yapp, Miss Alma Beatrice	infant teacher	1912	1914
Young, Miss Eva	assistant teacher	1914	1915

RULES

To be observed by the Parents of Children attending the National

*School at*_____

Parents who wish to get their children admitted into the above-named school, may do so by applying to the Master on any Monday morning, at a quarter before 9 o'clock.

Parents are requested to pay particular attention to the following rules :—

1. The children are to assemble at the school on every week-day morning at a quarter before 9, and every afternoon at a quarter before 2 o'clock, except Saturday, which is a holiday.

2. On the Sunday the children meet in the morning at   , and in the afternoon at   o'clock.

3. The school hours are from 9 to 12, and 2 to 5, in the summer; and from 9 to 12, and 2 to 4, in the winter.

4. The children must be sent to school clean and neat in person and dress.

5. No child may stay from school without leave from the Master.

6. Leave of absence will be readily granted, either by application personally or by note: this application must be made before, and not after, the child absents itself.

7. If any child come late or be absent, a ticket of suspension will be sent, requiring a reason from the parent.

8. If the ticket be disregarded, the child will not be allowed to attend the school until a satisfactory answer has been given by the parent.

9. Every child must bring   a week, to be paid in advance every Monday morning: if there should be three children in one family desirous of attending the school, the third will be admitted free.

10. No child will be admitted under the age of six years.

N.B. No child will be admitted until it has been vaccinated.

Sold at the *National Society's Depository*, Sanctuary, Westminster.

Rules for attendance at National Schools, 1850s

APPENDIX 3

SCHOOL NUMBERS

The information is taken from returns submitted to the County, and from the Bishop Sutton School logbooks.

The table below shows average attendance for Bishop Sutton and Stowey Schools. Figures for 1906 to 1927 are for September, from 1928 to 1956 for May:

	Av. attendance	
	Sutton	Stowey
1906	117	28
1907	108	29
1908	114	28
1909	112	24
1910	106	22
1911	107	29
1912	106	36
1913	109	38
1914	113	32
1915	116	28
1916	118	25
1917	117	31
1918	119	23
1919	n/a	n/a
1920	128	29
1921	125	29
1922	123	27

	Av. attendance	
	Sutton	Stowey
1923	119	26
1924	120	38
1925	119	42
1926	134	43
1927	127	40
1928	135	35
1929	132	20
1930	132	18
1931	132	15
1932	128	17
1933	125	17
1934	131	13
1935	135	15
1936	143	14
1937	139	13
1938	127	11
1939	122	11

	Av. attendance	
	Sutton	Stowey
1940	120	13
1941	107	14
1942	100	13
1943	95	13
1944	81	16
1945	90	14
1946	n/a	closed
1947	127	
1948	119	
1949	148	
1950	145	
1951	158	
1952	158	
1953	151	
1954	139	
1955	151	
1956	151	

Average attendance (as at April) for Bishop Sutton, Chew Magna and Chew Stoke Schools from 1957 to 1972. Figures for 1973 to 1979 were not available:

	Average attendance		
	Sutton	C Magna	C Stoke
1957	144	206	91
1958	73	47	80
1959	76	47	73
1960	76	52	67
1961	69	51	68
1962	74	53	66
1963	79	47	67
1964	88	46	63

	Average attendance		
	Sutton	C Magna	C Stoke
1965	83	47	62
1966	87	52	56
1967	96	57	53
1968	97	56	61
1969	100	52	68
1970	110	61	77
1971	125	66	70
1972	147	61	67

Threepenny bit 1909, 1936, 1940, 1941, 1967 (actual size)

WHERE DID ALL THE CHILDREN COME FROM?

The School Admission Register 1906 to 1935 listed any previous school attended by the pupils. Of the 728 children admitted to Bishop Sutton during those years, 408 had had no previous school and were therefore probably born in Bishop Sutton (or elsewhere within Chew Magna parish) or moved here before the age of around 5.

The remaining 320 came from schools in the following localities. The number after the name is the number of pupils involved:

Abercwmboi (Glam.) 1

Aberdeen 1

Abertillery 4

Avonmouth 2

Axbridge 1

Badminton 3

Banwell 1

Bath 2

Bedwas (Mon.) 1

Berkeley 4

Bournemouth 1

Blagdon 1

Bristol 43

Burrington 2

Cardiff 1

Charterhouse 2

Cheddar 3

Cheltenham 1

Chelwood 1

Chew Magna 13

Chew Stoke 5

Chippenham 1

Chipping Sodbury 1

Churchdown (Glos.) 1

Cleeve 3

Clevedon 3

Clutton 9

Compton Martin 5

Crewkerne 1

Dundry 9

Durham 2

East Brent (Somt.) 2

Eastbourne 2

Easton in Gordano 1

Emborough 1

Farmborough 1

Hackney 1

Harptree 32[1]

Harrogate 2

Haydon (Radstock) 1

High Littleton 2

Hinton Blewett 5

Kelston 2

Laverton (Wilts.) 2

Litton 2

Llanhilleth (Mon.) 1

Long Ashton 1

Longbredy (Dorset) 1

Lydney 1

Machen (Glam.) 1

Marksbury 1

Melksham 2

Mells 3

Midsomer Norton 3

Norton Malreward 1

Paulton 5

Pensford 6

Pontypridd 1

Porth (Glam.) 2

Portishead 1

Priston 3

Sheffield 1

South Wales 5[2]

Southampton 1

Stanton Drew 6

Stowey 62[3]

Temple Cloud 8

Timsbury 1

Treorchy 1

Twynyrodyn (Glam.) 1

Ubley 6

Wells 1

Westbury 2

----

[1] The records rarely distinguished between East and West.

[2] Sounds like a bit of a cop out! Perhaps the head couldn't spell the names.

[3] This figure should be treated with caution as children did tend to to-and-fro between Stowey and Bishop Sutton, and all Stowey children over the age of 11 had come to Bishop Sutton since 1927.

Appendix 5

School holidays

Holiday dates taken from the school logbooks.

	Half term	Easter	Whitsun	Summer	Half term	Christmas
1873	n/a	?	n/a	16 Aug – 19 Sep	n/a	24 Dec – 9 Jan
1874	n/a	3 Apr – 7 Apr	n/a	31 Jul – 4 Sep	n/a	23 Dec – 8 Jan
1875	n/a	26 Mar – 30 Mar	n/a	13 Aug – 6 Sep	n/a	20 Dec – 10 Jan
1876	n/a	14 Apr – 18 Apr	n/a	11 Aug – 18 Sep	n/a	12 Dec – 8 Jan
1877	n/a	30 Mar – 9 Apr	n/a	10 Aug – 3 Sep	n/a	21 Dec – 11 Jan
1878	n/a	24 Apr – 29 Apr	n/a	9 Aug – 6 Sep	n/a	23 Dec – 3 Jan
1879	n/a	11 Apr – 21 Apr	n/a	15 Aug – 15 Sep	n/a	26 Dec – 2 Jan
1880	n/a	26 Mar – 5 Apr	n/a	18 Aug – 13 Sep	n/a	24 Dec – 3 Jan
1881	n/a	22 Apr – 29 Apr	n/a	5 Aug – 5 Sep	n/a	23 Dec – 2 Jan
1882	n/a	6 Apr – 17 Apr	n/a	4 Aug – 4 Sep	n/a	22 Dec – 5 Jan
1883	n/a	22 Mar – 6 Apr	n/a	19 Jul – 20 Aug	n/a	21 Dec – 7 Jan
1884	n/a	14 Apr – 18 Apr	n/a	18 Jul – 18 Aug	n/a	24 Dec – 5 Jan
1885	n/a	2 Apr – 13 Apr	n/a	24 Jul – 24 Aug	n/a	24 Dec – 4 Jan
1886	n/a	22 Apr – 3 May	n/a	30 Jul – 30 Aug	n/a	23 Dec – 3 Jan
1887	n/a	7 Apr – 18 Apr	n/a	28 Jul – 28 Aug	n/a	22 Dec – 2 Jan
1888	n/a	29 Mar – 9 Apr	n/a	3 Aug – 3 Sep	n/a	20 Dec -30 Dec
1889	n/a	19 Apr – 29 Apr	n/a	2 Aug – 2 Sep	n/a	20 Dec – 6 Jan
1890	n/a	3 Apr – 14 Apr	n/a	1 Aug – 1 Sep	n/a	18 Dec – 5 Jan
1891	n/a	27 Mar – 6 Apr	n/a	17 Jul – 17 Aug	n/a	18 Dec – 4 Jan
1892	n/a	14 Apr – 25 Apr	n/a	29 Jul – 29 Aug	n/a	23 Dec – 2 Jan
1893	n/a	30 Mar – 10 Apr	n/a	28 Jul – 28 Aug	n/a	22 Dec – 8 Jan
1894	n/a	22 Mar – 3 Apr	n/a	3 Aug – 3 Sep	n/a	21 Dec – 7 Jan
1895	n/a	11 Apr – 29 Apr[1]	n/a	19 Jul – 19 Aug	n/a	20 Dec – 6 Jan
1896	n/a	2 Apr – 13 Apr	n/a	24 Jul – 24 Aug	n/a	24 Dec – 11 Jan
1897	n/a	14 Apr – 26 Apr	n/a	30 Jul – 30 Aug	n/a	23 Dec – 10 Jan
1898	n/a	7 Apr – 18 Apr	n/a	29 Jul – 29 Aug	n/a	22 Dec – 9 Jan
1899	n/a	30 Mar – 10 Apr	n/a	28 Jul – 25 Aug[2]	n/a	22 Dec – 2 Jan
1900	n/a	12 Apr – 23 Apr	n/a	27 Jul – 28 Aug	n/a	21 Dec – 7 Jan
1901	n/a	4 Apr – 15 Apr	n/a	2 Aug – 2 Sep	n/a	20 Dec – 6 Jan
1902	n/a	26 Mar – 7 Apr	n/a	25 Jul – 25 Aug	n/a	18 Dec – 5 Jan
1903	n/a	9 Apr – 20 Apr	n/a	31 Jul – 31 Aug	n/a	23 Dec – 11 Jan
1904	n/a	31 Mar – 11 Apr	n/a	29 Jul – 29 Aug	n/a	23 Dec – 9 Jan
1905	n/a	20 Apr – 1 May	9 Jun – 19 Jun	21 Jul – 18 Sep	n/a	22 Dec – 8 Jan
1906	n/a	12 Apr – 23 Apr	1 Jun – 11 Jun	3 Aug – 3 Sep	n/a	21 Dec – 7 Jan
1907	n/a	22 Mar – 29 Apr[3]	Monday only	30 Jul – 30 Aug	n/a	23 Dec – 10 Jan
1908	n/a	16 Apr – 25 Apr	5 Jun – 15 Jun	31 Jul – 31 Aug	n/a	24 Dec – 11 Jan
1909	n/a	18 Mar – 19 Apr[4]	n/a	30 Jul – 30 Aug	n/a	23 Dec – 10 Jan
1910	n/a	24 Mar – 5 Apr	13 May – 23 May	29 Jul – 29 Aug	n/a	23 Dec – 9 Jan
1911	n/a	13 Apr – 24 Apr	2 Jun – 8 Jun	28 Jul – 28 Aug	n/a	22 Dec – 8 Jan
1912	n/a	3 Apr – 15 Apr	24 May – 3 Jun	2 Aug – 2 Sep	n/a	20 Dec – 6 Jan
1913	n/a	19 Mar – 31 Mar[5]	9 May – 19 May	1 Aug – 1 Sep	n/a	19 Dec – 5 Jan
1914	n/a	9 Apr – 5 Apr	29 May – 8 Jun	31 Jul – 31 Aug	n/a	18 Dec – 4 Jan
1915	n/a	1 Apr – 12 Apr	21 May – 25 May	30 Jul – 30 Aug	n/a	17 Dec – 10 Jan[6]
1916	n/a	20 Apr – 1 May	7	28 Jul – 4 Sep	n/a	22 Dec – 8 Jan
1919	n/a	17 Apr – 28 Apr	6 Jun – 16 Jun	1 Aug – 8 Sep	n/a	19 Dec – 6 Jan
1920	n/a	31 Mar – 12 Apr	21 May – 31 May	30 Jul – 30 Aug	n/a	23 Dec – 10 Jan
1921	n/a	24 Mar – 11 Apr	13 May – 23 May	29 Jul – 29 Aug	n/a	23 Dec – 9 Jan
1922	n/a	13 Apr – 24 Apr	2 Jun – 12 Jun	3 Aug – 4 Sep	n/a	22 Dec – 8 Jan
1923	n/a	29 Mar – 9 Apr	18 May – 28 May	27 Jul – 27 Aug	n/a	21 Dec – 7 Jan
1924	n/a	16 Apr – 29 Apr	6 Jun – 12 Jun	1 Aug – 2 Sep	31 Oct – 3 Nov	19 Dec – 6 Jan
1925	n/a	8 Apr – 21 Apr	29 May – 8 Jun	31 Jul – 1 Sep	29 Oct – 3 Nov	18 Dec – 4 Jan
1927	n/a	13 Apr – 26 Apr	3 Jun – 16 Jun	29 Jul – 30 Aug	28 Oct – 1 Nov	23 Dec – 9 Jan
1928	n/a	4 Apr – 11 Apr	25 May – 4 Jun	3 Aug – 4 Sep	25 Oct -30 Oct	21 Dec – 7 Jan
1929	n/a	27 Mar – 9 Apr	17 May – 27 May	26 Jul – 27 Aug	24 Oct -29 Oct	20 Dec – 6 Jan
1930	n/a	16 Apr – 29 Apr	6 Jun – 16 Jun	1 Aug – 2 Sep	30 Oct – 4 Nov	19 Dec – 5 Jan
1931	n/a	1 Apr – 14 Apr	22 May – 1 Jun	31 Jul – 1 Sep	30 Oct – 3 Nov	23 Dec – 11 Jan
1932	n/a	23 Mar – 5 Apr	13 May – 23 May	29 Jul – 30 Aug	28 Oct – 1 Nov	23 Dec – 9 Jan

----

[1] extended by one week due to repairs

[2] one week deferred until 13-16 October

[3] school closed early due to whooping cough

[4] including extension ordered by Medical Officer due to measles outbreak

[5] extension 'by order' (no further reason given)

[6] closed early by order of Medical Officer of Health due to measles outbreak

[7] 'Whitsuntide holidays postponed'. No reason given.

	Half term	Easter	Whitsun	Summer	Half term	Christmas
1933	n/a	12 Apr – 24 Apr	2 Jun – 12 Jun	4 Aug – 4 Sep	?	22 Dec – 8 Jan
1934	n/a	28 Mar – 10 Apr	18 May – 27 May	3 Aug – 4 Sep	25 Oct -30 Oct	21 Dec – 7 Jan
1935	n/a	18 Apr – 30 Apr	7 Jun – 17 Jun	2 Aug – 3 Sep	24 Oct -29 Oct	20 Dec – 6 Jan
1936	n/a	8 Apr – 21 Apr	29 May – 8 Jun	31 Jul – 1 Sep	30 Oct – 2 Nov	23 Dec – 11 Jan
1937	n/a	24 Mar – 6 Apr	11 May – 24 May[1]	30 Jul – 31 Aug	29 Oct – 1 Nov	23 Dec – 10 Jan
1938	n/a	13 Apr – 26 Apr	3 Jun – 13 Jun	29 Jul – 30 Aug	28 Oct -31 Oct	23 Dec – 9 Jan
1939	n/a	6 Apr – 18 Apr	26 May – 5 Jun	28 Jul – 29 Aug[2]	n/a	23 Dec – 8 Jan
1940	n/a	20 Mar – 2 Apr	10 May – 14 May	2 Aug – 3 Sep[3]	25 Oct -29 10	20 Dec – 6 Jan
1941	n/a	9 Apr – 22 Apr	20 Jun – 30 Jun[4]	1 Aug – 2 Sep	3 Oct – 13 Oct	23 Dec – 5 Jan
1942	n/a	1 Apr – 13 Apr	22 May – 1 Jun	11 Aug – 7 Sep	n/a	18 Dec – 4 Jan
1943	n/a	?	11 Jun – 21 Jun	30 Jul – 31 Aug	29 Oct - ?	23 Dec – 10 Jan
1944	n/a	5 Apr – 18 Apr	?	4 Aug – 5 Sep	27 Oct -31 Oct	22 Dec – 8 Jan
1945	n/a	28 Mar – 10 Apr	?	27 Jul – 5 Sep	1 Nov – 2 Nov	21 Dec – 7 Jan
1946	n/a	11 Apr – 6 May	7 Jun – 12 Jun	26 Jul – 2 Sep	31 Oct – 1 Nov	20 Dec – 6 Jan
1947	21 Feb – 24 Feb	28 Mar – 21 Apr	?	25 Jul – 8 Sep	31 Oct -10 Nov	24 Dec – 5 Jan
1948	-	19 Mar – 12 Apr	15 May – 20 May	23 Jul – 6 Sep	29 Oct – 8 Nov	23 Dec – 6 Jan
1949	-	8 Apr – 2 May	3 Jun – 9 Jun	22 Jul – 5 Sep	28 Oct – 2 Nov	21 Dec – 4 Jan
1950	24 Feb – 27 Feb	31 Mar – 21 Apr	26 May – 5 Jun	28 Jul – 4 Sep	27 Oct – 6 Nov	19 Dec – 3 Jan
1951	19 Feb – 21 Feb	30 Mar – 11 Apr	11/5 – 21 May	27 Jul – 3 Sep	?	21 Dec – 7 Jan
1952	18 Feb – 19 Feb	4 Apr – 28 Apr	31 May – 9 Jun	25 Jul – 1 Sep	31 Oct -10 Nov	19 Dec – 5 Jan
1953	19 Feb – 26 Feb	27 Mar – 20 Apr	22 May – 4 Jun[5]	24 Jul – 31 Aug	30 Oct – 9 Nov	18 Dec – 4 Jan
1954	18 Feb – 24 Feb	9 Apr – 3 May	4 Jun – 14 Jun	22 Jul – 30 Aug	29 Oct – 8 Nov	22 Dec – 6 Jan
1955	17 Feb – 24 Feb	1 Apr – 24 Apr	26 May – 6 Jun	22 Jul – 29 Aug	28 Oct – 7 Nov	21 Dec – 5 Jan
1956	15 Feb – 22 Feb	23 Mar – 16 Apr	18 May – 28 May	27 Jul – 3 Sep	26 Oct – 5 Nov	21 Dec -14 Jan[6]
1957	14 Feb – 20 Feb	12 Apr – 6 May	?	26 Jul – 2 Sep	25 Oct – 4 Nov	22 Dec – 6 Jan
1958	18 Feb – 26 Feb	28 Mar – 20 Apr	23 May – 2 Jun	25 Jul – 1 Sep	24 Oct – 3 Nov	19 Dec – 5 Jan
1959	10 Feb – 18 Feb	20 Mar – 13 Apr	15 May – 25 May	24 Jul – 31 Aug	23 Oct – 2 Nov	19 Dec – 4 Jan
1960	18 Feb – 24 Feb	1 Apr – 25 Apr	3 Jun – 13 Jun	27 Jul – 29 Aug	21 Oct -31 Oct	21 Dec – 9 Jan
1961	16 Feb – 22 Feb	24 Mar – 17 Apr	19 May – 29 May	28 Jul – 4 Sep	27 Oct – 6 Nov	22 Dec – 8 Jan
1962	15 Feb – 21 Feb	6 Apr – 30 Apr	8 Jun – 17 Jun	27 Jul – 3 Sep	26 Oct – 5 Nov	21 Dec – 10 Jan[7]
1963	14 Feb – 19 Feb	29 Mar – 22 Apr	1 Jun – 10 Jun	26 Jul – 2 Sep	25 Oct – 4 Nov	20 Dec – 6 Jan
1964	20 Feb – 25 Feb	20 Mar – 13 Apr	15 May – 25 May	24 Jul – 30 Aug	30 Oct – 9 Nov	18 Dec – 4 Jan
1965	18 Feb -24 Feb	2 Apr – 26 Apr	?	23 Jul – 5 Sep	3 Nov – 8 Nov	21 Dec – 5 Jan
1966	17 Feb – 23 Feb	1 Apr – 25 Apr	29 May – 6 Jun	22 Jul – 5 Sep	2 Nov – 7 Nov	20 Dec – 4 Jan
1967	16 Feb – 22 Feb	14 Mar – 10 Apr	?	22 Jul – 4 Sep	31 Oct – 6 Nov	19 Dec – 4 Jan
1968	15 Feb – 17 Feb	29 Mar – 22 Apr	31 May – 10 Jun	19 Jul – 4 Sep	1 Nov – 11 Nov	20 Dec – 6 Jan
1969	20 Feb – 26 Feb	1 Apr – 21 Apr	24 May – 2 Jun	18 Jul – 3 Sep	24 Oct – 3 Nov	19 Dec – 6 Jan
1970	18 Feb – 25 Feb	20 Mar – 8 Apr	22 May – 1 Jun[8]	17 Jul – 2 Sep	23 Oct – 2 Nov	18 Dec – 6 Jan
1971	18 Feb – 24 Feb	2 Apr – 20 Apr	28 May – 7 Jun	23 Jul – 8 Sep	25 Oct – 1 Nov	17 Dec – 5 Jan
1972	15 Feb – 23 Feb	24 Mar – 12 Apr	23 May – 5 Jun	14 Jul – 31 Aug	27 Oct – 6 Nov	19 Dec – 9 Jan
1973	?	6 Apr – 24 Apr	25 May – 4 Jun	6 Jul – 21 Aug[9]	19 Oct -29 Oct	20 Dec – 8 Jan
1974	14 Feb - 20 Feb	5 Apr - 24 Apr	23 May – 3 Jun	19 Jul – 3 Sep	25 Oct – 4 Nov	19 Dec – 7 Jan
1975	14 Feb - 20 Feb	21 Mar - 8 Apr	23 May - 2 Jun	18 Jul – 2 Sep	24 Oct – 3 Nov	19 Dec - 6 Jan
1976	20 Feb - 1 Mar	9 Apr - 27 Apr	28 May - 7 Jun	23 Jul - 8 Sep	29 Oct – 8 Nov	21 Dec - 10 Jan
1977	12 Feb - 21 Feb	1 Apr - 19 Apr	3 Jun - 13 Jun	26 Jul - 7 Sep	21 Oct -31 Oct	20 Dec - 10 Jan
1978	3 Feb - 6 Feb	17 Mar - 3 Apr.	27 May - 5 Jun	20 Jul - 4 Sep	19 Oct -30 Oct	20 Dec - 8 Jan
1979	16 Feb - 26 Feb	6 Apr - 23 Apr	25 May - 4 Jun	20 Jul - 4 Sep	26 Oct - 5 Nov	21 Dec - 8 Jan

----

[1] extended for Coronation celebrations

[2] extended for most children for a further week as a result of commencement of war

[3] plus Bank Holiday Monday 3 August, remaining open until 11 Aug in case of need

[4] plus Whit Monday on 2 June

[5] including 3 days' Coronation holiday

[6] extended for a week due to the petrol shortage

[7] extended as a result of heavy snow and intense cold

[8] 'Whitsun' renamed 'Spring Holiday'

[9] plus Bank Holiday Monday on 27 August

Coronation 1953

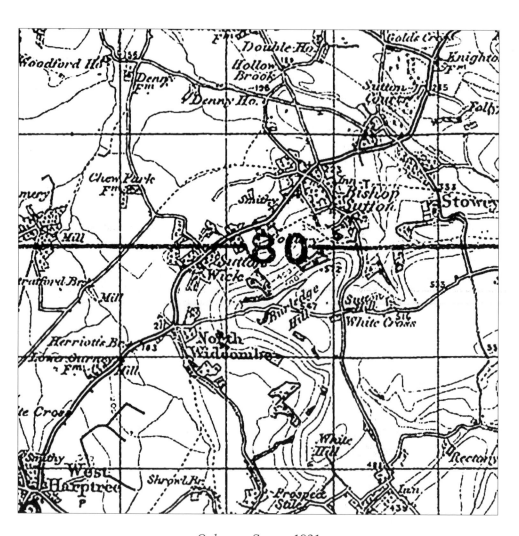

Ordnance Survey 1931

Appendix 6

Bibliography and sources

I am most appreciative of the permission given to me to reproduce documents, maps and wording where copyright has been involved, and will happily rectify any omissions - which are purely accidental - in any future issue. Information is from the following bibliography and sources:

Bishop Sutton School logbooks 1872-1979, Punishment Book 1900-1953, Cash Book, all courtesy of Mrs Bills, headteacher, Bishop Sutton School.

School Managers' Minute Books 1874-1929 and 1948-1975, Chew Magna School Board (and School Council) Letters Books 1874-1926, School Attendance Officers' Report Book 1891-1895, Stowey Parish Council minute book 1894-1949, Stowey Sutton Parish Council minute books 1949-1986, Sewage in Bishop Sutton 1894-1908, Highways Accounts Book 1844-1846, Bristol and Bath Regional Planning Scheme 1930, Chew Magna Vestry Books, Clutton Union Workhouse Master's Report and Journal, The Medical Officer's Record of Examination of Children (Clutton Union 1914-17), Clutton Union's Workhouse Punishment Book 1851-1898, Government Commission reports, sundry documents, all courtesy of Somerset Record Office.

The Light Railway Commission findings, courtesy of Bristol's City Record Office.

Department of Education and Science, Inspection Report of Chew Valley Schools - A Survey of Primary Education in the Chew Area of Somerset 1974, courtesy of Department for Children, Schools and Families.

Chew Magna Parish Council minute books 1894-1942, 1838 survey of Chew Magna, both courtesy of Chew Magna Parish Council.

Transfer deed 1844, courtesy of the Church of England archives.

Hunt's Directory of North Somerset 1850, Kelly's Directories, Pigots Directory of Somerset 1842, Post Office Directory of Somerset (E.R. Kelly) 1866, Post Office Directory of Somersetshire and Bristol 1861, Robson's Directory of Somerset 1839, Slater's Directory of Somerset 1852-3, all courtesy of various Record Offices and libraries.

Ordnance Survey maps (from author's own collection), all out of copyright although with the kind permission of Ordnance Survey.

- A Century of Childhood, Steve Humphries, Joanna Mack, Robert Perks, Sidgwick and Jackson, London, 1988, excerpts reprinted by kind permission of Pan MacMillan.
- A History of Blagdon Vol. 2, Neil Bentham, Blagdon Local History Society 2006, excerpts courtesy of Dr Bentham on behalf of the Blagdon Local History Society.
- Apparelled in Red, The History of the Red Maids School, Jean Vanes, Alan Sutton Publishing Ltd 1984, excerpts courtesy of The Red Maids' School.
- Before the Lake - Memories of the Chew Valley, Lesley Ross, Harptrees Historical Society, Antony Rowe Ltd 2004, excerpts courtesy of the Society.
- Bishop Sutton and Stowey Millennium Memories, Lesley Ross, Harptrees History Society 2000, excerpts courtesy of the Society.
- Collections of a Parochial History of Chew Magna, Frederick A Wood 1903.
- Diary of Francis Kilvert 1870-79 (Selections from the Diary of the Rev. Francis Kilvert edited by William Plomer, published by Jonathan Cape, excerpt reprinted by kind permission of The Random House Group Ltd).
- Geographical Readers of the Continents (Asia), Chambers, 1901.
- Highroads of History, Thomas Nelson & Sons, 1907.
- Highways and Byways of Somerset, Edward Hutton, Macmillan and Co. 1923.
- Histories and Antiquities of Somerset, John Collinson 1791.
- Imperial Gazetteer, W. D. Blackie 1855 (author's collection).
- Joseph Ashby of Tysoe, M. K. Ashby, Merlin Press, first published 1961, excerpts by kind permission of The Merlin Press.
- Methodism in Bishop Sutton - a Somerset Village Cause, Mair Price (unpublished), courtesy of Mrs Mair Price.
- 'Poor Little Hauve Timer', The Oldham Tinkers.
- Punch cartoons, reproduced with kind permission of Punch Ltd.
- Snip-Its, Mr A. H. Parsons (articles provided by various individuals).
- The History of Chew Stoke School 1718 to 1988, Zera Wilson, excerpts by kind permission of Mrs Zera Wilson.

- The Lore and Language of Schoolchildren, Iona and Peter Opie, Oxford Clarendon Press 1959, excerpts by kind permission of Oxford University Press.
- The Mid-Victorian Generation 1846 - 1886 by K. Theodore Hoppen, Oxford Clarendon Press 1998, excerpts by kind permission of Oxford University Press.
- Traveller's Guide or English Itinerary, W. C. Oulton 1805 (author's collection).
- Where the morning glories grow, words by Gus Kahn and Raymond B. Egan, music by Richard A. Whiting. Published Jerome H. Remick & Co, New York 1917.

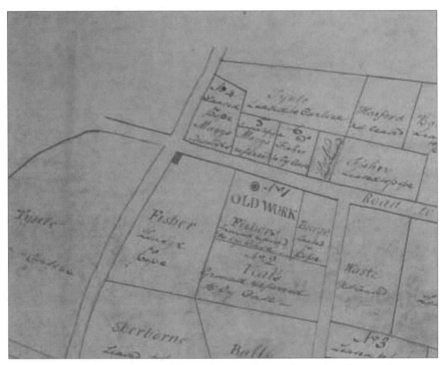

Top Sutton early 1800s. South is at the top. The road running diagonally top to bottom is Sutton Hill Road. Church Lane (annotated 'Road to Fields' on the full map) runs at right angles to the right. The Colliers' Arms is between the black rectangle at the crossroads and the then colliery ('Old Work'). The lane running down from a point to the right of the Old Work no longer exists.

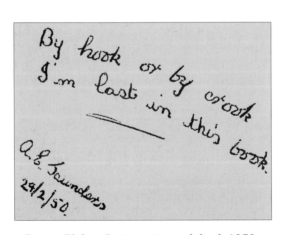

From a Bishop Sutton autograph book 1950